The
YOM KIPPUR WAR

The
YOM KIPPUR WAR

THE EPIC ENCOUNTER THAT
TRANSFORMED THE MIDDLE EAST

Revised and Updated Edition

Abraham Rabinovich

Schocken Books, New York

All rights reserved. Published in the United States by Schocken Books,
a division of Penguin Random House LLC, New York, and distributed in
Canada by Random House of Canada, a division of Penguin Random House
Canada Limited, Toronto. Originally published in slightly different form ·
in the United States by Schocken Books, a division of
Penguin Random House LLC, New York, in 2004.

Schocken Books and colophon are registered trademarks of
Penguin Random House LLC.

Library of Congress Cataloging-in-Publication Data
Rabinovich, Abraham.
The Yom Kippur War: the epic encounter that transformed the Middle East /
Abraham Rabinovich.
p. cm.
Includes bibliographical references and index.
ISBN 9780805211245 (paperback)   ISBN 9780307429650 (ebook)
1. Israel-Arab War, 1973. I. Title.
ds128.1.r33 2004 956.04'8—dc21 2003054353

www.schocken.com

Cover photograph courtesy of the Government Press Office, State of Israel
Cover design by Oliver Munday

Printed in the United States of America
Revised Paperback Edition, 2017

TO MICHAL AND GUY,
DANA AND ELAN,
YARDEN, DAVID, BENNO, TAL, AND ELIYA

On Rosh Hashana it is written and on the day of the fast of Kippur it is sealed . . . who shall live and who shall die . . . who by water and who by fire, who by the sword . . .

—from the Yom Kippur Prayer Book

CONTENTS

MAPS

Israel and Its Neighbors

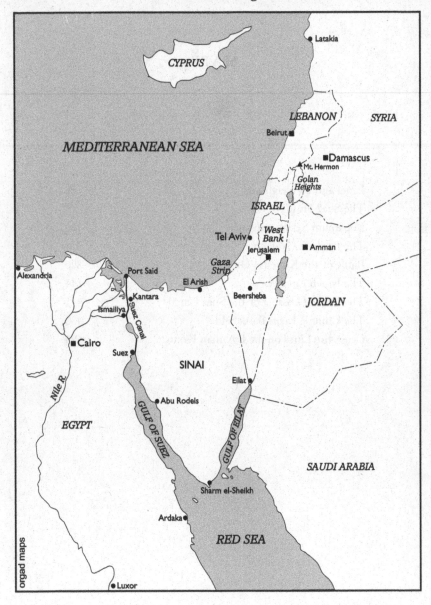

orgad maps

PREFACE TO THE REVISED EDITION

I N   T H E   Y E A R S   S I N C E   *The Yom Kippur War*'s first publication, in 2004, many of the war's deepest secrets have emerged, after more than three decades of censorship. These are spelled out in this updated edition. An invaluable new source is the official history of the Israeli general staff during the war, *Milkhama B'Yom Hakipurim (Decision Making in the Israeli High Command in the Yom Kippur War)* by Shimon Golan. Published forty years after the war, the 1,300-page volume, in Hebrew, is compiled from official transcripts and tape recordings and places the reader at the table where critical decisions are being shaped. Rare access to Israel's intelligence community during the war is provided by former Israeli intelligence analyst Uri Bar-Joseph in his books and articles. Other information has emerged in academic and military forums, military journals and the media. I have also profited from interviews with former Mossad chief Zvi Zamir and others.

Following are some of the revelations incorporated into this edition:

- Two Egyptian informants, working separately for the Mossad, provide information that dramatically affects the course of the war. A warning from one of them, the son-in-law of former Egyptian president Gamal Abdel Nasser, enables Israeli units to blunt the massive Syrian attack on the Golan Heights. The other agent provides a vital clue for Israel's crossing of the Suez Canal, the war's turning point.
- Israeli commandos, infiltrating into Egypt before the war, install sophisticated listening devices on key military communication nodes intended to provide a fail-safe warning of a surprise attack.

- The head of Israeli military intelligence refuses to activate these taps in the critical days before the war because he is convinced there will be no war. His superiors, however, are led to believe the devices are working and that they show no sign of a pending enemy attack. Only when the Israeli public learns this four decades later does it have an explanation for the bizarre complacency of Israel's leadership in 1973 as Arab armies mass on its borders while Israel's reserves remain unmobilized.

Happened again Oct. 7, 2023!

- We gain for the first time an insight into Israel's thinking on the nuclear option. As the army reels, Defense Minister Moshe Dayan seeks to prepare a nuclear "demonstration," presumably over the desert, to warn off the Arab armies. Prime Minister Golda Meir rules it out.

- On the fifth day of the war, Chief of Staff David Elazar concludes that Israel cannot win the war because of its heavy losses and its misreading of the Arab armies. He asks the government to seek a cease-fire. "No one knows how weak we are," he says. When Secretary of State Henry Kissinger is told of this, "he almost tore his hair out," according to the Israeli official who briefs him. "This means you lost the war, don't you understand this," exclaims Kissinger.

- Jordan's King Hussein, who had tried to warn Mrs. Meir of the planned Arab attack, is pressured by Arab leaders to send a tank brigade to Syria's assistance. He sends a message to Mrs. Meir asking Israel "to refrain from attacking this unit, if at all possible." In the end, combat is unavoidable but Israel pulls its punch.

- The Israeli command decides on a high-risk crossing of the Suez Canal in order to pressure Egypt into a cease-fire. We see how, amid the chaos of the battlefield, the army succeeds in pushing two armored divisions across the waterway at night through the heart of the Egyptian army. As it regains its psychological balance, Israel no longer seeks a cease-fire, but victory. Division commander Ariel Sharon spearheads the bold operation but his constant challenging of orders comes close to bringing his dismissal. We track the improvisations that lead to Israel's stunning reversal of fortune on the battlefield.

PREFACE

ON YOM KIPPUR AFTERNOON 1973, the Israeli army was staggered by a surprise attack on two fronts with its reserve forces—two-thirds of its strength—still unmobilized. As the front lines in Sinai and on the Golan Heights gave way before massive attacks, the nation was gripped by existential fear. When fighting ended less than three weeks later, however, Israeli tanks were threatening Cairo and Damascus. It was a turnabout of epic dimensions but Israel emerged from the war chastened rather than triumphant.

I covered the war as a reporter. When I reached the Golan Heights on the fifth day, the battlefield was eerily quiet. A vastly outnumbered Israeli force had just stopped a Syrian attack by close to one thousand tanks. A counterattack was to have begun this day but exhausted crewmen were falling asleep whenever their tanks stopped moving.

I would learn much of this only twenty years later when I wrote a magazine article on the battle for *The Jerusalem Post*. Although I thought myself well informed about the war, I discovered that what I knew were only disconnected episodes in a fuzzy matrix. In writing this book, I spent five years trying to understand the war as a coherent narrative in which everything connects. The research included interviews with more than 130 participants, from generals to tank gunners, and study of written sources. The deeper I got into it, the more fascinating it became.

I am indebted to Prof. Howard Sachar of George Washington University for his initiative in introducing me to my publisher. Particular thanks to Gen. (Ret.) Amnon Reshef, whose brigade was involved in the fiercest battles of the war, for making available his unit's war diary and for granting five long interviews. Also to American Gen. Donn A. Starry, who interviewed Israeli military leaders extensively after the war, for the insights he offered me in Washington. My thanks as well to the Israeli Armored Corps Center at Latrun for making available unit histories and to the Israeli Defense Forces Archives.

For all who lived through the war on either side, soldiers or civilians, the Yom Kippur War—or the October War, as Arabs know it—remains one of the defining moments of their lives. It is a defining moment too in the history of the region. Its reverberations are with us yet.

The
YOM KIPPUR WAR

The Suez Front

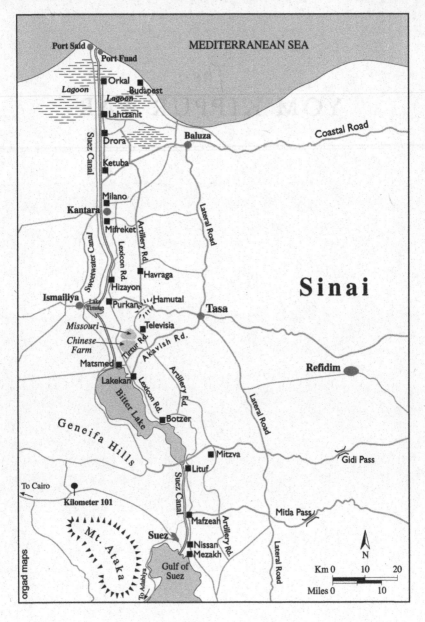

PROLOGUE

A MILITARY SATELLITE beaming images of the Middle East to earth late on the afternoon of October 5, 1973, would have shown a perplexing picture.

On the west bank of the Suez Canal, five Egyptian divisions—100,000 soldiers, 2,200 tanks, and 1,150 artillery pieces—were drawn up in full battle array. Bridging equipment and rubber boats positioned near the water's edge offered clear evidence of intent.

On the Israeli side, a few hundred men could be counted in strongpoints lining the canal. The Israelis were able to see the preparations for a crossing on the Egyptian bank but there was no sign that it troubled them even though they had fewer than 100 tanks and only 44 artillery pieces along the entire one-hundred-mile Suez front.

The satellite photos of the Golan Heights would have been even more puzzling. Here too five Arab divisions on maximum war footing confronted an absurdly thin Israeli defense line. If the Syrians chose to attack, there was no canal to slow them down. The disparity in tanks was 8 to 1 in Syria's favor, and far greater in infantry and artillery. On the Syrian side, secondary defense lines were carved into the landscape between the front and Damascus, forty miles to the east. On the Israeli side, there was no secondary defense line at all, as if the enormous disparity in forces was in Israel's favor, not the other way around.

In Israel itself this Friday afternoon, the satellite would likewise have detected no signs of alarm. There was hardly a person or moving vehicle to be seen on the country's streets. The setting sun would mark the onset of Yom Kippur and the country's three million Jews were at home preparing for this holiest of days. The only sign of unusual activity was at army headquarters in the center of Tel Aviv. Long after the lights went out in the rest of the building they remained on in the office of the chief of staff and in the military intelligence offices on the floor above.

In Jewish tradition, Yom Kippur is the climax of the Ten Days of Awe during which man makes accounts with his Maker. On this Yom Kippur, Israel's days of awe were only beginning.

I

FOOTPRINTS IN THE SAND

CAPT. MOTTI ASHKENAZI was not a man to accept a perceived wrong without protest. The outpost in Sinai that his unit
of reservists was taking over two weeks before Yom Kippur 1973 was
in an advanced state of neglect. Barbed wire fencing had sunk almost
entirely into the sand, trenches were collapsing, gun positions lacked
sandbags, and the ammunition supply was short. When the commander of the unit he was relieving asked him to sign the standard
form acknowledging receipt of the outpost in good condition, Ashkenazi balked. Without this formality, the unit being relieved could not
depart. When Ashkenazi refused an order from his own battalion commander to sign, the exasperated commander signed the form himself.

The battalion was part of the Jerusalem Brigade, which had never
before been assigned to a tour of duty on the Suez Canal. Unlike
the combat units that were normally assigned to the forts of the so-
called Bar-Lev Line, the Jerusalem Brigade was a second-line unit
which included men well into their thirties. Some were immigrants
who had received only a truncated form of basic training. A sprinkling
of younger reservists with combat experience stiffened the ranks and
officers too were generally veterans of combat units.

The assignment of such a unit to the Bar-Lev Line, once considered
hazardous duty, reflected the relaxed situation on the Egyptian front.
It was six years since Israel had reached the canal in the Six Day War
and three years since the intense skirmishing across the waterway—
the so-called War of Attrition—had ended.

The reservists grumbled as usual upon receiving their annual
call-up notices for a month's duty, particularly since their tour was
beginning on the eve of Rosh Hashana, the Jewish New Year, and

would last through Yom Kippur and the subsequent Sukkot holiday. However, by the time they boarded the buses that would take them to Sinai, many had reconciled themselves to a month of camaraderie, far from the routine of work and home. The men brought books and board games, finjans for brewing coffee, even fishing rods. Ashkenazi, a thirty-two-year-old doctoral student in philosophy at Hebrew University in Jerusalem, took along his four-month-old German shepherd, Peng, because he had nowhere to leave him.

Unlike the other Bar-Lev forts, which were built along the canal bank, Ashkenazi's outpost, code-named Budapest, was ten miles east of the canal on a narrow sand spit between the Mediterranean and a shallow lagoon. The outpost's purpose was to guard against an Egyptian thrust along the sand spit toward the coastal road leading to Israel. Budapest was the largest of the Bar-Lev Line fortifications, incorporating an artillery battery and a naval signals unit which maintained contact with vessels patrolling off the coast.

Toward evening on the day of his arrival, Ashkenazi, a deputy company commander, climbed the fort's observation tower and looked west along the sand spit. This northwest corner of Sinai was the only part of the Sinai Peninsula Israel had not gotten around to capturing in the 1967 war. Ashkenazi could make out a string of Egyptian outposts stretching toward Port Fuad, which, together with Port Said, straddled the northern entrance to the Suez Canal. The outpost closest to him was only a mile away. Since the canal did not separate them, the only thing that could inhibit an Egyptian raid was a minefield that Budapest's previous commander had pointed out to him during their tour that morning.

As Ashkenazi watched, a pack of wild dogs emerged from the Egyptian lines and trotted down the sands in his direction. They appeared to be heading toward Budapest's garbage dump at the western edge of the position. As they approached the minefield, Ashkenazi braced for explosions. But the dogs passed through unharmed. Tides washing over the sands had apparently dislodged or neutralized the mines. Ashkenazi decided to contact battalion headquarters in the morning to request additional fencing and sandbags.

Maj. Meir Weisel, an affable kibbutznik, was the most senior company commander in the battalion which moved into the Bar-Lev Line. In previous tours of reserve duty, his unit had clashed with Palestinian guerrillas along the Jordan River and taken casualties. "This time," a Jerusalem Brigade officer had told him when he reported for duty a few days before, "I'm sending you to the canal and you can rest." His company took over four forts in the canal's central sector. He positioned himself in Fort Purkan, opposite the city of Ismailiya on the Egyptian-held bank. The officer whom he replaced pointed out a villa across the canal that he said had belonged to the parents of Israeli foreign minister Abba Eban's wife, Suzie, who was from a prominent Egyptian Jewish family. It was not clear who lived there now but someone watered the plants every day. "As long as you see the gardener working there," said the officer, "everything is okay."

The limited forces Israel deployed on both the Syrian and Egyptian fronts opposite vastly larger enemy armies reflected a self-assurance stemming from the country's stunning victory in the Six Day War. Israel believed it had attained a military superiority that no Arab nation or combination of nations could challenge. The euphoria that followed that lightning victory in 1967 over the Egyptian, Syrian, and Jordanian armies gave Israel a sense of manifest destiny similar to that which impelled the United States westward in the nineteenth century. The Six Day War had been launched from within Israel's narrow borders that Eban had termed "Auschwitz borders," an allusion to their vulnerability. The post–Six Day War cease-fire lines for the first time provided Israel strategic depth.

Israel had twice as many tanks and warplanes in 1973 as it had in the Six Day War. Its largest armor formations were no longer brigades with a hundred tanks but divisions with three hundred. Veteran armor officers permitted themselves to fantasize commanding a division deploying into battle—two brigades forward, one to the rear, as they swept into the attack.

The armies of Egypt and Syria had grown more than Israel's in absolute numbers but the overall ratio in the Arab favor remained 3 to 1. Given the proven fighting ability of the Israel Defense Forces (IDF), this ratio was considered acceptable in Israel. The General Staff, in fact, was preparing to reduce the thirty-six months of service required of its conscript soldiers by three months. Convinced that it could hold its own against an Arab world thirty times its size, Israel was waiting for the Arabs to formally recognize the Jewish state and agree to new borders.

The Arab world, however, refused to accept the humiliation of

1967. In the War of Attrition launched by Egypt in March 1969, hundreds of Israeli soldiers died in massive artillery bombardments. Deep penetration raids by Israeli warplanes and commandos forced Cairo to accept a cease-fire in August 1970. Since then, the Suez front had remained quiet. On the Syrian front, there were periodic exchanges of fire—"battle days," Israel termed them—but no serious challenge to Israel's occupation of the Golan Heights.

The seeming docility of the Arabs encouraged a sense of invulnerability. In August 1973, Defense Minister Moshe Dayan, in a speech to army officers, said that Israel's strength was a reflection not only of its increasing military potential but of inherent Arab weakness. "It is a weakness that derives from factors that I don't believe will change quickly: the low level of their soldiers in education, technology, and integrity; and inter-Arab divisiveness which is papered over from time to time but superficially and for short spans."

A Mossad official, Reuven Merhav, who had been posted abroad immediately after the Six Day War, returned home five years later to find the country transformed. Israel was not just self-assured, he found, but self-satisfied, awash in a good life that seemed as if it would go on forever. Government and military officials traveled now in large cars and wrote off business lunches to expenses, a new practice. Arabs from the West Bank and Gaza Strip provided the working hands the fast-growing nation needed but were politically invisible. The sense of physical expanse was startling to someone accustomed to the claustrophobia of pre–Six Day War Israel. The border was no longer fifteen minutes from Tel Aviv or on the edge of Jerusalem but out of sight and almost out of mind—on the Jordan River, the Suez Canal, the Golan. People went down to Sinai now not to wage war but to holiday on its superb beaches.

The army had grown not just physically but in its prominence in national life. There was now a layer of brigadier generals, a newly created rank required by the army's expansion. The Mossad officer sensed arrogance in high places. Some generals ordered their offices redone to reflect their new status, some gave parties with army entertainment troupes singing in the background. All of this was foreign to the spartan ways Merhav had known as distinguishing features of Israeli public life only five years before. An attitude of disdain for Arab military capability had etched itself insidiously into the national psyche. The official was as yet unaware of the extent to which this disdain had led to distortions in the professional mind-set of the armed forces.

Sitting in a downtown Jerusalem café a few months before the war, Motti Ashkenazi told a friend that war was inevitable unless Israel accepted Egypt's demand that it pull back from the canal in order to permit the waterway to be reopened. Now, in command of Budapest, he took his own warning seriously. After two days of badgering battalion headquarters, he was informed that his request for sandbags and barbed wire concertinas was being met. The supply vehicle that arrived carried only a fraction of what he had asked for. Nevertheless, he was able to fortify the area around the fort's gate and the vulnerable approach from the beach.

A week before Yom Kippur, Ashkenazi was in a half-track making a routine morning patrol eastward along the sand spit toward his rear base when he saw fresh footprints in the sand on both sides of the road. Whoever made them seemed to have circled the area, as if examining the lay of the land. The road between Budapest and rear headquarters was closed off every night because it was vulnerable to commando landings from the sea. If anyone came down the road by day, Budapest was supposed to be informed beforehand, but there had been no such notification. The footprints, thought Ashkenazi, could have been left by Egyptian scouts landing from the sea, on one side of the road, or coming on foot through the lagoon, on the other side. He radioed headquarters and a vehicle with two Bedouin trackers arrived. They examined the footprints and concluded that they had been made by standard Israeli army boots.

"If I were an Egyptian scout, I would use that kind of boot," said Ashkenazi.

The trackers laughed. "Do you think they're that clever?"

"Why not?" asked Ashkenazi.

Twice more in the coming days he would find footprints along the route.

2

THE MAN
IN THE PEASANT ROBE

CIVILIAN CLOTHING DID LITTLE to mask the military bearing of the six men who descended from the Soviet passenger ship which docked in Alexandria on its regular run from the Syrian port of Latakia. Lt. Gen. Saad el Shazly, chief of staff of the Egyptian army, recognized his Syrian colleagues out of uniform as they came through customs with their false passports, trying to look like tourists. Shazly, in civilian clothing himself, escorted them to the Officer's Club and left them to settle in there. Toward evening, the Syrians were driven to a former palace serving as Egyptian naval headquarters. Eight Egyptian generals joined them, including War Minister Ahmed Ismail. The Syrians included Defense Minister Mustafa Tlass and Chief of Staff Gen. Yusuf Shakoor. In intensive meetings over the coming two days in late August 1973, the officers coordinated plans for a surprise, two-front attack on Israel. When they rose, all was settled except the timing of D-day. This would be left to the leaders of the two countries.

The humiliation of the Six Day War had cast its debilitating shadow over Egyptian president Anwar el-Sadat ever since he assumed office in October 1970. The largely static War of Attrition undertaken by his predecessor, Gamal Abdel Nasser, had not budged Israel from the Suez Canal. Nor had diplomatic efforts by the international community. Israel insisted on achieving border changes in direct negotiations with the Arab countries. The Arabs refused to recognize Israel as a legitimate state, let alone grant it border changes at their expense.

Prime Minister Golda Meir, confident that Israel's geopolitical situation had never been better, was content to wait for a change in the Arab position. She rejected Defense Minister Moshe Dayan's suggestion in December 1970 that Israel pull back twenty miles from the canal in order to enable its reopening and thereby reduce Egyptian motivation for going to war. Two months later, Sadat reshaped Dayan's proposal, without mentioning him, and adopted it as his own in an address to the Egyptian National Assembly. Unlike Dayan, the Egyptian leader saw a partial Israeli pullback as catalyzing, not indefinitely delaying, a final withdrawal.

Sadat astonished his audience by declaring his readiness to achieve a peace agreement with Israel, the first time an Arab leader had publicly suggested that possibility. But Israel, said Sadat, would have to commit itself to subsequent withdrawal from all of Sinai and from the other territories captured in the Six Day War—the West Bank, the Gaza Strip, the Golan Heights, and East Jerusalem. The Palestinian refugee question must be resolved as well. Dire as were Egypt's straits, economically and strategically, Sadat was not bidding for a separate settlement with Israel.

U.S. secretary of state William Rogers attempted to persuade Israel to agree to a limited pullback but found it unyielding. After a fruitless trip to Jerusalem, his assistant, Joseph Sisco, paid a courtesy call on the prime minister and handed her a bouquet of flowers before leaving for the airport. "Joe, you're saying it with flowers," Mrs. Meir said lightheartedly. "It won't do you any good."

Israel was determined not to return to the prewar borders, particularly on the West Bank, which dominated Israel's narrow waist, or in Jerusalem. It was certainly not willing to negotiate the return of Palestinian refugees, which it saw leading to the demographic demise of the Jewish state. A week after the Six Day War, the Israeli government asked the United States to inform Egypt and Syria of its readiness to evacuate Sinai and the Golan, except for minor border modifications, in return for peace treaties. There was no response from the two countries and an Arab summit in Khartoum two months later agreed unanimously on no peace with Israel, no recognition of Israel, and no negotiations with Israel. The following month, the Israeli government rescinded its offer. A chance for peace so long ago...

The international community made valiant attempts at a solution. In reply to a questionnaire submitted by United Nations envoy Gunnar Jarring in February 1971, Egypt declared its readiness to live in peace with Israel if it returned to the prewar border. In a parallel questionnaire submitted to Jerusalem, the reverse question was put—in return for peace, would Israel evacuate all Sinai? The reply was negative. Israel was prepared to withdraw to "mutually determined boundaries," not the prewar boundaries. Any peace achieved by pulling back to the vulnerable prewar borders, said Dayan, would be short-lived because it would make another war too tempting for the Arabs. "If we really want to honor all the sovereign rights of the past and all the desires of every Arab we won't be able to have a Jewish state here," he said. The possibility of an interim settlement in Sinai had sunk into the desert sands.

In Israel's view, it had twice in one generation—in 1948 and 1967—been forced into wars of survival by Arab states which wished to destroy it. It believed it had the moral right, the strategic need, and the military strength to demand border changes. The Arabs, for their part, regarded Israel as a usurper of Arab land. Sadat was willing to pay for Israel's withdrawal by offering it a sort of peace—one, he would later make clear, that did not include an exchange of ambassadors or normalized relations; in effect, a nonbelligerency pact. But he would not pay with territory.

Whether patient diplomacy could have won an Egyptian-Israeli peace agreement would remain a matter of conjecture, although the possibility seems in retrospect unlikely. The person who knew Sadat best, his wife, Jehan, would tell an Israeli newspaper in 1987 that peace could not have been achieved without the two countries first passing through the cauldron of war. "Sadat needed one more war in order to win and enter into negotiations from a position of equality," she said. Henry Kissinger would testify that Sadat himself told him years later that if the U.S. had been able in 1973 to broker an Israeli pullback to the prewar border without Egypt being required to sign a peace treaty, he, Sadat, would have accepted it, but only reluctantly, because it would not have restored Egyptian pride.

Sadat was regarded when he took office as a gray, interim figure filling Nasser's shoes until some more charismatic personality took power. He would metamorphose into one of the most imaginative and daring national leaders of the twentieth century. He reveled in his peasant origins and was imbued with a mystic view of himself as the embodiment of Egypt's destiny. As president, Sadat would often return to the poor Nile Delta village where he was born, Mit Abulkum, to meditate. His mother was the daughter of a freed African slave, an origin reflected in his dark complexion. Before pursuing a military career, he had attempted to become an actor. He failed to make it but the political stage would afford him far greater scope for his expansive sense of drama than any theater. His wardrobe attested to the variety of roles he pursued with flair; well-tailored Italian suits, medal-bedecked uniforms—of an admiral as well as a general—and peasant robes. In what seemed to some as ostentatious asceticism, he would accord interviews to visiting journalists as he sat on the ground under a tree in Mit Abul-kum dressed in a simple gallabiya. However, the sustenance he received from this link to his roots and from his Islamic faith was clearly genuine.

Sadat's desire as a young man to see an end to British hegemony in Egypt was accompanied by admiration for national leaders who fought for the liberation of their people. In this category he placed not only the likes of Mahatma Gandhi and Kemal Ataturk but Adolf Hitler. He held him in esteem as a charismatic leader who rebuilt a shattered nation. Sadat abandoned this assessment, at least publicly, only after he became president. From that point on, he used the term Nazi as a pejorative, usually directing it at Israel.

Although a visionary, Sadat well understood the hard rules of autocracy. Within seven months of assuming the presidency he had arrested his main political opponents and stabilized his regime. His declared readiness to make peace with the Jewish state, albeit on terms Israel was unwilling to accept, was a courageous departure from Arab political rhetoric.

With the failure of his call for a partial Israeli withdrawal, Sadat began preparing for war. His militant statements coupled with inaction rendered him a quasi-comic figure at home and abroad to many. Halfway through 1971 he declared it to be "a year of decision." But the year ended without decision. So did the following year. "We had already lost credibility in the eyes of the whole world and we had begun to lose faith in ourselves," Sadat would acknowledge in a television interview in 1974.

His declared readiness to sacrifice a million soldiers in the battle to recover Sinai made little impression on the Israelis. His army, as they saw it, was not ready for war.

Egypt and Syria were major Cold War assets for the Soviet Union because they provided port facilities, landing rights for reconnaissance planes, and bases for electronic monitoring stations. These facilities were needed by Moscow to keep track of the American Sixth Fleet, whose nuclear missiles were capable of striking the Soviet Union from the Mediterranean. Moscow had lost its previous foothold in the area when communist Albania shifted its allegiance to Red China. The Soviets were happy to cement relations with Egypt and Syria by selling them weapons for hard currency. Some fifteen thousand Soviet military experts were shaping the Egyptian armed forces into a modern army. A similar corps of advisers was attached to the Syrian army.

The Soviets attempted to discourage the Arabs from a military confrontation with Israel that would endanger Moscow's warming relations with Washington. Moscow refused to provide certain offensive weapons systems that Egypt demanded, such as long-range fighter-bombers. Transparent Soviet disdain for the fighting ability of the Egyptians strained relations. On one occasion, Marshal Andrei Grechko, the Soviet defense minister, lectured Sadat on the three prerequisites for a successful war—arms, training, and the will to fight. "The first two you have," said Grechko.

The closer that détente brought the superpowers together, the more despondent Sadat grew. The communiqué that followed the first summit meeting between President Richard Nixon and Chairman Leonid Brezhnev in Moscow in May 1972 was termed by the Egyptian leader "a violent shock." Its advocacy of military relaxation in the Middle East meant to him perpetuation of Israeli occupation of Arab land. The Soviets had even agreed to the possibility of border changes.

It took seven weeks before Soviet ambassador to Cairo Vladimir Vinogradov presented the Egyptian leader a report from the Kremlin on the Nixon-Brezhnev summit and its implications for Egypt. Sadat sat on a couch, he would later recount, leaning his head against his walking stick as the ambassador spoke. The message Vinogradov read out made no mention of Egyptian arms requests and ended by noting that Egypt was not yet ready for war. Sadat's reply was terse. He was herewith expelling all Soviet advisers from Egypt. Looking at his watch, he turned to an aide. "What is the date? I can't see without my glasses." Upon being told it was July 8, he turned to Vinogradov and said, "All right then, I'm giving you ten days. The old way of doing business between Egypt and the Soviet Union is at an end."

Sadat's action was no spur-of-the-moment whim. The outcome of the summit had made it clear to him that he could not rely on the Soviets for support in regaining Sinai. His stunning move—the kind of grand political theater that would become his hallmark—was received with dismay in Moscow and delight in Israel, where it was taken as a guarantee that Egypt would not be going to war in the foreseeable future. In Washington too, Sadat was seen as having left himself with no military option.

To one astute observer in Jerusalem, however, the expulsion did not mean the shelving of Sadat's war option but its possible activation. Gideon Rafael, director-general of the Foreign Ministry, after mulling over the expulsion for a couple of days, wrote a memo to his colleagues. It suggested that Sadat's move was intended to invite the Americans into the game in the hope that they would pressure Israel back to the international border. If this failed, wrote Rafael, Sadat intended to go to war and in that case the massive presence of Soviet advisers was an impediment, given Moscow's known opposition to Egyptian military adventures. Sadat's move, argued Rafael, meant that he was preparing both political and military options. Although not taken seriously in Jerusalem, Rafael's analysis was a precise reading of Sadat's intentions.

It was more than half a year before there was a significant response to Sadat's move from Washington, with which Cairo had severed relations after the Six Day War. In February 1973, Sadat's national security adviser, Hafez Ismail, was invited to the U.S. to confer with his American counterpart, Henry Kissinger. Meeting secretly for two days on a businessman's estate borrowed for the occasion, Ismail spelled out Egypt's position. His country was willing to make peace with Israel, he said, but the process must begin with a declaration by Israel that it would return to its prewar borders on all fronts.

It was Kissinger's impression that the Egyptians were leaving an opening for border adjustments on the West Bank and even for an Israeli presence along the Jordan River, aimed at preventing any Arab army from linking up with the West Bank. Once Israel declared its readiness for a pullback, said Ismail, demilitarized zones would be created on both sides of the Israeli-Egyptian border. Israeli vessels would be permitted to use the Suez Canal and Egypt would end its boycott of companies trading with Israel. There would, however, not be diplomatic relations or open borders. This would have to await an Israeli settlement with Syria—including full withdrawal from the Golan Heights—Jordan, and the Palestinians. Arab control of East Jerusalem and the Temple Mount was nonnegotiable.

Kissinger was skeptical about Israel agreeing to these terms even though they were far better than anything any Arab state had yet offered. Golda Meir was by now willing to discuss a partial Israeli pullback in Sinai but it was clear that Israel would insist on border changes in any final settlement. In the view of the Israeli government—at least Mrs. Meir's "kitchen cabinet," where policy was shaped—the Arabs had no military option and they would eventually have to accept the implications of that situation.

The message Ismail carried back to Sadat was that the U.S. could do nothing to change the situation. "My advice to Sadat is to be realistic," Kissinger had said, according to the report submitted by Ismail. "The fact is that you have been defeated so don't ask for a victor's spoils. Either you can change the facts, and consequently our perceptions will naturally change with regard to a solution, or you can't change the facts, in which case solutions other than the ones you are offering will have to be found. I hope that what I am saying is clear. I'm certainly not asking Sadat to change the military situation. If he tries that, Israel will win once again and more so than in 1967. In such a situation, it would be very difficult for us to do anything."

Sadat did not dispute this view; in fact, he shared it, except for the inevitability of another Arab defeat. "It was impossible," he would write in his memoirs, "for the United States or, indeed, any other power to make a move if we ourselves didn't take military action to break the deadlock."

This is what he was now preparing to do.

3

DOVECOTE

GOLDA MEIR WAS NOT in a position to judge Gen. David Elazar's military acumen but she was enough a judge of character to want him as her next chief of staff. He was, she felt, a resolute man who didn't compromise easily. He was also modest and easy to talk to. In addition, she would say, "he's a pleasure to look at."

Since the Six Day War, the military's annual intelligence assessment had deemed war unlikely as a near-term prospect. At Elazar's first meeting with the General Staff after taking up his post on January 1, 1971, he changed that. "The likelihood of war is strong," he said. Sadat had virtually no other option, Elazar believed, if he wished to get a political process started.

Israel had nothing to gain from another war, Elazar told the generals. Should it break out, the object would be to win swiftly, in order to reduce the impact on the economy, and decisively, to discourage the Arabs from trying it again.

The relevance of the Bar-Lev Line was one of the first subjects on Elazar's agenda. Built during the tenure of his predecessor, Gen. Haim Bar-Lev, its name conjured up an image of massive, interlocking fortifications like the Maginot Line. In fact, however, it was a string of small, isolated forts, each with garrisons of only twenty to thirty men. The igloo-like structures were surrounded by trenches and barbed wire. They had been built as protection from artillery fire during the War of Attrition. But they had come to be seen as having a defense role even though there were miles-wide gaps between the outposts. Some saw the Bar-Lev Line as a death trap—too thin to be a meaningful barrier, too thick to be an expendable tripwire.

Gen. Ariel Sharon, who became head of the Southern Command in 1970, proposed sealing the forts and maintaining Israel's presence in the Canal Zone with armored patrols and observation posts set well back from the waterline. A similar position was taken by Gen. Israel Tal, Elazar's deputy. The forts, he argued, should be evacuated the moment war began.

Elazar did not rest the defense of the canal area on the forts but on mobile tank forces. However, since the strongholds already existed and could interfere with an Egyptian crossing, he saw no point in dismantling them. They also provided ongoing observation of the Egyptian lines. In addition, he said, flying the Israeli flag on the canal was an important political statement. "Even if I thought that the strongholds were worthless from the military point of view, I would be in a quandary over whether to abandon them from the political standpoint. When I factor in that they do help to secure the line and provide a little intelligence I'm no longer faced with a dilemma." He had no objection, he said, to thinning out the line. Sharon interpreted "thinning out" in his own fashion. By the time he left Southern Command in the summer of 1973, fourteen of the thirty forts had been shut down. But the Israeli defense of the Canal Zone was still tied to this string of outposts which were left over from another kind of war. If the Egyptians were to stage a major crossing, Israeli tanks would have to be committed to defending or rescuing the garrisons along the canal before they could engage in mobile warfare.

The debate over the Bar-Lev Line reflected the paradox of Israeli military planning. Because of Israel's narrow boundaries, it was basic IDF doctrine before the Six Day War that in the event of war the fighting must be carried swiftly onto enemy territory. That war had pushed the cease-fire line into Sinai, 150 miles from Israel's border, but doctrine had not been changed to reflect this fact. Israel's objective in the event of an Arab attack was "to prevent the enemy from achieving any gain" in order to discourage future attempts. This was interpreted to mean that the Egyptians must be prevented from gaining a foothold on the Israeli-held Sinai bank.

But by drawing a political line in the sand at the farthest edge of Sinai, Israel was waiving the major military asset it had won in the Six Day War—strategic depth. With a broad desert to fall back into, the "no enemy gain" formula meant that the Israeli forces on the canal would be fighting with the same back-to-the-wall stubbornness as if defending Israel's heartland. It made eminent sense to instead draw the Egyptians into the desert in a war of maneuver, at which the Israeli armored corps excelled and the Egyptian army didn't.

. . .

Elazar was not indifferent to the merits of such a move. At a meeting of the General Staff in the spring of 1972, he permitted himself to fantasize. "If I know that they're going to attack in the morning, we could say—as an intellectual exercise—that under certain circumstances thirty kilometers in Sinai could be completely evacuated. We let them move five divisions into Sinai, and then we slam the door on them. Such a battle implies a number of political risks but it's a beauty and I'm sure it would make it into the military history books. We have no interest in war but if one breaks out, it's an historic opportunity to deal a crushing military and political blow that would last for a very long time to come." It was, however, merely a passing reverie. Neither in Sinai nor on the Golan, Elazar stressed, would there be tactical withdrawals. "We've got to kill them on the canal."

Intelligence believed that if fighting resumed it would likely be a renewed war of attrition consisting of artillery barrages and small-scale cross-canal raids. Another possible scenario was an Egyptian attempt to seize a limited foothold on the Sinai bank and hold it until a cease-fire was imposed.

To deal with these possibilities, the IDF drew up a defense plan code-named Dovecote. It rested on the three hundred tanks of the Sinai Division—the only armored division of the standing army—and on the air force. So confident was the Israeli command of coping with an Egyptian attack that the plan dealt only sketchily with the defensive battle itself and focused instead on a swift counterattack across the canal.

In the event that the Egyptians attempted a full-scale crossing with five divisions, a broader plan had been drawn up. Code-named Sela (Rock), it called for the mobilization of two reserve armored divisions before the war started on the basis of intelligence warnings, which were believed certain to come. Like Dovecote, Sela dealt only in passing with the actual defensive phase, as if the swift destruction of Egyptian forces crossing the canal was too straightforward to require elaborate planning. It left the task of dealing with the Egyptian incursion, in fact, to the Sinai Division and the air force, as in Dovecote, with reserve units helping out if needed. The reserve divisions focused instead on their crossing of the canal, a more far-reaching counterattack than called for in Dovecote.

In the highly unlikely event that intelligence did not provide sufficient warning for the reserve divisions to be mobilized before Egypt attacked, the Sinai Division was nevertheless expected to employ Dovecote to hold the Egyptian army off, with the assistance of the air force, upon which the bulk of the burden would fall until the reserves arrived. It was like expecting a napkin to serve as a tablecloth in a pinch. Only contempt for the fighting ability of the Egyptians could permit such thinking—one division holding off five divisions along a hundred-mile-long front. Given that only one of the Sinai Division's three brigades was normally manning the front line in the Canal Zone because of rotation and training exercises, a surprise attack would make the odds not 5 to 1 in Egypt's favor but 15 to 1. The planners did not provide a flexible alternative that would permit the defenders to fall back in a delaying action. The Sinai Division and the air force would in all circumstances stop the Egyptians on the canal. Despite the alarming toll that Soviet-made antiaircraft missiles had taken on Israeli aircraft in the War of Attrition, no thought was given to the possibility that the air force might find itself neutralized over the canal.

In a war game staged by Southern Command in August 1972, four Egyptian divisions were depicted crossing the canal, with only a forty-eight-hour warning provided by intelligence. In the exercise, the Sinai Division wiped out the Egyptian bridgehead in half a day. On the third day, the first Israeli reserve division reached the front and crossed the canal. The forty-eight-hour warning was regarded by participants as absurdly short notice given the known quality of military intelligence—which unofficially promised a warning of five or six days before an enemy attack. Sharon said that the exercise proved that the Sinai Division could meet any Egyptian threat. This confidence was shared by policymakers normally given to caution. Considering the way the Arab armies had fallen apart only six years before, it was hard to imagine otherwise. The notion that the Egyptians might stage a full-scale crossing with no warning at all was too far-fetched to waste time on in war games.

One Israeli officer thought it possible to thwart an Egyptian crossing before it even reached the Israeli side of the canal. Col. David Lascov headed a secret unit which developed special weapons and devices. At sixty-six, Lascov was the oldest Israeli officer on active duty. (He would still be on active duty in his eighties.) Born in Siberia and trained in architecture, his Zionist activities made him a target for the Soviet secret police. He fled via China to Haifa in the 1930s, served in the British army in the Second World War, and was an early recruit to the Israel Defense Forces. Over the years, he had come up with numerous ingenious solutions to operational problems. It occurred to him now that if the Egyptians attempted to cross the canal, Israel might deliver a blow comparable to that inflicted on Pharaoh's army when it tried to follow the Israelites through the parted waters of the Red Sea more than three thousand years before. Lascov intended to go the Almighty one better by setting the waters afire. It was a solution of biblical resonance but achievable with simple engineering.

Large fuel tanks were installed below ground at two of the canal-side fortifications, with pipes extended to the canal edge. From within the fort, the commander could release the fuel and ignite it with an electric spark. The system, dubbed Dusky Light, was tested in February 1971 at one of the forts. The flames and dense cloud of black smoke that covered the placid canal waters succeeded in alarming the Egyptians. The Israeli command was less impressed. The fire did not cover a large area and burned itself out too quickly. In addition, considerable maintenance problems would develop with the system. Sharon, as front commander, preferred to invest the funds allocated to Dusky Light in roads. Sixteen dummy installations were built—meant to be seen and serve as a deterrent. Gradually, the two real installations fell into neglect. But the Egyptians kept the threat firmly in mind.

Running parallel to the canal, about a mile inland, was a north–south road code-named Lexicon from which there was access to the canal-side forts. A second, thinner line of outposts was built on sand hills five to six miles east of the canal—the first high ground inside Sinai. These served as tank and artillery staging areas. In the event of an Egyptian attack, tanks would race from here to the canal-side forts. These outposts were linked to each other by a north–south artery called the Artillery Road. Fifteen miles farther east, another north–south road—known as the Lateral Road—was built to serve the rear area. The three north–south roads—roughly one, five, and twenty miles east of the canal and parallel to it—would be pivots around which future battles would unfold.

The post–Six Day War deployment on the canal and on the Golan Heights posed a challenge to military intelligence. Egypt and Syria had in the past kept the bulk of their armies well back from the borders. When Egypt began to move its divisions into Sinai before the Six Day War, Israel had ample time to mobilize and deploy. It lost this early warning buffer after the Six Day War since the Egyptian and Syrian armies were now drawn up in strength just opposite the Israeli lines.

The military attaché at the Israeli embassy in London perked up at the Arabic accent of the man on the telephone. The caller, identifying himself as an Egyptian, said he would like to meet with an Israeli intelligence officer at a neutral venue. The attaché said that a meeting could only be arranged in the embassy building. It was 1970, three years after the Six Day War, and there had been periodic calls since then from persons with Arabic accents professing to offer their services. Security considerations ruled out such meetings on non-Israeli turf. The caller said he could not come to the embassy but left his name and telephone number. The name meant nothing to the attaché.

He mentioned the conversation later to two visiting Mossad officers with whom he was being driven to the airport. Upon hearing the caller's name, they looked at each other and asked the driver to pull over. One of them took a taxi back to the embassy to call the number the man had left.

The Mossad officials knew Ashraf Marwan—the man who had called—to be no less than the son-in-law of Gamal Abdel Nasser, the Egyptian president who had died two months before. Under Nasser, Marwan worked in the Presidential Office, the nerve center of Egypt and of the Arab world. He had been kept on as a roving ambassador by Nasser's successor, Sadat, who saw the co-option of a member of Nasser's family helping to legitimize his own rule, which was being challenged by powerful political rivals. The Mossad kept a close eye on Egypt's ruling hierarchy and knew Marwan to be a political insider and a profligate spender, often short of cash. There had even been thoughts of trying to recruit him but they had not yet stretched that far into the heart of the Egyptian establishment.

Receiving the callback, Marwan was invited to a meeting in the lobby of a luxury hotel in central London. The Mossad officer who had called him, ostensibly reading a newspaper, sat close to the lobby entrance while along the street security men discreetly positioned themselves against surprises. At the appointed hour, a handsome, dark-complexioned young man carrying an attaché case entered and looked about him. The Mossad officer glanced at a photograph in a four-year-old Cairo daily concealed between the pages of his newspaper. It showed President Nasser beaming at his daughter in wedding finery and her young groom. The Mossad officer looked again at the new arrival, then nodded at a man with European features sitting across the lobby. The man, the deputy Mossad station chief in London, approached the Egyptian. "Mr. Marwan, good to meet you," he said in fluent Arabic. "My name is Alex."

The Israeli escorted Marwan to a room in the hotel that had been hastily reserved. After a brief chat, Marwan opened his attaché case and handed over a sheaf of documents. The Israelis had expected him at this initial meeting to bring up the subject of payment, but he did not. He wanted Mossad officers to first study the documents and grasp the nature of the information he was in a position to offer. (When compensation was eventually broached, the first thing the twenty-five-year-old asked for was a red Peugeot convertible.) The Mossad had not been sure what information Marwan had access to—military secrets, state secrets, information on other Arab regimes, perhaps the status of arms requests from the Soviet Union. A quick perusal of the documents "Alex" brought back from their first encounter showed that Marwan had access to all these areas, and more. The Israelis were stunned. They had never seen a high-level trove like this.

"This kind of material, from this kind of source," the Mossad officer who had contacted Marwan told colleagues, "is something that happens once in a thousand years."

In the coming months, Mossad officials would continue to be astonished at the flow of top secret documents that followed, including protocols of Egyptian cabinet meetings and meetings of the Egyptian army General Staff. Marwan even supplied a transcript of Sadat's meeting in Moscow with Soviet leader Leonid Brezhnev in which Egypt's arms requests were discussed. The document showed the skepticism of Soviet leaders about Egypt's ability to win a war against Israel.

A foreign "walk-in" offering his services as a spy inevitably raised suspicions that he might be a double agent, particularly if he was a citizen of the enemy country being spied upon. The Mossad would carry out intensive and repeated investigations into that possibility but find nothing to arouse suspicion.

The head of the Egyptian desk at Israeli military intelligence, Lt. Col. Meir Meir, a seasoned investigator, was dispatched to London after Marwan's recruitment to take his measure. In an intensive three-hour session, the Egyptian answered most of Meir's detailed questions on the Egyptian armed forces. He promised to bring answers to the rest at their next meeting. Before they parted, the Israeli asked Marwan if he could also bring two documents—Egypt's battle plan for the coming war and the armed forces' Order of Battle, which spelled out its command structure, including units, deployment, and weaponry. When Meir next met him four months later, Marwan handed over the documents requested. Their details checked out with what Israeli intelligence already knew and filled in much of what it hadn't known. For Colonel Meir, there was no longer any doubt about Marwan's authenticity and his importance to Israel.

His motivation would remain unclear. But with his appearance, the inner political and military workings of Egypt had become for Israel an open book. It was to Marwan that Dayan referred years later when he said that Israel's prewar intelligence on Egypt's strategic thinking was based on solid information. "I can say with total certainty that any intelligence service, chief of staff and defense minister in the world, having received this information and known its origins, would have come to the same conclusion."

In October 1972, after returning to Israel from posting as military attaché in Washington, Gen. Eli Zeira was appointed head of military intelligence, known by its Hebrew acronym, AMAN. Zeira, a former paratroop brigade commander, had once served as Defense Minister Moshe Dayan's aide-de-camp and was said to be the general Dayan most respected. The self-assured officer was already being mooted as a coming chief of staff. In some circles, however, his appointment caused unease. After Zeira addressed a forum of senior officers in his new capacity, a brigade commander remarked to a fellow officer as they left the hall that he was troubled by Zeira's overweening self-confidence. The colonel said he would have preferred an intelligence chief who was less certain about things.

AMAN was the leader of Israel's intelligence community. It was responsible for formulating the "national intelligence estimate" which served not only the General Staff but the government in decision making. The Mossad was responsible for intelligence collection abroad but, for all its reputation, it deferred to AMAN on assessments of Arab capabilities and intentions.

To ensure early warning in the new circumstances, AMAN under

Zeira no longer relied on analysis of what the enemy was capable of doing—he was now capable of attacking on very short notice from his forward positions—but principally on analysis of what he *intended* to do.

This could normally be equated with a reading of entrails, particularly when dealing with autocratic regimes where decisions lie mainly with a single man. But Zeira's belief that he understood Anwar Sadat's thinking rested on more than his own analytical abilities. The intelligence chief had discovered when he assumed his post that the Mossad had a supersource in Cairo—Marwan—who had provided the key to Sadat's strategic thinking. The Egyptian leader was prepared to risk war but he would not do so before two conditions were met. He wanted from the Soviet Union fighter-bombers capable of neutralizing the Israeli Air Force by attacking its bases inside Israel—a replay in reverse of Israel's preemptive strike against Egyptian air bases in 1967 that won Israel its swift victory. He also wanted Scud missiles capable of hitting Tel Aviv in order to deter Israel from air strikes against the Egyptian heartland. Israeli intelligence knew from other sources that the Egyptians were indeed negotiating with the Soviets for long-range planes and Scuds. The Soviets had not yet supplied them.

Zeira had inherited "the concept," as this assessment came to be called, but he embraced it, particularly since it was reinforced by other sources. It was Sadat's concept, not his, and from an Egyptian point of view it made sense. Zeira assured the General Staff that whatever angry noises Egypt might make, it would not go to war until those two conditions were met. Syria, which was far weaker, would certainly not go to war without Egypt.

Half a year after Zeira took over the intelligence branch, his analytical abilities and nerves were put to the test. Unprecedented movement was detected of Egyptian forces to the canal front. Generally reliable intelligence assets reported Sadat's intention to go to war in mid-May. As the date approached, Cairo placed its army on alert and expeditionary forces arrived from Iraq, Algeria, and other Arab countries. Libya sent a squadron of Mirages capable of reaching Israeli air bases. The IDF went onto alert status—code-named Blue-White.

On May 8, Prime Minister Meir was taken to army headquarters for a briefing. If the Egyptians intended to go to war, she was told, Israel would know about it. "How will we know?" she asked. "By the preparations?" If the entire Egyptian army was planning to cross the canal, Zeira assured her, the IDF would know. There would be tours of the front by senior officers, redeployment of units, and other signs. Syria was unlikely to join in, he said, unless it felt that Israel was in difficulty after the battle with Egypt was already under way. The Syrians had no barrier like the Suez Canal separating their capital from the IDF and their air force had no chance against Israel's. Therefore they would be very cautious. In any event, the chances of an all-out war with Egypt, which alone might bring in the Syrians, were "very low," said Zeira.

Mrs. Meir's simplistic-sounding question was more to the point than she realized because Zeira's analysis was *not* determined by Egypt's preparations but by his understanding of Sadat's thinking. His analysis was supported by, perhaps inspired by, his gut feeling that Sadat would not go to war because he simply feared the consequences.

Elazar did not accept Zeira's "low probability" assessment. War was not a certainty but he ordered the General Staff to prepare as if it were. This included the shifting of tank bases closer to the fronts, speeding up the creation of new units, paving roads on the Golan for tanks, and readying equipment to bridge the Suez Canal. There was no mobilization of reserves except for a small number of specialists.

The head of the Mossad, Zvi Zamir, did not share Zeira's assessment either. He believed that Sadat was ready for war, regardless of "the concept." He did not go so far as to forecast war but he supported the precautions being taken. Dayan also believed war a reasonable option for Egypt since it would bring the international intervention which Sadat wanted. But weeks passed and war did not come.

Zeira emerged from the Blue-White episode with his reputation, and his self-confidence, greatly enhanced. With alarm bells going off all around him and the nation's fate at stake, he had coolly maintained throughout the crisis that the probability of war was "very low." Even senior analysts on his staff challenged his assessment but he stuck to it, unperturbed. It was AMAN's task, he would say, to keep the national blood pressure down and not sound alarms unnecessarily. Otherwise, the reserves would be mobilized every couple of months with devastating effect on the economy and on morale.

Appearing before the Knesset Foreign Affairs and Defense Committee in May, Zeira said that even in their current deployment, poised to spring, there were a number of steps the Egyptians and Syrians would have to take before setting their armies in motion. Israel would be able to detect these steps, he said. The pledge was based, at least in part, on a secret eavesdropping operation that only he and a handful of others were privy to.

Zeira's triumph was an indirect rebuke for Elazar. He risked being viewed as an alarmist if he again cried wolf. In future, he would think twice before challenging Zeira's evaluations.

Zeira had proven right but for the wrong reasons. Sadat had indeed been ready to go to war but Assad asked for a postponement in order to await armaments from the Soviet Union, particularly new T-62 tanks and SAM-6 missiles.

In the general relief at the end of the crisis, little notice was given to a report that came across the Egyptian desk at intelligence head-quarters. Only some of the bridging equipment and artillery that the Egyptians brought to the canal had been returned to rear bases. The remainder was being left in storage areas in the Canal Zone.

4

BADR

GENERAL ZEIRA'S READING of Egypt's strategy, which he would cling to confidently over the course of a year, was obsolete even before he adopted it. The very month Zeira took over AMAN, Anwar Sadat revealed to his senior commanders that he had abandoned the concept on which the Israeli assessment was based.

Meeting with the Supreme Council of the Armed Forces on October 24, 1972, the Egyptian president said that he intended to undertake military action without waiting any longer for long-range aircraft and Scud missiles. "We have to manage our affairs with whatever we have at hand," he said.

When he expelled the Soviet advisers in July, he had ordered his minister of war, Gen. Mohammed Ahmed Sadek, to have the army ready for war by mid-November. At the October meeting, Sadat asked Sadek for a report on the army's readiness. Sitting next to Sadat, the general leaned over in embarrassment to whisper that he had not passed the order on to most of the generals for fear that it would be leaked. Two days later, Sadat dismissed him. "He didn't want to fight," Sadat would write in his memoirs. Also dismissed were two generals and an admiral who expressed reservations at the meeting about embarking on war.

The war minister had argued that only the conquest of all Sinai and the Gaza Strip—which Egypt had controlled until the Six Day War—would achieve Egypt's objectives. That, however, was a formula for doing nothing since it was clearly beyond Egypt's capacity. Sadat believed that simply gaining a secure bridgehead in Sinai would be sufficient to spark international intervention that would force Israel to abandon captured Egyptian territory. Dramatizing the point, he told his generals: "Just give me ten centimeters on the east bank." To achieve his goal, it was no longer necessary to neutralize the Israeli Air Force by attacking its bases, a dubious prospect in any case. Soviet-made SAMs (surface-to-air missiles) on the canal's west bank, whose reach extended six miles across the canal into Sinai, would protect the bridgehead.

This approach had been urged by General Shazly, whom Sadat had named chief of staff a year earlier. A charismatic paratroop officer, Shazly was selected for the post over thirty more senior generals. His appointment reflected Sadat's determination to go to war. Shazly's personal flair and his readiness to "eat sand" in prolonged stays with his men in the field made him an appropriate choice for restoring the self-confidence lost by the army after the disaster of 1967. Cairo newspaper editor Mohammed Hassenein Heikal, a shrewd judge of men, would conclude that Shazly was no military genius but that his energy and attention to detail would lead the army to success. "He knew what he was doing in using his glamour to achieve his military ends, above all raising the army's morale for the task it faced."

General Sadek rejected Shazly's proposal for a limited foothold in Sinai on the grounds that an Israeli counterattack could pin Egyptian forces against the canal, the very image Elazar had conjured up. Eventually, he authorized Shazly to draw up a plan, with the assistance of Soviet advisers, for an attack to the Gidi and Mitla Passes, some forty miles east of the canal—a plan known as Granite 2.

Even this was regarded by Shazly as unrealistic since it would take the Egyptian forces beyond the SAM umbrella. He was finally authorized to draw up a still more limited plan. Named High Minarets, it envisioned an advance of only five or six miles eastward from the canal, a range covered by the SAM batteries. In the chief of staff's view, this was Egypt's only realistic offensive option.

In the Six Day War, as a division commander, Shazly had barely escaped the Israeli onslaught. He had seen the devastation inflicted on the retreating army by warplanes operating with impunity over the battlefield. He did not want to risk exposing the army again to an unfettered Israeli Air Force.

At the same time, Shazly did not accept that Egypt could not go to war without upgrading its air force. He expressed this view at a meeting of the Supreme Council of the Armed Forces attended by Sadat. "If we are going to base our planning upon an adequate air force, we will have to postpone the battle for years and years," he said. "In fact, I believe the gap between our air force and the enemy's will tend to widen rather than narrow. We therefore have no choice but to prepare for a battle under conditions of enemy air superiority. We can do it by challenging that superiority with SAMs."

The new war minister named by Sadat, Gen. Ahmed Ismail, was the last man in the Egyptian army Shazly would have chosen to serve with, let alone under. The two men were longtime foes because of a squabble originating in the Congo in 1960. Ismail, heading an Egyptian military mission to the Congolese army, tried to interfere with Shazly's command of an Egyptian contingent that was part of a U.N. peacekeeping force. Shazly had thrown a punch at Ismail, who outranked him, and the two men thereafter maintained an icy relationship. Shazly submitted his resignation in 1969 when Nasser appointed Ismail as war minister. It was only Nasser's personal intervention that persuaded Shazly, then head of special forces, to remain. Six months later Ismail was dismissed following an Israeli armored raid on the Red Sea coast that met no resistance. Sadat now recalled him as war minister, to general surprise.

Thrown together in a working relationship, Shazly and Ismail managed to suspend their mutual distaste. Shazly showed Ismail both the Granite 2 plan for reaching the passes and the limited High Minarets plan. The minister accepted Shazly's opinion that only the latter was feasible and told him to proceed with detailed planning. Thus, an entirely new Egyptian strategic concept began to take shape even as Israeli intelligence held confidently to the old. In time, the name of the plan would be changed to Badr, the site of the Prophet Mohammed's first military victory in AD 624.

Shazly's battle plan was completed by January 1973 but would continue to be refined over the coming months. Its outline was simple but in the myriad, interlocking details lay its strength.

Five Egyptian infantry divisions had been deployed along the canal since the 1967 war. Three divisions, occupying the northern part of the line, constituted the Second Army. The southern two divisions constituted the Third Army. It was a basic premise that a canal crossing would be made all along the hundred-mile canal. This would play Egypt's best hand—its abundant manpower—against Israel's worst—its limited manpower.

The Egyptian army had been extensively revamped since the debacle of 1967. The heavily politicized General Staff was purged and new commanders chosen on the basis of competence. In the armored corps, illiterates, who had made up a significant percentage of tank crews, were replaced. The armed forces now had large numbers of university and high school graduates who could no longer evade conscription. Intensive training with modern Soviet military equipment and the guidance of thousands of Soviet advisers honed the army's skills.

Before coming to grips with the Israelis, the Egyptians would have to overcome the obstacle of the canal itself. Some 160 yards wide, it was subject to tides which rose and fell up to six feet. From the canal edge on the Israeli side loomed a steep sand barrier sixty feet high, forming the outer edge of the Bar-Lev Line.

The assault crossing would be carried out in rubber boats. Agile commandos in the first wave would carry rope ladders which they would secure to the top of the Israeli rampart to make it easier for the subsequent waves to climb. The bulk of the army would cross on bridges and ferries after openings had been cut through the Israeli rampart. Attempts to blow holes in sand ramparts with explosives had proved disappointing. A young engineering officer finally provided the solution. Water cannon, he noted, had been used during construction of the Aswan Dam to cut openings through sand dunes. Lighter pumps floated across the canal might do the same to the Israeli earthworks. Tests behind the Egyptian lines were successful and hundreds of pumps were purchased in Britain and Germany. Israeli intelligence was aware of the Egyptian plan to use water cannon but dismissed it as unfeasible.

High priority was given to neutralizing Lascov's "fire-on-the-water" system. An initial idea was to form fire-fighting units which would beat the flames out with palm fronds. Another proposal was to use chemical extinguishers. Shazly didn't think either approach efficient. He decided to use frogmen to block the fuel outlets on the Israeli bank just before the crossing or to rupture the buried fuel tanks with artillery fire. If these efforts failed, the crossings would be made upstream of the outlets, leaving the canal's current to carry the burning fuel away. In a worst-case situation, the crossing would simply have to be delayed until the fuel burned itself out.

In the back of every Egyptian's mind was the 1967 rout and the fear that it might be repeated. Whether or not this would happen depended largely on Shazly and his planning staff, headed by Gen. Abdel Ghani el-Gamasy, chief of operations. By not foraying beyond the SAM umbrella, the Egyptians believed they would be spared a concentrated air attack, provided the Israelis had not figured out how to foil the SAM missiles. But what of the Israeli tanks? Egyptian intelligence knew the outlines of the Dovecote plan from documents they had captured in cross-canal raids and from observing the frequent training exercises along the canal. Within less than half an hour of the opening barrage, Israeli tanks would reach the canal from the Artillery Road. Egyptian tanks could not cross to challenge them until openings had been sliced through the Israeli sand barrier and bridges erected, a matter of hours. Until then, the Israeli armor would have to be held off by foot soldiers with antitank weaponry.

There were two principal weapons the Soviets had supplied for this purpose. One was the shoulder-held RPG-7 (rocket-propelled grenade), a successor to World War II bazooka-type weapons, which was highly effective at close range. It had been developed by the Soviets in 1961 to penetrate the armor of NATO tanks and would still be in use in the twenty-first century. It could penetrate a target at three hundred yards but was generally used at closer ranges.

The other weapon, carried in what resembled a suitcase, was called the Malotka by the Soviets; in the West it was known by its NATO designation as the Sagger. The case opened to reveal a small missile connected to a length of thin wire and a joystick. The operator, looking through high-powered binoculars, would guide the missile to target with the joystick, which sent signals down the wire unreeling behind the Sagger. The missile's range was three thousand yards, about the maximum effective range of a tank gun, and its impact was as deadly as a tank shell. It would prove to be a game changer.

The Egyptian infantrymen would be fighting alone on the Sinai bank during the critical early hours but they would get covering fire from ramparts the Egyptians had built on their side of the canal. Instead of one continuous rampart the length of the canal, as on the Israeli side, the Egyptians raised separate ramparts at scores of strategic locations. The Israeli ramp had initially been higher and every time the Egyptians raised theirs the Israelis raised theirs as well. But in 1972, the Egyptians raised their ramps to twice the height of the Israeli barrier.

The Israelis conceded the race. Instead, they built tank emplacements, which they called "fins," a mile behind their canal-side strong-points. These were low earthworks shaped like inverted Vs, from behind which they could duel with the tanks atop the Egyptian ramp, relying on superior gunnery to overcome the Egyptian advantage in height.

The Egyptians had grasped Israel's operational mode and formu-lated an effective strategy to counter it. The Israelis would respond aggressively to an Egyptian attack, attempting to destroy the SAMs with air attacks and rushing tank forces forward to destroy the bridge-heads. The Egyptian response would be judo-like, letting the enemy's forward thrust be its undoing.

The SAM air defense system supplied by the Soviet Union was one of the strongest in the world. It was backed by hundreds of radar-guided antiaircraft guns defending against low-flying aircraft the SAMs could not lock on to.

In the ground battle, the intention was to let the Israeli armor break against a defensive wall that included thousands of Saggers and RPGs, an antitank array no army had yet encountered. Shazly ordered all units not crossing in the early waves to transfer their Saggers to those that were. Until the Egyptian tanks could cross, the infantry units in Sinai would form dense bridgeheads in order to concentrate their anti-tank fire. They would be supported by tanks and antitank guns firing from the Egyptian ramparts across the canal.

The Egyptian plan was impeccable. But there were two major unknowns. One was the ability of the Egyptian troops to stand up to whatever Israel was going to throw at them. The other was when Israeli intelligence would become aware of the impending attack and what steps the IDF would take to thwart it.

Mossad chief Zamir had taken to meeting with Marwan whenever they both happened to be in London. Intrigued by a personality he could not quite decipher, Zamir avoided discussion of operational issues, which he left to Marwan's case officer. He engaged instead in free-floating conversations, often over vodka, that flitted from Cairo political gossip and personal musings to strategic and political devel-opments in the Arab world and always came back to the mind-set of Anwar Sadat.

Marwan had been the first to spell out to the Israelis the rationale of "the concept." But early in 1973, he reported that Sadat was abandoning Nasser's strategy. Instead of trying to seize all of Sinai, which Sadat regarded as unrealistic, he would order the army to establish a firm bridgehead on the Sinai bank of the canal. This would be sufficient to shatter the political stalemate and oblige the superpowers to impose a peace process if they didn't want to risk being dragged into direct confrontation with each other by their proxies.

It was a stunning shift and Zamir, a retired general who had headed Southern Command, saw its far-reaching military implications. If the Egyptian army did not intend to venture beyond the protection of the SAM umbrella, it would not need to wait for additional aircraft. If Sadat gave up on Scuds as well, then war could be around the corner and not two or more years away, as AMAN contended.

"Beginning in February," Zamir would write, "the Mossad gathered information pointing to a substantial change in Egypt's direction. This information was passed on to AMAN immediately and in its entirety." However, there is no indication that the information was passed on by AMAN to the General Staff. When war came, the Israeli military command was braced for an immediate push to the Sinai passes by the Egyptian armored divisions, as in Nasser's plan, not for the creation of a powerful bridgehead against which, Sadat and Shazly hoped, Israeli armor would break. Zamir would say years later, "Intelligence that was of paramount importance was relayed to military intelligence, but never made it to the decision makers."

On April 18, the Mossad chief was invited to a meeting of Golda's kitchen cabinet in Mrs. Meir's official residence in Jerusalem's Rehavia Quarter. She served her guests tea and cake, fresh from her oven. Also attending were Defense Minister Dayan, Chief of Staff Elazar, AMAN chief Zeira, and several of Mrs. Meir's political advisers. The meeting had been called to explore the sharply diverging assessments of the Mossad, which was warning of a possibly imminent war, and AMAN, which rejected the notion. After hearing the two intelligence chiefs, almost all sided with the Mossad, including Elazar and Dayan, and the Blue-White alert was set in motion.

A month later, when the perceived danger of an Egyptian attack dissipated, Zeira's "victory" rendered him something of an oracle. He took the opportunity to declare his belief that Ashraf Marwan was a double agent. The Mossad source, he noted, had wrongly warned of war in this instance (as had other sources) and also in December (as had other sources). Such repeated crying of "wolf," he suggested, was intended to lower Israel's guard.

Sadat's new strategy, passed on to Zvi Zamir by Marwan and by Zamir to AMAN, was not internalized by the army command, if it was ever brought to its attention. Zeira himself, convinced that the only "logical" Egyptian plan was Nasser's—an attempt to capture all Sinai—did not relate to Sadat's plan brought by Marwan. Instead, Zeira's position, and the position of AMAN, was that there would be no war in the near future because Egypt did not have the planes and Scuds it wanted. The army's last major war game, executed in the summer of 1972, was based on Nasser's plan for capturing all Sinai and on this the IDF had built its own responses.

Mossad chief Zamir was unaware that his report on Sadat's plan was being ignored. He himself was not privy to the army's operational plans and could not approach Dayan or Elazar directly on strictly military matters without intruding on Zeira's turf. Zamir reported directly to Golda Meir and was not part of Dayan's weekly security forum. His meeting with Dayan and the military leadership in Mrs. Meir's apartment in April had been an ad hoc affair. But even without his report, there was ample evidence to indicate a change of thinking in Cairo. There were no more reports of requests by Sadat for new warplanes while the massive amount of Sagger antitank weapons and RPGs arriving in Egypt suggested far-reaching tactical changes. As the postwar Agranat Commission report would put it: "Intelligence didn't manage to understand the strategic logic and the operational implications of the possibility that Egypt would make do with limited gains on the ground in order to achieve political gains."

Whether or not Zeira was motivated by institutional rivalry with the Mossad, like that known between the CIA and FBI and between other security siblings in the world, he would continue to rebuff warnings that war was close. By virtue of his position and the credibility he gained during the May crisis, his view prevailed within the military command.

Sadat had abandoned "the concept" but Israel continued to embrace it.

5

ILLUSIONS

I T WAS OPERA, thought Benny Peled, and bad opera at that.

Reviewing contingency plans upon his appointment as Israeli Air Force (IAF) commander in May 1973, General Peled found the proposals for suppression of the SAM missiles absurdly complex.

Israel had encountered SAM-2s in the Six Day War and lost three planes to them. The missile batteries were few and vulnerable to low-level attack. In the War of Attrition, the nuisance became a nemesis. Deployed in large numbers, the batteries, each with six missile launchers, were now mutually supporting. The defenses had been reinforced by SAM-3s, which were more difficult to evade, and by conventional antiaircraft batteries effective against low-flying planes.

In July 1970, the air force tested a system devised by the Americans for countering SAM-2s over North Vietnam. It was based on electronic pods whose signals distorted the SAM's radar. Warplanes equipped with these pods were required to maintain formation at precise altitudes even if missiles were fired at them. The Americans, who lost two hundred planes to SAM-2s in Vietnam, did not know if the method was effective against SAM-3s. The commander of one of the IAF's two Phantom squadrons, Col. Shmuel Hetz, pressed for the system to be put to the test.

Hetz personally led a flight of twenty Phantoms into the missile zone. Activating the pods slung beneath their wings, the Phantoms held a steady course as the sky around them blossomed with exploding missiles. The planes got through to destroy four of the ten batteries targeted and damage three others. But one plane was downed on the way back. It was Hetz's, hit by a SAM-3. His navigator bailed out and was captured. Hetz did not manage to parachute. A Phantom flown by the other squadron commander, Col. Avihu Bin-Nun, was also hit and he barely succeeded in landing at a base in Sinai, his plane running off the runway and plowing into the sand for a hundred yards. Five Phantoms, the pride of the Israeli Air Force, were downed by missiles before the cease-fire went into effect three weeks later.

The air force was left with the queasy realization that it no longer held unchallenged mastery of the skies. The technological edge it enjoyed over the Arabs had been reversed almost overnight. The problem became even more acute when the Egyptians, flouting the cease-fire agreement, moved missiles into the Canal Zone from where their reach extended over Israeli-held western Sinai for several miles.

The best minds in the air force were put to work on the missile challenge. What Benny Peled found on his desk was a plan devised by a team headed by Bin-Nun that sought to make up with tactics what was lacking in technology. Code-named Tagar, it envisaged a complex aerial ballet executed by hundreds of planes performing exacting maneuvers at top speed and with stopwatch precision. A similar plan, code-named Dougman 5, was drawn up for the Golan front.

The Israelis succeeded in jamming the SAM-3s but the appearance in 1972 of the sophisticated SAM-6 posed a new level of threat. The electronic parameters of the missile were unknown to the Americans. The SAM-6 would therefore have to be attacked without electronic foreplay, greatly increasing the risks. Peled concluded that the air force could lose as many as one plane per SAM battery attacked. Given that there were eighty-seven batteries on the Egyptian and Syrian fronts—not to mention another ninety-five defending rear areas such as air bases—there was an immense price to be paid if this projection held, even if only the frontline batteries were attacked. Some air force officers maintained that Tagar and Dougman were too complex to work. But no one offered a better solution.

Ironically, Peled was the only senior airman in the IAF who had not experienced missiles close-up. He had joined the air force as a mechanic and only later became a pilot, rising to squadron commander, but the technical side of flying always intrigued him. He was an unexpected choice for the top command. In a clubby organization filled with superb pilots and fighter aces, Peled had never downed an enemy plane. He himself was shot down in the 1956 Sinai Campaign. His extended absences on special development projects made him something of an outsider. But his intellect, organizational brilliance, and ample self-confidence left no question once he took over about who was running the shop. He had an acerbic tongue and did not suffer fools.

The missiles had traumatized the air force. For long virtually invulnerable in dogfights, the fliers had seen Hetz and other top pilots suddenly brushed away by a new weapon system that threatened to drive them all from the sky. With most of the air force's energies and much of its budget dedicated to the missile question, attention was diverted from other critical subjects like strategic warfare and close support of ground forces. Meeting with the Tagar planners, Peled said he believed their scheme could work, but only in a perfect world. Success required good weather and fresh intelligence. Photos would be needed from the morning of the planned attack or the previous evening, fixing the exact location of the missile batteries. The air force would also need thirty-six hours' notice to prepare necessary accoutrements, some of them helicopter-borne, to foil the enemy radar. Above all, it required a government decision to launch a preemptive attack which alone could ensure these ideal conditions. This meant relying on politicians. Peled determined to find another solution but meanwhile Tagar and Dougman 5 remained on the books.

Shortly after taking command, General Peled was paid an official visit by Dayan, Elazar, and members of the General Staff. They had come to hear the new air force commander's war plans, particularly how he intended to cope with the missiles. With Peled were Bin-Nun and the other Tagar and Dougman 5 planners, who spelled out their "Star Wars" proposals, as Peled would sardonically label them. The visitors were impressed at the sophistication of the plans and were relieved to be told there was a solution to the missile problem. Before they left, Peled brought them back to earth. "You should know that these plans aren't worth the paper they're written on unless we get permission to strike first." As Peled would recall it, Dayan replied, "Do you think that if we have even a hint of an Arab attack we will not attack first?"

The visit by the heads of the defense establishment and the comfort they drew from the airmen's presentation betrayed one of the basic flaws of Israel's defense posture—overdependence on the air force. The IAF received fully half the military budget and had come to be seen as an almost mystical problem solver. The flimsiness of the frontline forces deployed opposite the Egyptian and Syrian armies rested on the presumption that in a worst-case situation the air force would bear the main burden of slowing the enemy down until the reserves mobilized and reached the front. But this now depended on prior suppression of the missiles. Tagar and Dougman 5 were only paper plans and the arrival of the SAM-6s rendered these already complex operations much more chancy.

Just as a sense of dolce vita had come to permeate the civilian sector, flabbiness of thought had overcome the senior military command. Israel had fallen victim to its own victory in 1967. A success of such dimensions, against such odds, evoked a sense of Israeli power and of Arab dysfunction that was too powerful to ignore. There were some who saw in this disparity a divine hand but most presumed a civilizational difference—a divide between East and West that would not be bridgeable for generations to come. "The Arab soldier lacks the characteristics necessary for modern war," then chief of staff Bar-Lev declared in 1970. These characteristics, he said, included rapid reaction, technical competence, a high level of intelligence, adaptability, "and, above all, the ability to see events realistically and speak truth, even when it is difficult and bitter."

However, the Egyptians had proven, as far back as the first Israel-Arab war in 1948, that in defensive battles they were stubborn opponents. The 1967 rout had been touched off by a premature fallback order by Egypt's high command on the second day of the war before 80 percent of its army had even been in contact with the enemy. A fleeing army may be dismissed as rabble. But that same army, infused with motivation, could prove formidable. In the War of Attrition, which saw daring commando raids behind Israeli lines, the Egyptian army showed that it also had another face.

Israel's tank corps was a particular victim of the victory syndrome. Its success in the 1956 Sinai Campaign and the Six Day War in breaking through heavily defended Egyptian positions reinforced the notion that the tank was king. The number of Israeli tanks had been doubled since 1967.

Israel's tank doctrine rested on a concept developed by General Tal during his seven years as head of the armored corps. It was called the "totality of the tank." Conventional doctrine, deriving from vast experience in World War II, called for a combined arms approach in which tanks advanced in tandem with infantry and artillery. The infantrymen protected the tanks from enemy ground troops wielding antitank weapons while artillery provided both with support.

Tal, however, believed that on the desert battlefields of the Middle

East the tank could for the most part manage alone. Visibility was far clearer than in hazy Europe and there was precious little brush for infantrymen with bazookas to hide behind. As for enemy antitank guns, these are easily spotted in the naked desert and could be hit at a distance with accurate gunfire. Tanks would move swiftly to reduce exposure to enemy fire, not stopping till they had broken the enemy line. Such a charge would create an effect of "armor shock." Infantry would follow to mop up. Since the charging tanks would outrun artillery, they would rely primarily on their own guns and on the air force. Tal stressed gunnery training, particularly accurate long-range fire. Israeli tank crews opened fire at longer range than in any other army. A senior American armor general who studied the Israeli armored corps would term its gunnery the best in the world.

This "totality of the tank" approach had its skeptics even within the armored corps but the results of the Six Day War appeared to confirm its validity. Several times, Israeli tank columns broke through fortified Egyptian positions by brazen, head-on attacks with virtually no assistance from artillery or infantry. Critics would note, however, that the fact that it worked in the context of that war, in which the surprise Israeli assault had stunned the Egyptians, did not necessarily prove its applicability in every war. There were other battles in the 1967 war which were won by effective use of combined arms, including battles led by Tal himself, but it was the dashing tank charge that seized the army's imagination.

In 1972 when the infantry corps requested better weapons, including rifles and antitank weapons, Tal—now deputy chief of staff—said the Belgian FN rifles it had were adequate. Spending on infantry upgrades meant fewer tanks. As for antitank weapons, he said, the IDF already had the best antitank system in the world, namely the armored corps.

The acquisition by the Egyptians and Syrians of the Sagger antitank missile in extremely large amounts made little impression. Israeli tank forces had encountered the missile in exchanges of fire across the lines during the War of Attrition and regarded it as just another antitank weapon along with conventional antitank guns, recoilless rifles, RPGs, bazookas, and tanks themselves, not a threat that required a basic revision of battle doctrine. AMAN printed booklets about the Sagger's characteristics based on information received from the U.S., which had encountered the missile in Vietnam in 1972. The armored corps command had even developed tactics for dealing with the missile. But neither the booklets nor the tactics had been circulated and few tank men were even aware of the Sagger's existence.

Its introduction, however, would change the battlefield equation profoundly. Unlike conventional antitank guns, the Sagger was wielded by a single soldier. He did not need bushes for cover; lying behind a small pile of sand or in a shallow foxhole, in a sand-colored uniform, would be enough to render him invisible at a distance to tank crews. The Sagger operator would find it much easier to hit a tank than the other way around—and at ranges that matched the tank's.

Israel was also aware that masses of RPGs had been acquired by the Egyptians and Syrians but did not find convincing the thought of Arab infantrymen standing up to charging tanks. The notion that they might do so in numbers large enough to break an armored attack did not arise.

Another technical advance in the Arab armies—the acquisition of infrared equipment for night fighting—was noted and dismissed. Night fighting had been Israel's preferred mode in the War of Independence in 1948. Its lightly armed troops used the darkness to close on the enemy, something that would have been costly in daylight. But as the army over the years acquired heavier weapons, daylight came to be seen as the best time to exploit this strength. The IDF continued to train in night fighting and to engage in it periodically and there remained a belief that the IDF preferred night fighting while the Arabs were afraid of it. However, by the 1970s few Israeli tanks had night sights. By contrast, Soviet tanks in Egyptian and Syrian hands were equipped with infrared projectors as well as infrared headlights and infrared sights for the crew. Night sights were also widely distributed among infantry units.

Israel had not turned its back on night fighting but it preferred not using infrared projectors, which could be detected by an enemy with infrared binoculars. The armored corps was planning to acquire night sights that magnified starlight. Meanwhile, however, the Arab armies had night-viewing equipment and the IDF did not.

The Israeli Navy had been spared the smugness which overtook the rest of the IDF after 1967. Its antiquated collection of ships took virtually no part in the Six Day War. The defense establishment regarded the navy as little more than a coast guard and would not expend funds to build a modern fleet.

In 1960, the service's senior officers assembled at naval headquarters to discuss the navy's future. From this two-day conclave, a revolutionary concept emerged. Israel's fledgling defense industry had developed a missile it was trying to sell to the air force and the artillery corps but neither was interested. The missile had to be guided onto target by a forward observer manipulating a joystick. If the missile could be adapted for use at sea, the naval officers fantasized, its large warhead would give an inexpensive patrol boat the punch of a heavy cruiser.

The navy invested prodigious efforts over thirteen years to develop the concept into a weapon system. The joystick was dropped along the way and the missile, dubbed the Gabriel, was provided with radar, enabling it to home in on a moving target.

Halfway through the project, it was learned that the Soviets had developed their own missile boats and were supplying them to the Egyptian and Syrian navies. Four months after the Six Day War, an Egyptian missile boat emerging from Port Said demonstrated the accuracy and lethality of seaborne missiles for the first time when it sank Israel's flagship, the destroyer *Eilat*. The Soviet Styx missile had twice the range of the Gabriel but after the *Eilat*'s sinking Israel installed on its boats electronic countermeasures that would, it hoped, divert the Styx. This could be tested, however, only in war.

Israel ordered twelve "patrol boats" from a shipyard in Cherbourg which were to be configured into missile boats in Haifa. For political reasons, France impounded the last five. On Christmas Eve 1969, in the midst of a Force Nine gale that kept even large freighters in port, Israeli sailors took the five vessels out into the roiling English Channel and ran for Haifa where they would be armed for a new form of naval warfare.

Like the Israeli Navy, the Arabs had been spared the self-satisfaction induced by victory. With the assistance of Soviet advisers, solutions were painstakingly hammered out for neutralization of Israel's superiority in air and armored warfare. Thousands of Arab officers were sent to advanced military courses in the Soviet Union and thousands of Soviet advisers were embedded at all command levels of the Egyptian and Syrian armies down to battalion.

If Israel's thinking had been lulled by hubris, Arab thinking was sharpened by desperation. The "on to Tel Aviv" bravado of earlier wars that led to disaster gave way to sober war preparations. Arab intelligence officers were trained intensively in Hebrew in order to permit them to monitor Israeli communications.

The bizarre disproportion of forces along the front lines reflected Israel's confidence that intelligence would provide warning of Arab war preparations in ample time. In the event of an intelligence failure, the fallback was the air force. Said Elazar: "That we dare to delay mobilization stems from our faith in the ability of the air force to halt the enemy."

To envision a failure of the air force on top of a failure of the intelligence services would be pushing imagination to the point of perversity. Even more difficult to imagine was Egyptian infantry stopping Israeli armor.

If any one of these scenarios became reality, it would pose a major challenge. If all three became reality—meaning neutralization of the IDF's intelligence, air force, and armor—Israel faced catastrophe.

6

SUMMER LULL

THE PHONE IN HENRY KISSINGER'S room at President Nixon's retreat in San Clemente, California, rang shortly after he returned from a farewell dinner for Leonid Brezhnev. The Soviet leader had asked to retire early in order to set out the next morning, June 24, 1973, for Moscow. The caller was a Secret Service agent who notified Kissinger that Brezhnev, in an unusual deviation from protocol, was asking for an immediate meeting with the president, who had already gone to bed.

Kissinger telephoned to waken the president and was with him when Brezhnev arrived forty-five minutes later. The Soviet leader said he wanted to discuss the Middle East, a subject he had failed to bring up during a week of talks in Washington and San Clemente. The proposal he spelled out was identical with Egypt's position—total Israeli withdrawal to its 1967 border in return for a nonbelligerency pact. If this was not accepted, warned Brezhnev, "we will have difficulty keeping the military situation from flaring up."

Though delivered almost as an afterthought, it was a clear threat that the Soviets could not, or would not, restrain their Arab clients from going to war if Israel did not meet their terms. Kissinger believed that Brezhnev's late-night maneuver was an attempt to catch Nixon off guard and elicit a verbal agreement in the absence of the president's advisers, principally himself. The Soviets, he would later deduce, had been told by their Arab clients that they intended to go to war and Brezhnev was hoping that Nixon, by agreeing to pressure Israel into concessions, would spare Moscow the embarrassment of seeing its clients suffer another ignominious defeat. If war did break out, the Soviets could at least say they had given warning. The president smoothly deflected the proposal with a version of "we'll look into it" and bid Brezhnev good night.

The Arabs and Israelis were not alone in the Middle East. Even while pursuing their own regional power games, they were doubling as proxies for superpowers engaged in global confrontation. The relationship between patron and proxy, however, was not one of commander-subordinate. To safeguard their foothold in Egypt, the Soviets had agreed to renew arms shipments to Cairo despite the expulsion of their advisers the previous year. Several hundred Soviet experts and their families had in fact already returned to Egypt together with the arms. It was nevertheless the Soviets' fervent hope that armed conflict could be averted. Middle East war risked the possibility that the superpowers would be sucked directly into the conflict.

In Israel, the amicable Brezhnev-Nixon summit was taken to mean that war had receded from the horizon. The Arabs appeared paralyzed while Israel was redrawing the map of the Middle East by establishing settlements on occupied land in Sinai and on the Golan Heights.

A major source of confidence was the charismatic Moshe Dayan, whose standing as a security icon went far beyond his function as defense minister. Chief of staff during the successful Sinai Campaign of 1956 against Egypt, he had on the eve of the Six Day War been forced upon a reluctant government by popular demand as defense minister when Israel appeared to be facing an existential threat. He became the symbol of Israel's astonishing victory.

Dayan's freebooter style and popular appeal were not appreciated by his cabinet colleagues. But they bowed to his judgment on defense matters. A rakish private life only enhanced Dayan's public aura, as did the general's black eyepatch; he had lost an eye when a bullet hit a telescope he was looking through in south Lebanon in 1941. He was scouting for a British force making an incursion into Vichy-held territory. Dayan did little to hide his extramarital adventures. He found solace too in the illicit embrace of the ancients, digging for archaeological artifacts in violation of Israel's antiquities law. He transferred some of the finds to his own home where he relaxed from affairs of state by gluing broken pottery together and mounting the artifacts in his garden. Pragmatic and no-nonsense in his daily life, he permitted himself a mystic identification with the ancient people who had shaped the clay vessels he unearthed.

It was Dayan who formulated policy toward the occupied territories. He was willing to envision the return of territory to the Arabs in exchange for peace treaties. But not all territory. In a reference to the southern tip of the Sinai Peninsula, which controlled maritime passage to Eilat, he famously said, "Better Sharm el-Sheikh without peace than peace without Sharm el-Sheikh."

Dayan would unashamedly change his mind when circumstance warranted—only mules don't change their minds, he would say. On May 21, during the Blue-White alert, he told the General Staff to prepare for war in the second half of summer. "We, the government, tell you, the general staff, 'Gentleman, please prepare for war in which those who threaten to start the war are Egypt and Syria.'"

By the following month, however, the perceived threat had receded and Dayan's tone changed dramatically. In a speech atop the historic mount of Masada, he said that Israel's geopolitical circumstances were of a nature that "our people have probably never witnessed." Interviewed by *Time* magazine, he predicted that there would be no war for ten years. To the General Staff, he now said, "We are on the threshold of the crowning period of the Return to Zion."

In Washington, a relatively junior analyst in the State Department's Bureau of Intelligence and Research, Roger Merrick, submitted a memo in May noting that Sadat's political alternatives were exhausted. Unless there was a credible U.S. peace initiative, he wrote, the chances of an Israeli-Egyptian war within six months were better than 50-50.

Many in the Israeli hierarchy held similar views but believed that war, while regrettable, would bring the Arabs closer to accepting Israel's terms. "We're not interested in war," General Elazar had said at the meeting in Golda Meir's home on April 18. But if war did break out, "I favor striking such a blow over a week or ten days that they'll need five years to lift their heads up again."

Mrs. Meir herself did not regard war as a strategic opportunity but as something to be avoided. If it appeared likely to break out, she said at the meeting, the Americans should be notified and asked to head it off. At this point, her closest political adviser, minister without portfolio Israel Galili, raised a delicate point. The danger of war, he noted, stemmed from Israel's unwillingness to withdraw to the 1967 borders. Referring to the meeting between Hafez Ismail and Kissinger in February, on which the Israelis had been briefed, he said, "If you take what Hafez said as a starting point—that [the Egyptians] are ready for peace . . . this is based on our complete pullback to the previous lines."

He later returned to this theme, as if fearing his previous remark may have been too oblique. "There is also a possibility that we can avoid all this mess [the danger of war] if we are prepared to enter into talks on the basis of returning to the previous border." From the protocol, Galili's remark sounds more like an observation than a proposal but the fact that he voiced it twice suggests that the veteran political adviser, although of hawkish bent, thought it worthy of exploration.

Mrs. Meir, however, declined to pursue it, either at this meeting with her political advisers and senior military officials or with the full cabinet. She was against war but she was also against total withdrawal from the territories. As she put it in a speech: "Neither war nor the threat of war" would move Israel from its insistence on defensible borders. "We will make every effort that these borders be accepted by our neighbors. We want defensible borders not only so that if we are ever attacked we will be able to defend them but so that the borders by their very existence will dissuade our neighbors from touching us."

Mrs. Meir had not informed the government about the proposals Ismail had floated or about the indications of Egyptian war preparations that led to the Blue-White alert. Galili suggested that she do so to forestall complaints from ministers later in case war did break out. But she did not.

Leading a nation into war was not a role Golda Meir would ever have wished for. But she was coping so far with the steadiness that had marked her long public career. Born in Kiev, she arrived in the U.S. at the age of eight with her family, the memory of pogroms still vivid. She trained as a teacher but in 1921 left with her husband for Palestine where they settled in a kibbutz. Strong-minded and articulate, she became in time part of the leadership of the Jewish state-in-the-making.

In May 1948, four days before the state of Israel was proclaimed, she was dispatched across the Jordan River to meet with Jordan's King Abdullah, Hussein's grandfather. In Arab dress and accompanied by a single male colleague, she passed through an area where an Arab army was preparing to invade the newborn state. Her attempt to persuade the king not to join in the attack failed. In 1969, Mrs. Meir was seventy-one when she was chosen prime minister. Her pluckiness, wry sense of humor, and simple lifestyle earned her widespread popularity. But her uncompromising mind-set left little room for exploring the chances of peace, however slim, with the Arabs.

In later years, an Israeli general would lament the fact that Mrs.

Meir had excluded the full cabinet from discussions on the crisis in the months before the war. "What we needed," he would say, "were ministers like [minister for religious affairs] Zerah Warhaftig [a Holocaust survivor], who was frightened by the prospect of war, saying 'Let's think this through again.'"

In July, Gen. Ariel Sharon stepped down as head of Southern Command, the most important of the IDF's regional commands, and retired from the army. He was replaced by Gen. Shmuel Gonen. The appointment by Elazar drew criticism, particularly from some of Gonen's peers. Apart from inexperience, they believed him clearly unsuited for the post. He had earned his reputation as a military leader in the Six Day War when he commanded the tank brigade that broke through the Egyptian lines in northern Sinai and was the first to reach the Suez Canal. While admired as a brave and competent field commander, he terrorized subordinates and jailed soldiers wholesale for minor infractions. On an inspection visit to one battalion, he reportedly ordered eighty-two men punished for minor infractions, such as buttons left unbuttoned. He maintained that discipline was indivisible and that sloppiness in minor matters could lead to indiscipline in battle. On speaking tours to American Jewish communities he had no objection to being billed as "the Israeli Patton."

Raised in Jerusalem's ultraorthodox community, Gonen had left that insular world as a teenager during Israel's War of Independence to take part in the fighting. He remained in the army and was among the first to join the armored corps. As a young officer, he trained Israel Tal and David Elazar, already senior officers, when they transferred from the infantry to armor. The connection with these important figures, who admired his expertise, influenced his subsequent rise.

Gen. Avraham Adan, commander of the armored corps, had long been disturbed by Gonen's crude behavior. Observing him during a desert exercise, Adan saw that Gonen's subordinates were afraid to report to him and did not give straight answers for fear of his reaction. Gonen shouted at subordinates and even threw things at them when he was angry. When the exercise was over, Adan told Elazar, "Gorodish has no place in the IDF," using Gonen's original name, by which he was still generally known. Elazar said only, "I'll speak to him." But Gonen's advancement was not halted and he was now commanding Israel's most important front.

The weeks passed uneventfully after the spring alert and tensions eased. Intelligence reported large arms shipments to Egypt and Syria in July but there was no sense of near-term conflagration, not even with the report on August 24 that the deterrence weapon long sought by Sadat, a brigade of Scud ground-to-ground missiles, had arrived in Egypt. With a range of almost two hundred miles, the missiles could hit Tel Aviv from the Nile Delta. It would take at least four months of training before they were to be handed over by the Soviets to Egyptian crews. Along the canal front itself, there was no change in the relaxed Egyptian deployment and soldiers were daily seen fishing in the canal.

Sadat, who had been hinting at imminent war since assuming office, was talking now of "an extended struggle." Intelligence counted four speeches during July in which he spoke of a "twenty-five-year strategy" to rectify the domestic situation and resolve the Israel-Arab question, a clear hint that the war option had been shelved for the foreseeable future.

Sadat's lowering of the rhetorical flames was part of an elaborate strategy embarked upon in May with the creation of an inter-ministerial committee for deception. Rumors planted about the poor maintenance of Egypt's weapon systems were picked up by the foreign press as were reports that Egyptian crews could not properly operate the SAM missiles. Rumors were also loosed about a falling-out between Egypt and Syria. War Minister Ismail, on a visit to Romania, let drop that Egypt's military strength was insufficient for a confrontation with Israel. Israeli intelligence would subsequently deduce that until late August only four persons in the Egyptian army knew when the war would begin.

Sadat's most brazen deception was of his ally, Syria. A two-front war against Israel was basic to any Arab strategy. However, Sadat and Syrian leader Hafez al-Assad had different goals. Assad aimed at taking back the Golan by force. But he would not risk war unless assured that Egypt would wage a campaign that would tie down most of Israel's military. Sadat, however, planned only a limited campaign.

Assad, a former air force commander, had seized power in 1970, a month after Sadat assumed the reins in Egypt. The two leaders had conflicting attitudes regarding Israel. The Egyptian leader was willing to contemplate a nonbelligerency agreement with the Jewish state while Assad refused to acknowledge Israel's right to exist.

Coordination between Egypt and Syria began in February 1973 when War Minister Ismail flew to Damascus to inform Assad of Sadat's intention to go to war. The minister cited three periods which Egyptian planners found suitable for attack—time spans in May, August, and September-October. On April 23, Assad flew secretly to Egypt for two days of talks with Sadat. The pair agreed on the establishment of a coordinating council made up of officers from both countries. Apart from the opening blow, however, the two sides did not set up machinery for joint command during the war.

Sadat assured Assad that Egypt would push for the Sinai passes in the first stage of the war. Assad hoped during this phase to regain the Golan. The Syrian leader was given to understand that the Egyptian army, after regrouping, would move on from the passes to capture the rest of Sinai. This ongoing pressure on Israel would inhibit a counterattack on the Golan before Syria had consolidated its position.

Sadat and his generals had already decided that the Egyptian attack would not reach the passes. Gamasy believed that Egypt should drive for the passes after an "operational pause," but Shazly did not want to venture out from beneath the SAM umbrella. The Egyptian planners did not believe they could push Israel from all Sinai at this stage and did not intend to try.

General Shazly was ordered by War Minister Ismail before Assad's visit to dust off Granite 2, the plan for reaching the passes, in order to show it to the Syrian leader. The order had come from President Sadat himself. The plan would be shown to the Syrians, Ismail said, but would not actually be implemented unless unforeseen circumstances developed, like a sudden Israeli withdrawal. Syria, he explained, would not take part in the war unless it understood that Egypt would push into the heart of Sinai.

In his autobiography, Shazly would write, "I was sickened by the duplicity." Granite 2 was duly updated but Shazly told his generals that there was no intention of actually implementing it. In instructing their subordinates, they were to remain vague about the second phase of the battle. "After an operational pause, we will develop our attack to the passes" was the way they would put it.

Jordan's King Hussein was on uneasy terms with both Egypt and Syria and could not be relied on by them to take part in the war even though his country shared the longest border with Israel. Reluctantly dragged into the Six Day War by Nasser, Hussein had placed his army under command of an Egyptian general and lost half his kingdom—the West Bank—as a result. It was now his supreme interest to avoid involvement in another war that would endanger what he had left. Other Arab countries were expected to join the battle but none would be made privy beforehand to the date of D-day.

Under the direction of General Gamasy, the Egyptian army's operations staff studied tide schedules and even the Jewish calendar in order to select the precise date for the attack. The planners wanted a long night for the canal crossing, half in moonlight and half in darkness. The bridges would be assembled in moonlight in the water and the tanks would cross in darkness, hidden to Israeli planes. One of the days within the optimal crossing period in October was Yom Kippur. It struck the Egyptian planners as fortuitous. Israeli reservists, they knew, were mobilized during emergencies by having unit code names broadcast on radio. On Yom Kippur, however, radio and television in Israel were shut down. The selection of D-day would be left to Sadat and Assad but the planners put a circle around October 6, Yom Kippur, noting its special advantage.

Yom Kippur, however, was the worst possible Arab choice. In the absence of radio, Israel had other ways of mobilizing its reserves—couriers, for instance. Unlike any other day in the year, it is certain on Yom Kippur where virtually every reservist in the country can be found—at his home or at a synagogue in walking distance. The total absence of traffic on this day would enable couriers to speedily reach the reservists and the reservists themselves to quickly reach their bases.

The October date also fell within the monthlong Muslim holiday of Ramadan. The Egyptian planners saw this as an advantage. The Israelis were less likely to suspect an attack during the holy month, when the Muslim faithful do not eat or drink during daylight hours. War then would come at the most sacred time of the year for both sides, with sanctity itself accorded a tactical role.

7

A ROYAL VISIT

FROM ATOP ONE OF THE volcanic cones on the Golan Heights, Maj. Gen. Yitzhak Hofi could see Syrian encampments straddling the road leading to Damascus to the northeast. The Syrians normally maintained three divisions opposite the Golan. They were pulled out in April for annual training and began to trickle back in midsummer. There were now, in mid-September, far more tanks and artillery out there than ever before.

Most worrying to Hofi, who headed Israel's Northern Command, was the presence since August of SAM-6 batteries. They covered the skies not only over the Syrian lines but over the entire Golan Heights and even parts of the Galilee inside Israel proper. This meant that the air force would not be able to operate against Syrian ground forces if war began until the missiles were eliminated. The air force had already stopped flying over the Golan; only low-flying light planes, such as crop dusters, were now permitted.

On September 13, two pairs of Phantoms returning from a photo reconnaissance mission over Syria were jumped by Syrian MiG-21s off the Lebanese coast and a flight of Israeli Mirages intervened. In the ensuing dogfight, eight Syrian planes and one Israeli Mirage were shot down. The downed Israeli pilot managed to climb into a life raft. As his comrades circled overhead, waiting for a rescue helicopter, a second wave of Syrian planes attacked. Four more were shot down. The helicopter picked up the Israeli pilot as well as one of the Syrian pilots in the water nearby.

At a meeting of the General Staff four days later, General Zeira tried to calm Hofi's concerns. Despite the Syrian buildup, the intelligence chief said, the Arabs understood they had no chance of winning a war against Israel. It would be another two years before Egypt had sufficient long-range planes and Scuds to even contemplate war. And it was axiomatic that Syria would not go to war without Egypt.

Hofi was not reassured. The Syrian deployment was growing more disturbing by the day. Artillery, normally deployed well to the rear, had been moved to forward positions. This made sense only if the Syrians intended to use the guns to support forces advancing into the Golan. The September 13 air battle was not the kind of blow Syria would take passively. Hofi did not believe the Syrians were thinking about full-scale war but they might attempt to capture one of the Israeli settlements on the Golan. There were now eight hundred Syrian tanks opposite the Israeli lines. All Hofi had was an understrength armored brigade with seventy-seven tanks. There were also two hundred infantrymen manning ten small outposts along the front line. The two armies were only five hundred yards apart.

The Blue-White alert in the spring had improved Hofi's defensive posture somewhat. A network of roads had been bulldozed through the rocky terrain for swifter deployment of tanks. The antitank ditch which had guarded only half the Israeli line was now almost complete. Minefields had been thickened. The Syrians could bridge the ditch and get through the minefields but these barriers would slow them down for a few precious hours. Firing ramps were prepared for tanks on high ground overlooking likely Syrian attack points.

The two spans linking the Golan with the Galilee across the narrow Jordan River—the Bnot Yaacov (Daughters of Jacob) Bridge and Arik Bridge—had their capacities doubled by widening. In an important move, some reserve tank brigades had their camps moved to the foot of the heights from the other end of the Galilee, enabling them to mount the heights an hour or more faster.

None of this made up for the loss of air support. Hofi had until now been able to reassure himself that despite the lopsided disparity in ground forces, the air force would, in the event of a surprise attack, keep the enemy at bay until the reserves arrived. However, with the forward deployment of the SAMs, including the SAM-6s, the air force would now be out of the picture for the critical opening day or two while it attended to Tagar and Dougman. The general decided to share his concern with his colleagues at the weekly meeting of the General Staff on September 24, which was attended by Dayan.

The main item on the agenda was the proposed acquisition of

American F-15 warplanes. Hofi was the first of the participants scheduled to comment. "Before I express my opinion I'd like to talk about something else," he said. The situation on the Golan was "very serious." The Syrians were in position to strike without warning and the Golan had no strategic depth that would permit his forces to roll with the blow. The introduction of the SAM-6s meant that he was now deprived of air support. "To my mind the Syrians are more dangerous to Israel than the Egyptians." Having painted this dire picture, he went on to give his opinion about the F-15s.

The discussion on the planes and other strategic issues proceeded around the table, without any reference to Hofi's remarks. It was Dayan who brought the generals back to it. "The General Staff can't let Khaka's [Hofi's nickname] remarks pass without comment," he said. "I ask that you explore this to the full. Either his scenario doesn't hold water or it does. If it does, we need a plan for dealing with it." Rosh Hashana, the Jewish New Year, was only two days away. Dayan said he could not permit himself to go on holiday without getting an answer.

The Syrian army was weaker than Egypt's, he said, but Hofi was right about it representing the greater danger. The Egyptian army would have to cross 150 miles of desert before it reached Israel's sparsely populated Negev in the south but the Syrians were less than twenty miles from villages and towns in the Galilee and two miles from settlements on the Golan itself. If the IDF was caught napping by a massive attack, the Syrians could be inside Israel proper in hours.

Elazar sought to downplay Hofi's concerns. "I don't accept that the Syrians can conquer the Golan," he said. Intelligence might not provide warning of a limited attack, the chief of staff said, but the forces already deployed on the heights were sufficient to deal with it. If the Syrians were planning full-scale war, intelligence was certain to pick up signals in time for reinforcements to reach the front. As for the SAMs, the air force was prudently keeping clear of their reach at present. In war, however, they would provide close support and pay whatever price necessary. "If it's a question of war, the missiles to my mind do not affect the ability of the air force to deal with the problem in half a day." It is not clear where Elazar got that impression but it would prove one of the major misconceptions of the war.

Dayan was not assuaged but did not wish to further interrupt the meeting. He asked Elazar to set up a meeting to decide on appropriate measures for the Golan. It was fixed for the morning of the 26th, two days hence, the day before Rosh Hashana.

On the night of the 25th, a helicopter landed at a security installation outside Tel Aviv and its occupants were led into a modest building serving the Mossad. Two of the visitors were conducted into a conference room where Golda Meir awaited them. "Your majesty," she said to the short figure who strode forward to shake her hand.

Jordan's King Hussein took a seat at the conference table opposite the Israeli prime minister. Alongside him was Jordanian prime minister Zeid Rifai. Alongside Mrs. Meir sat Mordecai Gazit, a veteran diplomat serving as director of the prime minister's office.

The Arab monarch had been maintaining secret contacts with Israel's leaders for years in order to avoid misunderstandings that could lead to armed conflict. He had requested this meeting without indicating what he wanted to discuss. In an adjacent room, Lt. Col. Zussia Keniezer, head of the Jordanian desk in AMAN, monitored the conversation through earphones.

The king began by raising a minor border problem north of Eilat. Both he and Mrs. Meir then offered a leisurely tour d'horizon of the political situation in the region. Mrs. Meir had grown up in Milwaukee but she had lived in the Middle East long enough to wait patiently for the king to get to what really brought him. From time to time, her longtime personal assistant, Ms. Lou Kedar, brought in hot drinks. It was close to an hour before Hussein came to the point. The Syrians, he said, were in a pre-jump-off position for war. Colonel Keniezer straightened up. Are they going to war alone against Israel, asked Mrs. Meir? No, said the king, according to Keniezer's report. In cooperation with the Egyptians.

Lou Kedar, who heard that part of the conversation, would remember it somewhat differently. When asked who else would join Syria, Hussein said "all of them." She had the clear impression that the king was saying that war was coming and that he was greatly disturbed by the prospect. Mordecai Gazit would afterward assert that Hussein did not warn about an imminent coordinated attack.

As soon as the king left, Mrs. Meir asked Kedar to get Dayan on the phone. It was already midnight. The prime minister gave Dayan a brief summary of the meeting and Dayan said he would call back. Mrs. Meir chain-smoked as she waited. When Dayan called ten minutes later, they spoke briefly. She then left with Kedar for the prime minister's official residence in Jerusalem. Mrs. Meir was supposed to depart the next day for France where she was to address a meeting of the Council of Europe in Strasbourg.

"I suppose we won't be going to Europe now," said Kedar as they drove.

"Why not?" asked Mrs. Meir.

It struck the incredulous Kedar that Mrs. Meir did not take Hussein's warning seriously. The prime minister's relaxed attitude stemmed from her conversation with Dayan, who had been briefed by someone in AMAN on the content and implications of the king's message. There had been other intelligence officers in the monitoring room besides Keniezer and the officer Dayan had spoken to evidently reported that there was nothing new in the king's remarks.

Colonel Keniezer's evaluation was the opposite. The king had met with Sadat and Assad in Alexandria two weeks before. Given the mutual suspicions prevailing among the Arab leaders it was unlikely that he had been told of any specific war plans. But it was probable that Sadat and Assad had raised the prospect of war with Israel in general terms to feel out the likelihood of Jordan joining in or at least preventing Israel from counterattacking Syria through Jordanian territory.

What electrified the intelligence officer was that for the first time a high-ranking source was suggesting that Egypt and Syria would be going to war together. Until now, it had been assumed that despite its warlike preparations, Syria would not undertake war without Egypt. And Egypt would not go to war because it still did not have long-range planes and Scuds. The import of Hussein's remarks was that "the concept"—the belief that Egypt would not go to war until it had new weapons systems—was no longer relevant.

Accompanying Keniezer as they emerged from the monitoring room was a longtime colleague, the senior officer in charge of field security in the IDF. "Stick with me," Keniezer said to him, "because I'm about to break field security and I'm going to do it twice."

He telephoned his direct superior, Brig. Gen. Arye Shalev, head of the Research Section at AMAN and second in the hierarchy to Zeira. "The bottom line of what Hussein had to say was that there's going to be war with Egypt and Syria. I'll give you details in the morning." Keniezer then called the head of the Syrian desk, Lt. Col. Avi Ya'ari.

Without revealing the source of his information, he told Ya'ari of the warning of a two-front war and suggested that he inform Northern Command.

The next morning at 8:15 Elazar met with the General Staff to discuss implementation of Dayan's demand two days before to beef up the Golan defenses—"if only to rest easy on Rosh Hashana," as Elazar put it. At Dayan's request, Elazar first sounded out the generals on Hussein's warning the previous night. "There's a report from a serious source that the Syrian army is prepared to launch war at any moment. It's not known if this is coordinated with Egypt."

Even Hofi dismissed the likelihood of the Syrians embarking on a full-scale war. Elazar summed up the consensus view by saying that the warning added nothing to what they already knew. It was unreasonable to think the Syrians would attack without Egypt. "I could almost say, I hope they try it. In any case, there's not going to be a war."

If the Syrians decided to react at all to the downing of their planes, it would most likely be with an artillery barrage, said Elazar. However, an attempt at a limited attack on a frontline fort or a settlement could not be ruled out. It was decided to dispatch to the Golan two companies from the Seventh Armored Brigade stationed in Sinai. This would bring the number of tanks on the Golan to one hundred. "We'll have one hundred tanks against their eight hundred," said Elazar. "That ought to be enough." In that sentence, Elazar summed up official Israel's reading of the Arab military potential.

An artillery battery was also sent to the Golan, and the air force was put on alert, as were a number of ground units.

At 9 a.m., Dayan joined them and Elazar spelled out the steps that had been decided on. "I think there could be nothing more idiotic on Syria's part than to attack alone," he said. "There won't be war on both the Egyptian and Syrian fronts. I believe all indications point to that. Therefore I would not go onto a war footing in order to prevent war on the Golan Heights."

Dayan agreed that all-out war was unlikely but noted that the Syrians did not have to cross a major barrier to reach the Israeli lines. "And we have to consider that there will be some clever Russian advising them."

The defense minister informed Elazar that he intended after the meeting to fly up to the Golan and transmit a message to the Syrians through the journalists who would cover the visit. He also wished to prepare the Israeli public for the possibility, however remote, of a flare-up in the north. He asked Elazar to accompany him. The chief of staff tried to dissuade Dayan from making the trip on the grounds that it would disturb the tranquillity of the Golan settlers during the holiday period. Dayan, however, insisted. "They have to be prepared for something, but we will do it in a positive way."

Dayan and his party, which included General Zeira, were helicoptered up to the Golan and driven to a hilltop overlooking the Syrian lines. They were briefed on the Syrian deployment by Maj. Shmuel Askarov, the deputy commander of a tank battalion on the front line. Pointing to the array of Syrian tanks and artillery positions in the distance, Askarov said, "War is certain." Dayan gestured to Zeira, giving him the right of response. "There will not be another war for ten years," Askarov would remember Zeira saying.

In his meeting with Israeli and foreign journalists on the Golan just three hours before the onset of Rosh Hashana, Dayan said that if the Syrians chose to strike at Israel in retaliation for the September 13 air battle, "any blow they land will hurt them more than it will us." His remark was duly picked up by the Syrian media.

The two-day holiday passed peacefully and Elazar was able to get in a brief beach holiday with his family at Sharm el-Sheikh, the southern tip of Sinai. Duty officers in the intelligence community, however, were kept busy monitoring new developments on the hitherto quiet Egyptian front. On September 25, troops were reported moving toward the Suez Canal. On the 28th, the level of alert in the Egyptian air force, navy, and some ground units was raised. AMAN at first attributed these moves to fear of an Israeli attack somehow connected to the air clash with Syria. However, a more cogent explanation soon emerged. The Egyptians, it was learned, were planning a large-scale exercise, called Tahrir 41, in the Canal Zone for October 1–7. The Egyptians held military exercises near the canal every fall, always letting the Israelis know beforehand through diplomatic channels. This time there was no such notice but Israeli intelligence gave that little significance.

On September 28, the anniversary of the death of Nasser, Sadat addressed the nation. The anniversary was normally an occasion for reaffirming the legacy of Nasser's struggle for restoration of the lost lands and Arab honor. Sadat made do with expressing hope for the nation's emergence from its present straitened circumstances "to a broad and glittering future." AMAN, in its analysis of the speech, interpreted it to mean that Sadat was indicating to the Egyptian public that there was at present no point in considering an armed struggle against Israel. But the fact that Sadat chose to keep silent about the struggle could have meant that it was not his own people he was seeking to lull.

8

SWORD FROM THE
SCABBARD

GENERAL SHAZLY HAD asked for fifteen days' notice before
G D-day to make final preparations. He got fourteen days. More
important, fourteen nights. It was at night that the convoys moved
across the desert from supply depots to the staging areas along the
canal.

Assad and Sadat, meeting secretly in Damascus on September 22,
agreed to launch the war on October 6. They differed over zero hour.
Assad wanted it at 7 a.m. so that the Israeli forces facing east on the
Golan would have the sun in their eyes. Sadat wanted the attack
launched just before sunset so that his air force could get in a strike
on Israeli bases in Sinai without the Israelis having time for a counter-
strike. His combat engineers could then bridge the canal under cover
of darkness. Assad, in an act of generosity about which he would
shortly have second thoughts, bowed to the Egyptian leader's preference. On his way to Damascus, Sadat stopped off in Saudi Arabia to
discuss with King Faisal the unleashing of an oil embargo against the
West as part of a coordinated effort by the Arab world to bring pressure on Israel and its supporters. Ashraf Marwan accompanied him
on the trip.

Shazly had 650,000 combat troops under his command. The Syrian army numbered 150,000. Contingents from Iraq, Jordan, and
other Arab countries would add another 100,000 soldiers. The Israeli
army numbered 375,000 soldiers, of whom 240,000 were reservists.

Israel's 2,100 tanks were half the combined number of Egyptian
(2,200) and Syrian (1,650) tanks. Iraq and Jordan would send 650
more tanks after war began. Israel had 359 first-line warplanes compared to a combined total of 680 for Egypt (400) and Syria (280).

The 100,000 Egyptian soldiers and 1,350 tanks drawn up west of the canal at the beginning of October were faced by only 450 Israeli soldiers in the Bar-Lev forts and 91 Israeli tanks in the Canal Zone. Another 200 tanks were posted deeper in Sinai, three hours away. In artillery and heavy mortars, the Egyptians outgunned the Israelis along the canal by a 40 to 1 margin on the first day. On the northern front, the Syrians enjoyed 8 to 1 superiority in tanks. The disparity in infantry and artillery was far greater. These odds would be greatly reduced once the Israeli reserves reached the battlefront. Until then, the young conscripts on the front line—nineteen- to twenty-one-year-old draftees—and their regular army commanders would bear the brunt of any surprise attack.

The first large-scale movement of Egyptian troops was picked up by intelligence on the night of September 24–25, an entire division proceeding from Cairo under heavy escort of military police. There were convoys every night following.

AMAN kept the military and political leadership abreast of ongoing developments through bulletins, issued several times a day. On September 30, it reported that a large-scale Egyptian military exercise would begin the following day and end on October 7. The exercise would involve mobilization of reserves, work on fortifications, troop movements, and mobilization of civilian fishing boats as troop transports. Henceforth, all moves by the Egyptian army would be depicted by AMAN in the context of the exercise. By discounting a priori all developments as part of a military exercise, Israel was in effect shutting down its early warning system.

The Syrians were raising their alert status and mobilizing reserves. This was attributed by AMAN to Syrian fears that the IDF might follow up the September 13 air battle with another blow or that Syria might be preparing to retaliate for the incident with a limited strike of its own. Fed by a double illusion—Egyptian exercise in the south, Syrian nervousness in the north—AMAN looked on unperturbed as two armies mustered for war in full view. The public was unaware of what was happening on the borders. So was the press. So was the cabinet, except for Mrs. Meir, Dayan, and ministers Galili and Yigal Allon. The army command, of course, was aware but as long as military intelligence, supposedly all knowing, was insisting on "low probability," there would be no mobilization.

Eleven warnings of war were received during September from

intelligence sources. But Zeira remained unmoved. War, he said, was not an Arab option. Not even Hussein's extraordinary warning succeeded in altering AMAN's composure.

Zeira was supported in his low-probability assessment by his second-in-command, Brig. Gen. Arye Shalev, who headed the powerful Research Section of AMAN, and by the head of the Egyptian desk, Lt. Col. Yona Bandman. The latter had won Zeira's high regard in the Six Day War as a young intelligence major. Asked his assessment of the Egyptian army on the eve of that war, he predicted that it would disintegrate in combat. He proved right and his opinion about the fighting quality of the Egyptian army had not changed much since.

AMAN's chiefs believed they knew a quiet truth—"the concept"— that rendered the cries of alarm going up around them irrelevant. Zeira and his top aides were to demonstrate in startling fashion how even intelligent and experienced men are capable of adhering to a false idea in the face of mountains of contrary evidence. Explaining away every piece of hard information that conflicted with their thesis, they embraced any wisp that seemed to confirm it. This included disinformation that should have been suspect since it came through channels the Egyptians clearly knew AMAN to be monitoring, such as the Arab press. The Egyptian and Syrian armed forces were being closely monitored as well and AMAN's "low probability" assessment clashed with the worrying evidence of war preparations that AMAN's own departments were daily gathering. The deception nevertheless succeeded beyond the Arabs' expectations because it triggered within Zeira and his close circle a monumental capacity for self-deception. Zeira clung with certitude to his view that war was simply not an Arab option.

Mossad chief Zvi Zamir, in his memoirs, writes that Zeira, in his frequent evocation of "low probability," even in official forums like the General Staff, never said on what that assessment was based. He himself, Zamir noted, always made reference to relevant sources when he gave the Mossad's assessments, accompanied by his evaluation of the credibility of those sources. "It would never occur to me in meeting with the prime minister or defense minister not to tell them on what my assessments were based," writes Zamir.

Eli Zeira's assessments, by contrast, were punchy but often short on relevant background.

"From a logical point of view it would be a mistake for Egypt to launch a war," was one of his standard lines, without spelling out what Sadat's logic might be.

"We know with certainty that he [Sadat] is afraid [of war]."

"Assad knows what his limitations are and the Syrians are aware of Israel's strategic superiority."

The self-confidence that Zeira projected and his correct (for the wrong reasons) prediction in the Blue-White episode when everyone else was wrong appear to have given him an aura that discouraged others from pressing him for explanations. Three decades after the war, Zvi Zamir would still be shocked at the failure of the military leadership, including Elazar and Dayan, to ask Zeira to spell out his analyses. The fate of the nation and thousands of lives hinged in good part on their accuracy. On the most critical issue—whether the Arabs would go to war—he was totally wrong. Absurdly wrong, given the profuse signs of war and the warnings from reliable intelligence sources. "I ask," writes Zamir, "how these assessments could have been put forth without any of the participants in the meetings asking what sources the assessments are based on."

The tempo of war drums became more insistent on the evening of September 28. American intelligence passed on a report from a source it considered highly reliable—in fact, King Hussein—that a massive Syrian attempt to reconquer the Golan Heights could be expected imminently. Hussein, of course, had delivered the same warning to Mrs. Meir three days earlier. The Americans were finding his warning worthy enough to pass on. The next morning, Elazar held a meeting of the General Staff to discuss it. Most of the generals were unimpressed. The most they expected from Syria was a limited strike in retaliation for the downing of their planes.

There was one dissenting voice, that of General Tal. All signs, he said, pointed to war on the Golan. These included the forward deployment of bridging tanks which could throw spans across Israel's antitank ditch. The Syrian divisions on the line were in emergency deployment, enabling them to attack without warning, and SAMs now covered the skies over the Golan. "The balance of forces has changed on the ground," Tal said at a General Staff meeting. "The only thing that can block a Syrian attack is the air force." He too believed the air force could cope with the SAMs. However, the weather was another matter, particularly now that the rainy season had begun. "If the air force is neutralized [by the weather], the Syrian army can sweep across the Golan. We can't take chances." He called for reinforcing the heights with the entire Seventh Armored Brigade and a battalion of artillery. Elazar disagreed with his deputy's assessment but agreed to send up several more tank companies from the Seventh Brigade in Sinai and the artillery as well.

Still troubled after the meeting, Tal telephoned Zeira and said he wanted to continue the discussion with him and Shalev in the intelligence chief's office, one flight up. When they met, Tal said the only thing preventing Elazar from ordering mobilization was AMAN's assessment of "low probability" of war. Zeira refused Tal's request to reconsider that assessment. As far as understanding enemy intentions, said the intelligence chief, he and not Tal was the expert. Tal replied that he was the expert on tank warfare and if the Syrians launched a surprise attack with three divisions the Israeli force on the Golan had no chance.

At 2 a.m. on October 1, the Mossad passed on to AMAN an alarming report it had received from a normally dependable source that war would break out this very day on both the Egyptian and Syrian fronts. According to the report, the Egyptian exercise, which was to begin at dawn, would unfold into an actual crossing of the canal that day. Zeira did not waken Elazar or Dayan to pass on the report. "I saved you a night's sleep," he told the chief of staff in the morning at a meeting of the General Staff. Elazar took it in stride but Dayan sent Zeira a note during the meeting taking him to task for not reporting the warning to him immediately. Zeira sent a note back saying he and his staff had spent the night checking the report and concluded toward morning that it was groundless. (It would later be said that the translation of the message from Arabic had been imprecise.)

Zeira noted at the meeting that Egyptian mechanized divisions had joined the exercise. So had bridging units and airborne troops. "There are several sources saying the exercise is not an exercise but is leading towards war," said Zeira. "This definitely does not seem likely to us, even though these are good sources." Egypt's mobilization of reserves and the cancellation of officers' courses did not change Zeira's assessment. He pointed out that similar moves in April had set off similar war alarms.

Zeira's fixation on "the concept" was a not unfamiliar phenomenon in the world of intelligence. Roberta Wohlstetter, writing about the American intelligence failure at Pearl Harbor, noted that on several critical occasions prior to the Japanese attack intelligence analysts failed to properly distinguish between irrelevant "noise" and "signals" hinting at enemy intentions. "Pearl Harbor, looked at closely, shows how hard it is to hear a signal against the prevailing noise, in particular when you are listening for the wrong signal," she noted.

Elazar and Dayan were unaware that the confident assessments given them by Zeira and Shalev were not shared by many in AMAN. Dissidents, including senior officers, insisted that the signs spoke clearly of war. Ever since monitoring King Hussein's meeting with Mrs. Meir on September 25, Lieutenant Colonel Keniezer was convinced that a two-front war was in the offing. He engaged in a shouting match on the subject with General Shalev, ignoring the rank that separated them.

The head of the Syrian desk, Lieutenant Colonel Ya'ari, had accepted AMAN's contention that Egypt was not going to war and that therefore Syria wasn't. This assumption was jarred by Keniezer's unauthorized report to him at midnight on September 25 about the imminent two-front war. Ya'ari would have been more upset had he known the source was none other than King Hussein. The warning had not been passed on to Ya'ari by his AMAN superiors, even though it directly concerned the Syrian front, his area of responsibility.

The warning of a two-front war passed on by the Mossad on October 1 finally convinced Ya'ari that "the concept" no longer held. Hussein's warning had been dismissed in AMAN as overwrought. But now another source was also making a connection between the Syrian and Egyptian fronts. Ignoring official channels and the late hour, Ya'ari telephoned the chief intelligence officer of Northern Command at his home and suggested that he alert General Hofi immediately to the possibility of war breaking out this day.

When Ya'ari arrived at intelligence headquarters in the morning for the daily staff meeting, he was roundly chewed out by General Shalev for having thrown Northern Command into an uproar by his unauthorized warning—a warning that contradicted AMAN's analysis. Shalev did not have to point out that war had not broken out; AMAN had been proven right again. Two days later, Ya'ari and the Northern Command intelligence officer were summoned to Shalev's office to have a formal rebuke entered into their records.

Col. Yoel Ben-Porat, head of AMAN's all-important SIGINT (signals intelligence) section, which monitored radio communications in the Arab world and beyond, was among those lulled by Sadat's September 28 speech, which he listened to on a radio as he relaxed on the Tel Aviv beach. "I heard Sadat's speech," he told a colleague the next day. "He talked about trees and stones, everything but war."

Ben-Porat was not a man normally lulled by events across the border. The essence of his professional being was edginess. His department was AMAN's prime bulwark against surprise attack. It was unlikely that an enemy could prepare for war without its radio signals leaving tracks. Ben-Porat had an obsessive personal interest in the possibility of surprise attack. As a boy of eleven living in Poland near the Russian border, he had witnessed the results of Operation Barbarossa in which the German army overwhelmed the Russian army after an elaborate deception. Ben-Porat lost his family in the Holocaust and spent part of the war years with partisan bands roaming the forests. He was sent by AMAN to Europe in 1969 to study the Soviet suppression of the Czech uprising the year before. In his report, he described the way Russian tank forces, carrying out what seemed routine maneuvers in neighboring Warsaw Pact countries, had suddenly descended on Prague.

"The only thing differentiating war from maneuvers is the last stage on the last day," he wrote. "The concentration of forces and the logistics is the same for both." He subsequently wrote a directive for the units under his command stressing this lesson. "Whenever there is a military exercise in the region of unusual scale, relate to the possibility that it cloaks intentions of war." Twice in the past two years he had put his men on emergency footing in response to Egyptian exercises.

The phone call that woke him at 3 a.m. on October 1 thus had special resonance. It was from an AMAN officer passing on the report from a Mossad source that the Egyptian exercise beginning this day would evolve into an attack across the canal before nightfall and that the Syrians would join in a two-front war.

"What does Research say?" Ben-Porat asked his caller, referring to General Shalev's section.

"They say it's just an exercise."

Information accumulated by Ben-Porat in the coming hours increased his suspicion that the Egyptians were up to something even though the exercise did not seem to be developing into a cross-canal attack this day. Failing to get Zeira on the phone, he spoke to Shalev and voiced his belief that the warning was significant. Shalev reminded him that he said the same thing during the Blue-White alert in the spring. "You're wrong this time too," Shalev said.

Shalev's refusal to relate to the evidence of war as serious, reflecting Zeira's position, infuriated Ben-Porat. But there was still one intelligence tripwire the Egyptians could hardly avoid falling over if they were on their way to war.

Nine months before, four Israeli helicopters bearing a commando unit and communications personnel had lifted off from Sinai at night and flown into Egypt. According to one account, they landed atop Mount Ataka, overlooking the road between Suez City, on the canal, and Cairo.

With the commandos securing the periphery, the technicians planted listening devices on communication lines leading to selected military and government offices that would be at the hub of any war preparations. The men were retrieved before dawn.

A description of the system has never been publicly revealed, nor the number of locations involved, but the devices were not ordinary taps. Minister Galili would describe them as "major achievements in electronics" and Mrs. Meir would say that their operation involved "fantastic sums of money." Installing and maintaining the taps involved risky penetrations into Egyptian territory. Those involved in the project regarded it as the nation's insurance policy, one that would warn of a surprise attack if all else failed.

Except for periodic tests, the listening devices remained dormant because their activation risked detection. They were to be turned on, by pushing a button in Tel Aviv, only when there was tangible fear of an enemy attack. The system was labeled "special means of collection" and was referred to by the few who knew about it simply as "special means." The taps were activated operationally for the first time in April when Egypt seemed about to attack. They provided evidence that the massed Egyptian forces across the canal were only conducting an exercise.

During the summer, the Egyptians discovered some of the taps. A fallen telephone pole, riddled with Israeli listening devices, would after the war be displayed in a military museum in Cairo. But other taps remained undetected.

In his telephone conversation with Shalev on October 1, Ben-Porat asked whether the "special means" had been activated. Shalev said he himself had asked Zeira to activate them, as had other senior figures in AMAN, but that the reply thus far was negative. It was the first time that Ben-Porat had heard Zeira's deputy indicating his own unease about the situation as well as a difference of opinion with Zeira.

After being wakened by the war warning at 3 a.m., Ben-Porat contacted the duty officer at SIGINT headquarters and asked to have his key staff assembled there in an hour. It was the consensus at the meeting that they would have to substantially increase monitoring of Arab communications. When Ben-Porat finally got through to Zeira, he asked permission to mobilize two hundred intelligence reservists for that purpose. Zeira's reply was firm. "Yoel, listen well. I don't permit you to think about mobilizing even a fraction of a reservist. It is intelligence's job to safeguard the nation's nerves, not to drive the public crazy, not to undermine the economy."

This definition of intelligence's role was one Ben-Porat did not accept. Despite the edge of annoyance in the voice on the line, he asked for activation of the "special means." Zeira refused.

"What do these 'special means' exist for," asked an exasperated Ben-Porat, "if not for situations like the one we're facing?"

"The situations you see," replied Zeira, "are not the ones I see."

Like others puzzled at the refusal of Zeira to bend to the accumulating evidence, Ben-Porat resigned himself to the notion that the intelligence chief must have other information which painted a different picture

SIGINT operations officer Shabtai Brill was also not assuaged by AMAN's litany of "low probability." A red light had flashed on for him on September 28 with a report that Syria had moved two squadrons of Sukhoi bombers to a forward airfield. Since the Six Day War, when much of its air force was destroyed on the ground, the Syrians had been careful to keep their warplanes well out of Israeli reach. The shifting of the Sukhois to a base where they could easily be hit made no sense unless they were intended to support troops advancing into the Golan. There were many other troubling signs. On the Egyptian front, a convoy of three hundred ammunition trucks had been detected making its way from Cairo to the Canal Zone. An exercise would not require that amount of ammunition, Brill argued. Most worrying of all was the shifting of SAM batteries from the Damascus area to the Golan approaches. If the Syrians were fearful of an Israeli attack, as AMAN's leadership maintained, why were they weakening the defenses of their capital? But his warnings had no more impact than those of other dissidents within AMAN.

The northern half of the line on the Golan Heights was held by a tank battalion commanded by Lt. Col. Yair Nafshi. Addressing his men the day he assumed command a year before, he announced his intention of transforming the battalion into the best in the armored corps. The only way to overcome the numerical superiority of the Syrian tanks opposite them, he said, was to shoot faster and straighter. Turning to a gunner, he asked, "How long would it take to hit three tanks coming at you at twelve hundred meters?" Four minutes, the gunner guessed. Others thought they could do it in half that time. "Seven seconds maximum," said Nafshi. He let the laughter die before saying he would demonstrate.

As the men walked with him to the gunnery range, he briefed a crewman on how to load the shells. The men sat on the ground to watch the demonstration, some of them holding watches. They could hear the tank commander give Nafshi, in the gunner's position, the order to fire. He hit three targets, spaced fifty yards apart, with three rapid shots and jumped down from the tank. Stopwatches showed 6.5 seconds.

Gunnery proficiency became the unit's hallmark. Nafshi cultivated "snipers" who could hit targets at long range. He had them wear gray uniforms instead of standard green to give them special status. Tanks which scored hits on Syrian tanks during skirmishes had tank silhouettes painted on their turrets. Nafshi instituted a series of written tests on subjects ranging from ballistics to the history of Israel's battles. His efforts were rewarded when the battalion was chosen to host the armored corps' Passover seder in April, attended by the defense minister and chief of staff. Following tradition, the afikoman matzah was "stolen" during the meal and Dayan, as the seder's "elder," agreed to buy it back with a present—in this case, a basketball court for the unit.

During the turmoil over the Golan front in September, the Suez front had remained calm. Apart from the small garrisons in the Bar-Lev forts, defense of the line was entrusted to an armored brigade commanded by Col. Amnon Reshef, who had been serving in Sinai since the Six Day War. The brigade had been on the line for three months after an intensive training period and was at the peak of efficiency. The young crewmen learned that modern tanks, properly handled, could cope better with the treacherous sands than did the tank armies which fought in North Africa in the Second World War. Even high dunes, previously thought impassable, could be climbed if approached straight on; attempts to take them at an angle risked throwing a tread. Before passing over a dune crest, crewmen had to remember to turn the tank gun sideways to avoid smashing it into the ground on the decline. The units exercised Dovecote day and night, the tanks rushing forward from rear deployment to take positions supporting the forts on the canal.

Reshef's tank brigade was one of three that made up the Sinai Division, commanded by Brig. Gen. Albert Mendler. The other two brigades were at training facilities in central Sinai. Mendler was scheduled to transfer out of the division on October 7 to assume command of the armored corps from Avraham Adan, who was to retire. Preparations were already under way for a series of farewell parties within the division and staff officers were searching Tel Aviv shops for appropriate gifts. However, a report passed on to Mendler informally by a friend in AMAN early on October 1 created a new agenda. "Fantastic," he wrote in his diary. "0515 hours. Intelligence. War tomorrow. Farewell, transfer."

Mendler ordered Reshef to have his brigade ready to move out on five minutes' notice. Crews were to sleep with their clothes and boots on and tanks ready for immediate movement, fully armed and fueled. In the fortifications on the canal, the men were to be roused half an hour before dawn.

It was only on this day—Monday, October 1—that the two senior Egyptian commanders on the Suez front, Gen. Saad Mamoun of the Second Army and Gen. Abdel Muneim Wasel of the Third Army, were summoned to Cairo and informed that D-day was set for Saturday, October 6. Divisional commanders were not to be informed until October 3. Brigade commanders would be told the day after that and battalion and company commanders only the day before hostilities commenced. With some exceptions, the soldiers themselves would not be told until six hours before the attack.

The Egyptian high command moved on October 1 to Center Ten, the underground complex in Cairo from which the war would be run. In the evening, the Supreme Council of the Armed Forces assembled there. Each commander in turn stepped up to an operations map, outlined his mission, and formally declared himself ready to carry it out. Sadat expressed his confidence in them and all joined in a brief prayer.

Sgt. Mahmud Nadeh introduced himself in his new notebook on the shore of the Bitter Lake. "We'll begin from the beginning. I serve as a sergeant in the armed forces. We'll be going to war in the next few days. I'm two and a half kilometers from the enemy. We've been told we will be the first to cross the canal to free our lands and expel the enemy." He promised, in the name of "historical truth," to keep an accurate account of the events that awaited him and of the heroism and patriotism of the Egyptian soldier.

The notebook, which would fall into the hands of Israeli intelligence, revealed that some units in the Egyptian army were aware at least three days before October 6 that they were going to war. The diary would offer an insight into the mind of a university-educated soldier whose kind was now to be found in the ranks of the Egyptian army alongside peasants and urban slum dwellers.

A third-year humanities student from Alexandria, Nadeh had trained as a commando but was now attached to an amphibious armored unit that was to cross the Bitter Lake. "We are to proceed with all possible speed to the Mitla Pass after an artillery barrage of fifty minutes," he wrote on Thursday. "I hope to emerge alive from the battle because I believe in God. There is a smile on everyone's face, even my officer's."

The tension on the borders had not prevented Mrs. Meir from departing for Strasbourg to address the Council of Europe. Comforted by AMAN's reports, she continued on to Vienna in an attempt to persuade Austrian chancellor Bruno Kreisky to rescind his decision to close down a transit center for Jews arriving from the Soviet Union, most of whom planned to continue on to Israel. He made his decision after two Palestinian gunmen seized a train and took five Jewish migrants and an Austrian border guard hostage. The meeting between the two leaders was tense and ended in disagreement.

Mrs. Meir's absence in Europe reassured the Arab command, since the Israeli government was unlikely to decide on mobilization as long as she was out of the country. Egyptian intelligence, closely monitoring developments in Israel and in Sinai, reported no indication that

Israel was taking cautionary steps. To the Egyptians' astonishment, the Israeli command seemed entirely unaware that the large armies on its borders were preparing for war. The preparations did not, however, go unnoticed by the soldiers on the front lines.

Four days before Yom Kippur, Sgt. Yoram Krivine's platoon took over Strongpoint 111, on the Golan cease-fire line. It was a routine rotation but it struck the twenty-one-year-old paratroop sergeant that the soldiers they were relieving seemed unusually happy about leaving. The outpost was one of ten fortifications along the forty-mile length of the line. The dark basalt fortifications were stout enough to withstand even direct artillery hits.

The hillock on which 111 was situated offered a view across the rocky Syrian plain. Krivine could see countless artillery pieces, tanks, and other vehicles nestling under camouflage netting. He had never before served on the Purple Line—a name given to the 1967 cease-fire line because of its color on the Israeli map—and did not know whether or not this massive deployment was routine. On a wall inside the fortification the men found a sign reading "111 Will Not Fall Again." Krivine learned that the post had indeed been captured by the Syrians and briefly held during a skirmish.

Opposite them was Tel Kudne, a Syrian military position on a volcanic cone that rose abruptly from the landscape. It was a mirror image of the positions on the Israeli side of the line. One hundred yards from the Israeli fortification was one of several U.N. observation posts situated along the line.

The day they arrived, Krivine's platoon was briefed by an intelligence officer belonging to the unit they had just relieved. The officer identified for them the Syrian units they were facing. "The whole Syrian army is out there," he said in conclusion. "I'm happy I won't be here when the war starts."

9

COUNTDOWN

HER CONTENTIOUS MEETING with Chancellor Kreisky was still on Golda Meir's mind when she met with her senior military advisers on Wednesday, October 3, the morning after her return from Europe. "He didn't even offer me a glass of water," she said. The newspapers carried extensive accounts of her trip and the closing of the transit camp in Vienna. In one or two papers there was passing reference to tension on the northern border.

The meeting in the prime minister's office had been requested by Dayan, who described it as a consultation. He could not shake off his concern over the Golan and wanted to share it with the prime minister. Military symbol though he was, Dayan related to the seventy-five-year-old grandmother even on purely military matters with the deference due her position. There were reports, he said, that Egypt was bent on war but the situation on the Syrian front was more troubling because of the immediate threat it posed to the settlements on the Golan. The Syrians had deployed their most advanced SAMs not around Damascus but opposite the Golan. "This is not a normal defensive deployment," he said. If the Egyptians crossed the canal, Dayan said, they would find themselves in open desert with Israeli forces attacking them from every side. But the Syrians, with one quick thrust, could hope to push Israel off the Golan and then be protected against counterattacks by the steep heights.

General Shalev, filling in for Zeira, who was ill at home, gave AMAN's appraisal of the situation. "There are troubling reports on Syria and also Egypt," he confirmed. The Syrians could attack without warning. They had deployed an unprecedented amount of artillery opposite the Golan. On the Suez front, the Egyptians were engaged in a large-scale military exercise. A worst-case situation, said Shalev, would be for Syria and Egypt to launch a two-front war. "Is this reasonable?" he asked rhetorically. "In my opinion, on the basis of much material received in recent days, Egypt believes it is not yet ready to go to war." And if Egypt was not going to war, then neither was Syria. Might Egypt not stage a diversion in order to let the Syrians attack, asked Mrs. Meir? Assad and the Syrians know their limitations, replied Shalev. "They're aware of Israel's great advantage in the air." In short, the probability of war remained low.

General Elazar agreed with Shalev's analysis. Egypt and Syria indeed had plans for a coordinated attack. "But I don't see a concrete danger in the near future." Should Syria attempt a full-scale attack on its own, he said, Israel would know beforehand. "We have good information. It's reasonable that if a big machine begins moving there will be leaks." He intended to keep the Israeli deployment on the Golan as it was, except for a slight beefing up. Despite her unease, Mrs. Meir did not take it upon herself to challenge a roomful of generals counseling calm.

Shalev's upbeat bottom line had succeeded in reassuring her, at least for the moment. As the meeting broke up, she shook his hand and said, "Thanks for putting my mind at rest." His words were so soothing that the security situation was no longer considered serious enough to be placed on the agenda of the cabinet meeting scheduled for the next day to hear Mrs. Meir's report on her European trip. The government thus had no idea that the possibility of war was even being mooted. Nor would the Arab buildup be referred to at Thursday's General Staff meeting. The sole item on the agenda—two days before Yom Kippur—was discipline, with emphasis on the need for soldiers to adhere to the military dress code.

This relaxed posture was grossly out of sync with what the men at the front were seeing or with what AMAN itself was picking up from its myriad sources. Lookouts along the canal were reporting a massive enemy buildup since the beginning of the week. Much of this information was not being passed upward by the chief Southern Command intelligence officer, Col. David Gedalia. Adopting AMAN's "low probability" thesis, he regarded such reports as irrelevant "noise" attributable to the Egyptian exercise. Some of the information which he did pass on to the Egyptian desk in AMAN was not passed on to Zeira and Shalev. Nor were the intelligence chief and his deputy themselves passing on to Elazar all the information reaching them. The reports about Arab preparations that did reach Elazar and Dayan were packaged with reassuring explanations—Egyptian exercise, Syrian fears of an Israeli attack—that sapped them of their menace.

Even as Mrs. Meir was consulting Wednesday with Dayan and the others, the Egyptian war minister, General Ismail, was flying into Damascus for final coordination with his Syrian colleagues. To his dismay, the Syrians requested a forty-eight-hour postponement of D-day in order to complete the draining of fuel tanks at Homs, which they feared Israel might bomb. Ismail refused on the grounds that any delay risked the secrecy of the operation. The Syrians dropped their request but asked that zero hour be changed back from 6 p.m. The two sides compromised on 2 p.m., which would give the Syrian sappers enough hours of daylight to breach the Israeli minefields.

The Syrian deployment had reached saturation point. The arrival of one armored brigade in particular, the Forty-seventh, raised eyebrows among Israeli intelligence officers. The brigade had been brought to their attention the previous year by one of the Syrian officers captured in a cross-border raid into Lebanon. The Syrians, reconnoitering the border area with a Lebanese escort, were seized in order to exchange them for Israeli pilots in Syrian hands. One of them, attached to the Syrian General Staff, mentioned that a new brigade, the Forty-seventh, was being formed to serve at Homs. The city was a hotbed of Islamic fundamentalist opposition to the regime in Damascus and President Assad wanted an armored brigade permanently posted there to suppress any uprising.

"If you ever hear that the Forty-seventh is being sent to the front, you can be sure it's war," said the officer offhandedly. On September 27, word was received that the Forty-seventh was heading toward the Golan. (In 1982 Assad would unleash his army against the Islamic dissidents in Homs, killing an estimated 10,000 to 25,000 of his own citizens.)

On the Bar-Lev Line, lookouts reported feverish activity across the canal. Descents to the water for boats were being prepared at dozens of locations and the Egyptians were working late every night to raise the height of their ramparts overlooking the Israeli canal-side positions.

General Mendler had begun holding staff meetings twice a day, instead of once, for situation assessments. It was becoming ever more apparent to him that the Egyptians were preparing for war. When the division commander passed his concern upward to Southern Command he was told that all was connected to the Egyptian exercise.

One junior intelligence officer in Southern Command begged to differ. Lt. Binyamin Siman-Tov was charged with monitoring the deployment of Egyptian forces. At a staff meeting on October 1, he submitted to Colonel Gedalia a memo suggesting that the Egyptian exercise was only a diversion. The memo listed a number of points:

-Why did the Egyptian army suddenly cancel training courses and postpone officers' examinations if this was a scheduled exercise?
-Why was Egyptian radio whipping up war fever if this was just an exercise and why were Egyptian officers being obliged to listen?
-Why have the Egyptians prepared some forty descents for boats along the canal?
-Why have tanks made an appearance along the canal in the (hith- erto quiet) northern sector?
-Why wasn't the Egyptian air force taking part in the exercise?
-Why were the Egyptians making such extensive preparations for an exercise only one week long?
-Why were they so assiduously stocking emergency ammunition and engineering equipment?

The last point struck others present as particularly telling. As for the Egyptian air force, its absence could mean that there was no real exercise going on at all.

Gedalia was not impressed. He was, in fact, annoyed; the lieuten- ant's appraisal ran directly counter to that of the intelligence chiefs in Tel Aviv. Gedalia first watered down the wording of the memo, then shelved it.

General Elazar, who was focused on the Syrian front and shielded by AMAN from troubling details, remained unaware that anything out of the ordinary was occurring in the south except for an extensive Egyptian military exercise similar to ones held in previous years.

No air photos of the Egyptian lines were taken between Septem- ber 25 and October 1, a week when large forces were streaming toward the canal every night. Reconnaissance flights were risky because of the SAMs but if there was a sense of urgency they would have been given top priority. A scheduled photo mission on October 2 was canceled because of poor visibility. It was rescheduled for the next day but when the plane returned it was found that the camera shutter had failed to open. It would not be until the afternoon of the following day, Thursday, October 4, that the mission would finally be executed.

It was precisely during this critical period that the CIA, which had been monitoring Egyptian and Syrian movements, was itself blacked out in Egypt. An Agena reconnaissance satellite which covered the Middle East was launched on a routine mission from Vandenberg Air Force Base in California on September 27 but Agenas could not transmit from orbit. Its pictures would not be developed until it landed in two weeks. A more sophisticated Big Bird satellite, which could send pictures from orbit, landed on September 28. Because of costs, these satellites were used sparingly and none was scheduled to go back up for a few weeks.

The blackout was extended to Cairo itself when Egyptian military headquarters suddenly switched from radio transmissions, monitored by the CIA, to landlines, which were not. The agency noted a number of oddities in Egyptian dispositions. Elite commando units were being deployed to forward bases, larger than normal stockpiles of ammunition were being prepared, and more divisions were getting ready for maneuvers than was normal. In addition, a communications network was being set up that was far larger than ordinary maneuvers would require.

The agency transmitted its concerns to Israel on September 30 through the office of Henry Kissinger, who had just been appointed secretary of state. The reply, transmitted by the prime minister's office in consultation with the Mossad, was that Israel was aware of the Arab moves and was studying their implications. Two days later, a fuller reply was sent to Washington. It expressed Israel's belief that Syria, for all its hostile intentions, did not believe itself capable of capturing the Golan Heights without Egypt's participation in a two-front war, although there was a small chance that it might try a limited attack. As for Egypt, Israel believed that the exercise being carried out along the canal was just that and not a camouflage for war. The Americans, respectful of the Israeli intelligence services, deferred to AMAN's assessment.

On Thursday, October 4, while the Israeli General Staff was discussing dress codes, the heads of U.S. intelligence agencies met in

Washington for the weekly meeting of the U.S. Intelligence Board's "Watch Committee." In reply to a query by Kissinger, the CIA and the State Department's Bureau of Intelligence and Research (INR), basing themselves largely on the Israeli assessment, reported that war in the Middle East was unlikely. The Defense Intelligence Agency went further, saying the Arab buildup was not even of a threatening nature, an evaluation that would cost three of the agency officials their jobs.

Direct superpower involvement in the looming crisis began on October 3 when Sadat summoned the Soviet ambassador in Cairo, Vinogradov, to inform him that Egypt and Syria had decided to go to war against Israel in order to break the Middle East deadlock. "What will the Soviet attitude be?" he asked. Sadat and Assad had agreed that the Soviets would have to be told beforehand since the Arabs would be dependent on them for resupply and political support once the war started. But they would discourage any attempt by Moscow to restrain them. When the ambassador asked when the war would start, Sadat said the date had not yet been decided. He and Assad had agreed that more information would be given the Soviets by the Syrian leader, whose relations with Moscow were better than Sadat's.

On Thursday, October 4, Assad duly summoned the Soviet ambassador in Damascus, Nuritdin Mukhitdinov, and told him the war would begin "in the next few days." Syria's object, he said, was Israel's eviction from the Golan Heights and restoration of Palestinian rights. Assad said that he had in mind a campaign lasting only one or two days, not a protracted war. The Syrian army, he said, would position itself to block an Israeli counterattack once the Golan was taken. In his report to Moscow, Mukhitdinov said that Assad was interested in having the Soviet Union initiate a cease-fire resolution in the U.N. Security Council immediately after the initial stage of the battle in order to forestall an Israeli counterattack.

Assad's request to the Soviets for an early cease-fire was made without Sadat's knowledge. Sadat had taken out his own insurance policy by ordering his army to stop well short of the Sinai passes, contrary to the plans shown Assad.

In Cairo, Ambassador Vinogradov passed on to Sadat an uneasy reaction from Brezhnev to Sadat's war plans. The Soviet leader reiterated Moscow's preference for a political solution. A decision on war was a matter for the Egyptian leadership alone, said Brezhnev, but it had best be thought through carefully.

Brezhnev asked permission to send aircraft to an Egyptian military base the next day to evacuate the families of Soviet advisers. Sadat was upset at the Soviet request, which he took to be a crude expression of nonconfidence in Egypt's military capability. However, he raised no objection.

The Soviet role in the developing conflict was ambiguous. In order to retain its standing with Egypt and Syria it had supplied them with large quantities of modern armaments and thousands of military advisers. However, Moscow did not want them to actually go to war since this would endanger the Soviet Union's warming relations with the West. Furthermore, no Soviet military or political leader believed the Arabs capable of winning. In 1967 the Israelis were armed with French weaponry. This time, they would be using American armaments against Soviet planes and tanks, and defeat would be an embarrassment for Soviet arms. In the unlikely event the Arabs won, their dependence on the Soviet Union would be reduced. War was therefore a terrible option either way Moscow looked at it but Egypt and Syria were its clients and, for better or worse, they would receive its backing.

In Moscow this Thursday evening, at almost the same time that Kissinger was being told by his intelligence advisers that there was no immediate prospect of a Middle East war, Foreign Minister Andrei Gromyko summoned aides to his study on the seventh floor of the ministry on Smolenskaya Square to tell them the opposite. What they were about to hear, he said, must be kept absolutely confidential. Egypt and Syria were to open war against Israel on Saturday at 2 p.m. Neither Sadat nor Assad had informed the Soviet ambassadors of zero hour, but the Soviets clearly had other sources. The prospect of war disturbed Gromyko. It would have a negative impact on détente and undermine the chances of a durable Middle East peace. He was skeptical about the Arabs' chances but acknowledged that a surprise attack might improve their odds. When an aide said that the evacuation of Soviet citizens might reveal the Arabs' intentions to the Israelis and Americans, Gromyko said, "The lives of Soviet people are dearer to us." As the meeting broke up, the foreign minister told the others to get a good night's sleep. "You'll need your strength very soon."

Through the night in Israel, teams of photo analysts worked on the films brought back by the reconnaissance plane which had carried out its mission late Thursday afternoon when the low-lying sun cast shadows that helped identification of objects. The analysts counted every tank and artillery piece in a twenty-mile-wide swath west of the canal and made note of changes since the previous photographs nine days earlier. The results were anxiously awaited by General Elazar and the rest of the high command. General Mendler sent one of his intelligence officers up from Sinai with orders to phone him with the first results.

Even before the reconnaissance plane had returned to base, however, AMAN's SIGINT branch picked up a report that would finally end the high command's complacency. A Russian-speaking monitor at SIGINT headquarters was taking a coffee break at 4 p.m. when he was hastily summoned back to his station. Putting on his earphones, he heard a conversation between a KGB official in Moscow and a Russian in Damascus. The voices were pressured. The man in Moscow was reading a notification which included pairs of numbers, the names of seaports and airports in Syria, and specific hours. He read the same notification to someone in Homs and then to someone in a third city who said he couldn't understand the message. "What don't you understand?" asked Moscow in an annoyed tone. "Twelve is women and seven is children."

Colonel Ben-Porat was notified that an emergency evacuation of the families of Soviet advisers was under way. The evacuation was only of the families, not the advisers themselves. The transmission had not been encoded, raising speculation that the Soviets might have intended that it be intercepted, perhaps to disassociate themselves from whatever was about to happen. A few hours later, it was learned that the evacuation also involved families of Soviet advisers who had returned to Egypt in the year since Sadat's expulsion order. This time, an encoded message had been sent to the Soviet embassy in Cairo more discreetly by telephone. Eleven Soviet planes were on their way to the Middle East, including six giant Antonov 22s, each with a capacity of four hundred passengers. The Soviet families were ordered to be at assembly points by midnight.

The hasty evacuation smacked of panic. What to make of it? AMAN's Research Section suggested that there had been a falling-out between the Soviets and the Arabs similar to the one that had led to Sadat's expulsion of advisers the previous year. Zeira himself offered this explanation when Ben-Porat called him at home. The SIGINT chief pointed out that the evacuation was not of the advisers, only of their families. "This can't mean anything except war," he said. This conclusion appeared to be supported by a report from Israeli naval intelligence that Soviet warships were hastily departing Egyptian ports.

Close to midnight Thursday, Egyptian informant Ashraf Marwan called a Mossad number in London. "I can't talk long," he said. Conversations in Arabic could be heard in the room behind him. He was in Paris with an Egyptian delegation but would be flying to London the next day. It was urgent, he said, that he meet "the general," as he called Mossad chief Zamir. "I want to talk to him about chemicals." Marwan was a chemical engineer by training and "chemicals" was the code word he was to use for war. "Lots of chemicals," he added. He had been given names of specific chemicals to indicate how imminent war was and the type of war to expect—a full-scale crossing of the canal or something limited, such as air or artillery strikes. Marwan, however, did not specify.

The Mossad chief was wakened by a call from his bureau chief, Freddy Eini, at 2:30 a.m. passing on the report from London about Marwan's call. It was the first time that Marwan had ever called to ask for him. The case officer in London had tentatively set up a meeting between Marwan and Zamir for 9 p.m. this coming night in London (11 p.m. Israeli time). Marwan said he could not make it earlier. Zamir and Eini discussed flight details and the security team that would be deployed for the meet.

Zamir remained sitting up in bed, mulling over the call. Marwan was not infallible. He had twice before sent war warnings—in December and in April—that proved wrong. It was still not clear whether his information then had been wrong to start with or whether Sadat changed his mind after initiating war preparations. The current Arab buildup, unprecedented in scope, and Zeira's puzzling dismissal of war warnings were increasingly weighing on the Mossad chief and he welcomed the chance to talk with Marwan. The urgency implicit in his call from Paris was somewhat offset by his failure to indicate the timing and scale of the Arab attack. This could mean that it was not imminent. But the fact that he had spoken of chemicals meant that something was supposed to happen.

Zamir was still sitting up when the phone rang again. This time it was Eli Zeira, who rarely called him at home. Zeira had been away from his desk for several days on sick leave, although in touch with his office. He was calling to pass on the report of the departure of the

Soviet advisers' families. For the first time, he sounded worried. Zamir told him of the call from Marwan. For both men the confluence of these two events—the evacuation of the Soviet families and the urgent call from the Egyptian informant—created a jarring resonance. The Mossad chief did not wish to waken the prime minister at this hour to inform her of Marwan's call and his decision to meet him. He asked Zeira to notify her in the morning that he was en route to London.

At 8 a.m., Dayan met in his office with Elazar, Tal, and other senior officers, including Zeira. The meeting was fraught with tension. Yom Kippur would begin at sundown but the transcendent nature of the holy day had been overshadowed by developments across the borders which had cosmic implications of their own for Israel. The air photos showed a stunning Egyptian buildup all along the canal. "You can get a stroke from the numbers alone," said Dayan. "There are 1,100 artillery pieces compared to 802 on September 25. You people don't take the Arabs seriously enough."

The air photos partially liberated Elazar from ambiguity. For days now, lulled by AMAN's "low probability" of war mantra, he had been forcing the evidence of Arab war preparations into molds—Egyptian exercise, Syrian nervousness—which were too shallow to contain them. Twice during the week he asked Zeira if the "special means" had been activated. He was given to understand that they were. In fact, they weren't. Zeira had not activated them because he was convinced that Sadat would not attack. To activate them unnecessarily, to his mind, risked exposing the taps to the Egyptians. Zeira had rejected pleas from his own staff to activate the listening devices and he did not hesitate to mislead the chief of staff about it. Zeira was acting as if he, not Elazar, was the ultimate decision maker. His extraordinary behavior meant that the "special means," which had been devised as a wake-up call in the event of an enemy attack, were being used instead to put the IDF to sleep.

Arrogance is an inadequate word to describe Zeira's behavior, given that the fate of the nation was at stake. He would contend after the war that the Egyptians had succeeded in bypassing the "special means" by avoiding use of the communication lines being tapped. However, even if true, he did not know this at the time because he had not turned the taps on. A psychological study into Zeira's behavior would conclude that he "had a high need for cognitive closure." This need, the authors conjectured, made him impervious to information that contradicted his conviction that Sadat was unlikely to risk war because of the IDF's clear superiority. Zeira himself would tell the Agranat Commission that he had spent most of his military career as a commander, not a staff officer, "and as much as my nature allows me, I do not pass responsibility upwards."

Israel's key decision makers—from Dayan and Elazar to Mrs. Meir and her ministerial advisers—were immobilized in the crucial week before Yom Kippur by their understanding that there was a fail-safe mechanism in place that would give them timely warning of war. Had they known that the taps were not turned on they would, of necessity, have focused on other warning lights flashing all about them. The Arab war preparations were clearly visible to the troops on the front lines and warnings of an imminent Arab attack were arriving every other day from credible intelligence sources.

It was only on Thursday night that Zeira was finally shaken out of his dogged complacency by the evacuation of the Soviet families, which he could not explain away. Close to midnight, he ordered that the "special means" be activated.

Elazar, who believed that they had been activated for nearly a week without signaling anything amiss, was nevertheless concerned enough by developments to order the armed forces onto a C alert Friday morning, the highest state of alert short of war. It was the first such alert since the Six Day War. The IDF's mobilization network was put on standby. Many soldiers had been scheduled to go home for the holiday in the coming hours but all leaves were now canceled, a critical move. Elazar ordered the remainder of the Seventh Armored Brigade dispatched to the Golan. There would be 177 tanks on the heights by the following morning. These, he felt, would be sufficient to cope despite the odds, which were now greater than 8 to 1 in Syria's favor. Staff and cadets at the army's Tank Training School were formed into a brigade led by the school's commander, Col. Gabi Amir, and flown down Friday night to Sinai to replace the Seventh Brigade, which had left for the Golan.

The evacuation of the Soviet families briefly shook Zeira's fixation on "low probability." Admitting for the first time to a measure of puzzlement about Arab intentions, he gave his blessing to the C alert. "The evacuation has introduced a new dimension," he said. It was not reasonable to assume the Soviets feared an Israeli attack, he acknowledged. If they did, they would have asked the United States to stay Israel's hand. But the Soviets might be aware of an Egyptian-Syrian plan to attack Israel. Although his analysis clearly pointed to an Arab attack as the most likely scenario, he did not say so. He would, in fact, continue to defiantly cling to his "low probability" assessment.

The nature of the Egyptian exercise was puzzling. No military radio traffic was being picked up except from outposts in the Aswan area five hundred miles to the south. The Egyptians along the canal were evidently confining their communications to landlines or messages delivered by hand. This could mean that there was no exercise at all. (Egyptian units had been ordered not to use wireless communications in order to prevent the Israelis from getting a fix on their identities and location.) Despite these admittedly troubling uncertainties, Zeira saw no reason to alter AMAN's basic assessment that Arab self-interest ruled out war as an option. "I don't see either the Egyptians or the Syrians attacking," he said.

Reporting Zamir's departure for London at the Friday morning staff meeting in Dayan's office, Zeira said, "It may be that by tonight we'll be a lot wiser." In extremis, he was putting faith in the man he had designated a double agent.

Despite Dayan's long-held confidence in Zeira's judgment, he had become uneasy at the intelligence chief's unyielding rejection of the numerous warnings of war. He now asked Zeira for the first time what the "special means" were showing. Like others privy to the secret, Dayan assumed the taps had been running since the Egyptian exercise began. "Absolutely quiet," responded Zeira. This time he was within the realm of truth. The technical officer in charge of the system had activated the taps at 1:40 a.m. Friday at Zeira's direction. They would remain on for nine hours, Zeira would say in a talk forty years later—his first-ever public reference to the subject—and then be shut down again. All that was picked up during this time, he said, were eleven conversations he described as innocuous.

It was not until the existence of the "special means" was publicly revealed four decades after the war that the Israeli public could understand the seeming complacency of the country's military and political leaders in 1973 as Arab armies massed on the borders. Confident of the high quality of the information the "special means" was capable of picking up, Dayan and the others assumed that Zeira's "low probability" of war assessments were solidly based. They believed that the "special means" would provide ample time for mobilization if that were necessary. It did not cross their minds that one of their own—the chief of military intelligence, no less—would make an error so grievous as to suspend Israel's "insurance policy" at this most critical of hours and then deceive them about it to boot.

By Friday, Zeira's self-confidence was no longer shared by his closest associates. Speaking to General Shalev by telephone midday, SIGINT chief Ben-Porat thought Zeira's deputy sounded like a man struggling with reality. Ben-Porat's assistant told him that Yona Bandman on the Egyptian desk likewise sounded uncertain for the first time about Egypt's intentions.

Against the background of massing armies, great power maneuverings, and cabinet deliberations, the events about to unfold were being pushed in opposite directions by two individuals gripped by deviant compulsions. Ashraf Marwan was betraying his people, giving away their deepest secrets to their bitterest enemy for reasons that could only be guessed at. General Zeira, with a blithe arrogance that defied rational explanation, was single-handedly blinding Israel's leadership to the coming confrontation.

What motivated Marwan to betray his country would remain a matter of conjecture to his Israeli handlers. Money was certainly a factor; he would receive millions of dollars from Israel over the years. But there was also a powerful psychological element of uncertain shape at play—perhaps addiction to the adrenaline rush of danger, or retribution for snubs from his late father-in-law, Nasser, or from his current patron, Sadat; perhaps a desire to play life's game at a more charged level than his social peers in Cairo. Zamir, who spent many hours with him, never asked him why he had chosen to spy for Israel. But the Mossad chief did sense a deep resentment toward Sadat, who, despite the sensitive assignments he gave to Marwan, allegedly treated him like a messenger boy. Whatever the motivations, Marwan and Zeira, each in his way, had key roles in a drama that would set the Middle East ablaze.

Following the meeting of the military chiefs in Dayan's office Friday morning, most of the participants proceeded to Mrs. Meir's office. "I still think that they're not going to attack," Elazar told her, "but we have no hard information." He was apparently referring to the silence of the "special means." Zeira, reverting to his previous stance, said that a joint Egyptian-Syrian attack was "absolutely unreasonable" and offered a new theory for the evacuation of the Soviet families. "Maybe the Russians think the Arabs are going to attack because they don't understand them well." In other words, the Russians who had been working alongside the Egyptians and Syrians for years, serving as their advisers and arms suppliers, did not understand the Arab mentality. Conceding that that was only speculation, Zeira said that in fact he could not explain the Russian move.

At 11:30 a.m., the generals briefed those cabinet members living in Tel Aviv. Ministers living in Jerusalem were not summoned because of the proximity of Yom Kippur, which would begin at sunset. Dayan and Zeira reviewed the fast-moving developments. The military options open to the Arabs, they said, were artillery bombardment of the Bar-Lev Line, limited raids into Sinai, or a massive Egyptian crossing. "All are low probability and the lowest of all is a crossing of the canal," Zeira said. "As long as they don't have the feeling they can achieve a reasonable situation in the air, they won't go to war, certainly not all-out war."

Zeira did not relate to Sadat's revised war plan that Zvi Zamir had passed on months before, a plan based on the SAM umbrella neutralizing Israeli air superiority over the battlefield. Sadat's far-reaching change negated "the concept"—that Egypt would not go to war without long-range planes and Scuds—which Zeira had been clinging to and which underlay his insistence on "low probability."

It was Mrs. Meir who challenged Zeira's reading of the situation, albeit obliquely. She expressed doubt that the Syrians, if they did intend to attack, would make do only with an artillery barrage, given the massiveness of their deployment. She found further cause for concern in the translations of the Arab press that had been laid on her desk that morning. On the eve of the Six Day War, she recalled, the Arab media was filled with false reports that Israeli troops were massing. Today they were writing the very same thing. "Maybe this should tell us something." Hers were the healthy instincts of a woman who knew nothing of military strategy but could recognize a bald fact staring her in the face.

Elazar said that if the Arabs decided to attack, there would be "indications" beforehand, apparently a reference to "special means." In response to a question by minister Galili, Mrs. Meir's closest adviser, Elazar said the IDF would not mobilize reserves without such indications. Mobilization was not something to be lightly undertaken since it could lead to events spinning out of control. Dayan firmly opposed mobilization unless the Arabs made the first hostile move.

With the Blue-White controversy the previous spring still vivid, the chief of staff ran the risk of being perceived as an alarmist if he mobilized the reserves on the eve of Yom Kippur, especially when AMAN was insisting on "low probability." He might well have felt otherwise had he been aware that Zeira's views were disputed by many in the intelligence hierarchy.

Ending the meeting, Mrs. Meir said the discussion would be resumed by the full cabinet on Sunday. At Galili's suggestion, the ministers formally authorized Mrs. Meir and Dayan to order mobilization on Yom Kippur if they deemed it necessary, without convening the cabinet. Mrs. Meir asked the ministers to leave telephone numbers with the cabinet secretary where they could be reached if necessary during the holy day. She herself would spend the holiday in her Tel Aviv apartment.

Mrs. Meir's assistant, Lou Kedar, had been growing increasingly distressed by the snatches of conversation she was picking up during the morning. On the staircase outside the prime minister's office she encountered a group of officers, including Zeira. Seeing her expression, he patted her on the shoulder and said, "Don't make a face like that. There won't be a war."

At that hour, Zeira's staff was preparing an updated intelligence bulletin which strongly indicated the opposite. In forty-two paragraphs, it spelled out details of unusual activity in Egypt and Syria that pointed to imminent war. But a forty-third paragraph negated the conclusion to be drawn from all the rest.

The details of the bulletin reveal something of the extent to which Israeli intelligence was monitoring the Arab armies:

Egyptian naval headquarters had the night before last ordered windows and car headlights at naval bases painted as a blackout precaution; soldiers had been ordered to break their Ramadan fast; military training courses were being canceled; in the past two weeks seventy-three of the eighty-five boat descents to the canal along the Egyptian bank had been improved; in the Gulf of Suez a force of naval commandos had been identified along with two dozen rubber boats; in Syria, ammunition was being transferred from Homs to the southern Golan front; several sources reported a feeling among Syrian soldiers and officers that a large-scale war was in the offing.

These reports, coming on top of what was already known about the Arab buildup, should have been enough to remove any lingering doubts about Arab intent. The item about the Ramadan fast alone should have set off every alarm bell in the country. Why would a Muslim country with a strong religious ethos order its soldiers to violate a central religious obligation just for an exercise? Israel, where religion played a much smaller role, would certainly never ask its soldiers to eat on Yom Kippur for an exercise.

Such conclusions were offset by the final paragraph inserted by Colonel Bandman: "Although the emergency deployment along the canal appears to show clear evidence of aggressive intent, our best assessment is that there has been no change in Egypt's evaluation of its relative strength vis-à-vis the IDF. Thus, the chances that Egypt is planning to renew hostilities are low."

In the General Staff command bunker in Cairo, Center Ten, Gen. Ahmed Fuad Havidi, head of the Israeli desk in Egyptian intelligence, studied the reports that had come in since mid-morning. Israel's Southern Command seemed to be showing signs of waking from the torpor which had gripped it for months. There had been no reinforcement in recent days of Israeli units in Sinai, no large-scale training exercises. Even the beginning of the Egyptian exercise had failed to stir the Israelis. But this Friday morning, bustle was reported by Egyptian signals intelligence and by Bedouin in Sinai serving as Egyptian spies. (Other Bedouin served as Israeli spies.) Senior Israeli officers were reported arriving at the large Refidim Air Base in western Sinai, tank formations could be seen on the move, mechanics were checking generators. At noon Havidi prepared a bulletin for distribution to the senior command. Its conclusion: Israel has discovered our intentions to attack and it also knows the scale of the attack.

General Gamasy, head of operations, was furious when he read it. The bulletin could raise fears of an Israeli trap precisely at a time when high morale was critical. Havidi said there was no reason for concern. The Israelis had only just begun to move and there was no chance of significant reinforcements reaching Sinai before the war began.

Despite the C alert, the Israelis had, in fact, hardly begun to move, apart from the last elements of the Seventh Brigade shifting north from Sinai to the Golan. In Tel Aviv shortly after noon, Elazar and Zeira hurried off to their fourth meeting of the day, this with the General Staff. The meeting had been scheduled weeks earlier in order to pass on holiday greetings. "But as long as you're here, we have some new information," said Elazar. Again, it was Zeira who gave the main briefing, including news of the Soviet evacuation and the results of the photo reconnaissance mission. "To sum up," he concluded, "I don't think we're going to war but there's a bigger question mark about it today, I would say, than twenty-four hours ago."

Elazar said that if the Arabs attacked without warning over Yom Kippur, the troops on the line, supported by the air force, would hold until the reserves were mobilized. Apart from the Jerusalem Brigade units on the Suez Canal, the troops on both fronts were young conscript soldiers with regular army officers. In conclusion, the chief of staff offered his generals the traditional greeting for the coming Jewish year—"May you be well inscribed in the Book of Life." In Jewish tradition, the heavenly book is opened on Rosh Hashana for the recording of one's fate for the coming year and it is sealed, after Ten Days of Repentance, on Yom Kippur.

Despite his attempts to be reassuring, Elazar was increasingly uneasy. In a departure from standing procedure, he authorized Air Force Commander Benny Peled to call up air force reservists without clearing the move with Dayan. If it came to a worst-case situation, Elazar wanted to have at least the air force at full strength.

A hush had descended over the land by late afternoon as the population prepared for the onset of Yom Kippur at sundown. Traffic halted completely and the streets were almost empty of pedestrians. Elazar, however, remained in his office, going through reports and thinking about whether he had done everything to prepare for whatever lay ahead. Within a few hours, Zamir was to report on his meeting with Marwan, which might finally clarify whether the Arabs were going to war. Unknown to Elazar, an answer to that question had already arrived and lay on a desk one floor above him.

SIGINT had that afternoon intercepted a message from the Iraqi ambassador in Moscow, who had learned from his sources of the evacuation of Soviet civilians in Syria. "The sources attribute it to the intention of Syria and Egypt to launch a war against Israel," he wrote. This message was what Elazar was waiting for—a signal of Arab intentions from a credible source that would justify mobilization. The message was passed on at 5 p.m. to a major serving as intelligence duty officer at army headquarters in Tel Aviv. The officer called his superiors and was bounced from one to another until he reached Zeira himself at home. Knowing that the report would probably trigger mobilization, the intelligence chief told the officer to delay distribution of the intercept. He wanted to first hear from Zamir in London.

It was, even for Zeira, a breathtaking display of intellectual arrogance, one that would have far-reaching consequences. Once again, he was preventing vital information contradicting his no-war thesis from reaching decision makers, even though he supported the C alert. Elazar would later say that if he had received the report shortly after it arrived, he would have set the mobilization process in motion. Instead, he waited fruitlessly in his office until 9 p.m. As he drove home through the deserted streets he wondered whether he had not overreacted by putting the armed forces on alert.

Footprints of intruders were detected by an Israeli patrol Friday morning in the central canal sector. The patrol tracked them to a barely perceptible opening in a sand dune. From it emerged an Egyptian intelligence-gathering team.

For the past week, the men in the canal forts had been reporting nightly convoys, sometimes numbering hundreds of trucks, entering the Egyptian lines. What were suspected of being ground-to-ground missiles were deployed at night and covered with tarpaulins. Egyptian officers were seen surveying the Israeli strongpoints every day with maps in their hands. SAM batteries were moved forward to extend their reach over Sinai.

The Egyptian rear, up to three miles from the canal, was overflowing with vehicles, pontoons, and equipment. The sound of tanks moving behind the Egyptian ramps had become commonplace. So too the sound of mines being detonated across the waterway. They had been laid as protection against an Israeli crossing. Their detonation meant either that the Egyptians intended to replace them with fresh ones, as had happened once before, or that they were clearing the way for their own crossing. Bulldozers worked late every night cutting openings through the Egyptian ramparts to permit vehicular access to the canal bank. The Israelis had grown accustomed to seeing Egyptian soldiers on the far bank over the years walking about at leisure without arms or helmets. For several days now, a new type of soldier could be seen—armed, helmeted, and with the purposeful look of combat soldiers. The soldiers who had previously been manning the positions along the canal remained in place, looking as indolent as ever and continuing to fish. Only now they seemed to be pretending.

Pvt. Menahem Ritterband of the Jerusalem Brigade participated in a motorized patrol each morning from Orkal, the northernmost fort on the canal, to neighboring Lachtsanit. The men in the half-track checked the dirt track alongside the road for footprints. The track was raked each evening so that infiltrators from across the canal during the night would leave fresh prints. Since the beginning of the week there had been footprints every morning. Almost all were heading inland, few returning. Unless the infiltrators were crossing back elsewhere during the night, this meant that the Egyptians were putting men into Sinai in significant numbers on long-range intelligence missions or as artillery observers. On Friday morning, there were so many footprints they couldn't be counted.

At Lachtsanit Friday morning, Ritterband chatted with its commander, Lt. Muli Malhov, who had briefly served with him at Orkal. Malhov had for days been voicing unease. Friday morning Ritterband heard him telling their battalion commander that the Egyptians were going to attack and that the forts didn't have a chance.

General Elazar remained oblivious to all of this. "For me, the week between October 1–6 in Southern Command is the most normal week," he would say. "I distinguish nothing out of the ordinary." This could only mean that the alarming things the men on the Bar-Lev Line saw had not reached him.

From the Purkan outpost opposite Ismailiya on Friday, men in the lookout tower saw Egyptian soldiers arguing with the gardener watering plants at the villa across the canal. A few moments later, the gardener was gone. So were other civilians normally seen in the area. Major Weisel, the fort commander, saw a group of Egyptian officers surveying his position. Through binoculars, he could see that their shoulder boards carried lots of rank. Some of the officers had turned their epaulets inside out so that the rank could not be seen. Weisel reported his sighting to battalion headquarters and an intelligence team was sent forward, but by the time it arrived the Egyptian officers were gone.

The group across the canal had included General Shazly. The Egyptian chief of staff had abandoned the claustrophobic atmosphere of Center Ten for a last look at the front line before the battle. He knew Weisel's fortification by its Hebrew name of Purkan, one of the strongest forts on the Bar-Lev Line. An Israeli map giving the code names of every position and road in western Sinai had fallen into Egyptian hands and copies were distributed to all units, particularly artillery batteries. Studying Purkan through binoculars, Shazly was relieved to detect no sign of special alert. When he saw it next, he hoped, the fort would be a ruin.

Officers from Reshef's and Col. Dan Shomron's brigades drove to General Mendler's headquarters in Refidim this day for a farewell party for the division commander, who was to hand over his command on Sunday. They found that Mendler had other plans. His departure was being put off, he said, until the present tension had resolved itself. From the air photos he had seen, it was clear to him that war was on the doorstep. Instead of raising farewell toasts, the general took the opportunity of his officers' presence to review the division's operational plans. He was interrupted by a call from a colleague in Tel Aviv reporting on the cabinet meeting. The caller said something that caused Mendler to stare into the middle distance and hang up wordlessly. Turning to his officers, he said, "They're not mobilizing."

Colonel Reshef had hoped to be back at his headquarters in Tasa by sunset in time for Kol Nidre, the opening prayer of the Yom Kippur service, at the base synagogue. When he emerged from Mendler's headquarters it was nearly dusk and his head was aswim with what he had just heard. Some fifteen Egyptian tank brigades were preparing to cross the canal. His brigade would be the only force standing in their way for hours along the hundred-mile length of the Suez Canal.

Walking to his jeep, Reshef encountered the armored corps chaplain, who suggested he put off his return to Tasa, an hour's drive. Stay and pray with us, he said. Snapped out of his reverie, Reshef looked at the rabbi, an old acquaintance, and for the first time addressed him not by his title but by his first name. "Ephraim," he said. "There will be war tomorrow."

In Center Ten, the absence of visible Israeli preparations had become a matter of concern. General Gamasy found it incomprehensible that the Israelis had been so completely deceived. The earlier intelligence assessment that Israel was aware of the impending attack did not appear to be substantiated. There was still no report of Israeli mobilization and the front line had not been reinforced. There was a gnawing suspicion among some officers that the Israelis had secretly moved forces into Sinai and were preparing a major surprise.

Late that night, Egyptian scouting parties were sent across the canal at several points. They landed well away from the canal forts and made their way to their vicinity stealthily to observe. The reports from the scouts when they returned before dawn all carried the same message: The Jews are sleeping.

One Jew wide awake was Zvi Zamir in London. He was not fasting and had not gone to synagogue to hear Kol Nidre but no Jew this Yom Kippur night was gripped by a greater sense of portent than he. Marwan, usually prompt, arrived late at the apartment hotel where Zamir and the case officer were waiting. Visibly tense, the Egyptian apologized, saying he had been busy getting updates from his sources in Cairo. It was only the day before, he said, that he learned in Paris by phone that the countdown had begun but his sources had no further details. Marwan was now updated.

"He [Sadat] is starting the war tomorrow," he said.

His sources had confirmed that the attack plan was unchanged. That meant that five divisions would cross the canal simultaneously and establish bridgeheads. Commando units would be helicoptered at night deeper into Sinai to ambush Israeli reserve units heading for the front. What Marwan's sources did not know was that that zero hour had been advanced to 2 p.m. He did not rule out the possibility that this warning might prove a false alarm like his two previous warnings. But he put the chances of war at "99.9 percent."

Until his telephone call from Paris the previous night, Marwan had not been in contact with the Mossad for a month. This at a time that reports were coming in from a number of other sources of imminent war. Uri Bar-Joseph, in his book *The Angel*, suggests that Sadat was confiding his plan only to those with a need to know. Another possibility, he writes, is that Marwan believed that Israel already knew enough from his previous reports to detect from certain Egyptian steps when war was coming. A third possibility, which Bar-Joseph says was raised by several intelligence officers, was that Marwan, despite having passed on myriad secrets in the past, hesitated to pass on this ultimate secret. Bar-Joseph gives this option the least credibility, given Marwan's past behavior.

Once or twice during their meeting, Marwan said to Zamir that he was sure the situation was clear to the Israelis and that they were taking the necessary steps. He sounded, in fact, like he wasn't sure. "How can you people not see that this is war?" he asked. The odd remark, Zamir reckoned, stemmed from something Marwan's sources in Cairo had said, possibly an expression of astonishment that there were as yet no signs that the Israelis were reacting. It was a remark that stirred Zamir's own deep anxiety about the Arab buildup.

The hour-long meeting ended at 12:30 a.m. (2:30 a.m. Israel time). After Marwan left, Zamir and the case officer walked to the apartment of the Mossad's station chief, about fifteen minutes away, while some of the security detail discreetly trailed Marwan back to his hotel. Zamir sat down at a desk with paper and pen to compose a message for Eini. He had told his bureau chief that he would phrase his message—whatever it would be—as a bland business note and they agreed on code phrases. Marwan's case officer, who had taken notes during the meeting, would transmit a fuller account to Tel Aviv from the Israeli embassy, properly encoded, at 7 a.m.

Zamir believed his message would trigger immediate mobilization if he did not express some reservation by pointing out Marwan's previous instances of "crying wolf." But too many troubling war signals had been ignored in the past week for this one to be downplayed. The discreet report he formulated was dry as dust. But the coded message at its heart was stunning—before the blast of the shofar marked the end of Yom Kippur this coming night, before the last invocation calling on God to open the gates of heaven and receive his people's prayers, Israel would be at war on two fronts.

YOM KIPPUR MORNING

ISRAEL'S WAKE-UP CALL came in the early hours of Yom Kippur, an insistent ringing at the bedsides of the nation's political and military leaders, rousing them into the same bad dream.

Zamir called Eini at his home outside Tel Aviv. It was a few moments before the Mossad chief heard the phone being lifted and then Eini's sleepy voice. "Put your feet in a tub of cold water," advised Zamir.

Dictating slowly, he described a business meeting he had with foreign executives. "They speak about the contract in terms we are familiar with." That meant the Egyptians would be implementing the battle plan Marwan had provided. The executives intend to arrive in Israel the next day even though they know it is Yom Kippur. "They think they can land before darkness"—an attack at dusk. "They don't have partners outside the region"—assurance that the Soviets would not be involved in the attack.

After translating Zamir's elliptical message into straightforward Hebrew, Eini made his first call at 3:40 a.m. to Mrs. Meir's military aide, Gen. Yisrael Lior. Next was Dayan's aide-de-camp. It was only at 4:30 that General Elazar, on whom time would press most of all, was wakened by his own aide-de-camp, Lt. Col. Avner Shalev (not to be confused with Zeira's deputy, Gen. Arye Shalev). Elazar asked that General Tal and other members of the General Staff be at headquarters by 5:15. The commanders of the Northern and Southern Commands were to be there by six.

Within ten minutes of being wakened, Elazar placed his first call from home. It was to Benny Peled. "We have information that there will be war with Egypt and Syria by tonight. Are you ready?"

"I'm ready," said the air force commander.

"What do you want to do?"

Peled gave priority to the Syrian SAM batteries since the Syrian front, close to the Golan settlements and Israel proper, was the more dangerous. Elazar agreed. "Roll it," he said. "I'll get permission." Authorization for a preemptive strike would have to come from Dayan and Golda Meir but Elazar had no doubt it would be forthcoming. Peled said the air force would be ready by 11 a.m.–noon.

As Elazar dressed, his wife, Talma, sleepily asked what was happening. "This is it," he said. "War." The look on his face—"almost ceremonial"—was one she had seen before. Driving through the empty streets, Elazar had time for a quick overview of the situation, which immediately registered on his subconscious as "extreme." It had been a basic assumption that intelligence would provide five or six days' warning of war. This would have permitted full mobilization and allowed time for reservists to adjust to military mode. Two days' warning was the least expected, but enough for mobilization. The present situation, just half a day's warning, was something he had never thought possible.

Zeira, who arrived at headquarters shortly after Elazar, was still maintaining that Sadat would not go to war. The chief of staff chose to humor him. "Let's act as if there *will* be a war," he said.

The imminence of war had at last cleared the air. Elazar was totally focused now on what lay ahead—"like a bulldog," his aide-de-camp would say. There was as yet no authorization for mobilization but Elazar told his deputy, General Tal, to activate the network that would carry it out, thus saving several hours. Without waiting for authorization from Dayan, he ordered the call-up of several thousand key personnel, including those filling staff positions at various command levels; also, some commando units.

At 5:50, Elazar met with Dayan in the defense minister's office. An officer who took the official notes of the meeting was surprised at Elazar's jauntiness. When he told Dayan he wanted to quickly smash the Syrians, Dayan asked what his hurry was. Elazar replied with a Jewish joke. An early riser in an eastern European shtetl is surprised to see a friend coming out of a brothel at 6 a.m. Why this early? he asks. I have a busy day ahead of me, says the friend. I just wanted to get this out of the way.

To Elazar's astonishment, Dayan rejected a preemptive strike. The Americans had made it clear that they had their own interests, including in the Arab world, and that an Israeli preemptive strike with American weapons would not be acceptable. In addition, Dayan was not at all sure war would break out. The CIA was reporting no sign of war. Marwan had told Zamir that Sadat might hold off if Israel let it be known that it was aware of Arab intentions.

"We're in a political situation in which we can't do what we did in 1967," said Dayan. To attack, particularly when the Americans were saying the Arabs were not going to war, would in the world's eyes be an act of aggression, not self-defense. There had been similar war warnings in the past that had proved false. The assurance he had given Peled that the government would authorize a first strike if the Arabs were seen preparing to attack did not stand the test of reality. The only circumstance in which he was prepared to approve a preemptive strike, said Dayan, was if information was received that the Arabs were planning to attack Tel Aviv, or to engage in something "hair-raising," an apparent allusion to the use of gas.

Thinking out loud, Elazar suggested that Israel counterattack the moment the first Arab shell exploded on its territory. Going him one better, Dayan said that he did not rule out striking the Syrians five minutes before their zero hour. "Who would know afterwards what happened?" The remark, however, was a wistful aside. Israel would not risk relations with the only country supplying it with weapons and political support.

The two men agreed that Israel would focus its counterattack on Syria. If Israel's thin line on the Golan Heights collapsed, the Syrians could be inside Israel in a day. An Egyptian army trying to cross Sinai, outside the protection of its SAMs, was unlikely to make it to the Israeli border. By focusing on Syria, there was a chance of quickly knocking it out of the war, leaving only Egypt to contend with.

Dayan also opposed Elazar's proposal for an "almost full" mobilization of 200,000 to 250,000 reservists. In the absence of active hostilities, mobilization on this scale would itself be perceived as an act of war. "We don't order full mobilization just on the basis of Zvika's report," Dayan said. At this stage, he said, only forces needed to buttress defenses, some 20,000 to 30,000 men, should be mobilized. The remainder of the reserves would be called up only if war actually broke out. Elazar said that defense alone would require 50,000 to 60,000 reservists, double Dayan's figure. Certain that war was coming, the chief of staff insisted that the entire reserve combat force be mobilized—four armored divisions plus ancillary units—so as to be ready to counterattack as soon as the initial Arab drive had been stopped. Dayan accepted the 50,000 to 60,000 figure. But the approval of Prime Minister Meir was needed for any mobilization. Since they would be meeting with her shortly, the two men left the overall decision to her, together with the decision on a preemptive strike.

Meanwhile, a preemptive strike had lost much of its relevance. Peled was at his desk at 7 a.m. when there was a knock on the door and his chief meteorologist entered.

"What are you doing here?" asked Peled. "I don't need you now."

"I'm sorry sir, but the Golan Heights are covered with clouds—base eight hundred feet, ceiling three thousand feet."

Peled called Elazar to inform him that the strike against the missile batteries could not be carried out. However, visibility over the rest of Syria was unlimited and Peled suggested hitting Syrian air bases instead. Elazar consented. The mechanics who had been arming the planes for the strike against the missile batteries now had to strip the armaments and replace them with bombs and fuses that would damage runways and penetrate the concrete shelters in which the Syrian warplanes were kept.

The day before, General Peled had summoned his base commanders to Tel Aviv to confer on Dougman, the plan to attack the missile batteries on the Syrian front. Since the downing of the Syrian planes on September 13, he had been expecting a sharp reaction from Damascus. Peled discovered at the meeting that important elements of Dougman were not yet completed. Some of the failings could be remedied within a day and Peled gave the order to do so. He warned his commanders, however, that if the ground forces were in difficulty, the air force might have to go to their assistance even if the missiles had not been destroyed. "Be prepared to go into the fire," he said.

Elazar put off the meeting with Mrs. Meir for another hour in order to confer with the generals who would lead the coming battles. He met separately with the commanders of the Northern and Southern Commands, Generals Hofi and Gonen. Once the war started, he would have limited opportunity to communicate with them and he wanted to be sure that they were all thinking within the same parameters. The warning of war, he told them, was shorter than they had ever imagined. The standing army, however, was already on full alert. "We'll mobilize whatever they permit. The rest we'll call up under fire."

Elazar asked them to return to their headquarters and set their commands in motion. They were to come back at noon to tie up loose ends with him. Elazar then met with the commanders of the air force, navy, and armored corps. He told them that war would break out about 6 p.m. Marwan had indicated in London that the Egyptian attack would be launched according to the war plan known to the Israelis. The first wave was to begin crossing the canal just before last light, which this day would be about 6 p.m., some forty minutes after sunset. Summoning the army spokesman, Elazar ordered him to attach foreign correspondents to both fronts so that they could report which side opened fire first.

Elazar told the generals that the reserve divisions would organize for a counterattack while the standing army held off the enemy with the assistance of the air force. The Syrian front was of immediate concern but Elazar was anxious about Sinai as well. Dovecote had not been designed to hold off an attack by five divisions; it was only a fallback in a worst-case situation, but the current case was far worse than had been imagined. "We're in for a difficult war," he said.

The meeting with the prime minister got under way at 8:05 a.m. Dayan began by saying that war was not a certainty. Children in the Golan settlements would be evacuated a couple of hours before the mooted Arab attack, he said, on the pretext that they were being taken on an outing. A reduction in tension during the day might make the evacuation unnecessary and thus avoid the ensuing public outcry at a government-organized excursion on Yom Kippur. Mrs. Meir, operating under her mandate as a grandmother rather than as prime minister, ordered that the children be brought down immediately. Dayan and Elazar then presented their respective cases on a preemptive strike and mobilization.

It was admittedly bizarre to have two generals, veteran war horses at the pinnacle of Israel's military establishment, bringing their differences over vital military matters to a seventy-five-year-old grandmother. Mrs. Meir lit one cigarette after another as they spoke, filling the room with acrid smoke that caused those present to squint. Elazar expressed readiness to compromise at this stage on 100,000 to 120,000 men. Gathering from Mrs. Meir's words that she was leaning toward his view, he dispatched his aide at 9:05 a.m. to make a phone call that would get mobilization started for two divisions.

Elazar argued for a preemptive strike against the Syrian airfields at noon and an attack on the missile batteries at 3 p.m., by which time the cloud cover should have dissipated over the Golan. "Then, at five, the air force can hit the Syrian ground forces and put them out of action." Aware of Mrs. Meir's sensitivity to casualties, he said that a preemptive strike would save many lives.

When the presentations were done, the prime minister hemmed uncertainly for a few moments but then came to a decision. She ruled against a preemptive strike. Israel might be needing American assistance soon and it was vital they know it was not Israel that started this war. "If we strike first, we won't get help from anybody," she said. As for mobilization, she agreed to Elazar's compromise proposal. "If war does break out, better to be in proper shape to deal with it, even if the world gets angry with us." Summing up the meeting, Dayan said, "The chief of staff will mobilize the entire force he has proposed." It was now 9:25 a.m. A sense of relief descended on those in the room despite the somberness of the moment. Indecision was over. The wheels had begun to turn. Elazar sent his aide to start mobilization of two more divisions. There was less time left than anyone knew.

Mrs. Meir made no pretense of knowing anything about military matters. She would confess to her military aide, General Lior, that she had no idea what a division was. When he had awakened her this morning with the report of imminent war, she asked him over the phone, "Yisrael, what do we do now?" Her step was heavy when she arrived at her office and her face gray. But she continued to function well. Her decisions at the meeting with Dayan and Elazar had been sound, based on common sense and political instincts, and they would determine Israel's operational profile for the critical opening phase of the war. There would be no preemptive air strike but the weight of Israel's reserve army would be brought to bear as quickly as possible. She left the running of the war to Dayan and Elazar but her instincts would continue to serve her well whenever her input was required, as it would be at critical moments.

Elazar called the air force commander at 9:30 to inform him that a preemptive strike had been ruled out. Even if the attack on the Syrian air bases had been carried out it would not have altered the outcome of the war. Unlike in the Six Day War, the Arab air forces were now protected in concrete shelters and difficult to destroy from the air. More important, it was not the Syrian air force but the SAMs that now menaced Israeli air superiority.

At 9:30, American ambassador Kenneth Keating and his deputy, Nicholas Veliotes, arrived at Mrs. Meir's office in response to her urgent summons. The diplomats were stunned when she described the situation. They had been assured by CIA reports and the Israelis themselves only the day before that there was no danger of war. Mrs. Meir told them that Israel would not carry out a preemptive strike. She asked that Washington, in the coming hours, try to stave off war by turning to the Soviets or directly to Cairo and Damascus. If the Arab moves were dictated by a misreading of Israeli intentions, the Americans were to assure them that Israel had no plans to attack. If the Arabs did initiate war, said Mrs. Meir, Israel would respond forcefully. As Veliotes rapidly made notes, the silver-haired Keating asked whether he could be sure that Israel would take no preemptive action. "You can be sure," Mrs. Meir said decisively. Keating said he would send his report to Washington with the highest security designation, which meant that Kissinger would be wakened to read it.

Israel's ambassador to Washington, Simha Dinitz, was in the corridor outside Mrs. Meir's office when Keating emerged, looking pale. Dinitz had arrived in Israel for the funeral of his father and was now in the weeklong mourning period. A former director of the prime minister's office, he enjoyed Mrs. Meir's confidence and was one of the first persons she summoned. "You've got to return to Washington immediately," she said. He was to first obtain from the defense ministry a list of armaments and equipment to be requested from the Americans. Washington would be a critical anchor for Israel in the coming storm. The prime minister asked her military aide to find a way to get Dinitz out of the country, no easy task because there were no commercial flights into or out of Israel on Yom Kippur. Lior arranged for the government-owned Israel Aircraft Industries to roll out an executive jet. It flew Dinitz in the afternoon to Rome where he boarded a commercial flight to the United States.

The brewing Middle East crisis jarred Henry Kissinger out of a deep sleep in New York's Waldorf-Astoria hotel. Without standing on ceremony, Assistant Secretary of State Joe Sisco burst into his suite at 6:15 a.m. New York time to announce that Israel and the Arabs were about to go to war. Sisco had just read the message from Keating. The ambassador quoted Mrs. Meir as saying, "We might be in trouble." Half an hour later, Kissinger himself roused Soviet ambassador to Washington Anatoly Dobrynin from sleep. He passed on Mrs. Meir's message that Israel was not planning offensive action and asked Moscow to urgently get this message to the leaders of Egypt and Syria. Kissinger then called the Israeli chargé d'affaires in Washington, Mordecai Shalev, to inform him of his conversation with Dobrynin and to urge Jerusalem to avoid any "rash move."

General Zeira's senior staff members, summoned to an urgent meeting in his office, took their places at the conference table. Zeira began by turning to his deputy, General Shalev, to his immediate left. "Tell me, Arye, will there be war today or not?" General Shalev did not look his usual confident self. "I have no reason to change my view that the chances of war are low," he replied. Zeira pointed at the next person in line, Yona Bandman, and asked the same question. The head of the Egyptian desk said he stood behind Shalev. Zussia Keniezer, who had come in late and taken a place on one of the couches along the opposite wall, rose angrily. "Say what *you* think, not that you stand behind someone." The two men had been rivals for the Egyptian desk and Bandman had won. Keniezer, head of the Jordanian desk, had been convinced war was coming since monitoring King Hussein's conversation with Mrs. Meir. He repeated that conviction now. AMAN's official assessment remained "low probability" but the awesome nature of their error was closing on AMAN's leadership.

At 10 a.m., Elazar descended to the underground war room—"the Pit," in popular parlance—to meet with the General Staff. Zeira offered a review of the Egyptian and Syrian war plans that Israel had obtained. The Egyptians, he said, would begin with artillery and air attacks followed by crossings in small boats along the entire canal front. They might also send helicopters bearing commandos into Sinai to cut roads and attack command posts. There would be five bridgeheads but only three of them—opposite the main roads leading into the heart of Sinai—would constitute major points of attack. On the Syrian front, the three enemy divisions on the line would send their infantry brigades forward to clear minefields and cross the Israeli tank ditch on foot, followed by bridging tanks which would lay spans across it. The tank brigades attached to each of these divisions would follow.

Dayan, who had joined them, asked for details of Israel's deployment in Sinai. Elazar said that one of the Sinai Division's armored brigades was presently positioned in the canal area and the two others were being held to the rear for use at Southern Command's discretion.

When will the reserves arrive? asked Dayan.

"At a very rough estimate," said Elazar, "three hundred tanks by tomorrow night, three hundred on Monday, and another three hundred on Tuesday." The total number of men already in uniform—conscripts (draftees), regular army personnel, and reservists who happened to be doing their annual service—was 100,000. Mobilization orders had already been issued for 70,000 reservists and the remainder would follow shortly.

Fully mobilized, the IDF numbered 350,000 men. Egypt had 650,000 soldiers and Syria 150,000. The Jordanian and Iraqi armies, if they were to join in, numbered 60,000 and 250,000, respectively, but not all were expected to reach the battlefront. Other Arab countries would also send contingents.

When Dayan asked Elazar what offensive action he planned, the chief of staff said the unexpected circumstances required revision of existing plans. In their previous discussion, Elazar had raised the possibility of reaching Damascus in a counterattack. The defense minister was not enthused by the idea. He now made it clear to his generals that if war came, Israel had no territorial ambitions.

"I want to remind everyone," he said, "that our main objective is destruction of enemy forces. Any move in the direction of Damascus would be in order to destroy forces, not to capture places that we will be obliged to pull back from. This is the line that will guide this forum."

Dayan was still not convinced there would be war. What will you do with all these reservists if war doesn't break out? he asked Elazar. If the threat is canceled and not just postponed, said Elazar, the men will be sent home.

"A hundred thousand men will hang around a full day before they're sent home?" asked Dayan. He sounded as if he was still annoyed that Elazar had won Mrs. Meir's vote for a large mobilization.

"They won't hang around," answered Elazar. "They'll go down to the front. If it turns out that there's no war, we'll release them in forty-eight hours." Tal thought it would be more like four days. In any case, the task at the moment was getting the men into uniform, not out of it.

For Health Minister Victor Shemtov, riding in a car through the empty streets of Jerusalem on Yom Kippur was an unsettling experience even though he was far from religiously observant. For his government driver, a religious man, it was excruciating. On Yom Kippur no vehicle normally moves unless it is carrying a pregnant woman or stricken person to the hospital. Shemtov had been called at home by the cabinet secretary who informed him that an emergency cabinet meeting was to be held at noon in the prime minister's Tel Aviv office. He was to tell no one of the planned meeting. Shemtov already had an indication Friday afternoon of something unusual afoot when his son, a reservist, was ordered to report immediately to his elite reconnaissance unit. Why on Yom Kippur eve? his son asked. Is anything happening? Nothing I know about, said the minister. Shemtov drove his son to his base in the Negev and got back to Jerusalem just before the onset of the holy day, puzzled over his son's call-up.

Military vehicles with high antennas were parked outside the prime minister's office when Shemtov arrived Yom Kippur morning. He bounded up the stairs and entered the cabinet room to find most of his colleagues already seated around the large table. Only the religious ministers from Jerusalem had not come. Faces were taut and no one was speaking, itself ominous, given this voluble collection of politicians. As Shemtov eased himself into his chair, the minister next to him leaned over and whispered, "There's going to be war." Shemtov was flabbergasted. He had not attended the previous day's abbreviated cabinet meeting in Tel Aviv and had received no hint over the past months of possible war, not even in intelligence briefings. Mrs. Meir had not yet emerged from her office by the scheduled noon starting time, which was unusual. When Shemtov went out to the corridor briefly, an army officer said to him, "They caught us with our pants down."

Mrs. Meir entered the cabinet room at 12:30, together with Dayan. She was pale and her eyes were downcast as she walked slowly to her chair. Her hair, normally neatly combed and pulled back, was disheveled and it looked as if she had not shut her eyes all night. For the first time, the ministers saw an old woman, slightly bent, sitting in the prime minister's chair. She lit a cigarette, leafed briefly through a pile of papers in front of her, and declared the meeting open.

She began with a detailed report of events of the past three days—the Arab deployment on the borders that had suddenly taken on ominous color, the evacuation of the Soviet families, the air photos, the insistence by AMAN that there would be no war despite mounting evidence to the contrary. The military men were divided, she said, over whether there would be a war or not, over whether there should be mobilization and a preemptive strike. She spoke in a monotone that sounded like a judge reading out a sentence. Then she reached the bottom line. In the early hours of this morning, word had been received from an unimpeachable source that war will break out at 6 p.m. this day on both the Egyptian and Syrian fronts.

The ministers were stunned. They had not been made privy to the Arab buildup on the borders. Furthermore, they had been told for years that even in a worst-case situation the IDF would have at least forty-eight hours to call up the reserves before war broke out. Now they were being told that a two-front war was less than five hours away, with the army still unmobilized.

Mrs. Meir asked Dayan to describe the situation along the two fronts. Despite her depressed look, her voice had been firm. But there appeared to be a tremor in Dayan's voice. He looked like a man whose certainties were in the process of crumbling.

At 12:30, Elazar met in the Pit with General Gonen with whom he had talked briefly five hours before. Although Gonen had assumed command of the southern front three months before, he had not bothered to familiarize himself with basic intelligence data. He was unaware, for instance, that the Egyptian war plans in AMAN's hands called for a crossing along the entire length of the canal. He was also unaware that the Egyptian plan specified that the preliminary artillery barrage would last thirty to forty-five minutes. He believed it would last several hours.

His counterpart on the northern front, General Hofi, had won significant reinforcement in the past two weeks by voicing concern over the Syrian buildup. But Gonen accepted AMAN's assessment of "low probability" of war and made no effort to beef up his front even after the Egyptian buildup across the canal had reached unprecedented levels. Nor had he replaced the second-line Jerusalem Brigade reservists in the forts with elite troops as called for in Dovecote. Neither did he attempt to form an independent judgment about whether the soothing estimates of "low probability" were justified by what the troops along the canal were reporting.

On Thursday evening, when the air photos were being anxiously awaited at General Staff headquarters and by Gonen's subordinate, General Mendler, Gonen himself chose to spend the night in Haifa.

When a member of the postwar Agranat Commission asked Gonen whether it was permissible to ask a gentleman where he had spent that night, Gonen said it had been with a friend.

Instead of moving Mendler's division to forward positions, as called for in Dovecote, Gonen decided to wait until 5 p.m., an hour before the anticipated Egyptian attack. He had heard Zeira say that morning that an Egyptian attack was far from certain. Gonen thought that an early deployment might be taken by the Egyptians as provocation. He also feared that premature movement of the tanks to the front would give the Egyptians time to adjust their preset artillery plans and hit the forward tank positions. Moving up only an hour before H-hour would not leave them time enough for that.

The day before, Gonen had ordered Dusky Light implemented Saturday. An engineering team reached the canal Saturday morning and found the two fuel installations, at Forts Matsmed and Hizayon, inoperable. With Marwan's warning now in hand, Gonen ordered repairs to the installation at Matsmed and fixed ignition for 6 p.m., the presumed time of the Egyptian crossing.

Dusky Light had largely slipped from the minds of the Israeli command over the years but it had remained a major concern of the Egyptians. They had reason to believe from commando surveys of the Israeli bank that many of the Israeli installations were dummies. They were, however, not sure about all. Late Friday night, Egyptian frogmen swam underwater across the canal to block the outlet pipes.

Soldiers in the Bar-Lev forts could hear activity across the canal all night and many did not sleep. Egyptian soldiers could be seen dragging objects down to the water's edge and work was going on intensively in the storage areas behind the lines. In the morning, stacks of orange life preservers could be seen alongside bridging equipment.

Throughout the morning, General Elazar had hoped that the American veto on a preemptive strike might be lifted as evidence mounted of the Arab war preparations. At noon, however, he notified Air Force Commander Peled that cancellation of the preemptive attack was final. The planes which had been held ready since early morning with full bomb loads in anticipation of an attack on Syria could be reconfigured for aerial combat at Peled's discretion. "Prepare for the possibility that the Egyptian and Syrian air forces [which together had twice as many planes as Israel] will attempt to simultaneously penetrate Israeli air space," Elazar said.

Peled said that despite the Mossad's warning of an Arab attack at dusk, zero hour could be as early as 3 p.m. since the Egyptian air force would likely want to strike at Israeli positions in Sinai and have the planes get back to their bases before dark. In the air force command center, several senior officers urged that the Phantoms, the heart of the air fleet, be kept in readiness in case an early Arab strike permitted Israel to attack the Syrian air bases in late afternoon. However, at 1 p.m. General Peled ordered the Phantoms stripped of their bomb loads and fitted out for interception. At 1:30 he began to send up other planes to patrol the nation's skies.

For Dr. Avi Ohri, this was the day his month of reserve duty at the canal was to come to an end. It had been a pleasant enough tour for the young doctor, rotating among the canal forts to relieve colleagues on leave. He had done a good bit of reading and when things got too boring he volunteered to fill in as a radioman or lookout. In some of the forts, men had fished in the canal and he had eaten his share of fish and chips. The heat and flies weren't pleasant but he usually wore short pants and a T-shirt rather than a uniform unless the lookouts reported a vehicle approaching.

Reaching Tasa mid-morning on his way back to Israel, he was informed that a C alert had been declared. In view of the sudden emergency, his superior asked whether he would mind staying an extra day. Fort Hizayon was without a doctor and none would arrive until tomorrow. Ohri agreed. He was the only passenger on the army bus that took him to Hizayon and was surprised at the haste with which the driver turned around and sped back after dropping him off. The guard at the gate directed him to a bunker. A few soldiers inside were lying on cots. They got up when the officer entered. He introduced himself—"I'm Avi, I'm a doctor"—and began to spread out his equipment. It was 1:30 p.m.

Col. Avigdor Ben-Gal, commander of the Seventh Brigade, which had arrived on the Golan piecemeal over the past ten days, was a commanding presence with a craggy face, large shock of unkempt hair, and tall frame. Born in Lodz, Poland, in 1938, he lost his family in the Holocaust and arrived in Palestine in 1944 with a group of orphaned children via the Soviet Union and Iran. In the absence of a family of his own, he adopted the army. To his officers and men, he radiated authority and professionalism. He had a cutting tongue but some saw his brusqueness as a mask. Since assuming command of the prestigious brigade the previous year, he had insisted that training exercises emulate war conditions as closely as possible. He drilled his men intensely in gunnery and held weeklong exercises in which the brigade operated only at night. Frequently, in the midst of an exercise, he would announce a change in mission, requiring rapid decisions by commanders and movement through unfamiliar terrain.

At 10 a.m. Yom Kippur morning, Ben-Gal was informed by Gen. Rafael (Raful) Eitan, the Golan divisional commander, of the war warning passed on by General Hofi. Ben-Gal ordered his battalion and company commanders to meet him immediately in an army camp in the northern Golan.

All present rose to their feet when he entered the room and he waved them back to their seats. "We don't have much time," he said. "Who's here and what's the state of your tanks."

"My deputy and five company commanders are in the room," said the senior battalion commander, Lt. Col. Avigdor Kahalani. "The tanks are under camouflage netting."

The other two battalion commanders, whose units had arrived during the night, reported that most of their tanks were in place but that some were still moving up from the supply depots at the foot of the Golan.

"All right," said Ben-Gal. "Let's get down to business. Gentlemen, war will break out today." The faces of the officers reflected disbelief. "Yes, just what you heard," he continued. "A coordinated attack by Egypt and Syria."

After issuing instructions, Ben-Gal told the battalion commanders to return to their units and prepare them for action. The men were to be ordered to break their fast. The officers would assemble again at 2 p.m. for a final briefing.

Unlike Ben-Gal, Col. Yitzhak Ben-Shoham, commander of the 188th Brigade, which was holding the Golan line, did not speak of war in alerting his officers to possible action. Colonel Nafshi, commanding the northern half of the line, thus assumed it would be the "battle day" he had been anticipating ever since the September 13 air clash. Most frontline units reported no unusual activity in the Syrian lines. An exception was a tank platoon commanded by Lt. Yoav Yakir at the southernmost end of the line. All night long the men had heard the movement of Syrian tanks opposite, as if new forces were arriving. In the morning, Yakir tried to persuade those crewmen observing Yom Kippur to break their fast. To encourage them to eat, Yakir and his first sergeant, Nir Atir, made breakfast for the platoon, a treat to which most of the men succumbed.

At Strongpoint 107 in the northern sector, 2nd Lt. Avraham Elimelekh spent an hour, twice as long as usual, reviewing with his men what each would do in the event of a Syrian attack. The garrison, normally numbering twelve, had been increased to nineteen in the past day. Of the ten strongpoints along the line, 107 was the only one not located on a rise that dominated its immediate surroundings. It sat flat on a plain that extended deep into Syria. The reason for the position's inferior siting was that it had been placed to cover the Damascus–Kuneitra road, two hundred yards away.

In the event of a serious attack, the strongpoint's survival would be dependent on the tank platoon posted to its rear. In the few weeks he had been at 107, Elimelekh had had intensive sessions with the tank platoon commander, Lt. Shmuel Yakhin, to work out cooperation in the event of an attack. The two officers identified elements of the topography together so that each would quickly understand what the other was referring to on the radio in a battle situation. They agreed that the tanks would deal with Syrian armor and the strongpoint with infantry. The battalion intelligence officer visited Yom Kippur morning and told Elimelekh that the Syrians might attempt to snatch a strongpoint in the coming battle day and take its garrison prisoner. A likely target was Strongpoint 107, said the officer, making a snatching movement with his hand.

Colonel Ben-Gal drove to the front at noon where he scanned the Syrian lines through binoculars. There was a large army out there but he could see nothing stirring. At the sound of chirping he lifted his head and saw birds on a nearby tree. There was nothing unusual about the birds singing. What was odd was that he could hear them. The unnatural stillness seemed final confirmation that war was imminent.

In Sinai, General Mendler was meeting with his commanders when Gonen telephoned at 10 a.m. Passing on Gonen's message to his officers, the division commander said that something was expected to happen at dusk but it was not clear whether it would be war or only the end of the Egyptian exercise.

Like most of their colleagues, Mendler and his officers assumed that if shooting started, it would be a resumption of the war of attrition, with massive artillery strikes and possibly raids. The prospect of the entire Egyptian army crossing was not raised. Mendler, indeed, focused the discussion not on defensive steps but on the offensive options embedded in Dovecote—a westward crossing of the canal by one or two brigades while Reshef's brigade dealt with any Egyptian forces which might cross eastward to the Sinai bank.

At 12:20 p.m., a listening post picked up a message from a U.N. observation post on the Egyptian side of the canal—"special time check." It was, the Israelis knew, code for an imminent Egyptian artillery barrage. The canal-side forts were ordered to pull back men from outlying observation posts and to prepare for heavy shelling. A sergeant at an outpost started toward the half-track sent to fetch his squad when he saw an Egyptian soldier across the canal trying to catch his eye. The Egyptian tapped his watch and spread his hands in a gesture of "Why?"

At 12:30, AMAN issued an updated bulletin noting extensive military preparations in Egypt and Syria. It acknowledged receipt of reports that war was imminent. However, noted the bulletin, "We assume that the strategic level in Egypt and Syria is aware of the absence of any chances of success." Even at this hour, AMAN was not to be stampeded by events into abandoning the logic of Sadat's strategic concept, as military intelligence understood it.

In the cabinet room, Dayan told his colleagues that if the Egyptians crossed the canal, they were heading for destruction. The situation on the Golan was more complex, he said. There was no significant barrier there to slow down the Syrians and the defenders were much fewer than those deployed in Sinai. But the IDF was confident it could hold the line. Justice Minister Yaacov Shimshon Shapira asked what would happen if the Egyptians detected the Israeli preparations and advanced their zero hour. Dayan said that the air force was already sending patrols aloft to guard against such a contingency.

For Jerusalemites, it was the sound of a plane that offered the first intimation of unusual developments. Early worshippers at the Western Wall Yom Kippur morning were startled by the sudden roar of a single Phantom low overhead, as if the air force was sending a wake-up call. As the morning progressed, the awesome silence of the holy day was increasingly broken by the burr of tires as military vehicles turned into residential neighborhoods. Military couriers carrying mobilization orders stepped out to scan house numbers. Generally, they were directed by neighbors to a nearby synagogue. When the soldier entered, services were halted to permit him or a synagogue official to read out names from the podium. It was apparent to all that if mobilization was being carried out on Yom Kippur it must be because of a surprise Arab attack.

At a synagogue in Jerusalem's Ramat Eshkol quarter, a young man wearing a prayer shawl rose from his seat when his name was called. His father, seated next to him, embraced him and refused to let go. The rabbi approached and said gently to the weeping father, "His place is not here today." The father released his son and the rabbi placed his hand on the young man's head to bless him. In the Bait Hakerem quarter, the courier consulted with a sexton. Mounting the podium, the sexton called on the congregation for silence and then read out the names handed him by the courier, pausing almost imperceptibly as he reached the name of his own son. Rabbis told their congregations that it was permissible for all those mobilized to break their fast and drive a car, something strictly forbidden on Yom Kippur except in life-or-death situations.

Throughout the country, men wearing skullcaps and prayer shawls could be seen incongruously driving cars, something they had never done in their lives on Yom Kippur, or trying to hitchhike to assembly points. Many family men drove their wives and children to relatives before heading to their units. Resonant in the minds of all—those being called up and those left behind—was the "Unetanai Tokef" prayer with its poignant melody that they had chanted this morning. "On Rosh Hashana it is written and on the fast of Kippur it is inscribed . . . who shall live and who shall die, who in his allotted time and who not, who by water and who by fire, who by the sword."

In Cairo, President Sadat donned his military uniform and was waiting at home when War Minister Ismail arrived in a jeep at 1:30 to drive him to Center Ten. The officers of the Supreme Command sat on a low dais overlooking the operations room where the commanders of each branch of the armed forces and their senior staff sat by communication consoles. The room was dominated by situation maps projected onto a large screen. Echoing the directive to Israeli soldiers this morning to break the Yom Kippur fast, the Egyptian high command repeated the order to break the Ramadan fast. Clerics ruled it permissible also to smoke. Sadat could see no one in the room doing either. He ordered tea and lit up his pipe and soon others were doing the same. All eyes now were on the clock.

At 1:30 on the Israeli side of the canal, the soldiers in the forts were ordered to don flak jackets and helmets and to enter bunkers. Only fort commanders remained as lookouts, mostly in tiny "rabbit holes" built into an outer trench wall, safe from anything but a direct hit, where they could observe the surroundings through a periscope. At Fort Matsmed, the commander chose to mount the observation tower. The only thing he could see moving on the other side of the canal were farmers in a distant field working the land. At Budapest, Motti Ashkenazi also climbed the tower. The enemy lines opposite were devoid of movement. For the first time, the Egyptian lookout towers were empty.

On the Golan Heights at 1:30, an artillery observer on Mount Hermon reported to Nafshi that the Syrians were removing the camouflage netting from their artillery and tanks. Nafshi recalled that the Syrians were wont to start their battle days at 2 p.m. He ordered the tanks on his half of the front line to pull out of their regular positions and move some distance away. If the Syrians opened fire they would hit every fixed Israeli position marked on their maps.

At 1:50, the voice of an intelligence officer monitoring Syrian communications was heard over the intercom at air force headquarters: "We have liftoff at Damir [a Syrian air base]." Within moments reports came in of planes rising from Egyptian bases.

In the cabinet room, Dayan was nearing the end of his briefing a few minutes before 2 p.m. when an aide entered and handed him a note. The defense minister announced that Egyptian airplanes had begun to attack in Sinai. As Mrs. Meir declared the meeting closed, a siren began to wail in the street outside. A senior officer saw General Zeira walking toward the war room. He had become markedly pale.

Galvanized, General Elazar descended immediately to the air force control center to ask Peled if he could attack the Syrian airfields in the three hours of daylight remaining. To Peled's infinite regret, he had to say no. An hour before, the most formidable concentration of power in the Middle East was awaiting his command—more than three hundred fully armed warplanes and air crews primed to go. Now, at bases around the country, the Phantoms resembled plucked chickens as swarms of ground crewmen stripped them of bombs and other accoutrements and began to convert them to interceptors, a task that would take another three hours.

There would be no Arab attempt to enter Israeli air space this day, and the aircraft would engage in uneventful patrols instead of undertaking a meaningful counterattack. It was the first glitch of the war for an air force which just six years before, under the command of Motti Hod, had achieved one of the most stunning air victories in history when it destroyed hundreds of Arab planes within a few hours on a June morning and established Israel's air superiority.

Before handing over command of the air force to Benny Peled, Hod had devised a bold plan to deal with an emergency situation precisely like the one Peled faced this Yom Kippur day—an Arab surprise attack. The idea had come from studying a military exercise across the canal the previous year in which the Egyptians simulated a crossing of the Suez Canal without actually trying to cross. From air photos, Hod saw the Egyptian divisions massed on the canal approaches as if waiting for bridges to be built. The chosen crossing points made tactical sense and it was a fair assumption that they would be used by Egypt when war came.

Hod's plan, labeled Srita (scratch), called for an air armada to attack these concentrations. The planes would come in low over the desert floor, on the Israeli side of the canal. Some two miles short of the waterway, they would pull up sharply and fling their bombs across the canal. This "toss bombing" technique was notoriously inaccurate when aimed at small targets. However, the concentration of Egyptian tanks, trucks, and troops would be so deep and dense and the number of bombs so great that it would be hard to miss. Each plane would carry up to 24 small bombs to make for a wider spread, which meant 2,400 bombs in a single run by 100 planes. Hod's plan called for at least two attack cycles, perhaps three. If 200 warplanes were used, the damage on the Egyptian side, physical and psychological, would be that much greater. The Israeli planes were not entirely out of reach of the missile batteries but losses, Hod would maintain, would have been minimal compared to those actually suffered in the war.

In an interview decades later, Hod would still be lamenting Peled's failure to order the attack which, Hod believed, would have thrown the entire Egyptian attack off stride, taken the wind out of their psychological sails, restored Israel's sagging spirits, and enabled a robust IAF to move on to attack the missile sites. "He had only to say 'Srita, execute.'"

II

THE EGYPTIAN CROSSING

THE EGYPTIAN PLANES WENT IN FIRST, skimming low over the canal and then rising briefly for orientation before diving at their targets—Israeli command centers, Hawk antiaircraft missile batteries, artillery batteries, air bases, radar stations, the main intelligence base in Sinai. One of the first Egyptian fatalities in the war was the half brother of President Sadat, a pilot shot down in an attack on Refidim Air Base. The main runway at Refidim was knocked out for several hours and the control tower damaged.

When the planes had passed, artillery opened up. In the first minutes, more than ten thousand shells fell on the Israeli lines, mostly on and around the canal-side forts. With the Israeli defenders driven into their bunkers, flat-trajectory weapons and tanks were moved into position atop the Egyptian ramparts and began firing directly at the forts opposite. The lookout towers in the Israeli forts were all shot away. Heavy mortars lobbed 240mm shells into the fortifications with thunderous explosions, causing bunkers to shudder and trenches to collapse.

Fifteen minutes after the start of the bombardment, four thousand commandos and infantrymen comprising the first wave slid down to the water's edge along the length of the canal where 720 rubber and wooden boats awaited them. Screened by smoke shells, they started across the waterway—some paddling, some propelled by outboard motors—to the chanting of "Allahu Akbar" (God is great). General Shazly had arranged for loudspeakers to be set up at crossing points, repeatedly broadcasting the ancient battle cry, which was picked up by the soldiers.

In the forefront of the first wave were engineering teams which checked the "fire-on-the-water" outlets to ensure that they had been properly blocked by frogmen during the night.

Landing on the Sinai shore, generally out of sight of the Israeli forts, agile soldiers made their way up the steep sand embankment and affixed rope ladders to the top. Tank-hunting teams climbed after them and raced inland. Many carried the suitcase-like Sagger containers. Many more wielded RPGs. Ammunition and equipment too heavy to be carried was dragged in wheeled carts. One cart could hold two Saggers or four mines. Thousands of carts had been produced at the order of Shazly after he had seen one left behind by an Israeli raiding party on the Red Sea coast in 1970. ~~A cart could hold two Saggers or four mines~~.

In many places, soldiers managed to reach the "fins"—the earthen barricades a mile inland—behind which the Israeli tanks intended to take up firing positions. Dust clouds to the east indicated that the tanks were fast approaching.

On the Bitter Lake, an amphibious force consisting of twenty tanks and eighty armored personnel carriers (APCs) began churning its way eastward. Lake Timsah to the north was crossed by an infantry company in amphibious vehicles. The Sinai shores of these lakes were largely undefended. On the northern end of the Suez line, a diversionary force of Egyptian tanks and APCs prepared to make its way along the sand spit that led to Fort Budapest.

South of the Suez Canal, in coves along the western shore of the Gulf of Suez, scores of fishing boats had been assembled to transport commando forces to southern Sinai under cover of darkness. Other commandos were waiting to be helicoptered behind Israeli lines at dusk.

With the crossing of the canal by the first wave, seventy engineering teams equipped with pumps and water hoses began scouring holes in the Israeli embankment. The engineers had been allotted five to seven hours to open passageways.

The crossing would be carried out by 100,000 men in exemplary order. Large signs bearing luminous numbers were planted on the Israeli-held shore by the first wave. These matched the numbers on the color-coded signs along the routes taken by units moving up to the canal. Military police ensured that units did not go astray or become entangled with each other. Within two hours, 23,000 men had crossed and five tenuous divisional bridgeheads had been established on the

Israeli bank, each one mile deep and five miles wide. Artillery now shifted to targets deeper in Sinai.

Large transporters bearing bridge sections backed up to the water's edge on the west bank and slid them into the canal where engineers waited to assemble them. Other units began assembling thirty-one prefabricated ferries capable of carrying tanks. Monitoring the reports in Center Ten, Shazly sensed that the vast machine constructed for this day was working superbly. The Israelis appeared to have been taken by total surprise.

At 5:30 p.m., the twelfth and final wave of the initial assault force crossed the canal, bringing the total on the Sinai bank to 32,000 men. The bridgeheads were now two miles deep. The Israelis were reeling, and this before even a single Egyptian tank had crossed the canal. At dusk, dozens of helicopters crossed into Sinai bearing commandos. Many were downed by Israeli planes and ground fire but hundreds of commandos were landed behind Israeli lines in southern Sinai.

At 6:30 p.m., water hoses opened the first breach in the Israeli sand barrier. Within another two hours, sixty passageways had been opened. In the southern canal sector, the claylike embankment dissolved into thick and slippery mud which made passage impossible. Ten planned openings in this sector had to be abandoned. But the remainder along the canal's length were now open to tanks and supply vehicles crossing by ferry.

The first bridge was completed at 8:30 p.m., six and a half hours after zero hour. Two hours later, all bridges were open—eight heavy bridges which could take tanks and four light bridges for personnel and supply vehicles. The bridges would be periodically disassembled and floated opposite different breaches opened in the Israeli barrier in order not to provide a fixed target for artillery or air attack. The way into Sinai was open and Egyptian armor and infantry were pouring through. Not since the construction of the pyramids—at least not since construction of the canal itself—had Egypt witnessed such a massive and well-executed enterprise.

Capt. Motti Ashkenazi, atop Budapest's observation tower, had seen the planes before he heard them, four Sukhois flashing low over the lagoon to his left as they headed for the Israeli rear. He heard the Egyptian artillery, however, before the shells began crashing on his compound. The fort commander slid down the tower's ladder and dove into a rabbit hole from which he could survey the surroundings through a periscope. The ground shook beneath him. This, he imagined, was what it would have been like at Normandy or Stalingrad. Shell smoke obscured everything. Budapest was the only fort that Egyptian vehicles could reach without crossing the canal since the Egyptians still retained a foothold on the Sinai bank in this sector. Fearing that enemy forces might already be advancing under cover of the shelling, Ashkenazi ran toward the western edge of the position where the smoke was thinner. The barbed wire, he saw, had been blown apart by the shelling.

Ashkenazi returned to the main bunker and told the men to remain under cover until he summoned them by radio. He did not want to risk losing anyone before the enemy was close enough to engage. Returning to the western perimeter, he saw personnel carriers emerging from Egyptian positions three miles to the west and forming up on the road. He could make out tanks as well and jeeps mounted with antitank weapons. The vehicles began slowly moving in his direction along the sand spit.

The bazooka shells he had asked for had not arrived and Budapest was without antitank weapons of any kind. Ashkenazi believed, however, that he still had a fighting chance. The Egyptian tanks carried exterior fuel tanks. They would have to pass below the elevated fighting positions of the fort and it might be possible to ignite the fuel tanks with grenades. He was about to summon his men when the guard at the main gate reported two Israeli tanks approaching along the shore from the rear. Ashkenazi ran across the compound and climbed aboard the closest tank. Its hatch was closed and when he banged on it he was not heard above the noise of the shelling. Ripping off a shovel strapped to the side of the turret, he rapped again. A sergeant poked his head out. "Who's in command?" shouted Ashkenazi. The sergeant pointed at the other tank. By the time Ashkenazi reached it, its turret hatch had opened and Lt. Shaul Moses was looking in his direction.

Ashkenazi guided the tank officer westward along the shore to a point where the smoke began to thin. Moses made out the approaching Egyptian column. Five tanks, old T-34s, were in the lead, the closest 1,200 yards away. Infantrymen had already descended from the personnel carriers and were forming a skirmish line. There was sufficient smoke around the Israeli tanks to cloak them from the Egyptians' view. The two tanks opened fire. Within minutes all the Egyptian tanks were burning. When the sergeant's tank reported a turret malfunction, Moses continued firing alone, methodically working down the

Egyptian column as the other vehicles frantically tried to turn on the narrow sand spit, some of them colliding. He hit all of them—five APCs and three trucks. Soldiers abandoned the vehicles and ran back toward the Egyptian lines. Moses let them go.

In Fort Purkan, midway on the canal, Major Weisel saw through his periscope rubber boats crossing to the north. A call for artillery fire drew no response. The few Israeli batteries on the front could not respond to all the calls coming from the Bar-Lev forts. The noise of the incoming Egyptian artillery was deafening. A tank on the ramp across the canal swiveled its gun in Weisel's direction and fired. The ground around the company commander's observation post shook. A moment later, two shells exploded nearby, emitting red smoke. Weisel thought at first it was gas but the Egyptian artillery lifted and he understood that the smoke was a signal to the infantry to close on the fort. Weisel summoned his men by radio into the trenches. Racing from the bunkers, they repulsed the Egyptian attack. Scattered shelling resumed. As the awesome thump from a 240mm mortar shell died away, Weisel said to the men around him, "Fellows, that's as bad as it gets. The next heaviest thing is an atom bomb." Despite the massiveness of the shelling, the bunkers had held and the only casualties were two wounded.

At Hizayon, north of Purkan, the commander, Lt. Rami Bareli, sank several boats with machine gun fire. Other boats, however, made it across. From his post at the other end of the fortification, Sgt. Pinhas Strolovitz could see flames arching over the top of the positions facing the canal where the Egyptians were wielding flamethrowers. Strolovitz's own position was being heavily assaulted. The barrel of his machine gun had grown hot and had to be changed because of the danger of blockage but the sergeant was afraid that if he stopped firing, even briefly, he would be overrun.

Bareli, a former paratrooper, ran from position to position to encourage his men, most of whom were not combat soldiers. An hour after the battle started, a shell exploded alongside him, killing his radioman and virtually severing Bareli's left arm. He was carried to the medical bunker and had enough presence of mind to notice the unfamiliar face of the man leaning over him. "Who are you?" Bareli asked. Dr. Avi Ohri introduced himself. "I've just arrived." The arm was beyond saving. Ohri cut it off and stilled the pain with morphine. The agony of Hizayon had begun.

At Fort Milano alongside the abandoned Egyptian town of East Kantara, the commander, Capt. Yaacov Trostler, a twenty-nine-year-old geology teacher, was cut in the head by the opening salvo. He resumed command after his wounds were dressed but much of the responsibility now fell on his young deputy, Lt. Micha Kostiga, twenty-one, who had recently finished his regular army service. Less than an hour after the start of the shelling, a soldier reported hearing voices in Arabic outside the western perimeter fence where the ground fell sharply away toward the canal. Kostiga heard it too, someone shouting, "Enter, enter." He climbed out of the trench. Just downslope were ten Egyptian soldiers moving toward the lip of the position, an officer urging them on. Kostiga fired before they did, emptying his Uzi in their direction. He jumped back into the trench, took his radioman's Uzi, and climbed back onto the sandbags to fire at the retreating Egyptians. Returning to the trench, he threw a dozen grenades downslope. As he did, he saw additional boats crossing the canal straight for the fort. The garrison sank them or drove them off. But attacks were coming all around the perimeter. Trostler had the noncombatants load magazines and bring up crates of grenades for the dozen men in the fighting positions.

An Egyptian flag went up on one of Milano's outposts five hundred yards to the south, which had been evacuated that morning. Kostiga called down artillery fire on it. With darkness, the men heard the hammering of a bridge being erected to their south. A few hours later they heard the rumble of tanks crossing on it. The men would later hear a bridge being constructed to their north. Israeli artillery groped for the spans but neither could be seen from Milano so the fire could not be adjusted.

At Lituf, south of the Bitter Lake, the fort commander was wounded in the first Egyptian assault; his deputy and the first sergeant were wounded in the second. The attackers reached within five yards of the outer fence before being driven back.

It was apparent from the radio net that the Egyptians had crossed in strength. The men of the Jerusalem Brigade, regarded dismissively as second-line troops, were fighting well. So were the paratroopers from the standing army manning the three southernmost forts. But their impact on the Egyptian crossing was negligible. Not even the best fighting units could have made a difference given the wide gaps between the forts through which the Egyptians passed unimpeded. The role of the Bar-Lev forts as a barrier against an all-out Egyptian attack was a blatant failure. The besieged forts had instead become bait that would lure General Mendler's division to its near destruction.

12

THE HUMBLING
OF THE TANK

IN THE TANK STAGING AREAS along the Artillery Road, company commanders were giving final briefings when a wailing on the radio net signaled enemy air penetration. Bombs struck the compounds before the tanks could get away but none was hit.

Speeding toward the canal, they covered the distance in twenty to thirty minutes but in most cases lost the race. The sand barriers behind which they were to take up firing positions—the "fins"—were already covered by figures in sand-colored uniforms. From observing Dovecote exercises, the Egyptians knew exactly where the tanks would be heading.

"Infantry to the front," shouted tank platoon commanders. "Attack." It was a drill they had rehearsed repeatedly—racing forward to shoot, stampede, and literally crush the enemy. The Egyptians, however, had prepared a scenario of their own. Commandos rising from shallow foxholes with RPGs on their shoulders hit the lead tanks. Some of the commandos were cut down but others held their ground. Surprised at the resistance, tank commanders pulled back beyond effective RPG range, about three hundred yards. It was not far enough.

A platoon commander saw a red light waft lazily past him and explode against a nearby tank. The commander of the impacted tank was propelled from the turret by the pressure, like a cork from a bottle. Other lights floated in from the Egyptian rampart across the canal. The platoon commander had no idea what they might be. The answer came over the radio net. "Missiles," said the company commander, the first to recognize the Sagger. Their three-thousand-yard range was ten times that of the RPG and their impact more deadly.

For the first time since tanks lumbered onto the battlefields of the

First World War, the greatest danger they faced was not from enemy tanks or antitank guns but from individual infantrymen. Bazookas had been used by infantrymen in previous wars but never in such quantity as the RPGs were being used now or with the range and lethality of the Saggers. The Egyptian troops had been provided antitank weapons in prodigious numbers. At Shazly's orders, Saggers were stripped from rear units and transferred to the spearhead forces. Each of the five attacking divisions had 72 infantrymen armed with Saggers and 535 with RPGs. In addition, 57 antitank guns and 90 recoilless weapons added a more conventional but no less deadly tank-killing capability. This added up to close to 800 antitank weapons per division apart from the 200 tanks attached to each division. Never had such intensive antitank fire been brought to bear on a battlefield. In addition, Israeli tank commanders, who rode with their heads out of the turret for better visibility, were vulnerable to the massive Egyptian artillery fire and to rifle and machine gun fire from infantrymen all around them. The profusion of fire was stunning. So was the grit with which the infantrymen defied the charging tanks.

The decision by Israel not to raise the embankment on its side of the canal to mask the Sinai bank from the Egyptian ramparts severely aggravated its situation. Tanks, Saggers, and antitank guns on the ramparts opposite dominated not only the Israeli forts but an area up to two miles inland from the canal. Israel's idea of neutralizing the ramparts with long-range fire from the shelter of the fins had no validity now that Egyptian RPG teams were dug in all around them.

The air force, on which Elazar had rested his confidence, was unable to stem the Egyptian tide. Because of the SAMs, the planes could not circle over the battlefield and choose targets. Where defenses were heavy the planes resorted to "toss bombing," in which the aircraft pulled up sharply at a calculated distance, speed, and angle to release their bombs without overflying the target itself, which could be as much as four miles away. The IAF carried out 120 sorties on the Egyptian front this day and lost four planes but the snap attacks had little impact. The Egyptian infantrymen were more vulnerable to artillery but the IDF had only a few dozen artillery pieces along the hundred-mile-long front and these were under heavy counter-battery fire.

The Bar-Lev strongpoints proved virtually useless as a defense line. For the most part, the boats simply crossed between them, out of view.

The Egyptian high command had been prepared for 10,000 dead in the crossing operation but the number killed, according to the final Egyptian count, would be 280.

Defense of the Suez front fell in the opening hours on Colonel Reshef's 91 tanks, constituting the forward brigade of General Mendler's Sinai Division, and the 450 men in the sixteen Bar-Lev forts. Mendler's two other brigades were at their base in central Sinai, fifty miles away, and would not reach the front for three hours.

The four northern forts on the canal were strung along a causeway between the canal and a lagoon. The northernmost, Orkal, was because of its remoteness the only one to have tanks permanently assigned—a platoon of three. With the onset of firing, pairs of tanks were dispatched by the northern battalion commander, Lt. Col. Yom Tov Tamir, to the three other causeway forts via a road through the lagoon. The pair rushing to Fort Lachtsanit, just below Orkal, were ambushed. An RPG hit the lead tank, killing its commander, but the driver bulled through and reached the entrance to Orkal. There the tank was ambushed again and another crewman killed. Soldiers came out of the fort and led in the two surviving crewmen. The second tank reached Lachtsanit but was destroyed there.

Pairs of tanks managed to reach the two causeway forts south of Lachtsanit but each pair was ordered in turn to proceed to Lachtsanit, whose radio had gone silent. All four tanks were ambushed. One crew managed to escape on the road through the lagoon on foot. The crewmen came across a downed Israeli pilot with a broken leg who refused to be carried so as not to slow them down. He was taken prisoner before a rescue vehicle reached him.

Battalion commander Tamir led the rest of his force toward two forts south of the lagoon. Several tanks bogged down in marshes, difficult to discern because they were covered by sand. Others were disabled by surface mines or hit by RPGs or Saggers.

Responding to distress calls from Fort Milano, Tamir dispatched three tanks to its assistance. Milano lay alongside the ghost town of East Kantara, abandoned in the Six Day War. Egyptian soldiers, who had now returned to the town, knocked out two tanks.

As dusk approached, Tamir was ordered to send tanks again to Lachtsanit. He sent almost all his remaining tanks together with infantrymen on half-tracks. This force too was ambushed. The war was only four hours old and Tamir's battalion was almost entirely wiped out.

The fortunes of Reshef's two other battalions on the line were better, but not by much. In the central sector, where most of Egypt's Second Army was crossing, Israeli tanks scored some initial successes. Destruction of four Egyptian tanks on the enemy ramparts sent a surge of optimism along the radio net. At 4 p.m. Egyptian infantrymen were spotted already three miles east of the canal. A small armored force stopped them just before darkness and drove them back.

In the southern sector, where Egypt's Third Army was crossing, Lt. Chanoch Sandrov halted his tank company six hundred yards from Fort Mafzeah and surveyed the terrain. There was no enemy in sight and no sign of activity on the rampart across the canal. As the company started forward again, RPG squads rose from the sand and set the lead tank afire. Sagger missiles erupted from the Egyptian rampart and an artillery barrage descended.

A rescue tank approaching the burning tank was hit by a Sagger which killed the loader. The tank's commander was cut down in the turret by bullets. The gunner rose to take his place and was hit too. The driver turned back with his three dead or dying comrades.

Sandrov was blinded in an eye by shrapnel and pulled back briefly to have a crewman apply a bandage. Resuming command, he ordered his deputy, Lt. Avraham Gur, to comb the area south of the fort with half the tanks while he swept north with the rest. When Gur passed close to the Israeli embankment, an Egyptian with an RPG rose on the slope above. Gur, standing in the open turret, ordered his driver to turn right. As the tank swung, throwing up a cloud of dust, the RPG shell exploded alongside. "When the dust settles," Gur shouted, "fire." A moment later the gunner said, "I see his face," and fired. Gur saw the Egyptian soldier lifted into the air and disintegrate.

Gur rejoined Sandrov's force just as a missile coming off the Egyptian rampart struck the company commander's tank. Gur ran to it and found Sandrov and his loader dead. The lieutenant took the other two crewmen, both wounded, into his own tank. A tank fifty yards away was struck by a missile and Gur climbed onto that too. The tank commander was slumped inside. Gur took his wrist but there was no pulse. Calling for artillery cover, he began evacuating the wounded.

In late afternoon, the canal-side embankment began to fill again as Egyptian infantry clambered up from boats. Lt. Col. Emanuel Sakel, commanding the southern battalion, formed armored personnel carriers into line with Gur's remaining tanks and led a charge.

The Egyptians broke, many of them throwing away their weapons. The waterline had been regained in this sector but only two tanks remained in action, Sakel's and Gur's. Sakel told Gur to begin towing damaged tanks to the rear. The battalion commander's tank remained near Mafzeah to cover the fort against infantry attack.

Five miles south, another of Sakel's companies, commanded by Capt. David Kotler, broke up an infantry attack on Fort Nissan. But no matter how many Egyptians were hit, others sprouted in their place. Kotler's deputy, Lt. Yisrael Karniel, saw a Sagger wafting toward his tank just as he was shot in the shoulder. Falling back into the turret, he shouted "hard right" and passed out. The tank swerved sharply and the missile exploded harmlessly beyond it. A platoon leader went to Karniel's aid but his own tank was struck a blow that brought it to a shuddering halt. A Sagger had hit just above the gun, where the metal was thickest. It did not penetrate and the driver was able to restart. Reaching Karniel, the officer tied a stretcher to the hull of his own tank and strapped him on it. As they started toward nearby Fort Mezakh, the tank was hit again, this time by an artillery shell. The stretcher was lifted into the air and slammed back down. The platoon leader was certain that Karniel was dead until he heard him groan. They reached the fort without further incident.

Toward evening, the doctor at Mezakh asked for urgent evacuation of the wounded. The fort, the southernmost on the Bar-Lev Line, was located on an artificial spit of land projecting into the Gulf of Suez. Kotler headed there together with Lt. David Cohen. As they approached, Cohen's tank hit a mine. The commandos who had placed it rose from foxholes and fired at the stricken tank. Kotler drove them to ground with machine gun fire and closed up behind Cohen's tank. At Kotler's signal, Cohen and his crew leaped aboard while Kotler kept the Egyptians' heads down. At a rear staging area, Cohen took over a tank whose commander had been wounded. By now, all that remained of the eleven tanks Kotler had started out with three hours before were his and Cohen's.

Reshef's brigade was being relentlessly eroded as it tried to enforce Elazar's dictum of "killing them on the canal." The aim was to deny the Egyptians territorial gain and thus discourage future attacks. But this was turning out to be a grievous miscalculation, particularly in view of the enormous disparity of forces. Instead of demonstrating the power of armor, the Israeli tanks were engaging in a wild brawl they could not win. They were up against masses of infantry armed with weapons that could kill a tank as easily as a tank could kill them.

A report half an hour before sunset of bridge sections being assembled in the water near Purkan was the first clear indication to Reshef that the Egyptians were intending to put their army into Sinai. He dispatched a newly arrived company led by Lt. Moshe Bardash to attack the bridging site. The setting sun was in Bardash's eyes as his eight tanks approached the canal. There was an indistinct vision of infantrymen on the road, then a hail of RPGs. Several tanks were hit. The tankers fired blindly into the haze. Bardash, wounded, ordered his tanks to pull back.

At a safe distance, the tanks halted and Reshef's operations officer, who had been guiding Bardash's force to the bridge site, assembled the tank commanders to explain what they were up against—the copious use of RPGs, the boldness and overwhelming number of enemy infantry, and, particularly, the Sagger missile.

Such impromptu lessons were going on all along the front as new units took the field alongside tank crewmen who had survived the day.

Saggers, the "veterans" explained, were a formidable danger but not an ultimate weapon. They could not be used close-up since they required several hundred yards of flight before they "acquired" their target. They could be seen in flight and were slow enough to dodge. It took about ten seconds for a missile to complete its flight—at extreme range it could be twice that—during which time the Sagger operator had to keep the target in his sights as he guided the missile by the bright red flare on its tail. From the side it was easy for the tankers to see the flare. As soon as anyone shouted "Missile" on the radio net all tanks would move back and forth in order not to present a stationary target. The movement would also throw up dust that would cloud the Sagger operator's view. Simultaneously, the tanks would fire in the operator's presumed direction, which in itself could be sufficient to throw him off his aim.

The RPG would prove deadlier this day than the Sagger. As long as the Israelis were fighting near the water's edge, the Saggers were fired during daylight from the Egyptian rampart. But RPG teams lying in shallow foxholes were a close-up threat day and night as the tanks attempted to reach the canal-side forts. The profusion of RPGs took the Israelis aback. Tank commanders learned to examine the terrain for possible ambushers before moving forward. There could be no such precaution at night.

Even before the sun set on Yom Kippur day, it was clear to the tank crews on the front line that something revolutionary was happening—as revolutionary, it seemed, as the introduction of the machine gun or the demise of the horse cavalry. Tanks, which had stalked the world's battlefields since the First World War like antediluvian beasts, were now being felled with ease by ordinary foot soldiers. It would take time before the implications of this extraordinary development were grasped by higher command. Meanwhile, the tankers were figuring out for themselves how to survive.

Emerging from a rabbit hole when the shelling lifted, Sgt. Shlomo Shechori saw soldiers trying to get through the barbed wire surrounding his outpost near Fort Lituf. He thought they were reinforcements from the main fort until he noticed the sand-colored uniforms and heard shouts in Arabic. When the Egyptian squad was ten yards away in the winding trench, he rose and emptied his magazine at them before slipping through a hole in the fence. Halfway to the main fort, he dropped to the ground. Lituf was surrounded by an Egyptian company pouring fire into it.

Shechori made his way to the nearby road and saw three Israeli tanks racing toward the fort, firing as they came. His dark uniform identified him as Israeli and the lead tank stopped alongside. Capt. Boaz Amir beckoned Shechori aboard. The officer, who commanded the northernmost of Sakel's three companies, posted the sergeant in the turret alongside him. Shechori tried to hug him but the officer stopped him. "Save the kisses till this is over," he said, handing the sergeant a grenade. Other grenades were stashed within reach. "Anyone you see is Egyptian," said the officer. "Throw grenades and use your Uzi."

The tanks swept through the fort compound, spewing fire and running over enemy soldiers who tried to hit them with RPGs. Within minutes, the surviving Egyptians had pulled back. Amir decided that he too would have to withdraw because of fire from the Egyptian rampart.

As he left the compound, he saw three Soviet-make APCs. Soldiers aboard them waved in greeting. The IDF had units made up of Soviet vehicles captured in the Six Day War but these vehicles were the sand color of the Egyptian army. On the other hand, the Egyptians could not have put up bridges across the canal this quickly. Captain Amir radioed headquarters and reported what he saw. Is there any Israeli unit with Soviet-made APCs in the vicinity? he asked. "No," came the reply. A moment later the three APCs were smoking hulks.

Lifting his gaze, the company commander saw a mass of APCs and tanks approaching. They constituted the southern wing of the amphibious brigade which had crossed the Bitter Lake. Amir was moving his tanks into firing positions when Lituf called again for assistance. He sent two tanks to the fort and with the four remaining opened fire. In the ensuing exchange, twenty-six Egyptian vehicles, mostly APCs, were set aflame, with the loss of one Israeli tank.

The Egyptian infantrymen who escaped the APCs deployed with Saggers and RPGs. His ammunition depleted, Amir ordered the three remaining tanks to fire short machine gun bursts to keep the infantrymen at bay until reinforcements arrived.

The Israeli command would conclude that the amphibious force was intended to link up with commandos landing at the Gidi Pass in order to block Israeli reserve forces on their way to the front. The large number of personnel carriers may have been intended to bring the commandos back after completing their mission. But most of the helicopters had been shot down.

The sounds of Amir's battle reached 1st Sgt. Haim Yudelevitz on the roof of a building in the Mitzvah staging area, several miles to the rear, where he was keeping lookout. A dozen soldiers, mostly technicians and medics, sheltered in a bunker from the intermittent shelling. A tank had returned from the front earlier with its wounded commander. A second tank arrived now from a maintenance workshop at the rear. It had no machine guns and no crew except for the driver, Sgt. Moshe Rosman, who joined Yudelevitz on the roof. Toward evening, the pair saw a cloud of dust heading in their direction. As it drew closer, the sergeants identified ten Egyptian amphibious vehicles, including at least one tank.

Sergeant Rosman told the crew of the wounded officer's tank that he was taking command. He removed the tank's two machine guns for use by the men at Mitzvah to defend the post and set out in the tank with the rest of the crew to meet the approaching force. Yudelevitz had meanwhile gathered two nonfunctioning machine guns from a storeroom and, cannibalizing parts from one, made the other operable. He hauled it up to the roof along with ammunition belts. The Egyptian APCs halted a mile away. Officers formed the soldiers into line and then advanced, first slowly and then at a trot. Yudelevitz opened fire at two hundred yards. Many Egyptians went down, either hit or taking cover. Others began to edge around to the flank. Yudelevitz descended and deployed the men along the perimeter fence, ordering them to fire short bursts at random in the gathering dusk from the machine guns Rosman had provided.

Rosman meanwhile spotted a line of APCs at 1,500 yards. His gunner hit two. The others dispersed among the dunes. Rosman took up pursuit and hit two more. Yudelevitz returned to the roof and ranged him in by radio on a tank a mile away which Rosman's gunner set aflame.

Darkness now descended. It seemed that the Egyptian force, what was left of it, had pulled back. Rosman and his crew remained in their tank seven hundred yards from the compound. After half an hour, Yudelevitz reported that he could hear vehicles nearby. Rosman turned and saw two armored personnel carriers at the entrance to the compound. His gunner dispatched them with two shells. Flames from the burning vehicles briefly lit the area.

Rosman positioned the tank at the compound entrance and remained there with the engine off, the better to hear. Half an hour later, he sensed movement to his front. Thirty Egyptian soldiers appeared out of the darkness, the closest only three yards away. They plainly regarded the silent tank as incapacitated. In a whisper, Rosman told the driver to start the engine. As it sprang to life, he tossed grenades and shouted, "Run them down." Those Egyptians left alive pulled back into the desert.

Two tank maintenance sergeants, acting on their own initiative with a pickup team of soldiers, had broken the Egyptian drive in this sector.

Anticipating an Arab air strike well before dusk, Air Force Commander Peled had ordered patrol planes aloft at 1:30 p.m. His move quickly paid off. A reservist Mirage pilot patrolling over the Mediterranean shortly after 2 p.m. saw what seemed a MiG heading toward the coast. It moved sluggishly and when he fired at it and sent it spinning into the water, it blew up with a ferocious bang. He had hit a Kelt air-to-ground missile fired from well offshore by an Egyptian Tupolev bomber which had already turned back to Egypt. A Kelt fired by a second Tupolev had fallen into the sea. In lieu of Scuds, the Egyptian command was using the Kelt, homing on a radar in the center of the country, as a warning that it could retaliate in kind if Israel struck its hinterland. With the sounding of the sirens, some planes at air force bases still armed with bombs were ordered to take off immediately and drop their bombs in the sea so that they could move into their patrol sector.

The most notable air battle this day took place at Sharm el-Sheikh, the remote southern tip of the Sinai Peninsula, where Israel maintained small military bases. The IAF had allocated only two Phantoms to its defense. The two pilots and two navigators, all fresh out of flight school, were in their cockpits on the runway at 2 p.m. when the flight controller reported numerous aircraft approaching. The Phantoms took off and plunged into a formation of twenty-six MiGs from opposite ends. Within half an hour, the rookies had together downed seven planes, far better than any of the numerous aces in the Israeli Air Force would do this day. Although the runway had been holed by bombs, the pair managed to land safely. The Egyptians had succeeded in firing Kelt missiles which destroyed the naval station's radar and damaged communications.

Col. Oded Marom, a former Phantom squadron commander recently transferred to a desk job at air force headquarters in Tel Aviv, found himself superfluous Yom Kippur afternoon and drove to an air base in search of gainful employment. Two Mirages on standby were waiting at the end of a runway when his car passed. The pilots recognized him and one, who had to attend to a call of nature, signaled him to take his place. Marom did not recognize either of the pilots because of their helmet visors but he hurried to a dressing room to don flying gear and returned to relieve the pilot. The latter had just disappeared from view when the control tower ordered the Mirages to take off. The air controller started the pair toward Sinai but then ordered them to turn north on full power. Over the Golan, the Mirages jumped four MiGs attacking Israeli ground forces, shooting down one apiece. Marom only now recognized his wingman from his voice as Mirage squadron commander Avi Lanir. Twenty minutes after taking off, they were back at base where Marom handed over the plane to the original pilot, who was furious at having missed his first chance at a combat sortie. (Marom would continue flying for a few days with his old Phantom squadron, scoring more kills, before being recalled to duty at air force headquarters. Lanir would be shot down within a few days over the Syrian lines. He would die under interrogation.)

The main contribution of the air force to the ground battle in Sinai this day was the downing of helicopters trying to land commandos. Of forty-eight commando-bearing helicopters that crossed into South Sinai, twenty would be downed by the IAF and by ground fire, many loaded with troops.

A photo reconnaissance plane, flying at thirty thousand feet well inside Sinai to keep out of range of the SAMs, took photographs of the Canal Zone and beyond for AMAN. Although the air force took the photos, it was military intelligence which decided on distribution.

The canal photos taken on Yom Kippur afternoon were not seen by General Peled until two weeks later. To his astonishment, they showed Egyptian tanks and other vehicles lined up for miles, virtually bumper to bumper, waiting to cross the bridges. Had he known of this stationary target in real time, Peled would say, he would have attacked despite the profusion of SAMs in the area. It would have meant the loss of two to four planes, he estimated, but it would have wrought greater destruction than the fleeing Egyptian army had suffered in Sinai in 1967. It was precisely this picture that Motti Hod had envisioned in drawing up Srita, the plan that was never executed.

Reshef's battered brigade had been holding the line alone for more than three hours when Mendler's two other brigades reached the battlefield shortly before dusk. Dan Shomron's brigade took over the southern sector from the remains of Sakel's battalion. Gabi Amir's brigade, made up of staff and cadets from the Armored Corps School, moved to Reshef's northern flank, where Yom Tov Tamir's battalion had been destroyed. Each of the brigades detached units to reinforce Reshef's depleted force in the center.

Shomron had been unable to make radio contact with division headquarters while traversing the Gidi Pass. Emerging, he telephoned Mendler from a small army base.

"What's the situation?" he asked.

"Grave," replied Mendler. "The Egyptians are crossing along the entire front. Do the best you can."

The brigade commander pressed for details. What was the status of Sakel's battalion, which was now to come under Shomron's command? How deep had the Egyptians penetrated?

Mendler said he didn't know. "Do the best you can," he repeated.

Shomron ordered one battalion under Maj. David Shuval to continue to Fort Lituf, near where Boaz Amir was still holding out. Emerging from between high dunes, Shuval's battalion came on a score of Egyptian APCs and tanks, the northern wing of the amphibious brigade. The Israeli tank commanders were surprised to encounter Egyptian armor already more than six miles inside Sinai and made quick work of them. Captain Amir's three remaining tanks were down to their last machine gun bullets when they saw Shuval's battalion topping a rise two miles to their rear with lights on. Shuval continued past them and engaged more than a score of intact Egyptian APCs closer to the shore of the Bitter Lake. By 9 p.m. all were burning and Shuval's tanks stood at the water's edge, without having suffered a loss. The sense of easy victory would not last long.

Shomron's other battalion had meanwhile proceeded south along the Lateral Road for an hour in the darkness and then turned west toward Mezakh, the southernmost fort on the Bar-Lev Line. Surface mines and RPG teams blocked the way.

At Mafzeah, a newly arrived company linked up with Sakel, who had been maintaining lone vigil for hours. Sakel led the tanks forward in a sweep of the embankment.

What concerned Reshef most was the unmonitored gaps between the forts. Some were wide enough to put an army through, which was precisely what was happening. At dusk, he ordered a newly arrived company to reconnoiter the twelve-mile gap between Matsmed and Purkan in the center of the line. Reshef sent one of his officers as a guide. It was almost dark when the guide, in the lead, called out, "Infantry to the front. Break right." The day's experience had already amended the standing order of "Infantry to the front, charge." Infantry now merited a respectful distance.

The company commander, Maj. Avraham Shamir, saw figures rise from foxholes. His tank was hit glancing blows by RPGs three times but none penetrated and he kept pressing westward. The fourth time, he was wounded. Reshef contacted him to ask what was happening. The company commander was too dazed to respond coherently. The officer guiding them was dead, the tanks were scattered, and radio contact had been lost with most. Reshef ordered him to pull back. Shamir retired a short distance and lit his projector. The remaining tanks, all with wounded aboard, assembled on him. Scorched by this baptism of fire, the company moved off to the rear. With the failure of the patrol,

Reshef ordered a tank platoon guarding Fort Matsmed to reconnoiter northward. It too was driven back, its commander wounded.

A newly arrived company commanded by Lt. Zeev Perl resumed the attack toward Hizayon. Drawing fire, the tanks charged toward the source. Most were hit, including Perl's. He was temporarily blinded and the gunner took his place in the turret. Perl ordered his tanks to pull back but the driver lost his direction. The tank was still traveling toward the canal when it was hit again. Perl called to the loader and the gunner but got no response. Reaching out, he touched their bodies. When the driver slowed to get his bearings, Egyptian soldiers leaped on the tank in an attempt to drop grenades through the open turret. The driver swerved sharply, throwing them off, and then ran over them. The tank stopped only when it went into a bog. The driver extricated Perl, who told him to take the maps and canteens. They proceeded east on foot, the driver leading the blinded officer by the hand for eight hours. Close to dawn they reached a staging area where Perl was evacuated to an aid station. (His sight would return.)

As the night wore on, units were ordered to disengage and tow disabled tanks to the rear. Repairs were imperative if there was to be anything left of the division in the morning.

Meanwhile, in South Sinai as night descended, Israeli forces braced for more Egyptian commando landings along the two hundred miles of coastline south of the Suez Canal. The commander of naval forces at Sharm el-Sheikh, Capt. Zeev Almog, kept patrol boats at sea in anticipation of an Egyptian attempt to land supplies and reinforcements for the commandos helicoptered across the Gulf of Suez. At 10 p.m., two of the vessels picked up radar images of dozens of small craft approaching across the gulf. In the light of flares dropped by a patrolling plane, they saw rubber boats filled with commandos and opened fire. The rubber boats fled into an area of reefs where the Israeli vessels could not follow and succeeded in making their way back to the far shore.

The MiG attack in the afternoon had knocked out radio communications between Almog and two patrol boats at the northern end of the gulf. At 10 p.m., the patrol commander, Ensign Zvi Shahack, was startled to be called directly by the commander of the navy, Adm. Binyamin Telem, speaking from the navy's war room in Tel Aviv. Intelligence had reported Egyptian plans to transport commandos to the Israeli-held shore this night in fishing boats. The admiral ordered the ensign to cross the gulf and attack any craft he found.

Feeling his way down the dark desert coast, Shahack entered a small anchorage at Marse Telemat while the other patrol boat remained outside. Switching on his projector, he saw fishing boats anchored around the rim of the bay. In the center was a large patrol boat attached to a buoy. Two rubber boats alongside it were filled with commandos in wet suits. Shahack and his crew opened fire as they moved counterclockwise around the anchorage, setting boats ablaze. Points of light showed where Egyptians were shooting back.

The boat shuddered to a stop when it ran onto a reef. Shahack switched off the projector and summoned the other boat to sweep the harbor. Shahack's chief mechanic, taking off a boot and shoving his sock into a hole in a water pipe, managed to get the engine started. Shahack worked the boat off the reef. The other boat also hung up briefly on a reef but freed itself. The two vessels left the anchorage with half their crews wounded and one man dead but the sky behind them had turned red from burning boats.

Although beginning to grasp the magnitude of the Egyptian attack, the Israeli command had still not absorbed the disastrous nature of its preplanned response—Dovecote. The Egyptians had converted an offensive initiative—the crossing of the canal—into a defensive battle, with the odds on their side. The Israeli tank crews and commanders were fighting with exceptional bravery but their erosion was inevitable as they hurled themselves again and again at the masses of Egyptian infantry waiting for them to do precisely that. The concept of armor shock had been reversed by the Egyptians' new weapons and tactics—it was armor that was being shocked by infantry.

At 6:30 p.m. Elazar held his first staff meeting of the war. The IDF, he noted, had never before begun a war on the defensive, something it knew about only in theory. Zeira said that according to the Egyptian plan they would push eastward the next day with their armored divisions and hope to reach the Sinai passes in three to five days. The intelligence chief made no mention of the revised plan that the Mossad had passed on from Marwan to AMAN which called for an advance of only five to six miles, not forty miles.

Elazar authorized Gonen to evacuate canal-side forts that were not an impediment to a major canal crossing. However, Gonen did not issue evacuation orders. Instead of pulling back to reorganize, Mendler and Gonen continued to try to stop the Egyptians on the waterline in adherence to a political directive whose wisdom was dubious when conceived and which made no sense at all now. Unlike the tank crews who were adjusting to the Saggers, neither the division nor front commanders were coming to grips with the new realities. They clung mechanically to Dovecote when it should have been clear that a single division could not hold the waterline against a five-division crossing and that the air force could not take up the slack.

The surprise attack had a paralyzing effect on much of the Israeli command. "You break into a cold sweat and your mind freezes up," a deputy division commander would later say. "You have difficulty getting into gear and you react by executing the plans you've already prepared, even if they're no long relevant." Mental circuits shorted as commanders tried to simultaneously grasp what was happening, how it could have happened, and what had to be done.

The men in the field, soldiers and officers, were spared these excruciating deliberations. They only had to figure out how to stop the enemy and stay alive. Battalion commander Emanuel Sakel would relate that his men went through the difficult battles "like Prussians," without despair. "If your men see you in your turret, everything is all right." A brigade commander would later say that officers in his category, even when they continued to function and seemed unaffected, generally needed two days before the shock wore off.

General Gonen, still at his headquarters in Beersheba, more than 150 miles from the front, tried to discern from the reports pouring in where the main Egyptian crossing points were. Around midnight, he asked Elazar for permission to attack an Egyptian position half a mile north of Orkal. He was oblivious to the fact that the causeway leading to Orkal was a death trap that had consumed every tank that reached it. His proposal, which would have put Israeli forces in a better position to attack Port Said, was totally irrelevant to the desperate defensive battle under way along the canal. Permission was not granted.

At 1:30 a.m., with most of Mendler's tanks already knocked out, Gonen told the journalists attached to his headquarters that the Egyptian crossing was a failure since they had not moved their armor across the canal. In fact, several hundred Egyptian tanks attached to infantry divisions had already crossed, although they would not go into action until the morning. "Gonen arrived at conclusions without taking counsel," General Adan would write. "Instead of having his staff officers take part in the process of assessing situations, he relied on his intuition, based on his previous experience with the Egyptians, whom he held in deep contempt." Not until 2 a.m., twelve hours after the war's start, did Gonen fly by helicopter to his forward command post at Umm Hashiba.

Division commander Mendler did not share Gonen's illusions but he too did not draw the necessary conclusions from the picture unfolding before him. In the war room of the Sinai division, General Mendler sat quietly to the side, his eyes fixed on the large wall map which his staff was constantly updating. Having issued his brigade commanders their marching orders—basically, to defend the canal line—he gave hardly any further instructions and rarely spoke on the radio net. His injunction to Shomron—"Do the best you can"—was the last directive the brigade commander received from him this day. To an officer in the room, Mendler seemed to wear a thin, bitter smile as he stared fixedly at the map. "I said to myself," the officer would later recall, "why doesn't the man talk? A whole world that he built and trained for is collapsing in front of him and he keeps silent." The red circles and arrows his aides drew on the map were a parody of Dovecote, showing Egyptian bridgeheads expanding and Israeli units being pushed back. Periodically, Mendler would disappear into his office until the next staff meeting. He did not have the authority to order the evacuation of the forts but he did not request it.

The garrisons on the Bar-Lev Line could not understand why they were being asked to remain in the beleaguered forts when the circumstances were clearly hopeless. The decision not to evacuate them would prove calamitous for both the garrisons and the tanks trying to reach them. In some forts, most of the men were already casualties. Those who weren't were mostly service personnel, not combat troops. They pleaded with the tankers who reached them to take them out. The request was passed up the command chain but the response was negative.

Darkness provided cover for the Egyptian tank hunters who were now covering all approaches to the forts. Capt. Yaron Ram, commanding a force at Lituf, sent two tanks to locate a disabled tank. The rescue tanks were ambushed and communication with them lost. Shortly before dawn, one of their gunners came on the radio. Keeping his voice low, he said that only he and another crewman were still alive. They had been fending off Egyptian soldiers for more than an hour but ammunition was almost gone and they were now using grenades whenever enemy soldiers drew close. Captain Ram asked him to indicate his whereabouts by firing a shell. A moment later, a flash could be seen two miles away.

Three tanks were sent to the rescue. As they drew close, one was disabled by an RPG and the others driven back. Ram asked Major Shuval for permission to go himself with the three tanks remaining. Shuval refused. Ram's tanks were the only force blocking the road to the Gidi Pass. Ram told the trapped gunner that his only chance was to play dead when the Egyptian soldiers climbed aboard. Two minutes later, the tank's radio went silent. When the tank was recovered the next day, the gunner and his comrade were dead inside.

Reshef received the last of the division's reserves at 1 a.m., a battalion under Lt. Col. Amram Mitzna. On its way toward Hizayon, fire was opened from the side of the road. The tanks' projectors revealed several dozen soldiers firing from shallow foxholes. "Attack," ordered Mitzna. The Egyptian infantrymen rose with RPGs as the tanks charged. They were tall black men, apparently Sudanese. Some managed to get off shots but all were cut down. One tank officer was killed.

Close to the canal, the battalion passed between two rows of stationary tanks, some of whose crews were sitting on the ground drinking coffee. It was an encampment of Egyptian T-55 tanks which had just crossed. The surprise was mutual. After a brief exchange of fire, Mitzna broke contact.

Air attacks on the bridges were called off at midnight. It was more dangerous flying at night because the pilots could not gauge the distance of the SAMs fired at them in the dark and thus could not outmaneuver them.

Twice during the night, Israeli tanks broke through to the canal and inflicted damage on bridges and ferries. "Through the night, commanders of [Israeli] sub-units, even individual tanks, fight on," General Shazly would write in his war diary. "They are evidently made of better stuff than their senior commanders."

A battalion commanded by Lt. Col. Amir Yoffe was ordered to link up with Forts Mifreket and Milano in the northern sector. The thirty-three-year-old Yoffe, nephew of a distinguished general, had a reputation as a hard-bitten, punctilious professional—the kind of officer, General Adan would say, whom you would not want to serve under in peacetime but to whom you would readily entrust your life in war. During the hasty organization of combat formations at the armor school the day before, he had not noticed that his younger brother, Eyal, a cadet in an officer's course, had been assigned to him as a tank commander.

Yoffe was guided through the boggy terrain by Yom Tov Tamir, whose battalion had been destroyed a few hours before. Yoffe first proceeded with half his tanks to Mifreket where they engaged RPG teams swarming over the approaches. Entering the fort, Tamir found that the radioman was now in command. Tamir's request by radio that the garrison be evacuated was denied.

Firing at a bridge north of the fort, a tank stalled on the canal embankment but continued shooting even though it was now a sitting target. The gunner, Sgt. Yadin Tannenbaum, a flautist, had been hailed before his army service as a musical prodigy. The nineteen-year-old had been singled out for praise by conductor Leonard Bernstein. After hitting the bridge, Tannenbaum knocked out a bulldozer widening a passage through the Israeli rampart and then hit an Egyptian tank coming through the opening. A shell hit his tank, killing him and his tank commander.

Sgt. Eyal Yoffe's tank followed that of his platoon commander, Lt. Michael Vardi, through a narrow, S-shaped entrance into the Mifreket compound. He could hear shouts in Arabic in the trenches. He and his men fired into the darkness around them with their machine guns and Uzis. As they approached the main bunker, members of the garrison ran out and climbed atop Vardi's tank. The officer descended and led them back to the bunker. He had orders, he said, to evacuate only wounded. He tried to assure the remainder that rescue would shortly come. Eyal Yoffe, in his tank outside, heard his brother on the radio ordering Vardi to join him north of the fort. Without identifying himself, Eyal said he would pass on the message.

It was difficult for him to grasp that this was reality, not an exercise. Darkness added to the disorientation. As Eyal followed Vardi northward, he saw an Egyptian tank thirty yards away. In his excitement, he forgot the protocol for issuing a fire command. "Ehud," he shouted to his gunner. "Quick. A tank to the right. Fire." The first shot hit. In the light of the burning tank, its four crewmen descended and ran toward his tank. Eyal stopped them with his machine gun. His tank hit an Egyptian bulldozer and fired at the bridge. Reality had begun to disentangle itself.

From time to time, Eyal Yoffe and Vardi reentered Mifreket to strike at Egyptians who had returned and to encourage the men in the bunker with their fire. Before dawn, the garrison's wounded, together with wounded tankers, were placed aboard Eyal's tank for evacuation. One man had lost both legs and an arm. Eyal saw his brother issuing orders nearby. The battalion commander did not recognize him in the darkness until he heard his voice. He was startled to discover that his kid brother was serving under him.

"How you doing, Ili?" he asked.

"Doing fine," responded Eyal, taking off his tanker's helmet for this moment of intimacy.

Transporting the wounded to the rear, he returned to Mifreket as it began to dawn. Lieutenant Vardi, he discovered, was dead. Most of the remaining tanks were either mired in marshes or trying to extricate others which were.

The Yoffe brothers, together with another tank commander, fired on enemy vehicles moving inland until Eyal's tank was hit by a Sagger. His brother placed him inside his own tank. Eyal had suffered burns on his face and could not speak but nodded to indicate to his brother that he would be all right.

As Tamir had done, Yoffe requested evacuation of the Mifreket garrison. Colonel Shomron was likewise asking permission to evacuate the forts in the southern sector. "If we don't do it now we won't be able to do it in the morning," he said. Mendler said he had not been authorized to evacuate the forts.

Tamir had gone back to guide brigade commander Amir and the rest of Yoffe's battalion to Milano. The fourteen-tank column moved through East Kantara, a ghost town since its abandonment in the Six Day War. But Egyptian troops had now returned. Two tanks became lost in side streets and were destroyed by RPGs.

Reaching Milano, Colonel Amir found the situation surprisingly calm. The fort commander, Captain Trostler, said they had beaten off several attacks during the day and had sunk a number of boats crossing the canal. He had lost four men but the defenses were intact and he was not in need of help. Tamir led the tanks out before first light by a route that avoided Kantara. Of the fourteen tanks, only five returned. Of the eighteen tanks Yoffe had brought to Mifreket, another five returned. Had they been authorized to evacuate the forts there would have been purpose to their sacrifice.

In the southern sector, the commander of a lone tank reported that he had stalled. He was told to put his gear into reverse and fire a shell. The recoil succeeded in starting the engine and the tank rejoined the remnants of Shomron's brigade, which had fallen back to the Artillery Road.

Mendler finally received permission late Sunday morning from Gonen to evacuate the forts, more than twelve hours after Elazar had authorized evacuation of most of the Bar-Lev Line. But it was too late. All the forts were surrounded now by masses of Egyptian infantry, and tanks as well. Mendler asked Shomron if he was able to evacuate the forts in his sector. "Any attempt will cost a battalion," replied the brigade commander. "It's your decision." The decision was negative. The battle for the waterline was over and the Egyptians had won it.

The conceptual failure of the Bar-Lev Line had been brutally exposed. By the early hours of Sunday, the import of the past day's events was beginning to be absorbed by the IDF command. In twelve hours, almost two-thirds of the Sinai Division's tanks had been knocked out, the bulk by Egyptian infantry. Of the division's 280 tanks, only 110 were still operational. Reshef's brigade had only one-quarter of its tanks left.

Virtually every assumption by the Israeli command about the nature of the coming war had proven wrong—that AMAN would provide ample warning, that the air force would somehow cope with the SAMs and save the day, that the IDF could get by with limited artillery and infantry, that "armor shock" would stampede the enemy, that the Arab soldier was a pushover and the Arab military command inept.

The Israeli command had permitted itself to believe that given the nature of the enemy—"we're facing Arabs, not Germans," as one officer put it—Dovecote could somehow cope with a five-division crossing. The General Staff failed to think through the implications of the massive amount of antitank weapons known to be in the hands of Egyptian infantry. Duels at fifty paces between tanks and individual soldiers wielding RPGs was not what armored warfare was about.

The tank crews, conscripts mostly aged nineteen to twenty-one, and their field commanders had fought with supreme courage and exemplary skill. But they had been thrown into a meat grinder. The Bar-Lev garrisons, including those of the Jerusalem Brigade, had fought outstandingly but their situation was hopeless from the start.

Of all the fuzzy thinking in the high command, reliance on air support was the fuzziest. Air Force Commander Peled had made clear that he would need the first forty-eight hours of war to deal with the SAMs. Yet Elazar and his generals permitted themselves to believe that the air force, still wreathed with the magical aura of the Six Day War, would somehow find a way to deal with enemy ground forces as well. Compounding the problem, the IDF deployed only a few dozen artillery pieces and heavy mortars on a hundred-mile-long front because it relied on the air force. Without meaningful artillery and air support, the IDF lacked firepower even more than manpower.

AMAN's failure went deeper than the failure to warn of war. It failed to prepare the IDF for the kind of war that might overtake it. It failed to suggest the innovative tactics the Egyptian army would employ or point to the motivation and training that would make the Egyptian soldier of 1973 different from the soldier of the Six Day War. A common factor behind all these failings was the contempt for Arab arms born of that earlier war, a contempt that spawned indolent thinking.

The surprise of the Arab assault would be a staggering psychological blow for Israel that would impact on the rest of the war. However, it was not surprise that was most responsible for the debacle on Yom Kippur day but basic unpreparedness and inept generalship on the southern front. Even if there had been no surprise, the IDF was not prepared to cope with the Egyptians' new antitank tactics, the air force was unable to provide assistance to the ground forces in areas dominated by SAMs, and Dovecote would still have been a suicidal response.

For Israel, there was one bright spot—the performance of the tank crews and their field commanders despite the disastrous tactics imposed on them.

The Sinai Division had been mauled but not destroyed. Most of its damaged tanks would be returned to action, some within a day, and its command structure was largely intact. Many of the wounded would return to duty, replacements would fill the gaps, and appropriate lessons would be drawn.

The reserve divisions now approaching the battlefield would have to learn these lessons for themselves.

. . .

Exhausted by the day's battle, the surviving tank crews pulled back before dawn to refuel and rearm. The men had hardly eaten since the onset of Yom Kippur, which seemed a lifetime ago, and they had not slept. Thinking about what they had been through and what the morrow might bring, thinking about their dead and wounded comrades, they fell into a brief and troubled sleep.

In the Egyptian lines this night, soldiers who could doze off did so on the wings of euphoria. There had not been a feat of Arab arms like this since Saladin defeated the Crusader army near the Sea of Galilee in the twelfth century. No matter what was yet to come, Egypt's soldiers had restored Arab honor.

13

MOBILIZATION

A GROUP OF WOMEN sitting in front of their apartment building Saturday afternoon in the port city of Ashdod watched with mounting unease the extraordinary sight of vehicles moving through the streets on Yom Kippur. The husbands of all had received emergency call-up orders in the past few hours, except for one. It was she who stepped forward ruefully when a car pulled up and a courier emerged with a brown envelope in his hand. Her husband had returned from a month's reserve duty just two weeks before and she had permitted herself to hope that he might be spared. She found him already packing his kit bag. As a member of a mechanized infantry battalion, he had no doubt that he would be called.

Other men from his unit were already at the nearby assembly point. He could read in their eyes the same surprise and apprehension that he felt. The consensus among them was that whatever was happening would be over in a couple of days. If the Arabs had forgotten the lessons of the Six Day War after only six years, they would be reminded soon enough. Nevertheless, the prospect of war was sobering. Two buses arrived at 6:30 p.m. As they moved off, the men began singing. Passersby waved and applauded.

Army bases seethed with activity as reservists arriving from around the country reported to their units. First, the men were formally mobilized, handing over their reservists' identity cards to company clerks who asked for the name of relatives to be informed "in case something happens." After receiving uniforms and personal weapons—not having to sign for them as they did during reserve stints—the men dispersed to the sheds of their respective battalions to equip and arm the tanks and personnel carriers.

More than 200,000 civilians were being transformed overnight into an army. The process had been set in motion shortly after nine that morning with the transmission of code words to brigade mobilization centers. Designated couriers from each brigade were summoned by telephone and provided with civilian vehicles that had already been mobilized to deliver call-up orders. The car owners were permitted to drive the couriers if they preferred not handing over the keys to the army. Most of the civilian bus fleet had been mobilized to pick up reservists from assembly points. Some reservists reached their bases by early afternoon. Others, living in remote parts of the country where the buses had to stop at many rural settlements, did not arrive at their bases until after midnight. Some men, impatient at not having received their call-up notice, came on their own, sometimes even by taxi. Veteran warhorses long since mustered out of service showed up at their old units and asked to be taken on, a request usually granted.

While the mobilization process went smoothly, the scenes at the tank bases were of barely controlled pandemonium. The tanks had been stripped when put into storage after their last use and they now had to be equipped and armed from scratch. Tanks assigned to reserve brigades were used in training by various units and, like borrowed books, they were not always returned in their original condition or returned to their proper place. The army assumed that even in an emergency it would have at least forty-eight hours' warning in which to replace missing or damaged equipment. The depots were not ready to handle a call-up of the entire reserve army in one day. Sometimes the tanks themselves were missing and officers had to scurry among army bases to track them down or find replacements. Brigade commander Haim Erez had to send men to six different bases to retrieve his unit's tanks. Officers from one battalion almost came to blows with quartermasters who refused to release tanks the quartermasters believed designated for another unit. Small but important pieces of equipment like binoculars and flashlights were missing almost everywhere while the availability of other items ranging from crew helmets to projectors was spotty. Far more grave, entire brigades had to set off for the front without machine guns, which would be more important than tank guns in the encounters with infantry that lay ahead.

Some problems were solved by local initiative. At the request of army officers, police in Beersheba, around which many army bases lay, summoned storeowners at night to open their shops for the sale of items like binoculars and flashlights. At a base in the south where no forklifts could be found to transfer crates of shells from ammunition bunkers, soldiers "borrowed" forklifts from an adjacent industrial area after breaking through a fence. In the north, a battalion commander borrowed forklifts from his home kibbutz which was near his unit's assembly area. General Sharon telephoned a millionaire friend in the U.S. for binoculars. A shipment would arrive by air within a few days and be rushed to the front.

The men worked feverishly into the night to turn the metal behemoths into fighting machines. Technical teams swarmed over the tanks. Optical sights, drivers' periscopes, radio sets, and other equipment were fitted into their places. Water and battle rations were put aboard and shells, passed from hand to hand, were stored in the turrets and bellies of the tanks. Officers constantly pressed the men to move faster. "We'll lose the war because of you" was a standard spur. "Hurry. Hurry."

Despite the problems, 85 percent of units would reach the front within the time planned. Some would reach it in half the time despite missing pieces of equipment.

News from the front was scant but the reservists were aware that the small forces holding the line must be fighting a desperate battle.

Gen. (Res.) Yeshayahu Gavish, who commanded Israel's Southern Command in the Six Day War, drove down to his old headquarters in Beersheba on Yom Kippur afternoon to see whether the current commander, General Gonen, could use his services. He found him in his office going through papers. "How's it going, Shmulik?" he asked.

"We're going to screw them," said Gonen.

Gavish went into the war room to monitor the radio net. What he heard shocked him. Cries of desperation were coming from the forts, and tank crews were engaged in fierce battles. Gavish returned to Gonen and urged him to come out and listen for himself. "Things aren't going well," said Gavish.

Gonen waved dismissively. "We're on top of it," he said. "Don't worry about it." Gavish gathered that Gonen had no assignment for him.

Shortly afterward Col. (Res.) Uri Ben-Ari arrived at the Beersheba headquarters to take up his reserve assignment as assistant to Gonen. He too suggested that the front commander come out of his office and listen. "It'll be over soon," Gonen had replied, remaining behind his desk, 150 miles from the front.

In giving Ben-Ari his assignment, Elazar was balancing Gonen's limited experience and sometimes volatile behavior with the steady hand of one of the most respected veterans of Israel's armored corps. The strapping, German-born Ben-Ari looked like a Prussian officer. His grandfather had in fact been an *ulan*, a member of the Kaiser's bodyguard. Ben-Ari himself was born Heinz Banner in Berlin. His father, a prosperous textile merchant, had sent him to Palestine at age fourteen, half a year before the onset of the Second World War, in order to get him out of Germany. All of Ben-Ari's relatives, some ninety persons, perished in the Holocaust. He himself served in the elite Palmach strike force in Israel's War of Independence—he was Elazar's commander at San Simon—and was one of the first to join the armored corps. In the 1956 Sinai Campaign, he commanded the Seventh Armored Brigade, which spearheaded the Israeli breakthrough. Gonen had served under him in that campaign. Ben-Ari left the army shortly afterward, but as a reservist in 1967 he led a mechanized brigade in the battle for Jerusalem. Recalled to duty on Yom Kippur, he was surprised to find that Gonen had not yet moved to his forward command post in Sinai, Umm Hashiba.

When they did fly there twelve hours after the war began, Ben-Ari found the underground facility barely functioning. He would devote his first day to putting it in working order. The most important task he assigned himself was keeping an eye on Gonen. It was clear to him that Gonen was totally unsuited for his post. Elazar, in countering critics of Gonen's appointment, had said that he would gain experience over the course of time. But Ben-Ari believed that waging a multidivisional war on a broad front was simply beyond Gonen's intellectual and emotional capacity.

Ben-Ari was repelled by Gonen's coarse behavior—cursing, shouting, throwing telephones at personnel when he couldn't get a line. In Beersheba, Gonen had been relatively relaxed but upon arriving at Umm Hashiba, charged with running a war, he went out of control. Staff officers hesitated to call unpleasant facts to his attention for fear of his outbursts. "It was very difficult for him to formulate a position about anything," Ben-Ari would say, "or to make an appraisal of the situation because of the atmosphere of tension and fear. There was no orderly staff work." Ben-Ari decided that as long as the war lasted he would not go to sleep before Gonen and not waken after him. He asked his driver to be sure to waken him if he saw Gonen waking first. The front commander, he felt, must not be left alone.

The two reserve divisions assigned to Southern Command were commanded by generals whose rich military careers had seemed behind them—Avraham Adan and Ariel Sharon.

Adan, known to all as "Bren," was scheduled to retire in a month. The public knew him best from the photograph of him as a handsome, young officer climbing a pole to raise the first Israeli flag in Eilat during the War of Independence twenty-five years before. He had now been commander of the armored corps for five years. In that time, he had overseen the doubling of the armored forces. There was a shyness about him that made him seem cold to some but he was regarded by his peers as a consummate professional.

Sharon was cut from different cloth. He had won fame as a commander of special forces but his assertive character brought him into conflict with superiors and peers at virtually every stage of his military career. He was accused of being overaggressive, disobedient, and divisive. When Sharon transferred to the armored corps, Adan and other veteran tank commanders saw him as burdened by an infantryman's mentality. "He did not seem cut out to be an Armored Corps soldier," Adan would write in his memoirs. Adan found Sharon's views on strategic-political issues simplistic, if not extreme in their hawkishness.

However, Israeli military analysts would credit Sharon with having conceived and executed the one classic set-piece battle in Israeli military history—the night battle for Abu Agheila in Sinai in the Six Day War. The complex operation involved paratroopers landing by helicopters in the enemy rear to silence artillery, flanking movements by infantry that avoided the enemy's main defenses, effective use of artillery, engineers clearing enemy minefields, and frontal assaults by tanks. Each unit's combat potential was exploited to the maximum. The meticulously timed operation was executed almost exactly as planned, a model of a combined arms operation that was nevertheless overshadowed in Israeli military thought by the notion of the totality of the tank.

A general who knew Sharon since serving as his company commander in the War of Independence would say of him that "Arik can never execute someone else's plan, only his own." It was a trait not bound to endear him to superiors. In the waiting period before the Six Day War, General Gavish had prepared a tentative plan calling for two divisions to attack while the third, commanded by Sharon, remained in defensive positions. Sharon objected strongly to his role and Gavish made a point of coming to the briefing Sharon gave the next day to his division staff. A look at the maps on the wall showed that Sharon was planning to attack, not defend. Gavish asked him to come outside. If Sharon did not intend to carry out orders, then he should "get on your jeep and go home," Gavish said. Instead of being put down by the rebuke, Sharon said, "Let's speak to Yitzhak," a reference to chief of staff Yitzhak Rabin. Calling Rabin in Gavish's presence, he said that Gavish was proposing a plan that made no sense. Sharon then proceeded to outline his own plan. Rabin did not even ask to speak to Gavish. "Obey Gavish's order or hand over your command," he said. From that moment, Gavish had no problem with Sharon. In the end, plans were changed and Sharon got to execute his own at Abu Agheila.

Even Sharon's bitterest opponents acknowledged that he was a superb field commander—the best Israel had, in the view of many— a daring and imaginative officer who could read a battle as it unfolded and inspire his troops. He remained a field soldier even in high command, capable of studying a photostat of unfamiliar territory for a quarter hour, as a staff officer would testify, and then lead his unit through the terrain for an entire night without further reference.

He had reluctantly retired from the army after it was made clear to him that he had no chance to be appointed chief of staff and that his term as commander of the Southern Command was ending after three and a half years. On the morning of his retirement, he telephoned Dayan to plead for another year as front commander. War with Egypt was a real possibility, he said, and his battle experience and familiarity with the front were assets not to be cast aside lightly. Sharon heard a pause before Dayan replied, "There won't be war in the coming year."

Despite opposition by Elazar, Sharon had with Dayan's support been granted a commission as commander of a reserve division. Dayan appreciated Sharon's qualities as a fighting general even though he was well aware of his excesses. In the Sinai Campaign of 1956, Dayan, then chief of staff, had considered court-martialing him for launching an attack at the Mitla Pass in defiance of orders that cost the lives of thirty-eight paratroopers. "Better a noble steed that you have to restrain," said Dayan, "than a lazy ox you have to beat." In the three months Sharon had been a civilian, he had proved himself no less vigorous in the political arena. He was the driving force behind the formation of the new right-wing Likud Party headed by Menahem Begin and was himself a candidate for the Knesset in elections scheduled for the end of October.

Telephoning Gonen in Beersheba on Yom Kippur afternoon, Sharon urged him to move to his forward command post to get a better feel of the battle. Gonen did not appreciate the advice. Until three months before, he had been subordinate to Sharon. The delicate command situation made for a charged atmosphere and Sharon realized he would have to be cautious. Both Sharon and Adan had far more combat experience than Gonen, who they were now serving under, and both had more seniority. Both were also extremely skeptical about his command abilities. Neither, however, wanted his job. They were grateful to be leading divisions in the field rather than sitting behind a desk in rear headquarters.

As armored corps commander, Adan attended the meeting at 7 a.m. with Elazar and Zeira in the Pit where he learned of Marwan's war warning. He proceeded from there to his own headquarters where, in his capacity as commander of a reserve division, he met with his three brigade commanders. Adan's division was assigned the northern canal front and would proceed there along the Mediterranean coastal road. Sharon was assigned the central sector and would proceed through the heart of Sinai to Tasa. Mendler's remaining tanks would confine themselves to the southern sector after the other divisions arrived.

Meeting with Elazar later in the morning, Adan found the chief of staff calm and coping. They agreed that Mendler, who was to have been replaced the next day by Gen. Kalman Magen, would remain at his post for the duration of the war.

The first tank transporters, bearing a reserve company from Adan's division commanded by Maj. Yitzhak Brik and accompanied by a small force of infantry in half-tracks, set off for the front Saturday night at 10:30, just thirteen hours after mobilization had been set in motion.

Sitting in the radio-less cabin of the transporter as it moved through the desert darkness, Brik was cut off from the outside world in the borderland between sleep and wakefulness. He reviewed the frantic events of the day which had begun with the sound of warplanes over-flying his kibbutz in southern Israel. He and a fellow kibbutz member belonging to his battalion had driven to their assembly point, assuring each other that whatever was happening would be over in a day or two. The storerooms in his mobilization depot were in good shape, which accounted for the swift readiness of his unit. But the haste and the unclear orders with which he was dispatched to the front did not bode well. He was told to proceed along the road to Baluza, on the approaches to the canal, until he was flagged down. There he was to await further orders. His battalion commander, Assaf Yaguri, said that the Egyptians were staging a major crossing.

At dawn, Brik's transporters reached the environs of Baluza. The road was empty and no one flagged them down. The Canal Zone was not far ahead and Brik was wary. Should they encounter Egyptians while still aboard the transporters they would be helpless. "We're unloading here," he said to the driver.

The tanks and APCs descended from the transporters and formed up behind the company commander. They had only proceeded a mile when Brik heard an explosion behind him. At the rear of the column, an APC was burning. Fire suddenly opened on the entire length of the column. Some 150 Egyptian commandos, who had landed by helicop-ter at dusk the day before, were dug in on either side of the road and under camouflage. Most of the fire was coming from the right. Brik ordered his driver to turn in that direction. Commandos rose from the sands all around him, firing and throwing grenades. Brik and the other tank commanders fired their machine guns and the drivers tried to run the commandos down. The tanks moved with difficulty through the dunes and commandos tried to clamber aboard from the rear in order to drop grenades through the open turret hatches. Brik and the com-mander of a tank forty yards away fired their machine guns at each other's tank to knock commandos off.

The other tank commander was hit and his crew pulled back, leav-ing Brik's tank alone. He fired his machine gun without pause until a rocket-propelled grenade literally brushed him, its heat igniting his shirt. Shouting to his gunner to take command, he leaped from the tank and rolled in the sand to extinguish the fire. The gunner rose into the turret and turned the machine gun on Egyptians closing in on Brik. One commando fell dead near the company commander. Brik was intact except for a badly singed face. Crawling back to the tank, which had meanwhile halted, he scrambled aboard. Several other tanks and an APC now joined him in pursuit of the Egyptians, who were pulling back.

Cautiously resuming movement westward, Brik saw a solitary Israeli tank and stopped alongside. The crewmen appeared stunned. They were young conscripts who had survived the battle at Mifreket the night before. From their account, and from what he himself had just experienced, Brik began to grasp that they were not up against the Egyptian army they knew from the Six Day War.

The other reserve forces streaming toward Sinai still had no idea of what awaited them. Many, anticipating an upgraded replay of the Six Day War, were afraid they would miss the action. Others were afraid they wouldn't. A company commander assembled his men and said that reports from the front indicated that a tough battle awaited them. All were veterans of the War of Attrition, a gritty conflict that evoked no nostalgia. "Be careful," he said. "Use your heads. Good luck." To brigade commander Haim Erez of Sharon's division, luck was a flimsy crutch in the face of a surprise so total. "We're in a mess," said Colonel Erez prophetically to one of his battalion commanders, Ami Morag. "This is going to end with 2,500 to 3,000 dead."

As Sharon's division passed through Beersheba on the way to the front, people on the streets applauded. At an intersection, a tank clipped a civilian car waiting at a red light. The car driver, a soldier, got out to examine the damage and waved reassuringly to the tank commander. "It's all right," he said. "It's a mobilized car, not mine." There would be compensation. Passing out of the city, the vehicles were swallowed up by the desert, which stretched all the way to the canal.

The convoys grew longer and slower as the night progressed and units joined from camps dotting the Negev. Men drew reassurance from the long line of tanks, their commanders upright in the turrets. "The Egyptians have made the mistake of their lives," said one soldier, contemplating the sight. Others, however, sensed that this war was different. It was the Arabs who had seized the initiative this time.

The men fell silent as they traveled west. A doctor with Sharon's division was struck by the surreal nature of what had overtaken them. "Only yesterday," he would write, "it was high-rise buildings, grassy lawns, synagogue, and children. Now it's armored vehicles, desert, khaki, and an endless road leading to war."

At times, the convoys had to pull over to make way for vehicles heading back to Israel. These were for the most part empty tank transporters or buses carrying young women soldiers ordered out of the war zone. The girls made the V sign to the soldiers moving up to the front.

For Egyptian sergeant Mahmud Nadeh, the first day's encounter with war had been enough to remove all illusion about a stirring adventure. His amphibious battalion, which crossed the Bitter Lake, had been savaged by Boaz Amir's tanks. "The amphibious tanks proved worthless beyond the crossing of the lake itself," Nadeh wrote in his diary the next morning. "Most of the tanks with me were set on fire, the rest scattered. It was the cruelest night we've ever experienced—death, hunger, thirst, fear, and cold. All of us fellows from Alexandria have gotten into one foxhole at the edge of the lake, so that we can die together. Some of the news they're broadcasting on the radio caused us to laugh out loud."

However, the broadcasts on Cairo Radio about Egyptian successes were truer than Nadeh and his comrades were in a position to appreciate in their isolated corner of the battlefield. Surveying the field reports Sunday morning in Center Ten, General Shazly could declare the battle of the crossing won, and by an astonishing margin. By 8 a.m. Sunday, 90,000 men had been put across the canal. By 2 p.m.—twenty-four hours after the war's start—the number had grown to 100,000 men. Also across were 1,020 tanks and almost 14,000 other vehicles in what Shazly would describe as the largest first-day crossing of a water barrier in military history.

Bridges had been hit during the night by Israeli planes but damaged modular sections were replaced within an hour. Shazly permitted himself a touch of ironic regret at the failure of the Israelis to have mobilized on time. Had their reserves been fully deployed, he thought, they would have rapidly followed up the Sinai Division's attack, repeating the same mistakes and suffering the same fate. It was an opinion that not a few Israeli officers would come to share.

General Adan had reached Baluza at 6:30 a.m., shortly before the Egyptians sprang their ambush on Brik. Fortunately for him, the commandos were waiting for heavier prey and did not reveal themselves by hitting the light vehicles carrying the divisional command. After reporting his arrival to Gonen, Adan set off to meet Gabi Amir. He found the brigade commander, an old comrade, and Yom Tov Tamir

in a half-track alongside a handful of tanks. The faces of the two officers were enough to convey the harrowing nature of what they had
been through. Colonel Amir gave a chilling description of the night's
battles. Tamir was offended that Adan offered no words of solace
about his battalion's destruction but the general was too busy absorbing the dimensions of the setback to empathize. Instead of scattering the remains of Amir's shattered brigade among other units, Adan
decided to keep it intact, in order not to destroy the morale of its men,
and to attach fresh forces to it.

Gonen raised Adan on the telephone. "Good that you've arrived,"
said the front commander, sounding weary. "The situation along the
canal is rough. Move your forces to prevent a breakthrough." Elazar
had urged Gonen to move back from Umm Hashiba for fear that commandos might be preparing to attack it. Commando units had been
spotted on hills nearby. "I don't want a general taken prisoner," said
Elazar. Gonen assured him he would never permit himself to be taken
prisoner.

The command post was a bunker built into a high hill fifteen miles
from the main IDF base in Sinai at Refidim. From the hilltop, the
canal could be made out on a clear day but the post itself was entirely
underground. Gonen ordered machine gun positions set up on its
approaches and told his officers to be prepared to repulse an Egyptian
commando attack should it come.

As Adan deployed his units astride the east–west roads in his sector,
he was informed that the commando force dispersed earlier by Brik
had returned to block the coastal road. The commandos had fired
on a convoy of half-tracks traveling from Baluza toward the rear for
refueling. The vehicles got through except for the last half-track, which
had engine trouble, and a jeep at the rear of the convoy. The thirteen
men in the two vehicles dismounted. Nine were Israeli commando
officers.

At the direction of Lt. Rafi Sa'id, who took command, they began
moving toward the ambushers. On the way, Sa'id saw an Israeli tank
sheltering in a fold in the ground. He signaled it to take the lead. As
they closed on the Egyptians, Sa'id split his force into two squads
which proceeded under the covering fire of the tank toward the enemy
flanks. This time it was the ambushers who were taken by surprise.
The tank driver ran down enemy soldiers while Sa'id's men hit the
disoriented Egyptians with precise fire. When the battle was over, the

tank commander was dead and several Israelis were wounded but the bodies of ninety-two Egyptians covered the ground. The Egyptian commander was taken prisoner. All told, twenty-one Israelis were killed in the two phases of the battle on the coastal road. Five tanks and five other vehicles had been knocked out. Lying on the roadside, they would constitute a warning to arriving forces that this was going to be a different kind of war.

Another Egyptian commando force had landed by boat before dark Saturday on the sand spit leading to Budapest. The two-hundred-man force placed mines and waited for Israeli reinforcements to try to reach the outpost. Close to midnight, eight Israeli tanks started up the road. When the first hit a mine, the Egyptians sent up flares and unleashed a volley of Saggers, hitting two tanks. The Israelis pulled back but resumed movement at first light. They were again stopped by mines and Saggers, losing another tank.

The commandos were well dug in overlooking the road. A belt of mines and the narrowness of the sand spit prevented flanking. The Egyptian scouts whose footprints Motti Ashkenazi had evidently seen had chosen the ambush site well. An Israeli force made another attempt at 9 a.m. after shelling the area with mortars. The foot soldiers were exposed as they moved along the shore and in the ensuing battle fifteen Israelis were killed and thirty wounded. Budapest remained cut off.

On the coastal road, Adan's division was tied up in traffic jams all the way back to El Arish, ninety miles from the canal. The deep sand alongside the road made it difficult to push stalled vehicles off. An order was finally given for tanks and APCs to be off-loaded from transporters so that they could continue forward on their own tracks through the sand. Fighter planes circling overhead guarded against air attacks.

The approach of Sharon's division to the front went smoothly. The Egyptians had intended commando ambushes along this route as well but Israeli planes had downed most of the helicopters carrying them. Sharon himself left for the front at 2 a.m. Sunday in a mobilized pickup truck painted with the sign "Ray of Light Solar Heaters." The owner of the vehicle had chosen to stay with it as driver. With Sharon was an old friend from his paratroop days, Zeev Amit, who had decided to come along for the war. Sharon's wife found a pair of her husband's old boots to lend him. Reaching the Refidim base, Sharon entered the underground war room. Officers and men inside instinctively rose, as if he were still front commander.

General Mendler was relieved to see Sharon and to hear that the lead elements of his division were not far behind. Mendler was visibly weary. The situation on the front was unclear, he said. What remained of Reshef's brigade was confronting the forward elements of the entire Second Army. Shomron's brigade was opposite the Third Army. Amir's brigade barely existed. Overall tank losses were heavy. So were casualties. The Egyptians were now three to five miles east of the canal and their forces were streaming across the waterway without hindrance.

For Sharon, this succinct account was verification of his worst nightmares about the Bar-Lev Line.

Arriving at Tasa, which would be his headquarters, he moved forward in a jeep to a point overlooking the canal area. Smoke from artillery fire rose all along the front in the distance. Sharon flagged down several withdrawing tanks and talked to their commanders. "I saw something strange on their faces," he would write. "Not fear but bewilderment." For the first time in the soldiers' lifetimes, an Israeli army was being driven back and they could not fathom what was happening.

It was clear to Sharon what had to be done—a swift and concentrated blow by at least two divisions before the Egyptians fortified their bridgeheads. The attack could be launched the next day, Monday, when his and Adan's divisions would be in place. It was vital, Sharon believed, that the Egyptians be denied the feeling of success. The psychological factor was critical in war and the Egyptians had to be thrown off balance by a swift counterattack. His aim, he would write, was "to create in the Arabs a psychology of defeat, to beat them every time and to beat them so decisively that they would develop the conviction that they would never win."

Another thought taking shape as he looked out over the battlefield was the need to rescue the men in the forts. Returning to Tasa, he asked to be put in radio contact with the forts in his sector. Identifying himself only by his radio code number, 40, he sought to get a feel of the tactical situation and the mood.

In Purkan, radio operator Avi Yaffe, who had brought a tape recorder to reserve duty from his Jerusalem recording studio, recorded Sharon as he spoke with Major Weisel, the fort commander.

"Do the Egyptians seem tired or do they have momentum?" asked

Sharon. He himself sounded tired and was plainly unclear about the situation. "How many tanks do you see? Are they moving towards Tasa?"

Weisel, sounding unruffled, said the Egyptian tanks were deployed on Lexicon, the road paralleling the canal. "They seem to be waiting for our tanks to attack," he said.

Weisel noted that Israeli planes had attacked the Egyptians in his area earlier. "It reminded me of six years ago," he said, referring to the Six Day War.

"Were you in that war?" asked Sharon.

"I've been in four, well three," said Weisel. "You're talking to an old man of almost forty-one."

Sharon laughed politely but his voice remained deadly serious. "I just got here. I'm going to try to get you out. What vehicles do you have?"

"Two half-tracks and a truck."

The radioman at Fort Hizayon, Max Maimon, a Jerusalem bank clerk, cut into the conversation. He had been issuing desperate calls for assistance since the day before and he recognized Sharon's voice. "Forty, forty. We know you. We know you will get us out of here. Please come to us."

Sharon was deeply moved by these conversations. A soldier on his staff saw his eyes grow moist. Contacting Gonen, Sharon said it was a moral duty to try to rescue the men trapped in the forts. He proposed that tanks move forward after dark on a narrow front with a heavy artillery bombardment creating a "fire box" on their flanks and front to keep off the RPG teams. Simultaneously, the men in the forts would emerge under the cover of darkness in vehicles or on foot to meet the tanks at predetermined points. Sharon believed it was still possible to rescue them because the bulk of the Egyptian army, particularly the tanks, had not yet crossed. However, the danger was the infantry, which was already deployed in force. Gonen, whose sangfroid had given way after seeing most of Mendler's division dissolve in fruitless attacks, rejected Sharon's proposal. The men in the forts would have to wait for a general counterattack, which he was planning for the next day.

Sharon had no hesitation about going over Gonen's head and calling Dayan directly to ask for his intervention. The defense minister said the subject of the forts would be discussed at a meeting that night at Gonen's headquarters. Sharon and the other division commanders would also be attending.

Mitzna's battalion, on high ground five miles east of Hizayon, watched the Egyptians pouring across a bridge just south of the fort. After the enemy units formed up, they moved across the sandy plain and climbed the hills toward the Artillery Road. Mitzna's battalion blocked their way, destroying dozens of tanks in daylong skirmishing. Like the units that had encountered Saggers for the first time the day before, Mitzna's tank crews improvised responses to the threat—firing directly in front of their own tank to create dust, moving back and forth and firing toward the presumed location of the Sagger operator. These techniques would in time be adopted by NATO forces adjusting to the newly perceived threat of Warsaw Pact Saggers.

By late afternoon, ammunition and fuel were nearly exhausted and many of Mitzna's tanks had been hit. During a lull in the firing, company commander Rami Matan climbed out of his turret and sat on the hull to smoke a cigarette. In the distance, another Egyptian wave was forming up. Reconciled to death, the twenty-two-year-old captain reckoned that he would be able to fire off his last few shells before being overrun. The Egyptians had not yet attacked, however, when a dust cloud to his rear indicated tanks approaching. Mitzna ordered his men to prepare to pull back. The reserves were moving into the line.

Sgt. Chemi Shalev, a member of a medical unit in Adan's division, drove north on the Lateral Road Sunday to the army base at Baluza on the Mediterranean coast. He had been asked to locate casualties from his battalion. A soldier in the Baluza base pointed to a nearby building when Shalev told him what he was looking for. The sergeant assumed he was being directed to the base infirmary. When he opened the door, he saw a room filled with soldiers. Most were lying on the floor, some on tables, some propped up on chairs. All were dead. Shalev instinctively recoiled but then entered the makeshift morgue. He was astonished at the sight of so many bodies in this one remote corner of the battlefield just one day into the war.

"I spent long minutes peering at their faces, some of which were disfigured and others in perfect shape," he would write decades later as a veteran journalist with *Ha'aretz*. He checked dog tags. "Then I started all over again, gazing at them anew, even after I realized that none of them were from my unit. There were young soldiers among them, but mostly older reservists. I started guessing who they were, what they did, where they came from, who would miss them. An angry officer burst into the room, shouting at me to get out at once. I was grateful." Shalev's father, Mordechai, was himself coping with the war from the diplomatic front line as chargé d'affaires at the Israeli embassy in Washington where he was holding the fort until Ambassador Dinitz returned from Jerusalem.

Returning to his unit, Sergeant Shalev saw a personnel carrier parked at an awkward angle near the medical tent, its motor running. A doctor whom he asked about it said that a soldier had driven it in at high speed and then run off into the desert. "We were too tired and too busy to ask why."

Examining it now, members of the unit saw that it had a hole in the side where an RPG had penetrated. A doctor warily opened the rear door. He stepped back and let out an unearthly wail.

With darkness Sunday, there was time for the men on the line to listen to Israel Radio and try to make sense of what was happening. Fighting seemed to be heavy everywhere. It would have been no consolation to the Israeli soldiers in Sinai to know that as bad as things seemed for them, the situation on the Golan front, three hundred miles to the northeast, was far worse.

14

SYRIAN BREAKTHROUGH

SYRIA EXPECTED TO REGAIN the Golan Heights within the course of a single day, and with good reason.

Opposite the 177 tanks Israel had on the heights Yom Kippur morning, Syria had 1,460. Opposite Israel's 11 artillery batteries, Syria had 115. Opposite 200 Israeli infantrymen manning ten strongpoints along the forty-mile-long front were 3 Syrian infantry divisions with 40,000 men.

That the Israeli command was willing to accept this dizzying disparity reflected a contempt for Syrian arms even more than it reflected Israel's limited manpower. As Elazar had said a few days before, 100 tanks on the Golan should be sufficient to deal with the 800 Syrian tanks. Had it not been for the arrival of Ben-Gal's brigade, the ratio of tanks would not have been 8 to 1 but 18 to 1. Unlike on the Egyptian front, there was no substantial physical barrier the Syrians had to overcome to reach the Israeli line; only a tank ditch and minefields.

The Syrians assumed it would take the Israeli reserves twenty-four hours to reach the front. They intended to conquer the Golan before then. The broad outlines of the Syrian plan were known to Israeli intelligence for at least two months; an updated version was acquired a week before Yom Kippur. As in Sinai, this foreknowledge played little role in the battle itself where it was rendered irrelevant by the overwhelming disparity in forces. The three Syrian infantry divisions on the line—the Seventh in the north, Ninth in the center, and Fifth in the south—would attack simultaneously. Despite their infantry designation, the divisions numbered 900 tanks among them. Two armored divisions with another 470 tanks were deployed to the rear, a few hours' drive from the front. They would support the attack if it stalled and would anchor the defenses against the anticipated Israeli counterattack after the Golan was captured.

Engineering units were given three hours to bridge or fill in the tank ditch and clear the minefields. Infantry would then move through to capture the Israeli frontline strongpoints and the tels—dormant volcanic cones—which served as observation posts behind the Israeli front line. The tank formations would follow and overwhelm the Israeli armor within three to four hours. According to the Syrian plan, the army would penetrate five to six miles during the night. The armored divisions would complete the conquest of the Golan and then brace for the Israeli counterattack.

A key element in the Syrian plan was the landing of commandos by helicopter at the Jordan River bridges ten hours after zero hour. They would block, or at least delay, the reserve Israeli divisions that would try to reach the heights. By dawn, less than sixteen hours after zero hour, the entire Golan would be in Syrian hands and the major approaches across the Jordan would be cut. There were no operational plans for continuing on into Israel itself but the option of continuing on to the Israeli Arab city of Nazareth was left open. Israel's counterattack would be of limited strength, Damascus believed, because its forces would be occupied primarily on the Egyptian front.

The Israeli military command was divided as to where the main Syrian thrust would come. AMAN believed it would be in the southern Golan where the terrain was relatively flat. Northern Command believed it would come in the northern sector near the abandoned town of Kuneitra. The terrain here was more difficult but a breakthrough would swiftly bring the Syrian forces to Nafakh, the main Israeli base on the Golan, and to the Bnot Yaacov Bridge over the Jordan, the main route into Israel.

A valley winding through the hills just north of Kuneitra—the Kuneitra Gap—was considered by Northern Command the most likely avenue for a Syrian thrust. General Hofi had over the summer ordered a series of tank ramps built on the hills overlooking the valley. They permitted tanks to fire with only their turret and gun exposed, giving them a substantial advantage over fully exposed tanks in the valley. Tank ramps already existed alongside the infantry strongpoints on the front line. Kuneitra itself was empty except for a limited Israeli military presence on its periphery.

The Israeli line was normally held by two tank battalions, total-

Maximum Syrian Advance

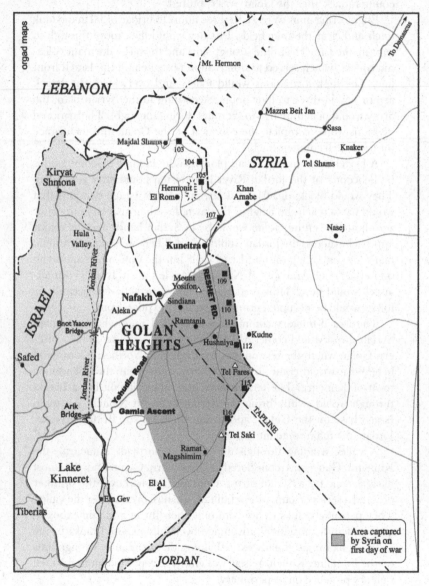

orgad maps

To Damascus

LEBANON

Mt. Hermon

Mazrat Beit Jan

Sasa

Majdal Shams
103

SYRIA

Knaker

104
105

Tel Shams

Hermonit
El Rom

Khan
Arnabe

Kiryat
Shmona

107

Nasej

Hula
Valley

Kuneitra

Jordan River

Mount
Yosifon

RESHET RD.

109

Nafakh

Sindiana

110

ISRAEL

Aleka

Ramtania

111

Bnot Yaacov
Bridge

GOLAN
HEIGHTS

Hushniya

Kudne

112

Safed

Tel Fares

113

Jordan River

Yehudia Road

Arik
Bridge

Gamla Ascent

116

TAPLINE

Tel Saki

Lake
Kinneret

Ramat
Magshimim

El Al

Tiberias

En Gev

JORDAN

Area captured
by Syria on
first day of war

ing seventy-seven tanks, from the 188th Brigade commanded by Col. Yitzhak Ben-Shoham, an amiable, Turkish-born officer who had taken command only two months before.

As with the Bar-Lev forts, the main purpose of the ten frontline infantry outposts, each garrisoned by twelve to twenty men, was observation, artillery spotting, and warding off minor probes. The five northern strongpoints were manned by the Golani Brigade and the southern by the Fiftieth Paratroop Battalion. In the event of a Syrian ground attack, it would be upon the tanks that the main burden of defense would fall, not the strongpoints. The arrival of the Seventh Brigade, dispatched piecemeal to the Golan following Moshe Dayan's intervention on Rosh Hashana eve, more than doubled Israeli strength on the heights. The last of the brigade's 105 tanks arrived on Yom Kippur morning and joined the others in holding areas.

Unlike in Sinai, where an intercepted radio message from a U.N. outpost had alerted the Israelis to an impending Egyptian artillery strike, the opening barrage on the Golan came without warning. Lt. Oded Beckman, a platoon commander in Ben-Shoham's brigade, was trying to persuade a crew member to break his fast when the barrage hit with a deafening roar. He could see the ground rippling as the Syrian guns methodically worked their way across preplanned target areas. His tanks managed to scramble out of the way just in time.

Smoke blanketed every crossroad, military camp, strongpoint, command center, tank park, and communications facility on the heights. The battalion commanders from the Seventh Brigade were just arriving at Nafakh for their scheduled 2 p.m. meeting with Colonel Ben-Gal when four MiGs dropped bombs on the camp. "Everyone to your tanks," the brigade commander shouted. A sentry already lay dead at the gateway.

As he moved off in his half-track, Ben-Gal was contacted by Ben-Shoham and told to move two of his battalions to the nearby Wasset junction and await further orders. General Hofi, before flying to Tel Aviv at noon for his second meeting of the day with Elazar, had given Ben-Shoham temporary command of the Golan. Unaware of this, Ben-Gal balked at receiving orders from another brigade commander of the same rank. He decided to return to Nafakh to straighten out the chain of command. Entering the underground command bunker, he found so many men sheltering from the shelling that he could not push through to Ben-Shoham at the far end. Spotting the Northern

Command operations officer, Lt. Col. Uri Simhoni, Ben-Gal shouted, "I'm moving the brigade towards Kuneitra," and hurried out to his half-track.

The surprise attack had created a command vacuum. Not only was Hofi absent from the Golan; so were his deputy, his bureau chief, and his division commanders. Ben-Shoham had nominal command but apart from the problem of giving orders to Ben-Gal he had his hands full commanding his own brigade now that the battle had begun. He sat with earphones in front of radio sets communicating with his two battalion commanders who were engaging Syrian forces all along the line. Although Colonel Simhoni was of lower rank than the two brigade commanders, who were full colonels, he was the channel through which orders were normally passed from General Hofi. Ben-Gal therefore did not hesitate to accept orders from Simhoni, who did not mention their source. In a curious command transformation, the source had become Simhoni himself.

As Simhoni saw it, the absence of Hofi and his senior staff left the reins in his own hands. It was a responsibility he embraced. He chose not to seek instructions from his superiors at northern front headquarters. He knew more about the swiftly changing situation than they and he felt more competent in the circumstances than they to exercise command. Thus it was that a lieutenant colonel effectively took upon himself the role of a major general commanding the most sensitive front in the critical opening hours of Israel's most difficult war.

Simhoni's first order would be one of the most important issued in the war. Military analysts would still be debating years later whether it was the right one. Barely half an hour after the opening barrage, he directed Ben-Gal to send one of his three tank battalions to the southern Golan and to deploy the other two battalions north of Kuneitra. These forces would back up the two tank battalions from Ben-Shoham's brigade which were holding the line—Yair Nafshi's in the north and Oded Erez's in the south. Ben-Gal's earlier decision to head for Kuneitra on his own had no legitimacy and could readily have been revoked. It was Simhoni's order, delivered under the mantle of Northern Command, that committed the bulk of Israel's reserves on the Golan Heights to the northern sector.

His decision was based in part on information coming in from the front. The southern sector reported that it was keeping the Syrians at bay. Reports from the northern sector were more alarming because observers there had a better view of the approaching Syrian masses from high ground, including Mount Hermon. But the major factor influencing Simhoni was past war games by Northern Command which had concluded that the Syrian main effort would be in the Kuneitra area.

The battalion taken from Ben-Gal to reinforce the southern sector was commanded by Maj. Haim Barak. Simhoni briefly considered keeping back one of Ben-Gal's two remaining tank battalions as a reserve in case the situation in the southern sector deteriorated but decided against it. His decision to deploy three tank battalions in the northern sector and two in the southern, with nothing held in reserve, dictated the course of the coming battle, for better or worse. By committing all his reserves in the opening hour, before the battle had truly been joined, he was violating one of the basic principles of warfare. He feared, however, that failure to commit all available forces might lead to a Syrian breakthrough; and of the two sectors, he viewed the northern as more critical.

In a curious dichotomy, half the Israeli forces on the Golan were braced for all-out war and the other half for a limited "battle day." Ben-Gal told his battalion commanders that war would break out this day on two fronts. He had so been briefed by division commander Eitan, who heard it from Hofi. The deployment of Ben-Gal's forces reflected this assessment. His units operated at no less than company strength, the better to deal with large-scale incursions. But Ben-Shoham, in passing on Hofi's alert, had not mentioned war. "Something's going to happen today," he told his officers. The brigade's tanks were thus dispersed thinly as on battle days, which usually involved only static exchanges of fire. Ben-Shoham believed that "war" was an imprecise designation for what could be expected. Indeed, Hofi himself did not anticipate an attempt to drive Israel from the Golan even though he had dutifully passed on the war alert.

Ben-Gal's tanks were positioned two miles behind the front line, overlooking it from high ground. One battalion was deployed at the southern end of the sector, near Kuneitra, and the other at the northern end, just beneath the slopes of Mount Hermon. Between the two, on a ridge called Hermonit, Ben-Gal created a new force with tanks taken from the other battalions. Thus he once again had three tank formations to maneuver even after Haim Barak's battalion had been sent south.

Nafshi's battalion from the 188th constituted a forward screen, positioned mostly in support of the infantry strongpoints on the front line. Nafshi himself was near Kuneitra when the Syrian barrage began. Even inside his tank, he could feel the ground trembling. "This is 10," he said on the battalion radio net, giving his identity number. "Capital. Repeat, Capital. Good luck." "Capital" was the code word for the battle day they had been awaiting. As his units headed for their predetermined positions, Nafshi drove to Booster Ridge near the southern edge of the sector. His tank ran over the mess kits of tankers who had been breaking their fast when the shells hit. Syrian planes returning from bombing runs roared low overhead. One flew so close that Nafshi could see the pilot grinning.

Ben-Gal drove along the front in his half-track to see if the Syrians were attacking but dust and smoke reduced visibility to virtually zero. Near Kuneitra he ordered his driver to stop. From across the line he detected a distant clanking and the sound of engines. Abruptly, the shelling ceased and from the settling dust cloud emerged a mass of Syrian tanks.

In Nafshi's tank, his operations officer had taken out a notebook to record reports from the battalion's tanks of hits on assigned targets, such as enemy tanks and positions. This was the routine record keeping of a battle day. However, what Nafshi was looking at as the dust settled was like no battle day he had ever seen. All along the broad front, hundreds of Syrian tanks and APCs were on the move. Leading them were bridging tanks capable of throwing a span across the tank ditch. At his order, his tanks opened up on the bridging tanks at long range, as much as 3,500 yards.

At Strongpoint 107, two miles north of Kuneitra, Lieutenant Elimelekh could not tell if the Syrians were advancing toward him because of the smoke and dust. His men had taken shelter from the shelling in a bunker, as called for, but Elimelekh and his radioman remained outside, in a sheltered observation position. The lieutenant asked battalion headquarters, atop a hill to his rear, whether they could see Syrian movement. But artillery was hitting the hill as well, obscuring the view. However, Lt. Shmuel Yakhin, commander of the tank platoon moving forward to cover 107, reported to Elimelekh that Syrian vehicles were advancing.

When the bombardment ceased, Elimelekh could see through binoculars a mass of tanks and trucks coming down the Damascus

Road. Infantrymen aboard the trucks held their rifles in the air and pumped them up and down in exultation. Yakhin's three tanks took positions on two firing ramps a few hundred yards on either side of the strongpoint and opened fire at two thousand yards. The tank gunners methodically worked their way down the line of Syrian vehicles. After the first ranging shots, the second shots almost always hit. Elimelekh pinpointed for Yakhin enemy tanks the tank officer couldn't see clearly because of folds in the ground.

At one point, Yakhin pulled back to load shells from the belly of his tank into the gun turret. The loader was outside the tank when Yakhin looked up to see a column of enemy tanks four hundred yards away. The lead tank was pointing its gun at him and he lowered his head to await the blow. However, the loader managed to scramble back into the tank and get a shell into the breech. Yakhin's gunner fired, holing the Syrian tank before it got off a shot. The reaction time of Israeli crews compared to that of Syrian crews would prove a major factor offsetting the disparity of forces, the Israelis getting off two or more rounds in the time it took for the Syrians to fire once.

Seven other tanks under Capt. Zvi Rak took positions alongside Yakhin's platoon, adding to the bonfires along the Damascus Road. To the Israelis' astonishment, Syrian tanks kept coming, swerving around those which had been hit. It was not until some thirty tanks were knocked out that the column veered south out of range.

When Strongpoint 109, a mile south of Kuneitra, reported Syrian tanks approaching, Rak dispatched his deputy, Capt. Oded Yisraeli, with three tanks. Following a narrow track along the border, Yisraeli came on a company of Syrian tanks crossing the tank ditch on two spans laid by bridging tanks. Yisraeli's tanks had caught the Syrians on their flank and within minutes destroyed them all. A mile further on, he saw a second company crossing. These tanks were accompanied by a bulldozer which had filled in the tank ditch. Alerted by the fight with their sister company, the Syrian tanks were waiting for Yisraeli. He called on Rak to send him reinforcements. "It's like a movie out here," he said.

Leaving Yakhin's three tanks at 107, the company commander started south with his remaining four tanks in Yisraeli's wake. As they skirted the border, there was an explosion and Rak found himself covered with blood. It was a moment before he realized the blood was not his. His loader had been standing with his head out of the loader's hatch when an RPG decapitated him. While the other three tanks continued on to join in the fight, Rak returned to Kuneitra to extricate the loader's body and change tanks. His gunner and driver became hysterical at the sight of their comrade's body. Rak slapped them and threw water on them and they calmed down.

Yisraeli's force, meanwhile, had destroyed the second Syrian company. An Israeli officer was killed in the fight. As Yisraeli continued on, he hit two more tanks coming up a small wadi from the border. These were the spearhead of a third company. The Syrian tanks had crossed in dead ground not visible from the Israeli strongpoints and were attempting to filter up wadis running between a series of low hillocks. But Yisraeli and a handful of tanks, in an almost offhand manner, had destroyed the better part of a Syrian tank battalion.

Taking position near 109, one of Rak's platoon leaders, Lt. David Eiland, noticed antennas behind trees on the border. He took his tank down the nearest wadi. Fifty yards to his front was a Syrian tank with its gun pointing in his direction. Just behind it was a second and one hundred yards beyond, a third, facing in the opposite direction. Eiland's gunner hit all three. In the distance, other tanks could be seen pulling back, the remnants of the Syrian battalion.

As with the Egyptians, the Syrian strategy was to stretch the limited Israeli defenses by attacking on as broad a front as possible and exploiting weak points. The Ninth Division in the center of the Syrian line sent forces against Kuneitra in the northern sector and also attacked in the southern sector. When the latter proved more porous, more forces were directed there.

Maj. Shmuel Askarov, the deputy commander of Oded Erez's battalion in the southern Golan, was the officer who had predicted war to Dayan and Zeira during their visit to the Golan ten days before. At twenty-four, he was the youngest deputy battalion commander in the IDF. Awaiting the Syrian attack, he had driven at noon to battalion headquarters at Hushniya, and left his tank parked next to his office door.

A few minutes before 2 p.m., the stillness gave way to the roar of aircraft and explosions. As MiGs pulled away, artillery shells tore into the base. Askarov and his crew mounted their tank and, with half a dozen others, headed through the barrage to join the tank platoon posted at Strongpoint 111 opposite the Syrian fortifications at Tel Kudne.

Moving on to one of the frontline tank ramps, Askarov could at first see nothing because of the smoke. As the Syrians lifted their barrage, a mass of tanks came into view. Five bridging tanks were the first to reach the Israeli ditch. Askarov managed to hit the three within range.

He noticed for the first time that the tanks he had come with had not mounted the ramp. He called on their commanders by radio to move up but got no clear response. Askarov told his driver to reverse down the slope. They braked alongside the nearest tank and Askarov climbed aboard. Pulling out his pistol, he pointed it at the commander's head. "Get up there or I shoot," he said.

Within a minute, all the tanks were on the ramps firing. Given the number of tanks and APCs passing under the Israeli tank guns it was like shooting fish in a barrel. Except that the fish were sometimes shooting back. For the most part, the Syrians simply swerved around their crippled tanks and pressed on, ignoring the Israeli fire. Some, however, detached themselves to engage the tanks on the ramps. One after another, the Israeli tanks were hit and most of their commanders killed. Askarov's tank was hit four times but remained operational.

He could not help admiring the Syrians' determination. They seemed indifferent to their losses as they pressed forward. He moved from ramp to ramp in order to throw up dust and create the impression of a large force. He had no illusions about surviving the day intact.

Askarov's gunner, Yitzhak Hemo, from the northern border town of Kiryat Shmona, was regarded as the finest tank gunner in the brigade. Askarov would pick a target and turn the turret, roughly aligning the gun. Hemo did the rest. Within two hours, Askarov would claim thirty-five tank kills, in addition to APCs.

At 4 p.m., Hemo hit a tank fifty yards away which had come up from the Kudne track to the left of the ramp. Looking to the right, Askarov saw another tank thirty yards away. He swung the turret and shouted to Hemo, who fired the same instant as did the Syrian gunner. Askarov was blown out of the turret by the Syrian shell. Retrieved by men from the strongpoint, the wounded officer was carried into a bunker. A few tanks remained on the ramp but the Syrians found a way to pass out of range to the south. With darkness, they would pour through unhindered into the southern Golan.

As the tanks of Capt. Uzi Arieli's company sped from Hushniya toward their preassigned positions on the front line, Lieutenant Beckman found himself unable to control the shaking of his limbs, even though his mind functioned clearly. The tanks were to support a platoon at Juhader, where the 1,200-mile-long Tapline oil pipeline entered Israeli-held territory. The buried pipeline stretched from Saudi Arabia to Lebanon, cutting diagonally across the Golan Heights. The tank platoon at Juhader had been pushed back and Arieli's tanks engaged Syrian T-55 tanks trying to come around the ramps. Pressure was unrelenting but the small Israeli force held. Beckman, on the left flank, saw a Syrian column led by a bridging tank approaching the tank ditch a few hundred yards away. He let the bridge be laid and then hit the first tank to mount it when it was halfway across. When a second tank came onto the bridge in order to push the first across, he hit that too, effectively blocking passage. A second bridging tank approached and Beckman hit it before it reached the ditch.

Toward dusk, he was dispatched to Strongpoint 115 where a high ramp offered a good view along the front. Beckman approached the lip of the ramp on foot. Immediately below him were four Syrian tanks and two APCs with mounted Saggers waiting to cross the cease-fire line. Lying down, the platoon commander summoned his gunner forward and showed him their prey. Beckman said they would undertake rapid fire, with the loader assembling shells for quick insertion and the gunner shifting swiftly from target to target. Beckman's tank moved forward and in less than half a minute the six Syrian vehicles were burning. The last in line managed to get off a Sagger that missed, leaving Beckman covered with a length of its guide wire.

After dark, Beckman and Arieli saw green flares fired to their rear. These were signals used by Syrian commanders to indicate their location to their scattered tanks. The Syrians, it was clear, were filtering through.

Second Lt. Yossi Gur, a paratrooper commanding Strongpoint 116 at the southern end of the line, had arrived only the day before to fill in for the regular commander who had gone home for the holiday. He found the strongpoint unready. There was little small arms ammunition and only five bazooka shells. The fort had been built two hundred yards on the Syrian side of the cease-fire line because of the site's elevation. The Syrians had swallowed this intrusion but it meant that the fort lay forward of the Golan tank ditch. There was thus no barrier separating the strongpoint and its fourteen defenders from the Syrian army except for the mines and barbed wire surrounding the position itself.

The opening Syrian barrage hit the position dead center. Gur ordered the men to the bunkers while he kept watch from a rabbit hole. The view through the periscope was limited and he periodically entered a trench to scan the surrounding terrain. On one such foray late in the afternoon he saw two long columns of Syrian tanks approaching the tank ditch four hundred yards away. Bridging tanks were already laying spans. He reported his sighting to Lt. Yoav Yakir, who commanded the three tanks assigned to the defense of 116.

Yakir was several miles away. With the opening barrage, he had led his platoon south to stop twenty-five Syrian tanks crossing the cease-fire line along an old Roman roadway that had once led to Damascus. The accuracy of the platoon's fire reflected the fact that the gunners in both Yakir's tank and that of his first sergeant, Nir Atir, had won a number of battalion gunnery contests. Firing from the ramps overlooking the ancient roadway, they hit the bulk of the Syrian tanks during a two-hour exchange.

Receiving Gur's report, Yakir led his tanks back toward 116. Dozens of Syrian APCs and tanks were already on the Israeli side of the tank ditch. Yakir's platoon fired on the move from open terrain at distances ranging from two hundred to a thousand yards. Two tanks from a neighboring platoon joined them but both were soon knocked out. When darkness fell, Yakir asked Gur to fire flares from a mortar. In their light, the platoon continued to score hits.

At 9 p.m., Yakir informed Gur that he was out of ammunition and would have to pull back to rearm. Two of the tanks had fired all the shells they had—seventy-two each—and only five shells remained in the third tank. Yakir and Gur, both aged twenty, realized that withdrawal put the outpost's survival in doubt. Yakir's platoon had hit dozens of tanks and APCs but the Syrians were still pouring across. When he requested permission from his company commander to pull back, the reply was negative. So desperate was the hour that Yakir was told to use his machine guns against the Syrian tanks in the hope that this sign of an Israeli presence, however pathetic, would give the enemy pause before advancing.

Shortly afterward, Yakir was killed by machine gun fire. Sergeant Atir, assuming command of the platoon, ordered Yakir's gunner to tie the fallen officer to the gunner's chair and to take command of the tank. At this point, brigade commander Ben-Shoham cut into the radio net to talk directly to Atir. He ordered the sergeant to fall back for ammunition. Strongpoint 116 would have to hold out on its own.

The Syrians, although pressing home a bold plan, were beginning to display telling deficiencies in tactics, training, and command. Time and again, Israeli tanks would whittle down the odds by engaging formations larger than theirs while shooting faster and straighter. The professionalism of the Israeli tank crews—their tactics, gunnery, and coolness in action—were compensating in good measure for the failures of the Israeli leadership that had exposed them to the Arab assault. But they could not compensate entirely.

Haim Barak's battalion sent south by Ben-Gal theoretically doubled Israeli strength in the southern Golan. In fact, however, the battalion would go largely to waste this night. Even as Erez's battalion was fighting a desperate war of survival nearby, Barak's saw limited action.

Erez's thirty-six tanks could not hold a twenty-mile-wide front which was being attacked in strength along its entire length. Instead of splitting the southern sector between the two battalions, Ben-Shoham kept Barak's tanks in reserve, to be fed into the battle as needed. This would prove highly inefficient. Barak, whose tanks had arrived on the Golan only this morning, had no idea of what was happening on the front line, a mile away. He was in communication with both Simhoni at Northern Command and Ben-Shoham but Erez did not even know there was another tank battalion in his sector.

Barak's battalion was an odd mix. Two of its companies were only halfway through their basic, four-month, armor training course. The third, commanded by Capt. Eli Geva, was a veteran unit considered one of the best companies in the armored corps. One of the trainee companies ended up at Strongpoint 111, but only after the Syrians had bypassed it. The other was dispatched to Strongpoint 116 and was ambushed along the way, losing most of its tanks. The one effective battle waged by the battalion this day was when Geva's company, moving at dusk along the main north–south road half a mile from the Purple Line, was fired on by Syrian tanks that had infiltrated. Geva's tanks quickly deployed and engaged the Syrians. Air photos the next day would show that Geva's gunners destroyed some thirty tanks while losing only one.

To observers on the Israeli-held spur of Mount Hermon, 6,600 feet above sea level, the battle on the Golan was grand opera viewed from the upper balcony. Although there were Syrian troops higher up the crest—the Syrian Hermon, as it was known—the Israeli position seemed detached both from them and from whatever was happening on the plateau below.

The Hermon had been occupied as an afterthought in the Six Day War when it was realized that it made a superb intelligence platform and early warning station. A large outpost was built atop the mountain, part of it underground. Its electronic equipment monitored Syrian activity along the front line and as far as the Syrian capital forty miles to the east.

There were fifty-five men in the Hermon outpost on Yom Kippur. The bulk were army and air force intelligence personnel and technicians. The outpost was in the final stages of extensive reconstruction, and the defensive positions around it had been temporarily stripped away. The security detail consisted of a dozen infantrymen from the Golani Brigade, three of whom were detached to an observation post a mile away. The fact that such a valuable installation would be without defense positions, even temporarily, and its security left to a single squad of soldiers reflected a belief that the Syrians, so easily routed in the Six Day War, could not muster the will or ability to attack it.

The Syrians had in fact placed the Israeli Hermon at the top of their target list. Lt. Ahmed Rifai al-Joju, a company commander in the Eighty-second Paratroop Battalion, the elite combat unit of the Syrian army, was given a final briefing on his mission Saturday morning. He and his men would be landed by helicopters half a mile from the Israeli structure. They would take positions covering the outpost and the single road leading up to it from the Golan. The rest of the battalion, some two hundred men, would set out by foot from the Syrian Hermon. This force would attack the outpost, with Joju's men providing covering fire.

Four Syrian helicopters lifted off at 2 p.m. and headed toward the Israeli position. One of the craft crashed when its rotor struck a slope but the others landed their troops safely. Artillery fire was placed on the Israeli outpost to keep the defenders' heads down. At 2:45 p.m., the attack force from the Syrian Hermon reached the outpost. In the absence of trenches or firing positions, the Golani soldiers could only fire from the narrow entranceways to the structure. After an exchange of fire lasting forty-five minutes, the surviving defenders pulled back into the building and slammed shut the metal door. By 5 p.m. the attackers, dropping grenades and smoke canisters through air ducts, had forced their way in.

Eleven men managed to escape but thirteen were killed and thirty-one taken prisoner, four of them after hiding in a basement for seven days. Soviet and East German experts who arrived to dismantle the electronic equipment were exultant to discover most of it intact. For the Syrians, an even greater windfall was the information elicited from Israeli intelligence personnel during interrogation, particularly from a lieutenant named Amos.

When his commander at SIGINT headquarters learned that the Hermon had fallen, he prayed that Amos had not been taken alive. In Arab hands, the young officer was a threat to some of Israel's most guarded intelligence secrets. He had a curiosity about things, important or trivial, that was obsessive. He read everything at headquarters he could get his hands on. He also had a photographic memory and a compulsion to display it. He would challenge his colleagues to ask him the car license number of any officer on base and his answers were inevitably right. His analyses of Syrian systems were brilliant but his commander found his obsessiveness and nerdiness annoying in the extreme.

In the days before the war, as tensions in SIGINT headquarters mounted, the commander decided that Lieutenant Amos was too much of a distraction and ordered him transferred to the Hermon listening post. An aide pointed out that IDF policy barred the assignment of soldiers like Amos, the only son of a widowed mother, to dangerous posts. The commander said that the Hermon was unlikely to be attacked and insisted that he did not want him at headquarters.

It did not take long after Amos's capture for the Syrians, and their Soviet mentors, to realize that a treasure had fallen into their hands. Held separately from the other prisoners, he was told that Israel had fallen and that any information he gave would not harm his country because it no longer existed. It was not an implausible claim to prisoners who had witnessed the stunning collapse of Israel's defenses in the opening hours of the war. His interrogator displayed a gun and told Amos he would be killed if he did not cooperate but, unlike the other prisoners, he was not tortured. He answered all questions at exhaustive length—in Arabic, which he spoke fluently. He gave the names and duties of SIGINT's officers, revealed which Syrian communication lines were being tapped, where Israeli commando units placed listening devices on Syrian territory, how Israeli intelligence was organized. As Amos's bounty poured forth without pause, his interrogators found it difficult to keep up. In the end, they gave him paper and a pen and told him to just write down whatever he knew. Which he did over the coming days. He had far more answers than they had questions. When he was done, drained of secrets, he was taken to a large cell where he was astonished to find some thirty other Israeli prisoners—pilots and tank crewmen—sitting in a circle on the floor. They made room for him. When he learned that some had been captured days after Israel had supposedly fallen, he covered his face with his hands and said, "It will take twenty years to repair the damage I've done." The effect of his revelations was felt almost immediately by SIGINT whose listening devices lost track of Syrian command and intelligence personnel.

When the Israeli prisoners in Syria were returned home eight months later, Amos was separated from the rest and taken for debriefing over the course of three months in a Tel Aviv apartment where he was asked to spell out exactly what he had revealed. Appalled and intrigued by his story, Prime Minister Meir asked to see him. She reportedly expressed pity rather than anger after talking to him. Instead of being court-martialed, as some officers urged, the Israeli military command decided to designate him as a war casualty who had suffered psychological damage. His story was not publicized, although it was whispered here and there. Forty-three years after the war, in 2016, he appeared on Israeli television to make his story public in an interview, for reasons he did not make clear. Viewers learned that he married after the war, had children, and taught international relations. Asked about his life since the war, he described it as "living on the margins."

The fall of the Hermon was for Israel the single most humiliating episode of the Yom Kippur War. From the Golani Brigade to the General Staff, a grim determination took shape to regain it at any price.

General Hofi returned to Nafakh from General Staff headquarters two hours after the war began, bringing with him as air force liaison Gen. (Res.) Motti Hod, who had commanded the air force until a few months before. Hofi did not take exception to Simhoni's earlier decision to commit all the reserves, and to send most of them to the northern sector. He divided the front into two separate commands. The Seventh Brigade was given responsibility for the northern half of the line, taking Nafshi's battalion from the 188th under its command. Ben-Shoham's brigade would be left with responsibility only for the southern sector. This force was now made up of Oded Erez's battalion and Haim Barak's, transferred from the Seventh Brigade.

By late Yom Kippur afternoon, the Syrian offensive appeared to have ebbed and Israeli commanders were reporting that they were in control all along the front. This soothing assessment would not last long.

Just before darkness, the Syrians threw two brigades against the northern sector and four against the southern. Oded Erez's battalion had lost twelve tanks during the afternoon's fighting—a third of its strength. Two of his three company commanders were dead and his deputy, Major Askarov, wounded. As dusk descended and the Syrians began to press their attack more vigorously, Erez called futilely for massive air and artillery support. The situation in the Golan's northern sector, by contrast, was under control. Nafshi's battalion had lost seven of its thirty-three tanks but had blocked Syrian penetration. Ben-Gal's brigade to the rear had yet to engage.

At Strongpoint 109 just before darkness, Major Rak asked his officers to join him at his tank during a lull in the shelling. "There's a war going on," said the company commander. It was not an idle comment. Despite the company's destruction of some fifty Syrian tanks and the intensive artillery bombardment they had experienced for the past hours, the general assumption was that this was a battle day—more intensive by far than any they had ever experienced but a one-day event. What made Rak realize that it was something more were the reports on Israel Radio he heard now for the first time on a crewman's transistor radio about battles in Sinai. A two-front war was raging and it was not going to end with nightfall.

Late in the afternoon, Colonel Kahalani led his Centurion tank battalion through the shell-pocked fields of Kibbutz Ein Zivan near Kuneitra toward Booster Ridge. The drivers, still with a peacetime mind-set, attempted to avoid irrigation equipment left by the kibbutz farmers. The Booster, behind Strongpoint 107, was the southernmost of the ridges on which Ben-Gal deployed his units. Kahalani saw clouds of dust being thrown up by Syrian armor far to the east moving down the Damascus–Kuneitra road.

All afternoon, the attackers in the northern sector had been kept at bay by Nafshi's frontline battalion. With darkness, Syrian tanks began to infiltrate between the strongpoints toward Ben-Gal's brigade on the ridges beyond. When they struck, it was in the center of the line—

the Hermonit Ridge, defended by a force commanded by Lt. Col. Yos Eldar. He called for flares but the supply was soon exhausted. In planning for a battle day, which always ended by nightfall, the Israelis had failed to prepare for combat that would continue after dark. The seemingly trivial oversight would prove a major handicap.

Kahalani could make out additional Syrian tanks moving toward Eldar's position. He ordered his men to fire on them but the range was too great.

"Brigade commander," he called to Ben-Gal on the radio. "This is Kahalani. I'm firing at the tanks attacking Yos but I'm afraid it's a waste of ammunition. I suggest that I move up to join him."

Ben-Gal assented but ordered him to leave a small force on Booster. As Kahalani approached Eldar's position, he heard him addressing Ben-Gal on the radio net in a strained voice.

"Brigade commander, this is Yos. Over."

"This is the brigade commander," replied Ben-Gal. "Over."

"I'm wounded. I'm evacuating myself to the rear."

Eldar had been hit over an eye by shrapnel. Kahalani reached Eldar's position and took command. The Syrians had for the first time this day penetrated the sector in some strength. The attack on Eldar's position appeared to have been repulsed but the Syrians were now hitting the battalion at the northern end of the line, commanded by Lt. Col. Meshulam Rattes. They were also attacking in the vicinity of Kuneitra where Nafshi's tanks were positioned. With no artillery flares available, Kahalani ordered his men to fire two of the few mortar flares available. As these slowly descended he could see no enemy tanks to his front.

"Battalion commander, this is Emi." It was Capt. Emi Palant, a company commander who was positioned on Kahalani's northern flank. "About fifteen tanks moving in my direction. I'm waiting for them."

Through infrared binoculars, Kahalani could make out a line of infrared headlights in the distance, still inside Syrian territory. When he looked in the same direction with his naked eye he could see nothing. Some of the tank commanders also had infrared binoculars but the tanks themselves were not equipped for night fighting. The Syrian tanks had infrared headlights to illuminate the terrain and infrared projectors to light up targets without the Israelis knowing that they were being illuminated. No special importance had been given by the

Israeli military to the night vision equipment in Arab hands since it was assumed that they would not initiate night fighting. The Arabs were now doing a lot of things the Israelis had not expected.

The moon had risen higher and was offering a misty light. Bushes moving in the wind downslope and the ruins of an abandoned village took on a menacing aspect. At one point, Kahalani thought he could make out a pair of infrared lights moving in his direction and ordered his gunner to fire. But it proved another night mirage. As he raised his infrared binoculars to check on the Syrian tanks to the north, he suddenly saw his own tank as if in daylight. When he lowered the binoculars he could see nothing but when he put them back to his eyes there it was again. He raised the binoculars higher and, with a chill, found himself staring straight into an infrared projector a few dozen yards away.

"Driver, back up," he shouted. "Quickly." The tank shot backward down the slope, not stopping until it reached bottom.

Kahalani took it back up to a different position. As he scanned the other tanks on the line, he saw that one had its rear lights on. By radio, he ordered officers to make sure the tanks in their platoons had their lights out. All reported back to confirm. But Kahalani could still see the taillights. He ordered engines cut but the lights of the single tank stayed on and he could hear its engines working.

It was mad to think that an enemy tank had deployed among them. It was possible that a tank from a neighboring unit, not on their radio frequency, had blundered in. But Israeli tanks did not have infrared projectors. If it was a Syrian tank its commander must realize, after having studied Kahalani's tank, that he had wandered into an Israeli position. But the intruder had taken his place in line, his gun facing toward the Syrian lines. Kahalani told an officer near the stranger to have one of his tanks prepare to flash a projector on it. If it were Syrian, said Kahalani, only his own tank would fire. He ordered his gunner, David Kilion, to be prepared. The commander of the tank with the projector reported himself ready.

"Light," said Kahalani.

The white shaft that broke the darkness illuminated a Syrian T-55 fifty yards away.

"Fire," barked Kahalani.

The Syrian tank burst into flames.

"Battalion commander, a suspicious tank in my area," called an officer on the right flank.

"Confirm that it's an enemy tank before firing," replied Kahalani.

In the light of the burning tank, Kahalani made out another Syrian tank backing away into the darkness. He ordered Kilion to fire but another tank hit it first.

Kahalani ordered his men to keep their motors off in order to be able to hear the sound of approaching tanks. Captain Palant said the enemy column had reached the tank ditch a mile to his front. Scanning his map inside the turret, Kahalani told his artillery officer to call down fire on the crossing point.

Things quieted down after midnight and Kahalani permitted the men to take turns sleeping.

The danger to the Southern Golan was not immediately grasped by the Israeli command because the Syrians were infiltrating between the strongpoints. Despite the ferocity of the Syrian attack, and despite Elazar's warning of war, Hofi was still thinking in terms of a limited territorial grab by the Syrians. His objective remained the one Elazar had outlined—to deny the enemy any territorial gain. This meant spreading his forces so as to prevent incursions. At 9 p.m. Hofi was still telling his commanders that "we must make an effort to block every attack, even the smallest." The cherished principle of armor—concentration of force—was being ignored here as it had been in Sinai in order to cling to territory.

In the command bunker at Nafakh, the chief intelligence officer for the division, Lt. Col. Dennie Agmon, permitted himself to make an operational suggestion directly to the front commander, General Hofi, who was sitting at the same long table. The Syrians, said Agmon, might be attempting to recapture the entire heights, not just a settlement or strongpoint. If so, they would try to seize the Bnot Yaacov Bridge to block the arrival of reserves, using special forces. Hofi doubted that but he ordered that an engineering unit near the bridge be alerted to the possibility.

At the far end of the table, General Eitan had been standing for hours, his back against the wall and one foot propped up on a chair, saying little. From a farming village in northern Israel, Eitan was an earthy, taciturn paratrooper who had a colorful turn of phrase when he did speak. One hand was wrapped in a bandage. He had a few days before lost the tips of two fingers to an electric saw in his workshop at home. (According to a longtime associate, Eitan had an extraordinarily high tolerance for pain. "He didn't know he lost his fingertips," he said, "until he saw them on the floor.") As long as Hofi and his senior officers remained in Nafakh directly running the war, Eitan was outside the loop. But he did order Colonel Ben-Shoham at one point to leave the bunker and join his brigade in the field. Ben-Shoham still considered this to be a battle day, not a full-scale war. Eitan believed otherwise.

Ben-Shoham left Nafakh at 6:30 p.m., heading south on the Tapline Road in an APC serving as a mobile command post. It passed a mile from Hushniya without incident but was halted shortly afterward by a heavy artillery barrage. Pulling back to a sheltered wadi, Ben-Shoham asked that his tank be sent to him from Hushniya. When it arrived, the driver said he had passed many tanks in the darkness. It was a puzzling remark since Ben-Shoham's tanks were deployed four miles to the east along the Purple Line.

For hours after nightfall, reports of Syrian penetration in the southern sector were dismissed at Northern Command because the tank forces on the line were reporting that the Syrians had not gotten past them. But the absence of flares and night sight devices meant that the Israelis were blind to what was going on beyond their immediate front. When a radio monitor heard a Syrian brigade commander reporting that he was in Hushniya, Ben-Shoham was asked by Northern Command if that could be true. Having passed near Hushniya himself not long before, Ben-Shoham said the Syrian commander must be confused.

However, Maj. Yoram Yair, commanding the paratroop force manning the southern strongpoints, was receiving reports from his men that said otherwise. A five-man paratroop observation team atop Tel Saki, just behind the line near Strongpoint 116, reported Syrian tanks moving on the Israeli border road below heading south toward the settlement of Ramat Magshimim. Yair learned from Strongpoint 111 that Syrian tanks had penetrated the line near there. Another report spoke of a penetration between 115 and 116. When the paratroop officer passed on these reports to Ben-Shoham, the brigade commander was dismissive. "You don't know what you're talking about," Yair would remember him saying. When Major Barak had earlier informed Ben-Shoham that his men heard Syrian tank engines from the area of Hushniya, the brigade commander said that it was probably the tank he had summoned from the Hushniya camp.

The collapse of the southern sector stemmed in part from the relatively flat topography, which made it easier to penetrate and in part because there were one-third fewer Israeli tanks defending here than in the northern sector. But ineffective command played a key role. In the north, Ben-Gal was positioned just behind the front, in constant radio contact with his commanders. Ben-Shoham, by contrast, conducted the battle in the critical opening hours of the war from the bunker at Nafakh. It was initially the logical place to be since he had overall command on the Golan while Hofi was in Tel Aviv. But when Hofi returned at 4:30, Ben-Shoham remained in Nafakh for another two hours. Prevented later from reaching the front by artillery fire, he maintained radio contact with his units from his isolated APC off the Tapline but was unable to properly read the flow of the battle from there.

The first confirmation of Syrian penetration came from the commander of a supply convoy dispatched down the Tapline Road with ammunition and fuel for Erez's force. When the convoy came abreast of Ben-Shoham's personnel carrier, its commander alighted from his jeep to speak to him. Ben-Shoham said it was too dangerous to take the trucks forward because of the shelling. Only tanks could navigate the area safely. Raising Erez on the radio, Ben-Shoham asked him to send his tanks back one at a time to rearm and refuel at the convoy's present location. Erez said he could not remove even a single tank from its position without risking a Syrian breakthrough.

As they talked, two tanks approached Ben-Shoham from the south and stopped twenty yards away. The brigade commander asked Erez if in fact some tanks had not pulled back. Erez, sounding surprised, said he would check. A few moments later, he said no tanks had been sent to the rear. Ben-Shoham concluded that the two crews had fled the front. He asked an officer to order the tank commanders to get their carcasses back to the line. The officer walked toward the tanks and began shouting at the nearest commander, whose outline he could make out in the turret. The figure dropped into the tank without a word, pulling the hatch closed, and the tanks roared off. As they did, the officer distinguished the silhouettes of Syrian T-55s.

Ben-Shoham ordered the supply convoy to return immediately to Nafakh. A few minutes after setting off, the convoy commander radioed that he had just passed the intersection with the Hushniya Road and found himself driving through a mass of Syrian tanks. "I don't know how I got through," he said.

Hofi ordered Ben-Gal, whose sector was relatively calm at the moment, to dispatch another battalion to Oded Erez's aid. The Seventh Brigade commander dispatched one of his battalions but recalled it before it got far. He told Hofi that his brigade was coming under attack and that he could spare no one. Hofi did not argue the point. Ben-Gal's sector was not in fact under heavy attack but the brigade commander had lost confidence that his superiors were in control of the battle and was determined to keep his force intact. "If I don't look after myself," he would contend later, "who will?" The southern sector was left to make do with what it had.

For Lieutenant Gur in Strongpoint 116 that meant having to hold out without tank support. An hour after Yakir's tank platoon had gone, Gur saw the dark shapes of three Syrian tanks approaching down the narrow track linking the fort to the Israeli border road to his rear. The tanks moved slowly, one behind the other, but did not fire, as if the commanders were uncertain whether or not the position had been captured. Gur had earlier ordered a soldier to place two rows of mines on the surface of the track. A soldier with a bazooka crouched alongside Gur in a trench. As they watched, the lead tank went over the mines but there was no explosion. Powder from the crushed mine spilled into the roadway and Gur realized that the soldier who had placed the mine had failed to arm it. He could see a red light emanating from somewhere inside the tank as it crashed through the gateway ten yards from him and entered the fort's courtyard. The tank commander, who had not opened his hatch, had a limited range of vision and his tank ran into an inclined basalt wall surrounding the fort's mortar position. The tank rose up at a 30-degree angle, as if trying to climb the wall. Gur told the bazookist to fire. The soldier had difficulty making out the odd silhouette in the darkness. "Fire in the general direction," said Gur. A moment passed and the bazookist shouted, "Misfire." Following the drill for such a situation, Gur told the soldier to take his hand off the firing mechanism. The lieutenant removed the defective shell from the back end of the weapon and inserted a new one. The bazooka fired, striking the tank in the turret. As the Syrian crew leaped out, Gur fired at them, hitting two of the four crewmen.

The second tank had now reached the entrance and the bazookist, without prompting, set it aflame. This time Gur hit all four of the crewmen as they emerged. The third tank turned and made off as Israeli artillery shells, called down by Gur, struck the area. Fearing that two crewmen from the first tank might still be inside the compound, he ordered his men to stay inside their positions. Together with one of his men, he ran through the trenches firing to his front but encountered no enemy soldiers.

The area outside the strongpoint was alive with Syrians on foot, many of them crewmen from disabled tanks. Gur's fear was that Syrians would infiltrate the strongpoint in the darkness. The operator of the garrison's heavy machine gun cut down enemy soldiers in the immediate vicinity. Wounded Syrians cried out on the barbed wire fence surrounding the strongpoint. One of them near the gate could be heard weeping all night.

About 2 a.m., a large Syrian supply convoy approached the tank ditch and halted. Gur called for artillery but the overtaxed batteries could fire only a few shells. With first light, the convoy crossed over the ditch. As it did, ten Syrian soldiers detached themselves and approached the strongpoint. They appeared to believe that the position had been captured. Gur prayed they would turn away but they kept coming. The garrison opened fire at thirty yards, cutting them down.

As Gur feared, the firing stirred the hornet's nest. APCs disgorged infantrymen; some provided covering fire while others crawled forward. The strongpoint's machine gun raked the vehicles in the convoy and a mortar fired on APCs attempting to approach. With rifle ammunition low, Gur ordered his men to hold fire until the Syrian infantrymen reached the fence.

After a protracted battle, the attackers pulled back. Three of Gur's men were wounded, one of them seriously. But there were no fatalities. The garrison had won this round.

At Tel Saki, two miles to the south, the paratroop observation team was joined by three tanks from Haim Barak's battalion, survivors of the ambush which had destroyed the rest of their company, and by Sergeant Atir's three tanks, which had fallen back from 116 without ammunition. During the night, the men on the tel fired at Syrian tanks and APCs below, setting a number of vehicles aflame. Most of the Israeli tanks were hit by RPGs. Half an hour before dawn, the paratroop commander on Tel Saki, Lt. Menahem Ansbacher, reported to Major Yair that a large Syrian force was preparing to attack. There were now thirty men on the tel, mostly crews of disabled tanks.

In a desperate move, Yair dispatched three half-tracks from his command post at the settlement of El Al just before dawn to evacuate the position, despite the Syrian forces besieging it. The vehicles were ambushed and most of their occupants killed. With first light, Syrian tanks and infantry attacked up the slopes. Ammunition exhausted, the defenders fell back toward a bunker near the summit. At 6:30 a.m., Yair received his last message from Ansbacher. "This is Menahem. The Syrians are at the entrance to the bunker. This is the end. Say goodbye to the guys. We won't be seeing each other again."

Although now recognizing the danger to the southern Golan, Northern Command was still misreading the battle. A Syrian mechanized brigade reached the religious settlement of Ramat Magshimim less than an hour after students at a yeshiva there had been evacuated. Unaccountably, the Syrian force halted. Except for the handful of men with Major Yair just five miles down the road at El Al, there was nothing to prevent them driving south another twenty miles into Israel's Jordan Valley. Alternatively, the Syrians could continue ten miles west and descend to the shore of Lake Kinneret, the biblical Sea of Galilee.

These, however, were not the scenarios the Syrians had in mind. Their objective was the main Israeli base at Nafakh and the Bnot Yaacov Bridge. The direct approach through the Kuneitra Gap was blocked by the Seventh Brigade but the Syrian plan had a built-in alternative—breaking through into the southern Golan and then turning north. The Fifty-first Brigade, with one hundred tanks, was ordered to reach Hushniya and then turn north along the Tapline straight to Nafakh. A parallel thrust would be made by the Fifty-third Brigade, which would turn north as soon as it crossed the Purple Line and proceed on the Golan's main north–south road, code-named Reshet, parallel to the border. Only seven Israeli tanks guarded the Reshet Road. There were no tanks at all on the Tapline Road.

Enter Zvika Greengold. Waiting to begin a course for tank company commanders, Lieutenant Greengold, twenty-one, was unattached to any unit when the war began. When the sirens sounded, he was at home in Lokhamai Hagetaot (Fighters of the Ghettos), a kibbutz founded by Holocaust survivors, including his parents. Donning a dress uniform, the only one he had at home, he hitchhiked to Nafakh, which he reached in late afternoon. There were no tanks immediately available but when three damaged Centurions arrived from Kuneitra, Greengold was told to lead them back to the front as soon as they were repaired.

He oversaw the removal of dead crewmen and helped wash the

tanks of blood. At 9 p.m., with two tanks ready, Greengold was ordered to move out and take command of the scattered tanks remaining near Strongpoints 111 and 112. All officers there were casualties, he was told, and a sergeant was in command. On the way, Greengold was to pass through Hushniya. There were unconfirmed reports of a Syrian presence there. Greengold was to destroy any enemy he encountered.

The mission seemed straightforward enough to the lieutenant. He was given the frequency of the brigade radio net and assigned a code name, "Force Zvika." It was a designation that would enter Israeli military lore.

The two tanks set off down the Tapline Road. It took a while to adjust to the darkness but Greengold knew the area well. The Tapline was a service road, not an artery. Until a few years before there had only been a narrow dirt track marking the route of the oil pipeline buried below. After Palestinian guerrillas blew a hole in the line in the early 1970s, the American owners of Tapline built a ten-foot-high chain-link fence on either side of the track at Israel's request, creating a fifteen-yard-wide corridor, and laid a narrow asphalt patrol road just outside the fence. It was down this patrol road that Greengold proceeded. He kept one tank track on the dirt shoulder to minimize damage to the asphalt, a constraint reflecting the lingering civilities of peacetime. Given the boulders strewn about the area, tanks generally stuck to the roadway, particularly at night, rather than venture cross-country. The Tapline ran arrow-straight between Nafakh and the Hushniya turnoff for fifteen miles through a landscape of dips and rises.

Greengold proceeded cautiously, halting every time he topped a rise to examine the surroundings. He ordered his gunner to load a shell into the breech and keep the gun off safety. Greengold kept watch to the front and left. The other tank commander, thirty yards behind him, was responsible for the rear and right.

The two tanks had proceeded only three miles when Greengold saw a column of vehicles approaching with headlights on. The jeep in front stopped when its lights illuminated the tanks and an officer ran forward. It was the convoy commander whom Ben-Shoham had sent back to Nafakh. He told Greengold of having just passed among many Syrian tanks at the Hushniya intersection.

Proceeding even more cautiously, Greengold passed the halfway point to the intersection when he topped a rise and saw a tank speeding toward him.

"Fire," he shouted.

The gunner, whose nerves were hair-trigger-taut, squeezed the trigger. The approaching tank exploded, barely twenty yards in front of them. Greengold had not had time to identify the tank before firing, relying on the convoy commander's information that any tank to the front was hostile. In the light of the burning vehicle, he saw with relief that it was a T-55. His driver pulled back into the darkness. The vibration from the firing had knocked out the electricity in the tank turret. Greengold switched tanks, telling the other commander to return to Nafakh for repairs.

Beyond the burning Syrian tank, the night was swarming with "cat's eyes"—tiny running lights the Syrians placed on the edges of their tanks. The impression Greengold had was that the Syrian formation was organizing, perhaps refueling, rather than in movement. The tank he had encountered could have been a forward picket. From time to time, the Syrians sent signal rockets skyward. Taking his tank up a low hill, Greengold came on three Syrian tanks with their lights on. He destroyed them before they could return fire. Half an hour later, he opened fire on a convoy of some thirty tanks and trucks. Their running lights and the flares they periodically sent up provided him with illumination. He could sense that fire was being returned but it was ineffective, as he kept shifting position. In this cat-and-mouse game he had one advantage. Every tank he saw was a target. The Syrians, on the other hand, had difficulty identifying him, even with night sights. Greengold took care to keep his tank on rear slopes, only the gun and turret projecting over the crest. He plowed back and forth through the chain-link fence as he shifted from position to position. Parts of the fence caught on the tank treads and he was soon dragging a long train of fencing, including fence poles, wherever he turned. He would not be able to remember how many tanks he hit in this skirmishing.

Listening to the radio during lulls in the fighting, he began for the first time to grasp the enormity of the situation. Tanks in Oded Erez's battalion were reporting that they were almost out of ammunition and fuel. Supplies were not getting through and desperate calls for reinforcement were met by replies that no tanks were available.

On the radio net, Colonel Ben-Shoham made contact with Force Zvika and attempted to ascertain its strength. Aware that the Syrians were probably monitoring communications, Greengold evaded a direct answer so as not to reveal that his was the only tank between the

Syrian force and Nafakh. Ben-Shoham, believing the Syrians to be a small raiding party, ordered Force Zvika, which he assumed to be of at least company strength, to press forward to the western end of the Hushniya Road. Battalion commander Haim Barak was told to position himself at its eastern end. When Force Zvika pushed the Syrian force back, Barak would be waiting for them. Greengold attempted to signal his inability to undertake offensive action by saying "the situation isn't good." After an hour of solitary skirmishing, Greengold, to his relief, was informed that another force was on its way to join him.

Ten tanks, belonging to a "rapid-reaction" reserve battalion commanded by Lt. Col. Uzi Mor, had begun moving from their base camp at the foot of the Golan at 8 p.m. toward Nafakh. The tanks had not been stripped of their equipment after their last mobilization exercise and were thus ready to move out as soon as crews were organized. They were directed down the Tapline Road where they linked up with Force Zvika. At 10:30 p.m., little more than twelve hours after mobilization began, Mor's force became the first reservist unit on either front to enter into battle.

It would be a devastating baptism by fire. Greengold briefed Mor on the situation and the battalion commander ordered an immediate advance. Mor's tanks moved in column on the asphalt road. Greengold moved parallel to them on the dirt track between the fences. As the tanks descended the first deep dip in the road, a waiting Syrian force unleashed tank fire and RPGs.

All eight tanks that had begun the descent were hit. Mor was blinded and lost an arm but his men managed to extricate him under fire and carry him back up the hill. Some men who managed to escape their burning tanks, including a badly wounded company commander, were captured by Syrian infantrymen. Greengold's tank was hit too, apparently by friendly fire, but he did not feel it. The gunner, whose clothing was afire, lunged for the turret and for an absurd and terrifying movement he and Greengold filled the narrow aperture and were unable to move. Greengold finally forced his way back down into the tank as the gunner scrambled out. Something inside the tank exploded, peppering Greengold's face with shrapnel, and his clothes caught fire. He leaped out and rolled on the ground to extinguish the flames. Fearing that the tank was about to explode, he clambered over the fence and found himself lying among boulders alongside his gunner and loader. The driver had been killed.

The three men made their way back up the hill shouting, "We're Israelis, we're Jews, don't shoot." Wounded and dead were being loaded for evacuation aboard two of the three remaining tanks in Mor's force that had not been hit. Greengold himself climbed onto the hull of the third tank and sat there while he slowly regained touch with himself. The pain from his shrapnel wounds and burns was now registering but he did not feel incapacitated. He signaled to the commander of the tank to take off his helmet with its earphones so that he could talk to him. "My name is Zvika," he said. "I've been fighting here all night. I know the area. Let me take your tank." The reservist looked at him for a moment and then handed him his helmet, climbing out of the turret to find a place on another tank.

Greengold introduced himself in the darkness to the crew. "I'm Zvika. I'm now your commander. What are your names?"

The two other tanks pulled back with the casualties, leaving Greengold alone once again on the Tapline. He put the tank's radio onto Ben-Shoham's wavelength. "This is Zvika," he said. The brigade commander's sigh of relief was audible. All Ben-Shoham had known was that the relief force had been pummeled. He had not been sure that anyone was left on the Tapline to stop a Syrian drive toward Nafakh. He asked Greengold for a status report. The lieutenant declined once again to go into details beyond reiterating that the situation was not good. This time, however, he added, "We need a general here." The remark was intended to indicate both the scale of the challenge and the paucity of resources to deal with it.

Ben-Shoham got his drift. He told Greengold to assume a secure firing position. "Don't initiate any firing. Shoot only at tanks that try to move up the road towards Nafakh. Wait for reinforcements."

It was now 2 a.m. Greengold pulled back a few hundred yards. It would be another hour before reinforcements arrived. Among the things that passed through his mind, he would later say, was an awareness that the Holocaust his parents had survived was suddenly relevant again. He sensed that he stood between an enemy and the prospect of his people's annihilation.

Maj. Meir Zamir, commander of Tiger Company, posted near Kuneitra, was ordered by Ben-Gal at 3 a.m. to block a Syrian tank force moving north up the border road, according to a report from the commander of a disabled Israeli tank who had seen them go by. Zamir set an ambush near Strongpoint 110. His deputy deployed 800 yards east of the road with four tanks and reported himself in place. Zamir, with four tanks, took position 1,200 yards to the north, two tanks on either side of the road. He told the officer across the road from him to be ready to throw on his projector.

Within a few minutes they heard the sound of tanks. In the moonlight, Zamir could make out a long column approaching from the south. He waited until the lead tank was close. "Light," he commanded. The projector lit up the column and Zamir's tanks opened fire, setting close to a dozen tanks and APCs aflame. The Syrian force was the spearhead of the Forty-third Armored Brigade, heading toward Nafakh. Most of the ambushed force turned back to Syrian territory but part of it scattered on the Israeli side. Tiger would take up pursuit at first light.

It was not until midnight that Hofi began to grasp the scale of the Syrian penetration. Three hundred Syrian tanks had broken through in the southern Golan and there were fewer than thirty Israeli tanks left there to oppose them—almost out of ammunition and fuel after ten hours of battle. Substantial reserve forces would not arrive until the afternoon. Hofi expressed doubts to Elazar that the heights could be held. "Only the air force can stop them," he said. Disturbed by Hofi's tone, Dayan, who heard the conversation, told Elazar he was flying up to Northern Command in the morning "to see if we're going to lose the Golan."

At the forward command bunker in Nafakh, radios crackled with reports from embattled units along the front. Hunched over maps, Hofi and his staff officers issued orders and debated the enemy's moves.

Motti Hod was a relatively detached observer. He had himself directed numerous air actions from command bunkers but never from one where he could hear artillery shells exploding outside. Just six years before, as commander of the air force, he had sat in the air force war room consuming jugs of water as he orchestrated the strikes that destroyed the Egyptian air force and determined the outcome of the Six Day War. What alarmed him now more than the explosions outside or the dismaying reports from the front was what was going on in the bunker itself. Everybody was reacting—to events, to each other—but it was plain that nobody, from the tank commanders in the field to Hofi and his staff, had time to think. How can you conduct a war without thinking? Hod asked himself.

Shortly after midnight, the airman's unpracticed ear detected what he took to be direct Syrian tank fire on the Nafakh camp. Turning to Hofi, he said, "The army's going to need you tomorrow. I suggest we get out of here." Hod was wrong about Nafakh being attacked by Syrian tanks. But only by a few hours.

The collapse of the southern Golan front would, paradoxically, prove the mettle of the individual Israeli soldier and field commander more strikingly than any other battle in the war. The sheer weight of the Syrian attack accounted for the breakthrough. Unlike in the northern Golan, where brigade commander Ben-Gal and his battalion commanders were waging a tight, disciplined fight, effective battle control was lost in the south. But the surviving defenders did not pull back. They fought tenaciously in small, isolated groups guided less by direction from above than by the skills and motivation they had brought with them.

"You have a choice—to succumb to shock or to become a tiger," a tank platoon leader would later say. "It became clear in the first hour that the battle had been left to the company and platoon commanders and individual tank commanders. The adrenaline rush was tremendous. Orders from some officer in the rear didn't matter much. We were alone and we made the decisions."

Though there would be scattered cases of battle shock, the tank crews and the soldiers in the frontline outposts performed superbly, breaking the impact of the Syrian onrush, slowing it down, and inflicting heavy losses.

Close to 1 a.m., Hofi handed over command of the Golan to General Eitan and drove back into Israel in a jeep with Hod. Crossing the Hula Valley, they drove up to Northern Command headquarters on Mount Canaan outside Safed, a city which had been the center of Jewish kabbala in the Middle Ages. Hod looked back across the valley and saw the Golan dotted with fires. Some were brushfires but others were burning tanks. Barely twelve hours into the war, the Syrian army was already deep into the Golan Heights.

15

DARKEST AT DAWN

REPORTS FLOWING into the Pit from the Syrian and Egyptian fronts this first night of war competed with each other in their unrelenting bleakness. "The worst thing is the reporting from the field," Elazar told the cabinet Saturday night. "It keeps changing all the time. First they say the enemy is here, then they say he isn't. We're trying to grope our way through the fog of war."

The chief of staff would have to decide before dawn which front had more need of the two powerful instruments that were his to allocate—the air force and a reserve armored division commanded by Gen. Moshe (Moussa) Peled. The impression gained during the early part of the night was that the Syrian drive had slowed while the Egyptians were making rapid headway. It was thus decided to unleash the air force against the Egyptian missiles in Operation Tagar in the morning.

Elazar had also intended to send Moussa Peled's division to Sinai before Hofi began signaling distress. The division constituted the main General Staff reserve. Its deployment also affected the Jordanian front. The division was mobilizing in camps on the West Bank, positioned to meet an attack from Jordan if King Hussein decided to join in the war. Elazar summoned Colonel Keniezer, the head of AMAN's Jordanian desk, for his appraisal of the king's intentions. Keniezer's firm opinion was that the king would not attack across the Jordan River and thereby open his kingdom, undefended by SAMs, to the wrath of the Israeli Air Force. Accepting this appraisal, which echoed his own, Elazar ordered Moussa's division north, leaving the Jordanian front virtually naked. It was, he acknowledged, a high-risk gamble but in the circumstances every move was a gamble. Meanwhile, he ordered

Hofi to evacuate endangered infantry strongpoints on the Golan front line—the fate of the Bar-Lev strongpoints was trauma enough—and prepare a fallback line near the western edge of the plateau.

Summoned to the meeting of the full cabinet, its first since the war started, Elazar attempted to calm the ministers' nerves. The IDF was at this stage undertaking a defensive battle. "We know how to do it from the books but we've never actually done it before. We have to simultaneously block and mass forces and only afterwards go over to the attack." The blocking stage was going "reasonably well," he said. Dayan also tried to be optimistic. The crisis should bottom out by the next day when the reserves began to reach the battlefield, he said. But he could not avoid pointing to a danger that lay beyond the horizon. If Syria and Egypt appear to be winning, he said, Iraq, Jordan, and Lebanon might enter the war.

Commanding a reserve tank brigade assembling in a camp at the foot of the Golan Heights was Col. Ori Orr, who had returned from a year's study in the U.S. just two months before. The thirty-four-year-old colonel had never before commanded reservists and had not been enthusiastic about the prospect of leading a collection of paunchy soldiers with civilian mind-sets into battle. However, he had received a young brigade, most of whose members had finished regular service only two or three years before.

The brigade's mobilization base had been moved during the summer from the opposite end of the Galilee as part of the Blue-White preparations, a shift that saved critical hours now. As buses arrived with reservists, officers arbitrarily matched up tank commanders, drivers, gunners, and loaders into crews even though they had never served with each other before. Orr had been surprised during his stay in the U.S. to learn that the American army, instead of rotating entire tank units to Vietnam, rotated tank crewmen individually. It was gospel in the IDF that men fought best in the company of comrades whose good opinion they valued. Now Orr found himself forced to scrap that valued principle precisely in a war situation. There was no time to wait for each crew's organic members to assemble.

One tank commander, recently returned from six years in Los Angeles, was surprised to find that his three crewmen were yeshiva students. "Fellows," he said, "I want you to know who you're going to war with. I'm an atheist." He acknowledged to the younger crewmen

that he had forgotten how to operate a tank. "By the time we get up
to the heights," he said, "I'll remember how to close the hatch and
how the radio works. Meanwhile, check the firing circuits and load as
many shells as you can."

A sense of urgency enveloped the base as mobilized buses and private vehicles deposited reservists through the evening. The brigade
would be the first reservist unit to mount the heights except for Uzi
Mor's rapid-reserve force, which had been mauled on the Tapline.
Shortly after midnight, Colonel Orr dispatched a platoon up to the
southern Golan, the only reservists to be directed there this night.
Lt. Nitzan Yotser was arbitrarily chosen from the milling crowd of
reservists as platoon commander. He was to ascend the Yehudia Road
and proceed to its intersection with the Tapline where he would block
any enemy advance. The whereabouts and strength of the Syrians
was not known and it was not clear if the conscripts on the Golan
were holding on. One of Yotser's four tanks broke down before exiting
the camp. A reconnaissance jeep guided the remaining three to Arik
Bridge, just north of Lake Kinneret, and took leave of them at the foot
of the heights.

As the tanks started climbing, the young officer was gripped by
the surreality of the moment. Only twelve hours before, he had been
spending a leisurely Yom Kippur afternoon with his girlfriend in his
student apartment in posh north Tel Aviv, remote from any thought
of war. Drafted two months after the Six Day War, he had been convinced that he would never see war in his lifetime except in the cinema. Israel's army was so demonstrably powerful that the Arabs, so
demonstrably ineffective, would never dare take up arms against it
again. Since completing his three years of military service in 1970,
he had been studying economics at Tel Aviv University and dutifully
done his annual reserve duty. But he had grown his hair long and
permitted himself the hedonistic fancies of the Sixties generation that
had belatedly reached Israel. This Yom Kippur afternoon, he had not
even bothered opening the radio or making a phone call when the
sirens sounded, assuming it was a technical glitch. When his mother
telephoned to inform him that a two-front war had begun, he was
certain she had misunderstood the radio announcement. On the bus
carrying him to base, he admitted to himself that he had misgauged
the Arabs. But he was certain too that they had misgauged their own
strength and that "we'll soon show them."

Now, leading a tank platoon up the Golan Heights, he was no longer sure it would be easy. The pandemonium in the camp, the hasty way the tanks were being armed, and the random formation of crews suggested to him that the IDF was not entirely prepared for this war, and not just because it had been surprised. There had not been enough time to take on a full load of shells and he had not even been issued an Uzi before being sent off. Only as his tank began to move did someone throw him an extra box of ammunition for his machine gun. This was not the way to be going to war. There had not even been time for the crew to learn each other's names. He addressed his men by their job designations: "Driver, straight ahead."

He had no idea that his three tanks were the spearhead of the Israeli counterattack in the southern Golan—in fact, for the next few hours, the entire Golan. Nor did he know that hundreds of Syrian tanks had broken through to his front. His immediate concern was to remember how to command a tank. His three tours of reserve duty as a deputy company commander were spent dealing with logistics, generally the lot of deputy commanders, and he had forgotten basic tank skills. Almost any of the officers in the teeming camp below had more recent experience handling a tank than he. He was not sure, for instance, which way to push the radio switch in his helmet if he wished to speak only to his crew and which way to speak to the other tanks. He had forgotten the proper way of issuing orders, a basic requirement if he wanted the crews of three tanks to act in coordination. Unlike the Six Day War, when the reserves had a three-week waiting period in which to hone their skills, get their equipment ready, and prepare themselves mentally, the reserves were going into this war stone-cold.

Looking at the road in the moonlight and listening to the sound of the tank engines, he found himself undergoing a strange metamorphosis. Imperceptibly disconnecting from his "make love, not war" mind-set earlier in the day, he began to focus on the task at hand—namely, making war. He was a civilian wearing a uniform when he started climbing the heights. By the time the tank topped the plateau, he was a soldier.

Yotser saw a large fire in the distance and assumed it was a brushfire touched off by artillery shells. The road carried the tanks in the direction of the fire. Drawing close, he saw that it was on the road itself—a column of burning ammunition trucks. The trucks were facing east, which meant they were Israeli vehicles on their way to the front when hit. When Yotser's tanks drew close enough to the fire to be visible in its glow, shells exploded around them. The Syrian tanks that had ambushed the trucks were still out there.

The instincts drilled into Yotser during his army service now kicked in. He barked a litany of commands directing the tanks to pull back into the darkness and take up defensive positions. For the next three hours, Yotser and his men exchanged spasmodic fire with the Syrian tanks, aiming at gun flashes. They could not see the Syrians but had the feeling that the Syrians could see them. A shell hit Yotser's tank a glancing blow at one point but caused little damage.

Meanwhile, Orr had begun dispatching tanks to the northern Golan up the Bnot Yaacov Bridge as fast as they could be readied. Tanks that had even half an ammunition load were sent up in make-shift platoons of three without regard to battalion or company affili-ation; sometimes even individual tanks were dispatched. Before first light, Orr himself set out, leading twenty tanks.

Northern Command was at the same time preparing for the Golan's evacuation should the defenses crumble. At 4:30 a.m., it ordered documents brought down from army bases. Trucks began evacuating ammunition from a large depot at Snobar above the Bnot Yaacov Bridge and engineers assembled a cache of antitank mines on the southern shore of Lake Kinneret in the event that tank obstacles had to be created. Bulldozers were ordered to stand by to cut the roads leading down from the heights.

On the front line in the southern Golan, the remnants of Erez's battalion continued their lonely battle. Four tanks under Captain Ari-eli had been holding off enemy tanks at Tel Juhadar since dusk. At 1 a.m., Colonel Ben-Shoham ordered them to pull back half a mile to a small army camp where the tanks would be better protected behind earthen berms. The camp controlled the intersection of the main north–south road, Reshet, and the Tapline. The crossroad was soon lit with burning Syrian tanks and APCs.

In the predawn hours, combat tapered off all along the line. Syrian forces continued to flow through unguarded sectors into the Golan but there was no dash for the Jordan River and no commando landings at the bridges. At some places, tanks continued for a while to exchange desultory fire but gradually the situation become static. Both sides were resting for the new day.

Arriving at Northern Command headquarters by helicopter at

dawn, Dayan was taken aback by the gloom. Hofi told him bluntly that the heights might have to be abandoned. There were no forces capable of preventing the Syrians from pushing south from Ramat Magshimim to the Jordan Valley. One of the first settlements the Syrians would encounter in that direction was Kibbutz Degania, where Dayan was born. The kibbutz still preserved a Syrian tank stopped on its perimeter fence by Molotov cocktails during the War of Independence in 1948. Degania had also been Motti Hod's home. "We can't let it happen," said the former air force commander, who joined the conversation.

"Only the air force can stop them," said Hofi.

Gen. Dan Laner, commander of a reserve division making its way to the front, shared Hofi's pessimism. "The fighting is over in the southern part of the Golan and we've lost," he told Dayan. "We don't have anything to stop them with." The commander of Syria's Forty-seventh Brigade had just reached the edge of the Golan escarpment and was heard reporting that he could see Tiberias and Lake Kinneret, five miles away.

Dayan's physical appearance dismayed Colonel Simhoni, Hofi's operations officer. The minister was pale and his hands were shaking. "It was not pleasant to see the hero of your youth like that," Simhoni would recall. The relentlessly grim picture confronting the defense minister in the hours since the war began had touched an apocalyptic chord which would resonate in him for at least two days.

But it did not impede his ability to make quick, and generally insightful, tactical and strategic decisions. As defense minister, it was not within his authority to issue operational orders to members of the armed forces—except to the chief of staff. But he would do so frequently, generally offering it as nonobligatory "ministerial advice" if he encountered raised eyebrows, but sometimes skipping that legal nicety.

He told Hofi to prepare the bridges across the Jordan for detonation. Sappers were to be posted alongside them with orders to blow them upon command and antitank guns were to be positioned there as well. Dayan asked Hofi to send a senior officer to organize defense of settlements in the Jordan Valley.

Unable to get Elazar on the phone, he had himself patched through to Benny Peled at 5 a.m. "What are your plans for this morning?" asked Dayan.

Israeli soldiers look across the Suez Canal at Ismailiya shortly after the Six Day War. Israel and Egypt had not begun to fortify their respective banks.
Photograph courtesy of Israeli Government Press Office

The narrow Jordan River, with the Golan Heights in the background.
Photograph courtesy of Israeli Government Press Office

Syrian tanks at Israeli antitank ditch on the Golan. A tank, hit by Israeli fire, has fallen off one of the two bridges the Syrians laid across the ditch. Another knocked-out tank lies in the ditch. To the left is the roadway the Syrians later succeeded in opening through the barrier.
Photograph courtesy of Israel Defense Forces Archive

Israeli long-range artillery piece firing on the Golan.
Photograph courtesy of Israel Defense Forces Archive

Reservists arriving on the Golan in half-tracks.
Photograph courtesy of Israel Defense Forces Archive

Gen. Yitzhak Hofi (seated at center of table), head of Northern Command, on the second night of the war. Sitting next to Hofi is Gen. Haim Bar-Lev. Between the two men, looking over their shoulders, is Gen. Motti Hod, former commander of the Israeli Air Force.
Photograph courtesy of Israel Defense Forces Archive

Israeli Centurion tanks attacking on the Golan early in the war.
Photograph courtesy of Israel Defense Forces Archive

Israeli tanks moving to the front in the Sinai.
Photograph courtesy of Israeli Government Press Office

Lt. Cols. Avigdor Kahalani (right) and Yossi Ben-Hanan
after the battle for Kuneitra Gap.
Photograph courtesy of Israel Defense Forces Archive

Ashraf Marwan (far right) alongside his bride, Mona, at their
wedding, shaking hands with his father-in-law, Egyptian
president Gamal Abdel Nasser.
Anonymous/AP

Zvi Zamir, head of the Mossad.
Photograph by Abraham Vered.
*Photograph courtesy of
Israel Defense Forces Archive and
Israeli Defense Ministry*

Israeli chief of staff
Gen. David Elazar.
*Photograph courtesy of
Israeli Government Press Office*

Israeli Air Force commander
Gen. Benny Peled.
*Photograph courtesy of
Israeli Government Press Office*

Col. Amnon Reshef. The brigade he commanded during the war was the only Israeli armored unit on the Bar-Lev Line when the Egyptians attacked. *Photograph courtesy of Israel Defense Forces Archive*

Gen. Shmuel Gonen, head of Southern Command. *Photograph courtesy of Israeli Government Press Office*

Gen. Eli Zeira, head of Israeli Military Intelligence. *Photograph courtesy of Israel Defense Forces Archive and Israeli Defense Ministry*

General Gonen (with glasses, second from left) sitting alongside Brig. Gen.
Uri Ben-Ari (face toward the camera) in Southern Command headquarters.
Photograph courtesy of Israeli Government Press Office

General Elazar (seated, center, with hands touching) at a briefing in South-
ern Command headquarters. Behind him, holding a cigarette, is Yitzhak
Rabin.
Photograph courtesy of Israeli Government Press Office

"I'm going after the Egyptian missiles," said Peled. "Tagar."

"Forget it," said Dayan. "There's only sand in Sinai and the Suez Canal is 250 miles from Tel Aviv." The situation on the Golan was grave and only the air force could hold the Syrians off until the reserves arrived. If planes were not attacking by noon, said Dayan, the Syrians would reach the kibbutzim in the Jordan Valley. For the first time, Dayan used a phrase that he would repeat in the coming days to the dismay of all who heard him. "The Third Temple," he told Peled, "is in danger." The First Temple, built by Solomon, was razed by the Babylonians in 586 BC and the Second Temple, built by Herod, was destroyed by the Romans in AD 70. The Third Temple was a metaphor for the modern state of Israel.

When Peled tried to argue, the minister snapped, "This is not a request. It's an order."

Final squadron briefings on Operation Tagar began at air force bases at 6 a.m. The aircrews were given files containing the latest air photos of their targets, radio frequencies, code words, navigation instructions, and updated intelligence.

The four-stage attack was aimed at the sixty-two SAM bases in the Canal Zone. The first wave would target not the missile batteries themselves but the antiaircraft guns defending them. In addition, seven air bases whose planes might attempt to interfere with the Israeli blitz would be hit. The missiles themselves were to be dealt with in three follow-up attacks during the day.

Most of the planes in the IAF were to be involved in the spectacular operation—hundreds of them attacking in precisely orchestrated sequence. The heart of the plan was the low-level approach. The planes would skim the ground until almost upon their targets. At a precise point, they would pull up steeply to six thousand feet and dive directly into the attack. The few seconds during which they would be exposed to the SAM batteries were too brief, theoretically at least, for the missiles to lock on. The flying had to be so finely calibrated that when the planes rose up and dove the targets would be right in front of them since there would be no time for adjustments.

The attack was to be augmented by an elaborate assault on enemy radar screens which were to be flooded with false targets. Chaff— aluminum strips that can be mistaken for airplanes by radar—would be fired into the missile zone with rockets. Similar images would be sent electronically from dozens of helicopters and other aircraft on the fringe of the missile zone. Unmanned drones would further clutter the screens. In among this multitude of false targets would be the Israeli warplanes. If the radars were activated, planes would drop American-made Shrike bombs which home on radars. If the radars remained dormant so as to foil the Shrikes, low-flying planes would sweep in and hit them with "dumb" bombs. The operation demanded clockwork choreography and precision flying.

It was a brilliant plan with two problematic aspects. One was the mobility of the SAM-6s. Half a day would probably elapse between the last air photo mission and the attack. The cumbersome SAM-2 and SAM-3 batteries could not be transferred to a new site in that span of time. The SAM-6s, mounted on tracked vehicles, could easily be moved. This was somewhat less worrying in Sinai, where only ten of the sixty-two batteries were SAM-6s. On the Syrian front, fifteen of the twenty-five missile batteries were SAM-6s.

The second problem was the low-level approach itself. It protected the planes from missiles but exposed them to the masses of radar-controlled antiaircraft guns deployed by both Arab armies. There was also danger, in flying low over an area dense with troops, from thousands of rifles, machine guns, and tank guns firing into their flight paths. As random as this kind of shooting was, it threw up a curtain of fire that could be lethal. For this reason, Tagar called for a preliminary attack on the antiaircraft guns guarding the missile batteries and on troop concentrations in the area. This was to be done by tossing cluster bombs from several miles away rather than diving on the targets directly. With the first stage already under way, General Peled decided to let it be completed.

Col. Ron Pekker, commander of Tel Nof Air Base, flew with the first wave of Phantoms Sunday morning. All base commanders, and many officers at air force headquarters, would leave their desks periodically to participate in combat missions during the war. As his flight approached the Canal Zone, Pekker saw a cloud of dust rising east of the canal. With a start, he realized that it was being churned up by tank battles and that the Egyptians must have already crossed the canal in strength. He had never thought he would see such battles on Israeli-held territory.

The navigators in the rear seats of the Phantoms pressed their stopwatches as the planes passed over stacks of white barrels serving as markers. The aircraft roared low across the canal at 540 knots as the navigators counted down. At a precise second, the pilots pulled their sticks back and hit the afterburners, sending the planes thrusting skyward at 60 degrees. The bombs were released at a predetermined height and flew like stones from a slingshot at their distant targets. The planes themselves meanwhile looped in the opposite direction. Toss bombing was less accurate than conventional bombing but it reduced exposure to ground fire. Two planes were nevertheless lost in the attack.

Arriving back at their bases, the squadrons were to be quickly refueled, rearmed, and turned around for the first attack on the missile batteries themselves. But a major surprise awaited them. In the wake of Dayan's order, Peled himself had called to notify base commanders that Tagar was being called off. Instead, the Phantom squadrons were to execute Dougman 5—the attack on the Syrian missile batteries— before noon.

Elazar had also ordered Peled to cancel Tagar and go to Northern Command's assistance after a phone conversation with Hofi, who told him about Dayan's call. (Elazar may have called to give legal backing to Dayan's order, since the defense minister had no right to give direct orders to anyone in the military except the chief of staff.)

Senior officers in the air force war room were appalled. Peled had passed the order on to his staff in a brief phone call from the Pit and he was unavailable when staff officers tried to get back to him. They were incensed that two years of intensive preparations were being thrown out the window just as the operation had gotten under way. More energy and creativity had gone into formulating Tagar than had gone into the preemptive strike in 1967. Intelligence on the Egyptian missile sites was freshly updated. All the devices that had been prepared to deceive the SAM radars were in place. The aircrews, at their fighting edge, were ready to go. If successful, it could have undone the success of the Arab surprise attack and led to a stunning Israeli victory. But this was not to be.

When Peled returned from the Pit, he assembled his senior staff around a table and explained that the northern front was crumbling. Operations chief Col. Giora Furman and others pointed out that a squadron of Skyhawks at Ramat David Air Base in the north had been deliberately excluded from the Tagar operation in order to be available over the Golan Heights for just such contingencies. This, they argued, was sufficient to provide the ground forces on the Golan any close support needed. In addition, there was simply no room for the entire air force over the Golan, which was only forty miles long and seven to fifteen miles deep. There was therefore no logic in calling off an attack that promised to destabilize the Egyptian armed forces, Israel's principal enemy, before sundown. Colonel Furman engaged Peled in a heated argument that, as he would recall it years later, almost came to blows.

Col. Avihu Bin-Nun, heading the team planning air strikes and a future commander of the IAF, was the primary architect of Tagar. He believed Peled had made a snap judgment in response to Dayan's call. If he had only asked for ten minutes to consult with his staff, Bin-Nun believed, they would have convinced him that the availability of the Skyhawk squadron in the north fulfilled Northern Command's needs. Because of the constant changes made to Tagar during planning updates, Bin-Nun believed that Peled may have been unaware of the northern squadron's availability. Col. Amos Amir, Furman's deputy and a future deputy commander of the air force, was among those at the table who believed that Peled, brilliant though he was, lacked the operational experience to fully grasp the inappropriateness of the order.

Logic may have been on the side of the staff officers, but Peled was the only man in the room who had heard Dayan's voice that morning. He forcefully closed off the debate. "I understand you all," he said, smacking the table. "The air force goes north."

So great was the sense of urgency that the operational orders for Dougman were a caricature of the carefully structured plan that had been exercised so diligently. The helicopters bearing the electronic equipment needed to deceive the Syrian radars had been flown to Sinai for Tagar and they could not be brought north in time for Dougman. There was no time for a softening-up attack on the Syrian anti-aircraft guns and ground forces in the path of the attacking squadrons, like the one just carried out in Sinai. Worst of all, there was no time for a photo mission to ascertain that the SAM-6s were still where they had been when photographed the previous afternoon. Weather conditions did not permit photo reconnaissance early in the morning. Given that the Syrian army had moved forward, it was likely that the mobile SAM-6s had moved as well.

Sixty Phantoms raced eastward over the Galilee in late morning and skimmed low over the Golan Heights. The advancing Syrian troops were now massed on both sides of the Purple Line. When the planes thundered over their heads at one hundred feet, the Syrian infantrymen and tanks joined the antiaircraft guns in throwing up a wall of small arms fire, shoulder-held missiles, and machine gun bullets. The planes pulled sharply up as they neared the presumed battery sites. As they gained altitude, the pilots saw that almost all the SAM batteries were gone. Only one battery was destroyed, another damaged. Six of the Phantoms were shot down by conventional ground fire.

The day's results were devastating for the air force and for Israel's entire defense posture. Tagar had been aborted and Dougman had failed miserably. The IAF, normally so meticulous and decisive, had been jarred into sloppy haste. In a single day, its reputation for invincibility had been shaken, a startling turn of events that affected the self-confidence of the decision makers and of the air force itself. Its role as a powerful, quasi-independent strategic entity at Israel's cutting edge had given way to that of a harried subcontractor for the ground army, rushed from front to front in a fruitless attempt to stem the Arab tide. The toll would be heavy. In the first four days of war, Israel would lose 83 planes—a quarter of its combat aircraft—half shot down, the rest seriously damaged.

When the war started, Israel had 317 serviceable combat aircraft and another 82 in maintenance or repairs. All 82 would be returned to service during the war, largely offsetting the loss of 102 planes. The erosion of pilots, who flew three or four sorties a day, was heavy, too: 53 would be killed in the war and 44 captured.

Of all the "what if's" of the war, the decision to call off Tagar was perhaps the most weighty. If the Egyptian army had been stripped of its SAM cover, the IAF would have had little problem eliminating the conventional antiaircraft batteries. The planes would then have been free to hit the bridges and ferries and methodically attack those ground forces that had already crossed.

Not all air force officers were confident that Tagar would have succeeded, given the mobility of the SAM-6s and the uncertainty about suppressing conventional antiaircraft fire by toss bombing. But Bin-Nun, Furman, Amir, and other senior officers would remain convinced decades later that the operation would have worked and that Tagar's cancellation denied Israel an early and decisive victory. There was no question that the Egyptian missiles would have been eliminated, Amos Amir would say in an interview. The only question was how many planes would have been lost. This, he expected, would have been in the dozens. (The IAF would lose 102 planes in the war.)

As for Dougman, Gen. David Ivri, Peled's deputy and successor, would later say that if the attack had only been delayed by two hours there would have been time for a photo reconnaissance mission to determine the location of the SAMs and time to bring up the helicopters with the electronic equipment from Sinai.

The mood in the air force Sunday was morose. Peled had warned his commanders two days before that they might have to "go into the fire" if the SAMs could not be destroyed. They had indeed gone into the fire and were rapidly being consumed. The Arab missile defenses remained almost entirely intact and their ground forces had hardly been impacted by the air force except for the helicopter-borne commando forces destroyed on the first day.

The IAF would score impressive successes in the war. By persistent attacks on enemy airfields, it kept the Egyptian and Syrian air forces busy defending their airspace. Air force cover permitted Israel's reserves to reach the fronts in miles-long convoys without interdiction and the skies over Israel itself would be kept almost totally clear of enemy planes. (Three Syrian planes that attempted to attack a radar station on Mount Meron on the first day of the war were downed and two others would fail in their attempt to attack the Haifa oil refineries later in the war.) In dogfights, the IAF was shooting down enemy aircraft by the bushel.

These successes, however, meant little to the beleaguered Israeli ground troops on both fronts who kept looking skyward and asking, "Where's the air force?" But the IAF could no longer roam freely over the battlefields, looking for prey.

General Peled would ruefully note in an interview long after the war that the air force controlled the skies over all the Middle East during the Yom Kippur War, even over Syria and Egypt, with two exceptions—the small rectangular patches over the Suez and Golan battlefronts.

16

THE FALL OF THE
SOUTHERN GOLAN

REFRESHED BY A few hours' sleep in his tank, Avigdor Kahalani rose in the turret at first light Sunday to breathe deeply of the
chill morning air. A rumbling emanating from the landscape sounded
like the distant roar of lions preparing to feed. It was the sound of tank
engines revving up. Dark smoke rose from vehicles on both sides of the
line. In the distance, clouds of dust were already being thrown up by
Syrian tank columns on the move. Raising his company commanders
on the radio, Kahalani wished them good morning and told them to
prepare for a Syrian attack.

One hundred yards to his front were two tank ramps he had not
seen in the darkness. He ordered his tanks to take up positions there.

"Move carefully," he cautioned. "There are Syrian tanks on the
other side."

The tanks descended in a broad line, the commanders standing
in the turrets. Kahalani stayed behind to check their deployment. A
moment after the first tank reached the top of the main ramp it began
firing.

"Battalion commander, this is Yair," came a call from the right
flank. "A number of enemy tanks heading in my direction. I'm moving into position and opening fire."

Kahalani ordered his driver to move forward. "Kilion," he called
to his gunner, "be prepared to fire." As his tank edged up the ramp,
Kahalani braced. "Stop," he called. Before him was a brown, barren vale. This was the Kuneitra Gap through which the Syrian tanks
would move if they were heading for Nafakh and the Jordan River. At
first Kahalani could detect no movement. Then he noticed a single
tank throwing up black smoke. In a moment, other tanks could be seen

detaching themselves from the landscape and moving forward. The Syrians were commencing their attack.

"Our sector," he called to his tank commanders in a litany straight from a training exercise. "Range 500 to 1,500 meters. A large number of enemy tanks moving in our direction. Take your positions and open fire. Out."

The tank guns began barking almost immediately. Kahalani's own tank joined in, his operations officer, Gidi Peled, directing the fire. Unlike the other tanks, which had four-man crews, command tanks shoehorned in an operations officer as well.

As Syrian tanks began to burn Kahalani called encouragement to his men. "We caught them with their pants down," he cried. "We've got good positions and they're in the open. Finish them off."

"Kahalani, this is Yanosh." The voice of the brigade commander, who was monitoring the radio net, was crisp. "Report."

"I'm in contact with Syrian tanks moving towards me from the east."

"Do you need help?"

"Not for the moment. I'll report later. I'm personally in contact."

Ben-Gal did not intrude further.

The large bowl below Kahalani was now aswarm with tanks. The Syrian tank commanders were buttoned up with hatches closed. Periodically, they halted and fired two shells at the Israeli turrets on the skyline before starting forward again.

Exultant cries were coming from Israeli commanders along the line. "Battalion commander, this is Emi. We're pounding them. They're burning like torches. I'm being heavily pressed."

The Israelis were taking hits too. Kahalani could see burning Centurions and the radio brought first reports of casualties. One of his company commanders was already dead.

Kahalani scanned the deployment of his battalion. The tanks were well positioned and delivering rapid fire. Syrian tanks were burning all over the slopes. Sometimes an internal explosion sent a Syrian turret flying skyward.

"This is the battalion commander. You're doing great work. This valley is beginning to look like Lag B'Omer," a reference to the bonfires lit on that Jewish holiday. "Keep firing. We've got to stop them." Accurate Syrian artillery fire struck the ramps.

From time to time, tanks backed off to permit crewmen to load ammunition into the turret from the belly of the Centurion. Kahalani watched the tank commanders move unhesitatingly back up to the firing line. Emi Palant on the left reported more of his tanks knocked out. Kahalani ordered two platoons from the opposite flank to go to his assistance.

"Brigade commander, this is Rattes." It was the battalion commander on the brigade's left flank talking to Ben-Gal. "It looks like a lot of tanks attacking Kahalani."

Ben-Gal raised Kahalani. "Do you see anything?"

"It's not clear to me what he's talking about," said Kahalani.

The report worried him. He did not know if Rattes was referring to the tanks already attacking or to yet another force hidden by the terrain.

"There are a lot of Syrians coming at me, Yanosh. I'll manage."

Ben-Gal sent Kahalani the three tanks which protected his mobile command post, the brigade's only reserve. Moving constantly around the battlefield, the brigade commander fine-tuned the defense as he shifted companies and even platoons from one sector to another in anticipation of shifting Syrian pressure. It was his principal task, as Ben-Gal saw it, not to react to specific Syrian moves—his commanders on the ground would attend to that—but to imagine what the problems were likely to be in another fifteen minutes or two hours. To effectively command, it was important to be near the heart of the action. Only thus could he detect weak spots on both sides and understand the flow of the battle.

Like Askarov in the southern Golan, Kahalani was struck by the courage of the Syrians. They kept on coming, passing around their burnt-out tanks and pressing on. But it appeared to him a mindless courage. If he were attacking, he thought, he would have slowed the pace and attempted to find another opening. The Syrians just continued banging their head against the same wall. However, with a wall as thin as the Israeli line and a force as large as the Syrians' there was no telling how the story would end.

From Booster Ridge on the right flank overlooking Kuneitra, the officer in command requested permission to send one of his tanks back to bring up ammunition. Kahalani could see Syrian personnel carriers with infantry moving in that direction. "I don't want any tank leaving the line now," he said.

Palant on Kahalani's left flank cut into the radio net. "The Syrians are trying to break through my company."

"Are there any points you don't control?" asked Kahalani.

"I'm controlling everything. I just wanted you to know. Over."

The message being passed on to him by his commanders was the same that he was passing on to Ben-Gal—the situation was serious but meanwhile under control.

As his own tank pulled back for a few moments to load shells into the turret, Kahalani glanced along the line. The tanks were no longer the neat fighting machines they had been in the morning. Pieces of equipment had been knocked ajar by shell fire and the sleeping bags and other personal accoutrements lashed to the exterior of the tanks were riddled with shrapnel. One of Palant's tanks was burning. The gun of another tank hung askew. All the faces in the turrets were dark with powder and dust. He could sense, however, an easing of the pressure. Here and there, enemy tanks continued to fire but when he mounted the rampart he could see that the great armored wave had broken.

"Kahalani. This is Yanosh. What's happening?"

"We've managed to stop them. The valley below me is full of burning and abandoned tanks."

Ben-Gal asked if he could estimate their numbers. "Eighty or ninety," said Kahalani.

"Well done. Well done." Coming from a hard case like Ben-Gal, the warm words were not a compliment Kahalani took lightly.

The fight was not yet over. MiGs appeared overhead and dropped bombs. The explosions were deafening but the bombs hit a hundred yards behind the rampart. "Where's our air force?" Kahalani asked Ben-Gal. Neither had any idea of the desperate situation on the southern Golan or Sinai.

By noon the Syrian artillery had abated. For the first time in twenty-four hours, men got out of the tanks, one at a time, to relieve themselves. The tanks pulled back in rotation a mile to the rear for fuel and ammunition. Kahalani drove to Ben-Gal's command post.

"I've lost a lot of men," he reported. He sensed that the brigade commander did not want to talk about it.

"I want you to know," said Ben-Gal, "that the Syrians are not stopping. They've got enough tanks and they'll try to break through again."

Kahalani was taken aback by the thought that they might have to go through this once more. As he started back to his vehicle, the brigade operations officer, who had followed the progress of the battle on the radio net, embraced him. "You were great, brother," he said.

As grim as was the prospect of another round, Kahalani and Ben-Gal had less cause for anxiety than did General Hofi. The front commander knew that the grueling but controlled battle the Seventh Brigade had waged this day was the one bright spot in Israel's entire military picture, on the ground and in the air. The southern Golan was being overrun by the Syrians. In Sinai, the Egyptians had destroyed the Bar-Lev Line and were pushing inland. In the air, Israeli planes were being knocked down with frightening frequency by Soviet missiles. Something had gone terribly wrong.

Skyhawks began flying over the southern Golan at 7 a.m., despite their vulnerability to the SAMs, in a desperate bid to slow the Syrian tanks. Ben-Shoham's intelligence officer, Maj. Moshe Zurich, saw the first four Skyhawks come in low from the southwest. Within seconds, a volley of missiles rushed at them and all four appeared to be hit. A few minutes later another foursome appeared and two were downed. It was apparent to Zurich that salvation would not be coming from the skies.

Skyhawk pilot Shlomo Kalish circled over Lake Kinneret with the other three planes in his flight, waiting for the planes which had gone in ahead of them to vacate the area. It was still unclear to the young pilot why the mission in Egypt they had trained so extensively for had been abruptly called off and why they had been hastily dispatched, with virtually no briefing, to the north. Whatever was happening on the Golan was obviously serious. Just how serious became apparent when the flight leader told them as they started in to stay low to avoid missiles and to "hit anything you see." Kalish realized this meant there were no more Israeli forces in the southern Golan. As they swept in over Ramat Magshimim he saw a large number of tanks parked in rectangular formation. He started to dive when a shoulder-held Strela missile exploded near his tail. A light on his instrument panel indicated a fire. Lieutenant Kalish continued his dive and unloaded his bombs. He managed to land his plane at the Ramat David Air Base in the north a few minutes later. Instead of receiving kudos when debriefed, he was rebuked for not having headed immediately for base when the warning signal went on. Six Skyhawks had been downed in the desperate bid to halt the Syrian tanks and eleven planes, like Kalish's, were hit but managed to get back. Any impact of the air attacks on the Syrian tide was not visible.

Maj. Yoram Yair, commanding the paratroop contingent manning the five southern strongpoints, had also seen the Skyhawks devoured by the Syrian missiles. When he reported that the Syrian tanks at Ramat Magshimim, five miles to his north, were starting to move in his direction, he was ordered to leave El Al immediately. He told the men at his command post to descend to the Kinneret and to take all the vehicles with them. Unwilling to leave while his men were cut off in frontline strongpoints, Yair told headquarters he was remaining to report on Syrian movement. Two of the men volunteered to stay with him. The Syrian tanks reached seven hundred yards from El Al and halted.

General Hofi ordered the evacuation of the frontline strongpoints as Elazar had directed and Yair passed the order on to the commanders of the five strongpoints manned by his paratroopers. Col. Amir Drori, commander of the Golani Brigade, which manned the five northern strongpoints, objected to the order. He told Hofi that his men were holding their own and inflicting heavy losses on the Syrians. Hofi relented. A similar protest was made by AMAN chief Zeira when he learned of the order to evacuate an important intelligence post overlooking the Syrian lines near Kuneitra. Reinforce it with tanks and protect it with planes, said Zeira. Here too the evacuation order was rescinded.

At Strongpoint 111, a radioman picked up a transmission from the commander of a Syrian unit at dawn. "I see the whole Galilee in front of me. Request permission to proceed." The answer that came back was "Negative." The paratroopers manning the position had developed a measure of fatalism after beating off infantry attacks and enduring hours of shelling. During a lull, they heard a vehicle approaching from the rear. An Israeli APC swung into the compound. "We're getting out," shouted the platoon commander. "Leave everything. You have one minute to get in." The bodies of two dead paratroopers were placed on the vehicle floor. Sgt. Yoram Krivine tried not to step on them as eighteen men crowded in. The APC commander stood with his head out of the turret so that he could guide the driver cross-country, well away from roads. At some points, the men had to get out to enable the APC to cross steep wadis. Krivine felt so stifled by the crowding that he asked his officer for permission to find his way back to the Israeli lines on foot. The request was denied.

The APC commander calmly described to the men inside what he was seeing, including occasional Syrian tanks in the distance. At one point, the vehicle turned a sharp bend and the men heard tank engines very close. "Two Syrian tanks," said the officer. No one was visible in their hatches, and the crews, after a day and night of battle, may have been asleep. The officer's body twisted as he flung a grenade. The men could hear a muffled explosion. "Got it into the turret," said the officer. "The other tank's taking off." When the APC finally stopped and the men tumbled out, they found themselves in the Nafakh camp. Although he had never before been claustrophobic, Yoram Krivine would be ever after.

Dawn brought the end to an agonizing night for Colonel Ben-Shoham. Cut off in a remote wadi, he had attempted to conduct the battle by radio without a coherent picture of what was happening. Daylight made his personal situation precarious. A large dust cloud indicated that Syrian units were beginning to get under way in his area. The dust trail moved westward toward the Gamla Ascent, Ben-Shoham's only escape route since the Tapline to his rear was cut off. He requested permission from Northern Command to descend the heights into Israel in order to come back up to Nafakh via the Bnot Yaacov Bridge. Permission was granted. Syrian tanks came into view two miles to the rear as Ben-Shoham's tank and APC crested the escarpment and began the descent.

His last order to Erez before departing was to fall back with all his remaining tanks on Tel Fares. Concentrating them on the high mound was the best chance of surviving the day. "All we can do now is hang on until the reserves come up," said Ben-Shoham. "We've done our bit."

17

THE BEANSTALK

To the reservists approaching the Golan Heights Sunday morning, the Hula Valley at its foot was mocking in its serenity. Cotton fields tufted the valley floor in festive white but the men who should have been harvesting them were fighting on the heights above or in far-off Sinai. Except for wisps of smoke seeping over the edge of the escarpment from brushfires, there was hardly a hint of war—no enemy planes, no bombs, no sound of artillery except for a few long-range artillery shells which hit the town of Rosh Pinna. To those familiar with Jack and the Beanstalk, it was easy to imagine the winding roads climbing the escarpment as ascents from an innocent garden to the high place where the ogre dwelt.

It was beginning to dawn when Col. Ran Sarig and twenty-five tanks crossed Arik Bridge and began to climb the Yehudia Road. The force was the first to be dispatched to the southern Golan since Lieutenant Yotser's platoon had gone up in the early hours of the morning. Contact had been lost with Yotser and his fate was unknown. "There's no Jew responding to radio calls south of the Tapline," General Eitan radioed to Sarig, in his picturesque style. "Find the Syrians and start fighting."

The ogre was waiting for Sarig a few miles up the road, masked by the rising sun. The Israeli column topped the Katsbiya Ridge and came upon an open area teeming with a hundred tanks and scores of APCs, trucks, jeeps, and fuel tankers. The burnt-out remains on the road of an Israeli supply convoy showed that the Syrian force had been there for hours. This was the convoy Yotser had seen burning the previous night. Had the Syrian force, the Forty-sixth Armored Brigade, moved just a few hundred yards farther west and taken positions on

the ridge that Sarig's tanks had now reached, they would have dominated the Yehudia Road. Unbeknownst to Sarig, Lieutenant Yotser
had already engaged the Syrians. Yotser's three tanks now descended
from the positions they had taken during the night and joined Sarig's
column. Before the Israelis could go into action, two of their tanks
were hit from the right flank and set aflame. The lead company piv-
oted to confront the attackers.

The hurried mobilization had left no time to bore sight the tank
guns, a procedure in which the gunner's sights are aligned with the
barrel of the gun so that what he sees through his sights is what the
gun is pointing at. The deficiency became immediately evident to
Sarig when his gunner fired at a Syrian tank only two hundred yards
away and missed. Backing briefly out of the fray, Sarig conducted an
abbreviated form of bore sighting that provided a rough alignment.
Returning to the battle, he found the tank he had previously missed
and his gunner set it alight. A flanking force sent by Sarig reached
high ground overlooking the Syrian ambushers and took them under
fire. Sarig could see hatches on the Syrian tanks being raised one after
the other as the crews escaped. Hofi, anxious to avoid further erosion,
ordered Sarig to proceed cautiously.

Riding in Sarig's tank was his operations officer, Maj. Giora Bierman, who had the day before checked himself out of the hospital
where he was being treated for a severe case of jaundice. His illness
did not prevent him from carrying out his duties but as smoke and the
smell of cordite filled the tank he felt himself losing consciousness.
Telling Sarig that he needed air, Bierman climbed out of the tank and
lay down in a ditch alongside the road. There, with shells exploding
about him, he passed out.

When he woke an hour later, the battle was still going on over his
head—tank shells, artillery, machine gun fire. The brigade had moved
forward slightly. He ran to the nearest tank and looked inside. It was
empty but blood spattering the tank's innards told its tale.

The next tank he climbed was commanded by Sgt. Dan Meridor, a
Jerusalem lawyer who would, in a few years, become cabinet secretary
under Menahem Begin and then a minister. Bierman could make out
the brigade commander's tank two hundred yards away but Sarig was
not in the turret. Borrowing Meridor's binoculars, Bierman focused
on the flat surface projecting from the turret—a map rest installed on
brigade commanders' tanks. There was no map there but Bierman

could see blood. He ran to the tank and learned from the crew that Sarig had been wounded in his neck and shoulder by shrapnel. Bierman climbed onto the tank and, in the absence of any other senior officer, took temporary command of the brigade.

The advance of Sarig's force marked the reopening of the battle for the southern Golan. The area south of Ramat Magshimim had not been captured by the Syrians only because they had not chosen to move in that direction, which was devoid of Israeli forces except for Major Yair and the two paratroopers at his command post at El Al. On the west, the Syrians had stopped near the edge of the escarpment above Arik Bridge, where Sarig met them, and on a parallel road, the Gamla Ascent, within sight of the Kinneret. There were no other Israelis left in the southern Golan except for small enclaves cut off along the Purple Line.

Hofi feared that the situation in the northern sector might deteriorate as well. He suggested to Eitan at 8 a.m. that he and his staff evacuate Nafakh. Maps in the command bunker were hastily pulled off the wall and burned. Eitan left on a half-track for the Aleka base, a mile closer to the Bnot Yaacov Bridge.

The task of reconquering the southern Golan was delegated to Dan Laner, a veteran armor general who had retired in February from the regular army to his home kibbutz in the Galilee. He had been asked in the spring to form a reserve division to supplement General Eitan's division on the Golan in time of war. The framework of the new division had been partially completed but Laner did not have a mobile command post from which to operate. On Yom Kippur morning, one of his first orders to staff officers was to lay hands on six half-tracks and provide them with radios and maps. Thus equipped, he set off for the Golan approaches.

Laner positioned himself early Sunday near Arik Bridge and channeled the reserve units streaming in from camps around the Galilee toward the southern Golan. All were arriving understrength because they had hurried toward the front before their mobilization was completed and because of tank breakdowns along the way. Almost all went into battle lacking basic equipment, from maps to machine guns. Pressed to make all possible speed, virtually none took time to bore sight their guns before reaching the battlefield, a procedure that normally takes up to half an hour. Commanders assumed there would be time to do so before going into battle but there almost never was.

The movements resembled less those of an army going to war than a fire brigade responding to a five alarm fire. Laner was the fire chief, directing units to the shifting centers of conflagration. He hijacked a reserve tank battalion assigned to Eitan's division when it passed through his area and sent it up the Yehudia Road to meet an urgent need by Sarig's battalion. Sometimes, he fleshed out understrength forces by attaching other units to them. Sometimes, he split units in order to plug dangerous holes. The fluidity with which the Israeli tank forces, from companies to divisions, changed their organizational shape in battle permitted them on both fronts to reorganize themselves almost instantaneously, according to shifting operational needs.

A brigade led by Col. Yaacov Hadar was directed by Laner up the Gamla Ascent. Nearing the top, Centurion commanders in the lead were taken aback to see T-55 tanks silhouetted against the skyline. The Syrians had reached the edge of the escarpment and were reveling in the splendid view of the Kinneret and the Galilee until Hadar's tanks appeared. Although the Syrians occupied the high ground, they were at a disadvantage since they could not lower their guns sufficiently to hit the Israeli tanks coming up the steep road and had to come forward on the slope, exposing themselves. The Israeli force pushed the Syrians back three miles by darkness, knocking out a dozen tanks without a loss.

Major Yair was on the roof of his command bunker at El Al at 9 a.m. watching the Syrian tanks to his north through binoculars when his sergeant shouted, "Tanks behind you." The paratroop commander instinctively threw himself flat and rolled off the low roof. The tanks were Israeli, a column of Centurions approaching from the south. Yair flagged them down and ran to the officer in the lead tank. There were men trapped at Strongpoint 116, said Yair, and he wanted a platoon of tanks with which to skirt the Syrian force up the road and rescue them. But the tank officer, Lt. Col. Yossi Amir, a battalion commander in Sarig's brigade, had other orders from Laner. The terrain here formed a narrow waist, only a mile wide, between two ravines, forming an ideal blocking position. For the first time since the war began, there was a force in place to block Syrian movement south toward the Jordan Valley. Amir's nineteen tanks started forward and engaged the Syrians just north of El Al.

In the early afternoon, a second armored force of reservists arrived at El Al, a mechanized brigade led by Col. Mordecai Ben-Porat. The trip from the mobilization base near Haifa had taken nine hours. Of forty-four tanks which started, eighteen broke down on the way. The tanks were Korean War–vintage Shermans which had been upgraded. Half were fitted with 105mm guns capable of penetrating Syrian tank armor. The other half had 75mm guns, which could not penetrate but could disable with a well-placed hit. It had been a brigade joke that if war came they would be posted with their old Shermans to guard the Haifa oil refinery. But they were about to take their hoary tanks into a real war. Colonel Ben-Porat took Amir's Centurion battalion under his command. By dusk the combined force had advanced two miles.

Meanwhile, Ori Orr had arrived at Nafakh at 8:30 a.m. with his twenty tanks, the largest reinforcement yet to reach the northern heights. General Eitan, who had returned to Nafakh after briefly evacuating it, directed Orr to the Kuneitra area to protect the southern flank of Ben-Gal's brigade. From there, Orr's tanks sparred with Syrian forces across the Purple Line but the brigade commander was surprised at the relative tranquillity of the area. He had, during the night, conjured up a desperate picture from monitoring Ben-Shoham's radio net. From this vantage point, it did not seem so bad.

Reservists were slowly taking over the fight in the southern and central Golan but the standing army units which had been fighting since Saturday afternoon remained in action. Major Zamir set out with Tiger Company in pursuit of elements of the Forty-third Syrian Brigade, which had remained on the Golan after the previous night's ambush on Reshet Road. In a series of running battles, he knocked out ten more tanks as well as APCs and trucks, again without loss.

On the Tapline, Lieutenant Greengold's lone vigil had been reinforced during the early morning by other tanks from Colonel Mor's rapid-reaction battalion. At 3 a.m., Colonel Ben-Shoham ordered his deputy, Lt. Col. David Yisraeli, to leave the command bunker at Nafakh and take command. When Yisraeli arrived, Greengold descended from his tank to brief him. Although no longer under Greengold's command, the force, which now numbered sixteen tanks, was still being referred to on the radio net as Force Zvika. With first light, Yisraeli led the tanks forward. They had topped two rises when they saw Syrian tanks coming toward them over the next, a mile away. The Syrian advance on Nafakh had resumed.

In the ensuing clash, the Israelis benefited from the shape of their tanks. The British Centurion and the American Patton had higher profiles than the Soviet tanks used by the Arabs. On flat ground this made them more prominent targets but in rolling landscape it offered a decided advantage. The Western tanks could position themselves hull down on rear slopes—that is, with only the turret and gun projecting over a hilltop or embankment. The Soviet tanks, on the other hand, could not depress their guns sufficiently and had to fire from the forward slope, exposing themselves completely as had happened at the Gamla Ascent.

Arriving back at Nafakh after his escape from the southern Golan, Ben-Shoham dropped off his intelligence and communications officers who had been with him during the night and picked up the brigade operations officer. "The brigade doesn't exist anymore," Ben-Shoham said to him. "Let's go fight." He turned down the Tapline and took command of Force Zvika.

In a brisk battle, the Israeli tanks drove the Syrians back a mile. The Israeli tanks dropped back in rotation to refuel and rearm. When it was the turn of Greengold's tank, he and the crew dismounted to stretch their limbs. It was the first time that they had a chance to see each other in daylight. Greengold was startled to see that one of the reservists was still in civilian clothing. The crewmen, in turn, were shocked at Greengold's appearance. His face was covered with burns, cuts, and soot and he looked as if he'd escaped from a hospital bed. He had almost passed out during the night. The crewmen insisted that he sit while they loaded shells. One man climbed onto the tank and extracted from his knapsack an apple he had brought from home the day before. He handed it to Greengold, who accepted it gratefully.

Meanwhile, Golani troops on the front line were repulsing repeated attacks. At Strongpoint 107, the defenders watched infantrymen descending from trucks a mile away and advance toward them in skirmish lines. When Lieutenant Elimelekh reported the advance to his battalion commander he was told to let them reach the outpost fence before opening fire. However, Lieutenant Yakhin, still riding herd on the outpost with his three tanks, did not want RPGs getting that close and opened fire at five hundred yards. The strongpoint's machine guns joined in. The forward line of Syrian infantrymen suffered heavy casualties. Those behind went flat and after a few minutes began to pull back. There had been no attempt by the Syrian infantry at fire and maneuver and no coordination with their tanks which mounted a failed attack from another direction.

At Strongpoint 104 beneath the Hermon, Syrian troops succeeded in occupying an empty firing position. Colonel Drori summoned a platoon from the Golani's reconnaissance company, which retook it. Watching the fight from an adjacent ramp, Drori saw enemy troops counterattacking. There was something odd about their appearance. Their glistening helmets and their uniforms were not anything he had seen on Syrian troops before. Their attack was also oddly unprofessional. They ran in a straight line up a path and were easily shot by the defenders. A few of the attackers were captured and identified as Moroccans by some of Drori's men, who were themselves Moroccan-born. The attackers were from a Moroccan brigade which was operating on the Syrian northern flank. Israel would discover in the coming days that it was up against more of the Arab world than it expected.

18

THE BATTLE FOR NAFAKH

THE SYRIAN COMMAND received two unexpected reports from its forces in the southern Golan early on Sunday, the second day of battle. Part of the Forty-seventh Brigade had erred in navigation and instead of reaching Ramat Magshimim found itself on the upper switchbacks of the Gamla Ascent. Turning a bend, they saw below them to their left the bright expanse of Lake Kinneret, with the city of Tiberias clinging to the slopes on the far shore. The glittering sighting, however, was overshadowed by a message from the commander of the Forty-sixth Brigade on the Yehudia Road. Israeli reserves had reached the battlefield, said Col. Walid Khamdoon.

It was Khamdoon's brigade that encountered Sarig's tanks shortly after sunrise, well short of the twenty-four hours that the Syrians had believed a minimum for the arrival of Israeli reserves. Uzi Mor and his rapid-reaction force had in fact entered battle on the Tapline only nine hours after the war began, but the Syrians had no reason to suspect that this was a reserve force. Yotser's platoon encountered Khamdoon's tanks three hours later and likewise was not distinguishable as a reserve force. But the appearance of Sarig's tanks moving in column on the road leading up from Arik Bridge clearly suggested the arrival of reserves only fifteen hours after the war's start.

In mid-morning, the Forty-seventh Brigade had the same unpleasant surprise when their view of the Galilee and Lake Kinneret was marred by the appearance of Hadar's brigade.

If the Israelis were ahead of schedule, the Syrians themselves were behind theirs. They had not yet descended from the plateau, let alone seized the bridges over the Jordan as their plan called for by zero plus ten hours. The consequence of their failure to press home their advan-

The Battle for Nafakh

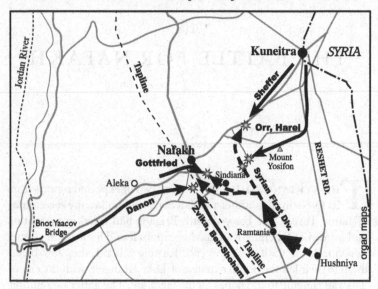

tage at night when all lay open before them would become steadily more apparent.

It is not clear whether the Syrians would have attempted to continue toward the river during the night if they had not encountered Israeli forces. The Forty-third Brigade was indeed in movement toward the Nafakh area when it was stopped by Tiger Company after midnight but the Fifty-first Brigade on the Tapline and the Forty-sixth Brigade on the Yehudia Road both appeared to be stationary when Lieutenant Greengold and Lieutenant Yotser, respectively, made contact with them. The Syrian brigade at Ramat Magshimim stopped about 4 a.m. without encountering any Israeli opposition and the supply column near Strongpoint 116 likewise halted until dawn of its own accord.

In the absence of any account of the war by authoritative Syrian sources, the reason they did not press home their attack at night after breaking through in the southern Golan is one of the major remaining mysteries of the war. The northern axis, on which they had hoped to quickly seize the Golan jugular—Nafakh and the Bnot Yaacov Bridge—was blocked by Nafshi and Ben-Gal. But in the southern sector, despite fierce resistance which threw their schedule off by hours and shattered several battalions, the Syrians had nevertheless succeeded in inserting hundreds of tanks capable of reaching the Jordan bridges virtually unopposed. Yet they had not done so.

A possible factor was the change in zero hour, just three days before the war. The Syrians had originally wanted 7 a.m. but eventually agreed on 2 p.m. as a compromise with Egypt. This meant that the bulk of the Syrian fighting would be done at night, which they had not planned for. Although their possession of tanks with night sights appeared to give them a major advantage over the Israelis, they had not trained extensively in night fighting and avoided it if they could. Their gunnery at night, all along the line, had proven grossly deficient. On the Seventh Brigade's northern flank, tanks from Rattes's battalion were positioned on the edge of the Druze village of Bukata and in its vineyards when they came under fire from a sizable Syrian force attempting to cross the border. Rattes had no flares and could not see the Syrian tanks, but from the shells that hit nearby it was clear to him that they could see his tanks. Nevertheless, the Syrians failed to score hits. Rattes's tanks, firing at the flare of the Syrian tank guns, managed to hit several and the light from the burning tanks permitted them to hit several more. In the southern sector, Major Barak, whose tanks engaged the Syrians in the darkness, was surprised to find the Syrians missing by a wide margin. Greengold too had managed to avoid being hit in duels on the Tapline and so had Tiger Company in the Reshet Road ambush. In all these cases, the Israeli tanks, even without night sights, managed to score numerous hits. The only clash in which the Syrian gunnery had proved effective was in the ambush of Uzi Mor's force on the Tapline where the Israeli tanks were confined to a narrow roadway. Even here, however, RPGs appeared to play a major role.

If the Syrians' original zero hour had been adhered to, they would have gotten in more than ten hours of fighting before darkness. The commandos would have been landed by helicopter near the Jordan bridges at dusk, which would have given them just enough time to locate their landing sites and secure the area before being cloaked by darkness. With the revised schedule, the Syrian tanks had only three hours of daylight fighting before night descended—barely time enough to get across the antitank ditch and minefields—and the commandos would have had to be landed in difficult terrain near the river at midnight. But Syrian helicopter pilots had little or no training in navigation at night.

A map found later in a captured tank on the Tapline included a written order stipulating that the Fifty-first Brigade would make its way to the abandoned customs house, above the Bnot Yaacov Bridge, where it would link up with a unit that would be waiting there. This was almost certainly a commando unit that was to have blown the bridge.

Defense Minister Mustafa Tlass would say after the war that Syria had agreed to the postponement of zero hour in order to permit the Egyptians to cross the canal under cover of night. Noting that the afternoon start time meant that Syria would be entering the war with the sun in their troops' eyes, he said, "We paid a price." The price, however, may have been much higher than poor visibility.

The Syrians had thrown 720 tanks into the battle as of Sunday morning, including the tanks blocked by the Seventh Brigade in the northern sector. Israeli tanks numbered only 250, including the first of the reserve units to arrive, but as the morning wore on, dust clouds in the Hushniya area attested to a further buildup of Syrian armor in the heart of the Golan.

By mid-morning Sunday, reports that the front in the southern Golan was stabilizing measurably improved the mood at Northern Command. But not for long. It was still assumed that the Syrians were preparing to push south past El Al or west toward the Jordan River. The first reservist forces had been thrown across these routes. But the main Syrian objective lay to the northwest—Nafakh and the Bnot Yaacov Bridge. Blocked on the Tapline by Force Zvika, now led by Ben-Shoham himself, and on Reshet Road by Tiger Company, the Syrian command chose a route between the two. It passed through the abandoned villages of Ramtania and Sindiana, a mile east of the Tapline.

It was battalion commander Haim Barak, riding with Eli Geva's company, who first made contact with this force. After destroying the Syrian battalion at dusk Saturday, the company was spared for the rest of the night by the furies sweeping the area. Barak's second company, commanded by Capt. Yaacov Chessner, spent a relatively quiet night guarding Strongpoint 111. The companies were only two miles apart but, unknown to them, Syrian forces had passed between them in the darkness.

Sunday morning, Barak was ordered to proceed to the Sindiana Road where a small tank force, part of Uzi Mor's rapid-reaction battalion, was in trouble, its commander in apparent shock. The unit had found itself at first light facing a mass of Syrian tanks. With no time to bore sight their guns, the Israelis' fire was ineffective. The Syrians knocked out two tanks and the Israeli force hastily withdrew. Barak found the reservist commander indeed disoriented by the clash and asked him to attach himself to Geva's company with the few tanks remaining to him.

Looking south, Barak saw large dust clouds moving from the border area toward Hushniya. Barak obtained Ben-Shoham's permission to proceed to Ramtania, overlooking the large base. The boulder-strewn terrain confined passage at points to a single navigable track. The battalion commander led the way, pausing at every rise to scan the terrain ahead. After three miles, his tank crested a ridge and he saw below hundreds of tanks—some fueling, some in defensive positions, some preparing to move out. It was the Hushniya base. Thrown off stride by the Israeli resistance and the early appearance of the first Israeli reserves, the Syrians had sent in the First Division, one of their two armored divisions, ahead of schedule to bolster their forces.

Barak ordered his tanks to take position on the ridge and open fire. "Just point the gun anywhere and shoot," he said to his gunner. "You're sure to hit something." Barak's tank managed to get off two rounds, setting a Syrian tank afire, before itself being hit. Barak was blown out of the turret by a Sagger missile and temporarily blinded. His operations officer, who had been standing alongside him, and two crewmen were killed.

Captain Geva had the casualties lifted into a half-track and ordered his men to pull back as an angry swarm of Syrian tanks began to climb toward them. Fighting a delaying action, he peppered the pursuing Syrians with long-range fire and attempted to raise Ben-Shoham. There was no response. With no one else to turn to, he switched to the radio frequency of his home brigade, the Seventh, and relayed his predicament to Ben-Gal. The brigade commander was immersed in his own battle and had no idea of what was happening elsewhere. He told Geva to fall back on the Seventh.

Meanwhile, Chessner had been ordered to meet a logistics convoy at Mount Yosifon to refuel and to replenish ammunition. Moving north on the border road, his company destroyed four Syrian tanks on the way and dispersed an infantry concentration. The surprise Chessner detected in Ben-Shoham's voice when he reported his arrival at

Yosifon, and the heartfelt "Well done," made him realize that the area he had passed through was now effectively under Syrian control.

He had not yet loaded ammunition when Geva notified him of the clash at Ramtania and the wounding of their battalion commander. Looking south, Chessner saw a mass of enemy tanks heading in his direction. His tanks opened fire at long range. Down to his last shells, Chessner decided to join Geva in falling back on the Seventh Brigade's logistics depot at Wasset, north of Nafakh.

The Syrians were striking at precisely the right place and time to splinter the Israeli defenses. If Nafakh and the high ground to its northeast were seized, the Israeli position in the northern and central Golan would be untenable. The First Division would be in position to turn right and strike the embattled Seventh Brigade from the rear or turn left and swoop down on the Bnot Yaacov Bridge. Or do both. The Israeli command at Nafakh was not even aware that a Syrian armored division was moving in its direction.

As Chessner passed Nafakh, he saw a newly arrived reservist artillery battalion parked at the side of the road, its men leisurely sprawled on the ground. Chessner fired a machine gun into the air to get their attention. "Start shooting or get out," he shouted. "The Syrians are right behind us." He spotted his battalion's logistics officer at the head of an ammunition convoy; Chessner told him to turn around. As far as he knew, there were no other Israeli tanks in the central Golan.

He was mistaken. Besides the tanks on the Tapline, Ori Orr and a score of his tanks were five miles east, near Kuneitra, protecting the Seventh's southern flank while other tanks from Orr's brigade were drifting up from the Bnot Yaacov Bridge to the west at the tail end of the mobilization process. Twelve tanks led by Lt. Col. Ron Gottfried had reached the outskirts of Nafakh when Chessner's and Geva's tanks darted across the road to their front, heading north. Startled by the sight, Gottfried halted the column. Before he had a chance to call Orr, he was contacted by division headquarters inside Nafakh and told to stand fast. A jeep emerged from the camp and took him to the command bunker.

General Eitan seemed relaxed when Gottfried entered and even smiled, but personnel were milling about in apparent confusion and the blare of military radios made it difficult to hear anyone. Eitan told Gottfried he was detaching his force from Orr's command and sending it down the Sindiana Road. "Ben-Shoham's in trouble," he said. Gottfried asked about the general situation but got no clear reply. From the atmosphere in the bunker, Gottfried guessed that Eitan didn't really know. In order to test the general's sense of urgency, Gottfried asked whether he should proceed in column—the fastest way—or to move with his tanks deployed for possible combat. In column, said Eitan. "Get there fast." This suggested that Eitan did not believe enemy tanks were in close proximity. However, Gottfried's glimpse of the retreating Israeli tanks and the confusion at division headquarters made him opt for caution.

Turning into the Sindiana Road, he deployed his tanks to either side of him and told the commanders that they would pause at every rise to survey the terrain before advancing. Topping the very first rise, they saw the spearhead of the First Division bearing down on them. The T-62s were a thousand yards away and closing fast. "Fire," Gottfried barked. Syrian tanks began to burst into flame but the rest kept coming, returning fire without pausing to aim. The range was too short and the Syrian advance too swift and massive for the dozen Israeli tanks to stop them. Gottfried counted eight or nine Syrian tanks burning before his turret was blown off and he was flung unconscious into the air.

He woke to find his face so puffed by burns that he could barely see. His driver lay nearby, with similar injuries. The two other crewmen were dead. It was not clear how much time had passed. Half a dozen of his tanks lay gutted around him. There were Syrian hulks as well. Gottfried took the stunned driver by the hand and walked back to the Nafakh–Kuneitra road. As they turned left toward Nafakh, a mile away, Gottfried heard tanks approaching from that direction. He planted himself in the middle of the road and raised his hand, palm outward. The lead tank stopped just in front of him. Gottfried's vision was blurred but he could make out the tank commander in the turret, a man of about thirty with a mustache. He appeared to be amused at the sight of the two soot-covered tankers hitchhiking. It was a moment before Gottfried realized that the tank he was leaning on was a T-62. Grabbing the driver, he scrambled into a ditch. The Syrians recovered from their own surprise and began spraying machine gun bullets in their direction, but the two men were not hit and the tanks moved on.

Other tanks from Orr's brigade were meanwhile arriving at Nafakh from the direction of the bridge, finding themselves without warning in the middle of the war. Since they were not yet in the framework of organized units, tank commanders reacted according to their individual temperament. Some leaped into the swirling fight which by this time had reached the perimeter of the camp. Others pulled back to await orders.

Lt. Hanan Anderson had found the mood lighthearted among the men in his makeshift platoon which reached the heights at 12:30 p.m. At the edge of the Nafakh base, the platoon was flagged down by an officer. "You're in a battle area," he said. "Don't go any further." He was Maj. Hanan Schwartz, communications officer of Ben-Shoham's brigade. Schwartz told the tank commanders to switch to Ben-Shoham's frequency.

Through the trees, Anderson could make out Syrian tanks five hundred yards away, two of them burning. On the radio net came an order to enter the camp's garage area and stop tanks approaching from the direction of the Tapline. Anderson was not sure for whom the order was intended but he was familiar with the base and climbed a steep road to the garage area with another tank. He saw six to eight Syrian tanks approaching and hit one. The others took cover and exchanged fire. Next to the camp's perimeter fence was a sentry dog attached to a long wire leash. Anderson, a farmer's son with an eye for dogs, noticed that every time his tank fired, the dog—a beautiful Shepherd—was propelled by the blast into a somersault. After a lengthy exchange, the last of the Syrian tanks to Anderson's front was knocked out. The commander of the tank next to him was dead. The dog was still on its feet, its barking inaudible in the battle din.

In the command bunker, the air conditioner had been knocked out and the air was stifling. Periodically, intelligence officer Dennie Agmon made his way to the entrance for a breath of fresh air. As he mounted the steps about noon, the sound of incoming artillery gave way to a sharp new sound—the explosion of tank shells. Venturing out, Colonel Agmon saw a score of Syrian tanks outside the camp fence, some as close as fifty yards, the farthest five hundred yards away. As he watched, a tank at the fence swiveled its gun and hit one of two half-tracks parked outside the command bunker. It was his own half-track. The other was that of division commander Eitan. The only Israeli tank in the vicinity, immobilized by a broken tread, was parked next to a helicopter pad. Its crew was aboard and the gunner destroyed the Syrian tank. Another Syrian tank destroyed the Israeli tank.

Agmon hurried into the bunker and described to Eitan what he saw. "It's a minute before midnight," said Agmon. "We've got to get out." The general thought otherwise. "From what you tell me," he said, "it's a minute after midnight. We can't go out now."

Eitan raised Orr on the radio. Soviet advisers were known to be handling radio intercepts for Syrian intelligence and it was assumed that their monitors recognized the voices of Israeli commanders. Eitan therefore kept his message elliptical so as not to let the enemy know that the Israeli divisional commander was trapped inside Nafakh. "Listen," he said to Orr. "I've got lice in my hair. Maybe you can help me scratch." Orr got the message and started his tanks toward Nafakh. Eitan also called on Ben-Shoham to break off his fight on the Tapline and return swiftly.

Orr left three tanks behind under a battalion commander, Lt. Col. Rafael Sheffer, to block any attempt to hit the Seventh Brigade from the rear. His main force, fifteen tanks under Lt. Col. Moshe Harel, proceeded with Orr himself on high ground south of the Kuneitra–Nafakh Road. From there they had a view of the terrain which the Syrians would have to cross to get to Nafakh. They soon spotted forty tanks heading northwest. The tanks were a shiny green and looked as if they were fresh off the factory floor. The Israeli tanks split into two groups. Attacking from the flank, they knocked out most of the Syrian force.

As Orr's tanks approached Nafakh from the east and scattered tanks like Anderson's and Gottfried's were blocking from the north, Ben-Shoham came up from the south with Zvika Greengold falling in close behind. Most of the other surviving tanks of Force Zvika remained to block the Syrian brigade on the Tapline. From high points on the undulating road, Ben-Shoham and Zvika could see Syrian tanks outside Nafakh's fence firing into the camp. Abandoning the road, they cut cross-country together with a reservist lieutenant who had joined them, pausing at every rise to fire. As they drew closer to the camp, they passed burned-out Syrian vehicles—tanks and APCs—as well as Israeli hulks. Dead and wounded from both sides were scattered on the ground. These were remnants of Gottfried's battle.

At one point, Ben-Shoham's tank disappeared from Greengold's view. On the radio net, the brigade commander could be heard calling for support. "I'm in the lead alone. Close up on my right and left." When Greengold regained the road a mile from the camp, he saw a tank lying on its side. It was Ben-Shoham's. The brigade commander and his operations officer had been cut down by machine gun fire from a disabled Syrian tank at the side of the road as they stood with their heads out of the turret. Their distraught driver had swerved sharply and turned the tank over. Not far behind them, Ben-Shoham's deputy, Lt. Col. David Yisraeli, lay dead alongside his own tank. With the Syrians at the gates of Nafakh, Greengold had no time to pause.

By now, another small Israeli force was converging on Nafakh, this time from the west. Three tanks led by Maj. Haim Danon were among the last of Orr's brigade to cross the Bnot Yaacov Bridge. Danon was unable to make radio contact with Orr as he climbed the heights but the sight of half-tracks and trucks heading down toward the river gave him an uneasy feeling. A senior divisional officer in a jeep stopped alongside. "Get up there fast," said the officer. "The Syrians are in Nafakh."

Danon left the main road and headed east cross-country with the other tanks. Approaching the Tapline two miles south of Nafakh, they saw a force of Syrian tanks beyond it near Sindiana and opened fire at long range, hitting eight. Coming on the remains of Force Zvika on the Tapline, Danon took them under his command.

Meanwhile, Greengold and the reserve lieutenant reached Nafakh's perimeter. They fired on the Syrian tanks outside the fence until there were no more targets.

Absorbing the silence for a moment, Greengold called the command bunker. It was all right to come out, he said. Soldiers began appearing from different corners of the camp. Eitan's staff piled into his half-track, which had been spared, and headed down to the bridge with documents they had scooped up. Eitan himself drove off in his jeep, together with Colonel Agmon, and headed north to set up a command post in an open field a few miles away.

Eitan had earned a reputation as a fighter since his days in the pre-state Palmach when he jumped one of two armed Arabs who had intercepted an unarmed group of friends as they crossed a creek in the Galilee. Eitan drowned the man in the creek. At the battle for San Simon Monastery in the War of Independence, he was shot in the head but insisted on remaining in the fight. His comrades propped him up on a chair set on a table from where he could fire through an upper window at Arabs trying to come over a wall. In the Six Day War, leading a brigade of paratroopers on the Egyptian front, he was shot in the head again. The surgeons extracting the bullet also extracted fragments of the 1948 bullet. He was not accustomed to retreats but he had now evacuated Nafakh twice in one day. The base was clearly too unsafe to serve as a divisional command post. But Eitan resolved in his own mind that, come what may, he himself would not retreat from the Golan.

Greengold got through to Uri Simhoni at Northern Command and informed him that there were "no live Syrian tanks" in the immediate proximity of Nafakh. Believing that the rest of Force Zvika had been destroyed, he said there were also no Israeli forces any longer on the Tapline. "And I think number one was killed." Shocked at the report of Ben-Shoham's demise, Hofi's operations officer asked Greengold to verify it by checking the overturned tank. Greengold, his strength gone, passed the request on to the reservist lieutenant.

Meanwhile, tank commanders unable to raise Ben-Shoham started calling Zvika, a name they had been hearing on the radio net since the previous night, to ask for orders. The lieutenant asked them to contact Major Zurich, the brigade intelligence officer, in Camp Aleka.

On his tank intercom, Greengold suddenly heard strangled breathing. "What's wrong?" he asked. The sounds were coming from the driver's compartment. With the assistance of the other crewmen, Greengold helped lift the driver out. There were tears in the reservist's eyes and he was breathing with difficulty. Nothing was physically wrong with him, it was soon apparent, but the stress of the past hours had finally overcome him. Without a word, the soldier walked to a half-track evacuating wounded and sat down inside.

Stranded, Greengold radioed Zurich and requested a driver. An officer drove up from Aleka with a young soldier who volunteered for the job. Faint from his wounds and emotionally drained after twenty hours of battle, Greengold asked the newcomer to drive to Aleka. The lieutenant was unaware of any other Israeli forces in the vicinity. It was clear to him after the death of Ben-Shoham that the fall of Nafakh and of the Golan was imminent and that there was nothing more he could do about it.

Seven members of the Golani Brigade armed with two bazookas had decided on their own to stay on at Nafakh after their unit pulled out. They fired five shells—all they had—at the Syrian tanks but scored no hits. As Greengold drove out of the camp, he saw several of these infantrymen at the entrance. An officer among them signaled to Greengold. Above the noise of the tank, he mouthed the words "Don't leave us." But Greengold could no longer carry on. (The Golani lieutenant would in time become a general and a Knesset member.)

The scene along the road to Aleka reminded Greengold of films from the Second World War—burned-out vehicles, wounded men walking toward the rear supporting each other, trucks filled with soldiers escaping the Syrian onslaught. His new driver's volunteering spirit proved greater than his driving skills. Wildly weaving, he bumped into almost everything in their path but finally managed to brake awkwardly at a roadblock outside Aleka. Zurich was waiting there. Greengold descended from the tank and collapsed but Zurich caught him. "I can't anymore," said Greengold. He was placed in a jeep and driven to hospital in Safed. His performance would win for Greengold the country's highest medal for valor.

The death of Ben-Shoham and his two most senior officers and the pullback of the divisional staff from Nafakh left a command vacuum. Major Zurich had been dismayed at the sight of vehicles, including tanks, passing Aleka and continuing down the road toward the bridge. The pungent smell of panic hung in the air. The tanks were apparently manned by makeshift crews and not part of coherent units.

Zurich ordered his driver to block the road with their armored personnel carrier. Old Syrian minefields on either side made this a perfect choke point. A Golani mortar platoon was waiting at the roadside and Zurich ordered its commander to have his men flag down all vehicles approaching from Nafakh. "From here, no one retreats," Zurich said. "If anyone tries, we shoot." The lieutenant responded enthusiastically and within an hour a dozen tanks, including the one Greengold left behind, were deployed with guns pointing up the road toward Nafakh. But no Syrian tanks appeared.

Toward evening, Zurich returned to Nafakh and found that some men had remained in the camp. Syrian tanks with hatches open were scattered outside the perimeter fence. Some were intact, their engines running, but the crews had fled. As with Greengold's driver, they had reached the end of their tether.

The main Syrian force had pulled back under the pressure of Orr's tanks, although not far. By the time darkness fell, Orr, bolstered by stray tanks from other units, succeeded in establishing a thin, four-mile-long defense line on high ground parallel to the Nafakh–Kuneitra road, the first semblance of a line in the central Golan since the war's start.

. . .

The Israeli forces on the Golan had been staggered by the Syrian attack, whose scope was beyond anything they had imagined. Unlike on the Egyptian front, however, the type of battle they engaged in was the kind they had trained for—tank versus tank. The Egyptians had resorted to infantrymen wielding Saggers and RPGs in massive numbers in the opening battles in Sinai because their own tanks were not able to cross the canal in time to meet the initial rush of Israeli armor. The Syrians were no less well supplied with RPGs and Saggers but had not resorted to them on a large scale because they did not need them as a stopgap. The Syrian tanks were able to cross the barriers separating them from the Israeli line—the antitank ditch and minefields—with relative ease and meet the Israeli tanks with overwhelming strength. Saggers and RPGs were used in small numbers but for the most part the Israeli tank crews on the Golan had to contend only with crushing odds, not a new form of warfare.

The battle at Nafakh exemplified the characteristics that would permit the Israeli forces to regain their balance despite the awesome nature of the blow they had been dealt. Small groups, operating independently of each other in a situation of near-chaos, had displayed high motivation—lunging at a more powerful enemy; and superb professionalism—shooting faster and straighter, and making better use of the terrain. The battle had crescendoed in the spontaneous convergence of tank forces at Nafakh in which Ori Orr and his reservists had lifted the sword from Colonel Ben-Shoham even as he fell.

At a staff meeting that night at Northern Command headquarters, General Hofi would give a terse appraisal of the battle. "Ori saved us today."

19

CUT OFF

Fʀᴏᴍ ᴛʜᴇ ʜɪɢʜ ɢʀᴏᴜɴᴅ of Tel Fares on which he had fallen back, Colonel Erez could see Syrian tanks flowing freely into the Golan Sunday morning. Apart from his twelve remaining tanks, there were no other Israeli tanks intact along the southern half of the line. Since the war broke out the previous afternoon, Erez had lost two-thirds of his battalion. Also on the tel were sixty unmounted personnel—paratroopers evacuated from nearby strongpoints, crews of disabled tanks, intelligence personnel manning the lookout post atop the tel. They were now cut off behind Syrian lines. From time to time, Israeli Skyhawks dove on Syrian tanks. Erez saw a few tanks hit but it made no impact on the armored tide. He counted five Skyhawks shot down.

The Syrians mounted several attacks during the day by platoons of tanks and by infantry-bearing APCs which were easily driven off. At 2 p.m., six helicopters bearing commandos approached from the north. Tanks and paratroopers downed three with machine gun fire and drove off the rest. With the heights in danger of falling, Northern Command ordered Erez to try to make his way back to Israeli lines with his isolated force as soon as darkness set in.

Elazar spoke with Hofi late Sunday afternoon and urged him again to form a second line of defense at the edge of the plateau. It was vital, he stressed, to maintain a foothold on the heights until Moussa Peled's division reached it in the morning. Hofi was not certain he could do it. The Syrians had almost overrun Nafakh and they had still not committed all their armor.

The conversation disturbed Elazar. He respected Hofi and was aware that without his warning about the Syrian buildup the heights would have fallen by now. But Hofi, he told his aides, was exhausted and needed a senior officer at his side to share the burden. Dayan had expressed uneasiness about Hofi's mood when he returned from Northern Command in the morning and Elazar had already decided to send up Gen. Yekutiel Adam, a former commander of the Golani infantry brigade, to serve as Hofi's deputy. He now had another idea—to send up Haim Bar-Lev, his predecessor as IDF chief of staff, to assess the situation.

Bar-Lev, commerce minister in Mrs. Meir's government, was a boyhood friend of Elazar's in Yugoslavia where they were both born. His famously slow drawl enhanced his reputation for unflappability, a characteristic sorely needed in these hours. When Elazar put the idea to Dayan, the defense minister responded enthusiastically. So did Mrs. Meir. Bar-Lev accepted the proposal immediately. Meeting with Dayan before heading north, he asked what was wanted of him. Dayan said that the original intention was for him to replace Hofi, who, he said, was "collapsing, tired, worn out." Elazar had in the end ruled that out. "But in practice," said Dayan, "the intention is that you do replace him, with an official appointment or without." Dayan repeated his principal directive—no descent from the Golan.

At Northern Command headquarters near Safed, the situation seemed only marginally less tenuous with the arrival of the reserves. These units too were beginning to be ground down by the unending flow of Syrian armor. As the day progressed, a question increasingly being asked was "Where's Moussa?"

Gen. Moussa Peled had taken leave of his reserve division the day before Yom Kippur for a year's study at university. He was at home when the deputy division commander, Col. Avraham Rotem, telephoned Yom Kippur morning. "You might want to get here," suggested Rotem. Peled stepped back into harness without further ado.

As a strategic reserve, the division had the luxury of a more thorough mobilization process than other units since the general staff needed time to decide which front to send it to. It was not until 10 a.m. Sunday that Peled was summoned by Elazar, who told him the division was to go north. "The Syrians have broken through," he said. "Get up there quickly." Peled ordered Rotem by phone to start the division moving. Peled himself drove to Northern Command headquarters with staff officers in two jeeps.

The war room on Mount Canaan had been hastily set up the previous night in a movie theater whose seats were removed. Cubicles and soundproofing had not yet been installed and the din from military radios echoing in the large space was jarring. Peled was unable to get a clear briefing from anybody. He found Hofi lying on a cot in a darkened side room, trying to nap.

"My division arrives tonight," said Peled. "Where do you want me?"

Hofi asked him to form a defense line along the Jordan, at the foot of the Golan. Peled was shocked by the order, which implied abandonment of the heights. He was disturbed to learn that engineers had already prepared the bridges on the river for demolition. Hofi looked calm but Peled presumed him to be laboring under the strain of the apocalyptic events of the past day. Peled himself was fresh and untraumatized and he had an armored division at his back.

"I don't believe in defense," he said. "I believe we have to attack." Hofi asked him to return in the evening to join a scheduled meeting of senior commanders.

With a few hours at his disposal, Peled drove toward the Golan. A veteran warhorse, he wanted to smell battle once again as he prepared himself for the task ahead. Near Almagor in the Galilee he saw a familiar figure sitting on a roadside boulder looking across the Hula Valley at the Golan. It was Moshe Dayan. Aides stood at a discreet distance as General Peled joined him. Smoke and flashes could be seen in the distance and the sound of explosions reached them. Peled had grown up on the farmstead adjoining Dayan's in the village of Nahalal, Peled being eleven years younger. This longtime relationship permitted Dayan now to let down his guard. As Peled would remember it two decades later, the defense minister spoke despondently of the destruction of the Third Temple. Peled placed a hand on Dayan's shoulders, a gesture only a very old acquaintance would make, and saw tears start to flow from his eyes. The harder he pressed, Peled would recall, the more tears that flowed.

Continuing on, Peled crossed Arik Bridge and found what he was looking for after a brief drive—the familiar low profile of Syrian tanks in the distance and the sound of artillery and tank fire.

His division was meanwhile straggling into Tsemach, at the southern end of Lake Kinneret. Almost half the tanks had broken down on the drive from their camps on the West Bank and maintenance crews had gone out to repair them. No fuel trucks were waiting at Tsemach but officers persuaded the proprietor of the gas station there to fuel the tanks in return for IOUs. Instead of holidaymakers who normally lined up at the pumps on weekends, tank crews now patiently waited their turn.

When Bar-Lev arrived at Northern Command headquarters in late afternoon he was appalled at the din and sense of confusion. He ordered all radios shut off. In the ensuing silence, he ordered anyone whose task did not require them to be there, such as drivers, to leave. The radios were then put back on, one at a time.

It was dark when Moussa Peled returned to Hofi's headquarters. Bar-Lev wanted to hear his thoughts. Peled proposed pushing straight north from El Al toward Rafid, twenty miles northeast. This move would cut across the main Syrian points of entry into the southern Golan. Once their logistic lines were threatened, the Syrian command would be obliged to withdraw their forces, fight, or risk their annihilation. It would be a terrible mistake to have his division form a defense line along the river, he argued. It would also be a mistake to have it continue north to the Bnot Yaacov Bridge in order to counterattack from the central Golan, as was also being proposed. That would mean losing at least eight hours in transit and risk additional tank breakdowns along the way.

Bar-Lev favored Peled's approach and called Elazar. The chief of staff questioned Peled on the phone and gave the plan his blessing. Hofi received the news as he conferred outside the building with his staff. "The plan is approved," said Bar-Lev. "We're going to counterattack." He handed Peled a cigar. "Smoke it when the time is right," he said.

At Tel Fares as darkness fell, the twelve remaining tanks formed into column and foot soldiers climbed atop them—five or six per tank. Dead and severely wounded were placed in a half-track. Company commander Uzi Arieli took the lead, followed by Lieutenant Beckman. With hundreds of Syrian tanks and tank hunters between them and the Israeli lines, they proceeded with extreme caution, avoiding roads and making use of their intimate knowledge of the terrain. Stopping before every rise, the drivers shut their engines to permit Captain Arieli to listen for sounds of enemy tanks. He and Beckman would then walk forward to look over the top of the rise. The way proved clear until they reached the last rise before the Tapline. Straddling a dirt track, just short of the Tapline fence, were four Syrian tanks, facing in their direction.

"What do we do?" asked Beckman.

"We go quietly," said Arieli.

He called the tank commanders forward to explain the situation. They would pass between the Syrian tanks without firing but keep their guns trained on them. In the darkness, the Syrians might not identify them or, if they did, might choose not to challenge them. They would then plunge through the Tapline fence and proceed west cross-country. It was wild, trackless terrain but Arieli knew it well.

Moving slowly, Arieli's and Beckman's tanks reached the Syrian tanks and passed between them, with just a few yards' clearance. It was as if the Syrian crews in the buttoned-up tanks were sleeping. As the third Israeli tank approached, however, one of the Syrian tanks fired. It had not raised its gun to aim and the shot hit low, damaging the Israeli tank but not disabling it. The Israeli tanks responded with a volley that set the Syrian tanks aflame. Arieli smashed through the Tapline fences and led the tanks into a wadi beyond as Syrian tank formations nearby sent up flares.

Arieli navigated cautiously through the rough, boulder-strewn terrain. The wadis began to deepen toward the edge of the plateau and precipices appeared. Regaining high ground, the column was confronted by a mile-deep stretch of brushfires. Arieli could have gone around the flames but feared that if he did the tanks would offer a perfect silhouette to any Syrian tanks in the area. It would be safest, he decided, to pass through the fire.

Lieutenant Beckman could smell the scorched earth as they plunged into the flames. Soon he could smell scorched rubber from the tank bogies, near the treads. Between patches of fire, the charred earth glowed. The soot-covered riflemen clinging to his tank's superstructure were invisible except for the whites of their eyes and the orange light of the flames reflected by the ammunition bandoliers draped across their chests. Looking back, Beckman saw the tanks forming a half crescent—a line of armored behemoths plunging through a field of fire like the riders of the apocalypse. It was a scene that would still be vivid decades later.

With their frequent pauses to look and listen, it took close to ten hours to cross the width of the Golan. Nearing the edge of the plateau, they fired on the silhouettes of four Syrian tanks which proved to have been knocked out earlier in the day, apparently by aircraft. Finally, they reached the last rise before the descent to Arik Bridge. Arieli and Beckman went forward on foot again and, seeing nothing, returned to their tanks. As Arieli led the column over the rise, his tank was hit. The shell killed the battalion operations officer riding alongside him and wounded the company commander himself. The driver hastily pulled back.

The column had reached the outskirts of the night encampment of Colonel Hadar's brigade at the upper stretch of the Gamla Ascent. The forward pickets of Hadar's force had positioned themselves with only their guns projecting above a rise and were virtually invisible. Hadar himself had heard the tanks approaching and notified General Laner, saying that they sounded like Centurions. Laner had not been informed of the breakout from Tel Fares. He asked Hadar to try to raise the tanks on the emergency radio wavelength to which all tanks were supposed to be tuned. When there was no response, Laner told him to open fire. Northern front headquarters, monitoring both sides, realized belatedly what was happening and ordered everyone to cease firing. Lieutenant Beckman told Northern Command he was switching on his headlights and moving forward. He topped the rise and friendly lights flashed back at him.

The abandonment of Tel Fares left Strongpoint 116 as the only Israeli position along the southern part of the cease-fire line still manned. Heavy artillery fire had resumed with darkness. Feeling the evening chill, Lieutenant Gur donned a flak jacket for warmth. It was the first time he wore one since the fighting began. At 8 p.m., five Syrian tanks turned off the border road toward the fort. The lead tank pushed aside disabled vehicles and stopped to fire. After every round, it moved forward a few yards and stopped to fire again, showering the men in the trench with bits of sharp basalt. With only two bazooka rounds left, Gur decided to try a rifle grenade, about whose efficacy he was uncertain. He told the bazookist to be prepared to back him up. When the lead tank reached the entrance to the compound, Gur rose and fired. He could not tell what physical impact the grenade had but the tank stopped moving and stopped firing. He hit the second tank in line with another rifle grenade. It too stopped but the other three tanks opened heavy fire.

Gur called down artillery on the strongpoint and its surroundings. A shell exploded directly behind him. The flak jacket absorbed most of the impact but shrapnel gouged a deep hole in his right shoulder where the jacket ended. He lost feeling in his arm and then passed out.

Soldiers carried him to a bunker where a medic bandaged the wound and Gur regained consciousness. He had already decided that if he were to be hit he would pass command to a private who had been fighting alongside him since the battle began. The young soldier was outranked by everyone else but he had shown the stuff of a natural leader—courage, a sharp eye, and the ability to analyze a situation quickly. Gur wanted to say "Take command" but the phrase struck him as too theatrical. "Go back up and make order," he said.

Through the night, Gur felt himself floating near the tempting shores of death but toward dawn his mind began to clear. From time to time, the private and others would come down to see how he was and to seek advice. They reported driving off several attacks by Syrian infantrymen. There were only ten men still on their feet. Haunted by the thought that Syrians might penetrate the outpost, Gur told the three other wounded men with him that they had best place their weapons alongside them. One man eased the safety on the grenades so that those who could not use one hand, like Gur, could detach the pin easily with their teeth if need be.

In mid-morning, Syrian tanks began methodically pounding the fort. Dust coming in through the air vents filled the bunker and stone chips fell from the ceiling. The shelling was interminable but, released from responsibility, Gur felt strangely calm until he heard what he feared most—shouts in Arabic. The Syrians were inside the fort.

The lieutenant pulled himself to his feet and together with one other wounded soldier who could walk moved to the bunker exit, gripping his rifle in his left hand. It was drizzling outside and the sky was gray. In the courtyard to his front, near a basketball hoop, were three Syrian soldiers. One, a tall, mustachioed figure with a bandolier of bullets across his chest, held a machine gun in both hands and sprayed bullets in a random arc. None of the men in the garrison could be seen. Propping his left leg up on a jerrican of water just inside the entrance, Gur rested the rifle on it and fired on automatic with his left hand. The Syrians were not hit but disappeared from view. At the fort gateway, he saw Syrians with RPGs. One fired in Gur's direction and basalt splinters from the bunker wall hit him in the back. Suddenly, he heard exploding grenades and small arms fire. The other soldiers in the garrison had been sheltering in the deep trenches from the pounding of the tanks and were unaware that there had been a penetration until they heard the gunfire in the courtyard. They now counterattacked, killing some of the attackers and driving off the remainder. With his adrenaline flowing, Gur resumed his post at the gateway.

Shortly after dark Sunday, Major Yair heard a muted voice on the radio. "Everyone's dead or wounded. Hurry and get us out." The caller identified himself as a tank commander on Tel Saki. It was Sgt. Nir Atir, whose platoon commander had been killed while supporting Outpost 116. He was calling from a disabled tank near the bunker in which the Israeli survivors on the tel had taken shelter. He kept his voice low so as not to be overheard if Syrian soldiers were still in the area. Yair had given up hope of anyone remaining alive on Tel Saki after Lieutenant Ansbacher had made his farewells more than twelve hours before.

Close to thirty men were sheltering in the inner room of the unfinished bunker Sunday morning. The Syrians had fired a shell through the wall of the bunker, then tossed two grenades inside. Almost all the men were hit, some fatally. But the Syrians did not enter for fear that there might be armed survivors. Ansbacher was among the badly wounded. "Somebody go out and surrender," he said. A tank crewman took off his white undershirt and held it aloft as he left the bunker. Two bursts of automatic fire outside were heard. "The bastards aren't taking prisoners," said someone. But the soldier had not been hit. Taken prisoner, he told his captors that he was the last one alive in the bunker. They chose not to check.

The Israelis lay all day where they had fallen. One man shouted for a while in pain. The others tried to silence him. However, he had been deafened by the explosions and could not hear them. A soldier said the shouter would have to be killed or they would all die. Someone wrote a note on a cigarette pack and held it in front of the wounded man who read it by the light of a match held for him. "You must keep quiet," it said. He stopped shouting. Spirits rose after Sergeant Atir returned with half a jerrican of water and a message from Yair about the coming counterattack.

As darkness approached Sunday, the battle in the Golan's central sector tapered off. Ori Orr asked a contingent of Golani infantry to scour the battlefield for disabled tanks and to check them for wounded and dead. There were many missing, including two battalion commanders. The infantrymen found Colonel Sheffer and his crew lying wounded next to their tank on the road between Nafakh and Kuneitra. The officer had been blinded in one eye. The second battalion commander, whose disabled tank had been found earlier, arrived on foot after eluding Syrian troops. He too was wounded.

In view of the heavy casualties, it was necessary to rebuild the brigade from scratch. Orr appointed virtually every officer to a new task. Apart from the wounded battalion commanders, two of his company commanders were dead and two others wounded. Some officers whom he had not regarded highly had performed superbly under fire and others had disappointed him. Altogether, the men had fought well despite the psychological wrench of being thrown into battle straight from civilian life and despite the random way the crews had been formed. They had gone into battle unbonded with their fellow crewmen, which made the unnatural deed of moving into the way of death even more harrowing. Orr decided not to reorganize the crews but to leave them as they were, now that they had fought together.

General Eitan, operating from his command half-track in a field a few miles north of Nafakh, ordered Orr to attack in the morning on the Sindiana Road. With his tanks deployed on full alert, Orr could not summon his officers for a briefing and he spent much of the night moving along the line to talk to them individually. Sometimes he paused in the darkness to listen to the conversations of the men on the tanks. It was apparent that the common rallying point was Orr himself. He recognized that his voice on the radio net and the sense of him as an authority figure were central to the brigade's functioning.

In a book written by Chaim Sabbato, a yeshiva student who served as a gunner in Orr's brigade, the author describes Orr climbing onto his tank in the darkness after the first day of battle. The book is fiction but based on Sabbato's experience. Introducing himself—"I'm your brigade commander"—the colonel pulls a bar of chocolate from his shirt pocket and distributes it among the crewmen. "I know it's difficult for you. You're young. It's difficult for me too. I've fought in a tough war [the Six Day War, in which Orr was commander of a reconnaissance company in Sinai under Gonen] but this is something else altogether. We've lost a lot of tanks. You're without a battalion commander and company commander. But we're going to win. Whoever hangs on longer wins. We've got no choice. Before dawn we're going to attack towards Hushniya. Your company will provide covering fire." Taking his leave, the brigade commander says, "It's going to be a tough day tomorrow. Get some rest."

It was still dark when Colonel Rotem started up the Gamla Ascent with two half-tracks and a jeep. The vehicles traveled without lights. Moussa Peled had ordered Rotem, his deputy, to take command of the left wing of the counterattack that would get under way in the morning. Hadar's brigade, incorporated into Peled's division, constituted the left wing. Hadar was not responding to Rotem's radio calls, adding to the sense of unease about what was happening up there. Hadar was maintaining radio silence so as not to risk his unit's presence being picked up by Syrian directional finders.

As they rounded a bend, Rotem heard the sound of approaching tanks. He ordered the drivers to pull over and cut engines. In a few moments he detected with relief the familiar sound of Centurions. Dark shapes loomed ahead and he flashed a recognition signal. It was the tanks from Tel Fares. As they came abreast Rotem saw that they were covered with soldiers, some of them wounded. He had the disturbing impression of an army in flight.

It was dawning when the Tel Fares convoy reached Arik Bridge. Reservists heading toward the Golan waved and called out to the approaching column returning from the front. They fell silent when they drew close and saw the exhausted, soot-covered faces on the tanks. After unloading their passengers, the tankers were ordered to refuel, rearm, and return to the battalion's rear base, Camp Jordan, on the heights. Their war was not over.

In two days of battle, the conscripts posted on the Golan had succeeded, with the help of the first reserve units, in blunting the enemy onrush. The Syrian attack had not yet peaked but a thin line of reserve units was beginning to form around the enormous hole gouged in the Israeli lines. Northern Command, which had Sunday morning made preparations for withdrawal from the Golan, was preparing by Sunday evening to counterattack.

After midnight, Moussa Peled briefed his officers in a eucalyptus grove at the southern end of Lake Kinneret. There was no intelligence available about the Syrian deployment, he said. However, the division's attack was not dependent on intelligence. They would drive north regardless of what lay in their path and cut the entrance points into the Golan south of Kuneitra, hitting the Syrians on their flank. By concentrating on a narrow front, said Peled, they would wield a clenched fist powerful enough to smash through anything the Syrians put in their way.

By the light of a pocket flashlight, the division intelligence officer showed on a map what their line of attack would be. They would be going into battle, he said, against three Syrian divisions. General Peled advised the officers to get a few hours of sleep. As they started to move off, Peled called them back. "Just a móment. We have a guest who wants to say a few words."

The officers could not make out the figure standing alongside the division commander in the darkness but they immediately recognized his voice. "You're Israel's last hope," said Haim Bar-Lev. "The eyes of the nation are upon you. Get up there and good luck."

20

HAND ON THE TILLER

FOR GOLDA MEIR, the descent into the Pit Sunday for a briefing could have served as a metaphor for what she would experience this day—a descent into a trough of despair, deeper and more charged than any in her experience.

The visit to the war room itself was less devastating than it might have been, thanks to the positive slant put by General Elazar on reports from the battlefield. He made it sound like the situation, while serious, was in the process of being resolved, or at least stabilized.

Moshe Dayan knew otherwise. His visit to Northern Command at dawn had colored his mood darkly. With his visit to Southern Command later in the morning, concern turned to despondency. The war room at Umm Hashiba was better organized than Northern Command's and Gonen was far more confident than Hofi, his northern counterpart. That, however, was the problem. "He was too sure of himself," Dayan would write, "about knowing what was happening and understanding the situation as it really was." With the arrival of the reserve divisions, Gonen told him, it would be possible to drive the Egyptians out of Sinai and perhaps to cross the canal as well.

Annoyed at Gonen's easy optimism, Dayan told him that top priority must be given to forming a fallback line that could be held if the front gave way. The Bar-Lev forts must be abandoned; too many units had been eroded trying to reach them. Garrisons that were surrounded should attempt to make their way out on foot after dark and there must be no further attempts to break through to them with tanks. Immobile wounded would be left behind to be taken prisoner. The defense minister recommended that a defense line be set up along the Artillery Road, six miles from the canal. Gonen said that was unfeasible because of the topography. "It is within my authority," said Dayan, adopting an uncharacteristic formality, "to order you to form a line that you can hold. Otherwise we will end up on the [pre–Six Day War] border. Let the line be the Artillery Road or the Lateral Road." The defense minister advised Gonen to consult with Elazar on where the line should be drawn.

On the helicopter flying back to Tel Aviv, Dayan pondered the implications of what he had seen on his visits to the two fronts this day. Like everyone else, he was stunned by the surprise Arab attack. Unlike anyone else, except Elazar, the major responsibility for dealing with it fell upon him. His colleagues knew him to possess personal courage that seemed to reflect indifference to death. What he sensed now, however, was Israel's mortality and it shook him. He was gripped, he would later write, by an anxiety he had never known.

An unspoken premise on which Israel had built its defense strategy—and he its prime architect—was that the Arabs they would face in the next war were the same Arabs they had so handily defeated in the Six Day War and the Sinai Campaign of 1956. It was a premise that invited strategic corner cutting, like maintaining disproportionately small forces on the front lines. A single day's battle had now demonstrated that these were not the same Arabs. Both the Egyptians and Syrians were attacking according to a well-thought-out plan—better thought out, clearly, than Israel's own. They had been massively supplied with modern weapons by the Soviets, including weapons Israel had no answer for, like the SAM-6 and the Sagger. More troubling still, they were infused with a fighting spirit they had never before shown. They were not running, even when hit hard. Israel had not calculated the psychological boost the Arabs would derive from seizing the initiative. Nor did it calculate the negative psychological impact the surprise would have on Israel.

What concerned Dayan most was not the immediate battle, troubling as that was. Beyond Egypt and Syria lay the rest of the Arab world. Israel's three million Jews were now facing eighty million Arabs who were beginning to smell blood. Syria and Egypt might accept a U.N.-imposed cease-fire but they could renew the fighting at any time with expeditionary forces from other Arab countries and fresh arms while Israel would be steadily worn down.

The breadth of Dayan's vision had become the depth of his despair. Before the helicopter landed at Sde Dov Airfield on the Tel

Aviv seafront, he determined to share his dark vision with Elazar and Mrs. Meir.

Most Israelis had little doubt that while the situation was difficult, the IDF had the resilience to recover and to win the field. The day before, with the war only two hours old, Dayan himself had spoken optimistically at a meeting with Israeli newspaper editors. "The Egyptians have embarked on a very big adventure they haven't thought through. After tomorrow afternoon [when the reserves begin to reach the front] I wouldn't want to be in their place." Now it *was* tomorrow afternoon and it was Israel that was in trouble, not the Arabs. "Do you know what I fear most in my heart?" he said to Elazar in the Pit. "That Israel will be left without sufficient arms to defend itself, regardless of where the new line is drawn. That there won't be enough tanks and planes, that there won't be enough trained personnel." The war was not against Egypt and Syria, he said. "This is the war of Israel against the Arabs"—that is, the entire Arab world. This was the message he intended transmitting in the coming hour to Mrs. Meir. "If you take exception to anything," he said to Elazar, "tell me now." He was not advocating an immediate retreat but a fallback line had to be prepared, he said, perhaps along the Lateral Road.

Elazar did not address Dayan's apocalyptic vision, only his operational recommendations. The chief of staff agreed that the Bar-Lev forts should be abandoned and that a second line of defense be established along the Lateral Road where Sharon's and Adan's divisions were already forming up. However, Elazar favored a counterattack once the reserves were ready. The difference between himself and Dayan, he said, was that he, Elazar, believed it possible to block the Egyptians. What they did not know was that the Egyptians had no intention of pushing inland beyond the range of the SAMs, some five or six miles. This had been spelled out in the revised Egyptian war plan that Ashraf Marwan, the Egyptian agent, passed on to the Mossad earlier in the year and that Zvi Zamir had passed on to AMAN.

Dayan departed for a meeting with Golda and her inner cabinet, leaving behind a cavernous gloom among the officers who heard him. For them, as for the general public, Dayan was a military icon embodying the nation's self-confidence and its ability to meet any challenge. He was now probably the most depressed man in the country, certainly the most depressing.

Meeting with Mrs. Meir in the afternoon he offered his stark assessment of the situation. The IDF's lines on both fronts had broken. Israel must cut its losses and pull back—in Sinai to the Lateral Road or the passes; on the Golan, to the edge of the plateau. There the troops would hold out "until the last bullet." Those strongpoints (on the Bar-Lev Line) that could be evacuated, should be. As for the rest, the garrisons should try to infiltrate back through the Egyptian lines at night or surrender.

The impact of Dayan's words on Mrs. Meir was predictable. She heard them "in horror," she would write, and the thought of suicide crossed her mind. Her longtime assistant, Lou Kedar, was at her desk in the room next to the prime minister's when Mrs. Meir rang. "Meet me in the corridor," she said. The discussion was continuing in her office but she wanted a private space. Although she had the country's top military and political advisers on call, she would share her deepest feelings, and fears, only with her old friend. When Kedar emerged into the corridor, Mrs. Meir was already waiting for her. Kedar was shocked at her pallor, which matched the gray jacket she was wearing. There was despair in her face. Leaning heavily against a wall, Mrs. Meir said in a low and terrible voice, "Dayan is speaking of surrender." If Dayan had used that word, it is inconceivable that he used it in the conventional sense. But he *had* spoken of beleaguered garrisons surrendering and of surrendering territory—pulling back from the Bar-Lev Line. (Years after Mrs. Meir's death, her old friend, Ephraim Katzir, a distinguished scientist and a former president of Israel, said that Mrs. Meir told him that "a senior officer," evidently Dayan, had suggested at an early stage seeking international intervention to end the war.) Dayan offered Mrs. Meir his resignation, which she refused. When she asked what his reaction would be if the U.N. ordered a cease-fire, he said he would grab it, even if this meant the Egyptian army remaining on the Sinai bank of the canal.

Mrs. Meir stared hollowly at Kedar, her mind elsewhere. Slowly, the expression on her face began to change and color seeped back into her cheeks. "Get Simha," she said. Kedar heard the familiar determination once again in her voice. Through Ambassador Simha Dinitz in Washington, Mrs. Meir would start putting pressure on the American administration for arms. As a stopgap measure, the Americans agreed to permit unmarked El Al airliners to land at American military bases to load up on vital electronic items, ammunition, and other matériel. Many excruciating days still lay ahead, but psychologically the prime minister had touched bottom and begun to regain her balance. However, her encounters with the unthinkable on this first full day of war were not yet over.

Many would be going through similar emotional buffeting as the country reeled from the war's opening blows. Senior officers realized with a stab that they had prepared for the wrong war, that basic assumptions on which their confidence had rested were illusions. The Arab soldiers were not running—they were attacking and they were fighting well with new weapons and new spirit. The Israeli Air Force was hardly being felt on the battlefield and it was losing planes to the SAMs at an alarming rate. Israeli tank forces had been unable to hold the line on either front except for the northern Golan. Israeli intelligence, presumed to be all-knowing, was responsible for an incredible glitch, still unexplained, that threatened to bring disaster on the country. Everything was coming apart and the war was hardly a day old. If the Arabs had succeeded in accomplishing so much in this span of time, what else lay in store?

Soldiers in the field were generally too busy to spare thoughts about national survival. Sometimes, however, they too were gripped by dark thoughts, particularly airmen who had a broader view. A Phantom pilot who returned from a mission over the Golan was asked by a female operations clerk at his base what it was like. He described to her columns of dark Syrian tanks rolling slowly across the Golan Heights like hordes of giant ants, with nothing to stop them. Alarmed by his description, the clerk said that her brother, a tank crewman, "is up there." She wanted the pilot to tell her that things would be all right. Instead, he said absently, "*was* up there," as if nothing could survive the Syrian juggernaut. The acting commander of a Phantom squadron, Ron Huldai (future mayor of Tel Aviv), briefing his pilots after their first day's encounter with the SAMs, said, "Take a good look at each other. When this war is over, a lot of us won't be here."

On the Golan Heights, paratroop battalion commander Yoram Yair saw Israeli planes falling out of the sky with unnerving frequency. There was no indication of a counterattack that might reach his men trapped behind enemy lines. As far as he could tell, the situation in Sinai was no different. "I was thinking," he would recall years later, "that the episode of the Jews here in the twentieth century had reached its end."

For civilians too, the abrupt switch from tranquillity and national self-confidence on Yom Kippur afternoon to all-encompassing war and existential alarm—without what psychologists would call "the positive process of anticipatory fear"—was a shock that would not quickly heal. The distress was amplified by realization that the battle lines were not holding.

In this, the most perilous period in Israel's history, the effort to avoid national disaster hinged in good measure on the steady nerves of one man. Given the gloom all about him, given the debacle on the battlefield and the abrupt collapse of the military doctrine on which Israel rested its security, given the appalling prospect of national annihilation that suddenly loomed, David Elazar merits a niche in history's pantheon of great military leaders just by virtue of not losing his head.

He was hardly without sin. He had accepted and propagated a doctrine that left the IDF unprepared for this war, a doctrine resting on scorn for the enemy. He bore responsibility as chief of staff for overly deferring to AMAN and not seeking at least partial mobilization in the days before Yom Kippur. He had advocated a static defense on the canal against basic military sense, and it was he who appointed the woefully unsuited Gonen to Israel's major field command. Nor would he be without occasional error in the conduct of the war itself. But in the cruel testing, with basic concepts giving way and strong men about him faltering, his was the stable hand on the tiller. The protocols of his meetings show the steadiness, and even good humor, with which he directed operations, although there were moments when he too was close to despair. Around his firm presence a calm space emerged where issues could be objectively analyzed and sensible decisions made. In the circumstances, it was not a foregone conclusion that Israel's center would hold, but it did hold, and David Elazar was the center. "He was a rock," Golda Meir would later say. It would be on him, rather than Dayan, that she would primarily rely for the difficult decisions that had to be made in the early days of the war.

Elazar's coolheadedness in crisis had been noted in 1948 when, as a junior officer in the elite Palmach strike force, he took part in the battle of San Simon Monastery in Jerusalem against hundreds of Arab militiamen. In the battle, which lasted sixteen hours, Elazar moved from breach to breach to drive off attackers. "He had a special tone of voice during a battle," recounted an officer who was there, Mordecai Ben-Porat, "quiet-like, as if he were singing, as if he were having a friendly chat or explaining something. I didn't know him before but I remember saying to myself: 'What a character that one is.'"

Toward the end of the battle, he was among only 20 of the 120 Palmach fighters still on their feet—40 were dead and 60 wounded. A decision was made for the walking wounded and able-bodied to retreat when night fell. Instead of leaving the remaining wounded to the mercies of the Arabs, it was decided to bring the structure down on them by blowing it up. Elazar and two other officers were to remain behind and detonate the explosives. Before that happened, the Arabs pulled back.

The harrowing battle helped shape those who survived it. Several were now senior officers serving under Elazar—among them General Eitan; Uri Ben-Ari, now acting deputy to Gonen; and Ben-Porat, leading a mechanized brigade on the Golan. Elazar was still blessed with a calm temperament and his upbeat assessments would provide encouragement and guidance to the embattled front commanders and to the inner cabinet with which he met every day. Unlike Dayan, who served up the cruel truth cold, Elazar warmed it to digestibility with his innate optimism. Things, after all, had looked much worse at San Simon and they had come through.

After Dayan left the Pit, an important decision had to be made regarding the two reserve divisions now forming up behind the front in Sinai. Dayan had demanded a pullback to a new line. Sharon, on the other hand, was urging an immediate crossing of the canal. So was Gonen. Elazar's instincts placed him somewhere between the two approaches—it was too early to attempt a canal crossing but he did not want to pull so far back that it would be difficult to reach the canal in a counterattack. Intelligence reported no sign that Egypt's two armored divisions were preparing to cross the canal. Elazar was still hoping they would cross into Sinai where they could be whittled down in a major tank battle before the IDF crossed to the other bank.

Dayan was still conferring with Mrs. Meir and ministers Galili and Allon when Elazar arrived to lay out three choices confronting the IDF. The army could fall back to the Lateral Road to create a stable line for a day or two, and then counterattack in an attempt to win back the territory captured by Egypt. Or it could fall even farther back to the passes and dig in, a suggestion Dayan himself had raised. But that would mean abandoning two major installations—the air base and logistics center at Refidim and the Umm Hashiba command and intelligence post. The third possibility was to try to cross the canal, as Sharon and Gonen were proposing.

Dayan responded a bit less gloomily than he had in the Pit earlier. His visit to the fronts, he said, left him skeptical about the prospects of a counterattack. But he agreed that Elazar should fly to Southern Command to explore the possibilities. If the chief of staff concluded that a counterattack within Sinai was realistic—not Sharon's cross-canal gamble, Dayan said—the cabinet would authorize him to carry it out.

Elazar's presentation was cut short by a call summoning him back to the Pit; there was more bad news from the Golan. His hasty departure from Mrs. Meir's office left the prime minister with Dayan and her two ministerial advisers. Dayan rose to leave but as he grasped the handle of the door, he said, "Oh, I forgot the most important part. Because we don't have a lot of time or many options, I thought we should be prepared to demonstrate the nuclear option too. So as not to waste any time, I decided before coming here to call Shalhevet Freier. He's waiting outside." Freier was director-general of Israel's Atomic Energy Commission. A nuclear "demonstration" required the permission of the prime minister and defense minister and it was evident that Dayan had already given his green light.

To Galili, it was clear that Dayan had waited for Elazar to leave the room because he believed the chief of staff would oppose his proposal and might influence the prime minister. By waiting until the meeting was almost over and framing the option in an offhand way as "preparation," Dayan was seeking to downplay the significance of the move.

"If you authorize it," Dayan said to Mrs. Meir, "[Freier] will make all the necessary preparations so that if we decide to deploy, it can be done within a few minutes, rather than spending half a day trying to do the preparatory work." What Dayan had seen on his visits to the two fronts had traumatized him. In his view, preparation for a worst-case scenario was urgent.

Both Galili, a pre-state Haganah commander, and Allon, who commanded the Palmach strike force in the War of Independence, objected. The reserves were on their way to the fronts, they said, and the situation would soon stabilize without any need for flexing nuclear muscles. Mrs. Meir welcomed their advice. Turning to Dayan, she said decisively, "Forget about it."

"Fine," he said. "If that's your decision, I accept it."

Galili's longtime assistant, Arnon Azaryahu, had been sitting on a bench in the corridor outside waiting to go to lunch with his boss. Hearing footsteps, he saw Shalhevet Freier, whom he had known for years, coming down the corridor. When Freier saw him, he stopped and, without acknowledging Azaryahu's presence, sat down on a bench some distance away.

Galili came out of the office but when he saw Freier he went back in. Mrs. Meir's military attaché opened the door a moment later and beckoned the nuclear physicist inside. When Gailili finally emerged, he and Azaryahu went to lunch. According to Prof. Avner Cohen, who would conduct a video interview with Azaryahu in the course of writing a book about Israel's nuclear history, Galili indicated to Azaryahu that he did not wish to talk. He ate absently, his mind somewhere else. Only after the meal did he tell Azaryahu what happened. "The whole time," Galili related, "Dayan was hanging on to the door handle, as if we're just standing around, chatting." The reason Galili had gone back inside after seeing Freier in the corridor was to ensure that the physicist was called in and heard directly from the prime minister that there was to be no nuclear demonstration.

Azaryahu's testimony is the only account we have of the episode. He did not mention the type of demonstration Dayan had in mind, but Professor Cohen suggests the possibility of high-altitude detonations over unpopulated desert areas in Syria and Egypt shortly after sunset so that the explosion could be vividly seen and the thunderclap heard in Cairo and Damascus.

Although Mrs. Meir rejected the idea of making a nuclear threat, she had already approved steps to protect the country's nuclear infrastructure against attacks. Prof. Yuval Nee'man, one of Israel's leading physicists, who served during the war as an aide to Dayan, would say afterward that "it would have been normal" for those in charge of the nuclear program to come to the prime minister when war broke out and obtain her approval for a number of basic steps. These would include "shutting down the reactors to minimize risks from bombardment."

After Elazar had left for Mrs. Meir's office, the mooted pullback was discussed by officers in the Pit. The proposal angered Benny Peled. Returning to the air force war room, he ordered an immediate attack on the canal bridges "at all costs." When Elazar returned, he was informed by the air force commander that seven of the fourteen bridges on the canal had been knocked out. The bombing, in fact, had little impact because the damaged bridge sections were swiftly replaced. However, it did give the Israeli commanders the impression that the Egyptian crossing was being contained, encouraging them to think more boldly in terms of counterattack.

Elazar set off in late afternoon by helicopter to Sinai for a meeting that was to decide the battle plan for the next day, Monday, October 8. Accompanying him was former chief of staff Yitzhak Rabin. The latter had no official standing but provided a sympathetic ear for the chief of staff, whose relations with his deputy, General Tal, were becoming increasingly strained by differences of view. Tal was consistently urging caution while Elazar was seeking a bold stroke that would shift the tide of battle.

Southern Command's senior officers were waiting for Elazar in the war room at Umm Hashiba when he arrived at 6:45 p.m. but the blare from radio equipment was so intrusive that they repaired to Gonen's office, a small room with a map covering one wall. The only person missing was Sharon. Gonen said there was a misunderstanding about where a helicopter was to pick him up. Adan was struck by Elazar's seeming serenity. Gonen and Ben-Ari looked weary. So did Mendler, whose division had borne the brunt of the fighting for the past two days. In response to Elazar's question, Adan said the Egyptian commandos encountered on the coast road that morning had fought surprisingly well. They held their fire until the Israeli troops were almost upon them and they did not flee when they came under mortar fire or even from a head-on tank attack.

After waiting awhile for Sharon, Elazar started the meeting without him. He presented an overview of the situation on both fronts and asked those present for their thoughts. Gonen proposed that Sharon and Adan cross the canal the next night at Suez City and Kantara, in the southern and northern sectors, respectively, on captured bridges. Mendler proposed that the two divisions attack together in the central sector. Sharon, according to Gonen, wanted to send his forces this night to rescue the men in the forts in his sector. Adan said that any rescue attempts would be costly and probably not succeed. He recommended a limited counterattack to prevent the Egyptians from advancing farther. There should be no attempt to reach the canal until sufficient strength had been built up. Ben-Ari said that no canal crossing should be attempted at this point.

Agreeing with the cautious approach of Adan and Ben-Ari, Elazar ordered a limited attack the next day. Adan, in the northern sector, would start the operation by sweeping southward parallel to the canal. He would keep at least two miles from it to stay out of range of the tank guns and Sagger missiles on the canal-side embankments. The force should by noon reach a point inland from Fort Matsmed, halfway down the canal. If all went well, Adan would then halt and Sharon's division would move out, executing a similar sweep parallel to the canal to a point opposite Suez City at the canal's southern end. Both attacks would be supported by artillery and planes. Mendler's battered division would hold fast in the southern sector.

A basic element of the plan, which Elazar voiced repeatedly, was that it be carried out "with two feet on the ground." Only one division would move at a time while the other two remained in place, ready to support it if necessary. Gonen would have to request approval before dispatching Sharon southward after Adan completed his sweep. The object was not to uproot the Egyptian bridgeheads or to cross the canal, Elazar said, but to seize the initiative and blunt any Egyptian attempt to advance. The IDF's counterattack would come later, preferably after the Egyptian armored divisions had been engaged on the Sinai side of the canal. He left open the possibility of reaching, or even crossing, the canal the next day if the Egyptian army should suddenly collapse, as happened in 1967. But that was not part of the plan, only a contingency to be kept in mind. On the other hand, if some catastrophe should occur to the Israeli side, it would be possible to pull back to a secondary defense line.

It was now 10 p.m. and Elazar had to return to the Pit to monitor developments on the Syrian front. He told Gonen that he wanted to receive from him during the night his detailed operational order for tomorrow's attack. As Elazar, Rabin, and Adan emerged from the command bunker, they encountered Sharon, who was hurrying from the helicopter that had finally brought him. Furious at having missed the meeting, Sharon hurriedly made his pitch to Elazar. The men in the forts were waiting for rescue. The IDF never abandoned its men, Sharon said, and he had a plan for breaking through to some of the forts this night.

Elazar asked Sharon whether his division could mount an attack in the morning if the rescue effort were made this night. Sharon replied in the negative and Elazar said there could therefore be no rescue attempt. Sharon told Elazar that a concentrated attack was needed against the Second Army bridgehead. The Egyptians were heady from the scent of success and only the shock of a combined attack by at least two divisions could restore a psychological balance.

"I can't risk the only two divisions I have between Sinai and Tel Aviv," said Elazar. He did not refer to Mendler's depleted division.

"The Egyptians aren't heading for Tel Aviv," replied Sharon. "That's beyond them. Their target is the canal and the line of hills. They can't afford to go beyond their missile cover."

Sharon had precisely read the thinking of the Egyptian command but Elazar was unwilling to risk an all-out attack in view of the heavy losses and unpleasant surprises of the past two days. He told Sharon that Gonen would brief him on the plan that had been decided on.

Sharon missed the meeting because the airstrip near Tasa, where he would normally have boarded the helicopter, was a potential target of Egyptian commandos believed to be prowling the area. He gave Gonen's headquarters the coordinates of a site in the dunes some distance away where the helicopter was to pick him up. He waited for close to two hours before it arrived. Sharon was convinced that the delay in reaching him had been ordered by Gonen to keep him from presenting his plan for the rescue of the garrisons.

Ever the tactician, Sharon did not show his anger when he entered the bunker. Instead, he took Gonen aside and attempted to persuade him that he was not trying to usurp his authority. "Look, Shmulik," he said, using the diminutive of Gonen's first name, "I've left the army already. My life is going in an entirely different direction. I'm not coming back to take your place here. The only goal I have is to defeat the Egyptians. Once we're finished with them, I'm gone. Shmulik, you can win this war. You can come out a winner. All you have to do is to concentrate your forces against them. You don't have an enemy in me. You don't have to deal with me at all. Just deal with the Egyptians." His words touched a chord in Gonen, who nodded.

Adan believed that Sharon, whose division had not yet been seriously engaged, did not realize the nature of what they were up against and that he had been overly influenced by his radio contact with the men in the forts. It was clear to Adan that the only solution for the beleaguered garrisons was for them to try to get out on their own.

At Orkal, the northernmost Bar-Lev outpost, permission for a breakout came this night. The Egyptians had captured the entrance to the sprawling compound and only the presence of the three tanks stationed at Orkal prevented the rest of the fort from being overrun. One tank had been knocked out. As soon as darkness set in, the garrison survivors climbed onto a half-track sandwiched between the two remaining tanks and into the rearmost tank. The three vehicles charged toward the exit and broke through the surprised Egyptians. They still had to travel five miles on the causeway before reaching the road leading to their base. Commanding the first tank was Sgt. Shlomo Arman, who had been leading the platoon since his officer was killed at the beginning of the war. The convoy stopped after two miles to pick up several men at observation posts who had been cut off when the fighting broke out. They had found shelter in the lagoon just off the road and maintained radio contact.

One of them, Yitzhak Levy, a thirty-three-year-old reservist, climbed into Arman's tank. The twenty-one-year-old tank commander patted Levy on the shoulder and said, "Soldier, you're saved. There's nothing that can stop this tank." Levy recognized the confident voice as that of the tank commander he had heard on the radio conducting the battle in Orkal. Shortly after the convoy started forward again, the half-track and rear tank were hit by RPGs. Arman reported the ambush to a company officer by radio and said he was going to their assistance. "Negative," came the response. "Keep moving." Arman protested but the officer at the other end said, "Negative. They'll kill you all. Move out of there fast. Out."

The tank resumed movement but after four hundred yards it too was hit. The crew leaped out to the left and Levy, their passenger, jumped to the right. He landed among a group of Egyptian soldiers. They struck at him with rifles and he punched back. Suddenly, he heard Arman's voice: "Reservist, where are you?" Levy managed to get away in the dark and joined the tank crew plunging through the lagoon.

After a few hours, Levy's strength gave way and the young tank crewmen supported him. But Levy felt he could no longer go on. Leave me, he said. I'll continue later by myself. "No one stays in this swamp," said Arman. "If we make it, we'll all make it. If we don't, it'll be all of us." As they continued on, Arman asked Levy to talk about his wife and children. "We'll soon be there," he said.

Close to midnight they saw the outline of Israeli tanks to their front. "Hey tankers," shouted Arman. "We're from the forts."

"Don't move," came the reply. "Who are you?"

"We're from Orkal."

"Who knows you?"

Arman gave them the names of his battalion and brigade commanders. "Where in Israel are you from?" A series of other questions followed. And then: "What company are you from?" L Company, said Arman. There seemed to be a consultation among the dimly visible figures to their front. One of the tank officers would later say that the unit had been told there were no Israeli forces in front of them, only Egyptian commandos. "What company did you say?"

"L Company."

A tank shell exploded alongside the five men, killing Arman and another crewman. Levy, who was not hurt, shouted, "Nazis. Nazis. Why don't you kill us all?" From the tank position, he heard shouts of "Cease fire."

Other soldiers were also trying to escape through the lagoon to the Israeli lines. One of them, Yeshayahu Mor, was alone when he was challenged in Arabic.

"Who's there?"

"Me," replied Mor in Arabic.

"Who are you?"

"A soldier."

Mor, of Yemenite origin, had come on an Egyptian outpost on a dry elevation. The Egyptians could not make out his uniform in the dark and took him for one of their own. They saw that he had been shot in the arm and they dressed the wound. Lying on the roadside after the ambush, Mor had pretended to be dead when the ambushers closed in. One shot him twice in the arm to see if he was faking and he had not moved. The Egyptian soldiers in the lagoon offered him coffee, the first hot drink he'd had since the onset of Yom Kippur. Mor managed to avoid saying anything during the night that would give away his identity. With dawn, however, the Egyptians discovered that the brother-in-arms with whom they had spent the night was the enemy. He was taken prisoner and brought to the rear.

At Fort Milano, the war had settled into routine for Captain Trostler by Sunday night. His men had fought well, beating off several attacks. The garrison had been reinforced by eight crewmen from Gabi Amir's brigade, whose tanks were disabled nearby during the night. The young tankers manned gun positions inside the fort with enthusiasm.

A tank had thrown a tread 150 yards from the front gate. Trostler asked its crew to remain in the tank in case its gun were needed.

A few hours later, two Egyptian APCs loaded with infantry approached the gate. Trostler's deputy, Lt. Micha Kostiga, knocked one out with a bazooka. The disabled Israeli tank, which the Egyptian APCs had ignored as battlefield litter, destroyed the second from behind. With darkness, the Egyptian attacks ceased but Trostler could see in adjacent East Kantara lanterns, flashlights, even the glowing ends of cigarettes. The ghost city had come to life.

The company commander adjusted to the idea that they might have to hold out for days before being rescued. At 10 p.m., however, brigade headquarters in Baluza ordered the garrison to set out for the Israeli lines on foot this night. Trostler was given map coordinates of a point seven miles to the southeast where Israeli forces would meet him. The garrison would have to start within the hour in order to make the rendezvous before dawn. Trostler wanted to take the four dead with him but headquarters ruled that out.

The garrison organized for departure, checking weapons and filling canteens. When someone called "What about the wounded?" the answer that came back was "Whoever wants to live, assemble here now." There were six wounded, three of them seriously. All insisted on walking rather than being carried on a stretcher.

The men, forty-two in all, formed up inside the main gate. The wounded were put in the middle of the column. Trostler decided to move through the town itself, rather than around it, since it offered cover. Entering East Kantara, they heard voices in Arabic in buildings they passed. The town was serving as a divisional headquarters and the sound of military radios could be heard. Anyone seeing the men moving through the side streets could presume they were Egyptian.

The group passed through the town without incident and emerged into the open desert, whitish in the light of the moon. After a few hundred yards, Trostler saw dark shapes to the front, tanks or artillery pieces. As he tried to find an opening, his group was spotted. Flares lifted into the air and there were random shots. Trostler pulled back and led his men due east, where passage seemed clear. But fire was opened on them again and the men went flat. Lieutenant Kostiga, who knew Arabic, shouted, "Are you crazy? Why are you shooting at us? We're Egyptian."

After a pause, a voice shouted, "They're not Egyptian." Kostiga had pronounced the Arabic word for crazy, *majnoon,* as it is pronounced by Palestinians, with a soft "j"; in Egypt it is pronounced with a hard "g." Fire was opened again, this time more intensely. The Israelis responded in kind. Several more men were wounded. Trostler looked back at the town and could see the tree line broken by the silhouette of a large house. "Everybody back to Kantara," he shouted. "To that house we can see."

Reaching it, he raised Baluza on the radio and described their situation. Headquarters gave him a new rendezvous point, this time to the northeast. He told the men crouched around him that they would move through the town to the cemetery at the other end before striking off into the desert again. As they went, they could hear vehicles moving on nearby streets as if search parties were out. In the seclusion of the cemetery, Trostler counted the men. To his dismay, there were only twenty-four, including all four officers. Eighteen men were missing. He had to decide quickly whether to go back and search for them. To do so, he decided, would be to risk the lives of all. He announced his decision and they set off into the desert. With his group were several of the wounded. There was little more than two hours left before first light and they would have to move fast. Kostiga and the tank crewmen formed a rear guard. They helped the wounded and some of the older reservists winded by the forced march.

Meanwhile, the missing men were trying to assess their options. The last man to leave the ambush site, Sgt. Shalom Chala, fired a light machine gun to cover the retreat. He found the other seventeen men taking cover in a bomb crater. At twenty-one, Chala was the youngest man in the unit, which included men well into their thirties. But as a product of the Golani Brigade he was one of the few with serious combat training. As he listened to the others discussing what to do next, he saw it becoming a pointless symposium. In the absence of any officer, he told them, he was taking command. No one argued the point. The group included several who had just been wounded as well as some who had been wounded in the fort. It was apparent that they could not get far walking. Chala led them into a one-story house just inside the city and the wounded were put into an inner room.

With first light, a lookout at one of the windows spotted Egyptian trackers following their footprints in the sand. Shortly afterward, bullets were fired through the windows. An Egyptian officer appeared in the doorway holding a pistol. "Throw your weapons down," he said in Arabic, and ordered the men outside. Some left the building; others, including the wounded, didn't. The Egyptians threw grenades inside, killing all who remained. Chala and seven others were taken into captivity.

When dawn came, Trostler and his men had not yet reached the site where the tanks were to pick them up. The area was a sandy plain offering no cover. An Egyptian artillery battery was firing not far away and the ground was pocked with the prints of boots. Trostler led the men toward a marshy zone indicated on the map. A dark shape that looked like an Egyptian tank loomed ahead of them. Through binoculars, it proved to be a patch of brush. They took shelter there, hoping to remain undiscovered until nightfall. In mid-morning, two tank shells exploded nearby. Tank crewmen in the group listened to the sound of tanks in the distance. "They're ours," they said. An Israeli tank commander had fired at the brush because it looked to him too like an Egyptian tank. The men did not rush from cover. Any Israeli tanks in the area would presume that foot soldiers approaching from the direction of the canal were Egyptian. One of the tankers said he had an idea. Borrowing a prayer shawl from a religious soldier, he said he would wave it at the tanks from a distance. "If it works, we'll be back soon," he said before disappearing down a dune with a comrade. "If not, so long." Not long after, a tank came roaring up the dune, with the two men sitting atop it, one of them waving the prayer shawl.

In Tel Aviv, the cabinet met at 9 p.m. Sunday night. Mrs. Meir regretfully noted that Elazar had not yet returned from Sinai. She had come to rely on his upbeat tone as a balm against the gloom projected by Dayan. However, the defense minister, aware of the demoralizing impact his words were having on his colleagues, made an effort to sound positive as he outlined the military picture. His own mood had improved considerably since his difficult meeting with Mrs. Meir in the afternoon. He was no longer talking about the Third Temple. He had not abandoned his demand for a fallback line in the event the Sinai front gave way, but he now advocated a quick counterattack across the canal. "The chief of staff's optimism about a counterattack has gotten to me," Dayan acknowledged to the ministers. "We've got to smash the Egyptian armor as soon as possible and also [to smash] the new legend that's beginning to be woven about the Arabs having become phenomenal warriors. There may be some narrowing of the gap but a nation doesn't change in six years. Individuals change. Not nations. This is not just a war of armor but a serious war of nerves." He seemed to be regaining his. On the northern front, he said he was looking for a breakthrough that would put the IDF on the road to Damascus. "We won't capture Damascus but we want to oblige the Syrians to dance to our tune."

A colleague who had worked with Dayan for many years knew him to be an instinctive pessimist, despite the cavalier, self-confident air he projected. However, the colleague said, Dayan was a "constructive" pessimist. "Instead of saying 'everything will be all right,' he would say 'everything won't be all right unless we do something, so let's figure out what we're going to do.'" Even though he had lost his composure, Dayan had in fact been in constructive mode from the beginning of the war, rationally trying to identify the holes in the dam and the ways best to plug them.

The change in the Arabs' ability to make war was indeed not due to an overnight change in national character. In 1967 they seemed totally inept because they were stunned by Israel's opening blow and were ordered into a catastrophic retreat. Now, they were executing a meticulous plan that they had been exercising for half a year. They had seized the initiative, they were well prepared operationally to meet the Israeli counterattack, and psychologically the wind was at their back. It was Israel that had taken the opening blow this time and it was still struggling to find its feet. But it had not broken.

At midnight, Dayan stopped by the Pit to hear Elazar brief his staff after his return from Sinai. The atmosphere was taut with antici- pation and Elazar addressed his officers as if they were about to set off into battle themselves. There would be counterattacks tomorrow morning on both the northern and southern fronts, he said. This was the turning point they had all been waiting for. He outlined Moussa Peled's battle plan in the north, and the plan he himself had dictated to Gonen in the south. There should be six hundred battle-ready tanks on the southern front by morning. In a clerical oversight that would prove telling, Elazar's battle plan was not written down by the operations branch and transmitted to Southern Command as a formal order, which was standard procedure.

Dayan was swept up in the enthusiasm pervading the war room. "From tomorrow we would begin to lift our head out of the water," he wrote later, in recalling his own thoughts. "The initiative was ours and we could pick the battleground and assemble our forces accordingly. Why shouldn't we win? The divisional and brigade commanders were the best of our soldiers. Arik [Sharon], Bren [Adan], Albert [Mendler]—the major league of the IDF. The entire chain of command up to the chief of staff was from the Armored Corps. All of them are experienced in combat, all of them know the Sinai well. Tomorrow will be the day of armor."

Tomorrow, however, would be the day of Shmuel Gonen. Despite the blows his forces had suffered over the past two days, the front commander nurtured the thought that he would repeat, on an even grander scale, the rout he had helped inflict on the Egyptians in 1967 as a brigade commander. Elazar repeatedly told him that the counterattack must be a limited one, that his forces should not get closer than two miles from the canal, that only one division was to move at a time, and that there was to be no canal crossing or attempt to rescue the Bar-Lev garrisons except in the unlikely event of a sudden Egyptian collapse. Gonen would proceed to act as if Elazar had said exactly the opposite.

He had gone to sleep without sending off to Tel Aviv the detailed attack plan Elazar had asked for. Ben-Ari woke him half an hour later when headquarters in Tel Aviv called to ask for it. It took only thirty-five minutes for Gonen to complete a plan—consisting of a sketch and a brief text. It was dispatched by air to Tel Aviv at 2:45 a.m. "The objective," it read, "is to clear the area between the canal and Artillery Road, destroy enemy forces, rescue of men in the forts, retrieval of disabled tanks." Instead of distancing the attack forces two miles from the canal, Gonen was proposing rescue of the men in the canal-side forts, which Elazar had specifically ruled out. In addition, the forces were to prepare themselves for crossing the canal, which Elazar had also ruled out.

In conversations with Sharon and Adan by radio later in the morning, Gonen would spell out his thoughts in greater detail. Sharon was to destroy the Third Army in the southern canal sector, then cross over on an Egyptian bridge and establish a defense line twelve miles farther west, toward Cairo. Adan would do more or less the same in the northern sector. There were variations on these themes that Gonen would set forth in a series of contradictory communications with the divisional commanders through the morning. One proposal called for the day's operations to begin not with a north–south sweep by Adan, as

Elazar had stipulated, but by an east–west thrust by Sharon's division to the waterline to rescue the men in the forts. At 6:17 a.m., Gonen dropped this plan and reverted to the north–south sweep.

His optimism was untempered by the fact that the Egyptian army had, less than forty-eight hours before, put five divisions across the canal, destroying two-thirds of General Mendler's tank division, mostly with infantry, while suffering minimal losses. Gonen also gave little weight to the fact that Egypt had two armored divisions and other forces on the west bank which had not yet come into action. Nor did he take into consideration his paucity of artillery, more essential than ever now because of the need to neutralize foot soldiers wielding antitank weapons, and the virtual absence of air support due to the SAMs. Artillery had lower priority than tanks on the few roads into Sinai; the bulk of the guns would not reach the front till late in the day.

Staff officers in the Pit noticed that Gonen's plan deviated from the one outlined to them by the chief of staff in his midnight briefing but they did not raise an alarm, perhaps because of the pressure of events. In a few hours, counterattacks were to be launched on both fronts.

Elazar was shown the attack plans submitted by the front commanders. He made changes to the plan submitted by Hofi regarding the attack by Moussa Peled's division; but he made no changes to Gonen's plan, evidently assuming it was based on what he himself had dictated to him the night before at Umm Hashiba. Elazar would later testify that he had no recollection of having seen Gonen's plan; that he did not have time to read all the papers laid on his desk during the battle. One way or another, he had permitted Gonen's delusional plan to get past him.

Shortly after 6 a.m., Gonen informed him that Adan would begin his attack in two hours. He requested permission for Adan to cross the canal after completing his north–south sweep. Elazar was less dismissive of the possibility than he was the night before. He was exultant over the arrival of the reserves on the battlefield in half the time allotted and over the fact that a counterattack was to be launched on both fronts less than two days after the IDF was staggered by the Arab surprise attack. With some six hundred Israeli tanks expected to enter the battle during the day, the possibility of an Egyptian collapse seemed less remote to him than it had the previous evening. He discussed a crossing this time with Gonen as a reasonable possibility. If one is undertaken, he said, it should be at Matsmed where one flank would be protected by the Bitter Lake. Only one brigade should be sent across and it would then take up defensive positions five miles to the west. Elazar expressed doubt that the Egyptians would leave an intact bridge for Gonen to capture. The Israelis were not aware that even if bridges were captured they could probably not support their Western tanks, which were fifteen to twenty tons heavier than the Soviet tanks for which the Soviet-made bridges were intended.

But Elazar had not changed his position from the previous night that a crossing would be considered only if there was a general collapse of the Egyptian forces. The chances of that happening might be a little less unlikely now but it was hardly certain. Elazar's objective at this stage was not relieving the forts or crossing the canal but destruction of the Egyptian tank formations believed to be moving inland from the Sinai bank. Whether or not there would be a crossing, he said to Gonen, depended on the results of Adan's sweep. And only the General Staff, he reminded him, could authorize a crossing.

"Shmulik, be careful not to go too close to the ramparts," cautioned Elazar again. "Good luck."

21

FAILED COUNTERATTACK

ADAN'S DIVISION BEGAN rolling westward at 2 a.m. Monday from the Lateral Road, twelve miles from the canal. The launching of a counterattack by the reserves only thirty-six hours after the war's start, and on the most remote battlefront, boded well.

The tanks moved slowly in broad deployment, uncertain where they might encounter the enemy. A single tank platoon had been posted since sundown on a ridge near the Artillery Road, six miles from the canal, as a forward listening post. Its commander reported hearing intense vehicular activity to the west where tanks were crossing the canal but the Egyptians had not pushed appreciably inland.

Only two of Adan's three brigades were involved in the advance, the third having not yet freed itself from the traffic jam on the Sinai coastal road. The two, Gabi Amir's battered brigade from the armored school and a reservist force commanded by Lt. Col. Natan (Natke) Nir, had 120 tanks between them, just over half their allotted strength. Missing tanks were still making their way to the front. The clashes at Kantara and Mifreket and with the commandos on the coastal road induced caution among Adan and his commanders as they moved toward the coming encounter.

At Gonen's headquarters, however, caution was on indefinite leave. The southern front commander had, like everyone else, been shocked by the surprise attack and by the determination displayed by the Egyptians. He quickly recovered, reverting overnight to the bravura mind-set of the Six Day War. General Elazar's careful, two-feet-on-the-ground attack plan—appropriate to the uncertain circumstances—was dropped by Gonen, who was planning to kick the enemy with both feet.

Adan understood his mission to be the one outlined by Elazar the night before at Umm Hashiba—to sweep south for some thirty miles from Kantara to Fort Matsmed while keeping a safe distance from the canal embankments. At 4 a.m., he was contacted by Gen. Kalman Magen, who had taken command of the Baluza sector, with new orders from Gonen, who was unable to make direct radio contact with Adan. The latter would head for the canal, after all, and link up with Forts Hizayon and Purkan. If he found an Egyptian bridge intact, he would send a brigade across and have it take up defensive positions twelve miles to the west of the canal. If there was no bridge available, he would continue south to Matsmed and cross there on a captured bridge, likewise sending a brigade westward twelve miles.

This gross deviation from Elazar's plan—and from reality—was enough to alert Adan to a major problem at Southern Command. But that was only the start. Fifteen minutes later, Gonen sent a correction via Magen: Adan would link up with Hizayon and Purkan but would not attempt to cross there, only at Matsmed, farther south. And the defense line would be established six miles west of the canal, not twelve. When Magen ventured that Adan would have difficulty effecting a linkup with the forts and had made no preparations for it, Gonen immediately changed his instructions. The linkup, he said, would be carried out by Sharon. Adan would pause in his southerly progress to permit Sharon to dash in and rescue the two garrisons. Sharon would then pull back to get out of Adan's way.

At 4:30 a.m. Gonen was finally able to make direct contact with Adan. This time he put both options to the division commander: either link up with the two forts on the way down to Matsmed or let Sharon carry out the rescue operation. Adan said he would not be able to answer until daylight when he could assess the opposition confronting him.

"Prepare for both options," said Gonen crisply.

By dawn, Amir's and Nir's brigades had descended the low hills overlooking the plain fringing the Suez Canal. Here they halted prior to beginning their southward sweep. At 8 a.m., Adan gave the order to advance. Amir's brigade took the lead, with Nir following several miles behind.

The division had encountered no Egyptian tanks on the way west and encountered none now as it headed south, two miles from the canal and parallel to it. Several teams of Egyptian artillery spotters along the way were killed or captured. The third brigade, commanded by Lt. Col. Arye Keren, had arrived with sixty-two tanks during the night and moved parallel to the rest of the division on the Artillery Road as a reserve force.

As Nir's brigade came abreast of Kantara, he was ordered to halt. Photo interpreters examining the results of a fresh reconnaissance flight had identified a brigade of Egyptian T-62s under camouflage netting at the edge of the city. Unwilling to ignore the threat to his rear, Adan ordered Nir to remain in place.

It was Nir's men who would pick up the escapees from Milano. Major Brik, who had been involved in the clash on the coastal road the day before, spotted two men approaching from the direction of the canal and prepared to fire. Looking again through his binoculars, he saw them waving something white and recognized it as a prayer shawl. One of the pair was Lt. Ilan Gidron, a tank platoon commander and, like Lieutenant Vardi who was killed at Mifreket, the son of a general. He asked for command of a tank, declining Brik's suggestion that he rest from his ordeal for a day or two before going back into battle. The officer was sent to the brigade's maintenance unit in the rear and would join Brik's company later in the day with a repaired tank.

Adan's swift advance was taken both in Umm Hashiba and the Tel Aviv Pit as a portent of Egyptian collapse. However, the Egyptians had not sent forces forward from the canal in this sector and Adan was merely punching air. The mood in the Pit grew buoyant when Gonen asked the air force to stop bombing the Egyptian bridges so that his forces could cross on them. Gen. Rehavam Ze'evi, assistant to Elazar, suggested that tank transporters stand by to shift a division from Sinai to the Golan front as soon as the Egyptians had been driven back across the canal. The chief of staff accepted the proposal. Elazar had no desire to seize territory across the canal except perhaps small bridgeheads for tactical purposes. But on the Syrian front, he saw considerable room for territorial games. "If Gorodish can get back to the canal, I don't need more. But there, in the north, 'The sky's the limit,'" he said to his staff, using the English phrase. "It could be that I bring a division from the canal and go with it to Jebel Druze [a Druze enclave which some Israeli strategists saw ripe for breaking away from Syria] and with another division to Damascus and I don't know where else. Listen, if there's a place to exploit success, it's there."

Elazar realized, however, that he was indulging in fantasy. Talking with several former chiefs of staff, including Rabin, who had become an almost permanent presence in his office since the war's start, he said, "Listen, fellows. This army has launched a counterattack on two fronts thirty-six hours after the war began. Nice? That's first of all. Second of all is 'why isn't it nice enough?' Because the attacks haven't sufficiently developed yet. All it takes is a phone call from Northern Command or Southern saying that their attack has bogged down and we'll be in deeper trouble than we were yesterday."

Dayan urged the seizure of territory across the canal as a deterrent and a bargaining chip. He pressed Elazar to recommend to the cabinet the capture of Port Said at the northern end of the canal. Dayan planned to do so himself but the recommendation would bear more weight if it also came from the army. Elazar was reluctant. "It's too early to talk to the government about this," he said. "If I speak about Port Said, I'm committed. We're now beginning the counterattack. I hope our two divisions cave in their bridgeheads. But they haven't done it yet."

Elazar's caution was more warranted than he imagined. The counterattack by Adan's division that was supposed to begin turning the tide had taken on an oddly static, aimless character. The three brigades were widely separated and were not acting in coordination against any specific target. By ordering Nir to halt with his entire brigade opposite Kantara in case the T-62s emerged, Adan had left Amir's depleted brigade alone at the cutting edge of the southward sweep, with Keren's reserve brigade miles away. Adan agreed to Gonen's request to link up with Hizayon but in the absence of artillery he asked for massive air support. Gonen assured him it would be forthcoming.

Even though Adan had encountered no Egyptian tanks thus far, Gonen was already relating to the destruction of the Egyptian bridgeheads in Sinai as a done deed. With every passing hour, his focus was shifting from eliminating the Egyptian bridgehead in Sinai to launching a counterattack across the canal. Intelligence had passed on an unclear report that an Egyptian brigade commander in the Third Army sector was pulling back. This, combined with the untroubled progress of Adan's division to the Hizayon area, dispelled for Gonen any doubts that he would, on this very day, smash the Egyptian army. (The report from the Third Army of a pullback was connected to its difficulty in cutting openings through the clay soil of the Israeli rampart in that sector. Units were shifted northward to other crossing points.)

Gonen had not internalized the revolutionary nature of what was happening on the battlefield, something the soldiers in the field had quickly grasped. He was aiming to have the Second Army for lunch, as it were, and the Third Army for dinner this very day. His nightcap he expected to savor on the road to Cairo.

It was impossible for Adan to understand Gonen's intentions because his orders were unclear and constantly changing. At 9:20, Adan asked Gonen if he was just to evacuate the garrison at Hizayon or to cross the canal there.

"Before crossing, I want you to destroy all enemy forces that have penetrated," said Gonen, without responding to the question about evacuation.

"The process of reaching Hizayon will *be* a process of destroying forces," noted Adan drily.

"I mean that you should destroy all enemy forces from Milano [the Kantara area] to the end of your sector at Matsmed [a thirty-mile stretch]. After you've destroyed all these forces, cross over."

"I understand," said Adan. What he understood was that he was to break through to the beleaguered garrison at Hizayon but was not to cross the canal until he had reached Matsmed, fifteen miles farther south.

"It's very important that the movement south flows like a stream without a break," said Gonen. "When you get to Matsmed, that's where I intend for you to cross and form up on the Havit line," six miles west of the canal.

Adan said that his third brigade, under Arye Keren, was moving south on the Artillery Road toward the Matsmed area and would execute that part of the mission. "Do you want me to evacuate the men from Hizayon?" he asked again. It was not an idle question since on Saturday there had been an order not to evacuate the garrisons.

"Affirmative."

Gonen summed up the conversation: "So, two important things. To take small footholds, one or two, on the other side and to head south very quickly and cross at Matsmed. Out."

Within the space of a minute, Gonen had given Adan two conflicting orders—the first, to complete his drive south to Matsmed "like a stream" before crossing the canal, and the second, to first recapture at Hizayon and seize "one or two" footholds across the canal before continuing to Matsmed.

Gonen was behaving as if this was a sand-table exercise, with a virtual enemy whose movements could be dictated and an endless array of options for the home side to try out. His most far-reaching option was still to be played. Elazar's plan had called for Sharon to complete the north–south sweep after Adan had reached the midway point. Sharon would roll up the forward elements of the Third Army as Adan had supposedly done with the Second Army. Gonen, however, feared that the Egyptians would pull in their bridges as Sharon advanced south, making it impossible to reach Suez City on the other side. To avoid this, he proposed that Sharon travel around the Third Army bridgehead and strike it on its southern flank. This would make it more likely, he believed, to surprise the Egyptians and to find a bridge intact opposite Suez. Sharon would then send a brigade across to capture Suez City while his other two brigades rolled up the Third Army bridgehead on the Sinai bank from south to north, rather than the other way around. The problem was that it would take at least four hours to make the roundabout movement to the southern end of the line via the Lateral Road, leaving little more than an hour of daylight in which to fight.

When Gonen outlined his new plan to Elazar, the chief of staff tried to talk him out of it. He noted that Sharon would be wasting a whole afternoon in movement instead of engaging the main body of the enemy. Finally, however, he bowed to Gonen's enthusiasm. In the Pit, Rabin expressed surprise at Elazar agreeing to such a far-reaching change to the plan he had spelled out only the night before. "Since it's a borderline case," said Elazar, "let [Gonen] do what he wants."

It was, however, very far from borderline and Elazar's waiving of his own strong instincts out of deference to the commander in the field was a glaring error. Dayan was upset when he heard of the change and called Southern Command for an explanation. The reason offered by Gonen was that a large Egyptian force had crossed the southern end of the canal and was preparing to attack down the eastern coast of the Gulf of Suez toward the oil fields at Abu Rodeis. Speeding Sharon south would permit him to deal with this force, said Gonen, before carrying out the rest of his mission. It was not a reason he had given to Elazar.

Dayan had already begun to have an uneasy sense that the day's counterattack would achieve no significant results. "You don't get the feeling that [the Egyptians] are pulling back," he said in the Pit. "They're still pushing across forces." Elazar shared with his staff his own discomfort about the way the battle was developing. He was unable to get a clear picture of the situation from Gonen and had no idea what was happening with Adan's division. In fact, Adan was just marking time in the desert, waiting vainly for the air force to strike at the Egyptian forces blocking the way to Hizayon, as Gonen had promised, before sending his tanks forward.

Tired of waiting for Adan to complete his sweep southward, three commando officers at Sharon's headquarters drove two miles into the dunes to eat their rations away from the constant shelling and to discuss the situation. They gathered shrubs and had a fire going when shells exploded three hundred meters on either side. Hurrying back to their jeep, they drove two miles farther inland. This time, their coffee was already boiling when they were straddled again by shell fire. To Lt. Col. Amazia Chen and his two comrades, it was clear that Egyptian artillery observers in the dunes behind the Israeli lines were tracking them. Scanning the barren terrain as the jeep sped off, Chen's gaze settled on a saddle between two ridges in the distance that dominated the landscape.

Navigating the dunes on balloon tires, the jeep climbed toward the high ground. As they approached the saddle, Chen detected movement to his immediate front and opened fire with the jeep's machine gun. Descending, he saw a tarpaulin that was rendered almost invisible by a layer of sand that covered it, except for a small opening where he had seen the movement. Inside lay three Egyptian soldiers he had just killed. Fresh tracks led to the other side of the dune. Following them, the commandos spotted Egyptian soldiers fleeing at 120 yards. The Egyptians threw down their guns when they saw the Israelis and raised their hands. One of the Israeli officers, Maj. Danny Wolf, a cigarette dangling from his mouth, approached them from the side as Chen and the other officer—Maj. Meir Dagan, a future head of the Mossad—provided cover. With Wolf twenty yards away and the other two Israelis still upslope, the Egyptians recalculated the odds and dove for their guns. They were killed before they got off a shot. The Egyptians comprised one of the numerous artillery spotting teams that had been infiltrated into Sinai on the eve of the war. The Israelis retrieved the Egyptians' maps, codes, and radios and delivered them to intelligence officers at divisional headquarters.

Colonel Chen, known to all as Patzi, had been enrolled at Israel's Command and Staff College when the war broke out. He was a former commander of the Shaked reconnaissance unit, which had suppressed Palestinian resistance in the refugee camps of the Gaza Strip in a grueling campaign; Wolf and Dagan were also veterans of the unit. Returning from the encounter in the dunes, Chen proposed to Sharon setting up an ad hoc unit to guard the division's flanks and rear against infiltrators. Half the unit would man fixed observation posts and the remainder would ferret out Egyptian observers hidden in the sands. Sharon assented. In view of the bold use the Egyptians were making of commandos, caution was warranted.

At 10:45 a.m. Gonen ordered Sharon to prepare to disengage and move south as a follow-up to "Adan's success." Sharon was staggered. He had been observing Adan's forces from high ground and witnessed no success, only stalled movement. More to the point, the dominant ridges he himself was holding were critical both for blocking an Egyptian advance and as a jumping-off point for an Israeli counterattack toward the canal. The chances of finding an intact Egyptian bridge after a lengthy detour to the southern end of the canal, he believed, were close to nil. He protested in what he would describe as "the strongest terms" and urged Gonen to come forward to see the situation in the field. Gonen, however, insisted on Sharon carrying out his order. "If I didn't obey," Sharon would recall in his memoirs, "I would be dismissed immediately. Immediately. 'Then come down here and see for yourself,' I repeated. 'No,' Gonen shouted. 'You will be dismissed. I will dismiss you right now.'"

Gritting his teeth, Sharon ordered his staff to get the division moving. Unlike in Adan's sector, the Egyptians opposite Sharon's division had moved massive amounts of armor and infantry inland from the canal. His officers protested at moving out before Adan's forces reached them. At their urging, Sharon left behind the division's reconnaissance battalion to defend two key ridges.

Gonen now began urging Adan to proceed in haste to a map sector dubbed Missouri where large enemy concentrations were reported. He did not explain the reason—that he was pulling Sharon's division out of its positions opposite Missouri. "I'm not interested in stretching my forces too thin," replied Adan unhappily. "But if this is very important, I can do it."

"It's important," said Gonen. "And another thing, when you get to Hizayon grab the other side [of the canal] with a small force. It's very

important to me. Afterwards, carry out the main mission at Matsmed."
A few minutes later, he informed Adan that he was drawing up plans
to have him seize "many small footholds" west of the canal.

Thus, in a bewildering series of orders and counter-orders, bordering on the manic, Adan had been told in succession to roll up Egyptian
forces in a thirty-mile-long swath but to keep two miles away from
the canal, to reach the canal in order to cross either at Hizayon or
Matsmed or both on captured bridges, to post forces twelve miles west
of the canal, then six miles, to send entire brigades across, to send
small forces across, to capture Matsmed first, to capture Hizayon first,
to put "one or two" bridgeheads across near Hizayon, to seize "many"
bridgeheads, to proceed south to meet a major Egyptian tank force at
Missouri. All of this presumed that Adan had won the field whereas
he had not yet had his first encounter of the day with Egyptian forces,
which had not penetrated inland in his sector. Worst of all, Gonen left
out of this virtual war game the other player—namely, the Egyptian
army with its new spirit, its new competence, its masses of armor and
artillery, and its suddenly devastating infantry. Adan, with little more
than a half-strength division and no artillery or air support, was being
asked to subdue the better part of three fully intact Egyptian divisions
which had already demonstrated surprising fighting ability. He would
then, according to Gonen's instructions, cross the canal on bridges the
Egyptians would conveniently leave for him and deal with at least one
of the two powerful armored divisions waiting on the west bank. And
all this before nightfall.

Although he was only a short helicopter trip from the front, Gonen
remained in his command bunker at Umm Hashiba, oblivious to the
realities of the field and the perceptions of his field commanders. As
an Israeli analyst would put it, Gonen was commanding from a bunker, not from the saddle.

With the war having just started, Gonen had built-in credit, which
accounted for veteran fighters like Elazar and Adan going along with
his decisions despite rapidly deepening reservations. No one was prepared to acknowledge to himself that the commander of the southern
front was talking gibberish. Even if Gonen's orders seemed absurd or
quixotic, not to say fantastical, Adan assumed the front commander
knew something he didn't, like possible signs of an Egyptian collapse.
Gonen, indeed, had seized on such dubious "signs." In addition, Adan
did not care to begin the war by challenging the decisions of his nomi-

nal superior, regardless of what he thought of him, or to say he was unable to carry out an order. He had performed with distinction as a commander in all of Israel's wars and did not wish to end his military career, a month short of retirement, as someone pleading inability to carry out a mission. He chose to signal his discomfiture indirectly by refraining from expressions of optimism and by repeatedly noting that he had no infantry or artillery. It was a subtlety lost on Gonen. One of Adan's major failings this day was in not vigorously stating his reservations about the assignments given him. His laconic attitude permitted Gonen to continue building on his illusion that Adan's division was controlling the battlefield, an illusion the General Staff came to share. Adan's reticence about speaking his mind fed Gonen's fantasies.

Elazar, for his part, was distracted by the Golan front, where Moussa Peled had started his counterattack. The chief of staff had also spent an hour and a half with the cabinet in the morning during the most confused period of Gonen's decision making. Elazar was kept informed by notes passed into the cabinet room. It was a poor way to understand Gonen's thought process and Elazar was in any case inclined to give Gonen the benefit of the doubt as the commander in the field. It was Elazar, after all, who had appointed him and the chief of staff still thought of him as a tough, competent commander of armor.

Colonel Ben-Ari called Adan shortly after 10 a.m. to report "slight indications" that the enemy had begun to collapse and to urge him to complete his sweep down to Matsmed at maximum speed. "Otherwise they're liable to get away." Half an hour later, Ben-Ari called back. "After finishing with Missouri, we want you to cross at three places." At this point Adan, still a long way from Missouri, moderately balked for the first time. "I wonder what reports you've been getting. Here in the field it looks completely different."

The slack provided Gonen by his fellow generals would soon be cut, but not before October 8 would register as the most ignominious day in Israel's military history, a day in which the IDF in Sinai defeated itself in a dreamlike succession of errors that dashed whatever chance it had of smashing the Egyptian bridgeheads.

The movement of Gabi Amir's brigade toward Hizayon was more drift than purposeful march. While waiting for air support, the force bided its time for close to two hours under heavy artillery fire, constantly moving to avoid presenting a stationary target on the open plain. One of Amir's two battalions was commanded by Colonel Yoffe, which had been savaged Saturday night at Mifreket and Kantara. It came under long-range fire now from tanks and Sagger teams positioned around a palm grove near the canal, two miles north of Hizayon, the brigade's first direct contact with enemy forces this day. The other battalion, a reservist unit commanded by Lt. Col. Haim Adini, a lawyer in civilian life, slowly moved closer to Hizayon. The fort had inscribed itself on the consciousness of those listening to the radio net because of the plaintive pleas by its radioman for rescue. The Egyptians had erected two bridges adjacent to Hizayon and the area was a major crossing point.

With the trauma of Saturday night's battles still fresh, Colonel Amir was uneasy about trying to break through to a canal-side fort again with his depleted brigade. He asked Adan to arrange for a tank battalion from Sharon's division, visible on an adjacent hilltop, to be attached to him for the attack. Adan passed on the request to Gonen, who approved. However, when Amir approached the battalion commander, Maj. Ami Morag, the latter checked with his superiors and was told that Sharon refused. The division was moving south and Sharon wanted to retain all his units.

Accompanying Adini's battalion as it hovered on the Hizayon approaches was the deputy brigade commander, Lt. Col. Shilo Sasson, who was growing increasingly frustrated at marking time when there was a war to be fought. He sensed an opportunity to lunge eastward and capture a bridge. It was, he would later say, a commander's duty to take initiatives. Brigade commander Amir had gone off to search for high ground from which he could see the broad battlefield. In his absence, at 11 a.m., Sasson ordered both battalion commanders— Yoffe and Adini—to move toward the canal. Yoffe, however, broke off and led his tanks to the rear, saying he was out of ammunition and almost out of fuel.

For reservist Adini, Sasson's order was a trumpet blast. He ordered his twenty-one tanks to advance in broad deployment, two companies forward, one to the rear. Dust clouds lifted up around them as they picked up speed. It was a textbook charge and it looked for a while as if it was going to succeed. Adini would compare the experience of a tank charge to an orgasm. There was nothing, he would say, like the smell—a mixture of gunpowder, sweat, and grease—and the sight

from a tank turret of an enemy fleeing before you. He saw them fleeing now, hundreds of Egyptian infantrymen bolting toward the canal.

As the battalion raced across the sandy plain, missile and tank fire
erupted from the rampart across the canal and from the rampart on
the Israeli side. Four tanks on the right flank were hit and began to
burn but the others continued forward. Suddenly, from the seemingly
empty terrain to the front, Egyptian infantrymen rose out of shallow foxholes and unleashed RPGs and Sagger missiles at the charging
tanks.

Just five hundred yards to his front, Adini could see the canal. That
was as close as he got. An Egyptian soldier rose five yards in front
of his tank and hit the turret with an RPG before he was run down.
The explosion wounded Adini, who ordered the battalion to pull back.
Seven disabled tanks were left behind on the battlefield. Of the fourteen that returned, only seven were still fit for battle. Nineteen men
were dead, many others wounded.

Neither the division commander nor the brigade commander had
ordered the attack. There was no artillery or air preparation except
for bombs tossed without visible effect by two aircraft keeping their
distance from the SAMs.

Stunned when he learned what had happened, Colonel Amir
appealed again to Morag to "rescue us." Morag's battalion had already
begun to pull out in order to join Sharon. He halted and once again
contacted his own brigade commander. Amir cut into their conversation to say, "You people are arguing and my people are being slaugh-
tered." The tank commanders in Morag's battalion, who could hear
the exchange on the radio, began to turn their tanks back in order to
go to Amir's assistance. But the order that came down to Morag was
firm—disengage and join the rest of Sharon's division on the Lateral
Road.

When Morag caught up with the division, he saw Sharon on the
roadside and descended from his tank. The abandonment of Amir,
Morag told Sharon, weighed heavily on his conscience. Sharon replied
that he took the responsibility entirely upon himself. There was a
"holocaust" at the Mitla Pass and the division was needed there in all
its strength, he said. Reports of some kind of massive Egyptian incursion were indeed circulating within the division to explain the sudden movement south, but the origin of those reports was never made
clear.

From the hill on which General Adan had positioned himself, he could not see the location of the failed attack and he had only fragmentary radio reports. What he heard did not adequately reflect the blow Adini's battalion had received. Adan's reports to Southern Command thus did little to upset its complacency.

Sharon's division had by this time begun its planned sixty-mile run around the Third Army bridgehead. At 2:15 p.m., with the division strung out over thirty miles, Ben-Ari called the division's operations officer. "All units are to halt in place until further orders," he said. A helicopter from Umm Hashiba landed alongside Sharon's mobile command post shortly afterward and an emissary from Gonen informed him that he was to return to the positions he had abandoned little more than three hours before.

Gonen had received a warning from AMAN that the Egyptians were about to push forward all along the line. At the same time, the reality of Adan's situation was beginning to be grasped for the first time at front headquarters. The division was not destroying Egyptian tanks but was in fact bogged down.

Barely controlling his rage, Sharon ordered his division to execute an about-face, to the bewilderment of all. Gonen, for his part, had a new request for the air force—bomb the Egyptian bridges. He would not be using them.

Meanwhile, Act Two at Hizayon was about to begin, an uncanny repeat of Act One, except worse.

Deciding to attack Hizayon with two brigades, Adan ordered Nir to come down from Kantara, leaving one of his three battalions behind to guard against the T-62 tanks. He directed Nir and Amir to meet in order to coordinate but the division commander did not descend from his lookout point to join them. The brief meeting between the two brigade commanders would only be prelude to further misunderstanding. For reasons not clear, Amir did not mention Adini's failed charge even though Nir was about to attack in the same sector. Nir thought that Amir's brigade would be attacking too. Amir believed his role this time was only to provide covering fire. The absence of Adan's coordination was glaring.

Amir had lost the two battalions he had started out with—Adini's battered force had gone to the rear to reorganize and Yoffe's battalion had been dispatched to another sector. But a new battalion had arrived, commanded by Lt. Col Elyashiv Shimshi. Studying the fort's surroundings through binoculars, Shimshi could make out a mass of tanks and infantry. The Egyptians had seen the dust cloud marking the arrival of Nir's tanks and deduced correctly that the Jews were about to try for Hizayon again. This time the Egyptians would be waiting in even greater strength.

Shimshi was startled when Colonel Amir told him to be prepared to provide covering fire for one of Nir's battalions that would be attacking. How could a single battalion attack an enemy concentration like this? thought Shimshi. And without artillery or air support. Shimshi consoled himself with the thought that the forces in the field had already been fighting since Saturday and presumably knew things he did not. Perhaps they had learned that the Egyptians would collapse at the sight of charging tanks. It was not very convincing but he tried to hang on to the thought.

Battalion commander Assaf Yaguri and his officers had no such illusion. Part of Nir's brigade, they had been at the spearhead of Adan's division since its arrival the day before and knew that the Egyptians were not running at the sight of tanks. Nir had now assigned them the task of breaking through to Hizayon. Yaguri did not know that an Israeli force had only a few hours earlier failed on the same mission. His battalion had passed the survivors from Adini's battalion heading for the rear. They did not respond to Yaguri's gestures to stop but the look on their faces was enough to alert Yaguri and his men to trouble ahead.

As they waited for the brigade commander to return from his meeting with Amir, Yaguri and his company commanders scanned the Hizayon area through binoculars from atop Havraga Ridge, six miles away. It was difficult to make out details because of the glare. "I see something but I'm not sure what," said Yaguri. Over the radio, he heard Nir order the battalion to be prepared to send a platoon across the canal to "join up" with forces already on the other side, an order that had come down from Gonen. "Well, at least we won't be the first this time," said Yaguri's deputy, referring to their spearhead role until now. A report that Israeli forces had crossed the canal had been gaining increasing circulation. It apparently originated with a radio monitor in the Pit who misunderstood a remark on Adan's radio net. Elazar was informed of the report as he was briefing the cabinet and he passed it on to the delight of all present. Glasses were raised in a toast.

The unverified report, however, did not diminish the apprehension of Yaguri and his men. They could make out large clouds of dust near the canal. If a small Israeli force had indeed broken through to the other bank, the Egyptians seemed to have sealed off the passage. A group of Yaguri's officers approached him and said the battalion was being asked to carry out an unreasonable mission. "If you're going, I'm going with you," said a company commander. "But this is suicide." Yaguri believed so too and did not attempt to argue the point. He had urged that more forces be assembled and more information obtained on the enemy disposition before an attack was launched. But the front command was pressing for speedy action.

Upon his return from his meeting with Gabi Amir, Nir did not assemble his officers to brief them but ordered everyone to mount the tanks. To his operations officer, he called, "Bring a lot of cigarettes and get on." For Nir, getting on a tank was an unnatural act. Badly wounded in both legs in the Six Day War while commanding a battalion under Sharon, he had undergone numerous operations in Israel and abroad. His right kneecap was gone and he moved the leg in a stiff, semicircular motion. His left leg was sustained by a metal pin. Climbing into a tank turret was an effort and he sometimes needed help, but he had pressed for a return to field command and it had been granted.

Adan would later maintain that he had not ordered Nir to attack, only to prepare for it. Without artillery, Adan was still waiting for the air force to provide effective close support, not just two planes tossing bombs from a distance. Nir believed he had heard Adan order him and Amir to launch a two-brigade attack toward Hizayon. Once again, as in a bad dream, there was a fatal disconnect between the division commander and his forces in the field. Once again, a planned two-brigade attack would become a one-battalion attack. Once again, the division commander would be surprised to learn that one of his units was attacking.

Nir had intended to carry out a two-battalion attack but one of his battalions had been dueling with forces in the palm grove, as Yoffe had done in the morning, and had lost two tanks and a half-track. Nir told the battalion commander to remain behind and provide covering fire for Yaguri from behind the hillocks in his area.

Yaguri's tanks descended from the ridge and deployed, three companies abreast. Several tanks with mechanical problems fell behind as the force picked up speed. Yaguri told his men to maintain wide dispersal, to move fast, and to keep up constant fire as they closed range. Major Brik's company was on the left flank with Yaguri between him and the middle company. Colonel Nir, at the rear, noticed that Shimshi's battalion was not joining the attack and protested angrily to Colonel Amir on the radio.

Shells began to hit among the tanks and dust swirled up around them as they picked up speed. Yaguri glanced at his deputy in the turret of the tank alongside him. The officer smiled back. Whatever their reservations, they were launched into the attack. Almost a mile from the canal, Egyptian soldiers rose up out of foxholes around them. Sunday's ambush on the coastal road flashed across Brik's mind. With a deafening crash, tank and artillery shells, Sagger missiles, and RPGs exploded around the tanks. A dense cloud of smoke and dust closed in. From what Brik had been able to see, they were plunging into the center of a tight divisional defensive deployment with fire coming from three sides.

To Shimshi, providing covering fire from the south, the scene looked like a Soviet propaganda film from the Second World War—tanks racing heroically at the enemy across a broad front and spewing fire. A more apt comparison would have been to the Crimean War's "Valley of Death" into which the Light Brigade—"theirs but to do and die"—charged to its doom. In the lead were the tanks of Yaguri, his deputy, and one of the company commanders.

Shilo Sasson, Colonel Amir's deputy, who had ridden into the "valley" with Adini that morning after ordering the attack, followed a mile behind Yaguri's force out of curiosity even though this was not his brigade. He saw the battalion moving forward at high speed, well deployed, slightly north of the route that Adini had taken. The ambush this time was sprung eight hundred yards short of Lexicon Road, which Adini had crossed, and the fire was much heavier than that which hit Adini. Tank after tank was hit.

Yaguri survived the opening salvos but when he called his commanders on the radio only Brik responded. The battalion commander's worst fears had come true. His small force was attacking the main bridgehead of the Second Army with no artillery or air cover and was absolutely alone. "Pull back," he called on the radio. "Keep on firing and pull back." Amidst the smoke and noise he didn't know who besides Brik was left to hear him. His own tank lurched as it was hit in the treads and he ordered the crew to get out. With his operations officer, they were five. They raced toward a large bomb crater nearby. Three of them made it. They were joined by a crewman from another tank. APCs sped toward the crater, machine guns firing, but an Egyptian officer ran forward and signaled for them to stop. He took Yaguri and the others prisoner and placed them in an APC.

Brik had been confronting the most difficult dilemma of his life. On the one hand, he believed they were going to the aid of a force cut off across the canal and he was impelled to push through. On the other hand, it was absolutely clear that they could not make it. A battalion of tanks was not going to provide the "armor shock" to stampede an entrenched bridgehead. A shell hit Brik's gun early in the charge, rendering it inoperable, but he continued forward. It was with relief that he heard Yaguri's pullback order. He told his driver to go back in reverse in order not to waste critical seconds turning around. Through openings in the drifting smoke, he saw two men abandoning a disabled tank and took them aboard. Of the eighteen tanks that had charged, only four returned.

Pulling farther back, Brik came upon Nir's tank. The brigade commander was trying futilely to raise Yaguri on the radio. Brik asked for permission to go forward again to see if he could pick up more crewmen. "It's suicide," said Nir. He finally relented and Brik took his tank forward about a mile, sheltering in a depression from which he could scan the landscape. The central feature in the panorama before him was burning Israeli tanks surrounded by hundreds of Egyptian soldiers. Beyond them he saw a hundred Egyptian tanks as well as APCs being formed into line, plainly preparing to attack. Brik hurried back to Havraga Ridge where he rounded up four tanks and descended again to the edge of the plain with them to meet the Egyptians. He opened long-range fire as the enemy tanks came forward. Seven other Israeli tanks took up firing positions on the low hills behind him.

Nir and Amir had meanwhile been summoned by Adan who descended from his hilltop position this time to meet with them. For Adan, this was his worst crisis in four wars. Apart from the two disastrous attacks at Hizayon, his third brigade, under Arye Keren, had lost a strategic plateau called Hamutal five miles to the south to a large Egyptian force and was now staging a counterattack which was running into trouble. Looming ever larger in Adan's mind was the possibility of issuing an order he had never given in his long military career—retreat.

With Nir and Amir, he was bending over a map laid on the sand when aides of both brigade commanders called to report that the Egyptians were attacking. "Get back to your brigades fast," said Adan.

The Egyptians were moving forward with two mechanized brigades—infantrymen, many armed with Saggers and RPGs, flanked by tanks and supported by heavy artillery fire. It was the kind of combined arms operation that Israel had hitherto been unable to muster. The advance was slow and not well coordinated. The Israeli tanks opened fire at long range to keep the infantrymen at bay.

The reports Adan began receiving from his brigade commanders were alarming. "They're coming on a very broad front in huge numbers," said Amir. Nir called urgently for air support. "They're coming in masses," he said. "In masses. We don't have enough strength." The most effective weapon for dealing with the advancing infantry was artillery but there was none.

Nir feared that the Egyptians would overwhelm them and then reach the supply and maintenance units a few miles to the rear, effectively destroying the division. His fear went beyond that prospect; in view of the way the war had been going for the past two days, he feared now for the survival of the country.

Adan, in his command half-track, saw his staff looking at him as he weighed the options. In the end, there seemed only one. "We've got to pull back." Raising Amir and Nir on the radio, he gave the order. In the heat of action, there was no immediate response. Nir switched off his radio to avoid hearing the order repeated.

Brik's impromptu defense line thickened as Shimshi's battalion, Nir's second battalion, and stray tanks joined it. Some fifty tanks from different units, mixed in with one another, were now engaging the approaching Egyptians. The setting sun in the Israelis' eyes made aiming difficult. At one point, Shimshi made out three figures approaching his tanks on foot. They were shouting and waving their arms. He thought he heard Hebrew and told his men to cease fire. The three were survivors from Yaguri's battalion.

When Nir switched his radio back on after ten minutes, he heard Adan, surprised that they had not pulled back, asking him and Amir if they could hold on a bit longer. Both responded affirmatively and said that the Egyptian pressure appeared to be easing. Some Israeli tanks had pulled back on their own but were now returning to the line.

The moment the sun slipped below the horizon and out of the gunners' eyes, the Israeli fire accelerated and became more precise. Columns of smoke marked burning Egyptian vehicles all along the front. Israeli tanks were burning too, but in much smaller numbers. In the last remaining light, scores of Egyptian APCs wove their way around knocked-out tanks and approached the Israeli line. Many were hit and men could be seen leaping from the burning vehicles. The Israeli commanders braced for an infantry attack with Saggers and RPGs. But the Egyptians had had enough. Infantrymen could be seen fleeing to the rear, dark figures receding into a darkening desert.

Elazar had flown to Northern Command immediately after the morning's cabinet meeting and found the mood still depressed despite the relative success of the day's battles there. The Syrians were preparing to throw in more armor and officers were not certain how it would all end. Returning to the Pit at 3:30 p.m., Elazar was startled to hear what had been happening in the south. He had authorized Gonen's changes to his plan on the basis of the front commander's optimistic reports. He realized now that he had permitted his own solid plan to be gutted for naught.

"No, no, I don't want him to get near the rampart," he shouted over the phone at Gonen in a rare display of anger, when Gonen spoke of a renewal of the attack by Adan on Hizayon. Both were unaware of the attack by Yaguri that had occurred shortly before. Adan must stay out of range of the missiles on the ramparts, said Elazar, and confine himself to destroying tanks that had penetrated inland. "He [Adan] should not reach the canal at any point." Hanging up, he vented his anger to aides at the fact that Sharon's division had been sent on a futile runaround. "We've wasted a day," he said. "We've wasted a day." Elazar took comfort in the mistaken understanding that Adan had destroyed much Egyptian armor during his sweep south. As for Gonen, "I don't understand him," he said.

The battle at Hamutal had been no less desperate than at Hizayon. The plateau sat astride an important road leading from Tasa to the canal, opposite Ismailiya. Colonel Keren sent eight tanks there in the early afternoon under battalion commander Dan Sapir. Sapir reported 1,500 Egyptian infantrymen approaching from the direction of Missouri to the south. He fired at them but they kept coming and were joined by tanks. As the infantrymen began firing Saggers, several of the Israeli tanks pulled back. Sapir told the company commander that he had no permission to withdraw. The officer said he was on the verge of being overrun and that his tank commanders had begun to pull back on their own. "I'm not staying here by myself," he said. With his defenses compromised, Sapir received permission from Keren to pull back.

Half an hour before sunset, at Adan's order, Keren launched a counterattack. The force consisted of Sapir's battalion, numbering fifteen tanks, and Yoffe's battalion—comprising twelve tanks—now attached to Keren's brigade. Sapir was killed at the start of the attack and his disheartened force pulled back. Yoffe's tanks raced across the plateau, cutting their way through Egyptian tank formations and infantry. Yoffe's own tank was hit three times and his overheated gun barrel exploded but he continued to lead his men, wielding his machine gun. When only five of his tanks remained operational, he too pulled back.

With darkness, Adan's brigades left screening forces behind and fell back. It had been a long and desperate day marred by excruciating errors of judgment and abysmal battlefield management. The surprise this day was not the newfound capability of the Egyptian military but the bewildering incoherence of the Israeli command. There had been no field intelligence to provide basic information on enemy deployment, accounting for Adan's aimless north–south sweep and the false optimism that arose from his swift progress. The principal cause for the debacle, however, was the bizarre stream of orders issued by Gonen. These had thrown both Adan's and Sharon's divisions off stride and resulted in grievous tactical mistakes. Gonen was the day's choreographer but Adan's performance had been marked by a disastrous absence of control. There were puzzling performances as well at brigade levels. The shock of the surprise attack and the unexpected aggressiveness of the Egyptian army had thrown individual and collective mind-sets out of sync. Adan would recover quickly. His performance as division commander after this day would be regarded both by the high command and his own senior officers as superb. But the day's events had first to be internalized.

Adan's division lost some fifty tanks. More grievous was the profound blow to self-confidence. In this first attack initiated by the IDF in Sinai, failure had been total, except for the impromptu blocking action at sunset. At times during the battle Adan had wondered if he would still have a division when the day ended. Watching his tanks moving through the darkness to rear assembly points in orderly columns, the silhouettes of their commanders erect in the turrets, he was deeply moved. The division had been whipped but it had not broken.

It was clear to all that there were lessons to be learned from this agonizing day. The outcome of the war depended on it.

22

BOMB DAMASCUS

Mounting the podium of the Journalists Association in Tel Aviv Monday night for his first press conference of the war, Elazar sought to offer an anxious nation a measure of reassurance even if that required stretching the parameters of reality. The IDF had launched counterattacks this day, Elazar told the journalists, and was meeting with success. "This war is a serious one but I am happy to say we are already at the turning point." In response to a question about the war's likely length, he declined to commit himself but added: "I can foresee one thing: that we'll continue attacking and striking back at them and that we'll break their bones."

It was a remark that would, when the truth about the day's events emerged, draw criticism as baseless braggadocio that undermined the chief of staff's credibility. However, his words were aimed principally at discouraging the leaders of Jordan and Iraq from throwing in their lot with Syria by depicting the dire fate that awaited it. "Regarding ordinary clashes in peacetime we tell the truth," he would say later. "But in war, it's forbidden to tell the truth."

Given the swift pace of events and the slow ascent of information from the field, the picture Elazar had of the battlefronts much of the day was the reverse of reality. Still unaware of what had happened to Adan's division, he saw a wasted day on the southern front, not a calamity. His concern was focused on the north. The picture Hofi had presented during Elazar's visit to Northern Command was a desperate one when in reality his troops had found a tenuous footing and were beginning to push the Syrians back in places.

Referring to reports that Syrian tanks had almost reached the Upper Customs House, an old Syrian border post just above the Bnot

Yaacov Bridge, Elazar told aides: "There isn't a single [Israeli] tank from there to Haifa. And it's a quick enough drive from Haifa to Tel Aviv." It was urgent, he said, to create a fallback line on the heights and to direct all available resources to the Golan. The canal, he noted, was far from Israel's border, leaving ample room for tactical withdrawals. "As long as I have a few hundred tanks there, I trust the boys to maneuver their way back to the canal. But I don't have any breathing space on the Golan."

The only place on the northern front where Israeli troops this day had in fact fared badly was on the Hermon. Three soldiers who escaped from the outpost on Saturday reached the bottom of the mountain Monday morning, after hiding the previous day on the way down. They told Golani commander Amir Drori that the bulk of the men were still holed up inside the outpost when they escaped. However, their sense of time was distorted; they had not escaped the day before but two days before.

Believing that the men might still be holding out, the Israeli command decided on an immediate rescue operation. Colonel Drori ascended the mountain on its one road with a force of infantrymen in half-tracks, accompanied by several tanks and a bulldozer to clear obstructions. Another force, led by battalion commander Yudke Peled, ascended on foot. Peled's force was stopped by a commando battalion a third of the way up, sheltered behind boulders. Rifle fire at two hundred yards proved ineffective, the curve of the tracers showing how their flight was being bent by the powerful wind. To enable them to close range, Peled ordered his light mortars to fire smoke shells. Clouds scudding along the slope provided additional cover as the troops bounded up from boulder to boulder. At fifty meters, Uzis proved effective. The Syrian battalion finally pulled back, leaving the field to Peled's force, which suffered two dead and eight wounded. However, the vehicular force was ambushed and badly mauled. With a total of twenty-five dead and fifty-seven wounded, Drori ordered a withdrawal.

In the Tel Aviv war room, General Tal suggested dropping plans for a canal crossing and instead sending an amphibious force across the Gulf of Suez. Such a move would outflank the Egyptian army along the canal and threaten Egypt's major oil fields along the gulf. This was a long-standing contingency plan and the navy had tank landing ships

(LSTs) at Sharm el-Sheikh capable of ferrying an amphibious force across. Dayan was willing to consider it but still favored capturing Port Said at the northern mouth of the canal. One way or the other, he said, it was important to seize territory to offset the Egyptian gains in Sinai. Dayan had regained something of his wry humor. When Tal said that Sharon was determined to cross the canal, the defense minister said, "If I know Arik, he'll head straight for Cairo and try to get votes for Likud," a reference to Sharon's recent entry into politics.

Sharon himself was in no mood for levity. He was convinced that an opportunity to turn the war around had been lost this day by the failure to launch his and Adan's divisions against the Second Army bridgehead in a combined attack before the Egyptians had a chance to fortify their positions. Once the Second Army bridgehead was disposed of, they would have dealt with the Third Army. It was still possible, he believed, to collapse the Egyptians by bold action but he no longer had confidence that those running the war, including Elazar, were capable of it. He viewed their caution as reflecting a debilitating loss of self-confidence. The Egyptians, he pointed out, were digging in and laying minefields, not advancing. If they were broken at one point, he was confident that their whole line would collapse. But every passing day would make that more difficult.

Adan did not share Sharon's assessment. The understrength and still unorganized Israeli divisions would have suffered even greater disaster if they had undertaken an all-out attack, he believed. He would argue that on October 8 the army should have attacked only enemy forces which had penetrated beyond two miles from the canal. It would then have held that line until sufficient forces were organized for a breakthrough to the canal and a crossing.

Close to midnight Monday, Elazar flew south to discuss the day's events and determine immediate strategy. Dayan joined him as did Gen. (Res.) Aharon Yariv, Zeira's predecessor as head of AMAN. Yariv had agreed to unofficially assume the duties of army spokesman, a post made critical by the state of the nation's morale. Meeting with his staff before departure, Elazar spoke angrily about Gonen's performance. "I was taken in because I was fed overoptimistic information. If my plan had been carried out, I would be sitting with Arik in Suez [City] now." He was still unaware of the full extent of the day's failures.

The atmosphere in Gonen's headquarters at Umm Hashiba as

the division commanders assembled was heavy with unspoken anger. Adan was the last to arrive. The burden of the day's failure had fallen on him and he felt he had been put in an intolerable position. He was furious over the gross deviations by Gonen from the plan and over the fact that his brigades marked time for hours under heavy shelling while waiting for promised air support that never came. He was unhappy too about the contradictory orders he had received throughout the day. In his one angry aside, he told Gonen that he would wait until after the war before asking for an investigation into why he had been given false information about the Egyptians fleeing and why he had been pressured to cross the canal. Sharon was furious beyond words over his division's runaround and the fact that it had been prevented from coming to grips with the enemy.

The participants had not slept for three days except for brief cat-naps. Despite their exhausted state all recognized the urgent need for quick decisions. Gonen wisely kept the discussion from deteriorating into an angry analysis of what went wrong. Inept though his performance had been, he had not lost his nerve. He began with a terse review of the day's events and a report on current strength, 590 tanks. Sharon urged an attack across the canal. He said the crossing could not depend on the capture of Egyptian bridges, which he regarded as unlikely. The IDF must bring forward its own bridges. While avoiding direct criticism of Gonen, he said that if a two-division attack had been carried out this day, no Egyptian would have been left east of the canal. "Sometimes you've got to gamble," he said.

General Mendler agreed with Sharon's call for a canal crossing. Adan, however, said the IDF would have to build up its strength before attacking again. In addition, the use of the Israeli bridges was problematic. They would have to be towed at least five miles through the Egyptian bridgehead before reaching the canal. Gonen had been sobered by the day's events. "It may not sound popular, but I'm against crossing the canal with our present strength." Like General Tal, he now proposed attacking across the Gulf of Suez.

Elazar learned for the first time at the meeting that Adan had hardly encountered Egyptian tanks during his southward sweep, had suffered considerable losses, and at the end of the day had been forced to withdraw. Sharon's division had been run in circles and accomplished nothing. The battle, in short, had been totally bungled. After hearing out his generals, Elazar said that Southern Command would restrict itself in the coming days to defensive action and keep its losses to a minimum while repairing damaged tanks and building up its strength. The IDF would meanwhile focus on knocking Syria out of the war. Elazar left open the option of resuming the offensive in Sinai later in the week, perhaps by attacking Port Said, the easiest target of all across the canal. Sharon objected that Port Said, isolated on the marshy northern flank, was a sideshow that would have no impact on the outcome of the war. Victory, he said, could only be achieved by crossing the canal on the main part of the battlefield. Unlike Dayan, who wanted the port city as a diplomatic bargaining chip in postwar negotiations, Sharon was intent on going for the enemy's jugular—plunging into the center of his line and throttling him until he surrendered. He asked for permission to cross at Kantara in two days with his division. Elazar said he would keep that option open.

On the flight back to Tel Aviv, Dayan and Elazar lost themselves in their own thoughts, freed by the noise of the helicopter from any obligation to converse. The grievous failure of the counterattack in Sinai, whose full extent they had only now learned, together with the failure of the Golani Brigade to retake the Hermon earlier in the day, made it apparent that the strategy of the war had to be rethought. The high command had been thrown badly off balance and was facing the prospect of a prolonged conflict. Dayan had returned to his back-to-the-wall mode. This time, however, it was as a clearheaded war leader with a pragmatic agenda, not as a demoralizing prophet of doom. He spelled out his thoughts upon their return to the Pit before dawn Tuesday.

The nation was facing a major crisis, the defense minister said to the officers who gathered in Elazar's room, and it had to make painful adjustments. Large nations, like Britain and the Soviet Union, had undergone similar crises in war, he noted. The Israeli public would take it hard when it learned that the IDF could not throw the Egyptians back across the canal but there was no way around it. "We have to tell the nation the truth."

In order to knock Syria out of the war before Jordan and Iraq joined in, Dayan said, extreme measures were justified. The war had disproven many of the IDF's basic assumptions. "We thought our tanks could stop the Egyptians from putting up bridges but we didn't imagine the forest of antitank missiles. The air force had plans for eliminating the antiaircraft missiles but they didn't work. We have to learn life anew. The Arab world has gone to war. They have much power and we must understand that there is no magic formula."

To cope with the possibility of a protracted conflict, the IDF had to build up its strength swiftly, he said. The mobilization pool had to be expanded to include men in higher age brackets. The IDF should explore the possibility of giving seventeen-year-olds advanced training, particularly those youths qualified for pilot courses and those destined for the armored corps, so that when they were drafted at eighteen they would be ready sooner for active service. Additional armaments on a large scale were essential and request lists must be prepared for Washington. More immediately, antitank weapons similar to those which had proven so effective in the hands of the Egyptian infantry must be distributed "to the whole country" in the event that enemy armor reached Israel's heartland. This startling proposal indicated the magnitude of the danger Dayan saw confronting the nation.

As for the battlefronts, a suitable fallback position had to be prepared in Sinai, a line which could be held under any circumstances. This might be well to the rear of the Gidi and Mitla Passes, hitherto considered the ultimate fallback line—perhaps a line running from Sharm el-Sheikh to El Arish, two-thirds of the way back to the Israeli border. "It may be that I'm more pessimistic than Dado [Elazar]," said Dayan of his fallback proposal. "Maybe it's the age difference." On the Golan there was no room to pull back. "We fight there until the last man and we don't fall back a centimeter. If we lose all our tanks there we'll lose them but the Syrian force will be destroyed too." He would repeat this later. "Even if we lose all our armor we must bring the battle in the north to a decision."

Commanders at all levels who cannot carry out this mission must be replaced, Dayan said. After his visit to Northern Command Sunday morning, he told Elazar that Hofi was "tired and depressed" and that part of the problem was that he was a foot soldier, not a tank officer. Dayan had proposed that veteran commanders be sent north to bolster him. He now suggested that Elazar consider replacing Hofi—not dismissing him, but placing someone else alongside him in effective command.

Gonen clearly had to be replaced. Command of the southern front, said Dayan, was simply beyond him. One possibility was to have Sharon take over the post, which he had vacated only three months before. Dayan also proposed another candidate—Bar-Lev.

It was of paramount importance to knock Syria out of the war, the minister said, both because of the threat to northern Israel and because of the IDF's need to quickly push one of its enemies out of the war so that it could concentrate on the other. It was easier to get Syria out of the way first. To bring the war in the north to an end all possibilities must be examined, "even the wildest, including the bombing of Damascus. . . . My recommendation is to make a maximum effort—I permit myself to say brutal effort—till we force them to end the war. It is within our capacity to do this, which is not the case on the Egyptian front."

Although Dayan would in decision-making forums push for the army to reach within fifteen miles of Damascus so as to put the city within range of its long guns, he would indicate more than once in conversations with Elazar that he would not be averse to reaching Damascus itself if that were possible. (Kissinger was also encouraging Israel to move toward the Syrian capital in order to have more muscle at the negotiating table. "When you reach the suburbs you can use public transportation," he quipped to Dinitz.)

Dayan's unsparing remarks challenged any lingering illusions on the General Staff that the initial Arab successes were an unfortunate fluke that would soon be set right as the IDF regained its stride. This was a new kind of war and Israel would have to quickly refocus if it was to save itself.

After Dayan's departure, Elazar picked up on the theme of attacking the Syrian hinterland. The air force, he told his staff, should halt its attacks on Syrian air bases and instead go after four major cities—Damascus, Homs, Aleppo, and Latakia. "To destroy them. I need something effective and dramatic that will make the Syrians cry 'gevalt' [woe, in Yiddish] and stop shooting. To hit their power stations, everything." Despite the ferocious-sounding remarks, Elazar did not speak of attacking civilian quarters, and in fact none would be attacked.

Air Force Commander Peled, who had been scornful of the depressed mood among many in the Pit—the Holocaust Basement, as he would bitingly refer to it—was himself jarred by the report of the failed counterattack in the south. His colleagues in the air force war room found him pale when he returned from the meeting with Dayan and they shared his shock when he told them what had happened. Just as the ground forces expected the air force to sweep the skies clean and

provide close support, the air force never doubted that the tank formations, once unleashed, would demolish the Egyptians. The air force
was now as disappointed, and shaken, by the failure of the armored
corps—normally its rival for budgets and glory—as the latter was by
the air force's suddenly revealed inability to provide close support.

The hard truth about the country's military situation was presented
to Prime Minister Meir by Dayan, Elazar, and Zeira at a 7:30 a.m.
meeting Tuesday in her office. Also present were General Yariv and
Meir's closest advisers, ministers Galili and Allon. Dayan began by
saying that there was at present no possibility of approaching the
canal, let alone crossing it, because of the antitank weapons in the
hands of the Egyptian infantry. The IDF's immediate emphasis must
therefore be on persuading Syria to seek a cease-fire. Toward this
end, he proposed bombing military targets in Damascus. The Syrians had fired close to a score of FROG ground-to-ground missiles
at the Ramat David Air Base over the past three nights. FROGs hit
the air base and killed a pilot in a dormitory. But many of the missiles
hit nearby civilian settlements—like Kibbutz Gvat and the town of
Migdal Haemek—and wounded a score of people. This was enough
to justify an Israeli attack on Syrian urban areas and infrastructure.
"We've got to hit their General Staff headquarters, their Air Command, their electricity," said Dayan. "Our targets are military but we
can't rule out the possibility that civilians will be hurt."

Mrs. Meir was uneasy at the idea. "Can we begin by attacking targets on the periphery of the city, like the power station?" Elazar said
that was possible but the object of an attack was "to dramatize the
situation and bring a turning point."

Mrs. Meir expressed fear that an attack on Damascus might impact
on anticipated arms deliveries from the U.S. "We would be the first to
attack a city." Couldn't we begin by hitting something outside the city?
she repeated. Zeira said there were many targets outside Damascus,
including the largest power plant in the country in Homs, but that
nothing would have the impact of an attack inside Damascus. King
Hussein, he said, was weighing the possibility of entering the war and
he would not be deterred by an attack on a power station.

Dayan said an attack on targets in Damascus could shock Syria's
leaders into considering whether it was worthwhile continuing the war.
"Their situation is bad," he said. At least three hundred Syrian tanks
had already been knocked out.

Referring to the southern front, Dayan said a fallback position must be prepared but he was not recommending that the IDF retreat to it unless it became necessary. The defense minister said he believed it would be possible at a later stage to push the Egyptians back across the canal but the IDF must first reorganize. He proposed bringing back into service members of the "old guard"—retired officers with battle experience—to shore up the IDF command. Older persons must be drafted and even recruitment of Jews from abroad should be looked into. Victory, in short, was not around the corner.

Israel had prepared for a war lasting five days, said Elazar. "We are not built for a war that lasts months." Israel's military industries were working around the clock to produce ammunition but this was insufficient. The supply of arms and ammunition from the U.S. could make the difference between success and failure. Ambassador Dinitz had been pressing American officials but Washington had not yet shaped its policy regarding a major arms airlift. Meanwhile, seven unmarked El Al planes continued to ferry emergency supplies.

The prime minister raised what she called "a crazy thought"—that she travel incognito to Washington for twenty-four hours in the company of a senior officer to make a personal appeal to President Nixon to meet Israel's arms requests swiftly and in full. The administration, she believed, was not fully cognizant of Israel's situation. Not even the Israeli cabinet need know of her visit. Dayan supported the idea. (However, Kissinger, who doubted that such a visit could be kept secret, would veto the proposal when Dinitz broached it. "To have the prime minister of Israel leave the country in the middle of a war to plead for help could be interpreted by the other side as a sign of enormous weakness.") Before the meeting ended, Dayan proposed that he appear on television this night, the fourth of the war, to offer "straight talk" to the Israeli public.

Elazar, as usual, was not as gloomy as the defense minister. Instead of focusing on the possibility of retreat in Sinai, he concerned himself with holding firm on the present line. Nevertheless, he authorized preparation of a fallback line at the passes if retreat became necessary. A general would be dispatched to Sinai to oversee the work. Elazar intended to wait near the Artillery Road for the Egyptian armor to attack. He was confident that the encounter would significantly erode enemy tank strength. At that point—and not before, as Sharon was urging—the IDF would stage a canal crossing. There must be no more attempts, he said, to rescue garrisons holding out on the Bar-Lev Line. Elazar was not aware of it but more than a score of tanks and one hundred men had already been lost in the attempts to reach Hizayon with its twenty-one-man garrison.

Despite the urging of her generals, Mrs. Meir was still uneasy about bombing in Damascus. When she put the question to Minister Galili, he said, "We have to do it." Meir bowed to his judgment and had a message sent to Kissinger stating that the object was to knock Syria out of the war and dissuade Jordan and Iraq from joining in.

Returning from an early bombing run on the Egyptian front Tuesday morning, Maj. Arnon Lapidot stopped in at the Phantom squadron's operations room at Tel Nof Air Base to check the teleprinter. As deputy squadron commander, it was Lapidot's task this day to assign crews to the missions received from air force headquarters. The mission list had arrived and Lapidot was jolted to see that it included Damascus. Eight planes were to attack Syrian General Staff headquarters and the adjacent air defense headquarters in the heart of the city. Why us? was his first thought. The war until now had been brutal enough. But the air defenses around the Syrian capital would be more murderous than anything they'd yet seen. Even during the Six Day War when they were dealing only with conventional antiaircraft guns, the approaches to Damascus had been a rough ride.

There were only two pilots in the squadron with the experience to lead a raid as hazardous as this and one of them was Lapidot. Loath to dump it on his mate, the twenty-seven-year-old kibbutznik assigned himself the task.

In selecting pilots and navigators for the mission, Lapidot chose men not only for their skill but also their nerve. By now, everyone felt fear, unlike the first day of the war when it had been tally-ho and an eager rush for action. One eighth of the entire air force—forty-nine planes—had been shot down in just four days and almost the same number significantly damaged. Every time they went up—which they did three or four times a day—the airmen were narrowing their odds for survival. Some men coped with these odds better than others.

One of the pilots Lapidot chose was American-born Joel Aronoff, a graduate of the U.S. Air Force Academy, who had flown more than two hundred combat missions with Phantoms in Vietnam before mustering out in 1969 and emigrating to Israel. With the IAF just beginning to absorb Phantoms, his application to join was accepted in a rare departure from normal practice. Aronoff was the one pilot in the world able to compare firsthand the Soviet-made Arab air defenses with the Soviet-made defenses fielded by the North Vietnamese. After his first foray over the Suez Canal on Yom Kippur afternoon, he reported that ground fire was "much more than anything I ever saw in Vietnam." The Israeli pilots had listened with interest to his experiences evading SAMs over North Vietnam but he was the first to admit that they were far better pilots than he, particularly in air-to-air combat. Lapidot chose him because the cheerful American had demonstrated his coolness in combat in the past few days.

Examining the latest air photos showing the deployment of Syrian antiaircraft guns, Lapidot sharpened a pencil and drew a flight path that would avoid most of them. It was impossible to avoid all. The planes would fly low all the way to target to avoid revealing themselves to enemy radar. The main hazard would thus be the conventional antiaircraft guns, which were effective up to 4,500 feet. Lapidot decided that he would lead the planes in over the mountains north of Damascus, which meant a wide swing through Lebanon.

In case they went off-course for whatever reason and had to take new bearings, Lapidot chose a landmark recognizable from low level that would permit them to pivot toward their target without breaking stride. Otherwise, they would have to climb to see where they were and thus expose themselves. The landmark he picked on the map was a disused British airfield from the Second World War at Ya'at in the Bekaa Valley.

Lapidot completed the plan in forty-five minutes and briefed the crews. Their faces were somber and there were few questions. Before moving out to the aircraft, Lapidot left a little time as he always did for the men to commune with themselves. Some would be running through the attack plan in their heads, some might want to make a phone call, others had to make closure. From the time they climbed into their cockpits, there would be little time for thoughts beyond the business at hand.

Heading out to sea, the flight turned north. Off the coast of Lebanon, Lapidot saw a ship with large white containers on the deck, apparently a spy ship top-heavy with electronic equipment. He could not distinguish its nationality but made a worst-case assumption—that it was Soviet and that the Syrians already knew that eight planes would soon be penetrating their airspace. However, they could not know where the planes were headed.

Half an hour after takeoff Lapidot turned inland at Jounieh, a Lebanese Christian resort city just north of Beirut. From an altitude of three hundred feet, its hotels and casinos were clearly visible. As they crossed the coast, Lapidot saw in his mirror one of his planes turn back. Radio silence was being maintained and he assumed, correctly, that the plane had experienced a malfunction.

He led the planes eastward up a broad wadi cutting through the Lebanese mountains. Villas were perched on wooded slopes on either side, as in a Swiss postcard. Roaring up the canyon at 500 knots, the planes passed below high-tension lines spanning the tops of the mountains. Clouds were piling up, leaving little clearance above the mountaintops. As rain began to fall, visibility became difficult. Partway through the mountain barrier, the wadi lost its eastward orientation and turned north. Lapidot had planned to rise over the mountains at this point in order to continue flying eastward toward the Damascus basin. By skimming the mountaintops, he could avoid being picked up by Syrian radar. However, he would now have to rise above the clouds, which would put him on the Syrian screens.

The pilots behind him wordlessly took a spread formation aimed at avoiding collisions when passing through clouds. They had often drilled for this eventuality and needed no radio command. They broke into pairs, a mile between each pair. Within each pair, the planes took position two hundred yards apart, one above the other.

Lapidot, however, decided to stick with the wadi, even though it was now taking them off course. The other planes dutifully followed. The wadi debouched into the Bekaa Valley, still inside Lebanon, and the planes dove down to hug the valley floor. They were now well off course but Lapidot spotted the fading gray runways of the old Ya'at airport almost indiscernible amidst the green and brown fields worked by Syrian farmers. He turned gently and headed southeast toward Damascus on his new bearings.

One more mountain range lay between the Israeli planes and the Syrian capital—the so-called Anti-Lebanon. As they raced toward it, Lapidot saw that the mountains were completely covered with clouds. There was no wadi that would take them through the barrier and not even a squirrel hole between the mountaintops and the clouds through which they might squeeze.

To fly into a missile zone above clouds meant near-certain death. In a cloudless environment, a warplane—particularly an agile and powerful plane like the Phantom—had a reasonable chance of dodging a missile if the pilot began maneuvering when he spotted the missile far below. But in heavy overcast, the missile will emerge from the midst of the clouds, too close for the pilot to react.

For the first time, Lapidot thought about aborting the mission. But he suddenly recalled a lecture he heard from a meteorologist during his pilot training course. Humid air coming off the sea is pushed upward when it encounters a mountain mass and forms clouds. However, where the other side of the mountain falls away into desert, the relative humidity is lowered and the clouds on that side will soon dissipate. Lapidot also knew this from Mount Gilboa in northern Israel—the desert-edge mount on which King Saul died in battle against the Philistines and which subsequently bore David's curse, "Let there be no rain or dew upon you." On the other side of the Anti-Lebanon range, just beyond Damascus, was the Syrian desert. Might not the clouds on that side of the mountains be thinner than on this side? Making a quick calculation, Lapidot reckoned that if he went above the clouds he would have a minute's flying time before the missile radars picked him up. If the clouds didn't disappear in that time, he would turn back. He hoped at least to encounter some MiGs on the way home so that it would not have been a totally wasted mission.

Pulling his stick back, he climbed above the clouds and leveled off at twelve thousand feet. The six other planes tagged behind. The cloud cover was thin—only some two thousand feet—but it was full, offering no holes to dive through. Within half a minute, however, the clouds grew ragged and then disappeared, just like the meteorology lecturer had suggested. The planes dove, leveling off one hundred feet above the ground.

In going above the clouds they had been picked up by regional Syrian radar but not by the missile radars. Lapidot could see on his sensors that a SAM radar was groping for them but they were too low for it to lock on. According to the flight plan, a conventional anti-aircraft battery still lay in their path. There was no way to avoid it if they wished to remain on course. As it came into view, the pilots could see the gun crews below swiveling the barrels and firing but the shots missed. The planes swayed upward slightly behind Lapidot to pass over a high-tension line.

Damascus now lay dead ahead and there was no longer need for radio silence.

"Pull up," said Lapidot. In air force headquarters in Tel Aviv, where the flight's radio frequency was being monitored, it was the first sign of life.

As the nose of his plane rose, Damascus appeared below. The city was densely built, as ancient urban centers are, most of the buildings only three or four stories high. It was not a large city and it was surrounded by orchards and palm trees. Lapidot was enchanted. Asphalted streets glistened from a recent shower that had washed the city clean. Damascus, he would recall, glowed "like a bride in a church."

He had decided that the attack would be made from ten thousand feet, in order to keep well above the range of the antiaircraft guns. He had ten seconds in which to climb, pick out his target in the midst of the city, align his sights, and release his bombs.

"One going in," he said. Each plane would announce itself in numerical order as it began its run in order to ensure that they kept out of each other's way. As he climbed, Lapidot quickly scanned the cityscape for landmarks. He saw the stadiums he had circled on his map, Mazeh Air Base just west of the city, and then, in the midst of the urban matrix, his target, the V-shaped General Staff headquarters. Even though it was only seven stories high, it projected distinctly above the surrounding buildings. Antiaircraft guns opened on him as he entered his dive.

Buffeting from a strong side wind made it difficult for him to align on the base of the V as he intended. Heading toward the building at a slant angle of 30 degrees—an angle chosen to ensure that the bomb penetrates its target instead of bouncing off like a pebble thrown into a pond—he pressed the bomb release button on his control stick a mile from target. Eight 500-pound bombs fell away, giving the plane a slight bounce as it freed itself of their weight. Lowering a wing to clear his line of sight, Lapidot saw smoke blossoming on the northern wing of the building. There was smoke too in the street beyond, indicating that the wind had carried some bombs wide of the target. The detonators had been set so that the bombs exploded deep inside the building, down to the second floor where the main offices were believed to be.

"Two going in." The other planes were beginning their attack. Once their bombs were released, each pilot would have to wend his own way through the curtain of antiaircraft fire until the flight could re-form.

The exit route Lapidot had chosen followed the Damascus–Beirut highway. The antiaircraft guns had gone wild, attempting to make up for having been outflanked. Wherever Lapidot looked below, he saw the feverish sparkle of guns, all being fired at him. Unlike the antiaircraft ordnance of the Second World War which dotted the sky with dark puffs, these guns left few marks in the sky but their deadly outpouring was far more prodigious. Like a cornered animal fighting for its life, Lapidot hurled his plane, flying now at 4,500 feet, in wild gyrations, undertaking pendulum swings a mile wide as he dodged the fire.

From the start of his climb on the approach to Damascus to the point where he finally outran the gunfire on his exit only forty seconds passed. But they taxed every physical and moral fiber of his being. Dry mouthed, he headed into the calmer skies of Lebanon to catch his breath and await the others. The radio, however, brought a chilling one-word report: "Parachute." It was at once bad news and worse news. Parachute meant that a plane was down. Parachute in the singular meant that one of its two crewmen had gone down with it.

Lapidot asked the planes to report. Number Three was missing. In addition, the pilot of Number Five, Omri Afek, reported both engines aflame. Lapidot could hear Afek's wing mate, Joel Aronoff, describing the damage to Afek in his mangled Hebrew—"small fire left engine, big fire right engine." Afek closed the engines down in succession and then, despite considerable risk of explosion from leaking fuel, restarted one. Shepherded by Aronoff, Afek took the direct route back to Israel, risking ground fire along the way, rather than follow Lapidot and the others the long way around through Lebanon. Afek skillfully nursed the plane over the Hermon and descended toward Ramat David, Israel's northernmost airfield. The Phantom's hydraulic system and steering mechanism were defunct and so were the rear parachute that could have slowed the plane down and the emergency hook that could have grappled restraining wires. The burning plane hurtled down the runway, only partially slowed by the failing brakes. It was finally stopped by a net raised at the end of the runway.

In debriefing, it emerged that damage to the buildings in Damascus had been moderate. All the bombs that struck army headquarters had hit the northern wing.

Of the two planes which attacked Air Defense headquarters, one had had a malfunction and its bombs fell short by thirty yards, damaging a Soviet cultural center, where a number of Soviet personnel were killed and wounded. A television station was also hit accidentally.

But the attack on the military nerve center in the heart of Damascus, the most heavily defended patch of Syria, helped reestablish Israel's deterrent image. It mattered little that damage was limited and that the Syrian military hierarchy was anyway in underground war rooms elsewhere. There would be no more FROG missiles fired at Israel.

In the basement of Syrian army headquarters, Lt. Avraham Barber, a Phantom pilot downed in the Dougman operation two days before, was being interrogated when the bombs hit. The lights went out and dust filled the room. Barber was blindfolded and rushed outside. He knew there were other pilots in the basement and assumed they were being led out too. Rubble crunched under his feet before he was thrust into a vehicle.

According to information Israel later received, the Syrians believed that Israeli intelligence had known of the pilots' presence in the basement and had aimed their bombs so as to spare them. Barber also believed that Israeli intelligence must have known the airmen were in the building but he believed the mission planners were trying to kill them, not spare them. It was a dark thought based on what he had seen so far of the war. First had come the surprise of the Arab attack, then the sudden cancellation of Tagar and the squadron's hasty dispatch north to execute an improperly prepared Dougman. The first Syrian intelligence officer to question him said he had been listening to Israel Radio's Arabic service and it was clear that Israel was going under. You're lucky you're here, said the Syrian, not unsympathetically. Barber had arrived in Damascus blindfolded and did not know what building he was being taken to. But of all the buildings in Syria, it was the one the air force had chosen to bomb. He assumed that the desperate Israeli leadership had decided that the pilots must be killed to prevent them from talking. "Things must be in a bad way at home," he mused. The thought would dissipate within a few days. Unknown to Barber, the bombing had been carried out by his own squadron.

Returning to base, Lapidot and his crews had little time to dwell on the Damascus mission since they were scheduled to set out for other missions in a couple of hours. He learned for the first time that his was one of three squadrons that were supposed to attack Damascus this day. One flight had taken a different route and encountered the storm system that had just washed Damascus. Unable to find a chink in the clouds, the flight leader aborted. On his way back, he was directed to the Golan Heights where he dumped his bombs on Syrian positions. The third flight was canceled before taking off.

The attack on Syrian army headquarters would win Lapidot and his navigator the country's second-highest decoration. It was not, however, the pilot's most trying experience of the war. This would come two days later when he led a second attack in the area of Damascus, this time on the Syrian air force's wartime operations center, hidden beneath an orchard on the city's outskirts.

As they neared the area, Lapidot identified the target amidst a sea of orchards. All that was visible aboveground were eight air vents, each a square meter in size. As Lapidot was going into his attack, two SAM missiles were fired in the distance. Still dogged by the loss of his comrades over Damascus two days before, he turned to see if the SAMs were endangering the rear planes in the flight. When he turned back to his targeted air vent he could not find it and dropped his bombs aimlessly on the orchard. The only pilot to score a direct hit was the one who had aborted over Lebanon during the previous attack.

The attacks on the Syrian capital would be followed by 130 sorties against ports, refineries, power stations, bridges, and other infrastructure. These were only a tiny fraction of six thousand sorties the IAF would carry out on the Syrian front. The infrastructure attacks were painful for Syria but not enough for it to quit. The attacks deprived Syria of half its fuel capacity but replacement fuel was trucked in from Lebanon and Iraq. Roads and bridges were destroyed but alternate routes were organized. The worst damage was caused by the bombing of two power stations near Damascus, which knocked out 80 percent of the country's electricity supply. Although they doubtless had a psychological impact on the Syrian leadership and eroded the country's staying power, these strategic strikes would fail to knock Syria out of the war. The bombing brought home the cost of the war to the Syrian population at large—something that might be borne in mind in the future—but had no visible impact on the battlefield. In a relatively brief war, it would be developments on the front line, not limited strategic bombing, that would decide the outcome.

23

TOUCHING BOTTOM

TUESDAY WOULD BE FOR MANY in the Israeli command the worst day of all. It was when they learned the dimensions of the failed counterattack in Sinai and realized that their expectations of a quick turnaround in the war were an illusion. As General Tal would describe it later, "We didn't have any reserves left, there was nothing left. The war was perceived not just as at a critical, almost hopeless, stage but as a struggle for our very physical survival."

The low point came with the return of Dayan and Elazar from Umm Hashiba and the briefing they gave in the Pit. After their departure, a heated discussion developed among the officers who had heard Dayan's somber remarks. Two officers, one of them a general who in time would become a right-wing Knesset member, spoke of the need to take "extreme measures." According to accounts that emerged after the war, the pair spoke of resorting to emergency plans kept in the safe of the General Staff's operations section. Others, including General Tal, forcefully objected. In Tal's adjacent office, his bureau chief listened with some alarm to the rising tones until someone closed a door. Tal was the first to emerge. In his office, he related the gist of the discussion to his aide. An agitated staff officer, emerging half an hour later, said to Tal: "You've got to do something. They're going to destroy the country."

The deputy chief of staff calmed him down. Elazar would not go along with the hard-liners, he said, and neither would the government. None of the officers present was aware that Prime Minister Meir had rejected Dayan's suggestion two days before to consider a nuclear demonstration.

The editors in chief of Israel's daily newspapers were escorted into the depths of Moshe Dayan's gloom Tuesday evening. His background talk with them was part of his decision to "level with the nation." The IDF, he told them, was doing well on the Golan and would soon regain the territory it had lost there. But on the southern front Israel did not at present have the strength to throw the Egyptians back across the canal. Nowhere in the world, said Dayan, including the Soviet Union and Vietnam, was there such a dense deployment of modern Soviet weaponry. The war, he said, was against Soviet weaponry more than against the Arabs. Israel might have to withdraw deep into Sinai, and this carried far-reaching implications. "The world has seen that we are not stronger than the Egyptians. The aura, and the political and military advantage of it being known that Israel is stronger than the Arabs and that it would beat them if they go to war, this has not been proven here."

Dayan's harsh appraisal stunned his listeners. An editor asked whether the assumption shared by Israelis that the country could cope with any Arab attack, even one involving all the Arab states, was no longer true. "On the contrary," Dayan hastened to respond, recognizing the implications of his words. "We can stand against all the Arab states, against all the Soviet equipment."

Nevertheless, the editors were aghast when Dayan said he intended to address the nation on television this night. Even though he said he would speak in less stark terms than he had to them, they feared that his appearance would demoralize an already shaken nation. An editor close to Mrs. Meir called her to express his concern. She had already experienced the demoralizing effect of Dayan's unvarnished truth and asked him to let General Yariv appear instead. In a much praised television address that night, the former intelligence chief doled out the truth to the Israeli public in doses that could be swallowed. He offset the bitter taste not by fabrication but by offering optimism.

Inside Hizayon, Egyptian commandos penetrated the fort's trenches Monday afternoon and were driven off only after the garrison took cover in the bunkers and called down artillery on the fort itself. At 5:15 p.m. the acting commander notified his superiors that they could hold out no longer.

Radioman Maimon passed the word to the men in the bunkers on the intercom: "We're going to surrender." In the medical bunker, Dr. Ohri turned to the others with him and said, "Not yet." From the courtyard outside, Maimon could be heard calling on the loudspeaker in Arabic, "We surrender." In Sergeant Strolovitz's bunker, he and the four men with him likewise decided not to go out. One of the men suggested suicide, another that they go out shooting. The sergeant said that they would wait until night and try to get back to the Israeli lines.

With darkness, Strolovitz led his squad toward the gate. But as they approached, they heard voices of sentries and returned to the bunker. In the morning, Strolovitz left the bunker to surrender and was shot at. He tried again and this time he and the others were taken prisoner. As they were led away, they saw the bodies of the men from the command bunker lying in the courtyard, their hands tied behind their backs. Unaware of the fate of the others, Dr. Ohri remained in the medical bunker with the wounded commander of Hizayon, Lieutenant Bareli, and three other soldiers.

Most of the forts had by this time been abandoned or captured. The thirteen-man garrison at Fort Lakekan on the northern end of the Bitter Lake was ordered Sunday afternoon to pull back. When night fell, they and seven crewmen from disabled tanks who had joined them climbed aboard the post's solitary half-track and headed east. Avoiding roads, they climbed with difficulty through the dunes. Nearing Artillery Road, they stopped and moved forward on foot until they heard Hebrew being spoken. The tankers who received them were astonished that they had made their way through the Egyptian lines.

At Fort Matsmed, five miles north of Lakekan, hundreds of Egyptian infantrymen attacked Monday afternoon. The attackers reached the barbed wire but were driven back. When the attack resumed, the defenders hit two tanks with bazookas and the attackers pulled back again. The fort commander, Capt. Gideon Gur, called for artillery but few shells fell. This was the third day of battle and the thirty-five-man garrison had only one bazooka shell left. With night coming on, Gur thinned out his outposts to let as many men as possible get some sleep.

Thick fog covered the area Tuesday morning when the sound of tanks was heard again. Gur sounded the alarm and the men rushed to their posts. The tanks were no more than twenty yards from the main gate when they loomed out of the fog. Infantry followed close behind. This time the attack could not be stopped. Gur called again for artillery but there was none. He ordered the men into the bunkers. The Egyptians poured into the compound, throwing fragmentation grenades and smoke grenades into the bunker entrances. The defenders managed to throw some back but men began to choke. At 8 a.m. Tuesday, Matsmed surrendered.

Fort Purkan had been spared attacks since Yom Kippur afternoon except for occasional rounds from heavy mortars. With the Egyptians building up strength, rescue was becoming increasingly unlikely. Major Weisel spent much of Monday scanning the desert through binoculars to search for gaps in the Egyptian deployment. In late afternoon, he assembled all men who could be spared from their posts. The gathering resembled the communal meetings at his kibbutz where issues of the day were decided on by majority vote.

"Fellows, we're leaving here tonight on foot," said Weisel. He asked the men whether they were prepared to risk making their way through the Egyptian lines. His deputy objected. Without orders to abandon the fort, he said, he himself would not leave. Weisel said headquarters would be asked for approval but that meanwhile he wanted to know how the men felt about it. The overwhelming sentiment was to go. The garrison had been lucky so far. They could not expect luck to hold out much longer.

With darkness, Weisel contacted brigade headquarters and announced his intention of bringing the men out. Displaying a caution that even senior officers were neglecting, he assumed the conversation was being monitored by the Egyptians and used Yiddish for the more sensitive parts. Brigade's reaction was hesitant. Weisel sensed that the officers there were reluctant to authorize passage through the heart of the Second Army. "If you don't make a decision," he said, "I'll make it myself." When brigade continued to hesitate, he said, "Okay, we're going." The officer responding said, "No," then "Wait."

It was Sharon who came on the line next. Weisel outlined his intentions. "You haven't got much of a chance," said Sharon. "We can't come to help you."

"We're leaving anyway," said Weisel.

"If you think it will work, go ahead," said Sharon. He advised the major not to start out until the moon went down at 2:45. A rendezvous point was fixed at the foot of Hamutal Ridge, six miles east, where tanks would meet them.

"Take care of yourselves," said Sharon.

Weisel assembled the soldiers in the courtyard to outline the plan. They would burn documents but would not blow up anything so as not to alert the Egyptians. If they found their way blocked they might have to return and would want the radio and other equipment intact. To be less conspicuous, they would split into two groups—one under command of his deputy—and meet at designated map coordinates near Hamutal. Weisel told the men to eat and to fill their canteens.

As he spoke, a guard at the main gate announced an arrival. "He says he's a tank driver." A thin young soldier appeared. He related that his tank had thrown a tread while battling Egyptian tanks during the day and that the other three crewmen had been shot as they climbed out. The Egyptians had tried to kill him too but he closed his hatch and they couldn't get at him. They finally booby-trapped the exterior of the hatch and left. He had escaped through the emergency exit at the bottom of his compartment and had hidden until darkness. He was told to get some sleep before they set out.

After calling down artillery on the surrounding area, Weisel led the way out the front gate moments after the moon went down. They were thirty-two men in all. Crossing Lexicon Road, they found themselves in an empty Egyptian bivouac area. Sleeping bags on the ground were still warm. Less than a hundred yards away, Egyptian soldiers were hammering stakes into the ground for a tent encampment. Weisel and his deputy split up and the two groups hurried forward in the darkness.

Dawn revealed a desert glistening with gossamer sheen. Thin, silvery guide wires from Sagger missiles lay across the sands like spiderwebs. The two groups found each other in the early light. As they approached the foot of Hamutal, a fierce tank battle broke out above. They could hear the bark of guns and occasionally see tanks topping a rise. Weisel halted and reported his arrival on the radio.

Although Reshef's brigade had been shifted to another sector, he asked Sharon's permission to bring in Weisel and his men. Colonel Reshef admired Weisel's courage in coming out through the Egyptian lines. The commander of another fort to whom Reshef had suggested a similar escape had declined, even though there were no enemy forces in his vicinity. That garrison was taken prisoner after a battle. Reshef asked battalion commander Shaul Shalev to locate the men from Purkan and bring them in. Colonel Shalev set out in his own tank, accompanied by another containing an artillery spotter. Weisel's precise location was not clear and the area was swarming with enemy tanks and Sagger teams. When Shalev failed to find the men, Reshef ordered him to return.

Raising Weisel on the radio from a hilltop, Reshef asked him to fire a green flare. A flare rose above the dunes two miles away. This time, Reshef in his tank joined Shalev and the artillery officer. The three split up to widen the search area as they drove through the dunes. Following Shalev were several half-tracks bearing infantry.

Reshef was close to the approximate area of the flare when he saw thirty soldiers on a hill two hundred yards away. He halved that distance before he saw that they were Egyptians. Ordering his driver to charge, the brigade commander raked the enemy soldiers with machine gun fire. The Egyptians returned fire as Reshef fed a new ammunition belt into his gun. Sagger missiles fired from somewhere to the side passed overhead. The driver ran down the remaining enemy soldiers.

Shalev also encountered Egyptian infantry dug in on a hill and charged. As he did, his operations officer pointed to the left where the top of an antenna could be seen jutting out over a low dune. Shalev changed direction, leaving the Egyptians to be dealt with by the infantry following behind. Sweeping around the dune, he found Weisel and his men. The garrison's three wounded soldiers were lowered through the turret into the tank and the remaining twenty-nine clambered aboard the exterior, somehow finding handholds. A few minutes later, Reshef was startled by a monstrous apparition approaching across the sands. He finally recognized it as Shalev's tank covered with the Purkan garrison.

Two of the Israeli infantrymen in the accompanying half-tracks were killed but the report of the rescue on the radio nets sent a surge of satisfaction through the Israeli lines, hungry for good news.

In the morning, the Egyptians discovered Purkan evacuated. General Shazly, who was touring the front, asked to be taken to the fort which he had viewed from the opposite bank only four days before. Entering the gate through which Weisel and his men had passed a few hours earlier, Shazly said, "Alhamud lillah, allahu akbar"—"Thanks be to God, God is the greatest."

Lt. Col. Zussia Keniezer, head of AMAN's Jordanian desk, had been summoned Monday night to the office of Arye Shalev, Zeira's deputy. Shalev was standing before a large wall map of Sinai with the head of the Egyptian desk, Yona Bandman. Placing his hand on Keniezer's shoulder, Shalev told him he would be taking over Bandman's job.

"Dado doesn't want to see us anymore," Shalev said. The chief of staff would henceforth get intelligence briefings on the Egyptian and Syrian fronts directly from the heads of the respective desks. General Zeira would remain in place.

Emerging cautiously from his bunker in Hizayon Tuesday afternoon, almost a day after the fort's surrender, Dr. Ohri could see no sign of life. He searched the skies vainly for Israeli planes. The only things moving were Egyptian tanks heading deeper into Sinai. There was not even the sound of distant battle to suggest that Israeli forces were still out there. It seemed to the doctor as if Israel itself might already have fallen.

Nevertheless, he returned to the bunker, determined to put off surrender as long as possible. Apart from Lieutenant Bareli, whose arm had been severed, there were two lightly wounded soldiers. Another soldier had been with them but his nerves had snapped that morning. He had run into the compound, firing his Uzi. He was taken prisoner but the Egyptians had not come into the bunker afterward.

With nightfall, the bunker was totally dark except for faint starlight coming through the entrance. One of the wounded soldiers proposed suicide. He pulled the pin of a grenade and called on the others to stand with him around Bareli so that they could die together. Ohri firmly rejected the proposal. He had been trained in saving life, not taking it. "We'll get out of this," he said. The soldier did not reinsert the pin but sat on a cot gripping the grenade.

Over the past three days Ohri had gotten close to Bareli, the son of a Jerusalem judge. They were both twenty-five and found that they had a lot in common, even mutual acquaintances. The morphine Ohri had been giving Bareli had run out. Given the pain and the unlikeliness of rescue, the wounded man asked the doctor to kill him. Ohri refused. "We'll get out of this," he repeated.

Ohri had hardly slept since the war began. He was slumped on a cot at the far end of the banana-shaped bunker at 7 p.m. when the outline of an Egyptian soldier appeared in the entranceway. The soldier lit a piece of paper which he used as a torch. His eyes were on the floor and he appeared to be looking for loot. He saw a helmet and lifted it. Turning his head, the Egyptian found himself looking into a pair of eyes a few feet away staring wildly back at him. With a shout, the Egyptian bolted from the bunker. The Israeli who had been holding the live grenade leaped after him. Ohri heard the grenade explode

Arrow-straight Tapline Road, where Lieutenant Greengold met a Syrian brigade.
Photograph courtesy of Israel Defense Forces Archive

Gen. Moshe (Moussa) Peled (with mustache), division commander, leading the drive to recapture the southern Golan.
Photograph courtesy of Israel Defense Forces Archive

Defense Minister Moshe Dayan (with eye patch) and Gen. Ariel Sharon (with white bandage) on the west bank of the Suez Canal. Dayan visited both fronts regularly during the war. On the left is an armored personnel carrier.
Photograph courtesy of Israel Defense Forces Archive

Col. Ori Orr (right), whose brigade blocked the Syrian attack on Nafakh, and Lt. Col. Moshe Harel, a battalion commander who was wounded twice.
Photograph courtesy of Israel Defense Forces Archive

Maj. Arnon Lapidot led the air attack on Syrian military headquarters in Damascus.
Photograph courtesy of Israeli Government Press Office

Lt. Col. Ami Morag (left), tank battalion commander.
Photograph courtesy of Ami Morag

Soldiers from the Golani Brigade atop Mount Hermon after its recapture.
Photograph courtesy of Israeli Government Press Office

Israeli intelligence outpost on Mount Hermon after its recapture.
Photograph courtesy of Israel Defense Forces Archive

Israeli soldiers on the bank of the Sweetwater Canal.
Photograph courtesy of Israeli Government Press Office

General Bar-Lev (left), the former chief of staff who assumed command of the southern front. On the right is Gen. Rehavam Ze'evi.
Photograph courtesy of Israel Defense Forces Archive

Col. Danny Matt, commander of the reserve Israeli paratroop brigade that established the Israeli bridgehead on the west bank of the canal.
Photograph courtesy of Israeli Government Press Office

Egyptian president Anwar Sadat.
*Photograph courtesy of
Israeli Government Press Office*

Col. Ran Sarig in the Sinai. His
armored brigade was the only
one to be shifted from the Syrian
front to the Egyptian front during the war. *Photograph courtesy of
Israel Defense Forces Archive*

Israeli paratroopers breaking through an Egyptian commando ambush on
a sand spit leading to Fort Budapest on the Sinai front.
Photograph courtesy of Israel Defense Forces Archive

Israeli forces moving through the Sinai toward the Suez Canal.
Photograph courtesy of Israel Defense Forces Archive

The "Yard" from which Israel launched its attack across the Suez Canal.
The bulldozer in the foreground had helped open the breach in the ramp
where the first bridge would be built.
Photograph courtesy of Israel Defense Forces Archive

Crossing the canal on the pontoon bridge. *Photograph courtesy of Israeli Government Press Office*

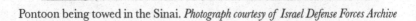

Pontoon being towed in the Sinai. *Photograph courtesy of Israel Defense Forces Archive*

Israeli-made "roller bridge" on the Suez Canal. *Photograph courtesy of Israel Defense Forces Archive*

and then the sound of guns. A few moments later a smoke grenade was tossed into the bunker and then a long tongue of fire from a flame-thrower penetrated the narrow space. Ohri passed out.

When he woke, he thought himself in hell. The heat was unbearable and it was difficult to breathe. He could smell burned flesh. With a pocket flashlight, he glanced at his watch and saw that it was midnight. He crawled out of the bunker, past Bareli's body, and reached the narrow trench outside. There he sat all night, his back against the trench wall, gripping his ankles and gulping the cold night air. There was something seriously wrong with his lungs. Hearing Arabic, he raised his head and saw soldiers moving about the courtyard but they did not notice him. After a while, there were no more voices.

With dawn, he could see that his skin was pinched, a sign of dehydration. Craving water, he rose and saw the men from the command bunker lying dead in the courtyard. There were no Egyptian soldiers. Almost all the bunkers had collapsed under the pounding of the heavy mortars, and all freestanding structures, including the kitchen, had been flattened. Amidst its ruins was a jerrican of water. It was, he feared, too good to be true. Ohri remembered a lecture he had heard warning that Egyptian raiders sometimes poisoned water supplies. His will to live overcoming his thirst, he turned away and continued out the fort entrance, hoping to find someone to whom to surrender.

As he staggered up the road, an armored personnel carrier approached. It stopped fifty yards away and a squad of Egyptian soldiers descended. Forming a line, the soldiers took magazines out of their pouches and slammed them into their Kalashnikovs. Ohri tried to shout that he was a doctor but no words came out of his burned throat. He felt like a gasping fish. Suddenly, a jeep dashed up the road and stopped between him and the soldiers. An Egyptian officer descended. He approached Ohri, who slid to the ground, his legs no longer able to support him. The officer tossed a canteen to the Israeli, who gulped down its contents and asked for another, then another. The officer came forward and offered him a biscuit but Ohri could not get it down his throat. "More water," he whispered.

Meanwhile, the soldiers from the personnel carrier had approached. One kicked Ohri, then a second. Others were about to join in when shells exploded around them. Everyone ran into the fort and took shelter in the trenches. Ohri was with the officer and his driver, the others some distance away. With his mouth close to the officer's ear, Ohri managed to whisper in English that he was a doctor.

"They want to kill you," replied the officer. "They may kill me too."

"But you're an officer," said Ohri. "They're just fellahin [peasants]."

The officer nodded. Then, signaling to his driver, he yanked Ohri to his feet and the three ran to the jeep amidst the falling shells. As they sped off, the officer, sitting in the rear, blindfolded Ohri, who was sitting next to the driver, and tied his hands behind him. They reached a place where, by the sounds, there were a lot of soldiers. The officer took leave of Ohri, who was led to a shell hole and told to sit. From time to time he was given water. Finally the blindfold was removed. Hundreds of soldiers, it seemed, stood around him. His face was blackened and his clothes covered with blood from the men he had treated.

Someone asked Ohri his name, rank, and serial number. When he said he was a doctor, a soldier was called forward, apparently a medic. The soldier spoke English well and said he would ask some questions to test Ohri's medical knowledge. "What do you take for heartburn?" he began. Ohri signaled that he could not speak and asked for a pencil and paper. These were supplied and he was able to furnish answers to the medic's satisfaction.

They were near the canal and Ohri was led to a boat which ferried him across. As he was being lifted out on the other side, he fell into the water, his hands still bound. Someone reached down and pulled him back up by his hair.

In a prison hospital in Cairo a few hours later, the Egyptian doctor examining him, a Christian Copt, correctly diagnosed bronchitis. An Israeli prisoner doctor was also summoned to the bedside. After examining Ohri, he said to the Egyptian in English: "He's not going to make it."

Forcing the words out of his mouth, Ohri said, "I'm going to live."

Television cameraman Mohammed Gohar was probably the first Egyptian civilian to cross the canal since the war began. He had been hastily dispatched from Cairo Tuesday morning to film Israeli POWs in Sinai before they were carried off to prison. The results were to be rushed to Jordan for showing on television in the evening. Israelis could not pick up Egyptian television but many did view television from Amman, which was in broadcasting range. Seeing their soldiers as prisoners would clearly be a devastating blow to Israeli morale.

The twenty-one-year-old cameraman crossed at Kantara and was led to a group of prisoners near the canal. They sat in rows—unshaven, heads bowed, with the vacant look of men who have surrendered to their fate. Egyptian soldiers were milling about watching the scene. Gohar told his military escort to have the soldiers moved away. Scanning the prisoners, he saw that some were wounded. They too were shifted out of camera range.

That done, he examined those remaining. There were sixteen in all and he made his calculations regarding light and camera angle. Before beginning to shoot, he raised his head to look at the prisoners again, this time not with the camera's eye but his own. It was, he realized, the first time he had ever seen Israelis. He had never even seen a photograph or a television image of one. All he knew of them were the grotesque cartoons in Cairo newspapers of Dayan and Golda Meir. He was surprised to see that the soldiers looked perfectly normal—in fact, like himself. They were about his age and many of them had olive skin like him and the expression they wore was what he expected his would be in their situation. All he had heard about Israelis, all he had learned about them in school, had not prepared him for this. As he studied them, he saw some raise their heads and look at him quizzically. They took in his stare, trying to understand what it meant. And they took in the camera. Having their picture taken—and shown on television—meant that they were likely to survive captivity. He understood what they were thinking and from the eye contact he believed they were beginning to understand something of what he was thinking. Gohar would in time become the official photographer of President Sadat. But from that brief encounter on the bank of the Suez Canal at the high point of Egyptian military achievement, he became a believer in peace with Israel.

Elazar ordered Gonen Tuesday morning to deploy defensively and build up strength in anticipation of the Egyptian armored divisions crossing. Tanks were to do no more than snipe at enemy armor from long range. "I can't risk erosion of our forces," Elazar said. He would repeat this warning several times during the day to make sure that Gonen understood him clearly. "We're sticking to the principle of a defensive battle, without too much maneuvering. The Egyptians are the ones who should get worn out while advancing."

Gonen passed the order on to Sharon and also to Sharon's brigade commanders since he did not trust Sharon to do so. Sharon, for his part, had no trust in Gonen's judgment, or in the high command's either, after Monday's fiasco. "This was not the time to sit back and allow the Egyptians to build up their bridgeheads and their defenses," he would write. "We should be pushing them, probing for their weak points."

Sharon had been cajoling Gonen since mid-morning to permit him to undertake a divisional attack on Missouri and the so-called Chinese Farm, an agricultural development area where the Egyptians were massing. When Gonen informed Elazar of Sharon's request, the chief of staff repeated his order: "No fight that can lead to loss of tanks."

Sharon interpreted the order in his own fashion. He would stage a "mobile defense," a concept that, to his mind, permitted forward movement. He got his chance when the Egyptians to his front launched a probe which was repelled in sharp skirmishing. One of his battalions destroyed thirty enemy tanks. Sharon told his commanders that he intended to "exploit our success" by sending two brigades forward. Gonen, who was monitoring Sharon's radio net, was alarmed. Keep your distance from the Egyptians, he said. "That's all right," said Sharon soothingly. "We're with you."

Sharon directed a battalion led by Ami Morag, to Hamutal, a strategic feature dominating the direct road between Tasa and the canal. Bitter battles had been fought there the day before but Morag found the three-mile-long plateau seemingly empty. "Hamutal is in our hands," he reported. A moment later, his tank was hit by a Sagger. The blow knocked him to the floor of the tank. He slapped his face to convince himself he was not dead. All three of his crewmen were wounded but said they could carry on.

Climbing back into the turret, Morag saw that a fold in the ground divided the plateau in two. His side indeed was empty but on the other side, sand was flying, indicating that troops there were digging in. It was from there that the Sagger had come. In the absence of machine guns, Morag ordered one of his companies to crush the infantrymen while another company provided covering fire. The attack force raced over the foxholes, the commanders firing their Uzis and throwing grenades. To Morag's astonishment, when the tanks passed, Egyptian soldiers rose up from foxholes which had not collapsed and resumed firing RPGs.

The second company was sent on the same mission but this time the company commander made a run along the edges of the foxholes so that the treads were better able to crush those inside. Even now, surviving infantrymen fought back. Egyptian artillery fire was so dense that the smoke made it difficult for the tank commanders to see each other.

The Israelis could now make out an extensive deployment of tanks and infantry at the far end of the plateau. Morag's men quickly dealt with the Egyptian tanks—sixteen were destroyed—but infantry was another matter. The swirling battle, involving Saggers and RPGs, was often face-to-face. An Egyptian soldier climbed onto a tank and with his rifle butt broke the jaw of the loader, whose head was projecting from his hatch. The loader succeeded in toppling him from the tank.

Morag pulled out of the battle to transfer a wounded crewman to a tank carrying casualties to the rear. When he returned, he found that in the five minutes he was gone all his company commanders had been wounded. So had almost all the platoon commanders. Morag contacted brigade commander Haim Erez and requested permission to pull back.

Morag asked one of the company commanders to lead the battalion back down. The officer had been wounded twice during the half-hour skirmish. His tank was burning, although not in apparent danger of exploding. Morag called on all tank commanders to "follow the burning tank." He himself meanwhile swept across the plateau to make sure no one had been left behind. He found a tank whose commander had not heard the pullback order and led it down. It was under cover of this battle that the Purkan garrison was rescued at the foot of Hamutal.

Of the twenty-four tanks that began the battle, three were destroyed on Hamutal and fourteen damaged but able to descend from the ridge. The twenty-seven-year-old Morag, in his first battalion command, was distraught as he looked at the casualties who had been laid out on the ground. Of the men he had led into battle for the first time barely an hour before, more than a quarter were casualties—eight dead and twenty wounded, including almost all his officers. Morag asked Colonel Erez to send the brigade's best doctors. "They fought too well for us to let them die," he said. As he watched, a doctor performed a tracheotomy to save the life of a company commander who was struggling to breathe.

"What do we do?" Morag asked his deputy, Maj. Yehuda Tal, an older reservist. Tal suggested that Morag go off by himself a bit while the wounded were being tended to.

Recovering his composure after a few minutes, Morag assembled his men. All were stunned by the violence of the encounter. "We took a beating on Hamutal," Morag began. "We didn't expect that infantry, especially Egyptian infantry, would stand their ground against charging tanks and that they would fire back with antitank weapons instead of running. We've taken casualties but we have no alternative. This is a battle for our existence. We'll screw them yet."

He ordered that the tanks still intact take under tow those which had difficulty moving. With that, he led the battalion back to Tasa where the damaged tanks would be repaired and needed crewmen chosen from the replacement pool.

Flying down to Tasa in a helicopter, Gonen drove into the dunes in a jeep and caught up with Sharon and the forward elements of his division. "Break contact," ordered Gonen. He waited until he heard Sharon give the order to his units to pull back and saw tanks begin to turn. When Gonen returned to his headquarters, however, he learned that one of Sharon's battalions had just attacked and retaken the Televisia staging area on the Artillery Road.

The move had been initiated by brigade commander Reshef after obtaining Sharon's permission. The crew of a disabled tank had found shelter in a building there, unnoticed by Egyptians around them, and made radio contact. Reshef sent forward the battalion of Shaul Shalev, who had rescued the Purkan garrison that morning. The missing crew was rescued but there was one Israeli fatality—Colonel Shalev himself.

Paratroop brigade commander Danny Matt, who arrived at Umm Hashiba during the day, was surprised to receive a fatherly embrace from Gonen, with whom he was not particularly close. On a wall map, Gonen pointed at Missouri and the adjacent Chinese Farm. Information was sketchy about the Egyptian presence there, he said. He wanted Matt to send out "silent patrols" this night consisting of officers to determine the Egyptian positions. The phrase "silent patrol"— scouting rather than fighting—struck Matt as something out of the First World War. On the basis of what the patrols found, said Gonen, Matt would attack the next night with his entire brigade. Using the paratroopers would permit Gonen to keep up pressure on the Egyptians while obeying Elazar's injunction against further erosion of the tank forces.

Gonen radioed Sharon and informed him that his "bearded friend" had arrived. Sharon understood that he meant Matt. Talking elliptically to confound Egyptian radio monitors, Gonen hinted at the mission he had asked Matt to carry out in Sharon's sector. Sharon's voice came booming out of the loudspeaker. "Do you know what you're talking about? There are ten thousand Egyptian soldiers there and at least a hundred tanks." Gonen dropped the idea.

Earlier in the day, a newly arrived officer had presented himself to Reshef for assignment. Lt. Col. Yoav Brom was traveling in Europe when the war broke out and had hurried home on the first available plane. The boyish-looking officer had given up a coveted position as school principal in his kibbutz, Shefayim, in order to return to the regular army two years before. General Adan, under whom Brom had served in the past, would term him "the best soldier I ever knew." Reshef suggested to Sharon that Brom replace the commander of the divisional reconnaissance battalion who had been killed the day before fighting for the vital ridges in Sharon's sector after the division had been sent off on its pointless run. He also suggested that the battalion be attached to his brigade. Sharon, as accommodating to subordinates as he was willful toward superiors, accepted both suggestions.

Lookouts reported that the area between Forts Lakekan and Botser on the shores of the Bitter Lake appeared to be empty. Reshef was concerned about the fate of the garrison at Matsmed, five miles from Lakekan, with which communications had been cut off since morning. Because of fog covering the area, his lookouts had not witnessed the fort's capture. Reshef asked Brom to check it out, avoiding contact with the enemy if possible. The reconnaissance force set out at dusk across the dunes which had been crossed two days before by the Lakekan garrison in their escape. The deep ditches of the Chinese Farm extended this far south and the tracked vehicles had to carefully navigate around them. It was dark when the battalion descended onto Lexicon Road. Brom sent a patrol to nearby Lakekan. Turning off their engines and hearing no sounds of life inside the fort, the tankers entered and found it empty. Matsmed was empty as well. Brom sent one company south to patrol partway down the shore of the Bitter Lake and started north with his other two companies on Lexicon. After passing the northern end of the Bitter Lake, the sound of out- going artillery grew loud and Brom detected movement to his front. His battalion had been provided the latest Patton tanks, which were fitted with night sights. Through them, Brom saw Egyptian soldiers eight hundred yards to his front digging foxholes at the junction of Lexicon and Tirtur Roads. Beyond, an Egyptian artillery battery was firing eastward. Brom summoned his deputy and one of his company commanders, Capt. Rafi Bar-Lev, nephew of General Bar-Lev. They could barely see each other's outlines in the darkness as they stood atop Brom's tank. Despite their distance from the Egyptian soldiers, they talked in whispers. Brom pulled the tanks back a bit and reported his findings to Reshef.

The Egyptian Second Army had crossed the canal north of the Bitter Lake and the Third Army south of the lake. The Second Army had negligently rested its southern perimeter not on the edge of the lake but on Tirtur Road, which formed a convenient boundary. But this left almost a mile of the Suez Canal, between Tirtur and the Bitter Lake, unguarded, as well as the northern half of the lake shore. It was as if the army's ankles had been exposed to mosquitoes by a blanket pulled up too high.

The report by Brom of his whereabouts electrified Sharon. He realized that the reconnaissance battalion had stumbled on the "seam" between the Second and Third Armies that would enable Israeli forces to reach the canal without having to fight their way through the Egyp- tian bridgehead.

Sharon saw an opportunity to continue straight across the canal into the Egyptian rear, a move that could change the course of the war. Contacting Gonen, Sharon said: "Shmulik, we're near the canal. We can touch the water. Request permission to cross." Sharon would subsequently maintain that he was only indicating a desire to cross after adequate preparations had been made, not on this night. As his superiors understood it, Sharon was proposing this very night to attack the Egyptian division deployed north of Matsmed in the Chinese Farm and then to cross the canal.

"Get him out of there," shouted Elazar when General Tal called from Southern Command to inform him of Sharon's location and intentions. "Get him out of there." The chief of staff was beside him- self with anger as his clear directives were once again being flouted. "I tell you he is not to cross. Not to cross. Not to cross."

Sharon was not put off when Gonen got back to him with Elazar's message. A bridge, said Sharon, could be moved up in a few hours. (It would, in fact, be a week before the bridges would be ready.) "I'm already here. The moment we cross, the whole situation will change. What if the Egyptians close the seam?"

Gonen remained adamant. Sharon tried unsuccessfully to reach Tal, then called back to Southern Command, but Gonen "couldn't be reached." With no other recourse, Sharon told Reshef to pull the battalion back in the morning.

At the same hour that the newspaper editors in Tel Aviv were being cast into a funk by Dayan's remarks little more than twenty-four hours after the debacle of the failed counterattack, the key had been found to reversing the course of the war on the southern front. But it was not yet time to turn it.

24

GOLAN COUNTERATTACK

T HE SYRIAN DIVISIONS OCCUPYING a bulge in the heart of the Golan Monday morning were ideally placed to punch a hole through the thin Israeli cordon around them wherever they chose to concentrate their forces. But the momentum had gone out of their attack. They had failed to push for the Jordan River Saturday night when only a handful of tanks stood in their way and they had failed to crack the hastily formed Israeli line on Sunday when the odds were still overwhelmingly in their favor. The odds would narrow significantly this day when Moussa Peled's division joined the battle.

A quiet night on Sunday had given the Israeli reserve units their first opportunity to organize. Tanks which had been thrown randomly into the battle in desperate bids to plug holes rejoined their organic units, casualties were replaced, and damaged tanks repaired.

Moussa Peled's division began climbing the heights before first light. Peled had only a single tank brigade commanded by Col. Yossi Peled (no relation), as well as a reconnaissance battalion and a brigade of infantry in half-tracks. Northern Command doubled his tank strength by attaching to him the brigades of Ben-Porat and Hadar already on the southern heights—each a mixture of Centurions and old Shermans.

While the division was making its way northward from the center of the country on Sunday, Yossi Peled drove ahead in a jeep to view the fighting zone. He was afraid the war would be over before he got to it. This feeling abated when he reached Kibbutz Ein Gev on the eastern shore of Lake Kinneret and saw antitank guns being set up on its perimeter. As his jeep turned up the Gamla Ascent, he was fired on by Syrian tanks at the edge of the escarpment. He led his brigade up the heights the next morning. At El Al, he received a briefing from Colonel Ben-Porat, whose tanks had been fighting there for twenty-four hours. Despite the Shermans' age and vulnerable armor, their upgraded guns were getting the better of the Soviet-made tanks opposite. Yossi Peled's brigade passed through Ben-Porat's formation and began driving the Syrians northward.

The Israelis in the bunker atop Tel Saki deduced from the sound of Syrian tanks pulling back that a counterattack had begun. At noon, an artillery barrage hit and the men heard the voices of two Syrian soldiers who took shelter in the outer room. A moment later a grenade exploded in the bunker. Virtually everybody was peppered with shrapnel again but no one made a sound. The Syrians chose not to enter. An hour later other Syrian soldiers likewise sheltering from a barrage threw two grenades into the room but again did not enter.

Not long after, the men once again heard footsteps. This time voices called out in Hebrew, "Is anyone alive?" At the response from the bunker, two officers entered. To one of the tank crewmen, the reservists seemed old enough to be his father. He could see tears in their eyes as they scanned the scene. All but five of the thirty men in the bunker were still alive, all of them wounded.

At Strongpoint 116, Lieutenant Gur, his arm in a makeshift sling, led soldiers out of the fort in the morning to collect Kalashnikov rifles and ammunition. The approaches were strewn with tanks, APCs, and bodies, testimony to two days of battle. Gur had no idea of what was happening elsewhere on the Golan.

There was no movement in their vicinity until close to noon when Syrians, recognizable by their overalls as tank crewmen, were seen fleeing eastward on foot. It was the first indication of an Israeli counterattack. In late afternoon a jeep turned down the track toward the fort. The men readied their weapons but someone shouted, "It's ours." Two reconnaissance personnel from Moussa Peled's division stepped out of the vehicle to tell Gur and his men that half-tracks would arrive in half an hour to evacuate them.

The conquest of Tel Juhadar near Strongpoint 116 opened a view toward Tel Fares, the highest tel on the Golan, from where Erez's battalion had pulled back the night before. Hunkered down in the folds of ground between the two volcanic cones were two battalions of Syrian infantry armed with Saggers and RPGs. The Golan battles had thus far been almost entirely tank versus tank but the Syrians now deployed large numbers of tank-killing infantry to guard their endangered southern flank.

Gen. Moussa Peled ordered artillery to lay down a rolling barrage just ahead of the tanks. This was the effective response to enemy tank hunters that had been missing in Sinai. Artillery was far more effective on the rock-strewn Golan, where the shells were shattered into lethal splinters, than in the Sinai where shell fire was muffled by the sand.

The Syrians had established dense concentrations of antitank guns and Saggers on main axes. Ben-Porat's brigade succeeded in overcoming the first one it encountered. While one battalion provided covering fire, another swept in from the flank and destroyed twenty-four antitank guns and numerous Sagger teams. However, an attack on another position was repulsed.

Maj. David Caspi, a deputy battalion commander, was shepherding a convoy of trucks to a forward logistics depot when a shell exploded alongside his half-track. Two Syrian tanks and three armored personnel carriers broke into the open six hundred yards away. Caspi, an elementary school principal in civilian life, ordered the men on the trucks to dismount and take shelter. His half-track and the one behind him turned toward the Syrians, now two hundred yards distant, and opened fire with their heavy machine guns. Caspi told the gunners to fire long bursts at the tank turrets. The effect was immediate. Machine gun fire could not harm the tanks but the hammering of the .50 caliber bullets unnerved the tank commanders whose view was limited by the closed hatches. The tanks halted and the crews bolted.

The advance of Peled's division in the southern Golan did not ease pressure on Ori Orr's brigade in the central Golan. The First Syrian Armored Division had resumed its drive on Nafakh at dawn along the Sindiana axis. Orr's brigade, which began the day with sixty tanks, blocked the advance in a brutal slugging match.

Erosion of personnel was merciless. Two more of Orr's company commanders—appointed only the day before to replace fatalities—were killed. The brigade was under heavy artillery and Katyusha attacks, the Katyusha rockets recognizable by their distinctive howl. During one barrage, everyone in Orr's command half-track ducked for cover as shrapnel rattled off the vehicle's sides. When they rose, the communications officer remained crouched on his seat. "You can get up now," said Orr, who was sitting alongside him. "It's over." When the officer did not rise, Orr touched his neck and his hand came away with blood. The wounded officer was evacuated.

The Syrians pushed hardest on Orr's right flank, anchored on a quarry near Nafakh. The battalion commander there, a replacement appointed the night before, had questioned his own fitness for the job, but Orr said there was no one else. At one point, the officer said his men could not hold on any longer. "I've got to pull back."

"Negative," replied Orr. "The Syrians don't know it's tough for you. They'll break soon." But the Syrians broke through and the officer was killed. Major Danon, commanding the battalion in the center of the line, ordered his tanks into an all-around defense as the Syrians swept around his broken right flank. Orr asked battalion commander Harel, on the left flank, to rush to Nafakh with his twelve remaining tanks. Wounded the day before, Harel had returned to action. He stopped the Syrians on the perimeter of the base.

Receiving six tanks as reinforcement, Orr counterattacked and reached Sindiana. Division commander Eitan, operating from a field in his mobile command post, ordered Orr to continue south to Ramtania. In a virtual replay of the incident with Maj. Haim Barak two days before, Danon's tank was hit in an exchange from the Ramtania Ridge with Syrian tanks in the Hushniya base below. Danon carried his badly wounded loader on his back through the village—deserted since the Six Day War—until he was picked up by a tank. Orr pulled his remaining tanks back to Sindiana to form a new line.

Sarig's brigade, on the western edge of the Syrian bulge, advanced a mile to the Tapline in heavy fighting. The brigade halted there in order not to get between Moussa Peled's division advancing northward and Orr's brigade attacking southward.

By evening, the Syrian enclave had shrunk but their divisions remained coherent, despite heavy losses. It was clear to both sides that the next day, Tuesday, would be decisive.

In Safed Hospital, Barukh Askarov, a high school senior from Tel Aviv, found his brother Shmuel lying in bed Sunday with his forehead and throat bandaged. Shmuel's vocal cords had been damaged by the Syrian shell which propelled him from his tank at Strongpoint 111 and he could only whisper. In the next bed lay an officer whose face and blond hair were blackened by burns and soot. He seemed to be sleeping but kept tossing and muttering, "What a mess, what a mess." Shmuel identified him to his brother as Lt. Zvika Greengold, with whom he had served in the past.

When Greengold opened his eyes he was astonished to see his girlfriend sitting by the bedside. She was from a kibbutz in the Jordan Valley. He had been certain that the Golan had fallen and that the Syrians had reached the valley. "How did you get here?" he asked.

During the day, Major Askarov received reports from visitors of an unending series of disasters; the brigade had been wiped out, Colonel Ben-Shoham was dead, and so were his deputy and the brigade operations officer. The remnants of Erez's battalion—Askarov's unit—were cut off behind enemy lines with almost no ammunition. Soldiers had begun to retreat on their own.

The deputy battalion commander had been told Saturday that he would have to remain hospitalized for two weeks. Early Monday morning, he slipped out together with Yos Eldar, the wounded battalion commander from the Seventh Brigade, and headed for the Golan in Eldar's jeep.

Askarov got off at a tank base at the foot of the Golan. With his brigade no longer functioning, he decided to organize a new force and lead it into battle. Rounding up four trucks, he assembled everyone he found at the base. There were about 150 men, including crewmen from disabled tanks. Speaking as loudly as his vocal cords permitted, Askarov said he was going back up the heights and wanted to take them with him. Every man was needed and he had trucks outside to transport them.

It seemed for a moment that they were with him but then an officer spoke up. "I'm a major and I ran away. You can put me in prison but I'm not going back to that hell." In the circumstances, that sounded to the others more like the voice of reason than Askarov's plea for heroics. He drove off to the Golan alone.

There, at Camp Jordan, he found the tanks that had returned from Tel Fares. Most were damaged. Oded Erez was there too. The battalion commander was emotionally drained after losing two-thirds of his tanks in a desperate battle and after the excruciating escape through the Syrian lines. The men were visibly dispirited, not just from the ordeal of the battle but from a sense that they had been exposed to impossible odds and left to their fate.

Askarov called them together. The situation was desperate, he said, and the tanks must be prepared for battle by morning. Despite his raspy whisper, his purposefulness came through. The response this time was enthusiastic. Mechanics were soon swarming over damaged tanks, cannibalizing some in order to repair others. Askarov's call for volunteers to replace dead and injured crewmen drew a ready response.

At one point, a colonel from Northern Command arrived. Shocked at Askarov's appearance, he ordered him to return to hospital. "I'm commanding the brigade now," replied the major, "and I'm giving orders here." The colonel relented.

Shortly before dawn, someone tapped Askarov on the shoulder. It was Lt. Col. Yossi Ben-Hanan, who had been commander of the battalion until a month before when he took leave to get married. He was in Nepal on his honeymoon when he learned from the BBC on Yom Kippur that war had broken out. He and his bride were on the first plane out. From Athens, he telephoned his parents and arranged to have his uniform and personal equipment, including binoculars and pistol, waiting for him at Lod International Airport (soon to be renamed after David Ben-Gurion). After stopping at Northern Command headquarters for a briefing from Hofi, he continued on to the Golan. Askarov readily handed over command of the force he had brought to life—eleven tanks and crews—to Ben-Hanan. Their old battalion was emerging from the ashes.

At Strongpoint 107 alongside the Damascus Road, Lieutenant Elimelekh was scanning the landscape when Syrian artillery opened up once again. The barrage continued without letup and the twenty-year-old officer decided to see how his men were faring in the bunker. Running the thirty yards from his observation post was a terrifying experience. In the bunker's sheltered entranceway, he drank a canteenful of water and smoked a cigarette. Only then did he enter with a casual "How you doing?" He found that his first sergeant had organized a strict regimen in order to keep discipline intact. One-third of the men were preparing for inspection—cleaning weapons, polishing boots, shaving. Another third was on alert status, prepared to rush to their positions if the alarm was sounded. The remainder were sleeping.

When the barrage lifted, Elimelekh summoned the men and deployed them in a 360-degree defense. Syrian commandos and

Battle of the Kuneitra Gap

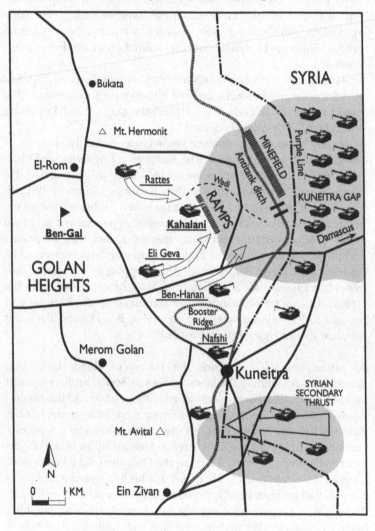

armored vehicles had penetrated the Purple Line in large numbers and an attack could come now from any direction. On Sunday night, a Syrian half-track had darted from the rear and skirted the strongpoint until it touched off a mine. On Monday, a Syrian tank heading back on the same path hit a mine 150 yards away. The explosion threw the tank commander from the turret and killed the others aboard. The wounded Syrian ran toward the strongpoint, waving a white undershirt. He passed through a minefield but the Syrian artillery fire had detonated the mines and he reached the strongpoint unhurt. Surprise at his safe passage turned to amazement when he shouted in Arabic, "Ana Shmuel [I am Shmuel]." The Israelis, none of whom spoke Arabic, believed him to be saying that he was a Jew from Damascus who had been drafted into the Syrian army. He was taken prisoner and eventually sent to the rear, but the garrison never learned his identity.

Monday night, the commander of the tank platoon that had been guarding the strongpoint, Lieutenant Yakhin, informed Elimelekh that he had been ordered to pull back. In three days, Yakhin's platoon and other tanks from his company had knocked out at least forty Syrian tanks on the approaches to 107. Elimelekh called battalion headquarters to protest at being left without tank support. Do the best you can, he was told. I don't have air support or artillery either, said Elimelekh. "The nation is behind you," the battalion command assured him. It was a phrase Elimelekh would become accustomed to hearing in the coming day.

The next morning, a single Syrian tank was stopped by mechanical problems a few hundred yards from the strongpoint, just out of bazooka range. The tank commander took advantage of the situation to methodically hit firing positions inside the strongpoint, destroying all its four mounted machine guns. When the tank finally made off, the garrison was left only with Uzis and two rifles. Elimelekh sent men out to the Syrian half-track that had hit a mine. It was filled with dead soldiers but also an abundance of weaponry. The men brought back machine guns, Kalashnikov rifles, and RPGs. The nation was behind them but the Golani troopers were getting their arms and ammunition from the Syrians.

For the Seventh Brigade, Monday was relatively quiet. Kahalani's battalion was ordered forward in the morning to ensure that manned Syrian tanks were not lurking among the knocked-out tanks littering the landscape nearby. They found that many tanks had been abandoned while still intact.

Ben-Gal ordered Yos Eldar, back from the hospital, to take command of the ramps in the center of the line, shifting Kahalani to the southern flank. A few officers who had served in Kahalani's battalion in the past and had no current combat assignment joined him after making their way to the Golan on their own. He assigned them to tanks whose commanders were casualties. As Monday night fell, Kahalani heard Eldar on the radio calling for flares. Something was stirring out there. When will it end? Kahalani asked himself. Where were the Syrians drawing their strength from?

Before dawn, Tuesday, Moussa Peled assembled his commanders to outline his plan to cut the main Syrian routes into the Golan. As they pushed north, clouds of dust signaled the approach of two tank columns, one from across the cease-fire line to the east and one from Hushniya to the west. The Syrians, recognizing the threat to their lifeline, were responding in force. For three hours, the two sides battled at close range. When the fight was over, fifty-five Syrian tanks lay inert on the battlefield and the remainder pulled back.

In late morning, Col. Yossi Peled was notified that eight Phantoms were approaching his sector with bombs to spare. This was the flight which had aborted the mission to Damascus because of heavy cloud cover. The air force offered to have them deposit their combined bomb load—thirty-six tons—wherever desired. Colonel Peled's satisfaction turned to horror when he saw the first bombs falling toward his own brigade. No damage was done and the planes dropped the rest of their bombs on Tel Kudne, the heart of the Syrian defenses across the Purple Line.

Ben-Porat's old Shermans attacked Hushniya frontally and were repelled. Shifting to the left flank, they broke through and reached the Hushniya base as dusk descended, knocking out armored vehicles and supply trucks. The Syrians re-formed and, when the Israeli tanks tried to make a return sweep, they were stopped.

Only seventy tanks were still operational when Moussa Peled's division compiled its status report Tuesday night. Maintenance crews working through the night would permit the division to begin the next day with two hundred tanks. On both fronts, the work of the maintenance teams was critical. The fact that the Israeli side was now advancing meant that tanks that had malfunctions or were damaged in battle could be reached by repair crews. Each night, the armored corps went to bed a cripple, and each morning it was born anew, shrunken only by a relatively small number of tanks beyond repair.

In the central sector Tuesday morning, Ori Orr braced for a renewed attack on Nafakh by deploying two battalions overlooking the anticipated Syrian route. In what was a make-or-break effort, the Syrians added elements of a third armored brigade to the two brigades that had been fighting in this sector for the past two days. The force included bridging tanks, indicating expectations of crossing the narrow Jordan River.

The early morning sun was in the Israelis' eyes but the Syrian attack was driven back in fierce fighting. The awkwardness of the first day, when tank crews were randomly thrown together, had been smoothed by three days of intensive fighting. Basic tank skills had been polished; the crews had bonded and so had the brigade. Orr drew comfort about the country's prospects from the motivation and skills displayed by this collection of reservists who were virtual strangers to one another only a few days before. Commanders reported that the numerous yeshiva students in the brigade's ranks had performed exceptionally well in combat.

On Sunday, Orr had seen a lieutenant standing in the middle of the battlefield in an apparent state of shock, the sole survivor of a tank crew. Instead of having him sent to the rear, Orr took him into his half-track. For the first day, the lieutenant sat in a corner saying nothing and staring blankly as the war raged around him. The second day, he began to display an interest in his surroundings and helped prepare food for the brigade staff. On the third day, he asked to be given command of a tank. Orr sent him back into battle.

After beating off the Syrian attack Tuesday morning, the brigade pushed south again toward Ramtania. Major Danon took the lead, his force moving slowly across the boulder-strewn slopes. In a battle fought at ranges as close as fifty yards, Danon conquered the village. His orders were to wait for another battalion to join him before attacking an adjacent tel with strong defenses. But dusk was descending and Orr told him not to wait. Danon's tanks were in secure firing positions and the tank commanders were reluctant to emerge once again in the face of heavy Sagger and tank fire. Danon, however, led the way and in a final rush his tanks took the tel, the last defenders fleeing down the hill toward Hushniya.

. . . .

To the north, the Seventh Brigade had been engaged in its own war for three days now, detached from what was happening elsewhere on the Golan. Theirs was a classic defensive battle, the kind that IDF doctrine virtually ignored. The brigade had already filled the Kuneitra Gap with masses of destroyed Syrian armor. In doing so, it had lost more than half of its own tanks but the critical juncture was only now at hand.

The Syrian high command, in a final effort, had assembled the largest force yet mustered in this sector. In addition to elements of the Seventh and Ninth Divisions that had been engaged there since the start of the war, a fresh brigade from the Third Armored Division, guarding the road to Damascus, was sent forward. So were seventy tanks from the Presidential Guard commanded by Rifat Assad, President Assad's brother. Syrian tanks in this sector now numbered 160, four times Ben-Gal's strength.

President Assad himself had been spending the war in the underground war room of the Syrian General Staff, taking an active role in directing the battle. Each morning, he emerged from the side room where he slept on a cot, exchanged salutes with his generals, and took his place at the operations desk. As his forces moved into position for the decisive battle, the Syrian president exhorted each of the division commanders separately by radio.

Ben-Gal's men were exhausted and emotionally numb on this fourth day of battle. A brigade staff officer fell asleep as Ben-Gal was talking to him. Here and there tanks were beginning to pull back without authorization. Seeing two tanks heading toward the rear, Ben-Gal asked their commanders on the radio where they were going. To refuel and rearm, they said. Ben-Gal ordered them back to the line. The contending armies had reached the endgame. One final effort, one minute more of endurance, could make the difference.

The day began with the most massive Syrian barrage the brigade had yet experienced. It was so fierce that Ben-Gal ordered the tanks on the ramparts, the focus of the Syrian shelling, to pull back a few hundred yards. Syrian artillery observers now had a clear view of the Israeli lines from the captured outpost on Mount Hermon.

Lieutenant Elimelekh at Strongpoint 107 was the first to see the enemy tanks. They came through a breach in an earth barrier two miles to his east at Khan Arnabe—two long columns heading for the

Kuneitra Gap to his left rear. The tanks passed within three hundred yards of the outpost, their hatches closed. Elimelekh ordered the bazookist on that side of the outpost to fire at them. The soldier had knocked out a Syrian tank two days before. He now hit five more. Ignoring the Israeli position, the other tanks thundered west toward the Hermonit Ridge, a mile away.

Ben-Gal called his battalion commander on the southern flank.

"Kahalani, this is Yanosh."

"This is Kahalani. Good morning." It was still quiet at his end of the line.

"Move out immediately and position yourself in my area. You will be my reserve."

"On my way."

Ben-Gal had taken up position near Kibbutz El-Rom on high ground two miles behind the tank ramps. Kahalani deployed alongside him. Ben-Gal told him that his tanks would serve as a second line. The battalion commander was surprised. Was Ben-Gal expecting the front line to break? Kahalani could see heavy artillery fire in the area of the ramps. On the radio, Eldar's tank commanders were reporting that their ammunition was running out. There could be no more than a dozen or so tanks left intact there.

Four Syrian helicopters passed directly overhead. Four others followed. One was shot down by ground fire but the others landed near Nafakh, disgorging commandos. Ben-Gal could not spare tanks to deal with them because his front was at this very moment cracking.

Lead elements of the Syrian tank force were approaching the empty ramps and Ben-Gal could not make contact with the tanks that had pulled back. He ordered battalion commander Rattes on the northern flank to move south to fill the gap.

After four days of hands-on direction, Ben-Gal's control was unraveling as officers were hit and orders were not passed on. There appeared to be no alternative but to have the tanks fall back. Even if they managed to outrace the Syrians to the new line, however, they would not be able to hold it for more than half an hour, he estimated, in the absence of proper defensive positions.

Ben-Gal decided on a last desperate bid to shore up the collapsing line.

"Kahalani, this is Yanosh. Move out. Fast. Over."

The battalion commander had been waiting impatiently for the order. Uncertain whether the front was still where he had left it the day before, he ordered his men to be prepared to fire without warning. As he moved forward, the ramp came into view straight ahead. It was empty except for the hulks of knocked-out tanks, Israeli and Syrian. The remaining Israeli tanks were now scattered five hundred yards to the rear.

Ignoring them for the moment, Kahalani cut across a plowed field toward a wadi to the left. It was through this gully, with its navigable incline, that Syrian tanks had penetrated onto the Israeli high ground from the valley on Sunday. Kahalani wanted to make sure it was empty before reoccupying the ramp. A fifteen-foot-high pile of dark basalt stones, cleared by kibbutz farmers, stretched across much of the field. As Kahalani's tank turned the corner of the stone pile, he came on three Syrian tanks. Two were static; the third was moving beyond them.

"Stop," he shouted.

His driver braked so sharply that everyone was thrown forward. Kahalani swung the gun at the nearest tank, just twenty yards away. Tank commanders could override the gunner's controls in order to roughly aim the gun but it was for the gunner to make the final adjustments.

"Fire," Kahalani shouted.

"What range?" asked his gunner, Kilion. They were so close he did not realize the dark object filling his scope was a Syrian tank.

"It doesn't matter. Just fire."

Kilion fired, holing the tank. Kahalani shifted the gun toward the second standing tank. "Do you see it?" he asked.

"Yes," said the gunner.

"Then fire. Quickly."

A hole appeared in the Syrian tank's turret.

Kahalani looked for the third tank. It had stopped and was pointing its gun straight at him. As he looked down the barrel, black and enormous, "T-62" registered in his mind. He had never encountered one before. "Fire, fire," he called.

"Misfire," shouted Kilion.

The casing of the previous shell was stuck in the breech. As the loader lunged at the shell to extricate it, Kahalani braced for instant death. He lowered his head into the tank and placed his hands on the lip of the turret in order to extricate himself if possible when the tank was hit. This was how he had saved himself from a burning tank in Sinai in the Six Day War.

When the explosion came, however, it was the comforting sound of an outgoing shell. Raising his head, he saw the T-62 aflame. A fourth Syrian tank was now racing toward them. Kahalani moved the gun slightly to the right and Kilion fired. The Syrian tank was hit but continued to charge like an enraged bull. Before Kilion could get off a second round, another Israeli tank which had moved forward delivered the coup de grâce. The vaunted T-62 was proving to be as vulnerable as the T-55.

Kahalani reported the encounter to Ben-Gal, who told him to take command of the sector, including the tanks of Rattes's battalion, which were on their way. Yos Eldar, who was operating from a personnel carrier rather than a tank, had had to pull back because the APC was too vulnerable to the intense artillery fire.

It was vital to regain the ramps if the Syrians were to be stopped. As Kahalani weighed the situation, another Syrian tank came up out of the wadi. He turned the turret and Kilion hit it. A few seconds later still another T-62 emerged and Kilion stopped it too. Kahalani looked around for a tank he could position at the head of the wadi. Seeing none, he ordered his driver forward to a knoll overlooking the length of the wadi. Within minutes, Kilion had notched up five more kills. This cleared the wadi, but from his position Kahalani could see into the valley beyond. Heading toward the Israeli line was a mass of tanks.

The Israeli tanks behind the ramp were scattered like lost sheep, their commanders unaware of the approaching danger. If they were to survive, it was essential to pull them together and get them up the ramp before the Syrians reached it. Only from there could the vast disparity in numbers be offset by superior firing position. When Kahalani called them on his radio he got little response. The tanks were from several units and operating on different frequencies. At his request, the brigade communications officer cut into every company's radio net to order the tank commanders to switch to Kahalani's frequency. When his calls continued to draw little response, Kahalani understood that most of the tank commanders preferred not to hear him. This was the fourth straight day of battle. They had been under constant artillery bombardment and the Syrian air force had had several goes at them.

Half their comrades were dead or wounded and they had hardly slept since the battle started. The tank commanders could no longer bring themselves to face the curtain of fire on the ramp. They had reached their breaking point.

Four miles away, Colonel Nafshi was monitoring a battle between Captain Rak's company and a Syrian tank force trying to cross the cease-fire line south of Kuneitra when Ben-Gal asked if he could see what was happening in the Kuneitra Gap. Nafshi could not. He gathered five other tanks, including Yakhin's platoon, and headed toward the Hermonit. On the radio, he could hear Ben-Gal giving Kahalani command of the area and imploring him to hang on. He turned up a slope for a look at what was happening in the valley beyond. As his six tanks started up abreast, Nafshi saw faint smoke rising above the ridgeline. He recognized it as exhaust smoke from tanks climbing from the other side. They could only be Syrian and they were plainly closer to the summit than he. He stopped and waited for them to come over the top. In the ensuing shootout, half a dozen Syrian tanks were knocked out. Three Israeli tanks were hit and two of their commanders killed. Nafshi's was the third tank hit but he was unhurt. He shifted to another tank and moved up to the summit. He could see the valley below dark with Syrian tanks on the move.

In the tank with Kahalani, Lieutenant Peled had since the start of the war felt fear knotted in his stomach. The operations officer had seen fear in Kahalani's face as well. Everyone was gripped by it. But until now the battalion had operated like a well-tuned racing car with fear along only as an unobtrusive passenger. Now, as he monitored the nonresponse to Kahalani's calls and noted that tank commanders were keeping their hatches closed, it seemed to the lieutenant that the passenger had moved into the driver's seat. Like many others, he had reconciled himself to the certainty that he would not survive this day intact. He permitted himself to hope that he would come out of it with no more than injury to an arm or leg.

A Syrian tank topped the ramp like some prehistoric beast, rising high to crest the front edge and then dropping down onto the firing position. As its snout swiveled in search of prey, Kahalani pointed his gun at it and Kilion set the tank aflame. When another tank from the Syrian spearhead force came over the top, it was knocked out by one of the Israeli tanks to the rear of the ramp.

Hope flared when Rattes arrived with his seven remaining tanks. The battalion commander's voice was weary. Kahalani had once served under Rattes as a crewman and he sought to cushion the fact that Rattes was now under his command by framing his directives as requests rather than orders. The sound of explosions was constant. Syrian and Israeli crews escaping from damaged tanks scrambled over the terrain, ignoring one another as they tried to make their way back to their respective lines. Suddenly, Rattes's tanks bolted for the rear. It was several minutes before Kahalani learned that Rattes had been killed by a direct hit. His deputy was also killed. The unit had gone through hellish days and the now leaderless tank commanders had panicked.

A nightmarish dilemma gripped Kahalani. Only he could see the approaching danger in the valley and only he could muster the tank crews to regain the ramp. Nothing but the personal example of the senior commander on the spot would get the paralyzed tank commanders, most of them nineteen- and twenty-year-olds, to move. But he could neither abandon the wadi, through which Syrian tanks could debouch at any moment, nor make radio contact with most of the tanks. Ten Syrian tanks had already topped the ramparts and been hit. In a little while, twenty or thirty would come over and there would be no stopping them. Kahalani weighed the possibility of ordering the men to fall back on the second line, but he feared they would be hit before they made it.

The same thought was occurring to Ben-Gal. He took the radio mouthpiece to issue the pullback order but then called instead to General Eitan to report his intentions. Eitan was watching the battle from a ridge just south of the Hermonit. He could see the small Israeli tank force sheltering behind the ridge and the mass of Syrian tanks surging across the valley toward them. Behind the Syrian tanks a line of APCs and supply vehicles stretched two miles east to the Syrian village of Ufana.

"Hang on five minutes more," said Eitan. "Reinforcements will be moving up to you." They both knew that the minutes Eitan asked for were not measured by the clock but by calculations of life and death, personal and communal. Eitan had himself been in this situation twenty-five years before in the battle at San Simon Monastery in Jerusalem where he fought alongside Elazar and Ben-Ari. The ability to hang on just a few minutes longer had made the difference then between victory and disaster and he thought of it now.

The division commander told Ben-Gal that a new unit had been put together in Camp Jordan by Colonel Ben-Hanan. The latter's father, a physical education instructor, delivered early morning wake-up exercises on the radio, therefore the patchwork unit's code name—Morning Exercise. Ben-Hanan's force was almost ready, said Eitan.

Calling Capt. Emi Palant, the senior officer behind the ramps, Kahalani told him to use a signal flag to get the tank commanders' attention and to lead them up the ramp. The company commander waved his flag but got no response. Seizing his machine gun, he fired at the side of the nearest tank. When the startled commander looked out, Palant passed on the message. He then ran from tank to tank, rapping on turrets to get the commanders' attention. Remounting his own tank, he started forward. When no tank followed, he returned to his starting point.

On the radio net, Kahalani heard a new voice addressing him, a tank commander from Rattes's unit introducing himself as "Sergeant, Platoon Four." It was a cool voice and Kahalani ordered the sergeant to come alongside. A solution to his dilemma seemed at hand. "Sergeant, Platoon Four, take my position and guard the wadi opening. Destroy any Syrian tank that tries to come up."

"This is Sergeant, Platoon Four. All right, but I don't have any shells left."

Kahalani tried to review his options but there didn't seem to be any. On the radio net he heard Major Zamir, flanking his position to the south, reporting a massive Syrian attack. Zamir asked permission to shift the few tanks remaining to Tiger Company to a better position slightly south. "Negative," said Ben-Gal, aware of the gap this would open. "Stay where you are. Kahalani, report."

"This is Kahalani. Not all the tanks here have made contact with me. I'm not managing to control them and they're constantly drifting to the rear." In his reports to Ben-Gal since the war started, he had tried to avoid sounding alarmist in order not to add to the brigade commander's burden. Even this report was phrased moderately but the facts were stark. Ben-Gal said he would try to get more tanks up to him.

"Sergeant, Platoon Four," said Kahalani into his mouthpiece. He had made a decision. "I know your situation. Stay here in my place and don't let anyone up from the wadi. Clear?"

"This is Sergeant, Platoon Four. I remind you that—"

"I know," he said. "Stand high in the position so that they see you. If they see you well they won't enter."

Starting toward the tanks behind the rampart, Kahalani addressed their commanders. "This is the battalion commander. Whoever hears me, raise your flag." There were ten tanks that he could see. Most of their commanders raised flags. "We must regain the ramp. Otherwise—" His remarks were interrupted by two planes diving on the cluster of tanks and dropping bombs. The explosions were powerful but none of the tanks was hit. As the second plane pulled up Kahalani saw a Star of David on its tail.

Despair threatened to overwhelm him. On the right flank, Zamir reported that he had only three tanks left and almost no ammunition. "Help is on the way," said Ben-Gal. "Just fifteen minutes."

"I don't know if I can hold on fifteen minutes," said Zamir.

Kahalani reached the tanks behind the ramps. "This is the battalion commander," he began again. "A large enemy force is on the other side of the ramp. We are going to move forward to regain the ramp. Move."

His tank started forward and a few followed, but with agonizing slowness. Two Syrian tanks came over the top of the ramp. Kilion fired along with other tanks, setting the Syrians aflame. The Centurions that had moved forward now pulled back to the more sheltered position from which they had started. Seeing how his own tank was exposed to any Syrian tank coming over the ramp, Kahalani now understood better the reluctance of the tank commanders to cross the open space.

Ben-Gal came on the radio to inform him that he was sending him a number of tanks under the command of Eli Geva. Morning Exercise was already on its way to relieve Tiger Company on the southern flank. Turning, Kahalani could see the dust cloud of approaching tanks in the distance. For the first time since the battle began this morning, points of light were beginning to appear.

"This is the battalion commander." Addressing his men, Kahalani realized that straightforward commands would no longer work. "Look at the courage of the enemy mounting the position in front of us. I don't know what's happening to us. They are only the Arab enemy we have always known. We are stronger than them. Start moving forward and form a line with me. I am waving my flag. Move." He had spoken in an even tone but shouted the last word.

A platoon commander two hundred yards to the rear had been sitting in his buttoned-up tank literally shivering from fear. The rest of his crew was in the same condition, their nerves shattered. He had not fled to the rear, the lieutenant told himself repeatedly, he had not fled. But he was unable to force himself to move forward or to stop shaking. To his front he could identify the battalion commander's tank by the markings painted on its turret—10 C. He had heard Kahalani's calls on the radio but had not responded. This time the battalion commander's words stung. Was he suggesting they were cowards? "Move," the lieutenant said to his driver. The other tanks had already started forward.

"Don't stop," Kahalani called, as he watched the tanks form into line. "Keep moving. Keep moving."

A Syrian tank came over the ramp and Kahalani swiveled his turret but the tank next to them fired first. Kahalani was exhilarated as he glanced at the formation.

"You're moving fine," he called. "Don't stop. Be prepared to fire."

The hatches were open now but the tank commanders kept low in their turrets, their eyes just above the edges. Everyone was fearful of what awaited them when they topped the rise. As they climbed abreast they had to make their way between burning Syrian and Israeli tanks. Not until they pushed up the final yards into the firing positions could the tank commanders see the valley.

The Kuneitra Gap was dark with vehicles. Most were static—tanks, personnel carriers, and trucks knocked out during the previous days of fighting and this day's battle. But among them a mass of tanks was moving doggedly forward. The farthest were a thousand yards distant, the closest only fifty yards.

The Centurions opened fire. Each tank commander unleashed his pent-up fury and fear on the approaching enemy.

"Aim only at moving tanks," called Kahalani. He was afraid they would waste scarce ammunition shooting at tanks already knocked out. Syrian crews could be seen jumping from damaged tanks and running to the rear. Eli Geva's Centurions now reached the ramp and joined in the shoot. For the first time, the Syrian tanks seemed to waver and search for a more protected approach but they kept coming. Finally, there were no more targets for the Israeli gunners.

A heavy Syrian artillery barrage descended on the ramps and the tank commanders pulled back into the turrets. When the shelling subsided, Kahalani put his head back out. Nothing was moving in the valley except flames licking at stricken tanks. When he reported to Ben-Gal, the brigade commander asked how many Syrian tanks had been hit. "We've destroyed sixty to seventy tanks," said Kahalani.

The Syrian attack on Ben-Gal's right flank was likewise moving toward its climax. Major Zamir, who had ambushed the Forty-third Brigade the first night of the war, was down to two tanks and again requested permission to withdraw. But Ben-Gal ordered him to stay. Help was on the way, he said. Just hang on a few minutes more.

Zamir, his ammunition exhausted, could wait no longer. The force led by Ben-Hanan arrived at precisely the moment that Zamir was pulling back. Ben-Hanan waved a nonchalant "shalom" to Zamir as they passed each other. Topping a small rise just ahead, Ben-Hanan saw a T-55 heading toward him just fifty yards away.

"Stop," he called. "Fire." His war had begun.

Askarov took up position alongside Ben-Hanan as the rest of the unit formed a battle line. Shell splinters cut Ben-Hanan's face and broke his eyeglasses. He passed command to Askarov and pulled back briefly to be treated by a medic. Askarov set ablaze a tank just forty yards from him but he was struck in the head by a bullet and seriously wounded. Once again, he was carried to the rear.

As Eitan watched the battle from the adjacent ridge, his intelligence officer, Lt. Col. Dennie Agmon, said, "The Syrian General Staff has decided to retreat." Eitan looked at him askance. Agmon had not been listening to any radio net and had no visible source for that far-reaching pronouncement. "Look there," he said, pointing with his binoculars. Vehicles which had been streaming past Ufana had stopped and were turning around. This was not a panicky retreat from the battlefield but an orderly pullback, beginning with vehicles at the rear, plainly a command decision. After a while, Strongpoint 107 reported Syrian tank crewmen in gray coveralls running toward the rear from the Kuneitra Gap. Finally, the last tanks still intact on the battlefield turned as well.

Ben-Gal came forward to watch from a ridgetop as the Syrian wave ebbed. In the valley lay 260 Syrian tanks as well as numerous armored personnel carriers, trucks, and other vehicles which his brigade, and Nafshi's tanks, had stopped during the past four days. Many of the tanks had been abandoned intact.

In the afternoon, Ben-Gal's tanks pulled back a few at a time for ammunition and fuel. Kahalani drove to the brigade command post to talk with Ben-Gal who had not slept for four days except for brief catnaps. In an upbeat tone that sounded forced, the brigade commander said, "We've been ordered to counterattack into Syria." Lieutenant Peled, the operations officer accompanying Kahalani, was horrified. After surviving the nightmare of the past four days, how could they be asked to undertake a counterattack? Were there no other units available?

Eitan wanted Ben-Gal to attack the next day, Wednesday, in order not to give the Syrians respite. But Ben-Gal asked for a day to permit the exhausted men to rest and to fill the enormous gaps in his ranks. "Phase One is over for us," he told Kahalani. "Phase Two is about to start."

Syrian commandos staged a successful ambush this day of a reconnaissance company at Bukata in the northernmost part of the Golan. Five Israeli APCs were hit by RPGs and twenty-four men killed. The helicopter-borne commando force which had overflown Ben-Gal fared less well. Israel's elite commando force, the General Staff Reconnaissance Unit (Sayeret Matkal), had been impatiently waiting at Nafakh for a role in the fighting. In a swift charge, its men killed forty of the Syrians, at a cost of two dead of their own. Other Syrian commandos who landed nearby were overcome by Golani troops.

Close to noon, Ben-Gal informed Nafshi that Strongpoint 107 was not responding to radio messages and had apparently fallen. Nafshi headed there through Kuneitra, accompanied by two other tanks. As he passed the town's cinema, the most prominent structure in Kuneitra, RPGs hit his tank and the one behind. The commander of the second tank was killed but Nafshi again escaped unhurt except for temporary deafness. Picking up a contingent of Golani infantrymen in two half-tracks, he drove through the part of town closest to the Syrian lines in the belief that the Syrian troops, who had apparently penetrated the town in strength, would not be expecting Israelis from that direction. Syrian soldiers appeared from side streets and waved at the dust-covered vehicles, assuming them to be Syrian. Nafshi, dust covered himself, waved back. Emerging from the built-up area, he took a cleared path he knew through an Israeli minefield that permitted an indirect approach to the strongpoint. Cautiously driving into the compound, he saw that the soldiers were all sound asleep at their posts.

Since the war's start, the Israelis had been struck by what they saw as a zombielike implacability with which the Syrians were hurling themselves at the Israeli defenses. But on Wednesday morning, electronic monitors picked up an order from the commander of the First Armored Division, Gen. Tewfik Jehani, to shell one of his own units, the Ninety-first Brigade, which had spearheaded the division's attacks. The order appeared aimed at stopping men from abandoning their tanks and fleeing on foot. In the end the order was canceled, but it pointed to a crisis in the Syrian ranks.

In a final push the next morning against the shrinking Syrian bulge, Israeli tanks reached the Purple Line along its length. Climbing a ridge overlooking Strongpoint 110, Major Bierman of Sarig's brigade saw hundreds of Syrian infantrymen besieging the post. A few tank shells dispersed them. The tanks also hit Syrian vehicles driving back across the line between strongpoints.

At the sight of the withdrawing enemy, the tankers cheered and fired their weapons into the air. When they descended to 110, the Golani troops, who had been under siege for four days, climbed the tanks to embrace them. There were now no more Syrians on the Golan. Moussa Peled lit up the cigar Haim Bar-Lev had given him with the injunction to smoke it "when the time is right."

For Israel, the nightmare of the first night of the war on the Golan had given way in four days to stunning victory. The Syrians left behind close to nine hundred tanks, the bulk of their armored strength. The scenario Elazar had once fantasized for Sinai—falling back from the canal and luring the Egyptian armor into a killing ground—had inadvertently transpired on the Golan. The Golan fallback had not been calculated—it was in fact a collapse—but the results were the same. Southern Golan became an enormous tank trap which snapped shut with Moussa Peled's drive north.

The return to the Purple Line was the first measure of consolation afforded Elazar since the war began. It also posed a major dilemma. What next? Should the IDF redeploy along the cease-fire line or should it push on toward Damascus? A choice had to be made quickly and it would be one of the most important in the war.

Nine hours of virtually continuous discussion began with a meeting Wednesday afternoon in the Pit between Elazar and his generals. The Syrians, for all their losses, had retreated in good order, noted Elazar. The troops manning their side of the cease-fire line had been reinforced by units retreating from the Golan. General Jehani had refused to leave the Golan until all his troops had exited. By the time he started back Israeli troops were between him and the cease-fire line. Israeli intelligence would later learn that the general and his aides had holed up in a culvert until nightfall before escaping.

The Israeli forces were exhausted. Officers reported entire battalions falling asleep whenever their tanks halted. Men were not responding to radioed orders because they had dozed off. Elazar ordered all operations halted for the rest of the day so that the troops could sleep.

The chief of staff inclined toward holding fast on the Purple Line. This would permit one of the three northern divisions, with 200 to 250 tanks, to be sent to Sinai to join in a major drive against the Egyptians. The Purple Line was more defensible than any other line they were likely to halt on if they advanced eastward.

The other alternative—a drive aimed at reaching Damascus, forty miles distant—offered the prospect of knocking Syria out of the war, but Elazar did not think that likely. With Iraqi forces expected to bolster the Syrians, it was questionable if Israel could get close enough to Damascus to impose a cease-fire.

The discussion moved after several hours from the Pit to Dayan's office where the participants continued exploring scenarios. Would an attack across the Purple Line cause the Iraqis and Jordanians to rush to the aid of Syria or would it deter them? If the IDF drew close to Damascus, would Moscow press for a cease-fire or be provoked to military intervention? Mossad chief Zamir had come to Elazar's office to inform him that the Soviets, who had tried to dissuade the Arabs from going to war, were replacing their enormous war losses with great speed now that battle had been joined.

Despite the return to the cease-fire line, Elazar's optimism was in retreat. Since the opening hours of the war, his upbeat tone had propped up sagging morale on the General Staff and in the cabinet. But now, with the immediate existential threat behind them, he permitted himself an unblinking assessment of Israel's situation.

Israel had been wrong-footed by the surprise attack and was having difficulty regaining its balance. It was fighting a war it was unprepared for, militarily and psychologically, against an enemy it did not know. Tens of thousands of Soviet military advisers had been training the Arab armies for years and Moscow had flooded Egypt and Syria with modern weaponry. Israel had no answer to the Sagger antitank missile or the SAM-6 antiaircraft missile. The Arabs were displaying not only superior weapons but new tactics and, above all, new spirit, leaving the Israeli command groping for an effective response.

After five days of combat, things looked bleak to Elazar on every front—in the south, in the air, even in the north. Although the Syrians had been pushed out of the Golan, Elazar was disappointed to learn on a morning visit to Northern Command that armored probes across the cease-fire line at Tel Kudne had met stiff resistance. Elazar was not sure it would be possible to break through. Intelligence was warning that a large Iraqi tank force was due to set out for the Syrian front within fourteen to thirty hours.

As for the Sinai front, "Every day we're doing the same thing, killing a lot of Egyptians and losing a bit of territory," Elazar said. Bar-Lev had informed him that Egyptian infantry was attacking Adan's division "like kamikazes." They were being cut down with machine guns but kept coming, wave after wave, firing Saggers. Elazar asked his staff to reequip the army in the south with mortars. In its exaggerated reliance on tanks, the army had virtually stripped its ground forces of this basic anti-infantry weapon.

Israel's situation was getting worse each day, he told his officers. The heavy losses suffered in the opening days had reduced the IDF's options. "Even if we get forty more Phantoms [which the Americans were promising], even if we get more tanks, it would not be substantial enough to change the balance of forces. We cannot today cross the canal or get close to Damascus." Within a few days, he said, the army might have to pull back deeper into Sinai. "There we'll be in for a long, indecisive battle—a defensive battle, just fending off disaster."

The air force would soon have only enough planes to secure the skies over Israel, not to provide substantial ground support. The logic of events was leading Elazar to a far-reaching conclusion: Israel could not win this war and must invest its energies in preparing for the next one. "I'm in a black mood if we're not heading for a cease-fire," he said to Dayan. "I'm only thinking out loud, and it may well be that I exaggerate, but I'm saying what I think right now. Things won't get better than they are now. We need a cease-fire so that we can rebuild the army." It could not be done, he said, while 400,000 men were under arms. The new army Elazar was contemplating would be twice as big and would have thought through the strategic and tactical implications of the current war.

In a reversal of roles, it was Dayan, recovered from his opening day shakes, who expressed optimism. The tide had turned in Israel's favor in the north, said the minister, and would do so in the south as well, as long as the IDF did not adopt Sharon's call for a major canal crossing. Dayan did, however, favor a limited crossing at Port Said and Port Fuad, the twin cities straddling the canal's northern entrance. The air force had succeeded in neutralizing the SAM batteries in that area and would be able to support a ground attack. The cities' capture would give Israel a territorial bargaining chip of symbolic weight in postwar negotiations.

If the Egyptians tried to advance in Sinai beyond the SAM umbrella, Dayan said, they would be trounced. In that case, countered Elazar, the Egyptians would stay under the umbrella and engage in a war of attrition, which was Israel's worst option, given that the Egyptian army was twice as big.

"Excuse me, Dado, but that's not the model," said Dayan. "If the Egyptians start a war of attrition, we send the air force on deep penetration raids." This is what was done during the War of Attrition in 1969–1970 when deep air penetrations against economic and military targets forced Egyptian acquiescence to a cease-fire.

Scud missiles had arrived in Egypt but the Soviets were maintaining operational control while they instructed Egyptian crews. If the Soviets handed over control, the Egyptians would have the ability to hit Tel Aviv in retaliation for deep air strikes but Dayan was prepared to risk it. After all, the air force could counter-retaliate more tellingly against Cairo. He suggested putting Egyptian economic sites even now on an attrition target list.

After Dayan left the room, Elazar turned to the other generals. "I tried to have a serious talk with him but I couldn't. I'll have it with you now. I doubt that we will be able to get out of our situation without some kind of territorial loss." A general noted that the defense minister had been on an "up." Said Elazar: "His 'downs' are too low and his 'ups' are too high."

A remark by General Tal led Elazar to reverse his position on the spot regarding an attack into Syria. Tal noted that if Israel deployed on the cease-fire line instead of advancing, there would be no forward movement on either front for four days while the division being sent south made its way to Sinai. "The Arabs will see after a couple of days," said Tal, "that we're on the defensive."

The observation by his deputy galvanized Elazar. "They'll see it after one day," he said. "We have to attack [on the Syrian front] tomorrow."

At 10:30 p.m., Elazar and his generals walked across a grassy patch separating the Defense Ministry from the prime minister's office. Waiting for them was Mrs. Meir, her inner cabinet, including Dayan, and advisers. This was the first meeting of the war cabinet since the war started.

"We're at the decisive point of the war," opened Elazar. He favored attacking into Syria rather than halting on the cease-fire line, he said. There was a chance that the Syrian army might suddenly crack, as it had unexpectedly done in the Six Day War when he commanded the assault on the Golan Heights as head of Northern Command. Apart from that, considerations of national image required Israel to advance. "The world believes that the IDF is strong and is waiting for it to attack. No one is aware of its [current] weakness—not the Israeli people, not the Americans, not the Arabs. If we are not attacking by tomorrow in Syria they will suspect something. After another day, they will know." Sadat would not accept a cease-fire, Elazar said, if he perceived Israel as weak. Ambassador Dinitz had reported that the Soviets were pushing for a cease-fire within forty-eight hours. It was essential to seize enemy territory before then. The possibility of a successful counterattack existed only on the Syrian front. "I favor an all-out attack into Syria tomorrow."

Dayan agreed. So did Mrs. Meir, who grasped the cardinal point. It would take at least four days to shift a division to Sinai. If there was a cease-fire before it could enter combat, the war would end with a territorial loss for Israel in Sinai and no gain on the Golan—an unmitigated defeat. This was a political, not military, consideration and her decision was unhesitating—to push immediately into Syria. At the very least, she wanted Syrian territory to bring to the postwar negotiating table, and it didn't have to be Damascus. Shortly after midnight, the decision was taken to attack in the morning.

Elazar's jauntiness was immediately restored. He asked to meet on the Golan in the morning with division and brigade commanders before the battle got under way. Calling General Hofi, he told him he would arrive at Northern Command headquarters at 5 a.m. "You're not going to the cinema tonight, right?" he said, alluding to the early hour and to the fact that Hofi's war room was located in a commandeered movie house. "We'll meet, go together to talk to the brigade commanders, come back [to Northern Command headquarters], and then, Yitzhak, we'll make war."

At Poriya Hospital near Tiberias where his life had been saved in an operation on Sunday, Colonel Sarig was feeling well enough by Wednesday for doctors to permit him a one-day visit to his nearby kibbutz, Bait Hashita. Anticipating that an Israeli attack into Syria was imminent, he joined the "escapees" fleeing hospitals for the front. Stopping home long enough to don a fresh uniform, he headed for the Golan. He had no feeling in his left arm and would need help getting on and off a tank. The doctors had warned him not to cough lest his neck stitches open. It was dark when he reached General Laner's command post on Mount Yosifon. Vehicles were burning from a Katyusha barrage moments before. One of the men killed in that attack, he was told, was from his kibbutz. No one told him that a few hours earlier his younger brother, a company commander in Hadar's brigade, had been killed.

Elazar came north at dawn on a helicopter flight that offered him a blessed hour of sleep. After reviewing the attack plan with Hofi, Elazar continued on with him to meet the divisional and brigade commanders at the Nafakh camp. It was his first meeting with them since the war began. The sight of the unshaven, bone-weary faces touched him deeply, particularly Ben-Gal's haunted visage. The coming battle, he told them, would be a turning point. It was doubtful that they could reach Damascus, but their aim would be to get close enough to threaten it.

The ground attack would begin with Raful Eitan's division skirting the foot of Mount Hermon whose slopes would secure the left flank. Kahalani's battalion would lead. A second force, under Ben-Hanan, would move on a parallel route a mile south. The attack had been set for 7 p.m. but Ben-Gal persuaded Northern Command to postpone it until 11 a.m. so that the sun would not be in their eyes.

Dan Laner's division would attack along the Kuneitra–Damascus road, code-named America. This was the obvious attack route, so obvious that the Syrians had long since made it the most heavily defended sector on any of their borders. The road lay under the guns of a major fortification at the village of Khan Arnabe. The IDF had not prepared a contingency plan for an attack along this route since it never intended a head-on assault here. But Hofi believed Syrian morale was at the breaking point and that an attack up America would work. The Syrians, he noted, had crumbled in the Six Day War when the Israelis gained a foothold on the Golan. However, Elazar said that the staying power of the Syrian forces in this war was unknown. General Eitan vainly urged that Laner's division follow him through the northern break-in point and then attack Khan Arnabe from the rear instead of challenging the formidable defenses on America.

Ben-Gal summoned his battalion commanders for a briefing. Three quarters of the brigade's tank crewmen who had started the war five days before were dead or wounded. But replacements overnight had brought the brigade back up to full strength, one hundred tanks and crews. When the briefing was over, Ben-Gal called Kahalani aside. "Listen," he said, placing a hand on Kahalani's shoulder. "I met the chief of staff this morning and I want you to know that I told him what you did." Ben-Gal seemed to have trouble expressing himself. "I told him you were a Hero of Israel [the name of Israel's highest medal for valor]. I wanted you to know this." Backing away from his emotion, Ben-Gal shook Kahalani's hand and said awkwardly, "It'll be all right. See you."

Lieutenant Peled, Kahalani's operations officer, watched the scene in astonishment. He had not heard the conversation but it was plain from Ben-Gal's body language and from the comradely hand placed on Kahalani's shoulder that the brigade commander was moved and was making personal contact. It was a view of Yanosh Ben-Gal the lieutenant had never expected to see.

Back at his battalion's staging area, Kahalani asked for the officers to be assembled. He scanned their faces as they sat on the ground in front of him. Most were new. "First, for all those who have just joined us and still don't know where they are, this is the Seventy-seventh battalion of the Seventh Brigade. Battalion commander Kahalani stands by chance before you." A hesitant smile appeared on the tense faces. "Before I explain our mission, I want to know who you are and what your tasks are."

Each new man was asked to tell which company he was assigned to, what he had done since the beginning of the war, and from what organic unit he came. A number were reservists. Kahalani asked each of the latter personal questions—what part of the country they were from, what they did in civilian life, whether they were married, how many children they had. Lieutenant Peled, accustomed to the spartan tone of briefings in the standing army, found these personal questions puzzling. What had they to do with the business at hand? Only later would he understand that Kahalani was spinning a human web, creating of this disparate group of strangers thrown together on a remote battlefield a cohesive team willing, in moments of danger that would shortly be upon them, to risk death because he asked them to.

Only when this bonding was done did Kahalani turn to Peled and ask him to unroll the map. "The brigade has been ordered to break through the Syrian lines," said Kahalani. "Our battalion will spearhead the attack." He pointed out their route and spelled out the order in which the units would move. "I wish you all success. And, the main thing, fight like lions. We're moving out in twenty minutes. On your tanks."

25

IRAQI INTERVENTION

THE MINEFIELDS CONFRONTING Kahalani's force lay behind a broad swath of agricultural land inside Syrian territory. The Syrian army had left openings in the minefields to enable Syrian farmers to access their land. The Israeli force passed unscathed by following these paths, which were known to intelligence.

In Ben-Hanan's area a mile south, the minefields lay directly on the cease-fire line and engineers cleared paths through it with bangalore torpedoes. With artillery providing a rolling barrage five hundred yards to their front, the two tank forces moved eastward on parallel routes, encountering no opposition except for artillery fire.

The easy success of the northern break-in encouraged belief that the Syrian defenses on the Damascus Road would collapse with the first shove. That confidence was not shared by the man who would be at the spearhead of Laner's force. Maj. Giora Bierman, who had passed out from jaundice on the battlefield four days before, was to lead a battalion against the Khan Arnabe fortification, which lay across two miles of flat terrain, by racing straight up the road with his sixteen tanks. A reconnaissance battalion commanded by Lt. Col. Hanani Tavori would attack to the left of the road with nineteen tanks across an open field.

Bierman regarded the mission as suicidal and said so to Colonel Sarig. But the brigade commander shared the belief that the Syrians were too dispirited to put up effective resistance. The tanks would rely on shock and speed, firing as they went. Most were bound to get through, he said.

Resigning himself to his fate, Bierman positioned his tank close to the head of his column and waited for the signal to advance. Sarig, in a thin-skinned personnel carrier, took position farther back.

The Israeli Enclave

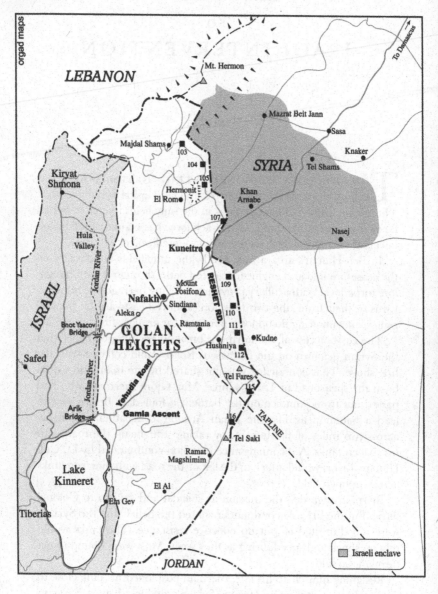

orgad maps

LEBANON

Mt. Hermon

To Damascus

Mazrat Beit Jann

SYRIA

Sasa

Knaker

Majdal Shams

103

104

105

Tel Shams

Hermonit
El Rom

Khan
Arnabe

107

Kiryat
Shmona

Hula
Valley

Kuneitra

Nasej

ISRAEL

Nafakh

Mount
Yosifon

Sindiana

109

RESHET RD.

Jordan River

Aleka

GOLAN
HEIGHTS

Ramtania

110

111

Kudne

Safed

Bnot Yaacov
Bridge

Hushniya

112

Jordan River

Yehudia Road

Tel Fares

115

Arik
Bridge

Gamla Ascent

116

TAPLINE

Tel Saki

Lake
Kinneret

Ramat
Magshimim

El Al

Tiberias

Ein Gev

JORDAN

Israeli enclave

The attack commenced under withering Syrian fire. Bierman's column started up the road but passage was soon blocked by knocked-out tanks. The sound of mine explosions marked the progress of Tavori's battalion across the field. All of Tavori's tanks had treads blown off except for a few which managed to gain the road. But all of these were soon hit by Saggers. The road became a cauldron of smoke and burning tanks. Instead of a swift dash up the road, those tanks still operational shielded behind tanks that had been knocked out and exchanged fire with the Syrians.

Finally, Bierman and a few other tank commanders managed to extricate themselves and charged the Syrian position. Bierman's tank was hit as it reached Khan Arnabe's outer trench. The gunner was killed and Bierman and his loader wounded. As he extricated himself from the turret, Bierman saw fire beginning to lick at the tank's innards. He and his loader sheltered behind the turret as Syrian infantrymen in the trench a few yards away tried to shoot them. Other tanks had made it inside the fortification and were firing machine guns into the trenches. Looking back, Bierman was relieved to see a fresh tank force starting up the road. He knew this would be Ori Orr's brigade. Swift exploitation of the breakthrough was essential if the Syrians were not to slam the door shut again. Orr had in fact been told to wait until evacuation of the casualties from the road and minefield. However, he feared that the sight was having a dispiriting effect on his men. He received permission to begin his attack immediately.

Bierman and his loader kept the turret between them and the Syrian trench. The major called on the driver, who had remained in his compartment, to begin driving in reverse. Unable to move one wounded arm, Bierman held on to the tank with the other and guided the driver toward the open field. After half a mile, Bierman called on the driver to stop and to get out before the fire touched off an explosion. As the driver emerged, artillery struck, killing him and wounding Bierman again—this time in the head, stomach, and lungs. Bierman would be retrieved unconscious by medics and helicoptered to a hospital.

Twenty-five tanks—two thirds of Sarig's force—had been knocked out. But the six tanks that made it to Khan Arnabe opened the way for Orr, who was followed by Mordecai Ben-Porat's brigade. The two reduced brigades moved off to the east and south and a force of paratroopers was sent in to clear the Khan Arnabe trenches of remaining

Syrians. During the night, Sarig received reinforcements and tanks that had been repaired. He would be able to notify Laner in the morning that his brigade was ready to continue.

On the northernmost axis, Kahalani's task force had by late afternoon reached a hill overlooking its objective, the village of Mazraat Bet Jann, without a single casualty. Abandoned Syrian tanks and damaged fortifications along the way showed the effect of three hours of artillery and air softening up, the kind General Adan had futilely called for at Hizayon in Sinai three days before.

In contrast to the stony landscape and bleak mud-hut hamlets to the south, Mazraat Bet Jann was a picturesque village in a well-wooded setting nestling at the foot of the Hermon. The thick vegetation could hide an ambush and Kahalani carefully studied the surroundings. Residents were fleeing the village on donkeys and on foot. Kahalani decided to give them time to get well clear before descending. But as he watched, Syrian tanks moved into the village and four helicopters disgorged troops. The Syrians were not giving up. With night almost upon him, Kahalani obtained Ben-Gal's permission to wait until morning before attacking.

Ben-Hanan's force was also just short of its objective, Tel Shams, when night fell. The fortified hill dominated the Kuneitra–Damascus road and was "the cork in the bottle," as Elazar put it, on the approach to Sasa. Hofi's mission was to reach at least as far as Sasa. From there, artillery would be able to shell Damascus's suburbs. Only if Israeli shells fell close to Damascus would the Soviets, on Syria's behalf, ask for a cease-fire in the U.N., Dayan told the front commander.

Hofi was uneasy, however, about ordering a head-on attack on Tel Shams after the grim results of his order to attack at Khan Arnabe. Studying the war map in the Pit, Elazar expressed concern that a handful of Syrian tanks on Tel Shams would be sufficient to repel an attack. "Our force has to climb up the valley. It won't get past it." Ben-Gal was also uneasy and was inclined to call off the attack. He acceded, however, to Ben-Hanan's request to let him go ahead with it in the morning.

Ben-Hanan moved out at first light with eight tanks. The road passed through the Leja, a dark plain covered with basalt boulders that severely impeded off-road movement. As they approached the tel, a volley of Sagger missiles was fired at them and Syrian planes attacked the formation. A rocket hit Ben-Hanan's tank, tearing off a piece of his ear and bursting his right eardrum. Remaining in action, he pulled his tanks back, but when out of sight of the tel he turned off-road into the Leja itself on a tortuous, mazelike route which brought him to the rear of the Tel Shams fortification in late afternoon. Ben-Hanan's tanks surprised the Syrians and destroyed more than a score of vehicles, including a number of tanks. As he began to ascend the rear of the hill, two Saggers hit his tank, propelling him from the turret and killing two of his crewmen. The rest of the tanks were either hit or pulled back.

Lying beside his burning tank, Ben-Hanan saw that his left leg was dangling. On a radio retrieved from the tank by his driver, Ben-Hanan contacted Ben-Gal. "This is Yossi," he said. "My leg's gone. I'm lying beside my tank. Get me out of here." The driver pulled Ben-Hanan to a pit that offered some shelter. Following a doctor's radioed instructions, he tied the officer's torn leg with a tourniquet.

Brigade urged the survivors of Ben-Hanan's force, who had pulled back into the Leja, to return to the hill. The radio exchange was overheard by Maj. Yoni Netanyahu, deputy commander of the General Staff Reconnaissance Unit (Sayeret Matkal), who broke into the transmission to offer his services. Ben-Gal gratefully accepted. Within three hours, Netanyahu and a small commando force reached the tel on foot and extricated Ben-Hanan and his driver.

Elazar was upset at the inability of Hofi's forces to continue on five miles to Sasa. Dayan visited Generals Eitan and Laner at their command posts bearing the same message. There was no intention to conquer Damascus, he said, as long as the Arabs did not bomb or shell Israeli cities. But it was important to impress on the Syrians that their attempt to capture the Golan would end with Israel on the approaches to Damascus. The division commanders replied with what seemed to the defense minister a pro forma "We'll try." After a week of intensive combat, the brigades were well under half strength and the men were exhausted. No less important, the existential threat to Israel had clearly passed, at least on this front, reducing readiness to take excessive risks.

At a mobile listening post attached to Eitan's division, a radio monitor turning the knob as he scanned Syrian radio traffic suddenly sat upright. Someone was transmitting with an Iraqi accent.

"Are you sure?" asked the commander of the unit, Capt. David Harman.

"I can tell you what village he's from," said the monitor, an Iraqi-born Israeli.

When Harman passed the report up to division, the reaction was skeptical. The Iraqis were known to be planning to send forces to Syria's aid but they were not expected this soon. Elazar conferred in his office with Air Force Commander Peled and intelligence chief Zeira on the possibility of interdicting them en route. Zeira said it would take the Iraqi tanks fourteen or thirty hours to reach the front, depending on where they were starting from. Given the uncertainty about the timing of the Iraqi convoy and the urgency of the missions his aircraft were already carrying out, Peled suggested that it might be preferable to insert a commando force by helicopter to lay an ambush on the long desert road from Iraq. Elazar accepted the proposal.

Iraq had not been made privy to the war beforehand by Sadat or Assad. But with its outbreak, Baghdad immediately notified Syria of its readiness to send an expeditionary force despite the uneasy relations between the two countries. Iraq simultaneously obtained Iran's agreement to keep their volatile border calm so that Iraqi troops could move to Syria's aid. A similar agreement was struck between Baghdad and the Kurds of northern Iraq. Israeli operatives had been training Kurdish guerrillas for years precisely in order to have them keep Iraqi troops tied down in the event of an Israeli-Arab war. But the Kurdish leadership decided at this moment of truth not to engage in a military adventure on Israel's behalf. The Iraqis started a division on the road to Damascus the next day, with a second armored division to follow. AMAN on Tuesday reported that the lead Iraqi brigade would probably reach Damascus that night after a trip of six hundred miles. However, AMAN lost track of the Iraqi force. It was dark when the lead elements of the Iraqi Third Division reached the outskirts of Damascus on October 11. The streets were deserted except for several armed civilians of the home guard. "Are you Iraqis?" called out one of them to the commander in the turret of the lead tank.

"Yes," replied the officer.

"In the name of God," said the civilian, "save our honor."

Despite the Iraqi tankers' fatigue, they were urged by the Syrian command to continue to the battlefront where the Syrian line was in danger of breaking.

Elazar urged Hofi to avoid attacking strongpoints like Tel Shams with tanks by day and instead to use infantry at night. Hofi had until now used infantry sparingly since he lacked an adequate supply of antitank weapons. But military supplies had begun to arrive from the United States in the unmarked El Al planes, including large numbers of LAW (light antitank weapon) missiles. The LAW had half the range of the RPG but was superior to the bazooka. And there were a lot of them. For the first time, Israeli infantrymen had an effective antitank weapon in quantity.

Orr's brigade was reinforced by a battalion of reservists who had returned from abroad after the war started. He let the unit take the lead, warning its commander not to be deceived by the seemingly empty landscape. "Move slowly," he said. "This isn't the Six Day War." An hour later, the battalion was ambushed and mauled. Orr sent forward one of his veteran battalions which drove the Syrians back.

Colonel Ben-Gal, who made a point of distancing himself emotionally in battle from the life-and-death decisions he was constantly making, was brought up short when the division's personnel officer notified him that both Kahalani's brother and brother-in-law had been killed on the Egyptian front. Deciding that he could not spare him, Ben-Gal did not inform Kahalani for twenty-four hours, at which point he left to mourn with his family.

Sarig's tank commanders had been traumatized by the Khan Arnabe attack. In a skirmish the next morning, only tanks commanded by officers responded when he gave the order to move into firing positions. When the battalion resumed forward movement, Sarig took the lead in his vulnerable personnel carrier to set an example. The men settled down and the going became increasingly easy. Moving through the boulder-strewn landscape and meeting little opposition, Sarig felt for the first time the way he had in the breakthrough stage of the Six Day War. Moving parallel to him was Ben-Porat's brigade. Their joint objective was Knaker, the last fortified position before the Damascus region. From Knaker, they could proceed either north toward Sasa or east toward Damascus itself, fifteen miles distant.

Monitoring their progress from atop Tel Sha'ar in the center of his divisional sector, General Laner could make out the dust trails of the two brigades moving northeast. They were to be joined at Knaker by Orr's brigade, presently refueling at Nasej village to their rear. Another brigade, Col. Yossi Peled's, which had remained behind on the Golan, was on its way across the Purple Line to join Laner's division in kicking open this outer gateway to Damascus.

As Laner idly shifted his gaze to the southeast, he was startled to see dust clouds there as well. A sizable tank force was moving swiftly toward his exposed flank. Intelligence had given no indication that the Syrians had forces capable of attacking from that direction. He thought at first that Moussa Peled's division, which was holding the line in the southern Golan, might have made a wide swing to join him. But when he checked with Northern Command he was told that Peled had not moved.

Sarig and Ben-Porat were only three miles from Knaker when they were ordered by Laner to halt immediately and return south. He did not say why. Both brigade commanders protested at being stopped just as the enemy was crumbling. "You're not listening to what I'm saying," countered Laner. "Stop and return with all your tanks."

Orr was told to stop refueling and prepare to meet enemy forces heading in his direction. His tanks deployed around the Nasej crossroads. The lead tank had just taken position when its crew saw two columns of tanks and APCs approaching from the southeast. They had an unfamiliar color but they were T-55s and thus clearly enemy. They appeared to be moving uncertainly, as if their commanders were not sure where they were. Orr's opening volley at four hundred yards took them by surprise and set the lead tanks aflame. The remainder pulled back. The Iraqis had arrived on the battlefield.

With darkness, Laner drew up plans to hit them in the morning before they had gained their bearings. As he conferred with his staff on Tel Sha'ar, an officer came in from an observation post to report dust clouds in the distance moving in their direction. The officer ventured that the Iraqis were resuming their attack. Laner was skeptical. The Syrians had not initiated a serious night attack since the first night of the war and it was unlikely that the Iraqis would do so only a few hours after having reached the battlefield, particularly after the bloody nose they had received this day from Orr. Laner asked the officer to take another look. The officer returned ten minutes later and repeated his finding. This time Laner asked his deputy, Col. Moshe Bar-Kochba, to have a look.

It was a bright, moonlit night, enabling visibility far across the landscape. Through his binoculars, Bar-Kochba could make out seven or eight parallel dust clouds, indicating a large tank formation moving in broad and deep deployment, four to five miles distant. The clouds appeared to be heading straight toward Tel Sha'ar. Upon receiving

Bar-Kochba's report, Laner ordered the division to prepare immediately to meet an attack.

Ben-Porat's and Yossi Peled's brigades deployed from Tel Sha'ar westward. Orr's and Sarig's brigades took position several miles to the east. The units thus formed a box with the southern end open toward the Iraqis. If the Iraqis moved into the center, both wings would converge on it. If they attacked either one of the wings, the other would hit the attackers in the flank or rear.

At 9 p.m., lookouts reported that the dust clouds had disappeared. The Iraqis appeared to have stopped to sleep. The Israeli tanks remained in position, tank crewmen taking turns dozing off. At 3:30 a.m., the men of a Sherman battalion heard engines approaching from the south. Lt. Col. Benzion Padan, the battalion commander, called for flares. In their light, the low silhouettes of Soviet-made tanks could be made out. Padan's tanks opened fire and the Iraqis fired back. The Israelis could detect no sign that the enemy shells were hitting anywhere close.

"Fellows, these are rookies," said an officer on the radio net. "They're shooting at the sky." Colonel Padan told his men to stop firing in order to encourage the enemy tanks to resume their advance. When the Iraqis did, the Shermans knocked out the six tanks in the lead. The rest of the formation halted.

With dawn, the Iraqis found Orr's brigade on their eastern flank and the Shermans, reinforced by a Centurion battalion, to their front. In a battle that lasted an hour and a half, twenty-five more Iraqi tanks were knocked out. Sarig's brigade was meanwhile sent on a wide sweep into the enemy rear and destroyed an additional twenty tanks. The Israeli units suffered not a single loss.

Despite the blow inflicted on the Iraqis, their swift arrival on the battlefield had changed the strategic situation in a fundamental way. The Israelis, instead of continuing eastward toward Damascus with their newly gained momentum, had now to deal with the challenge to their southern flank. The Iraqis' fighting ability was far inferior to that of the Syrians, General Eitan would conclude, but their numbers could not be ignored. Their swift arrival on the battlefield itself was an impressive achievement.

In the coming days, the Iraqi expeditionary force would come to number five hundred tanks, seven hundred APCs, and thirty thousand men, including commando units. It was a force that by itself matched

Israel's strength on the northern front. Unlike the bruised Syrians, the Iraqis were fresh and eager to do battle. Confrontation with the Israelis would cool their ardor but their massive presence tied Israel's forces down.

At the same hour that Colonel Bar-Kochba was watching the approach of the Iraqi force in the moonlight, Maj. Shaul Mofaz was looking down from a helicopter at the Syrian landscape one hundred miles northeast of Damascus. Mofaz commanded a twenty-five-man paratroop team whose mission was to ambush Iraqi reinforcements at a bridge on the road from the Iraqi border. The helicopter pilot, Lt. Col. Yuval Efrat, set the force down near a lonely stretch of road and returned to Israel to await the signal for retrieval. The paratroopers hiked to the ambush site and deployed but no convoy appeared, only occasional pairs of military trucks, which they let go by. With dawn not far off, the paratroopers prepared to blow the bridge and call it a night when a solitary tank trailer lumbered out of the gloom carrying a T-55. When it mounted the bridge, explosives sent bridge and tank crashing into the wadi. The paratroopers were supplied with LAW missiles but there had not been time for instruction. Two men who had read the training manual succeeded in hitting the upended tank with missiles. To their astonishment, however, instead of exploding, the missiles covered the tank with a white substance. The men would learn later that these were training projectiles filled with plaster. Colonel Efrat retrieved Mofaz's force before first light.

The night after the landing on the Baghdad road, Mofaz was dispatched again behind enemy lines, this time to blow a bridge on the road between Damascus and the northern city of Homs. The road was being used to transfer SAM missiles to the battle zone from Soviet transports landing at Aleppo Airport, farther north. Forty paratroopers were with Mofaz this time. Efrat was once again the pilot.

Because of a failure in a navigating device, he deposited the force several miles from the designated landing site. When Mofaz realized the mistake, he reoriented himself and led his men through a wadi in the direction of the bridge. A truck traveling without lights stopped on the road above. The Syrians had apparently seen the helicopter land and had tracked the force. Thirty soldiers alighted from the truck and opened fire at a distance of two hundred yards. The paratroopers fired LAW missiles, this time real ones, which exploded among the Syrians and sent them to cover. Mofaz led his men up into the hills and prepared to call for a rescue mission. From the higher ground, however, he could make out the bridge in the moonlight, not far away. Conferring with his officers, he decided to complete the mission.

As they started to move off, the paratroopers saw the road below filling with vehicles and soldiers. A Syrian plane circling overhead dropped flares and the paratroopers froze in mid-stride until the orange light died. There were now some five hundred soldiers below scouring the terrain with the aid of floodlights and search dogs. The bridge, Mofaz assumed, was probably swarming with soldiers as well by now. He led his men higher and called for rescue.

Efrat was more than halfway back to base when he heard the call. He did not have enough fuel to return for the men and then make it back to Israel. He continued on to Ramat David Air Base in northern Israel where he, his copilot, and flight engineer transferred to a fueled helicopter waiting for them. Exhausted after a week of action, Efrat fell asleep as soon as he was airborne again. Snapping awake, he removed his helmet and emptied a canteen over his head, letting the water soak his uniform and run down his back.

The Syrians on the Homs Road, certain that they had the Israeli intruders trapped but uncertain of their precise location, moved cautiously. At one point, some began to climb in the direction of the paratroopers. Mofaz ordered his men not to fire without his order. The Syrians still did not know where they were.

Two hours had passed since his call and the prospect of rescue before dawn was rapidly receding. Mofaz thought of breaking up the force and hiding out until a rescue attempt could be made the following night—a desperate plan with virtually no chance of success. A voice was suddenly heard on the radio. It was Efrat. "I'll be with you in fifteen minutes."

The moon offered Efrat a good view of the landscape—a gray, lifeless expanse he found depressing. It offered neither the greenery of Israel nor the golden sheen of the Sinai desert. When Mofaz activated an electronic signal beacon, one of Efrat's gauges flickered. They were only a few miles apart now but the beacon provided only a general direction. Getting closer, Efrat asked Mofaz to flash a light but the officer said he could not. The Syrians were only eight hundred yards away. Suddenly, Mofaz shouted, "They're firing at you." Efrat saw nothing but a moment later he heard the thud of bullets on the helicopter skin and smelled gunpowder.

Below was the Homs Road and beyond it a line of low hills. Mofaz, he guessed, must be there. Efrat took his craft on a wide swing so as to approach the hills from other side. Slowing down and lowering his wheels, he headed toward the back of a hill where he thought Mofaz might be, given the location from which the Syrians had fired.

"Give me a light just for a second," Efrat said.

Mofaz flashed a hooded light that projected a narrow beam not visible from the sides. Efrat was looking right at it when it came on a mile away. "I see you," he said. Keeping his eyes fixed on the spot, he asked his copilot to read the gauges and give him a running account of speed and altitude. Reaching the hill, Efrat spotted the paratroopers in the moonlight a hundred feet below. He set the helicopter straight down, without taking time to check whether the site was clear.

"Count them as they come in," he shouted to his engineer. The paratroopers swiftly entered the craft, officers last.

"Forty," said the engineer.

"Close it," said Efrat. "We're lifting off."

As the craft gained altitude, one of the officers yelped. A bullet penetrating the floor had hit him in the backside. A paratrooper looking out a side window saw a mortar barrage blossoming on the hilltop they had just left.

Touching down at his air base in an emergency landing an hour and a half later, Efrat and Mofaz walked around the helicopter and saw the rotor and skin peppered with bullets. (Mofaz would in time become army chief of staff and then defense minister. Efrat would become an El Al pilot.)

The same night—Saturday, October 13—a paratroop unit attacked Tel Shams on foot in accordance with Elazar's instructions and captured it after a five-hour battle, with only four wounded. Tanks moved past the hill the next day and reached a point halfway to Sasa where they were stopped by antitank defenses that had been hastily erected. The Syrians had taken advantage of the breather provided by the arrival of the Iraqis to reorganize their battered forces.

The commander of a long-range artillery battalion, Lt. Col. Aldo Zohar, was ordered to hit Mazeh Airport outside Damascus this night without waiting for the breakthrough at Tel Shams. Since the beginning of the fighting, the 175mm guns had been striking targets deep behind Syrian lines. But in the tumultuous battles they had also approached within a mile of the front and fired over open sights in direct support of ground troops. Studying his map, Zohar saw that to hit Mazeh not even the front line was close enough. With the road to Sasa blocked, the only way to reach firing range was through the Leja, which formed a boulder-strewn no-man's-land between the Syrians and Israelis. Air photos had shown that it was possible for tracked vehicles to weave their way deep into the volcanic field if they marked their path so that they could find the way back out. Ben-Hanan had followed such a path with his tanks for a short stretch in his foray through the Leja the day before.

Colonel Zohar—whose first name, Aldo, reflected the Italian influence that prevailed in his native Libya—moved forward with two guns after darkness. A Golani squad led the way on foot, marking the route with small fluorescent stakes while maintaining a lookout for Syrian commandos who might have penetrated the Leja from the other end. Reaching their predetermined firing position after five miles, Zohar ordered that the engines be kept running in case a commando attack or counter-battery fire required a quick getaway. Intelligence had learned that the prisoners captured on the Hermon were being held in a military prison at the airport and there was fear initially that they might be endangered. It was determined, however, that the prison was two miles from the runways.

The guns fired twenty-three shells before Zohar was ordered to pull back. Air photos the next day showed hits on the runways and terminal building. Far more important than the physical damage was the sound of artillery explosions wafting into Damascus's western suburbs. Zohar's two guns had provided the strategic card that Dayan had been eager to play.

The next night, Zohar was ordered to return to the Leja and hit targets in Damascus itself. This time the way was led by a reconnaissance team led by Yoni Netanyahu. Five military and government structures had been designated as targets but Zohar decided on his own to drop one because of its proximity to the Jewish Quarter. Thousands of Syrian Jews still lived in Damascus. The guns had just reached firing position when the mission was aborted. The Israeli political hierarchy had ruled it out, whether for fear of missiles fired in retaliation at Israeli cities or from Soviet warnings.

Moscow had let Washington know it was unhappy about Israel's proximity to Damascus and was reported to be mobilizing airborne divisions for possible intervention. Dayan did not take the Soviet threat lightly. "We must be careful not to bring the bear out of the forest," he said. He had never forgotten the implied threat to Israel's continued existence issued by Soviet premier Nikolai Bulganin in 1956 after the Sinai Campaign if it did not quit Egyptian territory. "I get nervous," Dayan once said, "if even the Red Orchestra is visiting the area."

There would be room in coming days to improve positions in the Syrian "enclave," as the captured area had come to be called, and a major effort was still in the offing to recapture the Hermon. But, further erosion of forces was to be avoided and dreams of Damascus put on the shelf. It was time, a week into the war, to shift focus to the Egyptian front. If there was to be a strategic turning, it would come there, against Israel's most formidable foe.

26

POWERS THAT BE

IN HIGH-CEILINGED OFFICES far from the battlefields of the Middle East, a parallel confrontation, no less fateful, was under way between the superpowers.

The attitudes of decision makers in Washington and Moscow had been almost identical when the war broke out. Both sides were convinced that Israel would quickly defeat the Arab armies. The Americans reveled at the prospect and so did Soviet officials, peeved at Sadat and Assad for ignoring their urgings to avoid war. Both in Washington and Moscow there was determination that the détente they had worked so hard to achieve would not be undermined by their unruly clients. However, realpolitik and developments on the battlefield steadily shifted the two powers' positions from shoulder-to-shoulder to face-to-face.

They could not stand aloof because the success or failure of their clients reflected directly on their status as superpowers. Already on Yom Kippur day, Kissinger proposed that the U.S. Sixth Fleet in the Mediterranean move closer to the war zone in case the Soviet Union felt called upon to flex its muscles on behalf of the Arabs. But from the opening hour, it was clear to him that the war could open a peace process. Support for this view came from Sadat's security adviser, Hafez Ismail, in a message delivered through intelligence channels on the second day of the war. On the face of it, there was nothing new in the Cairo note. It reiterated Sadat's call for total Israeli withdrawal from territories occupied in 1967 and rejected any interim agreements. Kissinger recognized that this was only an opening position. More important were the implications of the message. By secretly parleying with Kissinger, Sadat was risking the anger of the Soviets, who could cut off his arms supply and political backing. Likewise, the Syrians could opt out of the war and leave Egypt alone on the battlefield.

One sentence in the message bore particular resonance. "We do not intend to deepen the engagements or widen the dispute." To Kissinger, this meant that Sadat did not intend to pursue his military offensive into the depths of Sinai or to "widen the dispute" by attacking the U.S. verbally. Capable of sniffing diplomatic subtlety halfway around the globe, Kissinger sensed that something momentous was afoot. By not depicting America as the cause of his woes, as Nasser had done, Sadat was leaving open the possibility of Washington serving as a mediator following the war, rather than seeing itself primarily as Israel's patron. Kissinger now understood for the first time Sadat's dramatic expulsion of Soviet advisers as a move aimed both at clearing the way for war and for American involvement after the war. The message from Cairo also offered a revealing, almost touching glimpse of the psychological impulse behind Egypt's bold move. "[We want] to show we are not afraid or helpless."

"Until this message," Kissinger would write, "I had not taken Sadat seriously. [His] ability from the very first hours of the war never to lose sight of the heart of the problem convinced me that we were dealing with a statesman of the first order." Kissinger would come to understand that Sadat aimed both at shocking Israel into greater flexibility and at restoring Egypt's self-respect so that he, Sadat, could be more flexible. "Our definition of rationality," he would write, "did not take seriously the notion of starting an unwinnable war to restore self-respect."

The Soviet leadership was mustering far less empathy for the Egyptian leader. Moscow had all along tried to dissuade Sadat from war. At a Kremlin meeting three hours after the war's outbreak, Chairman Brezhnev predicted a speedy defeat for the Arabs. They would soon be sorry they had not followed Moscow's advice, he said. Nevertheless, the Soviet leader saw no option but to offer "our Arab friends" Moscow's support.

Foreign Minister Gromyko brought up Assad's request from October 4 that the Soviets seek a cease-fire in the Security Council forty-eight hours after the outbreak of war so as to secure Arab gains before the Israeli reserves could counterattack. In the circumstances, this was seen as a reasonable way out and Moscow's ambassador in Cairo, Vinogradov, was asked to obtain Sadat's consent. But the Egyptian leader adamantly rejected the idea. Moscow expected Sadat to reverse himself as soon as the tide of battle turned. But to general amazement, the tide was not turning, at least in Sinai.

Matters were different on the Syrian front. On Sunday night, October 7, Assad summoned Ambassador Mukhitdinov and described the situation as critical, with the Israelis about to counterattack. Looking anxious, the Syrian leader asked that the Soviets move immediately for a cease-fire. When Vinogradov approached Sadat the next day with Assad's renewed request, the Egyptian leader remained dismissive. If Assad wanted to end the war, he said, that was his business. Egypt intended to carry on. When Vinogradov asked what Egypt's goals were, Sadat said that its strategic goal was to exhaust Israel, its territorial goal was the Gidi and Mitla Passes, and its political goal was a peaceful settlement of the Middle East conflict. The military situation on both fronts was excellent, he said, and he wanted no Soviet proposal for a cease-fire placed on the U.N.'s agenda. Moscow had expected Sadat to be wringing his hands by now at having blundered into a war he could not win. Kremlin leaders expressed anger at his "stubbornness." Said Brezhnev: "His position is ridiculous."

The Soviets had, in truth, distorted Assad's request in depicting it to Sadat. The Syrian leader had linked a cease-fire to Israeli withdrawal to the 1967 lines but the Soviets had failed to mention that since they knew it would be a nonstarter if presented at the U.N. that way. When the omission was mentioned to Gromyko by an aide, he replied, "Don't make our life more complicated, please." A simple cease-fire held no charm at all for Sadat. When Vinogradov tried again the next day to persuade him, the Egyptian leader said the Syrian situation would resolve itself as soon as Iraqi forces reached the front line. As for Egypt, it would shortly begin moving forward in Sinai.

The Arab successes astonished military observers in both superpower capitals. The chief of the Soviet General Staff, Marshal Victor Kulikov, had not believed the Egyptians capable of crossing the Suez Canal without direct participation of Soviet advisers. Irritated at Sadat's expulsion of the advisers, he was looking forward with undisguised glee to the debacle he believed awaited Egypt. But three days after the outbreak of the war he acknowledged the Arab successes in an analysis he offered the Politburo. The Israelis had been surprised, he said, and had not put up the expected resistance. He pointed out with pride the central role played by Soviet weaponry, particularly the

SAM missiles and antitank weapons, in the Arab success. However, the veteran tank warrior who had fought in the Second World War denied that the success of the RPGs and Saggers meant the demise of the tank. Assisted by infantry and planes, he said, the tank would continue to rule the battlefield. It was the sort of encouragement Israeli generals could have used at the moment.

Kulikov complained that the Arabs had no clear-cut military doctrine and had failed to exploit the success of their initial tank attacks by using airborne troops against the Israeli rear. The Arab air forces had failed to gain control of the air, he said, and strategic cooperation between Egypt and Syria had not outlived their opening strike. For reasons he could not explain, said Kulikov, the Syrians had stopped their opening attack in mid-stride. When asked why Soviet advisers had not improved the Syrian performance, Kulikov said, "They don't listen to us. They pretend to be their own military strategists." As for the Egyptians, he said, they had made a fatal mistake by entrenching themselves on the Sinai bank and failing to move inland. The Soviet chief of staff cited enormous Arab losses thus far in weapons, ammunition, and personnel as reported by Soviet attachés in Cairo and Damascus. He had no information about Israel's losses.

The Arab success was likewise mystifying Washington. At the initial meeting of top policymakers on Saturday, October 6, to discuss Middle East developments, most participants presumed that Israel had started the war. When the initial Arab successes were verified, Pentagon experts predicted that Israel would seize the initiative within seventy-two hours when its reserves were in place. But as days passed Kissinger was increasingly puzzled by Sadat's refusal to consider a cease-fire. The secretary appreciated that the Egyptian attack had a political objective but believed that Sadat understood that he could not stand up for long against Israel and would want to quickly lock in his gains with a cease-fire. But it was not happening.

On Monday evening, October 8, Israeli ambassador Dinitz relayed to Kissinger an upbeat assessment of the war situation as seen in Tel Aviv. It did not incorporate what Elazar would learn during his late-night visit to Southern Command about that day's failure in Sinai. Kissinger was thus totally unprepared when he was wakened at 1:45 a.m. by a call from Dinitz. The urgency made no sense, given Dinitz's assessment a few hours earlier and given that almost all of Israel's arms requests thus far were in the process of being met. Kissinger told the ambassador they would talk about it in the morning. An hour later, the phone rang again. It was Dinitz once more, with essentially the same request. "Unless he wanted to prove to the [Israeli] cabinet that he could get me out of bed at will," Kissinger would write, "something was wrong."

Dinitz had been ordered to make the calls by Golda Meir—"I don't care what time it is," she said when he demurred. "Call Kissinger now. Tomorrow may be too late." Her demand reflected the alarm, if not to say panic, that seized her following the briefing Tuesday morning from Dayan and Elazar on Monday's failure in Sinai. At 8:20 a.m., Kissinger and aides met in the White House Map Room with an apologetic Dinitz, who was accompanied by the Israeli military attaché, Gen. Mordecai Gur. The Americans were stunned when Gur spelled out Israel's losses in the first four days of battle. They included forty-nine warplanes and five hundred tanks—one eighth its air force and a quarter of its armor. How did it happen? asked a flabbergasted Kissinger. Dinitz said he did not know. "Obviously something went wrong."

For the first time Kissinger understood the reason for Sadat's cockiness—his armed forces were doing amazingly well. He ordered his aides to provide Israel with the intelligence information Gur had asked for and told Dinitz he would see what could be done about increasing arms shipments. The seven El Al planes available were inadequate to meet Israel's needs and Kissinger said he would consult with his colleagues about ways to increase shipments.

Meeting with top administration leaders later on October 9, Kissinger found them skeptical about Israel's reported emergency. Some saw it as an attempt by Israel to gain more weapons just before it turned the war around. CIA chief William Colby said that Israel had ammunition for at least two more weeks. (The ammunition shortage, which baffled Israel's own logistics officers, turned out to be largely a function of faulty management. Ammunition in the pipeline between the center of the country and the battlefronts had been lost track of by the logistical command. The only real shortage was in long-range artillery shells.) Secretary of Defense James Schlesinger, unenthusiastic about rushing aid to Israel, said there was a distinction to be made between ensuring Israel's survival within its borders and helping it maintain its conquest of Arab lands. This view was shared by others at the meeting. Kissinger said that such calculations were now irrelevant. A defeat of American arms by Soviet arms wielded by Egypt and Syria would be a geopolitical disaster for America, he said. American assistance was essential, he believed, for Israel to pull itself together. Assurance of resupply from Washington would itself enable the Israelis to use their existing weaponry more freely.

Later in the day, Kissinger met with President Nixon to discuss the situation. The Watergate scandal was at its height and, in a separate scandal, the resignation of Vice President Spiro Agnew was to be announced the next day. Nevertheless, the president proved as focused and decisive as ever in foreign affairs, welcoming the opportunity to deal with matters of state rather than his own sorry situation. His decision on Israel's arms request was sweeping. Israel, he told Kissinger, was to be ensured that its battlefield losses would be replaced. Everything on Israel's wish list was to be filled except for laser-guided bombs, too new in the American inventory to be shared. Most important, all aircraft and tank losses were to be replaced. "The Israelis must not be allowed to lose," said Nixon. In his memoirs, Kissinger would describe the scandal-beset president as having "the composure of someone who had seen the worst and to whom there were no further terrors."

Anxious to avoid unduly angering America's friends in the Arab world, like Saudi Arabia, the administration sought to augment the El Al planes by arranging for private air charter companies to carry the supplies to Israel rather than American military aircraft. The companies, however, were unwilling to fly into a war zone or to risk an Arab boycott. Three days were spent in fruitless negotiations. On Saturday, October 13, Nixon cut the Gordian knot by ordering that supplies be flown directly to Israel in American military transports. The airlift, which got under way the next day, would soon come to be seen in Washington as serving America's own interests, apart from supporting an ally in trouble. The Soviets had begun an airlift to their Arab clients on October 10. It would not do, particularly after the failures of Vietnam, for the U.S. to be outdone in logistical muscle flexing. Abandoning his former discreet approach, Kissinger now wanted the American airlift to be visible as a "demonstrative counter" to the Soviet airlift.

European nations, alert to the threats of an oil embargo beginning to be heard from the Arab world, refused to permit the planes to refuel on their territory. Portugal was persuaded to extend landing rights in the Azores only after Kissinger sent its prime minister a scathing letter over President Nixon's signature "that threatened to leave Portugal to its fate in a hostile world," in Kissinger's words. Even aircraft sent from American bases in Germany had to be routed through the Azores because of the refusal of European countries to permit overflights on the way to Israel. The American warplanes were escorted on the final leg from airspace near Crete by Israeli fighters.

The change in political mood in the Kremlin was almost a mirror image of that in Washington. A request by Egypt and Syria for arms was initially greeted with skepticism by Gromyko and other officials who said the Arabs had sufficient weaponry and that additional supplies would only prolong the war. The military too was ambivalent, fearing that advanced weapons might fall into Israeli hands. Within two or three days, however, the Kremlin came to see its own prestige and interests inextricably tied to the side wielding Soviet arms. In addition, the surprising spirit of the Arab armies elicited a new respect. The unintended sinking of a Soviet merchant ship by Israeli missile boats during an attack on a Syrian port and the bombing of the Soviet cultural center in Damascus infuriated the Soviets, who claimed that thirty Soviet citizens were killed in the bombing. Some Soviet officials advocated retaliation but Brezhnev ruled out direct Soviet involvement. Threats, however, were another matter. "The continuation of criminal acts by Israel will lead to grave consequences for Israel itself," the Kremlin warned.

Soviet technicians provided direct support for the Syrian military effort. They repaired tanks and equipment damaged on the battlefield, assembled fighter aircraft that arrived by sea, and drove tanks from ports to Damascus. On both the Golan and Sinai fronts, Soviet military personnel retrieved American equipment left on the battlefield by the Israelis for shipment to Moscow.

As the war continued, the superpowers became increasingly militant patrons. Even as Kissinger was urging Israel to recapture the territory it had lost, Marshal Kulikov, the Soviet chief of staff, was pressing Sadat to resume his attack toward the Gidi and Mitla Passes. When the Soviets warned after the Damascus bombing that Israeli population centers would not remain immune, Kissinger let Ambassador Dobrynin know that "any Soviet involvement would be met by American force." Both nations reinforced their Mediterranean fleets. The Soviets placed seven airborne divisions on alert, knowing that the move would be picked up by American intelligence. Dobrynin hinted broadly to Kissinger over lunch that the alert was connected to the proximity of Israeli troops to Damascus.

Kissinger was willing to risk the collapse of détente if that was the price of maintaining America's position in the Middle East. "Once a great nation commits itself," he would write, "it must prevail." If

Soviet proxies won the war, he argued, it would be Moscow that controlled postwar diplomacy in the region. He was looking ahead to a postwar American role as the one mediator acceptable to both sides. In a message to Hafez Ismail, he said, "the U.S. side will make a major effort . . . to assist in bringing a just and lasting peace to the Middle East."

Even as they were rushing armaments to their clients and thereby feeding the flames of war, the powers realized that they might be caught up in the conflagration themselves if it continued unabated. Moscow was the first to acknowledge this by informing Washington in cumbersome diplomatic language on Wednesday morning, the fifth day of the war, that it was "ready not to block adoption of a cease-fire resolution" at the U.N. The Soviets were less prepared than Kissinger to risk the collapse of détente. Kissinger found the timing awkward for a cease-fire because it would leave Israel the clear loser. He told Ambassador Dobrynin that the proposal was "constructive" but that the administration needed some time to think about it.

Consulting with Dinitz, he said he would stall a cease-fire resolution in the U.N. as long as he could but urged Israel to fight its way back quickly to the prewar lines or beyond them, at least on one front. After Israel recovered the Golan, Dinitz told Kissinger that the government had not yet decided whether to cross the cease-fire line. "Why don't you?" was the response reported back to Tel Aviv.

"Our aim was to slow down diplomacy without appearing obstructionist," Kissinger would write in his memoirs, "to urge a speedup of military operations without seeming to intervene, and then to force a cease-fire before . . . impatience . . . or unforeseeable events could rip the whole finely spun fabric to smithereens."

This possibility was also heavy on Moscow's mind. Fearful of being drawn into a clash with the U.S. or of seeing its Arab clients suddenly collapse, Moscow had since the beginning of the war been encouraging Sadat to accept a cease-fire, even as arms shipments were stepped up. But the Egyptian leader had no intention of halting the war. His army was solidly entrenched in Sinai and the Israelis were unable to dislodge it. Israel's vaunted air force was helpless before his SAMs, and its armored forces had been stopped dead by his antitank weapons. It was now a war of attrition in which numbers would tell. And he had the numbers.

27

CHANGE IN COMMAND

FOR THE FIRST TIME since the telephone woke him on Yom Kippur morning eighty-three hours before, General Elazar lay down to nap Tuesday afternoon, October 9, on a cot in his office. Until now he had been getting by on adrenaline and catnaps on helicopter flights to and from the fronts. When he woke after three hours, it was to an unpleasant task—displacing Gonen as head of Southern Command. He discussed the matter with Dayan after asking everyone else to clear the room. Gonen, he said, was an able field commander but could not look beyond the battle in progress and prepare for the next day's battle. In addition, he was totally unable to control Sharon. This day, in defiance of explicit orders, Sharon sent his division forward again in a series of skirmishes aimed at putting it in position for crossing the canal. Fifty of his tanks had been hit, eighteen of them left behind in enemy territory beyond the reach of repair crews. The division had actually reached the canal, said Elazar—a reference to the reconnaissance probe sent by Amnon Reshef.

"What does Arik want there?" Dayan can be heard asking in a tape of the conversation.

"What does he want? He wants to cross."

"Cross how? How is he going to cross?" Israeli bridging equipment was still far to the rear.

Sharon wanted this very night to attack the Chinese Farm, held by an Egyptian infantry division, and cross the canal before dawn, said Elazar. "It borders on madness. I'm being sucked into a reckless adventure, a gamble I can't afford to risk." Dayan chuckled at Sharon's audacity but agreed that such insubordination could not be tolerated. During their visit to Southern Command, he said he had looked at Sharon and wondered what was going on in his head. "He would be asking himself, 'What will I be getting out of this business? That I should remain here in a blocking position? Together with Kalman [Magen], Albert [Mendler], Gorodish? How about Arik moving up to the canal and straightening things out? So, let's go. If we succeed great. If we don't, so the Jewish people have lost two hundred tanks. But Arik will have made a Rommel-type breakthrough.' He really thinks this is the way to go. He has a personal problem and it's called Ariel Sharon. It won't be for him to be sitting in a headquarters like other commanders."

This acerbic insight came from Sharon's major supporter—perhaps sole supporter—in the high command. "All this isn't to say he isn't making a contribution," Dayan hastened to add.

Thirty years later, when he was prime minister of Israel, Sharon would spell out his attitude regarding orders in a meeting with veterans of his division. A commander in the field, he said, can often grasp a situation better than his superiors at headquarters. "I believe that if there is no officer senior to you in the area, you can ignore or change an order, according to circumstance. As long as you are willing to accept responsibility for it afterward." As the war unfolded, this attitude would make his dismissal an increasing possibility.

Dayan wholeheartedly supported Elazar's proposal that Bar-Lev take over Southern Command and that Gonen be moved sideways, not down. Dismissal would be an acknowledgment of command failure and a blow to morale. Bar-Lev would be posted "alongside" Gonen, rather than in his stead, but it would be made clear at Southern Command that Bar-Lev gave the orders.

Gonen did not attempt to hide his dismay when Elazar called with the news. Had he run things badly, Gonen asked plaintively? "Not badly," said Elazar, trying to minimize the hurt, "but we're mobilizing all our talent so that things will go even better." Bar-Lev, he pointed out, was a former chief of staff who outranked Gonen, so it would be no disgrace to serve under him. Gonen would retain his title, O/C (Officer Commanding) Southern Command. The public announcement would simply say that Bar-Lev was assuming special duties as representative of the chief of staff and that this assignment was presently bringing him down to the Southern Command. "But he is the commander," Elazar made clear to Gonen.

Bar-Lev's visit to Northern Command on Sunday had been unofficial. He wore his old uniform but he retained his civilian status even though he made the key recommendation to have Moussa Peled's division attack from the south. He was now to be mobilized so that he could officially exercise command. This meant he had to give up his ministerial portfolio since the law did not permit a serving officer to be a member of the cabinet. Visiting the Pit before heading south Wednesday morning, he was told by Elazar that his first task would be to assess the situation and recommend a course of action. Sending his boyhood friend to take command of the most problematic front, Elazar felt his own load measurably lightened. If Sharon refused to obey orders, Elazar told Bar-Lev, he should be dismissed and Gonen named in his place as division commander.

Arriving at Umm Hashiba, Bar-Lev closeted himself with Gonen to make sure that the front commander understood that he, Bar-Lev, held ultimate command despite his amorphous title. "If we look around," he drawled, "it seems I'm the only one here who is a former chief of staff. To make life easier for everyone, let's agree that I'm in command." To soften the blow, he noted that he was now subordinate to Elazar, who had been subordinate to him. For that matter, Motti Hod, the former air force commander, was now serving under a man he formerly commanded, Benny Peled, and Sharon was serving under Gonen, who had once served under him.

Gonen was not mollified. "I've got my own private chief of staff." As soon as the war was over, he said, he would quit the army. In a telephone conversation with Elazar later in the day, Bar-Lev said Gonen had accepted the new arrangement, albeit "with a kvetch."

After spending much of the day reorganizing his headquarters, Bar-Lev announced that he was going to sleep. "A tired general is a dumb general," he told his staff. "Wake me only if Arik makes trouble."

Sharon was waiting for him when he woke three hours later. The replacement of Gonen by Bar-Lev was not glad tidings for Sharon. The two men had not gotten along when Bar-Lev was chief of staff and it required an effort for both to remain civil in their current incarnation. The relationship closely paralleled that of Shazly and Ismail. Following rejection of his plea for a canal crossing the day before, Sharon had come to request permission to attack the Third Army bridgehead. He flew up with two of his brigade commanders to try to persuade Gonen. When Gonen deferred to Bar-Lev, Sharon waited for him to waken. Bar-Lev heard him out and then asked Sharon's officers what they thought. Both disagreed with Sharon, who hadn't asked them. Brigade commander Reshef said they had to avoid further head-on attacks and find a better way to throw the Egyptians off balance—like crossing the canal. Bar-Lev agreed with him. Sharon's relations with Gonen had become strained almost to the breaking point since the war started. His relations with Bar-Lev would not be much better.

Bar-Lev's arrival was for Colonel Ben-Ari an act of grace. Discussions at headquarters would now be calm and decisions carefully calculated. Most important, there was now effective control of the forces in the field instead of organizational chaos. Each division was assigned a separate section of the war room with its own maps, logbook, and staff for follow-up and control. Gonen himself would settle down and perform competently as chief of staff to Bar-Lev. A visitor to Southern Command headquarters in Bar-Lev's absence might have thought that Gonen was still in charge. But the orders he now gave were within a framework fixed by Bar-Lev. At the personal level, he remained abusive but would no longer throw things or dismiss officers at whim.

At 8 p.m. the division commanders and other senior officers gathered at Southern Command headquarters for a review of options with Bar-Lev. Almost all had already changed their minds about the best course of action at least once since the war started. They would do so again as conditions on the ground changed and their perception of Israeli and Egyptian stamina shifted. Sharon repeated his call for a divisional attack against the Third Army bridgehead. Bren suggested that only one brigade be committed to such an operation. Mendler proposed crossing the canal south of the Bitter Lake. Some favored the capture of Port Said at the Mediterranean end of the canal.

Other proposals included pulling back into Sinai to lure the Egyptians out from under their SAM umbrella and an amphibious operation across the Gulf of Suez. General Tal added on to the latter suggestion the possibility of a long-range raid into the Nile Valley to throw the Egyptian command off balance and threaten Cairo from an unexpected direction. Gonen, no longer dismissive of the Egyptians, said that Southern Command had only six hundred tanks and needed one thousand for a major assault. Gonen and Ben-Ari proposed that no offensive action at all be undertaken until Southern Command had built up its strength. It was the latter approach that Bar-Lev adopted. The Egyptians, he believed, would continue to attack and erode their forces. Meanwhile, Southern Command would repair tanks, gather intelligence, and prepare plans.

Following Monday's failed counterattack, the ground war in Sinai had given way to vigorous skirmishing. The Egyptians pushed eastward every day, making incremental gains and reaching the Artillery Road at points. But there was no attempt to push toward the Sinai passes. Egypt focused efforts on solidifying its bridgehead defenses, along Soviet lines. On the Israeli side, the numerous tanks damaged in the furious first days of fighting were repaired and equipment shortages, such as machine guns for tanks, rectified.

Elazar had decided on the war's second day to relieve Southern Command of responsibility for South Sinai—the bulk of the penin-sula—so that it could focus on the canal front. Gen. (Res.) Yeshayahu Gavish, who successfully led Southern Command in the Six Day War, was recalled to duty and given command of the area. Gavish had found Gonen uninterested when he offered his services on the first day of the war but he now had an independent command which stretched for two hundred miles to Sharm el-Sheikh, at the southern tip of the peninsula. The area included the mountain regarded by tradition as Mount Sinai, where Moses received the Ten Commandments. Thou Shalt Not Kill had been temporarily suspended on Yom Kippur but the mountain was too remote from the battlefield to serve even as an observation post.

To assemble a staff, Gavish rounded up several neighbors in his Tel Aviv suburb, where many retired officers lived. Flying down to Sharm el-Sheikh, he took stock of his assets. To defend the vast area, he had only two battalions of second-line troops, a score of old tanks, a battery of heavy mortars, and two understrength battalions of para-troopers.

Hundreds of Egyptian commandos had landed in southern Sinai by helicopters on the first day, scattering into the mountainous areas just inland from the coast. The downing of many helicopters by the air force had thrown the commandos' operational plans out of kilter. Gavish put two helicopters at the disposal of a paratroop force, which hunted down the surviving commandos with the assistance of Bed-ouin trackers. Within three days almost all the commandos had been killed (196) or captured (310) at the cost of two Israeli dead.

Gavish and his staff organized the overage infantrymen and overage tanks for defense of the air and naval bases at Sharm el-Sheikh, which controlled the maritime passageway to Eilat.

What worried him most was the possibility that the Egyptians would send armored forces along the coast from the Suez Canal toward Sharm el-Sheikh. The best prospect of stopping them was at Abu Rodeis, fifty miles south of the canal, where a narrow passage between mountains and sea created a choke point. Paratroopers were deployed there with antitank weapons. Gavish ordered the evacuation of a small naval base and a Hawk antiaircraft battery at Abu Zneima, halfway between Abu Rodeis and the canal.

Air Force Commander Peled protested the pullback of the Hawks, which were under his control, and an angry-sounding Dayan was soon on the phone to Gavish. Did you order the evacuation of Abu Zneima? he asked. Gavish said he had. Dayan said he was flying down to Sharm to talk with him. Three hours later, a light plane landed at the Sharm air base. The pilot was General Peled himself, taking a break from the underground war room. The one passenger was Dayan. On what authority, he demanded of Gavish, did you order a retreat? Gavish explained his strategy on a wall map. He was not retreating; he was falling back in order to be able to fight on his own terms. Dayan studied the map with his one good eye and, with no further ado, turned back to the plane.

Gavish's strategy not only made sense; it was a microcosm of what could have been done on the Suez battlefront if the army had pulled back from the canal and waited for the Egyptians to advance. It was, in fact, what Gavish might have done himself had he bested Elazar in the contest for chief of staff almost four years before.

Peled had assigned a squadron of French-made Super Mystères to attack the Egyptians if they ventured down the Gulf of Suez coast beyond the umbrella provided by SAMs in the canal zone. A few hours after Dayan's visit to Gavish, an Egyptian infantry brigade supported by tanks started down the coastal road, just as Gavish feared and the air force hoped. The brigade had orders to move only at night but its commander chose to get a head start several hours before sunset. It was spotted, giving the Israeli Air Force its first chance to get at enemy ground forces without worrying about SAMs. Warplanes swooped in and knocked out dozens of vehicles, including tanks. The remnants scuttled back north. It was a pointed reminder to Shazly of the dangers of abandoning the missile umbrella.

. . .

The Egyptians were having more success at the other end of the battlefront where a tenacious Egyptian commando unit had been blocking the road to Budapest since Saturday night, the first night of the war. On Wednesday, an Israeli paratroop battalion under Lt. Col. Yossi Yoffe—cousin of tank officer Amir Yoffe—was ordered to break through to the beleaguered fort. Yoffe's reservists had had the major role in the conquest of Jerusalem six years before. Moving forward after calling down artillery, the Israelis found the Egyptians gone, having pulled back through the lagoon. Lt. Shaul Moses, the tank officer who had driven off the attack on Budapest Yom Kippur afternoon, could see the Egyptians moving through chest-high water about half a mile away, holding their weapons over their heads. Since they were not attacking the outpost, he did not expend his scarce ammunition on them.

With the road opened, an infantry unit from the standing army arrived to replace the Jerusalem Brigade reservists commanded by Motti Ashkenazi. Peng, his four-month-old German shepherd, which he had taken with him to reserve duty, had not only survived but contributed to the post's defense. It could hear the sound of outgoing Egyptian artillery and mortar fire before the soldiers could and its barking had provided them timely warning to take cover.

After dark, the new unit's sentries reported hearing noises outside the perimeter fence. Flares were sent up and the lookouts said they could see figures moving. The fort commander called for artillery fire. Moses thought the young soldiers were jumpy or just spoiling for a fight. The commander of his other tank, however, said he also thought he saw something outside the front gate. "All right," said Moses. "Fire." After the crack of the gun, there was silence for a few moments. Then an RPG was fired back from the darkness. Artillery fire was brought in tight around the outpost. With first light, Moses saw eight pairs of Egyptians lying dead outside the fort—RPG teams caught by the shelling, the closest only twenty yards from the gateway.

A sentry on the western side of the fort reported Egyptian tanks advancing from the direction of Port Fuad in what was plainly intended as a coordinated attack with the commandos. Almost out of armor-piercing shells, Moses sent the two tank crews to an ammunition bunker inside the fort. He was alone in his tank when he saw an amphibious APC outside the front gate. Behind it were three others coming up from the shore. The Egyptian personnel carriers unloaded infantrymen who passed through holes blasted in the barbed wire by artillery. Moses called the garrison commander on the radio. "Egyptians inside the fort. Get your men out." The soldiers scrambled out of the bunker and engaged the Egyptians. Moses's crewmen, meanwhile, rushed back with shells. The tanks destroyed the four half-tracks and joined in the fire on the attackers. The Egyptian tanks pulled back. Examining the body-strewn landscape after the battle, Moses deduced that the task of the RPG teams, which had come via the lagoon, had been to eliminate the two tanks at first light, before the infantry arrived. The well-planned attack had been thwarted by the alertness of the garrison and the precision of the artillery.

An Egyptian commando force of 150 men subsequently filtered back through the lagoon and ambushed a half-track-borne Israeli infantry force on the Budapest Road, setting their vehicles afire with antitank weapons. Eighteen Israelis were killed and sixty wounded. Yoffe's paratroopers were summoned back. After a brief battle, the Egyptians pulled back, leaving behind forty-five bodies. Others were killed as artillery fire followed them into the lagoon.

In a crisis of confidence that overtook the air force after the failure of Dougman, squadrons increasingly adopted their own tactics rather than rely on directives from air force headquarters. A Phantom squadron leader told his pilots that flight leaders should rely on their own good sense in deciding how to carry out their missions. Some squadrons employed low-level attacks. Others preferred to attack from high altitude and risk the SAMs—which they could see and attempt to evade—rather than run the murderous gauntlet of conventional antiaircraft fire at lower altitudes. The powerful Phantoms had a better chance than the Skyhawks of outmaneuvering missiles by turning on their afterburners. Each dodge, however, slowed the planes down and if the first few missiles missed, later ones sometimes didn't.

The commander of a Skyhawk squadron, attacking at first light in the Canal Zone early in the war, intended to come in low, rise briefly while remaining below effective range of the SAMs, then dive at his target. But the fire from conventional antiaircraft guns was so intense that twice he had to break off the attack. On his third try, he decided to go in at nine thousand feet, twice the effective range of antiaircraft guns, even though this put him in range of the SAMs. This system proved much safer—the missile crews could not react quickly enough in the brief time he was in their range. Although the airmen risked their lives daily in forays into missile zones, and often did not return, the impact of these quick attacks was hardly felt by the ground troops.

Improvisations at squadron level to the SAM threat echoed the way tank battalions were devising their own methods for dealing with the Saggers.

As the fighting raged in Sinai and the Syrian front, the high command was alert to the possibility of other fronts opening up, as well. Forty Katyusha rockets fired Tuesday, October 9, by Palestinian guerrillas from Lebanese territory at villages on Israel's northern border wounded several persons. Elazar requested permission to send forces into Lebanon but Dayan refused to divert strength from the Syrian front. The Palestinian threat tapered off in the coming days to border skirmishes in which twenty-three Palestinian fighters would be killed.

A more worrisome concern was that the Palestinians in the West Bank and Gaza Strip might rise up. Border police, a quasi-military force, were assigned to deal with such an eventuality but there were no incidents. Israel's own Arabs demonstrated remarkable restraint given a natural sympathy for the Arab side. A reporter driving past the Arab city of Nazareth found Arab women at the main road intersection handing out soft drinks and cakes to soldiers on the way to the Golan front just like Jewish women were doing outside Jewish villages. Scores of Arab men in the Galilee volunteered for farm work at kibbutzim where the adult males were almost all on the battlefronts. Arabs also donated blood for wounded soldiers. The mayors of Arab Nazareth and neighboring Jewish Upper Nazareth maintained daily telephone contact and cooperated in handling emergencies arising from the situation.

Parallel to Israel's grinding land and air battles, a war was being fought at sea. After more than a decade of intensive development, the missile boat flotilla had sailed out on its first full-scale maneuver on October 1. The boats returned to Haifa a day before the onset of Yom Kippur, ready at last for war after thirteen years in the making. On the first night, squadron commander Michael Barkai led five boats north to the Syrian coast. Their objective, he told his captains, was to draw Syrian missile boats out of their main harbor, Latakia. "If they don't come out," he said, "I mean to sail into the harbor and destroy them."

The Israeli vessels sank a torpedo boat and minesweeper on picket duty off Latakia. Before going down, the Syrian vessels managed to report the approach of the Israeli boats and three Syrian missile boats emerged from the harbor. The range of the Soviet's Styx missile, thirty miles, was twice that of the Israeli Gabriel. Barkai's boats switched on their antimissile electronic umbrella, designed to foil incoming missiles, and raced at top speed toward the Syrian vessels in order to close the gap in this first duel of missile boats in naval history. At naval headquarters in Tel Aviv, Admiral Telem heard Barkai report that the enemy boats had launched missiles. It was two minutes before the Styx completed their flight. Then Barkai was heard again. "Missiles in the water." The electronic countermeasures had worked. It was now the turn of the Israeli boats as the Syrian vessels turned and ran for harbor. The Syrians had no electronic umbrella. Their head-on charge had narrowed the range and the faster speed of the Israeli vessels closed it. A volley of Gabriels sank two of the Syrian boats. To avoid the same fate, the captain of the third boat deliberately ran it onto a beach, where the Israelis destroyed it by gunfire.

The success was repeated two nights later off the Egyptian coast. Three pairs of Israeli missile boats and two pairs of Egyptian missile boats charged toward each other, seeing each other only on radar screens. The Egyptians fired at maximum range and kept coming, firing three more salvos while still out of range of the Gabriels. On the Israeli boats, crewmen on deck could see red balls of fire descending toward them. The Israeli electronic devices sent out false images and the missiles, with their half-ton warheads, exploded in the sea, sending up large geysers. With the last salvo, the Egyptian boats turned and ran for Alexandria. The Israeli boats closed range and sank three of them.

From this point on, neither the Egyptian nor Syrian fleets, both far larger than Israel's, would venture beyond the mouths of their harbors, leaving Israel's coastline unthreatened and its vital sea routes to Haifa open. Two hundred vessels, many carrying much needed supplies, reached Israel during the war.

Meanwhile, far to the south, a different kind of naval war was being waged in the Gulf of Suez and Red Sea—old-fashioned cut-and-thrust raids by patrol boats and naval commandos. A week into the war, intelligence reported that the Egyptians were again building up a fleet of fishing boats—this time at Ras Arib, midway on the Gulf shore—for a commando landing in southern Sinai. Five Israeli patrol boats commanded by Lt. Cmdr. Ami Ayalon entered the anchorage after darkness. When they withdrew, they left behind nineteen sunk or sinking fishing boats loaded with supplies and ammunition.

The Israeli high command had since the beginning of the war contemplated sending an armored brigade westward across the Gulf of Suez on LSTs berthed at Sharm el-Sheikh. The option, however, was endangered by the presence of two Egyptian missile boats at Ardaka, on the Red Sea coast.

The boats were protected from Israeli aircraft by SAM batteries but Captain Almog, commanding naval forces in southern Sinai, believed that naval commandos could get to them. It would mean crossing sixty miles of rough waters in rubber boats at night and locating the anchorage on the dark Egyptian coast. Once they reached Ardaka, the commandos would have to penetrate a narrow, two-mile-long channel to reach the boat anchorage.

Lt. Cmdr. Gadi Kol, a burly commando veteran, volunteered to lead the mission. He set out in late afternoon with two boats, each with two frogmen and two backups. After a rough six-hour crossing the boats reached Ardaka but found a patrol boat barring the way in the channel. Kol returned to base but two nights later tried again. This time the channel was unguarded. Swimming underwater, he and his partner found a missile boat in the anchorage and attached limpet mines with timing devices. They returned to their boat and were already in open waters when the Egyptian vessel blew up.

At sea, at least, Israel was demonstrating its old military mastery.

28

DECISION TO CROSS

CLOSE TO MIDNIGHT Thursday, October 11, after another briefing to the cabinet and before another helicopter flight to the front, the unrelenting stress of running two wars simultaneously for six straight days caught up with Elazar. He was discussing the next day's battle plans with two generals and leafing through a pile of fresh reports on his desk when he turned pale and seemed about to faint. Alarmed aides brought him something to drink. "I don't want any pills," he said. He would need his wits for a major decision that had to be made in the coming hours.

Southern Command had been marking time since Tuesday while Northern Command drove the Syrians back across the cease-fire line. It was time now to weigh the next step in Sinai, a pivotal decision that would determine the outcome of the war. Instinct was irrelevant in matters as complex as this and there was no textbook solution. But with an orderly breaking down of the issues and a readiness to follow logic wherever it led Elazar would work his way through the problem. As with the decision to cross the cease-fire line in the north, the process would involve a daylong exercise in thinking out loud. In the end, after sharp changes in position and fresh intelligence supplied by the Mossad, the way forward would emerge.

The discussion began in the early hours of Friday morning, October 12, at a meeting in the Pit between Elazar and senior officers. Bar-Lev was due up from Sinai in a few hours to present his recommendations. Elazar wanted to informally examine the options before then. Northern Command's success in driving the Syrians off the Golan lightened the mood at headquarters considerably.

General Zeira opened by noting that the United Nations Security

Council was expected to pass a cease-fire resolution within forty-eight hours; he and Air Force Commander Benny Peled urged that the IDF cross the canal before then. The air force, which had already lost more than sixty planes, had the capacity to support one more major attack if it were launched by Saturday night, said Peled. Afterward it would have to confine itself to defending the skies over Israel.

"You don't have to convince me that we have to attack by tomorrow night," said Elazar. "The question is what happens afterwards?"

Expanding on the motif he had sounded in his talk with Dayan two days before, he said his goal was no longer victory but a stable cease-fire that would permit Israel to rebuild its armed forces.

Defeating Egypt was no longer a near-term option, he said. This was a painful admission for the commander of an army which until a few days before had been considered unbeatable by any combination of armies in the Middle East—an assumption he himself heartily shared. It was to Elazar's credit that he was not reduced to denial or paralysis by this startling turn of events.

The chief of staff was convinced that Sadat would not accept a cease-fire unless shaken by a dramatic military move, like an Israeli crossing of the canal. He was not sure that even a crossing would do it. Dayan in fact argued that the Egyptians would never agree to a cease-fire if Israel gained a foothold on the west bank, with Cairo no longer protected by the waterway. Even if the IDF did cross the canal and achieve a cease-fire, he said, the situation could quickly deteriorate into a war of attrition. In that event, the IDF would find itself holding a thin line on both sides of the canal against a far more numerous enemy. This, in fact, was Elazar's worst fear. He nevertheless inclined toward a crossing because he could think of no other possibility, however remote, of jarring Sadat into a cease-fire. "I would be happy, and you don't know how happy," he said to his officers, "if you have any better ideas."

They didn't. Peled expressed confidence that a crossing would bring about a swift Egyptian collapse. Elazar did not share that optimism. Northern Command had thrown all it had at the Syrians and made good progress but its offensive had run out of steam with the arrival of Iraqi forces. There was little hope now that the Syrians could be prodded into requesting a cease-fire. Elazar saw no reason to believe it would be much different on the Egyptian front. Nevertheless, he saw no better alternative.

If a crossing, then, where? Two formidable armored divisions remained on the west side of the canal plus a mechanized division and other forces. Together they fielded twice as many tanks as Israel could send across. Until now, the tanks that the IDF had confronted in Sinai were of lesser concern than the Saggers wielded by infantrymen. Confrontation with the armored divisions meant a major, World War II–type battle. This was precisely what the IDF wanted but not while crossing a major water barrier.

A possible solution to Elazar's dilemma lay in the Egyptian attack plan which Marwan had passed on. Knowing the plan had not helped the IDF stave off the surprise attack and proved useless once the war began imposing its own dynamic. But it might help now. According to the plan's "Phase Two," Egypt's two armored divisions were to be dispatched across the canal after the bridgehead in Sinai was secured and then attack immediately toward the Sinai passes. Unknown to Elazar, that plan had been rendered irrelevant by Shazly's more limited Badr plan. But events were about to make it relevant again.

If the Egyptian tanks crossed into Sinai this day or even the next, Saturday, there would still be time to defeat them and cross the canal westward before the anticipated cease-fire came into effect.

But would the Egyptian divisions cross? According to the Egyptian plan known to the IDF, they were to have crossed by now but intelligence was picking up no signs of movement. Elazar asked the air force to stop bombing the bridges in order not to discourage a crossing. If the Egyptian divisions did not cross into Sinai, said Elazar, the IDF would cross in the other direction, undertaking "a maximal, hazardous offensive" by Saturday night. The designation being used by planners for the land across the canal was Goshen, the biblical name for the part of ancient Egypt where the Israelites had dwelt until their exodus.

Three crossing proposals drawn up before the war were examined: a limited one aimed at seizing Port Said; a two-divisional attack from Fort Matsmed in the central sector; and a split attack by two divisions—one at Kantara in the northern sector and one at Matsmed.

Zeira, whose operational insights during the war would prove far more realistic than his intelligence assessments before the war, supported a two-divisional crossing from Matsmed. The Israeli forces, he said, would probably come up against the soft underbelly of the Egyptian army across the canal, an area called Deversoir, with its supply depots, artillery batteries, and SAM missile sites.

Others favored Port Said where the air force had knocked out the SAM batteries and could provide ground support. Elazar himself inclined toward a crossing at Matsmed but he suspended judgment until Bar-Lev had had his say.

The newly appointed Southern Command commander arrived at 9:30. The tense atmosphere he found reflected the fateful nature of the decision they were being asked to make. Bar-Lev had come to the same conclusion as Elazar. Only a canal crossing had a chance of salvaging something from the war. It was possible to destroy the Egyptian bridgeheads in Sinai, he said, but the IDF would exhaust its strength in the process, given the profusion of Egyptian antitank weapons. Standing still and not attacking was a futile option. The only viable choice was a canal crossing that might throw the Egyptians off balance and exploit Israeli tank mobility. He favored having Adan's and Sharon's divisions cross at Matsmed where their left flank would be protected by the Bitter Lake. "Regretfully," he said, "I don't have another solution."

Tal termed the proposal a dangerous improvisation. It was not certain that the bridging equipment could be brought intact through the Egyptian lines, he said. Even if the crossing were successful, the Israeli tanks would more likely encounter an armored fist in Deversoir than a soft underbelly. If the crossing were inconclusive, the army would have to remain fully mobilized and subject to constant attrition. Bar-Lev said he agreed with most of Tal's assessment. "But I see no alternative."

Whether a crossing would likely lead to a cease-fire or not was a political assessment, said Elazar, and he wanted the political level involved. Dayan, who was visiting Northern Command, had told him to bring the matter before the inner cabinet if he, Dayan, had not yet returned. But at the chief of staff's insistence the defense minister flew back to join the meeting in late morning. Elazar reviewed for him the discussion which had been going on for several hours now. The objective, he said, was to achieve a long-term cease-fire in order to rebuild the army "for a hundred years." Did Dayan believe a crossing would make a cease-fire more likely? Or did he not?

The defense minister bridled at the formulation. It was for Elazar to decide whether a crossing was a sound military move, he said. Political considerations were to be left to the political leadership. If Elazar recommended a crossing on its military merits, Dayan said, he would support it in the cabinet even though he believed the best hope for a cease-fire lay on the Syrian front.

"Have the forces advance another three to five miles to within artillery range of Damascus. The only thing that can bring about a cease-fire is if our shells hit inside the city." Benny Peled said the air force could easily bomb Damascus and already had. "There's a difference," said Dayan. "They know that planes don't conquer [territory]." Artillery, on the other hand, suggested an army at the gates.

Responding to Dayan's declaration, Elazar said, "Take this as a given: tonight our 175s will be able to hit Damascus."

After twenty minutes, the defense minister rose and said he was going to report to Mrs. Meir. He left behind his aide-de-camp, Gen. Yehoshua Raviv. Angry at Dayan's sudden departure, which he attributed to evasiveness, Elazar told Raviv to convey to the minister that he wanted the matter resolved this day. "This is a decision of tremendous military-political importance," he said. "The chief of staff will do whatever the defense minister decides."

Elazar proposed through Raviv that the matter be put to the inner cabinet. "I'm prepared to cross the canal if there's a chance of a cease-fire shortly afterwards; otherwise, there would just be continuous attrition and no chance to rebuild our forces." The decision was too critical, he made clear, to be left to him alone. "I want clearance from the political echelon today."

The chief of staff's blunt message brought a swift response—an invitation to the military chiefs to a meeting in Golda Meir's office with the prime minister and her civilian advisers, including Dayan.

For General Shazly too, this was a day for hard decisions. He had visited the front and returned eminently satisfied. The army was well dug in and in good spirits. Officers and soldiers were confident they could handle anything the Israelis could muster. The armed forces had given Sadat exactly what he had asked for, a firm foothold in Sinai from which he could begin leveraging Israel out of the rest of the peninsula through political means.

When Shazly returned to Center Ten, he found a message awaiting him in the operations room from War Minister Ismail asking him to stop by. The question put to him by Ismail was one Shazly had been dreading—could the army continue eastward to the passes?

A major reason the Badr plan had succeeded spectacularly so far was that it did not permit the army to go beyond the protective umbrella of the SAMs. The destruction of the brigade that had ventured down the Gulf of Suez shore outside SAM range demonstrated what could happen when this caution was abandoned. Shazly objected vehemently to Ismail's proposal and the minister did not press. By Friday morning, however, the suggestion had become an order. "It's a political decision," said Ismail. "We must develop our attack by tomorrow morning."

Sadat was responding to a plea from Assad, delivered by a Syrian emissary, to attack eastward in Sinai as a means of easing Israeli pressure on Damascus. Sadat could no longer ignore Assad. If Syria dropped out of the war Israel would turn all its might against Egypt.

The IDF counterattack on the Syrian front had failed to force Syria out of the war but it had succeeded strategically in an unexpected way by inducing Assad to call on Egypt for help. In responding, Sadat would provide Israel what it was waiting for—a major head-on battle with the Egyptian armored divisions.

The Egyptians had until now successfully tailored Soviet doctrine to their own needs. Soviet advisers had been involved in drawing up the plans for a canal crossing and a drive to the passes. In downsizing this plan to Badr, the Egyptians showed a healthy respect for Israeli capabilities and awareness of their own limitations. Soviet doctrine called for armored divisions to swiftly follow up the successful crossing of a water barrier but the Egyptian high command was refraining from attacking beyond the SAM umbrella. To Shazly's dismay, Sadat was now abandoning this basic tenet.

When he passed the attack order on to the commanders of the Second and Third Armies, Generals Saad Mamoun and Abdel Muneim Wasel, both protested. Mamoun offered his resignation, which was rejected. Shazly summoned the two generals to Cairo for a meeting with Ismail. The war minister was in no position to revoke Sadat's order. The most he could do was agree to Mamoun's request to postpone the attack by a day, until Sunday morning.

Not all Egyptian General Staff officers opposed an eastward drive. General Gamasy, chief of operations, believed it vital to push the Israelis back to the passes while they were still off balance. As for the danger of moving beyond SAM coverage, he argued that the proximity of the Egyptian and Israeli tank formations in battle would make it difficult for Israeli pilots to distinguish between them. He also believed that the Egyptian air force, under Gen. Hosni Mubarak, could acquit itself reasonably well against the Israelis. Furthermore, SAM batteries were being shifted into Sinai at night to extend the missile umbrella eastward. When he put his case to Ismail, Gamasy found the defense minister still haunted by the trauma of 1967. Voicing his concern about exposing the army to Israeli airpower, Ismail said, "We have to keep our armed forces intact." If any part of the Egyptian line broke, there was a danger that it would touch off a stampede. But Sadat had now decided to advance eastward and there was nothing Ismail could do but obey and pray.

To the critical meeting with the inner cabinet in Mrs. Meir's office Friday afternoon, Elazar brought Bar-Lev and members of the General Staff. Also present at the prime minister's invitation was Mossad chief Zvi Zamir. The inner cabinet consisted of Mrs. Meir, Defense Minister Dayan, and ministers Galili and Allon.

"I want to outline the next stage of the war," began Elazar. But before he made his operational recommendations, he said, he wanted to hear from the government whether it believed a canal crossing might lead to a cease-fire. "I am not avoiding my responsibility to make a recommendation but this crucial stage requires consultation." There might be alternative ways to achieve a cease-fire he had not thought about, he said—political alternatives, perhaps "threats." He did not spell out what kind of threats. In previous discussions he had raised the possibility of ratcheting up pressure by hitting civilian targets in Damascus and dropping bombs on Cairo in order "to dramatize the war." He downplayed this option now in view of Mrs. Meir's reluctance to hit civilian targets but he left it on the table. "It could be done at a later stage." Peled asked permission to create sonic booms over Cairo "so that when Sadat agrees to a cease-fire they won't butcher him in the presidential palace." Permission was denied.

Bar-Lev spoke in optimistic terms of what a crossing could accomplish, including severing of supply lines to the Third Army bridgehead and destruction of SAM missile batteries. There were serious risks, he acknowledged, including the possibility that the Israeli bridges might be knocked out, stranding the forces which had crossed. He spoke to his former cabinet colleagues of the high spirits of the men on the front and of the superb quality of their officers. "Our boys are fighting, bless them, with cool heads, a dash of humor, without panic. And they're *fighting*." But continuation of the status quo would erode the army's strength, he said. His own spirits had been uplifted at the front but ever since returning to Tel Aviv he felt himself drawn into the pervasive gloom.

Benny Peled's warning that the air force was almost at its "red line" beyond which it would not be able to provide ground support focused minds, particularly Elazar's. "Each day our situation is getting worse because we have no reserves," said the chief of staff. "Even if we received forty Phantoms [promised by the U.S.], even if we get tanks, that is not a substantial change in the balance of forces. We cannot today advance closer to Damascus or destroy the Egyptian forces facing us and force them to accept a cease-fire. Every day after the 14th [when air force ground support supposedly would stop] we'll be in a worse situation."

Peled would reveal decades later that he had lied about the red line in order to prod the military and political leadership toward an immediate canal crossing. The air force strength he cited referred only to planes capable of providing ground support, which was about 80 percent of actual operational strength.

A dissenting note was once again voiced by deputy chief of staff Tal, whose pessimistic tone was increasingly annoying his old friend Elazar. The risks of the proposed crossing were enormous, said Tal. If the crossing failed, the way to Tel Aviv would be open to the Egyptians. The armored corps had not been sufficiently trained in bridging operations, and it lacked sufficient bridges. The IDF never imagined that it would have to get through, or around, a five-mile-deep enemy bridgehead before it even reached the canal with bridging equipment. The troops had been in combat for close to a week and would have difficulty coping with the fresh armored divisions waiting across the canal. If there was to be a crossing operation, let it be on the less heavily defended flanks—Port Said or the Gulf of Suez.

As Tal was talking, the door opened and Mrs. Meir's secretary, Lou Kedar, entered to herald, unknowingly, the turning point of the war. Apologizing for the intrusion, she addressed herself to Mossad chief Zamir: "Zvika, your people want to talk to you urgently."

The phone was off the hook in Kedar's office down the hall. Zamir's bureau chief, Freddy Eini, was on the other end. The Mossad antenna had just picked up a radio message relevant to the subject of the meeting Zamir was attending, Eini said not all of it audible. The Mossad office was just a ten-minute walk from the prime minister's office. Zamir told him to hurry over. Eini arrived with another officer and a transcript of what could be understood. The message was not from Marwan but from another Egyptian informant. The Mossad chief read it and hurried back down the hall to the prime minister's office with the paper in hand, thinking about how he would phrase the message, including the part that wasn't there. All eyes turned toward him as he entered.

A report, he said, had just been received from a reliable agent in Egypt. Three Egyptian paratroop brigades were to land behind Israeli lines—near the Refidim Air Base and the Sinai passes—either Saturday night or Sunday night. By itself, the deep raid made little military sense. The message was garbled and the part that could be understood made no mention of the Egyptian armored divisions. However, according to the war plan the Mossad had obtained from Marwan early in the year, Zamir noted, the insertion by Egypt of special forces behind Israeli lines was to precede an attack by the armored divisions.

The atmosphere in the room was suddenly electric. Elazar could not have hoped for better news. "We will hold off on the [Israeli] crossing and organize for a defensive battle," he told Mrs. Meir. Elazar had been prepared to send his forces across the canal the next night even if the Egyptian armor was waiting for them. Zamir's report meant that the IDF would now have a chance to significantly reduce Egyptian tank strength beforehand, and on the Sinai side of the canal. Whatever trauma the Saggers and RPGs had inflicted, the IDF was still confident of its ability to deal with enemy tanks. Elazar and his officers hastened back to the Pit, elated by the prospect of the upcoming tank battle.

In Mrs. Meir's office after the generals left, Dayan drew the ministers' attention to the political dimension. Kissinger had told Ambassador Dinitz that he could not delay much longer a cease-fire resolution which the Soviets were pressing for. Under no circumstances, said Dayan, should Israel request a cease-fire, but he recommended informing Washington that it was withdrawing its previous objections to a cease-fire. Mrs. Meir agreed to send a message to this effect immediately to Kissinger.

After the meeting broke up, Dayan returned to speak with Mrs. Meir. Public criticism of the government was mounting, much of it directed at Dayan. To Mrs. Meir he acknowledged that he had erred in not anticipating the war and in underestimating the Arabs. He felt capable of directing the military effort in this difficult war, he said, but if the prime minister wanted him to resign for his failures he was prepared to do so. Mrs. Meir dismissed the offer. She had indeed lost faith in him in the opening days of the war when he was badly shaken, but his self-confidence had returned and she was once again relying on his broad military-political vision and pragmatic advice.

Flying to Southern Command later in the day, Dayan was pleased to receive from Uri Ben-Ari what Elazar had been unable to give him—assurance that the crossing of the canal was justified by military realities, irrespective of political aspects like a cease-fire.

The IDF was not built to fight in the constricted battlefield situation it found itself in, said Ben-Ari, the respected general serving as Gonen's deputy. The army, he said, did not have enough manpower, enough tanks, enough antitank weapons. The IDF's operational strength rested primarily on air superiority, which was largely neutralized over the battlefield by SAMs. It was therefore vital to cross the canal where it could break loose, destroy SAM batteries, and put the tank corps' mobility into play.

As for the pending clash that now appeared likely with the Egyptian armored divisions inside Sinai, Ben-Ari did not rule out pulling back into the desert where the IDF could maneuver, even if this meant giving up important bases, like Refidim and Umm Hashiba. In the end, he said, the Egyptian forces would be destroyed. Dayan was enthused. "I will tell the government that the desert is yours and recommend that you make war any way you see fit."

Zvi Zamir's warning was the second piece of intelligence with a critical operational impact that the Mossad had provided—the first being the all-important warning on Yom Kippur eve that war would break out the next day. The IDF would ready itself now for battle and the government would prepare the political context for a cease-fire. The initiative on the Sinai front, which for the past eight days lay with Egypt, was finally being seized by Israel.

29

STOUTHEARTED MEN

I T WAS QUIETER on the Sinai front Saturday, October 13, than it had been since the Egyptian crossing exactly a week before. But in both Cairo and Tel Aviv, decisions were being made this day that would determine the war's direction.

Sadat was wakened shortly before dawn and informed that the British ambassador had arrived with an urgent message. Kissinger had asked the British to submit a cease-fire resolution to the Security Council this day after being assured by Soviet ambassador Dobrynin that Sadat would welcome it. Dubious, the British instructed their envoy in Cairo, Sir Philip Adams, to verify Egypt's position. Israel had agreed to a cease-fire, the ambassador informed Sadat, and the superpowers supported it. Sadat rejected it out of hand. There would be no cease-fire, he said, unless Israel agreed to withdraw from all of Sinai.

Acceptance of the cease-fire would have achieved for Sadat the goals he set before the war—a firm Egyptian foothold in Sinai and international involvement in a diplomatic solution. But he hoped now to do even better.

Egypt was controlling the battlefield. The Israelis had not attempted to advance since Sharon's attacks on Tuesday while the Egyptians were making small-scale pushes eastward every day, with some success, as the Israelis sought to avoid escalation. SAM batteries were being sent across the bridges at night to extend the missile umbrella toward the passes. With every day, Arab strength was increasing as the Soviet arms airlift hit its stride and the Arab world dispatched reinforcements to Syria and Egypt. Contingents, some of them sizable, had arrived from Morocco, Algeria, Libya, Saudi Arabia, Kuwait, the Palestine Liberation Organization, Jordan, and Iraq. Even Pakistan sent pilots, and North Korean pilots were patrolling the skies over Egypt's hinterland. Israel was receiving no military supplies from abroad except for what the small El Al fleet could carry (the American airlift would begin only the next day); the only reinforcements were Israeli reservists returning from studies or travel abroad for the war. (Those in combat units were flown home free.) To Sadat, Israel's acquiescence to a cease-fire was a clear signal of weakness.

Israel's assessment of the situation was not far from Sadat's. The day before, the Mossad station chief in Washington, Ephraim Halevy, met in the morning with Kissinger and found him agitated. A message from Prime Minister Meir—sent Friday afternoon, Israel time—had just arrived saying that Israel was prepared to accept a cease-fire in place. Anticipating an Israeli counterattack that would reverse the course of the war, Kissinger had been stalling Moscow's efforts to lock in Arab gains with a speedy cease-fire. Now Israel was expressing readiness to accept a cease-fire without even attempting to condition it on Egypt pulling back across the canal.

"Kissinger almost tore his hair out," Halevy, a future head of the Mossad, would recall years later. "He said, 'You're declaring that you lost the war. Don't you understand that?'" The impression of an Israeli defeat, he warned, would undermine Israel's deterrence of the Arabs, not just now but into the future. The difference between requesting a cease-fire and not objecting to one was a subtlety that did not cloak Israel's dire view of its situation. However, Dayan believed that with the crossing of their armored divisions, the Egyptians would soon be receiving a bloody nose that would take the onus off Israel's readiness for a cease-fire.

Elazar himself had begun thinking anew. The looming set-piece tank battle held out for the first time since the war began the tangible prospect of a reversal of fortune, perhaps on a major scale. The battle might significantly erode Egyptian strength. If that happened, the Israeli crossing could turn out to be more than a desperate lunge aimed at persuading Sadat to stop the war. It could be the key to winning the war. This possibility was not yet being articulated by Elazar but was beginning to work its way into his thinking, as imperceptibly but inexorably as a tide turning.

Saturday, October 13, was Sergeant Nadeh's twenty-fourth birthday. The Egyptian soldier had survived a week of war, which was reason enough to celebrate. His unit was in Fort Botser, midway on the Sinai shore of the Bitter Lake, from which the Israeli garrison had managed to escape. Nadeh and his comrades found it an amazing oasis—a veritable underground city with a trove of canned goods and water, toilets, pinups, and cigarettes. "The Jewish cigarettes are really good," he wrote in his diary. A birthday, like the war itself, was occasion for reflection—the kind common to young men gone to war. "I've achieved many things which I thought impossible. I've reached the third year in humanities. Fate brought me to situations I could not have imagined. I used to be afraid and miserable. I became someone with strength. I tried to love and I passed through all the stages of love, from the pleasures of the flesh to real love, in which I failed. Now that I am in war I feel I need someone who would appreciate me."

Apart from Budapest at the northern end of the Bar-Lev Line only one fort continued to hold out after the third day of fighting—Fort Mezakh at the southern end. The paratroop garrison was augmented by the crews of several disabled tanks. Egyptian commandos and tanks had made repeated attempts to break in. With land approaches sealed off, Southern Command now proposed rescuing the garrison by water. The fort lay on a spit projecting into the Gulf of Suez. Naval officers were dispatched to General Mendler's headquarters Friday to examine the possibilities. They concluded that any rescue attempt was doomed. The closest point from which boats could be launched was six miles away. It would be a moonlit night and the Egyptians had the entire area covered by radar-controlled artillery. If the boats weren't spotted on the way to the fort, they certainly would be as they made their way back after what was bound to be a noisy shoot-out.

"I can't oblige you to do it," said Mendler. "But you're their last chance."

The naval officers bowed to his words. The plan they drew up called for six rubber boats to set out shortly after dark. They would halt offshore eight hundred yards from the outpost while frogmen swam ashore. Only at that point would radio silence be broken to inform the garrison of the rescue. As the boats closed on the shore, the commandos would eliminate any Egyptians between the landing point and the fort and the garrison would rush to the boats, carrying their wounded. Artillery would provide covering fire. The boats set out that night but were spotted before reaching the fort and were forced to pull back under heavy artillery fire.

Of the forty-two soldiers in Mezakh, five had thus far been killed and sixteen wounded. In Southern Command, surrender was seen now as the only option. Dayan objected to ordering the garrison to surrender and insisted that Lt. Shlomo Ardinest, the fort commander, be given permission to surrender if he so chose. Mendler was furious at the decision. If the high command had come to the conclusion that the men couldn't be rescued then they should be ordered to surrender, he told his staff, not left to make the decision themselves. By now, however, Ardinest had concluded that there was no alternative. There was not enough ammunition to resist another determined attack.

In his final radio report Saturday morning, the lieutenant passed on the names and health status of the men. Any deterioration would be attributable to their captors.

"Is our situation known to you?" an officer at Mendler's headquarters asked Ardinest.

"Negative."

"Our situation is good. The deed [the surrender] is being done because it would be too late by the time we reached you" (a hint that a counterattack was planned).

"We've taken it in good spirits. Give our regards home."

"This [surrender] is approved by higher authority."

"Otherwise," said Ardinest, "it would have been another Masada" (meaning the deaths of the entire garrison).

"We'll see you on the [television] screen," said the officer at division headquarters. "Keep your heads up. There will be Red Cross representatives."

"We're transferring the wounded and dead."

"Brief your men. Tell them to keep their heads up and smile. Anything to add?"

"Ask the fellows to see to our parents. Console them. I'm feeling fine. See you. We're doing it [surrendering] for the wounded."

As thousands of Egyptian soldiers on both banks watched, the garrison emerged, one man holding a Torah scroll.

The fall of Mezakh effectively concluded the saga of the Bar-Lev Line. Of 441 men in sixteen forts, 126 had been killed and 161 taken prisoner. The remaining 154, including 60 men at Budapest, which would hold out through the war, made it back without undergoing captivity.

Distressed by the surrender, Mendler left division headquarters to visit units in the field. He was talking on the radio with Gonen when an Egyptian shell hit his half-track, killing him, an aide, and an Israel Radio reporter.

Flying over the Israeli lines in a helicopter, Elazar had a view of the vibrant army that had sprouted on the dunes of western Sinai— thousands of vehicles, endless encampments, figures moving purpose- fully. Egypt had staggered the IDF but it had expended its bag of surprises. Arrayed against it now was an army whose fighting ability had been honed and its psychological balance restored. The energy and optimism became even more tangible after Elazar landed; main- tenance units were swarming over damaged tanks and Adan's division had begun moving into position behind Sharon's, ready to cross the canal once the bridges were up.

Sharon proposed not waiting for the Egyptian armor to cross. A cease-fire could be declared at any time, he argued, and it was best to begin biting into the Egyptian lines immediately. He was overruled by Elazar. If the Egyptians did not cross eastward, the chief of staff assured him, the IDF would cross westward tomorrow night, despite the risks.

Confirmation finally came after dark Friday that the Egyptian armored divisions were beginning to move. Elements of the Fourth Division were crossing over in the Third Army sector and the Twenty- first Division was crossing in the Second Army sector. "It's about time," Elazar said. "We need a big, beautiful offensive with lots of Egyptian tanks. Wipe them out east of the canal and then cross; that's the pro- gram." The Egyptians would need another day to position themselves for the attack.

Intelligence had picked up the movement of Egyptian paratroop units to forward air bases, presumably the units designated to land behind Israeli lines. Elazar weighed an air attack on the bases but Zeira argued against it. If the paratroop incursion was disrupted, he said, the Egyptian command might postpone the armored attack. Ela- zar agreed. It was decided to ask Egyptian helicopter pilots, if any had been captured, about likely landing sites. Israeli helicopter pilots were also asked their opinions.

Bar-Lev termed Israel's limited bridging equipment "a joke" and the crossing itself brazen. A few shells hitting the bridges and the army would find itself stranded west of the canal with no way to get back—at least, not the tanks. But, Bar-Lev reiterated, it was a risk he was ready to run. The Egyptians had at least a dozen bridges along the length of the canal; Israel would be lucky to have two.

Returning to Tel Aviv and the dour confines of the Pit, Elazar shared his uplift with his staff. "Anyone who feels depressed in these dark corridors should go into the field and see the boys. You'll come back in a grand mood. We're eight days into the war but when you meet the tankers they talk as if this is the third year of World War II. They know what the Egyptians are up to and have an answer for everything. The repair shops are working, the tanks are fine, there's ammunition. The best of our people are down there."

That night, Sharon tried to reach Dayan to argue his case for an immediate attack. Unable to track him down, he telephoned Dayan's daughter, Yael, who had served as a soldier in Sharon's divisional headquarters in the Six Day War. She didn't think her father would return home before morning, she said. "What, he's not sleeping at home again?" joked Sharon, a reference to Dayan's once notorious reputation for one-night stands. Yael took umbrage. "Come on, Yael, what happened to your sense of humor?" said Sharon, unfazed. He asked her to pass on a message to her father if she spoke with him this night. "Tell him the whole division here is stamping its feet. The horses are ready for battle. You remember the picture—like the eve of the Six Day War. Explain this to him. He must understand that there's enough spirit here to break the Egyptians. Otherwise, we'll enter a cease-fire in our present miserable situation." In a telephone conversation with Ezer Weizman the day before, Sharon had complained of the mood at the rear—"as if this is the final battle of the Warsaw Ghetto." To his right, said Sharon, was Adan. To his left, Mendler (who would be killed later in the day). The troops on the line were ready. "Believe me, we can finish everything quickly."

In Cairo, General Shazly contemplated the coming battle with trepidation. For five days, ever since Israel's failed attack of October 8, both sides had been hoping to see a major enemy assault. Egypt wanted Israeli armor to break against its defenses. Israel wanted a tank battle in the open field. Now, because of the Syrian pressure, it would be Israel that would get its wish. Egypt's Twenty-first Armored Division, which had already sent one of its two tank brigades to Sinai, now sent the other as well. Its commander, Gen. Ibrahim al-Arabi, found the canal crossing unusually easy. "I was surprised that the Israeli Air Force didn't attack us," he would say later. "They just let us in." The

Fourth Armored Division left 100 tanks behind on the west bank and crossed with the rest. Also remaining west of the canal were 250 tanks of the strategic reserve, including 120 of the Presidential Guard in Cairo. The Egyptian command believed this sufficient to cope with the threat of an Israeli crossing. The losses Israel had suffered in the war's first days and in the heavy battles on the Syrian front made it unlikely that it had enough strength left for a major crossing.

The Egyptian battle plan for Sunday, October14, was drawn up by War Minister Ismail himself. Attacking out of their bridgehead, two brigades would push separately toward Tasa in the center. In the northern part of the line, a brigade would drive toward Baluza and another would attack between Baluza and Tasa. In the south, an armored brigade would push for the Mitla Pass and a mechanized brigade for the Gidi Pass. In all, some five hundred tanks would participate in six thrusts across a hundred-mile front.

Shortly after 3 a.m. on Sunday, Lt. Col. Amazia (Patzi) Chen was notified by one of the observation outposts he had set up on the periphery of Sharon's division that four Egyptian helicopters had just passed overhead. Gathering the few men in his vicinity, the commando officer drove to the outpost for orientation. The observers pointed northwest in the direction of the Yukon staging area. That, Chen knew, was where Israel's major strategic asset at the moment, the main bridge that was to span the canal, was about to be towed to the waterway. It was beginning to dawn as he set out in that direction. Given that he had only twelve men, in two jeeps and a half-track, while the capacity of four helicopters was 130 men, Chen's intention was just to shadow the Egyptian force until reinforcements arrived. The Israelis advanced in wide formation from dune to dune until they saw an Egyptian soldier at five hundred meters scurrying for cover. Chen paused and radioed Sharon to give his position. "A tank platoon is on its way," Sharon said.

The commander of the half-track informed Chen that he saw the tracks of three men, presumably artillery spotters. Without waiting for the tanks, the Israelis started forward again cautiously. As they topped a hill covered by heavy shrubbery, the shrubs parted and Egyptian commandos from the helicopter force opened fire. Chen told his driver to back up, not make a U-turn, so that he could continue to fire forward with the vehicle's machine gun. The three vehicles managed to extricate themselves and joined up with the tanks, which soon arrived. After brief consultation, the combined force attacked from the flank. The tanks and Chen's vehicles fired as they wove through the Egyptian force until there was no return fire. About thirty Egyptians had been seen fleeing westward but all those on the hill were dead. Two Israelis on the half-track were also dead and four others wounded.

The battle was not over for Chen. Returning to his base in Tasa, twenty miles away, the colonel appropriated a reconnaissance company mounted on jeeps and led them back to the site of the battle. From there they picked up the tracks of the men from the helicopter force who had fled, as well as the tracks of the three artillery spotters, and hunted them down, apparently to the last man. In all, 129 bodies would be counted at the scene of the original clash and along the pursuit trail.

Still bruised by the extensive losses their commandos had suffered on the opening day of the war, the Egyptians were unable or unwilling to undertake the other commando operations planned for this night. (Of 1,700 Egyptian commandos sent into action, 740 would be killed—many in downed helicopters—and 330 captured. Their impact was marginal, except in the Baluza area.)

At 6 a.m. Egyptian aircraft darted across the canal for a bombing run. The Israelis were waiting with 350 tanks on the line and a similar number in reserve. Unlike the first days' battles along the canal when Egyptian tank-hunting teams lay in wait along routes they knew the Israeli tanks would take, it was the Israelis who were waiting now. They were on terrain of their own choosing and it was the Egyptians who would now have to cross a killing ground. Most of the Israeli tanks were deployed on high ground. Replacing Adan's division on the line was a reserve brigade commanded by Col. Yoel Gonen, younger brother of General Gonen. The unit, made up of Soviet T-55s captured in the Six Day War and upgraded, had not yet been in combat; one of Adan's brigades was deployed behind it as backup.

Colonel Reshef, whose brigade was deployed in the Israeli center, kept his tanks on the rear slopes of the Hamadiya and Kishuf Ridges. In the early light he and his battalion commanders moved up to observation positions, their tanks edging up the slopes until only the heads of the two officers, standing in their turrets, protruded above the ridgeline. The opening Egyptian artillery barrage was so heavy that, for the first time since the war began, Reshef closed his hatch.

At 6:30, tanks of the Twenty-first Division came into view, an enormous flow of fast-moving armor that reminded him of the flash floods that erupt in the Negev after a heavy rain and sweep everything before them. For a moment he wondered whether he too would be swept away. When the tanks were three thousand yards distant, Reshef said, "Firing positions." The empty ridges began to be dotted with dark shapes as company commanders moved up to stake out their sectors, then platoon commanders, then tank commanders. The ridgelines in Reshef's sector now bristled with a hundred tanks; with their first volley Egyptian tanks began burning. Some managed to reach the foot of Hamadiya where they were hidden from the Israeli tanks on the ridge above. The Egyptians lunged upward and engaged from as close as a few dozen yards. Reshef ordered tanks on Kishuf Ridge to his left to descend and hit the attackers on their flank and he called down artillery on the Egyptian rear, to impede their retreat. Within half an hour the battle in his sector was over. Scores of enemy tanks were burning. Five of his own tanks had been hit. The brigade's casualties were six dead and several wounded. At 7 a.m. Reshef radioed Sharon's deputy: "I broke their attack. Improving positions to the west." However, that innocent-sounding proposal for a pursuit was rejected by Southern Command, monitoring the radio net of Sharon's division.

Reshef's neighboring brigade commander, Col. Haim Erez, had raised his turret hatch at the end of the Egyptian barrage to find a tank coming at him through the shell smoke, barely twenty yards away. Erez's gunner stopped it. An Israeli tank commander spotted Sagger teams. He reported "tourists with suitcases" deploying in the sands. Erez sent a battalion to outflank this force, which was soon in retreat.

On the northern end of the front, near Baluza, a small Israeli force watched as a T-62 brigade advanced from the direction of Kantara. Two miles from the Israeli line, Egyptian infantrymen who had hidden in the sands during the night rose to join the attack. They walked between the tanks, which reduced the tanks' speed to the pace of the foot soldiers. At 1,200 yards the Israelis opened fire. Nine Egyptian tanks were hit and the attackers pulled back to reorganize. When they came again, twenty-one more tanks were hit and the Egyptian commander called it a day. The Israeli unit's losses consisted of a single tank hit by a Sagger.

Colonel Gonen's still unbloodied brigade fared less well. An assault by Egyptian Sagger teams and tanks cost him a dozen tanks—more than the losses suffered by all other Israeli units combined.

Gen. David Elazar, Israeli chief of staff (center), arriving by helicopter on the Golan. To the left, in civilian clothes, is Yitzhak Rabin.
Photograph courtesy of Israel Defense Forces Archive

Col. Avigdor Ben-Gal, brigade commander on the Golan.
Photograph courtesy of Israel Defense Forces Archive

Gen. Rafael (Raful) Eitan, division commander on the northern Golan.
Photograph courtesy of Israel Defense Forces Archive

Syrian tank knocked out in night battle by paratroopers at Strongpoint 116
on the Golan. In the background are other knocked-out tanks.
Photograph courtesy of Israel Defense Forces Archive

Lt. Yossi Gur, commander of Strongpoint 116 on the Golan Heights (with sling), shortly after an Israeli counterattack broke through to his beleaguered position. One of his men is being treated by medics. *Photo by David Rubinger/Yedioth Archive*

Lt. Col. Yitzhak Mordecai, who led a paratroop battalion in the battle for the Chinese Farm. *Photograph courtesy of Israeli Government Press Office*

Israeli paratroopers west of the canal.
Photograph courtesy of Israeli Government Press Office

Israeli vehicles rushing to retrieve an Egyptian pilot on the west bank of the Suez Canal.
Photograph courtesy of Israeli Government Press Office

Israeli soldiers in Sinai foxholes.
Photograph courtesy of Israel Defense Forces Archive

Exhausted artillerymen take advantage
of a lull in the battle.
Photograph courtesy of Israel Defense Forces Archive

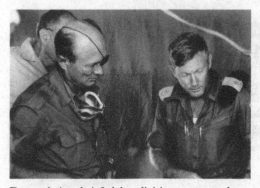

Dayan being briefed by division commander
Avraham Adan in the Sinai.
Photograph courtesy of Israeli Government Press Office

Tense meeting in the dunes. Sharon (with white bandage)
leans on map. Looking over his shoulder is Dayan. Facing him
is Bar-Lev. In left foreground is Adan. It was at this meeting
that Sharon thought of striking Bar-Lev.
Photograph courtesy of Israeli Government Press Office

SAM at captured base.
Photograph courtesy of Israeli Government Press Office

Egyptian soldiers loading jerricans of water onto boats on the Israeli-held west bank of the Suez Canal for transfer to the surrounded Third Army on the Sinai bank. On the opposite bank is one of the openings that was cut through the Israeli ramp on the first day of the war.
Photograph courtesy of Israeli Government Press Office

Gen. Ariel Sharon and troops after the battle.
Photograph courtesy of Israeli Government Press Office

Egyptian general Abdel Ghani el-Gamasy, chief of operations (in khaki uniform) and Israeli chief of staff David Elazar being saluted by U.N. guards as they emerge from the tent at Kilometer 101, where negotiations were held for the separation of forces.
Photograph courtesy of Israeli Government Press Office

Prime Minister Meir and Defense Minister Dayan meeting with troops during the cease-fire.
Photograph courtesy of Israeli Government Press Office

President Sadat and former Israeli prime minister Meir enjoy a joke during Sadat's visit to Jerusalem. On the right is Shimon Peres.
Photograph courtesy of Israeli Government Press Office

At the southern end of the line, where the Egyptians were trying to reach the Gidi and Mitla Passes, an armored brigade pushed up a broad, undefended wadi. Sighted by Israeli lookouts, the spearhead was stopped by small groups of hastily deployed tanks and paratroopers firing jeep-mounted recoilless rifles. The thrust carried the Egyptian tanks beyond the SAM umbrella and Israeli warplanes were soon taking a toll.

By late afternoon, Egyptian tanks had pulled back all along the line. Their losses would be estimated at between 150 and 250 tanks. A score of Israeli tanks were hit but most were soon repaired. For the first time since the start of the war on the southern front, the inherent strength of Israel's armor against enemy armor had come into play, without the distraction of Saggers. Elazar had hoped to destroy many more tanks but the Egyptians did not press their attack. "We blocked them too early," he lamented. But the day's battle, the first major Egyptian reversal of the war, had changed the psychological equation on both sides.

Until now, Egyptian field commanders—and to a large extent even the Egyptian media—had been sticking to more or less credible reporting, a far cry from the "oriental imagination" Israel chortled at in previous wars. This ability to deal with reality made Egypt a more formidable opponent. Toward the end of the day, however, wishful thinking could once again be heard on the Egyptian radio net, including reports of the capture of the Mitla Pass and other imagined successes. Bar-Lev would sum up the change succinctly in a telephone conversation with Golda Meir—"We've returned to ourselves and the Egyptians have returned to themselves."

Sharon would put it even more pointedly as he tried to cajole Bar-Lev into letting him take up pursuit of the retreating Egyptians. "I saw the Twenty-first Division today," he said, "and if I may use a crude expression in a conversation with a minister [a lighthearted reference to Bar-Lev's just vacated position as minister of commerce] they're the same old turds. They came, they were hit, and they ran." He himself would be reminded soon enough that the Egyptians were not to be dismissed so lightly. But after the most difficult week in the country's history, Israel could permit itself to celebrate its first clear battlefield victory in Sinai.

At Center Ten, Shazly tried to reach the commander of the Second Army, General Mamoun, by phone in late morning but was told that he was resting. Shazly found it odd that Mamoun would be resting at 11 a.m. in the middle of a major battle and that his aides would not summon him when the chief of staff called. But he did not press. Two hours later, Sadat asked Shazly to visit the front. He reached Second Army headquarters at Ismailiya in the late afternoon. This time when he asked to see Mamoun he was told the truth—the general had had a breakdown. Shazly found him lying on a cot. A doctor said that Mamoun should be hospitalized but at Mamoun's request Shazly delayed the evacuation by a day. Shazly continued on to the canal, with the intention of crossing into Sinai. He found that of the two bridges in the sector, one had been knocked out by artillery and the other was pulled in to avoid the same fate.

Returning to Cairo near midnight, he reported to Ismail and Sadat on "our most calamitous day." The attack was not only militarily disastrous, to his mind, but purposeless. It would not have drawn off Israeli forces from the Golan Heights to Sinai, as Assad hoped, because the Egyptian army did not pose the kind of threat to Israel's heartland that Syria did. In any case, Israeli airpower was sufficient by itself to prevent a crossing of the Sinai Peninsula by the Egyptian army once it moved beyond the range of the SAMs. Furthermore, the Iraqis had already joined the battle in the north and the situation there had stabilized. Shazly's analysis was perceptive but Sadat was not seeking to draw off Israeli forces from the Syrian front. His aim was to keep Assad in the war by a demonstrative show of support. Shazly would have been even more upset had he known that Sadat, in his conversation with the British ambassador Saturday, rejected a cease-fire which would have nailed down Egypt's gains on the Sinai bank.

Dayan expressed doubt that this was Phase Two of the Egyptian war plan—the push for the passes. Elazar believed it was, although more limited than originally planned. In order to encourage the Egyptians to try harder, Elazar held a radio conversation with Bar-Lev for the benefit of Egyptian monitors in which the two generals, sounding distraught, referred to the day's battle as a defeat. One of Bar-Lev's officers praised him afterward for his thespian talents, saying his choice of a military career had been a loss to the Israeli stage.

Sharon came up with a similar ploy. He told Reshef to lay down a smoke screen, as if to protect his tanks, and report on the radio that he was under heavy pressure and had to pull back. His battalion commanders would join in with cries for assistance. The bait was duly dangled but the Egyptians were not in the mood for amateur theatrics.

The battle had converted Dayan into an enthusiastic advocate of a canal crossing. When he returned to the Pit Sunday evening, Elazar told him that he had ordered the air force to halt operations for a day in order to let the pilots rest. "I'm concentrating on the main effort," he said. "Tomorrow night the breakthrough. The day after tomorrow, a day of battle. Not until we've established ourselves on the other side will we come down on the Egyptians with all our strength." Dayan again criticized Northern Command for not showing sufficient aggressiveness. Elazar noted that, unlike on the southern front, where there had been a relative lull for a few days and a rotation of units on the line, the troops on the northern front had been in almost constant combat for eight days. "The boys have been fighting night and day. They're bone tired."

The IDF had made almost every mistake possible. Its basic sin, one that grotesquely distorted strategic thinking, was to underestimate its enemies. Hubris lay behind the decision to stop the Egyptians on the bank of the canal instead of undertaking a flexible defense. Hubris had led the army to believe it could live with a worst-case scenario in which a single brigade tries to stop five Egyptian divisions crossing the canal on a hundred-mile-long front. The air force had been assigned the major role in the defensive battle even though its vulnerability in the SAM-saturated environment along the canal was known. How the ground forces would cope if the air force was neutralized was left unanswered. Confident that tanks would stampede the enemy, the planners failed to imagine that infantry—*Arab* infantry—armed with modern weaponry could stop a tank charge dead in its tracks. Israel knew of the unusually large number of Sagger missiles and RPGs the Arabs had acquired but failed to think through the tactical implications. Refusal to evacuate the Bar-Lev forts when that was possible turned them into death traps not only for the garrisons but also for their would-be rescuers. Hundreds of Israelis had died in futile battles along the canal bank.

That the IDF was still a credible fighting force a week later was due to the courage and skill of the soldiers on the line and their field commanders, not the foresight of the high command. The IDF had paid a painful price for its failures. But the ground had finally steadied under its feet. It was now Israel's turn for surprises.

· · ·

An hour before midnight Sunday, senior officers on the southern front gathered at Umm Hashiba to be briefed on the crossing operation. The packed conference room hummed with anticipation. All eyes were drawn to the large map covering the front wall and the code name of the operation that had been posted alongside—Stouthearted Men.

Gonen had drawn up the plan's broad outlines before the war. Bar-Lev reworked it to fit the present circumstances and intensive staff work was still under way to flesh it out. The two-hour presentation was begun by Gonen.

Wielding a long pointer, he said the crossing would be from Fort Matsmed on the seam between the Second and Third Armies. This meant that the canal could be reached without having to plunge through the five-mile-deep Second Army bridgehead. However, Matsmed was only eight hundred yards south of the Second Army's perimeter in the Chinese Farm. A major effort would be mounted to push the Egyptians northward at least two miles in order to create a corridor from the Israeli lines to the crossing point. The seam was wide enough to the south—fifteen miles—to rule out an immediate threat from that direction from the Third Army.

Sharon's division, already deployed in the area, would execute the actual crossing. During his term as southern front commander, Sharon had prepared a staging area alongside Matsmed for just such a contingency. Known as the Yard, it was surrounded by earthen mounds to protect units waiting to cross.

Sharon's division would seize the Sinai bank jump-off point and the opposite bank. Colonel Matt's brigade had been attached to the division for this purpose. The paratroopers would cross in rubber boats after darkness tomorrow, Monday, October 15, and establish a foothold in the area opposite Matsmed, known as Deversoir, site of a former British air base. Sharon's division would bring up the bridges from the rear and engineers would lay them across the waterway after the opposite bank was secured. The attack force would be plunging through a hole in the center of the Egyptian deployment and there would be enemy artillery within range on both sides of the canal. The best that could be hoped for was to secure the crossing point and the access corridor from direct tank and Sagger fire.

Once the bridges were up, Adan's division would cross and advanced toward toward Suez City at the southern end of the canal to cut the Third Army's supply lines. Sharon's division would follow when the corridor was secured. The two divisions were to capture a fifty-mile swath of territory from the outskirts of Ismailiya to Mount Ataka, south of Suez City. They would eliminate SAM batteries as they went, opening the sky to the air force, which could then begin providing proper ground support for the first time. The ground forces would then be prepared to move toward Cairo. Maps of the Egyptian capital would be distributed to all units. Bar-Lev, when he took over the presentation, made a particular point of blunting Sharon's fixation on leading the charge. His division would indeed execute the crossing but after the paratroopers gained their foothold across the canal, the rest of Sharon's division would remain on the Sinai bank to widen the corridor. "We must expand the bridgehead at least four kilometers to the north and this task, Arik, remains yours until the end."

"It remains what?" asked Sharon testily.

"Your responsibility. Securing the bridgehead remains your responsibility. Before you get to the Cairo Hilton you will need to be released from your assignment at the bridgehead."

The operation ahead of them was intricate, said Bar-Lev, but they would improvise solutions for problems as they arose. "We will show that we can do it and that we can do it right. On condition that everything agreed upon here is executed precisely. If we begin shoving one another, it will become a mess." It was clear to all about whom he was talking. Small tank forces, said Bar-Lev, would remain on the Sinai bank to contain the Egyptian bridgeheads there.

The Egyptians had trained intensively for their canal crossing with substantial Soviet input, and had executed it meticulously. The Israelis would be improvising under fire. (None of Israel's moves in the war, Bar-Lev would later say, came out of a drawer.)

Less than three days before, Elazar and Bar-Lev had viewed a canal crossing as a desperate attempt to win a cease-fire. No one in the army command was thinking in terms of victory; avoidance of disaster was the prime objective. But the aim now was to turn the war on its head. The erosion of Egyptian tanks in this day's battle had narrowed the odds but what brought the color back to the Israelis' cheeks was their own performance. "We've returned to ourselves," as Bar-Lev said.

When one of the briefing officers said that the objective of the crossing was to bring about the capitulation of the Egyptian army, Bar-Lev called out, "Our objective is destruction of the Egyptian army."

Absent from the briefing was General Elazar, who was in Tel Aviv to seek approval from the full cabinet for the crossing. Aware that some ministers regarded it as a high-risk gamble, he stressed that the operation was built on sound military principles. "If I thought there was a risk of disaster I wouldn't propose it. We're not going to all this trouble so that if a bridge is hit, the show is over." Nevertheless, he conceded, there was risk. "The outcome of a battle can only be presumed." The operation would be carried out in stages and it could be called off at any point. In a worst-case situation, where the bridges were knocked out after a small force had crossed, the men could be brought back in rubber boats even if tanks had to be left behind. "I believe that the chances of failing are pretty meager and the odds of success are good. How great the success will be I can't say but it may be very great."

It was not an easy decision for the cabinet. The worst-case situation Elazar described was not the worst imaginable—instead of a small force being cut off it could be a substantial part of the army. But Mrs. Meir trusted Elazar's judgment. The cabinet in turn relied on hers. She had recovered her composure and become a source of strength for the ministers, although her daily cigarette consumption had increased from two packs to three since Yom Kippur.

Elazar did not trouble the cabinet with his own nightmare—crossing the canal and getting bogged down in a war of attrition. He had ordered his staff that morning to prepare for such a contingency by drawing up plans for drafting older men, returning wounded men to their units, repairing damaged tanks, and acquiring new ones. They would also consider recruiting Jewish volunteers from abroad. Half an hour after midnight the crossing operation was approved by the cabinet. The Southern Command briefing ended half an hour later. The battle would begin in sixteen hours.

Getting across the Suez Canal had been on the IDF's mind since it came to an abrupt halt at the waterway in the Six Day War. Western countries sought to discourage a future Israeli crossing by refusing to sell it military bridging equipment. The best that could be acquired was a British system of floatable iron cubes that could be linked together into pontoons. Known as Unifloat, it was intended for civilian use in harbors. Israeli army engineers calculated that nine such cubes linked together would constitute a pontoon capable of carrying a tank. Twelve pontoons linked front-to-end would be sufficient to span the

160-yard-wide Suez Canal. To make them war-ready, the pontoons were filled with polyethylene to keep them afloat if hit by shells.

Also purchased in Europe, as scrap, were rafts called Gillois, after the French general who conceived the system. Their main advantage was that they were amphibious and could travel on their own to the water's edge, unlike pontoons, which had to be towed. Their disadvantage—and the reason they had been abandoned by all armies that tried them, including NATO forces—was their vulnerability. They were kept afloat by inflatable rubber belts that were easily punctured by shrapnel. There was a debate within the IDF about whether to invest in them at all. In the end, only half the junked rafts acquired were refurbished for possible auxiliary use in a crossing operation.

Not content with either of these options, the IDF developed a bridge of its own, a two-hundred-yard-long "assault bridge" conceived by the venerable David Lascov. Preassembled, it could be thrust intact into the Suez Canal and pushed across to the opposite bank without having to be put together in the water like pontoons. Deputy Chief of Staff Tal, himself a technical innovator, was enthusiastic about the idea and the two men developed a 450-ton construction that could be towed to the canal on its own floatable iron rollers.

Completed shortly before the war, the sections of the roller bridge, as it was called, were transported to a storage area, code-named Yukon, fifteen miles from the canal. In the event of war, the sections were to be moved to an assembly point five miles from the canal—far enough from the waterway not to be seen by the Egyptians yet close enough to be easily towed overnight to the canal across flat terrain. However, the intended assembly point fell into Egyptian hands at the beginning of the war and the bridge had to be assembled at Yukon itself. To reach the canal, the structure would now have to be towed three times the planned distance and over dunes. More problematic still, it would be towed along the edge of a battlefield, a target hard to miss.

On Saturday, October 13, assembly of the bridge was completed. Eli Geva's company had been trained for the complicated towing task, but it was fighting now on the Golan Heights. The assignment was given instead to a battalion commanded by Lt. Col. Shimon Ben-Shoshan of Sharon's division. It reported to the bridge assembly area Sunday night after participating in the day's tank battle. The men were astonished at the sight of a two-hundred-yard-long metal bridge in the midst of the dunes. Engineering officers who briefed them warned that the structure could run away from them when descending the dunes if not properly braked. Coordination was vital. They would pull together when the battalion commander completed his countdown: "Ready. Ready. Engage gears. Move."

Ten tanks were to pull from the sides and one in front while another was positioned at the rear to serve as a brake. Waiting for the preparations to be completed, the tank crewmen, who had risen before dawn to move into position for the tank battle, tried to fight off drowsiness. Ben-Shoshan asked each tank commander in turn to report his readiness. By the time the last had responded, crews in the first tanks had fallen asleep. Finally, the bridge convoy got under way. After a fitful few hours of stops and starts, they had managed to move less than two miles. The convoy halted at first light and the bridge was covered with camouflage netting. Mobile antiaircraft guns took up positions and from this Monday morning the air force would maintain a continuous presence overhead.

The pontoons, which were to comprise a second bridge, set out at dawn Monday in two convoys—from Baluza on the northern Sinai coast, sixty miles from the crossing area, and from Refidim, half the distance. The pontoons, each towed by a tank, were soon caught up in traffic. One of the tank officers asked the driver of an empty bus blocking his way to drive into the sands to let the pontoon pass. "I'll pull you out afterwards."

The bus driver balked. "If I go into the sands no one will pull me out."

After a fruitless exchange, the tank commander said he was going through. "Just do me a favor; don't stay inside."

With that he pushed the bus off the road, not before seeing the driver bolt. Traffic soon grew heavier. General Ben-Ari, overflying the road in a light plane, used a bullhorn to call on drivers to make way for the pontoons but his efforts were futile.

The Gillois rafts were about as far from the Suez Canal as it was possible to be in Israel when the war broke out. On a training exercise on Lake Kinneret, the crewmen watched occasional Syrian shells exploding in the water for two days until transporters arrived to carry them to Refidim. From there they proceeded on their own.

The pontoons and the Gillois would have to reach the crossing point on the same narrow road as the rest of Sharon's division. Code-named Akavish (Spider), the five-meter-wide asphalt strip ran southwest from

Tasa for twenty miles to the northern end of the Bitter Lake. It was the only road approach to the crossing area from the Israeli lines. Branching off from it midway was a dirt road named Tirtur which ran due west for six miles to the canal, paralleling Akavish part of the way. Tirtur had been built to carry the roller bridge to the waterway from its planned assembly point. It was, however, now the southern perimeter of the Egyptian Second Army. Its dual role—Egyptian defense line and would-be Israeli artery—would turn this nondescript desert road into a major strategic pivot.

Monday had not yet dawned when paratroop commander Danny Matt set out from the Mitla Pass, where his brigade was deployed, for Tasa to attend Sharon's briefing of brigade commanders. Matt had fought in every one of Israel's wars and in numerous skirmishes in between. Never in all his battles had he felt the weight of history that he did now. By crossing to the Egyptian bank, his brigade's assignment was to literally change the direction of the war.

The battlefield was still fitfully slumbering. Jagged flashes occasionally pierced the darkness and slowly falling flares decorated the night sky like Chinese lanterns. From the distance came an occasional rumble of artillery. Sitting in the commander's chair of his half-track, a small light illuminating a reading surface in front of him, the bearded commander set aside the map he was studying and removed from his breast pocket a tiny book of Psalms given him the day before by the chief army chaplain. Although no longer observant, Matt had a religious upbringing and still drew solace from the biblical verses. Turning to the first page, he read, "Happy is the man that hath not walked in the counsel of the wicked . . . he shall be like a tree planted by streams of water that bringeth forth its fruit in its season." As always, the words calmed him.

A sense that the turning point of the war was at hand was shared by all the commanders assembling at Tasa. Rarely—in modern times, at least—had a nation at war recovered from so massive a blow so swiftly and attempt to seize the initiative. The United States after Pearl Harbor and the Soviet Union after Barbarossa had had the territorial depth and the time to fall back on their resources and prepare a counterblow. Israel had neither resources to fall back on nor time, and it was pushing the conflict to a swift and decisive conclusion. The swings of fortune that in great wars often take place over months or years, as nations muster their energy and will, were taking place along the Suez Canal in days.

Southern Command had laid out the parameters of the operation but it was left to Sharon to devise the tactics. They would be going up this night against the Sixteenth Infantry Division in the Chinese Farm, he told his commanders at the early morning briefing. The adjacent Twenty-first Armored Division could be expected to join in. The battle would begin with a diversionary attack by Tuvia Raviv's brigade at dusk on the forward edge of the Egyptian bridgehead. While Raviv was kicking in the Sixteenth Division's front door, Amnon Reshef's brigade would quietly side-slip the Egyptian deployment via the seam for five miles and slip into the Chinese Farm through the back door. It was hoped that the dual attack would divert the Egyptians' attention from the seam itself where the forces undertaking the crossing would be moving up in the darkness. Meanwhile, tanks from Haim Erez's brigade would tow the pontoons and the roller bridge to the canal. In order to accomplish all this before the Egyptians realized what was happening, speed was essential.

It was a monumental operation in which the division would be engaging the Egyptians in the darkness simultaneously from several directions. "I looked at the faces of the commanders and wondered if, after all that had happened, they believed we could pull this off tonight," Sharon would write. "They believed."

At noon, Sharon repeated the briefing for Elazar and for the other division commanders and staffs in Southern Command. The paratroopers were to start crossing the canal this night at 8 p.m. If all went well, both bridges would be ready for Adan's division to cross on by dawn. Elazar approved the plan even though the timetable seemed much too optimistic. He would be happy, he said, if even one bridge was up by morning. Concern about the adequacy of the sparse road network weighed on all. An engineering officer present, struck by the audacity of Sharon's plan, would say years later, "If we had put all the details into a computer and asked it if the operation would work, the computer would have burned up."

As Sharon moved toward the front from Tasa with his mobile command post, he passed encampments embellished with wooden huts made from ammunition boxes and covered with palm fronds. The feast of Sukkot had arrived and the troops had found time to build the traditional holiday huts evoking the wandering of the Israelites in this very desert more than three thousand years before.

Meanwhile, in a ceremony at Umm Hashiba in the afternoon, Col. Uri Ben-Ari was promoted to the rank of brigadier general. Promotion of the reservist officer was acknowledgment of the key role he had been playing at Southern Command as a stable anchor, particularly during the hectic opening days of the war. For Elazar, who came down to Umm Hashiba for the occasion, it was a touching moment as he pinned general's rank on the shoulder of the man with whom he had fought, literally back-to-back, at the battle of San Simon twenty-five years before. When Sharon contacted headquarters and learned that Ben-Ari was being promoted, he said, "It's about time."

A traffic jam had already begun to form in early afternoon on the approaches to Akavish Road—tanks, ambulances, ammunition trucks, fuel trucks, jeeps, water trucks, personnel carriers. The excitement was palpable as the army moved up for the war's decisive battle. Vehicles bore freshly painted slogans like "Cairo Express." A chaplain stood on the roadside distributing copies of the Psalms, which were snatched up even by avowed agnostics.

Increasingly worried about the bridges getting through, Bar-Lev called Sharon in the early afternoon. "What do you want to do, go tonight or postpone until tomorrow?" Still sounding surprised years later, Sharon would write, "He left the decision to me." Sharon preferred sticking to the original schedule. He had his own doubts about the bridges getting through. But if the attack were delayed, he feared, either the Egyptians might discover what was afoot or the Israeli high command might have second thoughts. At 3 p.m. he informed Bar-Lev that the pontoons were trapped in gridlock and had not even reached Tasa, from where the road became even more constricted, with dunes on either side. Elazar, who had remained at Southern Command headquarters, said that if the pontoons did not get through in two hours, the crossing would be put off by a day. Bar-Lev objected. The Egyptians might take note of the activity in the area, he said, and plug the hole opposite the crossing point. Elazar relented.

The Gillois rafts had moved forward on their own from Refidim. Soldiers along the road looked quizzically at the amphibian vehicles, folded into mobile mode. When the troops grasped their purpose, they made the V sign and cheered the crews on. The raft commanders were directed to a holding area on upper Akavish.

However, all other units participating in the operation were still bogged down. The roller bridge, towed by tank crews new to the task, was crawling slowly across the desert floor like an invalid, which it would soon become.

Although Adan's division was bypassing Akavish, it was using the same feeder roads as the pontoons. At one point, a senior division officer ordered the cumbersome pontoons pushed off the road in order to let the division's supply vehicles through. It would take hours to haul the pontoons back out of the deep sands and reorganize. They would not reach the Tasa intersection, where Akavish Road began, until well after nightfall. One of the convoys arrived with only three of its twelve pontoons, the others having dropped out along the way. The second convoy arrived later but intact.

The paratroop brigade was having its own difficulties. The reserve unit had arrived in Sinai in civilian buses which were too vulnerable to enter a combat zone. Half-tracks had been promised but there was no sign of them. Capt. Hanan Erez, a company commander, was ordered to take a busload of drivers and rustle up half-tracks "by hook or by crook." He was to be back in the assembly area by 2 p.m., four hours away. If there were no half-tracks to carry them to the canal, there could be no crossing. "Don't come back without them," said his commander.

Captain Erez had seen rows of new half-tracks at the Refidim base two days before. Heading there now, he found them still in place. His drivers were getting into the vehicles when Erez was hailed by a white-haired lieutenant colonel who asked what he was doing. The vehicles were urgently needed by Colonel Matt's paratroop brigade, Erez explained.

"No problem," said the logistics officer. "Just show me your orders."

"We're the force crossing the canal," said Erez. "I don't have written orders."

"No orders, no half-tracks," said the colonel.

Erez attempted to persuade the officer, who remained unmoved. Running out of arguments, Erez cocked his Uzi. "Enough nonsense," he said. "If you try to stop me, I'll shoot."

Persuaded, the colonel stepped aside. "On the half-tracks and follow me," shouted Erez to the drivers.

Finding a line of vehicles backed up at the base's fueling station,

Erez took aside the officer in charge and confided to him the half-tracks' mission. The officer moved them to the head of the line. By now, military police were posted at every crossroad on the approaches to the canal, letting vehicles through according to priority. At each stop, Erez talked his way to the head of the queue. At 1:45 p.m. he led the half-tracks into the brigade assembly area and handed them over, with fifteen minutes to spare.

The half-tracks were not enough for the entire brigade. It was decided that one of its two battalions would continue forward in buses to upper Akavish, just out of Egyptian artillery range. They would remain there until the half-tracks carrying the first battalion returned from the canal to fetch them.

At 3 p.m., Col. Haim Erez, in command of the towing operations, told Sharon that neither the pontoons nor the roller bridge could make it to the canal on time. He recommended that the operation be put off by a day. Sharon repeated his concern "that the Egyptians will change their deployment or the Jews will change their mind."

At 3:45 p.m., Sharon received his first sliver of good news. His deputy, Col. Yehuda Even, reported that the Gillois rafts had gotten through the worst of the blockage. This meant that tanks could be ferried across. Sharon believed it essential to put tanks across, no matter how few. Contacting Bar-Lev, he informed him about the Gillois. "I'm attacking tonight," he said. The notion that the crossing would be staged with a handful of rafts rather than a bridge had never been considered. Sharon's decision was more brazen than any he had proposed, and been slapped down for, during the past week. This time, Bar-Lev said, "I agree."

Colonel Reshef spent the day going over maps and air photos with his officers and designing the choreography of the coming battle. The Chinese Farm, his prime objective, was an agricultural development site on which the Egyptians had begun work in the 1960s with U.N. participation. Israeli soldiers who reached it in the Six Day War mistook the Japanese writing on irrigation equipment for Chinese, hence the name. The area was cut by deep irrigation ditches, presently dry, which could double as trenches or tank traps. Reshef's brigade had lost the bulk of its tanks in the first twenty-four hours of the war, but it had been reconstituted and now had a full complement, almost one hundred tanks, as well as three paratroop and infantry detachments in half-tracks.

Late Monday afternoon, the brigade formed up by battalions off Artillery Road near the point from where they would cross the dunes after dark. Battalion commander Amram Mitzna tried to sound matter-of-fact as he outlined the unit's mission to his officers. After ten days of combat, however, they understood that a brigade attack into the heart of the Egyptian army was a venture from which many would not be returning intact. A radiotelephone had been made available and Mitzna asked every man to call his family. Afterward, they sat on their tanks waiting for darkness. Mitzna wrote a farewell letter to his wife which he left with his jeep driver, to be mailed if he did not get back. In it he mentioned offhandedly that she could give away the family dog, which was something she had long wanted to do.

Making the rounds of his units, Colonel Reshef first visited Brom's reconnaissance battalion, which would lead the force across the dunes. The battalion had been under Reshef's command for almost a week but he had not yet had a chance to meet the men. Addressing them now, he spoke of their key role in the coming encounter. Taking leave of Brom, he said to the former school principal: "What matters is stubbornness. *Stubbornness*. Do you understand what I mean?" Brom said he did.

General Adan took advantage of the respite to visit his three brigades as night fell. At each encampment, two thousand men rose at the shout of "Attention" and then sat back down on the ground as the division commander mounted a tank. In the light of jeep headlamps, Adan said he had often wondered how the younger generation, which had known only short wars, would bear up to the kind of setbacks he and his generation had known in the War of Independence. In the past nine days, he said, the men of the division had demonstrated their grit in a series of engagements more intensive than any experienced in 1948. It would be incumbent upon them in the coming battle to fight not only bravely but intelligently in order to overcome the disparity in numbers. They would wait for Sharon to establish the bridgeheads on both banks. They would then cross the canal and rip through the enemy rear.

The attack began at 5 p.m. with an artillery barrage along the entire Egyptian line. Raviv began his diversionary attack in the last light.

His brigade managed to penetrate the Egyptian defenses. Even after it withdrew, leaving behind four tanks in a minefield, the rattled defenders would keep firing for hours.

At 6:05 p.m. Reshef ordered Brom to move out. Following the reconnaissance battalion at fixed intervals were Reshef himself in a tank accompanied by two half-tracks serving as his forward command post; three tank battalions; followed by infantry and paratroopers in half-tracks. In the light of a large moon, the armored vehicles moved in line over the pristine dunes toward the canal, looking from a distance like a dark necklace undulating across the white sands. Sharon was gripped by the beauty of the scene. To help orientation, Reshef called for phosphorous shells to be fired at Fort Lakekan, six miles to the west, the point where they were to emerge onto Lexicon Road.

In the war room at Southern Command headquarters, General Gonen, the former yeshiva student, quoted to those around him a passage from the Talmud that compared the sweetly scented world of the spice merchant with the malodorous leather trade: "The world cannot function without perfumes and without tanneries," he recited. "Happy is he who works as a spice merchant and woe to him who works in a tannery." Reflecting his sense of the momentous nature of the enterprise they were embarking upon and his gratitude for being part of it, Gonen added, "As for me, I consider myself a spice merchant."

General Yariv, a central figure in the Six Day War as intelligence chief, reflected on the magnitude of the moment. "I don't remember a night this fateful in all our wars."

Elazar, studying the wall map, was moved to a reflection of his own. "If the history of how we pulled this off is ever written," he said, "it will be seen as the height of chutzpa."

30

THE CHINESE FARM

EXCEPT FOR PHOSPHOROUS SHELLS bursting around Fort Lakekan with a brilliant white light, all was quiet when Reshef's brigade emerged onto Lexicon Road, a mile from the canal and parallel to it. Five miles to the north was Tirtur Road. Beyond was the Chinese Farm where the Egyptian Sixteenth Infantry Division was entrenched. Reshef's mission was to throttle it before dawn.

He needed surprise on his side because the numbers weren't. The Twenty-first Armored Division, positioned just beyond the Sixteenth, could be expected to join in the battle. The two divisions together had half again as many tanks as Reshef. Of greater concern were the masses of infantry who would be wielding Saggers and RPGs. Military doctrine calls for an attacking force to have at least a 3 to 1 numerical advantage if it is to have a reasonable chance of overcoming an entrenched defense. Reshef estimated that the overall odds in the Chinese Farm, including antitank weapons, were on the side of the defenders, and by at least 5 to 1.

Reshef intended to penetrate the Egyptian lines as deeply as he could before opening fire. He wanted to explode in the very heart of their deployment like a grenade, with units bursting in all directions. The sudden eruption of Israeli armor in the darkness could stampede them.

At the Lexicon-Akavish intersection, two miles short of Tirtur, Reshef dispatched a tank company eastward to clear Akavish, down which the pontoons were to be towed. Akavish itself was clear but two tanks were damaged on the road by Saggers fired from Tirtur. A stretch of Akavish was within easy Sagger range of Tirtur, less than a mile. As the main column reached the Tirtur intersection, the reconnaissance battalion in the lead peeled off toward the canal. It overcame scattered

The Israeli Crossing of the Suez Canal

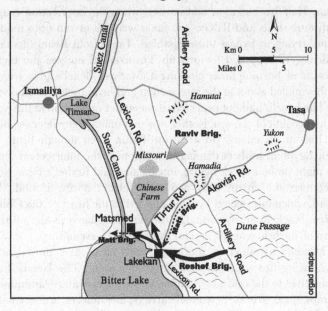

resistance and secured a two-mile strip along the waterway, including Fort Matsmed and the adjacent yard.

Mitzna's battalion took the lead of the main column as it crossed the intersection, Reshef's tank and the two half-tracks close behind. An officer in one of the half-tracks made out several Egyptian soldiers near the road. They appeared to be waving, evidently regarding the tanks as reinforcements. Mitzna's mission was to reach Usha Road, five miles to the north. Intelligence had located an Egyptian bridge where Usha reached the canal. If the Israeli bridges failed to get through the traffic jams, Sharon thought an Egyptian bridge might serve instead.

Next in line was a battalion under Lt. Col. Avraham Almog, who had replaced Shaul Shalev, killed after rescuing the Purkan garrison. The rear of the tank column was brought up by a battalion under Maj. Shaya Beitel. He had taken command earlier in the day from an officer who was sent home on compassionate leave after his brother was killed in action and his brother-in-law was reported missing. At the tail of the column were the half-tracks bearing paratroopers and infantrymen.

As Almog came abreast of the intersection, he thought he saw low silhouettes of tanks projecting above an earthen barrier to the right front. Half his battalion had crossed when the intersection erupted with tank shells and RPGs. Ten tanks were hit or ran onto roadside mines trying to bypass those disabled. Tanks from Beitel's battalion which were supposed to turn up Tirtur could not see the turnoff because of burning tanks blocking it. Many of Beitel's tanks were hit as they milled about at the intersection and he himself was wounded.

The Israelis had not expected to encounter opposition at this point. In his account of the war, Reshef says that military intelligence offered no hint of an enemy presence on Tirtur. Even though Brom had seen Egyptian soldiers digging trenches near the intersection during his night probe a week before, intelligence said Reshef's force would encounter the enemy only two miles farther north, around Shick Road, which intersected Lexicon and led to the heart of the Chinese Farm. Shick Road was roughly the line designated as the northern edge of the bridgehead corridor that was to be established.

Mitzna's battalion, in the lead, sowed havoc as it moved north, exchanging fire with Egyptian tanks as it went. The Israelis found themselves in the midst of a divisional logistical center—ammunition dumps, tanks, trucks, personnel carriers, fuel tankers, artillery batteries, SAM batteries. The tanks fired in every direction. SAM missiles, hit by shells, took off in wild gyrations, ammunition dumps erupted with a roar, and vehicles burst into flame. Egyptian soldiers could be seen running in the reddish yellow light of the fires and the flare of explosions. Some came out of foxholes wrapped in blankets against the cold desert night. The Israeli tank commanders hurled grenades from their turrets and used their Uzis against close-in targets.

Recovering from the surprise, Egyptian tanks and infantrymen began to challenge the intruders. It was almost impossible to distinguish friend from foe except in the light of fires. Company commander Rami Matan halted after knocking out an Egyptian tank fifty yards from him and was searching for others when a soldier climbed onto the tank, his rifle slung over a shoulder. "Do you have a cigarette?" he asked in Arabic. Matan tossed a live grenade. An Israeli medic made the same mistake when he climbed onto a tank to ask its commander to take aboard wounded. The Egyptian fired a pistol but the medic managed to leap off unharmed.

Encounters with enemy tanks occurred at ranges of a few dozen yards or closer when they suddenly became visible. An Israeli tank commander, fearful of losing touch with the rest of his battalion, was happy to be moving between two other tanks. At almost the same moment, the tanks on either side of him burst into flame.

Opposition dwindled as Mitzna left the Sixteenth Division encampment behind and reached Usha Road but only ten of his twenty-one tanks were still with him. Before he could check on the bridge, intelligence reported that an Egyptian tank battalion, which normally had some thirty tanks, was approaching from the Twenty-first Division encampment to the north. The ensuing melee in the darkness took a toll on both sides. Mitzna reported to Reshef that two of his three company commanders were dead and that enemy pressure was heavy. He requested permission to fall back. Reshef told him to join him at Shick Road, halfway back to the Tirtur intersection. As Mitzna headed south, three Egyptian tanks appeared to his front. He set one aflame but as he turned his gun toward a second his own tank was hit. Two crewmen were killed and Mitzna was hurled from the turret. His knee shattered, he pulled himself aboard another tank. Command passed to his deputy.

Meanwhile, battalion commander Almog had been knocked unconscious by an explosion after passing the Tirtur intersection. When he recovered, he found his tank alone. The tank that had been following was standing several hundred yards to the rear, blocking the tanks behind, which could not pass around it because of roadside mines. Almog could not raise the tank's crew on the radio. His operations officer, Lt. Zeev Lichtman, descended from Almog's tank and ran back on Lexicon, passing Egyptian soldiers likewise running in the dark. Climbing on the immobilized tank, he saw that the machine gun atop the turret was smashed. Inside, a company commander lay mortally wounded. The other crew members were in shock but otherwise unhurt. Lichtman appointed one to take command and ordered the driver to start forward.

With the four tanks that now joined him, Almog turned east on Shick, toward the heart of the Chinese Farm, spraying the trenches with machine gun fire. The tanks set ammunition dumps aflame and turned a radar station into an enormous torch. Egyptians drawing close with RPGs were cut down. After an hour, six other tanks joined Almog. He posted some facing north, others facing east.

One of the tank commanders glanced at a tank pulling alongside him and then looked again. It was a T-55. Its commander, believing he had attached himself to an Egyptian unit, scanned the landscape for Israeli tanks in the light of burning vehicles. The Israeli swiveled the tank gun at his new neighbor and told the gunner to fire. "Misfire," shouted the gunner.

For the first time, the Egyptian glanced over. He found himself looking down the barrel of a Patton tank and began swiveling his own gun. But by this time, the commander of the Israeli tank on the other side of the T-55 grasped the situation and backed off sufficiently to put a shell into it.

Reshef had halted across Lexicon Road from Almog's force. His brigade was scattered in pockets over several miles now and all units were reporting heavy casualties. The Egyptians had not been stampeded. They were resisting fiercely and calling in reinforcements. Reshef could see large numbers of Egyptian soldiers flitting between the darkness and the light of fires. The sound of bullets hitting the skin of his tank reminded him of hail on the windshield of a car. He ordered the foot soldiers in the half-tracks at the rear to dismount and retrieve casualties from the chaotic nighttime battlefield, particularly around the Tirtur intersection, which was littered with dead tanks. Climbing into them to check for survivors, the soldiers also retrieved radios and maps.

A tank officer spotted two knocked-out tanks from his own unit and sent his gunner out to search for survivors. The ground was strewn with wounded and dead, many lying in foxholes. The Egyptian foxholes were not vertical but horizontal, like shallow graves. Some seemed to contain both Israelis and Egyptians, whether live or dead was difficult to tell. The gunner, Bertie Ochayon, went from one foxhole to another, asking in a low voice, "Are you Jewish?" He got no reply until he came on a foxhole with a single figure lying partly in and partly out. His right arm was visible and Ochayon could see that it was badly injured. "Are you Jewish," he asked.

"Yes, I'm Jewish," came the reply, "and it's hard to be a Jew."

That phrase, "It's hard to be a Jew"—"*Iz shver tsu zein a yid*," in Yiddish—is the punch line for many a Jewish joke. The man with the wry sense of humor was Lt. Yiftach Yaacov, son of Yitzhak Rabin's sister. Ochayon's tank brought him to an aid station. Elsewhere, an Israeli medic coming across a wounded man with a torn leg instinctively began to bandage it. When the injured man reached for his holster, the medic looked up and saw that he was Egyptian. He bolted before the shot. A squad of Egyptian soldiers came on a wounded Israeli soldier, who pretended to be dead, lying in a trench. They rolled him in a tarpaulin and tossed him out in order to make room for themselves. He managed to crawl away in the dark.

When the tank carrying Mitzna reached Reshef, the brigade commander placed it alongside his own. An aid station was set up in the shelter of the two tanks and the two command half-tracks. Reshef asked Brom to send one of his reconnaissance companies to reinforce what was left of Mitzna's force. It was Rafi Bar-Lev's company that arrived. Within minutes, Haim Bar-Lev's nephew was killed by a tank shell.

As Reshef was talking on the radio, the brigade intelligence officer cut in with an urgent report from radio monitors. "We are now firing at the headquarters of an Egyptian brigade," the monitor said. "The shots just fired were fired at the headquarters of an Egyptian brigade."

Reshef looked over at Almog's tanks and saw them firing machine guns to the east. He raised the battalion commander. "It's you," said Reshef, his normally calm voice rising in pitch. "You're firing at enemy headquarters. Pour it on. Use your tank guns. Call down artillery."

Even as he was maneuvering his units by radio, Reshef was engaged in a personal battle for survival as Egyptian infantrymen periodically surged out of the darkness. He fired his machine gun so relentlessly that his hands were cut from the grip and from cocking the weapon. His force had penetrated a hornet's nest and the hornets were swarming, angry but disoriented. Flames turned the landscape lurid. Egyptian vehicles and infantrymen moved in every direction, some fleeing, some attacking. Five Egyptian tanks lumbered out of the darkness fifty yards from Reshef. Ordering his gunner to prepare for rapid fire, Reshef hit four. Raising Sharon on the radio net, he said, "Forty, this is Four," their respective code designations. "I've just destroyed four tanks." It was not customary to report tank kills on the radio but his men would be listening and Reshef wanted them to know that the brigade commander was fighting alongside them. His voice on the radio was important reassurance in a world that had lost recognizable shape. When he told Sharon of Mitzna's wounding, Sharon said that Reshef's counterpart—the commander of the Egyptian Fourteenth Armored Brigade whom Almog's tanks had been firing at—"has no such worries." Intelligence had just reported him dead.

Amidst the stress of the battle, which was turning out to be more difficult than the Israeli command had envisioned, communication between Reshef and Sharon was marked by an incongruous calm. Sharon did not sharpen his tone even when reminding Reshef that everything hinged on opening Tirtur, which would still be closed after hours of battle.

"The pressures we were under were enormous," Reshef would write in his account of the war. "The personal danger, the life or death battle, the terrible number of casualties, burning tanks and explosions, fire from every direction, fear that we won't succeed and that there won't be a crossing—all of this can break even a strong man. Against this background, I appreciated the communication with Arik—the tone, the courtesy—'I have a request.' 'Yes, please.' 'Thanks.' With all the killing and awfulness around us we remained human beings relating to each other with respect."

Reshef found himself, for the first time since the beginning of the war, free of fear. It was not denial of death that liberated him but acceptance of its inevitability. The chances of emerging alive from the Chinese Farm were so remote that he bowed to his fate, leaving nothing more to be afraid of.

That did not mean abandoning civilities. At one point, he was reinforced by a battalion whose commander spoke crudely on the radio net. Reshef brought him up short. "We don't talk like that here," he said. "If you do again, you'll be dismissed."

Sustaining Reshef and his men was the belief that they were changing the course of the war, that in reaping the bitter harvest of the Chinese Farm they were enabling a bridgehead to be created in the seam behind them. However, there was no bridgehead and with every passing hour the prospect of one was decreasing. The high command was in fact considering calling off the operation.

The optimism that had suffused Southern Command when Stouthearted Men got under way at sundown eroded as the hours passed. Dayan was the first to express fear that the crossing might have to be aborted. Elazar said more time was needed but he too had reconciled himself to the possibility. At 8 p.m., when the paratroopers were supposed to be putting their rubber boats into the water, they were hung up in gridlocked traffic fifteen miles from the canal and still had no boats. It had taken the brigade convoy of sixty half-tracks plus buses and jeeps three hours to cover just the last two miles. The pontoons were spread out even farther back, scattered hopelessly in the logjam.

It had been a nightmare trying to get the pontoons to make the sharp turn from the Tasa junction into Akavish without becoming bogged down in the sands. In a Sisyphean effort, tow tanks were decoupled from the pontoons in the darkness and then recoupled. As for the roller bridge, tank crews were still struggling to tow it over the dunes. Tirtur was still in Egyptian hands and the bridge's way to the canal blocked.

Elazar began to wonder aloud whether the paratroopers should be permitted to cross the canal, presuming they reached it. If the crossing had to be aborted the IDF would expand the foothold it had gained on the Sinai bank. If a cease-fire were declared, Israel would at least have regained a portion of the waterline.

Bar-Lev, however, had not reconciled himself to the possibility of failure. If Sharon's division continued to have difficulties opening Tirtur and bringing the bridges forward, Adan's division could be sent in to help. Committing it to the battle would erode the division's strength before it crossed the canal. But otherwise there might be no crossing at all. Adan himself had offered to take over the opening diversion from Colonel Raviv. This would have permitted Raviv's brigade, part of Sharon's division, to assist in the Chinese Farm itself. The thought had occurred to other senior officers as well but Sharon was unwilling to share the crossing mission with anyone else.

For the moment, Bar-Lev's proposal about Adan was in suspension while waiting to hear what tidings issued from the radio net. A dollop of good news came from intelligence intercepts which indicated that the Egyptians were viewing Reshef's attack as an attempt to roll up the Sixteenth Division's flank northward, not as a prelude to a canal crossing westward. The diversionary attack by Raviv's brigade at Missouri to the northeast reinforced that perception. A spate of radio messages being sent out by Mendler's division suggesting unusual activity southeast of the Bitter Lake was also diverting the attention of Egyptian intelligence. No notice was being paid to the black hole between those two points—the seam.

Matt was repeatedly reminded by Gonen that he was behind schedule. The paratroop commander still had no rubber boats. An engineering unit was supposed to meet them with the boats on Akavish but one rendezvous had already been missed. Matt had been given the code word Acapulco to transmit when he crossed the canal. That prospect was beginning to seem as remote as the Mexican resort itself.

About 9 p.m., the brigade finally forced its way through the traffic jam and linked up with engineers waiting at a roadside clearing with thirty-six rubber boats. It took an hour and a half to inflate them and lift them atop the half-tracks. The vehicles, which could carry no more than twelve soldiers comfortably, were already crammed with twenty-two or more. Two additional men were now added to each—combat engineers who would ferry the boats across the canal.

As the paratroop battalion, escorted now by a tank company, started forward again, the engineers aboard distributed life jackets and explained to the men how to carry the boats to the water and how to get in and out of them. The road cleared of traffic as they approached the battle zone. When they reached the stretch exposed to Tirtur, a few Saggers sailed overhead and bullets hit some of the boats without causing serious damage. Akavish was not yet secure and would be even less so in daylight. When the convoy neared the Tirtur intersection, the paratroopers saw grim evidence of the battle that had been raging there. In a torn Israeli half-track, twelve flaming corpses were still sitting upright.

Pathfinder teams from Matt's force were dropped off to stake out the route with signal lamps for the half-tracks following. Matt ordered the artillery batteries assigned to him to begin softening up the opposite bank and told the commander of the tank escort to position his company at the Tirtur intersection, which he presumed was clear. "Secure towards the north and keep an eye out to the east," he said.

Reaching the Yard—the staging compound at Matsmed—paratroopers in the lead company leaped from their vehicles and fired short bursts from their Uzis into dark corners. There was no return fire. The empty half-tracks started back to pick up the second battalion waiting in their buses on upper Akavish. Reaching Lexicon, the drivers saw some of the tanks that had escorted them only minutes before burning at the Tirtur intersection a few hundred yards to the north. In the light of the flames, Egyptian tanks could be seen moving at the intersection.

At the Matsmed crossing point, engineers used explosives to clear barbed wire concertinas from the edge of the waterway. Six rubber boats with outboard motors were dragged with difficulty over the sand embankment and eased into the water. There was no sign of life on the opposite bank as they started across the canal. Platoon commander Eli Cohen was the first man to climb onto the opposite bank. A few steps inland was a five-foot-high concrete wall, topped by a barbed wire concertina. Lieutenant Cohen tossed a sack of TNT with a timing device atop the wire and leaped back into the boat. It pulled out into the canal until the explosion.

Climbing through the hole opened in the wire, Cohen surveyed the terrain. To his left, barbed wire appeared to enclose a minefield. Straight ahead was a dirt path. There were no Egyptians in sight. One of the men inserted a stake with a green light into the canal bank to indicate the landing point. Another squad which had crossed a hundred yards north placed a red light. Monitoring the operation from a boat in the middle of the canal, the company commander radioed Matt on the Sinai bank that the landing points were secured. "Acapulco," said the brigade commander into his mouthpiece. It was 1:35 a.m. The one-word message was heard not just in Sharon's command half-track to which it was addressed but in Southern Command headquarters at Umm Hashiba and the Pit in Tel Aviv where anxious officers, monitoring the division's radio network, had been awaiting it for hours.

The crossing by the 750 paratroopers in the First Battalion proceeded rapidly, the men embarking from red and green "beaches" on the Sinai bank to their color-coded landing points across the canal. Once across, they moved swiftly inland to stake out a perimeter three miles wide and one mile deep.

Sharon reported to Umm Hashiba that Matt's force had met no opposition. "How's it going elsewhere?" he asked.

Dayan, gripped by the enormous gamble to which they were now committed, took the microphone. "Arik," he said, "there is no elsewhere."

Tirtur remained a bone in the throat. Not only was the road itself inaccessible to the roller bridge but Sagger teams on Tirtur were able to interdict Akavish, which the pontoons were to take. Egyptian infantry was deployed in the deep trenches abutting Tirtur, armed to the teeth with antitank weaponry and virtually immune to shelling.

All commanders from Elazar down were pressured by the blockage of Tirtur, none more so than Reshef. Time and again he had ordered units to open the intersection and Tirtur Road itself but every effort failed. The fact that intelligence had not warned about a potential problem there led Reshef to assume that resistance came from a random collection of tanks and infantry which had rushed to the site after he and the lead battalions had passed it. But he could not understand why they had not been overcome.

Determined to pry Tirtur open, Reshef ordered Brom to attack it with his two remaining companies. He asked the battalion commander to approach cautiously to see if he could determine what they were up against. Heavy fire was opened on the force as it drew near the intersection. Brom managed to hit two Egyptian tanks but thirty meters from the intersection his tank was struck by an RPG. The reconnaissance commander who had uncovered the seam was killed and the attack halted.

Reshef called forward a reserve paratroop unit commanded by Maj. Natan Shunari. The unit, one of the most unusual in the IDF, was something of an "old boys" outfit, made up of men who had served at one time or another in the same elite paratroop reconnaissance battalion. Almost half were over thirty. Among them were men whose names were legend to Reshef himself. Many were personal friends of the country's military leaders alongside whom they had fought in the past. The unit had arrived on Yom Kippur at the foot of the Golan Heights. Shunari called division commander Raful Eitan on the heights and asked him to "give us work."

"What color are your boots?" asked Eitan.

"Red," replied Shunari, the color of paratroop footgear.

"I need black," said Eitan, meaning tank crews.

Shunari prevailed on Eitan to bring the unit up to the heights, but after a couple of days the army dispatched it to Sinai where Egyptian commando operations were creating a demand within Southern Command for special forces. Shunari called Sharon, an old friend, to offer his services. Sharon immediately had Shunari's unit transferred to his division. It was placed under Reshef's command just as Stouthearted Men was getting under way. Within hours, Shunari and his men, who had feared being left out of the war, were dispatched to the most dangerous strip of ground in Sinai.

Reshef gave Shunari's paratroopers the task of opening Tirtur Road and placed the tanks of Capt. Gideon Giladi under his command. Giladi had taken over what remained of Major Beitel's battalion. He had been involved for hours in the melee around the Tirtur intersection and had already had one tank shot out from under him after losing one earlier in a ditch crossing the dunes. The wildness of battle was upon him. His tank constantly moved back and forth to avoid presenting a sitting target. When the commander of another tank company who had just arrived climbed on Giladi's tank for a briefing, he found him impatient. I have no time to talk, he said. I have to open the road. Giladi started his tank forward even before the officer leaped off.

Giladi had spotted the opening to Tirtur Road beyond the wrecked armored vehicles littering the intersection. But he was ordered not to enter until sufficient forces had been assembled. Now, he was told to lead the six half-tracks bearing Shunari's seventy paratroopers up the road.

Giladi, a former paratrooper, had switched to the armored corps after his brother was killed commanding a tank in the Six Day War. He was serving in his brother's old unit. At the intersection he had only two tanks, his own and his deputy's. The pair wove their way between the smoldering wrecks and entered Tirtur Road without being fired on, the first time the road had been penetrated since the battle began. "The intersection's open," Giladi reported to Shunari, who followed a few hundred yards behind. The veteran paratroopers could smell war—scorched rubber, cordite, smoke. The smell was familiar but not the intensity. A tank crewman ran toward them out of the darkness. His face was blackened with soot and he was weeping. All the other crewmen in his tank had been killed, he said. The young tanker vainly implored the men in the half-tracks to turn back.

On the radio, Giladi reported that he was encountering masses of infantry but was coping. Then silence. His deputy radioed that he was turning back but then his radio too went dead. Continuing forward, Shunari found Giladi's tank burning and the other disabled. Dead tankers were sprawled on the ground. Shunari reported the scene to Reshef, who told him to dismount and proceed on foot, for fear that the half-tracks would likewise be hit.

Shunari, however, preferred to keep his men inside the half-tracks, which offered a measure of protection against small arms fire. Within moments, Saggers and RPGs were exploding around them. Shunari managed to break through, together with the vehicle behind him, but the rear half-tracks were all hit. Shunari called on Reshef for artillery support. "They're slaughtering my unit," he shouted. The brigade commander said no artillery was available. "I'm in the same situation you are."

Shunari ordered his men to abandon the vehicles and head south on foot toward Akavish Road. By this time no one was alive in the rearmost half-track. Some of its men had attempted to charge the Egyptian positions but got only a few paces before being cut down. The others began pulling back but the Egyptians took up pursuit. As dawn broke, a group of Shunari's men including the unit doctor heard the treads of an Egyptian tank behind them as they made their way through the sands toward Akavish, carrying the wounded. There was nowhere to hide. As they prepared for death, fog draped itself over the desert with the suddenness of a shade being drawn. The tank passed within a few score yards. The men could not see it but they could hear its engine growing louder and then more distant.

Four men nearby took cover at the sound of incoming mortars. Three were killed by the explosions. The fourth, at forty-one the oldest man in the unit, turned to see a line of infantrymen heading toward him. He fired an antitank missile into their midst and succeeded in getting away. Of Shunari's seventy men, twenty-four were killed, including his younger brother, and sixteen wounded.

Close to midnight, the roller bridge was once again harnessed to the tanks of Ben-Shoshan's battalion in the expectation that Tirtur would soon be opened. "Ready," said Ben-Shoshan. "Ready. Engage gears. Move." The giant structure began moving across the dunes like a monumental caterpillar. On one of the first descents, the bridge ran up on two of the tanks. There was no serious damage but extricating the tanks took an hour. Hopes for reaching the canal before dawn faded. As the dunes became steeper, more tanks were put in harness. There were frequent stops and Ben-Shoshan's voice grew hoarse as he barked his litany. In the distance, Israeli artillery could be heard. It was 5 a.m. when they ascended the steepest dune yet. There were sixteen tanks pulling now. Two braked from behind.

Suddenly, a tank commander shouted, "Stop."

The noise of the engines abated and the officer said, "It's snapped."

"Then change the tow line," said Ben-Shoshan.

"It's not the tow line. It's the bridge."

Engineers rushed forward and saw that the bridge had indeed broken under the strain, as some tanks pulled and others braked. Informed that it would take twenty-four hours to repair, Sharon ordered Ben-Shoshan's tanks to disengage and move up to the canal. Another unit would take over when the bridge was repaired.

Sharon dispatched a reconnaissance officer to report to him on the bridge's condition. At its inception, it had been called the Lascov Bridge after its originator. When General Tal provided his input and pushed the project through to completion, it came to be called the Tal Bridge. When the reconnaissance officer returned to Sharon, he said, "You can call it the Lascov Bridge again," a hint that it was something a senior officer would prefer not to be associated with.

With dawn little more than an hour away, Sharon mordantly contemplated his options. The radio net had gone silent. No one had anything to report. It was as if the whole army had laid down to nap. The roller bridge was broken. The pontoons were scattered somewhere in the logjam. The silence itself broadcast despair. Nothing was moving except the clock. Exhaustion reigned. Momentum had dissipated. Sharon contacted his deputy, Colonel Even.

"What do we have?" asked Sharon.

"The Gillois."

"Where are they?"

"With me."

"Bring them to me, with their crews."

These retreads from a junkyard were his last hope.

Apart from being slimmer than the pontoons and not requiring towing, the Gillois were starting from a point closer to the canal and had a better chance of getting through. As they moved westward with Even, the amphibian vehicles picked up a tank battalion escort commanded by Maj. Giora Lev of Erez's brigade. When they reached a sheltered area, Sharon and the five APCs constituting his mobile command post joined them. Small arms fire was directed at the convoy when it moved into the stretch of Akavish exposed to Tirtur but no missiles. Sharon told Lev not to respond and to keep moving. Lev's mission, said Sharon, was to get across the canal "even with one tank."

As they moved forward, a bulldozer loomed out of the darkness and the driver flagged Lev down. "How do I get to Tasa?" he asked. Lev had no idea how a bulldozer could have reached this remote part of the battlefield but it occurred to him that he would need one. "Follow me," he said. The bulldozer driver obligingly turned his vehicle around, unaware that he was being led in the opposite direction from Tasa.

The convoy reached the Yard just before dawn. In preparing Matsmed as a base for a canal crossing when he was head of Southern Command, Sharon had ordered that a section of the Yard's enclosure wall facing the canal be kept thin, so that it could be easily broken through. He had red bricks placed in the wall to mark the spot.

Fifteen Gillois lined up abreast in the Yard. On command, the drivers inflated the rubber floats by having the engines pump in air, a process that took ten minutes. It was a pretty sight and the tank crews watched bemused in the blissful silence. Sharon's intelligence officer, who on Akavish had been listening to the startling, staccato-like firing of tank guns emanating from the Chinese Farm, was taken aback to be hearing morning birdsong on the banks of the canal a mile away.

At 6:30 a.m., the Gillois descended into the water where they were linked up by the engineers to form five rafts, each capable of carrying a tank. Through the breach in the enclosure wall, Sharon could see palm trees and lush growth on the far bank, like some desert mirage. It was a moment he had fantasized for years. In the command APC, a sergeant watched Sharon sit down in the commander's chair and fastidiously straighten the red paratrooper's beret tucked into his shoulder strap. After brushing back his hair with his hand he called his wife on a radio-telephone. "Lily," he said with excitement, "we're here. We're the first." Sharon asked the sergeant to make sure the men in the command vehicles were shaved. The crossing of the Suez Canal was an occasion that merited a bit of primping.

There was still no bridge but there was now a way to get tanks across the canal. Israel's major strategic move in the war, on the verge of being abandoned, was being literally kept afloat by recycled junk.

In the Chinese Farm, dawn wrapped itself in thick fog as if reluctant to reveal what had transpired in the darkness. Two armies which had hacked unrelentingly at each other for ten hours had fallen silent, resting for the moment on their swords. It had been a surreal night, given up to combat without lines separating "us" from "them." Death had become so familiar that it was meted out with a weary offhandedness. An Egyptian tank hurrying down Lexicon Road was followed by hollow eyes until someone, at less than fifty yards, put a shell into it almost as an afterthought.

The air was heavy with the smell of cordite and acrid smoke. Orange pulses in the mist hinted at fires all about. Were it not for the morning cold that set teeth chattering, the curtain seemed about to go up on a scene from hell. As the fog dissipated, hell revealed itself. Hundreds of gutted vehicles were strewn over the desert floor, many still burning. Shattered jeeps and trucks were scattered like chaff. But it was the remains of the heavy tanks that bespoke the violence of the night. Some had their turrets blown off. Some were upended like toys, their gun barrels embedded in the sand. Charred Israeli and Egyptian tanks lay alongside each other. Corpses were strewn on the sand. Many more were inside the gutted vehicles and in the ditches. There was no hint of the orderly lines of a divisional encampment which this had been a few hours before or the orientation of enemy formations facing one another on a battlefield. This was the all-around chaos of a murderous street brawl that left only an exhausted few still standing.

There had been madness here and none sensed it in the quiet of dawn more keenly than Lt. Yuval Neria. The twenty-one-year-old officer had been in combat since Yom Kippur afternoon, ten days before. The battalion he served with at the northern end of the canal was destroyed that day and he ended up joining another in one of the hopeless battles at Hizayon on October 8. In the ensuing days, Neria drifted like a vagabond warrior across the battlefield. Three times, the tank he was in was hit and he took over tanks commanded by sergeants, an officer's prerogative. After his tank was hit in the battle for Hamutal, he hitchhiked to Tasa. Coming across three tanks outside Fourteenth Brigade headquarters awaiting assignment, he told the crews he was their new commander and moved with them toward the front until he encountered Mitzna's battalion. Mitzna, whom he had not met before, assigned him three more tanks and appointed him a company commander.

Approaching the Tirtur junction at the opening of the battle, his tank ran onto a mine. Neria saw to the evacuation of his crew and set out on foot through the Egyptian lines to find his battalion. Holding his Uzi close to his body to mask its distinctive profile, he passed within a few dozen yards of Egyptian soldiers in foxholes, chatting or eating. They seemed oblivious to the battle raging a few hundred yards from them. Anyone noticing him could take him for someone bearing a message or obeying nature's call. To his front after a while he saw a line of tanks firing toward the north. As he drew close he could see that they were Israeli Pattons. He managed to climb aboard one from the rear without getting shot and discovered that the tanks were from Almog's battalion. The tank commander was not welcoming and Neria boarded another whose commander was happy to let Neria take over as gunner. For the next few hours, he fired as if in a trance, as the Egyptians staged local counterattacks. Ranges were so close that the tank sometimes had to back away from burning vehicles because of the heat. At dawn, Neria was surprised to find himself still alive. But the world itself seemed to have reached its end, reduced to charred metal, a shell-pocked desert, and numbed men at the limit of their endurance.

For Reshef too, dawn offered no balm. Tirtur remained blocked, Akavish was too dangerous for use, and the Egyptians were still stubbornly clinging to the Chinese Farm. He had lost fifty-six of his ninety-seven tanks. The brigade had this night lost most of the 128 dead it would lose in the Chinese Farm, together with 62 wounded—tank crewmen and paratroopers—without causing a noticeable dent in the Egyptian defenses. By objective standards, the attack was a failure, a bold enterprise that had come undone. Reshef, however, had no intention of writing it off. As he had told Brom the day before, the battle would go to whichever side was more stubborn. If he was hurting, so surely were the Egyptians.

At 5:50 a.m. he reported his situation to Sharon. His men were exhausted, he said, but he intended to renew the attack on the Tirtur intersection. In the absence of any indication from intelligence of an organized defense system at the site, he had assumed that the defenders were ad hoc groups of tanks and infantry. Yet they were still resisting after all he had thrown at them. He had called down artillery fire after Brom's failed attack with no visible effect.

Reshef asked that units from the division's two other brigades—those of Erez and Raviv—be temporarily assigned to him in order to try to force the road from its eastern end where elements of those brigades were positioned.

Daylight would have left Mitzna and Almog exposed on the open terrain, so Reshef ordered them to fall back to a high dune closer to the canal where they could deploy for all-around defense. The two battalions, which had had forty-three tanks between them when they set out the night before—little more than half strength—now had just ten between them. As he started down Lexicon in the fog, with Almog following some distance behind, Reshef's tank almost collided with an Egyptian tank traveling at high speed in the opposite direction. Before he could react, the tank swerved past him and disappeared into the fog. Reshef warned Almog, "T-55 coming straight at you." The battalion commander had barely absorbed the message when a tank burst out of the fog to his front. Its hatches were closed and two commandos with submachine guns were sitting atop it. Almog grabbed his machine gun but his operations officer, Lieutenant Lichtman, had his head out of the loader's hatch, blocking his line of fire. The Egyptian tank veered off the road and started to brush past them on the left. Before pulling his head back into the turret, Almog saw the commandos cocking and raising their weapons. Lichtman, who had ducked inside, came back up with his Uzi and sprayed it in an arc. Almog put his head back out in time to see the commandos toppling from the tank. As the T-55 disappeared into the fog, Almog turned his turret and pegged a shot in its direction. He was turning the turret back when an Egyptian jeep mounted with Saggers darted out of the fog and almost ran into the rear of his tank. "Back up," Almog shouted. The driver reversed and crushed the vehicle.

Meanwhile, an attack was launched on the intersection by a company led by Maj. Gabriel Vardi of Brom's reconnaissance battalion, the first attack undertaken after dawn. On his own initiative, Vardi approached the crossroad where his commander had been killed with three tanks, while four others provided covering fire. He could for the first time see something of the Egyptian disposition that had been hidden at night, including ditches that sheltered infantry and earthen mounds behind which tanks were positioned five hundred yards to the northeast. His force sheltered behind knocked-out Israeli tanks and dueled with the enemy tanks, hitting eight without suffering a loss. When a vehicle mounted with Sagger missiles appeared in one of the broad ditches, Vardi put a shell into it. A soldier ran from the burning vehicle, stopped, hesitated, and then ran back to lift out a wounded man. The tank commander swung his gun toward the two Egyptians. He too hesitated, then turned the gun away. He proceeded north for a mile, pumping shells into Egyptian positions, visible at last. With ammunition exhausted, he pulled back.

Reshef, meanwhile, had gathered the remnants of the reconnaissance battalion and personally led another attack on the intersection, passing Vardi's withdrawing force. This time, the defenders, who had stood all night against repeated attacks, raised white flags, presumably undershirts.

In the morning light, the mystery of the stubborn defense of the Tirtur crossroad revealed itself. Dug-in T-62 tanks, difficult to see and difficult to hit, were positioned to cover the intersection, as were jeeps mounted with Sagger missiles. There were well-placed machine gun positions, scores of foxholes for infantrymen bearing RPGs, deep trenches. The entire position was protected by mines. Reshef's forces had not dealt with a random collection of tanks and infantry but with the southern edge of a strong defense line.

The battle for the Tirtur-Lexicon intersection was over. But not the battle for the rest of Tirtur or for the Chinese Farm itself.

31

THE BRIDGES

A MI MORAG'S BATTALION had been serving since Monday night as outrider for the roller bridge, guarding it against commando attack. Keeping up with the bridge's slow pace grated on the tankers' nerves but Tuesday morning Morag was informed that his period of boredom was over. The battalion would be one of the two that would attack the Chinese Farm from its eastern end at Reshef's behest. Morag's assignment was to proceed down the length of Tirtur to its intersection with Lexicon and clear any pockets of resistance. Morag had little idea of the fierce battles that had raged around Tirtur all night. It was his understanding from Reshef that he would be encountering random bands of tank hunters. He was also to evacuate survivors of Shunari's unit, believed to be sheltering in ditches near the road.

Fog limited visibility to a few yards as Morag approached Tirtur at the head of two companies. He told his deputy, Yehuda Tal, to remain on high ground to the rear with a third company to provide covering fire. As Morag moved forward, two men emerged on foot from the fog—Shunari and one of his officers. They told Morag where they believed their comrades to be. As they conversed, the fog lifted like a theater curtain. On the vast stage that revealed itself was the Chinese Farm, veined with ditches. Two miles to the northwest were two large buildings housing pumping equipment, the major structures in the area. Out of the gray landscape, red balls of fire suddenly began to waft in their direction. "Missiles," shouted Morag.

He knew the area intimately from years of service in Sinai and led his tanks into the shelter of a shallow quarry. As the last tank entered, the slow-moving missiles passed overhead. To Morag's surprise, Sag-

The Chinese Farm Battlefield

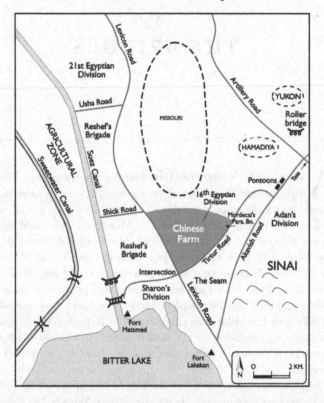

gers continued to overfly them. The missiles even appeared to be dipping.downward, as if searching out the tanks in the quarry. Morag realized that the Sagger operators were firing at the tank antennas and were attempting to guide the missiles down into the quarry with their joysticks even though they could not see the tanks themselves. Morag had his men lower the antennas and the firing ceased.

He remounted the road and led his tanks forward but a torrent of missiles sent them scurrying back. The second battalion requested by Reshef, from Raviv's brigade, moved into position a mile to the north to provide covering fire. Morag was concerned about the danger of friendly fire and asked the commander of the tank behind him to keep his eye on the nearest tank in the covering force. As Morag's tank mounted the road again, the tank commander behind him said, "He's swiveling his gun." Morag ordered his driver to pull back. As he did, a shell exploded where he had just been. Morag asked Reshef to have the other battalion withdrawn. "I have troubles enough with the Egyptians," he said.

To his left, he could see Ben-Shoshan's battalion, which had disengaged from the roller bridge, heading down Akavish toward the canal. It was escorting half-tracks bearing the second half of Matt's paratroop brigade. Morag warned Ben-Shoshan to beware of Saggers from Tirtur. "Thanks, I see them," came the reply. A moment later, a missile hit Ben-Shoshan's tank, wounding him. The tanks continued forward but the vulnerable half-tracks were ordered back.

Morag tried to move forward once again but the rate of missile fire had not slackened. Raising Reshef, he said it was suicidal to try to force Tirtur. We're not up against tank hunters, said Morag. There's an army out there. With the entire crossing operation dependent on opening the road, Reshef was unyielding. If Morag did not push down Tirtur, the brigade commander warned, he would face charges of disobeying orders. Reshef promised that when the tanks moved forward this time, Morag would have artillery support.

Major Tal, who heard Reshef's order, could see from his high ground a multitude of Egyptian infantrymen carrying Sagger suitcases moving into positions paralleling the length of Tirtur. He told Morag to refuse the order. It was madness to move down the road, he said. Morag, however, understood now that his mission was do-or-die. He would carry out the order but save what he could of the battalion. He ordered Tal's force to stay where it was. Of the eight tanks with Morag, three commanded by sergeants would remain behind at the edge of the quarry to provide covering fire in relative safety. The remaining five, all commanded by officers, would follow him down Tirtur. Morag told the officers that they would move fast, firing everything they had, and advance "at all costs."

Unaware of the importance of their assignment and of the fighting for Tirtur that had raged through the night, Morag's officers believed that Reshef was assigning them a doomed mission only because they were not part of his organic brigade. The battalion had still not fully recovered from the trauma of its baptism by fire at Hamutal, even though it had been in numerous skirmishes since. It had suffered another blow the previous night when a company assigned to escort

Matt's paratroopers to the canal lost four of its seven tanks at the Tirtur intersection. The dead included the company commander—a platoon commander who took over the company after all the company commanders in the battalion had been wounded at Hamutal.

As soon as Morag's force emerged into the open, a tank was hit by a missile but managed to limp back to the safety of the quarry. The remainder continued forward under an astonishing barrage of missiles. The unit had encountered Saggers on Hamutal and since but nothing like this. To one officer, it seemed as if some enormous machine gun was spraying missiles rather than bullets. From the heart of the Chinese Farm, Saggers were lifting off like fireworks.

Morag, in the lead, saw the ditches near the road dark with infantrymen. The tank commanders were exposed in the turrets but the Egyptian infantrymen in the trenches were too stunned by the armor thundering by them to shoot straight. The tank guns fired into the trenches and the tank commanders raked them with machine gun fire. The loaders worked like railroad firemen, feeding shells into the guns as fast as they could, pausing only to hand up machine gun ammunition boxes to the commanders in the turrets. There was no time to throw casings of the expended shells out of the loader's hatch so the hot metal tubes began to pile up inside the tanks.

The drivers weaved at speed along the narrow road to throw off the aim of the missile operators. Sagger guide wires from near misses wrapped themselves around antennas. Morag had given up any thought of staying alive. He called for artillery to be fired at the moving tanks so that shells straddling them would hit the enemy infantry. In less than two miles, the gunner in Morag's tank fired thirty shells. Morag himself, flinging grenades and firing his machine gun, went through three ammunition belts and resorted finally to his Uzi. "Wherever we fired, we hit," he would report. "There was infantry everywhere."

One tank was stopped by a Sagger. Major Tal could see the commander—who happened to be Amnon Reshef's brother-in-law—emerge from the smoking vehicle and carry a wounded crewman on his back. The other two crewmen followed. An APC manned by paratroopers dashed in from Akavish Road. It too was hit and its commander seriously wounded, but it managed to reach the tankers and make it back safely.

Nearing the Tirtur-Lexicon intersection, Morag found the road blocked by the two disabled tanks of Captain Giladi and his deputy and by Shunari's burned-out half-tracks. Deep trenches barred the way forward. Missiles were now also being fired at them from somewhere between Tirtur and Akavish. "Left," shouted Morag. They veered off Tirtur and found themselves racing alongside a ditch filled with Egyptian soldiers. Morag could see the frightened faces a few feet away. He also saw the RPGs. The tank gun fired point-blank into the trenches and the machine guns did not stop firing. They were so close that Egyptians in the trench were being burned by the flare from the tank gun, which was almost touching them. Morag kept using an override device to take control of the gun from the gunner in order to fire at RPG holders in the trench ahead. The gunner, feeling naked, kept calling for him to give the gun back.

To his immediate front, Morag suddenly saw a trench cutting across their path. "Stop," he shouted.

The driver, however, had from his seat lower in the tank been looking straight into the faces of the infantrymen they were passing. "I'm not stopping for anything," he shouted back. He hit the near lip of the trench at top speed and the tank spanned the void. Morag could hear the treads trying to grip the ground on the other side of the ditch and then find purchase. The other tanks all managed to get across or around.

For the first time since they had started out, there was no enemy in sight and no Saggers. To their front was a low sand hill. Morag halted alongside it and the other tanks pulled abreast of him in a swirl of dust. Silence descended. From their turrets, the tank commanders looked at one another in amazement. It made no sense but they were all still alive. Everyone's shirt was soaked with sweat. Someone let out a whoop. Then all began to cheer. The crews descended from the tanks to urinate and let their frayed nerves settle. As they luxuriated in a long pee, Morag heard voices speaking Arabic on the other side of the hill but it made little impression on him. As he would later describe his feeling, he was "beyond reality."

Climbing back onto his tank, Morag was contacted by Major Tal. "I see your tanks," he said. "Don't get off them. There are Arabs near you." Tal guided Morag back toward Akavish, steering him away from Egyptian forces scattered between the two roads. The route took them through a ditch wide enough for tanks. They had not proceeded far when they came on twenty soldiers. Morag recognized them as remnants of Shunari's force. The paratroopers were exhausted and without water. They climbed on the tanks and within moments had drunk dry the jerricans of water stored on the outside of the turrets.

When the tanks reached the safety of upper Akavish, Morag reported his position to the commander of his organic brigade, Col. Haim Erez. He did not want to get any more orders from Reshef, he said. He did not want to talk to him; he did not want to see him. If he saw him, he said, he would shoot him. (The two men would in the future work together amicably when Reshef was head of the armored corps and Morag served as his deputy.)

The tanks had penetrated almost the length of Tirtur, moving in line like ducks in a shooting gallery past an infantry brigade armed with antitank weaponry. They had rescued the remnants of Shunari's force and inflicted heavy casualties on the enemy. And they had survived. But the bottom line remained unchanged. Tirtur was blocked and Akavish too dangerous to be used.

Matt's paratroopers across the canal found themselves in an unreal world—green and tranquil. The west bank of the canal was a lush agricultural strip, dotted with palm trees and mud-hut villages—a striking contrast to the barren wastes of Sinai. The four-mile-wide strip was irrigated by Nile water fed through the narrow Sweetwater Canal, which ran down its center. The troops had begun to call the territory west of the canal "Africa," which quickly replaced "Goshen" as the common designation. Like the Bosphorus, which separated Asia from Europe on the other side of the Mediterranean, the Suez Canal in effect separated Asia from Africa.

The paratroopers were prepared to hold out alone against armor, if necessary. Equipped with three hundred newly arrived LAW antitank missiles as well as the forty bazookas organic to the battalion and a few recoilless rifles, they were prepared to do to Egyptian tanks what Egyptian infantry had been doing for the past ten days to Israeli tanks. For the first time, Israeli soldiers had an effective antitank weapon in quantity. The paratroopers did not remain alone for long. The Gillois which Lev had escorted to the canal returned the courtesy by ferrying his fourteen tanks across at dawn together with a company of infantry in APCs.

The Egyptians still had no idea what the Israelis were up to; not a shell had been fired at either bank. In this bucolic interlude, soldiers could imagine that they had left war far behind. A tank officer being ferried across, Capt. Yossi Regev, in a lighthearted gesture to the tank commander on the raft following, bent the antenna of his tank toward the water as if it were a fishing rod.

Major Lev led two tanks, each carrying a paratroop officer in the turret, to a former airfield shown on his map a mile from the landing point. It was now a base housing Egyptian logistics units. A sentry at the gate, assuming they were Egyptian, saluted as they entered. The tanks rolled down the runway, shooting up a score of vehicles and antiaircraft guns. Returning to the crossing point, Lev received a call from someone who identified himself with a code number he did not recognize.

"Who are you?" asked Lev.

"Do you know my voice?" asked the caller. This time Lev recognized the unmistakable drawl of General Bar-Lev.

"Yes, sir," said the major.

"I'm putting you under the command of the air force commander."

A new voice now came on the line. It sounded like Gen. Benny Peled.

"Do you see the flowers on your map?"

If the apparent transfer of his tank battalion to the air force was strange, this question was stranger still.

"What flowers?" Lev asked.

"Do you see numbers in red?"

On his map, Lev saw groupings of four red numbers in many locations on the west side of the canal. Now that he looked, he noticed that alongside each was a sketch of a daisy.

"Yes, I see them."

"Destroy all those in your area. Out."

Lev decided to wait for Colonel Erez, who was accompanying Ben-Shoshan's battalion. They were ferried across at 10 a.m. by the Gillois. Erez was as puzzled as Lev about what the flowers designated but he decided to find out.

Leaving seven tanks behind to protect the bridgehead, the brigade commander took twenty-one tanks and the infantry company and headed west. When they reached a bridge over the Sweetwater Canal, they encountered Egyptian tanks. The Israeli column had to remain in single file because of bogs straddling the road. Only the tank in the lead, commanded by Captain Regev, an Israeli diplomat recently returned from a South American posting, could engage. In an hour-long cat-and-mouse duel through the shrubbery, Regev destroyed four tanks. Urged by Lev to move forward, Regev said he believed a fifth tank was still lying in ambush. He spotted it at last, through the window of a hut. The tank had entered by breaking through the back wall. Regev put a shell through the front wall, setting the tank afire.

The Israeli raiding party drove across a flinty plain unsoftened by the dunes familiar from Sinai. They destroyed trucks which appeared randomly on the road, some of them carrying FROG missiles. At a desert encampment, they came on half a dozen tanks and a score of personnel carriers fitted with antitank recoilless rifles, a configuration the Israelis had not seen before. Erez's tanks destroyed them at a mile's range.

After half an hour, they approached the map coordinates of the first "flower." A mound appeared in the distance. As they drew closer, they could see earthen ramps, an antenna, a van, and the sleek outlines of SAM missiles pointing skyward. A reserve officer who was an engineering student at the Technion told Lev that the van was the brain center that controlled the system. The tanks fired and the missiles ignited, cavorting wildly before exploding in a puff of yellow-orange smoke. Two other SAM sites were hit later, the tankers looking forward each time to the pyrotechnic display. The tanks entered one missile base to top up their fuel tanks from drums of diesel fuel.

The raid took the force twenty miles west of the canal. Asked by Sharon on the radio how he was faring, Erez said, "I can go on to Cairo," about fifty miles distant. When an Egyptian truck convoy was spotted to the west, Colonel Erez sent the infantry company to deal with it. The APCs reached ten miles closer to Cairo before overtaking and destroying the convoy.

In late afternoon, Erez asked whether he should remain where he was in order to intercept enemy forces heading toward the bridgehead. He was told to come back; his force was not big enough for such a mission. The tanks returned before dusk after having completed a sixty-mile circuit, leaving behind burnt-out Egyptian vehicles and a small hole in the sky free of SAMs that the air force could begin expanding.

Matt's paratroopers had during the day destroyed trucks carrying Egyptian troops at the northern end of the perimeter. But overall, the bridgehead remained the calmest place on the southern front. Matt told his men to dig foxholes in anticipation of what was bound to come. With no one shooting at them meanwhile, the paratroopers and tankers got small fires going for coffee, well aware that their oasis holiday would not last long. In this relaxed atmosphere, the ebullient Lev, a future mayor of the city of Petakh Tikva, did a stand-up routine for Erez and Matt, in which he portrayed an angry Sadat upbraiding an apologetic Shazly for not knowing about the Israeli crossing. As a group of soldiers looked out at the Bitter Lake, into which the canal opened, one of them noted that some scholars believed this to be where the waters had parted for the Israelites more than three thousand years before on their way out of Egypt. "If they don't get a bridge up soon," said another, "we'll have to do it again in the other direction."

The absence of an Egyptian response to the crossing exhilarated Elazar, who had not had many causes for exhilaration since the war started. "I couldn't imagine things would go so well," he told his staff at 10 a.m. "The Egyptians haven't grasped what's going on. They don't understand that we're on the canal. They're thinking of it as a raid. We have a battalion of paratroopers over there and tanks."

Said Zeira: "What's happening now is not in accordance with the plan they've been practicing for years. They don't understand our moves. They don't know what to do."

At 10:20, radio monitors picked up an Egyptian report of five Israeli tanks on the west bank of the canal. The report assumed them to be amphibious tanks which had crossed the Bitter Lake the way Egyptian tanks had done, in the opposite direction, in the opening hours of the war.

Although the Gillois were performing nobly, headquarters was unwilling to rest a two-division attack across the Suez Canal on a handful of rafts. Apart from their limited capacity, the Gillois could easily be sunk once shelling started. Construction of at least one bridge was imperative. Southern Command began pressing Sharon late Tuesday morning when the dimensions of the problem became apparent. There was a growing feeling at headquarters that in his eagerness to cross the canal, Sharon had not applied himself to opening the roads and bringing up the bridges. It was an issue that would bring to the fore the latent antagonism between Sharon and other generals, particularly Bar-Lev.

"What we need," said Bar-Lev to Sharon on the radio, "is a bridge and a road. To my regret we have neither. Can you do this with your own forces or should we send in someone else [a reference to Adan's division]?" Sharon said he had no need for help. "Aha," said Bar-Lev, not hiding his skepticism. "You don't need anyone else right now. Arik, as long as there is no real bridge, we can't cross."

The warning was repeated to Sharon by Gonen. Without a bridge, he said, the crossing operation would have to be canceled. Telephoning the Pit, Gonen said, "I'm calling so that the mood where you are doesn't become too optimistic. What happened is that Sharon dashed for the canal and left behind unopened roads." Bar-Lev barred further transfer of tanks across the canal.

The order struck Sharon as madness. This was the time, he argued, to send over as many tanks as possible and turn them loose upon the enemy's SAMs and supply lines while the Egyptians still didn't realize what was happening. If the breakout was delayed, he argued, the Egyptians would have time to seal off the bridgehead. George Patton was described by Erwin Rommel's chief of staff as the only Allied general in the Second World War who dared to exceed safety limits in an attempt to achieve a decision, a description that applied to Sharon. He disagreed with Southern Command's contention that the forces across the canal were in danger of being cut off. We're not surrounded, he said. It's the Egyptians who are surrounded. A strategic victory was within Israel's grasp.

Southern Command was not persuaded. Gonen warned again that unless a bridge was put up soon, the forces west of the canal might have to be withdrawn. Bar-Lev put it differently to Dayan later in the day. If the roads were not opened, the APCs would be brought back but the paratroopers and the twenty-eight tanks already there would remain. In a worst-case situation, the men could be brought back by rubber boats and perhaps even the tanks could be evacuated if the Gillois were still afloat. As for now, the bridgehead would remain.

Sharon was not thinking in terms of Dunkirk but of blitzkrieg. He wanted to send a hundred to two hundred tanks across on the Gillois and strike before the Egyptians grasped the situation. Elazar agreed with Bar-Lev that such a large force could not be risked without a bridge, although he agreed to a slight increase in the number of tanks. The dispute stemmed from the basic difference in temperament that marked the relations between Sharon and his superiors throughout the war—the difference, as Bar-Lev would describe it, between calculated risk and irresponsible gamble. As Sharon saw it, this was the opportunity they had been seeking since Yom Kippur to unhinge the Egyptian army and it was being thrown away by timidity.

Stouthearted Men was hardly conservative. The IDF was taking an enormous risk in attempting to infiltrate the bulk of the army through the middle of the enemy lines, across a water barrier, with a single pontoon bridge (still not in place) and a handful of rafts and with only a narrow, still unsecured, corridor linking the bridgehead to the rear.

The situation was complicated by a major security slip perpetrated by none other than Prime Minister Meir. Unable to contain herself after eleven grim days of war, she decided to share the good news with the nation. "Right now," she said, in a speech to the Knesset broadcast live late Tuesday, "as we convene, an IDF task force is operating on the west bank of the Suez Canal." The military censor, to whom the speech had routinely been submitted, excised this passage but Mrs. Meir read it anyway. Public morale needed a boost and she assumed that she would not be telling the Egyptians anything they didn't know. She was mistaken. Dayan was furious but said nothing. Elazar was upset too. He was planning to bring back the forces which had crossed the canal unless Akavish and Tirtur were opened soon. In that case, the brief canal crossing could be passed off as a successful raid. After Mrs. Meir's upbeat remarks, however, evacuation would be a severe blow to national morale

Fortunately for Israel, the Egyptians didn't believe her. President Sadat was quick to dismiss Mrs. Meir's remarks as "psychological warfare." Reports of skirmishes west of the canal had reached the Egyptian command but they did not add up to a major crossing. If the reports were true it could not be more than a showcase raid by a small number of tanks the Israelis had somehow managed to get across the canal, probably amphibious tanks.

Shortly before Mrs. Meir's speech, as the Israelis were building up their bridgehead in "Africa" undisturbed, President Sadat, accompanied by War Minister Ismail, was driven to parliament through exultant crowds in what amounted to a victory parade. From the parliament podium, Sadat dictated his terms for a cease-fire—total Israeli withdrawal from Sinai.

The 890th Paratroop Battalion, which had one of the IDF's most illustrious histories, had thus far taken only a marginal part in the war.

Israel's oldest paratroop unit, it set combat standards for the IDF in the 1950s under its first commander, Ariel Sharon. With the onset of the current war, most of the battalion had been flown to the Gulf of Suez where it hunted down Egyptian commandos. But the battalion was still waiting for a major mission.

On Tuesday morning, eleven days into the war, the battalion commander, Lt. Col. Yitzhak Mordecai, was told to prepare his men for an amphibious operation. Landing craft would carry the battalion on a raid across the Gulf of Suez with half-tracks and tanks. The battalion was already at its embarkation point when Col. Uzi Ya'ari, commander of the brigade to which the 890th belonged, arrived to announce a mission change. The battalion was to board planes immediately for Refidim, rear base for the Suez Canal front.

With Sharon's division overextended and eroded by the battle for the Chinese Farm, Bar-Lev had transferred responsibility for opening the roads and bringing up the bridging equipment to Adan. Adan, in turn, assigned the task to his deputy, Dov Tamari. On the second day of the war, it was General Tamari who unclogged the coastal road, bringing the division down to the front after traffic was blocked for hours. When the division moved into position behind Sharon two days before, Tamari had scouted ahead and seen the traffic building up on Akavish. He advised Adan by radio to follow a route through the dunes he himself had scouted a few days before. Supply trucks that could not drive through the sand were towed by tracked vehicles.

Asked now to extricate the pontoons stranded on Akavish, Tamari assembled bulldozers and reconnaissance teams in half-tracks and descended on the road. The pontoons had been stuck since the day before in a twelve-mile-long, bumper to bumper traffic jam, the logistics tail of an army. Tamari ordered that vehicles blocking the pontoons be pushed into the sands. When the last of the scattered pontoons moved through, the vehicles were pulled back. It was an excruciating job but by nightfall a dozen pontoons—enough for a bridge—had reached upper Akavish.

Until the rest of Akavish was safe, however, the pontoons could not be towed to the canal. Until Tirtur was opened, neither could the roller bridge. If neither was opened, there could be no supply route to sustain a crossing. The prospect of the roads being opened seemed no closer after a day of heavy fighting. But if the Tirtur blockage could be broken, the pontoons were now in position to move to the canal.

Adan deployed tanks facing Tirtur from Akavish but after a few probes it was evident that the only way to get at the Egyptians in the ditches was with foot soldiers. Southern Command had come to the same conclusion. Colonel Ya'ari was ordered to put one of his battalions at Adan's disposal. The 890th Battalion would go into action this night.

After dark, ammunition and fuel for the Israeli force across the canal was dispatched over the dunes in tracked vehicles. The convoy included half-tracks carrying Matt's second paratroop battalion, which had been turned back on Akavish that morning. The convoy commanders oriented themselves this time not by phosphorous shells but by the lights of ships anchored in the Bitter Lake. The vessels were stranded when the canal was closed in the Six Day War. The foreign ship owners had rotated skeleton crews in the six years since to preserve their ownership rights.

Adan asked his chief ordnance officer, Lt. Col. Haim Razon, to examine the roller bridge, which engineers had estimated would take at least a day to repair. Razon said it could be done in three hours. Instead of repairing the broken section, he simply cut it away and welded the span back together. This shortened it by a few meters but it was still long enough to comfortably bridge the canal. Razon was in the midst of the task when he was informed that his son, a tank officer, had been seriously wounded. He wanted to rush to him but the doctor tending his son in the field told him by radio that he would be all right and was being evacuated to the rear.

Many senior officers were fighting the war with one ear cocked for news of their own sons on the battlefield. Uri Ben-Ari at Southern Command headquarters periodically had himself patched through to his two sons who were tank officers. General Tal took leave of the Pit early in the war to visit his seriously injured son in the hospital, the only survivor of a tank crew. Air Force Commander Peled learned of his pilot son being shot down over the canal from a note handed to him while giving a press conference with Dayan. After wordlessly scanning the message, he continued to answer questions in an even tone. A note handed him a few minutes later informed him that his son had been rescued by helicopter.

Danny Matt's son was a tank commander in Amir Yoffe's battalion. When Matt first arrived at Southern Command headquarters he was jolted to hear that only a handful of Yoffe's tanks had returned from their battles at Mifreket and Milano. He asked the chief medical officer at Umm Hashiba for a list of dead. Quickly scanning it, he saw that his son was not on it. He did not ask for the list of wounded and would never again during the war inquire about his son's status for fear that his own functioning might be impaired by bad news. (His son would be wounded toward the end of the war but recovered.) At the Yard, where Sharon had positioned his forward command post, a crewman descended from a tank and ran to Sharon's APC to embrace his father, the division's chief signals officer. An hour later, word was received that the son's tank had been hit and that he was in critical condition, paralyzed in both legs. Sharon urged the officer to take a brief leave to visit his son and console his wife but he refused to leave the front.

With Ben-Shoshan's battalion having crossed the canal, the task of towing the repaired roller bridge was passed to a tank battalion commanded by Lt. Col. Yehuda Geller. Pulled off the battle line, he found nobody in authority who could issue clear instructions about towing. The engineers present had lost their confidence after the previous failure. Geller had once seen a training film about the bridge and tried to remember the towing methods used there. The bridge at least had reached flat terrain. Geller was astonished when told it had been towed over dunes to this point. He and his deputy designed their own litany—"Prepare to move—one, two, three—move." With darkness, the towing began. The bridge had progressed less than a mile when Geller was ordered to halt. His tanks remained in harness and the men dozed off in their seats. About 3 a.m., those who were awake could hear the sounds of heavy firing to their front—infantry weapons, not tank guns. A battle was raging in the vicinity of Tirtur Road.

Colonel Ya'ari landed by helicopter at 10 p.m. near upper Akavish and was led to Adan's command post. The division commander explained the task briefly. Tirtur had to be cleared of Egyptian tank-hunting teams before dawn. Otherwise, the bridges could not get through. The paratroopers' mission was critical.

Mordecai and his battalion had been on the go since early morning. At Refidim Air Base, where they waited three hours beside the runways, they had to take cover from an Egyptian air attack. Buses finally arrived to carry them to Tasa. Mordecai descended repeatedly to talk the convoy through road jams. At Tasa, helicopters were found for them and the battalion was lifted to upper Akavish close to midnight.

Mordecai was led to Adan's tent for a briefing. The Egyptians were moving in deep trenches, he was told, so he could not be given specific targets. No air photos were available and there was no time to bring forward an artillery liaison officer. The paratroopers would simply move forward in broad deployment until they made contact. They had to begin moving immediately, Adan said, if the mission was to be completed by dawn, only five hours away. Foot soldiers moving across the open terrain in daylight would have no chance.

This was not the way the paratroopers were accustomed to work—no hard intelligence, no photos, no detailed plan, no artillery support. No one in Adan's command post knew anything about Morag's run that morning since he was part of Sharon's division, not Adan's. No one was aware of the masses of infantry Morag had seen in the trenches.

The battalion began moving after midnight. A young paratroop sergeant was elated as he set out in the moonlight on his first combat operation. Three companies, each with eighty to ninety men, moved abreast with a fourth company following in reserve. Attached to the latter were fifty officers who had formerly served in the battalion and had obtained Mordecai's permission to join him.

First contact was made at 2:45 a.m. by the company on the right flank, commanded by Lt. Yaaki Levy. When Mordecai asked what he was up against, Levy, sounding his usual confident self, said he could deal with it. He ordered a platoon to flank the enemy on the right. The platoon commander had not gone far when he caught a glimpse of the Egyptian forces opposite. He went to ground. "These aren't tank-hunting teams," he reported. "The area's full of troops." When Mordecai asked for more details, there was no reply. Levy had charged the Egyptian position and was dead. His deputy too was hit. The company was caught on flat terrain immediately to the Egyptians' front. The Egyptians were backed by tanks and supported by artillery and they had night sights, which left the Israelis totally exposed.

Mordecai ordered the company in the center of the line to outflank the enemy position on the left but it too was caught in the open and its commander killed. The paratroopers in the lead companies were two hundred yards from the Egyptian line, some soldiers as close as fifty yards. Almost all officers were hit. Mordecai called forward officers from the volunteer detachment to replace them.

Maj. Yehuda Duvdevani, one of the volunteers, was ordered to take over the company in the center. As he ran forward, shells exploded around him. The concussions buffeted him from side to side but the sand absorbed the shrapnel. Reaching the front, he heard cries from wounded paratroopers lying in no-man's-land. Duvdevani ordered men to bring them in but no one moved. The young conscript soldiers did not know him and did not respond to the gruff voice shouting at them above the din.

Grabbing a stretcher, he shouted, "Give me cover." The men did respond to this and laid down covering fire as Duvdevani started forward, sometimes crawling, sometimes on all fours. Three wounded men were lying fifty yards from the forward Egyptian trench. Duvdevani placed the most seriously wounded man on the stretcher and began sliding it toward the rear as he crawled backward. Periodically, he would leave him and pull the other two by their arms. "Help me," he said to them. The two managed to propel themselves a bit as bullets hit the sand around them but Duvdevani had to pull them much of the way. A bullet clanged off a smoke grenade on his pouch, another nicked his belt. At one point, the sand rippled from a machine gun burst that hit the stretcher. Duvdevani pulled the men a hundred yards before reaching a ditch serving as an aid station. Medics pronounced the man on the stretcher dead. The other two were rushed to the rear. Duvdevani reported to Mordecai on the radio. "I've brought in the wounded. I'm taking command."

The men in the company now responded to his orders. Hearing the sound of tanks just behind the Egyptian lines, he divided them into teams armed with LAW missiles. As the tanks started forward, one team rose and set the lead tank ablaze. The other tanks pulled back.

Meanwhile, the reserve company came forward to evacuate casualties. With dawn not far off, their commander told them not to waste time crawling. What mattered was speed. Every time he made his own way back carrying wounded, the company commander saw the trail to the evacuation point marked by more dead and wounded.

Mordecai set up a base of fire with machine guns to cover the rescuers. The man next to him was killed and he himself was cut in the chest by shrapnel but he covered the wound with sand so that his men would not see it.

At dawn, a tank battalion commanded by Lt. Col. Ehud Barak, future prime minister of Israel, was sent in. The battalion was made up of men who had been abroad—in Barak's case, studying at Stanford University—when the war broke out and had hurried home. Seven tanks advanced—not to rescue the paratroopers but to lead them against the Egyptian positions. Duvdevani told his men to prepare to charge. The tanks lined up abreast of the paratroopers but a barrage of Sagger missiles erupted from the Egyptian lines and five tanks were immediately knocked out. There would be no attack.

Lt. Shimon Maliach found himself at first light hugging the ground with casualties all about him and no cover. He and others began stacking the bodies of dead men to shelter behind. The brigade intelligence officer, lying nearby, addressed Maliach by his nickname. "Blackie, some mess we've gotten ourselves into." He didn't quite finish the last word. Maliach crawled closer and saw a bullet in his forehead. Men clawed at the sand in an attempt to dig shallow foxholes.

"Blackie, what's up?" said someone conversationally. It was one of the attached officers, a redhead whom Maliach knew only by his family name, Rabinowitz. The officer saw the radio Maliach was carrying and reached for it over a dead body in order to speak to Mordecai. As he did, he was hit in the back. Maliach put two fingers into the wound to staunch the flow of blood. Rabinowitz grew pale. He gripped Maliach's shirt and said, "Blackie, my wife's about to give birth. Don't let me die." Maliach said, "I'm staying with you. Nothing's going to happen to you."

An APC appeared behind them and a doctor leaped out. Ignoring the fire, he lay on his side alongside Rabinowitz and bound the wound. When one of Barak's tanks was hit nearby and crewmen emerged with their clothes aflame, Maliach and several others ran out to roll them in the sand and drag them behind the wall of bodies. The Egyptians fired mortars, killing several men, including the doctor. Everyone still alive crawled toward the rear except Rabinowitz, still groggy from the morphine the doctor had given him, and Maliach, who stayed with him. The mortar fire ceased and Maliach saw Egyptian troops coming out of their trenches. To remain was to die. Slapping Rabinowitz to waken him from his stupor, Maliach explained the situation. He was going back for help, he said. Egyptians were advancing. If they reached him before help came, he should play dead.

Maliach had gone only a hundred yards when he was wounded by mortar fragments. He reached an aid station and was evacuated to a hospital. Afflicted with guilt, he would remain there after his wounds were healed to be treated for severe mental stress.

. . .

Before Mordecai's paratroopers made contact with the enemy, Adan dispatched a reconnaissance company down Akavish in armored personnel carriers to test Egyptian reaction. The vehicles reached Lexicon and returned without drawing fire. Adan weighed the chances of the pontoons getting through. They were huge, lumbering targets—easy marks for the Saggers. Their destruction would virtually eliminate the chance of a canal crossing, given the difficulties the roller bridge was encountering. But with the battle around Tirtur growing more intense the attention of the Egyptians appeared to be fixed there.

Adan decided to take the risk. He ordered Dov Tamari, who had freed the pontoons from the traffic bottleneck, to now lead them down Akavish to the canal. The tanks towing the pontoons set off at intervals and drew no fire. The first pontoon arrived at Matsmed at 6:30 a.m. Wednesday, a full day after the Gillois. The rest would follow over the course of several hours. The crews could hear the sound of heavy firing on Tirtur as they passed it.

Elements of Mordecai's battalion remained pinned down until late afternoon. Seventeen hours after the battle began, APCs managed to dash in, with tank and artillery support, and extricate the last fighters known to be alive. Most of the dead had to be left on the battlefield.

A third of the battalion were casualties—forty-one dead and more than a hundred wounded. Grieving over their losses and angered at having to fight in such conditions, the paratroopers viewed the battle as an unmitigated disaster. But in enabling the pontoons to get through and loosening the Egyptian grip on Akavish, Mordecai's battalion had unknowingly opened the way to Africa.

32

CROSSING INTO AFRICA

INITIAL REPORTS ABOUT an Israeli incursion across the canal raised little alarm in Cairo. When newspaper editor Heikal passed on to Sadat an account from the wire services of Mrs. Meir's Knesset speech mentioning Israeli tanks on the west bank, the president telephoned War Minister Ismail, who said there were only "three infiltrating Israeli tanks." Later there were reports of a handful of amphibious tanks. Still later, the force was said to constitute a raiding party of seven to ten tanks. Chief of Staff Shazly contacted the acting commander of the Second Army, Brig. Taysir al-Aqqad, who said the intrusion was negligible and would be dealt with promptly. Nevertheless, Shazly ordered an armored brigade from his strategic reserve near Cairo to begin moving toward the canal.

Shazly proposed to Ismail that the Twenty-fifth Armored Brigade be pulled back from the Third Army bridgehead in Sinai to deal with the intruders. He also proposed that the Twenty-first Armored Division, in the Second Army bridgehead, send a brigade south along the Sinai bank to close off the gap in the Egyptian line through which the Israeli raiders had evidently crossed. The Egyptians still did not believe the Israelis had the strength for a major crossing.

Ismail refused to withdraw the Twenty-fifth Brigade or any other unit from Sinai. Any withdrawal, he feared, could trigger a collapse. In order to avoid panic the Egyptian command had refrained from issuing an alert about the Israeli incursion. Erez had thus been able to pounce on unsuspecting convoys and bases. There had been a number of clashes with Egyptian forces on the canal's west bank involving Erez's tanks and Matt's paratroopers but no one in Cairo—or Second Army headquarters—was fitting the pieces together. All reconnaissance units in the Second and Third Armies had been posted to the Sinai bank, so there was no designated force on the west bank to track down intruders.

Instead of pulling the Twenty-fifth Brigade back to the west bank, Ismail wanted it to attack northward along the Sinai bank and link up with the tanks from the Twenty-first Division pressing south in order to sever any Israeli crossing point. Shazly vehemently objected. Such a move, he argued, could prove a death trap. The brigade would have to proceed north for fifteen miles with its left flank confined by the Bitter Lake and its right flank exposed to possible Israeli attack. Ismail was unmoved. When Shazly raised his point with Sadat during a visit by the president to Center Ten, Sadat turned nasty. "Why do you always propose withdrawing troops from the east bank?" he asked. "You ought to be court-martialed. If you persist in these proposals, I *will* court-martial you." Stung by Sadat's words, Shazly did not argue the point. But he saw to it that a number of antitank infantry units in Sinai were sent back quietly to their mother units west of the canal with their Saggers. AMAN picked up on the goings-on at Center Ten and at 8 p.m. reported that Sadat had taken personal command at army headquarters.

The commander of the Third Army, General Wasel, was deeply distressed by the Twenty-fifth Brigade's marching orders. He telephoned Shazly at 3 a.m. to say that technical difficulties would prevent it from attacking at first light. Although sharing Wasel's fears, Shazly told him the operation would have to get under way as planned. In that case, said Wasel, the brigade was doomed. He pronounced a Muslim prayer signifying resignation to one's fate—"Man has strength for nothing without the strength of God." The brigade, made up of T-62 tanks, started north shortly after 7 a.m.

Adan began cautiously pressing north from Akavish with four tank battalions in an effort to widen the corridor beyond Tirtur. Egyptian tanks came forward as if to engage but then veered off to lure the Israeli tanks into range of infantry armed with Saggers. The advance was slow and contact with enemy tanks mostly at long range.

The attack by Mordecai's paratroopers, in addition to opening the way for the pontoons, had severed a final thread of fortitude among the Egyptian defenders on Tirtur. They had been subject to attacks for more than twenty-four hours from three directions. They had stood their ground but the pain was cumulative and Adan sensed that they were beginning to buckle. With Akavish still free of enemy fire, he permitted armored vehicles to proceed down the road toward the canal freely from 7:30 a.m. At 11 a.m., the road was opened to nonarmored vehicles as well. Supply and fuel trucks which had been backed up on Akavish for more than a day began to finally stream toward the Matsmed crossing where construction of the pontoon bridge was under way. The road jam was finally uncorked.

Adan notified Gonen that he intended to send the survivors of Mordecai's battalion to the rear. Gonen refused. The paratroopers, he said, would be needed to keep the Egyptians from infiltrating back into the ditches around Tirtur. Adan said the battalion had been savaged and needed to be pulled off the line to reorganize. There was no point, he said, in prolonging its suffering, particularly now that four tank battalions were involved in the battle. Gonen, however, insisted that they remain.

One of Mordecai's officers found the battalion commander sitting on the ground in the afternoon eating battle rations. "I saved some for you," said Mordecai, offering him a can of corn.

"What happens now?" asked the officer.

"What happens now? We go in again tonight. Isn't that obvious?"

If he had reservations, Mordecai did not show it. He intended to insist this time on artillery and tank support. And now that he knew the Egyptian disposition, he would attack from a flank.

The battalion commander ordered the men assembled. The ordeal they had passed through was imprinted on the faces of the young conscripts sitting on the ground in front of him. "We paid a heavy price," said Mordecai, "but the war isn't over. I tell you, soldier to soldier, that whoever doesn't have the spiritual resources to go on can opt out. I will not hold it against him. Whoever fought last night has done his share in this war. But I intend to fight until the war is over. Whoever wants to can fight with me. It may be that we will have to fight in the same place we did last night. Now, look to your ammunition, have something to eat and drink. Be prepared to move out in two hours."

No soldier backed out even though the thought of going in again to the Chinese Farm was appalling. When Bar-Lev arrived at Adan's command post shortly afterward, he overrode Gonen and agreed to the paratroopers' withdrawal.

· · ·

Ferrying vehicles and supplies westward and bringing back casualties, the Gillois continued to link the canal's banks. With the onset of Egyptian shelling Wednesday morning—after a grace period of more than twenty-four hours—one raft was hit. It did not immediately sink because its ramp was resting on the western bank but it was no longer usable. To limit casualties, the crews of each Gillois were reduced from twelve men to five. The remainder were ordered to remain in foxholes until summoned to take their turn.

In mid-morning, a flight of MiGs attacked the Yard, where Sharon had positioned himself. Sharon grabbed one of his APC's three machine guns and joined in firing at the aircraft. An artillery barrage descended, turning the Yard into an inferno. Anyone not in an armored vehicle or foxhole was hit. Sharon's best friend, Zeev Amit, who had come down from Beersheba with him as a volunteer, wearing a pair of Sharon's boots, was fatally wounded as he leaped from Sharon's APC to return to his own personnel carrier.

Sharon ordered his command vehicles out of the compound as shells burst around them. On the way, his APC fell into a shell crater and everyone was thrown. Sharon, whose head was outside a hatch, suffered a cut on his forehead. He was bleeding heavily and a crew member bandaged the wound. Emerging from the Yard, the APCs encountered a tank towing a burning pontoon. Half a mile away were several Egyptian tanks. They were facing the other way but Sharon was afraid that they might turn and enter the Yard where they could in minutes destroy the Gillois, the pontoons, and the rubber boats, bringing the enterprise to a close. There were no Israeli tanks in the immediate vicinity. Sharon called on Reshef to send help immediately and ordered his APCs to fire their machine guns at the Egyptians. The sergeant manning the heavy machine gun on Sharon's vehicle hesitated. "But they're tanks," he said.

"Fire," barked Sharon. The bullets would do no harm to the tanks but would distract their commanders.

Moving fast, the APCs opened fire and managed to scurry behind nearby dunes before the Egyptians turned their guns on them. Reshef's force arrived within a few minutes and destroyed the Egyptian tanks. Another pontoon had been hit but the remainder made it into the Yard intact.

Protecting the bridgehead from the north, on the high dune west of Lexicon, was Amir Yoffe's battalion, with fifteen tanks. Sharon had

contacted Adan to ask if he could borrow one of his battalions to reinforce Reshef's exhausted units in the Chinese Farm. Although Sharon
had refused two similar requests from Adan in the battle on October 8,
Adan immediately acquiesced and sent Yoffe's unit. During the night,
Yoffe had reported Egyptian infantry withdrawing from the farm, in
the wake of the paratroop attack on Tirtur. He was told not to interfere with their pullback.

The day began for the battalion with an attack by infantrymen firing Saggers. Well positioned behind the crest of the dune, Yoffe's tanks
dispersed the attackers with a single volley. Soon after, intelligence
warned of an imminent assault by sixty tanks from the Twenty-first
Division. When an hour passed without their appearance, tensions
eased. As the morning wore on, more Egyptian infantrymen were seen
withdrawing to the north, many of them carrying Sagger cases.

The only Egyptian vehicle to appear was a fuel truck which had
apparently lost its way. Several tanks fired at it and missed. Instead
of trying to get away, the driver stopped as if perplexed by the shots.
Sgt. Eliezer Barnea, the gunner in the tank nearest the road, was
ordered to hit it. Looking through his sights, he saw five men descend
from the vehicle. They lined up alongside the truck and faced in his
direction as if posing for a picture. The men apparently took the Israeli
tanks for Egyptian. This, Barnea said to himself, is an execution. He
took aim and paused—"to give them another second to live"—before
firing. He saw the man in the center disintegrate before the entire crew
disappeared in a ball of flame.

Barnea was acutely aware that death on the battlefield was a capri-
cious reaper and that he was as much its quarry as its instrument. Moving across the battlefield two nights before, he and the other crewmen
had told the driver to look through his periscope for the moon, newly
risen in the east, if they were hit. Drivers stood the best chance of surviving a hit and the crewmen wanted to be sure that he would carry
them back toward the Israeli lines and not the other way. This morning, the sergeant and his comrades had laughed when Egyptian MiGs
attacked an Egyptian tank formation. Not long after, Israeli Mirages
attacked Yoffe's battalion, wounding a tank commander. Barnea himself had fired the tank's machine gun at low-flying Mirages someone
said were Libyan. They turned out to be Israeli. In approaching the
position to relieve Almog's battalion the day before, they had been
fired on by one of the latter's tanks and a tank commander was killed.
It turned out that both tank commanders—the one who fired and

the one killed—were friends who had participated in the same tank course.

After hitting the fuel truck, Barnea climbed into the tank turret and lit a cigarette to steady his nerves. As he did so, he noticed on the ridge opposite dark objects that had not been there before. The objects took on the shape of tank turrets and were joined by many others. The box of matches dropped from his hand. There were flashes from the ridge and pillars of smoke and sand began erupting near the Israeli tanks. The Twenty-first Division tanks had arrived.

The Egyptian tanks descended and closed range. Yoffe ordered his men to commence firing at 1,500 yards. Barnea fired at the tank closest to him. He saw a flash on its skin and shouted, "Hit." His comrades cheered but the tank kept coming. He hit it again but the tank came on. Feeling the edge of panic, he wondered if the Egyptians were using some new kind of armor. He hit the tank a third time. It continued for twenty yards and stopped. No one emerged.

Barnea took aim at another tank but when he pulled the trigger nothing happened. "Misfire," he shouted. Looking through his sights, he saw an Egyptian tank aiming at him. He touched the Uzi at his feet. If he was trapped in a burning tank, he had decided, he would shoot himself. He saw the flash of the Egyptian gun and shut his eyes. It would take only two seconds for the shell to hit. He counted, "One, two." There was an explosion nearby. The tank commander shouted, "Reverse," and the driver took them to the safety of the rear slope where the loader cleared the breech and inserted a new shell. When they came back up, the tank commander ordered the driver to move forward of the battalion line to a better firing position. Colonel Yoffe ordered them back into line. The tank commander was a sergeant who had started the war as a loader. Barnea and the other crewmen chided him for bucking for a medal.

The Egyptian formation pulled back, leaving dozens of knocked-out tanks. No Israeli tank had been hit. Yoffe asked the tank commanders to report the number of tanks they had knocked out. Such reckonings were generally inaccurate, sometimes wildly so. Apart from human tendency to exaggerate, two or more tanks often hit the same target and each counted it as their kill. But the estimate offered at least a rough idea of enemy losses. One tank, commanded by a sergeant named Avi, claimed twelve tanks, an astonishing figure. The total for the battalion came to forty-eight. To general laughter, Yoffe noted drily that if Avi raised his estimate by two the battalion could claim an even fifty.

Meanwhile, Adan's forces were preparing to receive the Twenty-fifth Brigade. The night before, Uri Ben-Ari—now General Ben-Ari—had passed on to Adan an intelligence report that the Egyptians were planning to send the Twenty-fifth Brigade north. With the brigade's line of march apparent, Adan saw the making of a classic ambush. Tank ambushes are rare because tanks are not easy to hide, particularly in a desert. When staged, it is usually by small formations. But Adan intended now to stake out an ambush involving almost an entire division.

On the African shore this day, Matt's paratroopers, reinforced by their second battalion, expanded the bridgehead. A half-track-borne company led by battalion commander Dan Ziv approached the village of Serafeum, site of a major logistics center, and came under heavy fire from the village and wooded areas around it. Despite uneasiness expressed by his officers at the disparity in forces, Ziv pushed ahead. It seemed to a tank commander accompanying the force that the paratroopers had not yet learned what the tankers had learned: the Egyptians in this war were not to be taken lightly.

The lead half-track, containing fourteen soldiers including Ziv and company commander Asa Kadmoni, was cut off in the middle of the village by an Egyptian counterattack. The fight was led by Kadmoni, who took a position which covered approaches from several directions. Using grenades and ammunition passed to him by the others, he held off attackers at ranges as close as twenty yards for three hours. Several times he scored hits on Egyptian positions with LAW missiles. Kadmoni, who would be awarded the country's highest medal for his stand this day, was down to his last bullets when he heard the sound of tanks. A paratroop combat team, using smoke grenades to cover its approach, dashed in to retrieve the stranded men. In all, the patrol suffered twelve dead.

While this skirmishing was going on, another front was opening that Israelis would come to call "the War of the Generals." It had been in the making since Sharon's arrival in Sinai. No one projected greater charisma among the troops than he. They would paint "Arik, king of Israel" on their vehicles when there would be time for such things. An intelligence sergeant at Umm Hashiba noted the way the body language even of the other generals in the Southern Command war room changed when Sharon entered—a big man, with a heavy walk and a smile that exuded confidence and force. No one ignored him.

Sharon was fed up with Gonen and believed that Elazar and Bar-Lev were behaving timidly when the situation demanded daring. The three were unaware of the situation on the ground, he maintained, because they did not visit the front. A formative experience for Sharon had been the battle for Latrun on the road to Jerusalem during Israel's War of Independence. He was then a twenty-year-old lieutenant. Of the thirty-five men in his platoon, fifteen were killed in the battle, eleven wounded, and five captured. He himself was critically wounded. He would later say that the battle had gone amiss because no senior officer was on hand to make critical decisions.

His criticism of his superiors had always been acerbic and outspoken. And he was not always generous with his peers. What particularly infuriated Elazar were the attacks Sharon staged on October 9 after he had been ordered not to risk the loss of more tanks. When Sharon's superiors suspected him of deviating from orders and tried to reach him in the field, he was often unreachable because of "communications failure." More than once he told the commander of his mobile command post not to answer when Gonen, his direct superior, tried to reach him by radio. Elazar was angered during the night of the canal crossing at "the sloppy reports coming in from the crossing site [Sharon's reports], like nothing I've heard in all my years of warfare." The reports from Sharon about Tirtur referred to an "obstacle" or an "ambush," or "a position that will not surrender" without making it clear that it was a major problem endangering the entire operation. Sharon avoided terminology that might discourage the high command from continuing the attack. Four hours into the battle for the Chinese Farm he reported that he was almost finished cleaning Akavish and Tirtur Roads and that the enemy was "in total collapse." In fact, Egyptian resistance had not slackened at all and the battle for the roads would become even bloodier over the coming day.

Elazar complained to Dayan that Sharon wanted to continuously occupy center stage—to lead the crossing and lead the battle on the African bank in disregard of the original plan and in disregard of the fact that he had not yet secured the bridgehead corridor in Sinai. Dayan agreed that Sharon's behavior was regrettable. He admitted, however, that he could not help admiring Sharon's energy and his attitude that anything was doable.

Exacerbating professional differences and personality clashes between Sharon and the other generals was the bizarre—almost comic—intrusion of party politics. In the three months since leaving the army, Sharon had embarked on a full-blown career in politics and was managing the Likud's election campaign. He did not hesitate to contact politicians like Likud leader Menahem Begin to express his frustrations over the way the war was being fought and to ask for his intervention. He periodically called the defense minister himself, blatantly bypassing the chain of command.

His fellow generals believed that Sharon was after personal glory, in particular the glory that would come from being the general who led the attack across the Suez Canal. Politically, it was a winning ticket. Sharon warmly welcomed reporters who visited his division headquarters even though there were standing orders that no general was to grant interviews without permission of the army spokesman. Sharon supporters pointed out that he did not solicit these visits and that reporters sought him out because he was optimistic, friendly, and colorful. Even the large bandage around his forehead came to be seen as a contrived image enhancer. When Sharon was reported to have tossed oranges from his APC to troops as they waited to cross the canal, an officer who had served with him in the early days of the paratroopers smiled at what he saw as the populist gesture of a newborn politician. "It's not like him," the officer said. "He used to act like a general even when he was a major."

When Bar-Lev took over Southern Command, the political aspect took on added resonance. Bar-Lev was a politician now too, and from the opposite ideological camp at that. He had temporarily given up his post as commerce minister in the Labor government in order to return to uniform. When the war was over, he and Sharon would be on contending slates in Knesset elections. At first, the two "politician generals" joked about it with each other, even though they shared a personal antipathy since their time together in the regular army. There was lighthearted talk of a "Likud division," Sharon's, and a "Labor division," Adan's. Although Adan was not a political figure he was, like Bar-Lev and Elazar, a veteran of the pre-state Palmach strike force, which was identified with the kibbutz movement and the Labor Party. As differences over the conduct of the war deepened between Sharon and Bar-Lev, lightheartedness gave way. "He's a division commander who's a politician," said Bar-Lev after the tank battle on October 14, when Sharon sought permission to pursue the Egyptian tanks falling back on their well-defended lines instead of waiting for Israel's canal crossing operation that was to begin the next night.

"It's not the insubordination that's so astounding," Elazar had complained to Dayan when Sharon positioned himself for a canal crossing on October 9 in defiance of orders. "It's the logic of his plan." Dayan also heard from Bar-Lev that Sharon was not obeying orders. "Whatever I ask for is not executed. I don't know what he's doing."

Elazar seriously considered dismissing Sharon for insubordination—Ben-Ari was one of the officers mooted as a replacement—but he knew that Dayan would oppose it. Although Dayan was also disturbed by Sharon's insubordination, he could not help admiring his battlefield flair. Even Sharon's critics feared the adverse effect of his dismissal on morale, both in the country and among the troops. Sharon was adulated by his men and respected by his officers. Many of his senior commanders were members of kibbutzim whose left-leaning political views differed sharply from his. Even though these political differences deepened in later years, they would still count it a blessing that Sharon had led their division in the war. Reshef, who had not known Sharon well before, found him a superb field commander—able to read a battle, decisive, cool under fire, and able to delegate authority.

The tensions surrounding Sharon came to a head during an impromptu conference at Adan's forward command post at noon Wednesday, October 17. Dayan had helicoptered in to be briefed by Adan on the upcoming battle with the Twenty-fifth Brigade and his division's pending canal crossing. The minister invited Sharon to come up from the Yard to meet with him. Bar-Lev dropped in and Elazar soon arrived as well. Sharon had a few hours earlier come through the shelling of the crossing point in which he lost his best friend. He had not seen the other generals since the grueling battle for the bridgehead began two days before and he anticipated congratulations at having executed the crossing and good wishes for what lay ahead. But when Sharon descended from his APC, no one extended a hand to shake and Dayan was the only one to greet him. Bar-Lev's first words were: "Any resemblance between what you promised and what you've done is purely coincidental." Bar-Lev was speaking of the failure to open the roads and secure a corridor. In his autobiography, Sharon would write: "At that moment I felt tired to death. After all those terrible battles and casualties . . . when I saw this group of neatly dressed, washed, clean-shaven people, and I heard that sentence I knew there was only one thing to do. I had to smack Bar-Lev's face. I don't know how I kept myself from hitting him."

Adan, who had his own grudge against Sharon for having refused him assistance on October 8, spread a map on the sand and all gathered around it. When a journalist Sharon had brought along tried to get close, Adan waved him back. Tones were restrained but the tension hung heavy. Sharon said the pontoon bridge would be completed by late afternoon. He urged that four brigades, two from each division, be sent across the canal this night. The Egyptians were already building up a sizable force west of the bridgehead and it was important to smash them quickly, he said. This proposal upset Adan, whose division had been designated to execute the breakout into Africa. It would be a mistake, he said, to send four brigades across since substantial forces were needed on the Sinai bank to widen the corridor to the bridgehead. Sharon argued that if the IDF pressed hard enough on the west bank, the Egyptian forces on the east bank would collapse.

"I've been hearing about this collapse for the past week," said Bar-Lev. Sharon's expectations had not been fulfilled, said the front commander—neither the creation of a broad corridor nor the collapse of the enemy.

"Soon you'll be saying I wasn't even in this war," said Sharon.

Bar-Lev said that two brigades would cross this night, one from each division. The division commanders would cross with them, he said, leaving the bridgehead on the Sinai bank under the command of their deputies. It seemed like a generous gesture toward Sharon, who was supposed to secure the bridgehead, not participate in the breakout. But Bar-Lev would later tell Dayan that he preferred having Sharon cross because he believed that Adan's efficient deputy, Dov Tamari, would do a better job of securing the corridor than Sharon.

However, Elazar, who had been listening quietly to the debate, overruled Bar-Lev. Stouthearted Men would be executed as planned, he said, and there would be no splitting of the divisions. That meant that Sharon would remain to expand the corridor and Adan's division would cross to the west bank. Turning to Sharon, Elazar said, "Complete the task assigned to you and then you can cross too." With that, Adan left to oversee the ambush of the Twenty-fifth Brigade. It was time to put the War of the Generals aside, if only for a little while, and get back to war with the Arabs.

. . .

The killing ground Adan had chosen was a sandy plain bordering the northern end of the Bitter Lake. The desert might not have trees to shelter behind but it had dunes. Two of his brigades would hide among low hills east of Lexicon Road, along which the Twenty-fifth Brigade was proceeding. One brigade would be parallel to the head of the Egyptian column when the trap was sprung. The other would be at the rear, to cut off retreat. Four tanks from Reshef's brigade, already posted on Lexicon several miles south of Matsmed, would block the lead Egyptian tanks, at which point Adan's brigades would strike from the flank. The Israeli tanks outnumbered the Egyptians by 2 to 1.

It took time to get all Adan's units into position because of the distances involved and the deep sands, which made for slow movement. But the Egyptian brigade commander, Col. Ahmed Badawi Hassan, uneasy about his mission, halted frequently. When he reached Fort Botser, midway on the lake shore, where Sergeant Nadeh was posted, he stopped for three hours. The Israelis, monitoring his movements, were unsure whether he was contemplating going back or waiting for air cover.

Col. Natke Nir's brigade was to attack the leading half of the column. His brigade, which had been involved in the failed battle of October 8, included the reconstituted remnants of Assaf Yaguri's battalion. Approaching the ambush site, company commander Yitzhak Brik, a survivor of Yaguri's charge, looked out at the barren landscape with trepidation. He was reminded of that terrible day when he stood on a hilltop with Yaguri and the other officers, uneasy about what awaited them in the distant haze. Once again, there were telltale clouds of dust from vehicular movement in the distance. As at Hizayon, the Israeli tanks would have to descend into the plain in order to reach firing range. Brik prayed that there would not be Saggers and RPGs this time. In crossing over dunes, the tanks did not throw up dust that could be visible to the approaching Egyptians in the distance. The tanks halted two miles east of Lexicon. The brigade's reconnaissance jeeps, which had scouted the area, guided them into recesses where they would be hidden from the road by dunes.

At 1:30 p.m. the spearhead of the Twenty-fifth Brigade encountered Reshef's tanks on Lexicon. Reshef himself had joined the small blocking force. His tanks opened fire at long range and scored hits. This was the signal for Adan's tanks to spring. Brik led his company out into the open. The Egyptian column, which had not put out a screening force on its flank, continued north for a few moments, unaware of the tanks coming at them out of the east. Only when the Israeli force was a mile away, did the Egyptians halt and turn toward it. The Israeli tanks likewise halted. The Egyptian tanks were T-62s but Brik was relieved to see that there was no infantry. Facing each other in two long lines like mythic gunfighters on a dusty street, each side went for its guns. The Egyptian crews, shaken at the sudden apparition of enemy tanks on their flank, fired wildly. Brik could see his own tanks hitting with almost every shot. Egyptian crews began abandoning burning tanks, sometimes even tanks that were still intact. In a short time, the battle in Brik's sector was over without an Israeli loss. Egyptian tanks charged an adjacent Israeli battalion and reached within eight hundred yards before being stopped.

Several miles to the south, a battalion commanded by Elyashiv Shimshi topped a dune after a thirty-mile dash with Keren's brigade. Two miles to the front, the rear elements of the Egyptian brigade were proceeding northward with an odd nonchalance. "Enemy tanks to the front, three to six thousand meters," intoned Shimshi. "We will close range and destroy them." Designating the order of attack to his company commanders, he led the way forward. Most of the Egyptian force was spread out between Lexicon and the Bitter Lake, two miles beyond the road at this point. While some of Shimshi's tanks dealt with the vehicles on Lexicon itself, the battalion commander rushed across the road with the rest of his force to hit the main enemy body before it recovered from the surprise. The plain was soon covered with burning tanks and APCs.

Shimshi halted near the shore of the lake. The sun was about to set and visibility was difficult because of the dust glare and the smoke of burning vehicles. The Egyptians recovered sufficiently to call down accurate artillery fire. Egyptian MiGs attacked as well. The commander of Shimshi's southernmost company reported destroying numerous Egyptian trucks and APCs bearing infantry at the tail of the Egyptian column. Shimshi could see dozens of fires in that direction. As the sun went down on a burning desert, the battalion commander pulled his forces back. Some twenty Egyptian tanks, including that of the brigade commander, found shelter in Fort Botser together with two hundred soldiers. The battle had lasted only forty-five minutes.

The Egyptian brigade lost an estimated fifty to sixty tanks in addition to artillery pieces and scores of APCs and supply vehicles. Israeli losses amounted to four tanks, two of them to mines, and two dead crewmen. Together with the losses suffered by the Twenty-first Division tanks in the clash with Yoffe's battalion north of Tirtur, Egyptian tank strength in Sinai had been substantially eroded this day. As darkness descended, Adan ordered his commanders to refuel and rearm before they headed for the crossing point.

Dayan had accompanied Sharon back to the canal after the meeting at Adan's command post in the dunes. Army engineers were putting the pontoon bridge together and bulldozers on both banks were leveling ground at both ends of the bridgehead. The two men crossed on a raft and Sharon offered to take Dayan on a tour in an armored vehicle but Dayan preferred to feel Africa under his feet. When he returned to the canal at 4 p.m. he was able to cross on the just completed bridge. It had taken eight hours to construct, four times longer than in training. Tides, damage inflicted to the pontoons in transit, and periodic shelling had confounded the timetable. But the delay made no difference since Adan's forces were engaged with the Twenty-fifth Brigade and would not be ready for crossing until midnight.

In Tel Aviv that evening, Dayan reported to Mrs. Meir on the war situation and mentioned in passing his visit across the canal.

The prime minister was astonished. "You were there?"

"Yes," said Dayan. "There are a thousand soldiers there now. Tomorrow morning the whole state of Israel will be there."

Satellite pictures had been laid on the desks of decision makers in Washington and Moscow the day before showing a patch of desert with a score or so of antlike dots. The foray of Haim Erez's tanks beyond the agricultural strip at Deversoir had been spotted. Analysts in both capitals saw this as a raid. Israel described it as such to the Americans. Kissinger hoped it would prove to be more. Movement on a cease-fire had been in abeyance since Sadat rejected the proposal forwarded to him by the British ambassador to Cairo. But there had been meanwhile an extraordinary diplomatic development. Kissinger had sent a message to Hafez Ismail in Cairo in the hope that this back channel to Sadat's national security adviser which he had come to value would remain open despite the launching of the American airlift to Israel. "The United States . . . recognizes the unacceptability to the Egyptian side of the conditions which existed prior to the outbreak of

CROSSING INTO AFRICA   461

recent hostilities," said the message. "The U.S. side will make a major effort as soon as hostilities are terminated to assist in bringing a just and lasting peace to the Middle East."

Ismail's reaction to this measured show of empathy was an invitation to Kissinger to visit Egypt—this in the midst of a fierce war in which the U.S. was supplying arms and political backing to Egypt's enemy. Sadat was making his move, a political move no less audacious than his military initiative—turning from the embrace of the Soviets, on whose weapons he was dependent, toward an amicable relationship with the U.S., the entity best positioned to pressure Israel. As Sadat had hoped, the war had provided him with the wedge he needed to begin shifting political realities that had seemed as immovable as the pyramids.

Upon receiving the invitation, Kissinger understood that an endgame was in the offing. But before he joined in he wanted Sadat's hand weakened a bit. Those dots on the satellite photos held the promise of sobering the Egyptian leader, heady from his early victories, more effectively than any amount of diplomatic nimbleness.

The Soviets were frantically trying to keep up, unaware that Sadat had invited in a new player with whom he hoped to replace them. American intelligence learned this day, October 16, that a Soviet plane bearing a VIP was en route to Cairo. Premier Alexei Kosygin had abruptly canceled a meeting in the morning with the visiting Danish prime minister and it was believed that Kosygin might be the passenger. Mossad sources were able to confirm to their American counterparts that it was indeed him. He had been charged by the Politburo, after a seven-hour meeting ending at 4 a.m., with flying immediately to Cairo and persuading Sadat to accept a cease-fire.

Moscow's overwhelming interest was that the Middle East war not bring it into direct conflict with the U.S. For this, a speedy end was mandatory. Chairman Brezhnev noted at the Politburo meeting that the Soviet military was warning that an Israeli counterthrust was imminent. "Remind him [Sadat] that Cairo is not far from the canal," he said to Kosygin. The Soviet premier was to make it clear that Soviet troops would not become involved in the fighting. Foreign Minister Gromyko said that without an immediate cease-fire, prospects were dire. "The Arabs would be defeated, Sadat himself would be dismissed, and the Soviet Union's relations with the United States, as well as with the Arabs, would deteriorate." President Nikolai Podgorny objected to Kosygin's argument that the Americans would not let Israel lose—which the American airlift was specifically designed to hammer home. To acknowledge that, said Podgorny, "would be a recognition of our weakness." It was too good an argument, however, for Kosygin to forgo.

Before meeting with Sadat the following morning, Kosygin was briefed on the Israeli incursion by the head of the Soviet military mission in Cairo, just back from the front. Sadat greeted his guest courteously and listened patiently as Kosygin transmitted the Soviet leadership's congratulations on his military achievements. When Kosygin broached the subject of a cease-fire, Sadat said there would be none until he had received international guarantees that all territories captured by Israel in the Six Day War—not just Egyptian territory—would be liberated. Kosygin mentioned Israel's cross-canal operation and warned that Egypt's military situation might worsen if the war went on. Sadat dismissed the penetration as an Israeli "political maneuver," not a military threat.

The talks continued over three days without making headway. Kosygin said that the Soviets could not continue resupplying Egypt and Syria when their losses came to a thousand tanks a week. "Our resources are not unlimited." The Soviet military attaché told Kosygin that the best Egyptian troops were in Sinai and that Cairo, which had no defensive fortifications, lay open to Israeli attack. At the final meeting, on October 18, Kosygin produced photographs of the battlefield—not from satellites but from MiG-25 reconnaissance planes taken the day before. The photos revealed the seriousness of the Israeli penetration for the first time to Sadat but he professed to be indifferent. The "tactical" situation around the Bitter Lake, he said, would have no impact on the war itself.

The coin, however, had finally dropped. With Kosygin's departure for Moscow, Sadat hastened to Center Ten and authorized withdrawal of a limited number of armored units from the east bank in order to meet the Israeli threat. The IDF spokesman had been instructed by Elazar not to use the term "bridgehead" or "offensive" in talking about events west of the canal. Mrs. Meir's revelation could hardly be refuted but the spokesman would only confirm what she had already said, that troops were fighting west of the canal. Sadat, however, could no longer delude himself that this was merely a raid.

While maneuvering between the Soviets and the Americans, the

Egyptian leader also had to work his way around his Syrian allies. The speech Sadat had given in the National Assembly on October 16, a few hours before Mrs. Meir's speech in the Knesset, deeply upset President Assad. The Egyptian leader had said that he was prepared to accept a cease-fire if Israel agreed to withdraw to all its pre–Six Day War borders. Once the withdrawals were completed, Egypt would be prepared to attend a peace conference convened by the United Nations and would do its best to persuade other Arab states and Palestinian representatives to attend as well. Assad, who had no intention of ever making peace with Israel, sent Sadat a message expressing sorrow that he had not been informed beforehand of the nature of the speech. Sadat replied to "Brother Hafez" that there was nothing new in his remarks that required consultation. Despite the soft wording, the exchange was a reminder that the Egyptian-Syrian alliance was a marriage of convenience that might not survive changed conditions.

Sadat's speech to the National Assembly had included a warning to Israel that if it struck at Egypt's cities he would retaliate against Israel's cities with Al Kahir missiles. The Al Kahir was a highly inaccurate descendant of missiles Nasser had tried to develop with the help of German scientists in the early 1960s. But there were far more effective missiles in Egypt that could indeed reach Tel Aviv—two brigades of Scuds in the Port Said area. It was these that Sadat had in mind even though they were still under control of Soviet crews in the process of training their Egyptian counterparts.

The day after Sadat's speech, an American satellite photographed the missiles. There had been no attempt to camouflage them and the Scuds, with warheads attached, were clearly intended to be seen. When Elazar was informed, he ordered that a battery of Jericho ground-to-ground missiles be taken out of their shelters and left in the open. Soviet satellites which monitored the sites of Israel's strategic rockets would have no trouble picking up this counter-warning. Prof. Avner Cohen would write that nuclear warheads for the Jericho were apparently not yet operational. But the exposure of the rockets was warning enough. Israel had warplanes capable of delivery.

Mutual deterrence would prove effective. Sadat had publicly threatened to fire Scuds into Israel if his cities and economic infrastructure were attacked. Israel, in turn, warned Egypt via the U.S. not to fire missiles into Israel or use poison gas, which Egypt had used a few years before when it sent its army into Yemen. Except for two Kelt air-to-ground missiles launched in the opening hour of the war which failed to reach the radars that were their targets, Egypt did not fire missiles into Israel. Three Mirages transferred to Egypt by Libya were shot down over the Mediterranean as they appeared to be heading toward central Israel but their mission could not be confirmed. Sadat ignored a request from Assad to send his planes against Israeli cities in retaliation for the Israeli raid on Damascus.

Israel in turn refrained almost entirely from attacking Egyptian infrastructure. The one exception was an air attack carried out at Zeira's suggestion against underground communication cables at Banha in the Nile Delta. Destruction of the cables obliged the Egyptians to transmit messages via the airwaves where they could be intercepted. Elazar was informed that AMAN was being flooded with so much material it was having difficulty digesting it all.

Sergeant Nadeh, who had witnessed the ambush of the Twenty-fifth Brigade close-up from Fort Botser, was filling his diary now with battle scenes. "We saw the attack of the enemy which pursued the remnants of our brigade that had been well ambushed. But with God's help we managed to silence the enemy and opened our gates to the ambushed tanks." Nadeh was ordered the next day to clear a path in the minefield where two of Shimshi's tanks had blown off treads. He climbed into the tanks and found small El Al bags and canned food. He also found an Israeli army jacket which he wore on the way back. When a sentry challenged him, Nadeh responded in German for the fun of it. Before the sentry overreacted, Nadeh laughed and whipped off the jacket.

Listening to Sadat's speech to parliament, the sergeant found the president sounding quite confident. "We understood that we have won a victory but that the war will go on," he wrote. Nadeh visited his friend from Alexandria, Adel Halad, in his foxhole next to the canal to discuss the speech. Adel thought they would get a bonus for being in the first wave to cross the canal. "I wondered what I would do with the money. Adel told me, 'Nadeh, you're going to be a great man and you'll achieve all your desires.' I thought of buying a ring for my girlfriend. But I'll get that from my civilian salary when I'm released. With the bonus I'll buy a ring for my mother."

After one of his friends predicted that the war would soon be over and that they would be returning to Alexandria, Nadeh dreamed that he was returning home. "Father ran to me, even though he has suffered in his leg for years. I burst out crying and realized that we have to avoid such thoughts."

His platoon commander, wrote Nadeh, "sleeps all day and gives us hair-raising missions at night." Nadeh was ordered to plant mines in the dark.

Mood swings were wide. "I feel that we are facing great days. We've gotten used to the war and aren't afraid of anything."

The next day he wrote: "An hour doesn't pass without the soldiers arguing among themselves. The war is making us nervous."

Nadeh was asked by his battalion commander to throw grenades into the canal and bring in fish for dinner. "I feel like hearing Beethoven's symphony on courage—the Third, Eroica. Today we celebrated Muhsan's birthday. He's twenty-seven. We're fighting all the time with Mahmoud Rezek.

"Every time a shell explodes, I want to explode with it. God preserve us. War is the dirtiest word I know."

33
BREAKOUT

A DARK SHAPE SPANNED the shimmering waters of the Suez Canal when General Adan approached it close to midnight at the head of his division. "The bridge is a magnificent sight," he said to his brigade commanders on the radio. "It's waiting for you."

The way to Africa had been open for seven hours but the battle with the Twenty-fifth Brigade had delayed the crossing. Adan's driver handed him a bottle of whiskey he had been saving for the occasion. The general raised a toast to his staff. "Friends, we've come a long way. It won't be much longer before we break the enemy. L'haim."

Shortly after Adan's tanks started to cross the bridge, Egyptian artillery unleashed a furious bombardment. The unnatural lull was over. Shells exploded on both banks and straddled the bridge. A tank driver hurrying to cross drew too close to the tank in front of him, causing one of the pontoon sections to break under their combined weight. A bridging tank was summoned to lay its span across the broken section as a temporary measure.

The patch slowed movement on the bridge but passage continued on the faithful Gillois. The four remaining rafts had been linked into two double rafts, each capable of ferrying two tanks. The raft hulls had been punctured in numerous places by shrapnel but crewmen managed to plug the holes; pumps were working constantly to keep them afloat. The multilayered rubber floats had thus far absorbed shrapnel without deflating. Tank crews being ferried across were ordered to keep their hatches open and to be prepared to evacuate instantly if the raft was hit. Because of the heavy shelling two tank crews on one of the rafts closed their hatches. The raft was hit in mid-canal and immediately capsized, sending the tanks and their crews to the canal bottom, forty feet down. The Gillois crewmen were picked up by rubber boats but the tank crewmen perished. The remaining raft remained in use until the damaged pontoon was replaced. The "junk" rafts had constituted the sole link for vehicles to the western bridgehead for the better part of two days, ferrying across 120 tanks as well as scores of personnel carriers and supply vehicles.

According to Egyptian documents, 170 artillery pieces were zeroed in on the bridgeheads on both sides of the canal and scores of thousands of shells would be fired over the course of six days, in addition to mortar and Katyusha fire. One hundred Israelis would be killed and hundreds wounded. Among the dead was the bulldozer driver who had opened a breach in the enclosure wall of the Yard for the Gillois. Combat engineers remained in the open to maintain the bridge and keep traffic moving. When the bridge was hit, they ran out to fill the hole with sand and cover it with wooden planks.

Also in the open were paratroopers lying along the edge of the bridge and periodically throwing grenades into the water to guard against Egyptian frogmen. All duties at the bridgehead were assigned to pairs of men working in turn, so that if one was hit a replacement would be immediately available. After the initial barrage, in which some paratroopers were buried alive in collapsed foxholes and had to be dug out, Colonel Matt ordered his men to dig only shallow holes. If tanks were parked in the vicinity, the men preferred to shelter beneath them.

Elazar and Bar-Lev decided that Adan's division would bivouac for the night within the bridgehead and get a few hours' sleep before breaking out in the morning. The bulk of Sharon's division would meanwhile remain on the Sinai bank and widen the corridor. Sharon protested that the existing corridor was sufficient. He asked permission to bring over the two brigades he had in Sinai to join Erez's brigade west of the canal. Bar-Lev, who had lost patience with Sharon's constant challenging of orders, urged Elazar to replace him. "If you go back north without solving the Arik problem," Bar-Lev grimly joked, "I'm going with you." Elazar, however, had decided to leave Sharon in place.

Erez's officers, who had already spent a day in Africa, briefed Adan's brigade commanders about what to expect. Unlike in Sinai, fog did not come with first light but an hour later and could last until 9 a.m. They recommended waiting for it to provide cover before moving out in the morning.

Returning from its raid Tuesday, Erez's small force had pulled back behind the protective barrier of the twenty-yard-wide Sweetwater Canal in the middle of the greenbelt. By dawn Wednesday, Egyptian tanks and infantry had penetrated the outer edge of the greenbelt and were skirmishing with Israeli forces. Egyptian artillery spotters, some in trees, were ranging in guns on the bridgehead. An unhampered foray like Erez's was no longer possible. To get out of the bridgehead now, Adan would have to fight his way out.

Unaware of the extent of the enemy buildup, Adan planned to exit the bridgehead Thursday morning on two axes. Gabi Amir's brigade would move out the southern end and head for the Gencifa Hills where numerous SAM batteries were located. Natke Nir's brigade would head west across the Sweetwater Canal and then swing south into the open desert. The division's objective was the area of Suez City, thirty-five miles south, where the major supply routes to the Third Army converged. Adan's third brigade, Arye Keren's, was being retained in Sinai by Southern Command as a general reserve.

Not waiting for the fog, Nir and Amir pushed off at 6 a.m. and encountered resistance immediately. Egyptian tanks as well as Sagger and RPG teams had taken cover in the foliage and were blocking the narrow exits from the greenbelt. The Israeli armored units, no longer presuming to win the war by themselves, called for foot soldiers. A paratroop company went to the aid of Amir's brigade, which was held up by a fortified position. The paratroopers swiftly cleared the enemy trenches, killing forty-five commandos while losing three men. As at Tel Shams on the Golan, foot soldiers proved capable of rapidly overcoming resistance that had stopped armor. The paratroopers discovered that the Egyptian force had thirteen RPGs, or one for every three men, which accounted for their tank-stopping capability. Israeli platoons of almost similar size were issued only one bazooka. Many Israeli units had begun equipping themselves with captured RPGs in addition to captured Kalashnikov rifles, which the soldiers preferred to their old Belgian FNs.

After advancing a few miles, Colonel Amir's column encountered a formidable Egyptian position with dug-in tanks at a crossroad codenamed Tsach. Once beyond it, the Israelis would be in open desert but Adan decided to wait for Nir's brigade to join Amir in a coordinated assault. The division commander would avoid dissipating his strength as he had in the failed counterattack on October 8.

As Nir's tanks were passing through the seemingly abandoned Abu Sultan army camp, Major Brik, the survivor of Yaguri's charge, was fourth in line. Without warning, the three tanks in front of him were hit and burst into flame. Brik's tank was hit too but not disabled. He spotted tank guns protruding from the windows of mud huts six hundred yards away. The Egyptian tanks, which had broken through the huts' rear walls, were swiftly dispatched.

Beyond the camp, at a fortified crossroad, the column encountered a tenacious commando battalion wielding antitank weapons. A parachute company that had been attached to the armored brigade was summoned forward. Its commander, Capt. Benny Carmel, was in a personnel carrier when an RPG exploded inside. The company first sergeant, sitting next to Carmel, said "I'm finished" and fell over dead. Another officer toppled dead out the back door. Carmel was the only person still alive, though wounded. He threw grenades at a nearby enemy position from a hatch until another RPG hit his vehicle, setting it ablaze. Leaping out, he ran toward a small knoll with a bush on it, the only cover in the vicinity. He reached it together with an Egyptian soldier coming from the opposite direction. Carmel fired first and lay down behind the Egyptian's body.

The Israeli could see men from his company pinned down sixty yards away. Between them and him was English-born Max Geller, firing a light machine gun. From time to time Egyptian soldiers tried to move toward Carmel but Geller's fire stopped them. The other men kept throwing Geller ammunition. Finally, an APC dashed up and stopped next to Carmel. The back door opened and someone pulled him in. As they moved off, a machine gunner firing out of a hatch fell on Carmel with a bullet in his head and an RPG set the vehicle afire. Carmel once again managed to extricate himself, despite his loss of blood and dehydration. Nearby was a building where he had seen men from his company taking shelter. The entrance was blocked by a damaged APC so Carmel dove through the window. Among the men inside was a lieutenant who had been wounded ten days before in the battle against Egyptian commandos near Baluza. He had returned even though not completely recovered and had now been hit again. Outside, a wounded tank crewman saw three Egyptian soldiers running toward the building. He shot them dead and fell unconscious. Carmel and the others were retrieved later in the day but the unconscious tanker, lying among the dead Egyptians, was not noticed. He woke at night, not knowing where he was, and walked until he found an Israeli unit.

The two-brigade assault on the Tsach crossroad was launched at noon but enemy fire took a heavy toll. Adan stopped the attack and called for air support. Informed that SAMs prevented air activity in the area, he sent two battalions on raids twelve miles into enemy territory to destroy three missile bases. The SAM bases had adopted a new strategy to defend themselves. As the tanks approached, the anti-aircraft missiles were lowered and fired in a flat trajectory at them. In the first such encounter, the missiles overflew the tanks and exploded miles to their rear. At another base, a missile struck within ten yards of the command APC but did not cause injuries. Their mission successfully completed, the raiders returned as the sun was setting, towing one tank which had run out of fuel. In the first day of battle by Adan's division west of the canal, it had moved out of the agricultural strip but had not yet broken loose into the enemy rear because of stubborn resistance.

In an ironic turnabout, it was the ground forces that were providing close support for the air force by knocking out SAM batteries. But the air force had also begun helping itself. Instead of a Tagar-type assault on the entire SAM array, it began a series of attacks on SAM clusters. Over the course of several days, the air force had worked its way southward from Port Said, methodically opening up missile-free patches of sky, although not without cost. The Egyptian air force attempted to make up for the rapidly receding SAM umbrella by tripling its sorties. The IAF welcomed this opportunity to take on the Egyptian pilots.

Colonel Bin-Nun emerged from the air force's subterranean headquarters in Tel Aviv once every three days to return to a Phantom cockpit. As the chief planner of attack operations, he would on these days issue mission orders in the morning, drive to an air base where he would be briefed along with other pilots on the mission, participate in the attack, take part in the subsequent debriefing at the base, then return to Tel Aviv where he would receive the debriefing reports in the evening.

Staff officers at headquarters included many of the best pilots in the air force and they welcomed any opportunity to get back into the air. Col. Gad Eldar, who had been working out of a basement office, managed to return full-time to his old Mirage squadron where in two weeks he downed twelve planes, four of them during one sortie.

A reporter visiting a tank company on the Egyptian front which had pulled back to refuel found morale high. The men were supposed to have been rotated days before, said their commander, but they refused to come off the line. "As long as they want to stay, we'll let them." The unit had been in combat every day since Yom Kippur and had learned to cope with the Saggers. "We worked out a system in the course of the battle," the captain said. "The percentage of missile hits is just a fraction of what it was at the beginning." The officer praised the Egyptian infantry. "They fought like men." Their artillery had also improved since the Six Day War but not their tank corps, he said.

A group of young platoon leaders with stubbly beards knelt in the shade of a Patton tank listening attentively to a visiting information officer explaining on a map what was happening on the Golan front. Among them was a lieutenant whose right forearm was covered by a fresh bandage from elbow to wrist, an artillery observer attached to the tank unit. He was the son of a Beverly Hills doctor and had come to Israel on his own at age eighteen four years before. He would be visiting his family for the first time since then when he was discharged in a few months, he said. "I feel fulfilled." Crossing the canal that afternoon, he was killed by artillery.

The Israeli high command had begun to think about the endgame. As General Tal put it at a meeting in the Pit Thursday morning, the thirteenth day of the war, the battle-for-survival stage had ended. The IDF now had to determine where it wanted to be when the shooting stopped. A basic consideration was that Egypt pay a price for its attack. On the Syrian front, this had already been achieved by pushing the Syrians more than six miles beyond the former border. The idea of advancing toward Cairo was dismissed by Elazar despite the maps that had been distributed. Warnings sent to Kissinger from Moscow raised concern in Israel about Soviet intervention if the IDF drew close to the Egyptian capital. Elazar also wanted to avoid a cease-fire, which would leave the IDF on overextended lines.

General Yariv, the former intelligence chief, said there was now an option that hadn't existed before the crossing—breaking the back of the Egyptian army. Several proposals were raised for special operations on the margins of the battlefield. These included an amphibious attack across the Gulf of Suez, a takeover of Egyptian oil fields in the Gulf, and the capture of Port Said and Port Fuad, straddling the northern entrance to the canal. The most far-reaching plan was that put forward by General Tal—a raid by a tank force into the Nile Valley. LSTs capable of carrying a brigade across the Gulf of Suez were positioned at Sharm el-Sheikh and the operation could be launched within forty-eight hours. "I've been cultivating this dream for the past four years," Tal told Dayan. "To grab Cairo from the rear with a hundred tanks."

The special operations were intended to offset, politically and psychologically, Egypt's achievement in establishing a bridgehead in Sinai. However, once the Israeli crossing of the canal began at Deversoir, Elazar decided to focus all efforts on the main battlefield. The high command decided that encirclement of the Third Army would be the appropriate finale to the war. To achieve it, the Israeli presence in Africa would be bolstered with all units that could be spared.

General Magen, commanding Mendler's former division, was ordered to cross into Africa with half his force, some eighty tanks. Adan's third brigade was released from the general reserve in Sinai to join him across the bridge. Col. Ran Sarig's reduced brigade was ordered south from the Golan Heights, as was Maj. Yoram Yair's paratroop battalion. Sharon was told to bring over Reshef's brigade from the Chinese Farm to the west bank but Tuvia Raviv's brigade would remain to expand the bridgehead corridor in Sinai.

A small tank force had been deployed in Eilat since the beginning of the war to guard against a Jordanian move against the resort town which abutted the Jordanian port of Aqaba. A force of thirty Saudi light tanks was reported to be heading north toward Aqaba. Intelligence chief Zeira reported that they were still more than a hundred miles away. Instead of beefing up the tank force in Eilat, said Elazar, a message should be passed to the Saudi government that if they attack Eilat their capital, Riyadh, would be bombed. The Saudis did not draw closer to Eilat and most of the Israeli tanks there were dispatched to the Suez front. (The Saudi force, keeping its distance from the Israeli border, got lost as it cut through the southern Jordanian desert and was rescued by a patrol from Jordan's camel corps. A Saudi tank force, probably the same one, eventually made its way to Syria but there is no recorded mention of its involvement in the fighting.)

Stouthearted Men had originally called for Sharon's division, after crossing into Africa, to drive south parallel to Adan. Sharon now requested to attack northward instead, toward Ismailiya. Permission was granted on condition that he simultaneously press north on the

Sinai bank with Raviv's brigade to widen the bridgehead corridor. Sharon argued again that if supply routes in Africa were cut, the Egyptian bridgeheads in Sinai would collapse. Elazar rejected this approach. Tirtur, he reiterated, still needed to be secured so that the roller bridge could pass. In addition, strong Egyptian forces on Missouri, including artillery, remained a threat to the corridor.

In his memoirs, Sharon would bitterly attack Elazar and Bar-Lev for ordering him to expand the Sinai corridor, implying that the pair intended to prevent him from sharing in the laurels of the breakout. "I cannot free myself from the feeling that one of the reasons they were pressing me to attack the 16th and 21st Divisions [in Sinai] was not because they considered the corridor too narrow but because they wanted to keep my troops on the eastern side. My strong impression was that the antagonism of years between myself and those in command [Bar-Lev and Elazar], augmented now by political considerations, played a considerable role in the military decisions that were made at the time." Bar-Lev and Elazar in turn believed Sharon was motivated by politics and a desire for personal glory.

The antagonism toward Sharon was evident in complaints Elazar heard at Southern Command headquarters from its three senior commanders—Bar-Lev, Gonen, and Ben-Ari. All contended that Sharon did not carry out orders, that his reports could not be relied on, that he had failed to ensure that the bridges were brought up in time and failed to expand the corridor, that his main concern was having his division be first to cross the canal. One said that Sharon had "broken" the previous night but returned to himself in the morning. "He doesn't succeed in organizing anything."

Elazar said to Bar-Lev: "I understand from you that Arik wants to be in Africa and is therefore not securing the bridgehead in Sinai. That's why I'm giving him the job of expanding the bridgehead."

By contrast, the generals heaped praise on Adan for the destruction of the Twenty-fifth Brigade. "Bren is worth gold," said Elazar.

"He doesn't make excuses," added Bar-Lev, "no problems, quiet, executes everything." He could not help adding: "If the bridgehead holds, it won't be because of Arik."

Despite the efforts to deflate Sharon's ambitions, he would in the end achieve them. His division's deployment in the central sector made it natural that the crossing operation be assigned to him, including the tactical planning. The paratroop brigade that gained a foothold on the west bank had been attached to his division, which would give him, and his political supporters, the right to claim afterward that his division had been the first to cross. However, fortuitous developments would give him a much bigger role. According to Stouthearted Men, the bridges were to have been in place by dawn Tuesday at which point Adan's division would cross and begin the decisive battle of the war. With the delay in the arrival of the bridges, Sharon seized the moment by bringing forward the Gillois. His decision to send tanks across on the rafts to support the paratroopers was not challenged. Benny Peled's request to attack SAM bases beyond the bridgehead justified the crossing of more of Sharon's tanks. By positioning himself at the center of the drama—the crossing point—and employing bold-ness and tactical acumen to get tanks across, he played a central role in the turning point of the war.

President Sadat conferred Thursday with War Minister Ismail at Center Ten and agreed to transfer an armored brigade from the Third Army bridgehead in Sinai to the canal's west bank. To Shazly, this was a hopelessly inadequate response to the Israeli threat. Sadat did not ask his opinion. Instead, he instructed Shazly to proceed to the Second Army to assess the situation and shore up the front as best he could. The chief of staff set off from Cairo at 2:45 p.m. and arrived at Second Army headquarters at 5:30. He found that in addition to Adan's southward thrust from the bridgehead, Sharon's division had begun to advance northward. The only forces in position to stop the move toward Ismailiya were two commando battalions and a brigade of paratroopers.

Maj. Gen. Abd al-Munim Khalil had taken over command of the Second Army from General Aqqad, who had failed to perceive the seriousness of the Israeli incursion. The plan Khalil presented Shazly called for destroying all bridges across the Sweetwater Canal, which formed a barrier south of Ismailiya. Inside the agricultural belt itself, Sharon's advance would be resisted by the commandos and paratroop-ers. An armored brigade, with T-62 tanks, would be withdrawn from Sinai to Ismailiya. Commando raids and artillery fire would mean-while harass the Israeli crossing point at Deversoir. Shazly gave the plan his blessing. He remained at Second Army headquarters for the next twenty-four hours.

Dayan visited Adan's forward command post in the agricultural belt Thursday morning. Like many of the Israeli soldiers with a farming background, he was intrigued by the ancient wells, primitive duck coops, date palms, citrus groves, and peanut fields. When Dayan strolled away from the command post to study the vegetation, Adan said to the minister's aide-de-camp, "Keep an eye on your boss. There may still be Egyptian soldiers around." Two Egyptian helicopters suddenly appeared at treetop level and large drums filled with napalm were pushed out of their open doorways, exploding about fifty yards from Dayan in a dense cloud of black smoke. Machine gun fire downed both craft. The helicopters had been dispatched on a desperate mission to knock out the bridge. Others would succeed in getting closer but they too were shot down by ground fire. Dayan was impressed by the bravery of the helicopter pilots as well as that of the enemy infantrymen who had chosen to confront the Israeli tanks and whose bodies were now scattered about the area alongside their RPGs.

The defense minister went on to visit Sharon, who said he wanted to show him "something special." They drove back to the Sinai bank and turned left to the outskirts of the Chinese Farm. Dayan was stunned by the tableau—hundreds of blasted vehicles covering the landscape as far as the eye could see. He had been involved in every one of Israel's wars and had spent time with the American army in Vietnam as an observer. But he had never seen evidence of such fierce battle, not even in photographs or movies. In addition to the 56 Israeli tanks knocked out were 118 Egyptian tanks that had been hit and another 15 abandoned intact. There were also hundreds of destroyed APCs, trucks, and other vehicles.

Colonel Reshef, who joined them when they crossed the bridge, surveyed the scene as if seeing it for the first time. "Only now," he said, "do I understand what went on here." On the first night of the battle his Fourteenth Brigade lost 120 dead and 62 wounded, the highest price ever paid by the IDF in so short a time. The following night, the paratroopers of the 890th had 40 dead and 100 wounded in the fight for Tirtur Road.

As the personnel carrier carrying them started back toward the bridge, a solitary MiG appeared overhead and dropped a bomb. It exploded close enough to lift the vehicle and set it down, still rolling. Dayan was sitting with his head out of a hatch and a sergeant grabbed his leg to pull him back inside. The defense minister told him not to worry. "Do you know how many people are lined up for my job?"

. . .

Elazar summoned Air Force Commander Peled and his two senior aides to his office on the afternoon of October 18 for a dressing-down. The air force, said Elazar, seemed to be carrying out its own war, with little relation to the one that the ground army was waging. What was needed was close air support to prevent the Egyptians from forming a new defense line. His ground commanders had complained that the air force this day was busying itself with missions on the periphery of the battlefield instead of coming to their assistance.

Thirteen days into the war, the air force had already lost some eighty planes. The Americans had begun sending Phantoms and Skyhawks to replace them but they could not replace the crews. Peled noted that only seventy-two Phantom crews remained, a dozen or so less than the number of Phantoms. When Elazar asked if he could send his planes in the morning against Egyptian concentrations even though the SAM batteries in those areas had not been eliminated, Peled said he would. "But I wouldn't want to do it three or four days in a row."

The air force's aim, he said, was to methodically eat away at the SAM deployment and this meant working inward from the periphery. The pilots could not be asked to fly every day, he said, into missile concentrations entailing heavy losses. Periodically attacking relatively easy targets sustained pilot morale and could be considered "occupational therapy." Elazar did not dismiss this consideration, although it was new to him. However, he said, the air force would henceforth draw up its daily target list in closer coordination with ground commanders.

Mordecai's paratroopers had returned to Tasa drained emotionally and physically. The two companies most heavily engaged in the Chinese Farm had suffered more than 50 percent casualties. The men's faces were masked with soot and the vacant gaze of shock. Major Duvdevani, serving now as Mordecai's deputy, assembled the battalion and announced an inspection within an hour. He wanted, he said, to see shaved faces, polished boots, and cleaned rifles. His order was greeted with looks of incomprehension. A soldier protested and Duvdevani slapped him. He did the same to a second soldier who started to speak. The men drifted off to prepare. Duvdevani could hear the mutterings: "He's crazy."

"What does he think he's doing?"

He strolled through the encampment periodically, providing a countdown. "Forty minutes." "Twenty minutes." The men washed their faces, cleaned the sand from their weapons with brushes, and polished their boots. They lined up in formation after precisely an hour and Duvdevani walked down the ranks. He did not look closely at their boots or their shave but he saw what he wanted to in most of their eyes, which had taken on a semblance of focus. They were coming back to life.

On Thursday, the battalion was dropped off near the pontoon bridge and crossed on foot between artillery bombardments. The veteran reservists of Matt's paratroop brigade who received them on the other side of the canal were touched by the faces of the young paratroopers. Apart from the shock of the battle and the loss of comrades, the men of the 890th Battalion believed they had totally failed in their mission. They did not yet grasp that the very bridge they had crossed had been erected, in large part, because of their fight.

Brigade commander Raviv began Thursday morning to push north into the Chinese Farm from Akavish. He reached Tirtur without firing a shot. There he found the bodies of thirty of Mordecai's paratroopers left behind after the previous day's battle because they lay under the Egyptian guns. Among them was a wounded paratrooper still alive. The tankers were surprised at the extent of the defenses the Egyptians had managed to build.

With the road clear at last, battalion commander Geller, who had detached from the roller bridge during the paratroopers' battle, was ordered to reharness his tanks. The towing resumed, this time in daylight, with bulldozers moving ahead to clear a path—pushing aside destroyed tanks, evening out slopes, and filling in ditches. The procession moving majestically through the desert was now a hundred yards wide. At the center was the bridge itself, straddled now by sixteen tow tanks as it moved gracefully on its rollers over slight rises and dips. Flanking it were tractors and bulldozers. Personnel carriers and unharnessed tanks served as outriders, guarding the flanks against commando attacks. The cocoon was completed by planes patrolling overhead against Egyptian aircraft trying to reach the tempting target crawling across the desert floor. Seven MiGs fell to earth during the day around the convoy. Egyptian artillery reached for the bridge but there were no spotters to call down accurate fire. The convoy reached the canal bank a mile north of the pontoon bridge in the last light of day. By 6 a.m. Friday the bridge was anchored to both banks. The

Israeli bridgehead, established three days before with rubber boats and junked rafts, luxuriated now in two stable bridges.

Before crossing to join Sharon west of the canal, Reshef requested permission for a final attack on the Chinese Farm. The Egyptians were reeling after three days of incessant pounding. According to radio intercepts, the situation was desperate enough for the Sixteenth Division commander, Gen. Abed Rabb al-Nabi, to have personally led a company in a counterattack on the Tirtur Road. But Saggers were still keeping Raviv's brigade at bay as it tried to move north from Tirtur.

Attacking from the west, Reshef's tanks fired into the heart of the Chinese Farm. Foot soldiers cautiously entered the area and found that the Egyptian defenses had almost melted away. A reconnaissance company rushed the pumping station and captured it with the loss of two men. Another unit moved in the last light into the center of the farm without casualties and formed a defensive perimeter, together with tanks. All night long, they called down artillery on Egyptian units pulling back around them.

Reshef handed over the newly won positions to Raviv's brigade Friday morning and led his brigade across the roller bridge, the first unit to cross it. After three and a half days of battle, the Chinese Farm had fallen except for scattered pockets of resistance. But the Egyptian deployment on Missouri, on slightly higher ground to the north, was intact. It had, in fact, been substantially reinforced by the troops pulling back from the Chinese Farm.

In Africa, Adan's division prepared Friday morning for the breakout into the Egyptian rear. Thursday's tank raids on SAM sites had persuaded the Egyptians to pull back other SAM bases in the vicinity as well, opening the adjacent skies to the IAF. An air attack on the Tsach crossroad cleared the way Friday morning for Adan's tanks, as Elazar had requested. It was the first time in the war that close air support had opened a path for ground forces.

Breaking through into the open desert beyond, the division moved south on two axes, with battalions splitting off to attack missile sites and army camps on the way and rejoining to do battle with Egyptian tank formations. Spirits soared as the tanks raced across the scrub. A battalion commander in Nir's brigade, noting the name of their location on the map—the Aida Plains—serenaded his men with a rendition of the victory march from Verdi's opera, which had had its world premiere in Cairo in 1871.

Adan was thrilled at the sight of his division moving across the flat expanse, the first time in the war that Israeli armor had shaken loose. This was the vision that Israeli tank officers had conjured up for years—open terrain, immense clouds of dust thrown up by fast-moving tanks, smoke rising—in this case, from burning SAM bases and dummy missile sites. There were periodic halts for radio identity checks in order to enable commanders to establish their position and ensure that they did not fire on each other.

The rendering of the victory march had been premature. The battalion commander who sang it was wounded half an hour later by Saggers fired from a SAM site. Another battalion commander, who had lost an eye the day before, insisted on staying with his unit on a stretcher in a personnel carrier, offering guidance to his deputy. Ten miles west of the Bitter Lake, Nir's tanks came on an Egyptian artillery brigade which had been participating in the shelling of the bridge-head. At the approach of the tanks, the Egyptian guns were lowered and opened direct fire. Because of difficulty moving his legs, Nir had tried to avoid thinking about getting out of his tank quickly if it were hit. It was hit now but the explosion spared him the dilemma, propelling him intact from the turret onto the ground. Recovering, he ordered his tanks to charge. The Egyptians fired until the tanks were two hundred yards away and then broke. The tanks overran the position. Scores of artillerymen were killed and many more taken prisoners. Two Israelis were killed. One was Lt. Ilan Gidron, the general's son, who had been among the escapees from Fort Milano. It had been Gidron and another soldier who held up the borrowed prayer shawl that identified them to Israeli tankers.

Adan's division covered twenty-two miles this day, reaching the Geneifa Hills. Magen's reduced division, following behind, cleared pockets of resistance that had been bypassed.

Sharon's advance northward was within the agricultural strip, which made for slow going. Reshef, whose tanks were augmented by an infantry reconnaissance unit, attacked a sprawling logistics center defended by an Egyptian commando battalion. Moving methodically, the force avoided the kind of shapeless brawl that characterized the battle for the Chinese Farm. For the first time since the war began, the numerical odds were on Reshef's side. Surveying the enemy positions in daylight, he prepared a plan that gave foot soldiers the major role. As the infantrymen worked their way down the trenches, tanks moved parallel to them and raked the trench to their front. An officer reported the trenches packed so tight that he inflicted casualties every time he threw a grenade. The position was conquered before nightfall at a cost of eighteen Israeli infantrymen, seventeen of whom were killed when a Sagger struck a packed personnel carrier. When a search was made of the trenches and bunkers the next morning, more than three hundred Egyptian bodies were found. Fifty Egyptians sheltering in bunkers were taken prisoner.

Mordecai's paratroopers, participating in Sharon's drive, pushed enemy forces back this day far enough so that the bridges were for the first time out of sight of Egyptian artillery observers perched atop palm trees. But the crossing point continued to be pounded massively. As Sharon's troops moved north along the canal, they placed Israeli flags on the ramparts to undermine morale of the Egyptian forces across the canal in Sinai who could watch themselves steadily being cut off.

Elazar visited Sharon Friday near the Abu Sultan camp. Sharon had been in the thick of battle and was beaming. "Imagine," he said to Elazar, "you're commanding a division and suddenly there you are, you yourself, standing with your machine gun facing Egyptian tanks. I've fought in wars over twenty-five years but this is the first *real* war." One of his men had earlier given him a captured Kalashnikov rifle, which he reportedly used to fire at an artillery observer in a tree.

Elazar's message, however, wiped away Sharon's smile. The chief of staff wanted Missouri. He had fixated on it. The entire crossing, he feared, could turn into a disaster if the Egyptians, attacking from Missouri, closed off the corridor and stranded the forces on the west bank without ammunition or fuel. The Egyptian forces in Sinai greatly outnumbered the skeleton forces Israel had left behind. "I'm worried about Asia [the Sinai bank], not Africa," Elazar told the General Staff. Sharon argued again that Missouri would collapse once the Second Army was cut off. But Elazar did not believe Sharon had sufficient strength to cut off the Second Army. The chief of staff studied the faces of the frontline soldiers. They had been in combat now for two weeks. Their weariness was plain but spirits were high.

On the way back, the pilot of Elazar's helicopter made a navigational error and flew over an Egyptian position in Sinai. The Egyptians opened fire, hitting the craft's hydraulic system, but the pilot managed a safe landing at Umm Hashiba. There, Elazar told Bar-Lev and Gonen that the army's top priority was to expand the bridgehead northward on both sides of the canal, but particularly toward Missouri. So worried was he about the potential threat to the bridgehead that he gave only secondary priority to surrounding the Third Army. Friday evening, in areas where the battle had tapered off, men gathered to hear the Sabbath ushered in with the kiddush prayer over wine, a poignant reminder of home and other days.

Giora Lev's battalion was posted on the northern flank of Sharon's division. During the day it reached a point from which Ismailiya was clearly visible to the northeast, including the Hilton Hotel and the Tomb of the Unknown Soldier. With darkness, the battalion organized a night laager, the tanks forming a rectangle, guns pointing outward on all four sides, and the infantry APCs sheltering in the center. Lev was in his turret close to midnight when an infantry officer called up to him softly. The officer commanded the detail guarding the encampment and was equipped with a captured SLS night-viewing instrument that magnified starlight. Egyptian commandos, he said, were approaching. Looking through his own SLS, Lev saw a force of Egyptian soldiers two hundred yards away moving toward them. Lev told the officer to have his men alert the rest of the battalion, but not by radio, which the approaching enemy might hear.

Repelling an infantry attack on a night laager was an exercise tank units were trained in. It called for a massive response aimed at shocking the attackers. Lev had never experienced such an attack and had not expected that he ever would. But here it was. The Egyptians halted fifty yards away and began to deploy. Lev could make out RPGs and machine guns. "Attack," he called. Projectors flashed on, sirens sounded, and the tanks and APCs sprang forward, guns firing. The ensuing carnage was mercifully hidden by the darkness. But in the morning, the tankers could see what they had wrought. An Israeli officer came on an Egyptian major, apparently the commander of the force, clutching a map and a pistol. His legs were gone but he was still barely alive. As an act of mercy, the Israeli shot him dead.

During Elazar's visit to Sharon, he had been only a few miles from his counterpart, General Shazly, who was at Second Army headquarters in Ismailiya. The opposing chiefs of staff started back to their respective headquarters in Tel Aviv and Cairo about the same time late Friday afternoon, Elazar buoyed by his visit and Shazly shaken by the ominous turn the war had taken. Shazly was convinced that only a massive pullback of Egyptian armor from Sinai to the west bank could save the day. At Center Ten, he reported to Ismail on the dire condition of the Second Army and learned that the condition of the Third Army was even worse, with Israeli forces racing to cut it off. Shazly urged that four armored brigades on the Sinai bank, presently sitting idle, be withdrawn to the west bank, lest both armies be surrounded. Ismail refused to permit any more units to be withdrawn from Sinai. Shazly pressed him to invite Sadat to Center Ten to discuss the matter. It was 10 p.m. and Ismail was reluctant to call the president but he finally acquiesced.

Newspaper editor Heikal, a friend and adviser of Sadat, had earlier called on the president in his apartment in the Al-Tahira Palace. Ushered in, he found Sadat sitting alone on a balcony in the darkness. As they talked, the telephone rang. An aide said it was War Minister Ismail. "Do you want me to come over to Number Ten?" Heikal heard Sadat ask. "Well, all right then, I'll come." When Heikal asked what was happening, Sadat said that General Shazly had returned from the front with a full picture of the situation.

When Sadat arrived, he closeted himself with Ismail in the latter's office for half an hour. The minister relayed Shazly's request to bring back four brigades. According to Heikal, Ismail believed that any further withdrawal of forces from Sinai would, at best, severely undermine morale and, at worst, trigger a total collapse, as in 1967. Sadat agreed. Furthermore, Sadat believed that a reduction in Egypt's strength in Sinai would weaken its position in subsequent political negotiations.

Shazly had assembled five senior generals for the meeting, including Hosni Mubarak, commander of the air force and future leader of Egypt. When Sadat and Ismail joined them, the president asked each man to give his opinion in turn. General Gamasy opposed withdrawal of any forces from the Sinai bank on the grounds that it would be psychologically harmful to the army and because it was operationally unnecessary. When all present, except Shazly, had spoken, Sadat said, "We will not withdraw a single soldier from the east to the west." An officer next to Shazly whispered, "Say something." But the chief of staff saw no point in arguing his case after the president had already stated his position with such finality.

When the meeting was over, Ismail asked to have a word with Sadat in another room. He was now speaking for history, he said, and as a patriot. If the president saw a way open for a cease-fire on acceptable terms, he would support his decision. "I'm not pessimistic," said Ismail. "Our army is still intact. But in no circumstances should we get involved in any military development which will again face our armed forces with the threat of destruction." A week before, it had been Elazar who eagerly sought a cease-fire. It was now Egypt's senior command.

Sadat, in his autobiography, describes Shazly as having returned from the front "a nervous wreck." In the meeting at Center Ten, he writes, all the other generals present "were of my opinion—that there was nothing to worry about." After the meeting, he ordered Ismail to replace Shazly as chief of staff with Gamasy but not to announce it publicly so as not to harm morale. Gamasy, to his credit, would in his own account of the war refute Sadat's description of Shazly that night and indicate his respect for him as a soldier. "He was not dispirited, as President Sadat has described."

Sadat, despite his seemingly unruffled air, understood now that a cease-fire could no longer be put off if the scenario he had so artfully constructed was not to explode in his face. Hardly twenty-four hours before, in his final meeting with Kosygin, he had rejected the Soviet pitch for a cease-fire as he had rejected a cease-fire in his talk with the British ambassador, five days before that. But there was now no more room for posturing. Returning to Al-Tahira Palace close to midnight, he asked that the Soviet ambassador be summoned. Vinogradov was startled when Sadat told him that after conferring with his military commanders he had decided to ask the Soviets to seek an immediate cease-fire at the Security Council. "What are the conditions?" asked Vinogradov. Sadat said he would accept a cease-fire on existing lines, an about-face from his previous insistence on Israeli withdrawal to the 1967 borders. Hafez Ismail, Sadat's security adviser, who was also present, said the Israeli incursion was a serious threat to Cairo.

Vinogradov wakened Brezhnev at 4 a.m. Moscow time to inform him of the meeting. Brezhnev told him to return to Sadat and clarify several points, including the attitude of other Arab leaders, particularly Assad, to a cease-fire in place. To his colleagues in the Kremlin,

Brezhnev described Sadat's request as "a desperate appeal." Reverting to the Kremlin's attitude at the beginning of the war, Brezhnev said, "He [Sadat] got what was coming to him."

At 5 a.m., Vinogradov, who had just wakened the leader of the Soviet Union, appeared at the palace to waken Sadat. The Egyptian leader greeted him in pajamas, refreshed after a short sleep. He told the ambassador that he had just sent a message to Assad, informing him of his decision. In any case, he noted defensively, Assad himself had sought a cease-fire at the beginning of the war without coordinating with him. As for other Arab nations, said Sadat, their positions could be ignored.

Sadat's message to Assad was apologetic but firm. "We have fought Israel to the fifteenth day," he wrote. "In the first four days, Israel was alone, so we were able to expose her position on both fronts. . . . But during the last ten days I have been fighting the United States as well, through the arms it is sending. To put it bluntly, I cannot fight the United States or accept the responsibility before history for the destruction of our armed forces for a second time." He was therefore prepared to accept a cease-fire subject to guarantees from the Soviet Union and the U.S. He would insist, he said, on the convening of a peace conference to achieve an overall settlement. "My heart bleeds to tell you this, but I feel that my office compels me to take this decision. I am ready to face our nation at a suitable moment and am prepared to give a full account to it."

Assad was dismayed. If Egypt pulled out of the war, Israel would concentrate its forces on the Syrian front. Israeli artillery could already be heard on the outskirts of Damascus. In his reply to Sadat, he wrote: "I received your message with deep emotion. I beg you to look again at the military situation on the northern front and on both sides of the canal. We see no cause for pessimism. . . . My brother Sadat, for the sake of the morale of the fighting troops it is necessary to emphasize that although the enemy has as a result of an accident been able to break our front this does not mean that they will be able to achieve victory. . . . My dear brother President, I am sure you appreciate that I have weighed my words with the utmost care and with full realization that we now face the most difficult period of our history. God be with you." There would be no reply from Sadat.

Of all the Arab leaders, the most nuanced role was demanded of King Hussein. He had fervently hoped to stay out of the conflict and Egypt and Syria had initially indulged him. The mere presence of the Jordanian army along the Jordan River, they believed, was sufficient to pin down substantial Israeli forces in defensive positions on the West Bank. Israel, however, was aware of the king's reluctance to risk war and had left only a skeleton force opposite Jordan. As a worst-case contingency, army engineers planted explosive charges beneath the road leading from the river to Jerusalem, a half hour's drive, to delay any incursion until reinforcements could arrive.

Dayan had, in fact, ordered that the Jordan River bridges linking Jordan and the West Bank be kept open so that life for the Palestinians could go on as normally as possible. A reporter visiting Allenby Bridge, near Jericho, on the fourth day of the war saw the captain in command on the Israeli side walk out onto the span and call on his Jordanian counterpart by his first name to ask when the next bus was coming across.

When it became apparent that the Syrian drive on the Golan had been stopped and that Israel was counterattacking, Sadat and Assad urged Hussein to have his army take an active part in the fight. Sadat called to say that "the fate of the Arab world" depended on Hussein's joining the battle.

Israel had warned the king that if he attacked across the river into the Israeli-occupied West Bank, it would retaliate with devastating air attacks. Unlike Egypt and Syria, the kingdom was unprotected by surface-to-air missiles. Sadat urged that Hussein at least permit the Palestinian Liberation Army (PLO) back into Jordan so that its fighters could cross into the West Bank. Hussein had expelled the PLO in September 1970—Black September—after its bloody challenge to his regime. The notion of letting them back into Jordan was for him intolerable. Pressure also came from the Soviet chargé in Amman, who suggested to the king that "all Arab states should enter the battle now."

The king acquiesced to Baghdad's request to send it transporters to carry Iraqi tanks to the Syrian front. He also ordered the Fortieth Armored Brigade, Jordan's prime strike force, to be put on alert status.

When the hard-pressed Syrians pleaded with him to send an armored division, Hussein saw an opportunity. From Israel's point of view, he believed, the dispatch of Jordanian tanks to embattled Syria was less serious than opening a new front against it from Jordanian territory. He asked the British ambassador in Amman to inquire whether the Israelis would consider such a move a casus belli. Israel's uncompromising reply was that it would "crush" Jordan if it intervened in the fighting. The American ambassador, L. Dean Brown, told Hussein that "the Israeli generals are in a bitter, nasty mood," intelligence evidently gleaned by his colleagues in Tel Aviv. Elazar authorized a photo reconnaissance flight over Amman, visible to the Jordanians, as a warning.

Most of the king's advisers and family urged him to keep the country out of the war. Hussein's brother, Crown Prince Hassan, said that Jordan "could not dare even contemplate military action against the West Bank." But the king risked becoming a pariah in the Arab world, and among his own people, if he was perceived as fearful or indifferent to the Arab cause at this time of testing. Hussein dispatched liaison officers to Damascus in an effort to buy time.

On the fifth day of the war, he decided that he could wait no longer. "Before the Syrian war ends," he told the American ambassador, "Jordan has to be in." He ordered the Fortieth brigade, which had been largely destroyed in the Six Day War and reconstituted, to head for Syria at modest speed. Hussein hoped he could meanwhile negotiate a defensive role for it on the fringe of the battlefield where it could release Syrian forces for combat.

Prince Hassan suggested that his brother inform the Israelis of his decision and even provide them with the unit's coordinates to ensure that it would not be attacked as it moved toward the Syrian border. The American and British ambassadors in Amman readily agreed to serve as intermediaries. They assured Israel that "there was no intention of having the Jordanian unit come into contact with Israeli forces." The British ambassador, with Hussein's agreement, forwarded the brigade's route to the Israelis.

Committed now, the king sent a detailed letter through the American embassy to Prime Minister Meir, whom he had met in Tel Aviv little more than two weeks before, spelling out why he was obliged to send a brigade to Syria. He asked Israel "to refrain from attacking this unit if at all possible." It was, he explained, a relatively small force and would be confined to an area adjacent to the Jordanian border. "This would not affect the outcome of the fighting and would give Jordan the political cover it needed for remaining outside the present conflict."

The Israelis understood that the unit's dispatch to Syria, rather than across the Jordan River into the West Bank, was the least Hussein could do as a belligerent. Nevertheless, the Jordanian brigade constituted a potential threat. "It's worth two or three Syrian brigades," said General Tal, who was Israel's foremost expert on armor. With Israeli forces having moved eastward across the Purple Line, he said, the Jordanian tanks could slip around the southern flank and reach the Bnot Yaacov Bridge linking the Golan to Israel proper "in no time."

Kissinger asked Israel not to attack the brigade. The unit, he said, would not fight "but just stand there." In his memoirs, Kissinger would write that "only in the Middle East is it conceivable that a belligerent would ask an adversary's approval for engaging in an act of war against it."

Changing its tone, Israel asked Hussein through diplomatic channels for "the best assurances possible that you will not open fire," a far cry from the warnings of devastation a few days before.

On Saturday, one week into the war, the king notified Kissinger and Mrs. Meir that the Fortieth Brigade had reached the Syrian border and that its moves henceforth "are to be slow and deliberate." Hussein himself drove north to join the brigade, which crossed into Syria but remained largely stationary. At the suggestion of Mossad chief Zamir, the king was informed via Washington that as long as the unit remained within an area near the border, which Israel delineated, it would not be attacked.

An Israeli artilleryman told a reporter visiting the battlefield that the attention of his battery had been drawn to a group of men scanning the terrain from a hilltop just inside the Syrian lines. "We were told that King Hussein was there and that we were not to fire at them." General Hofi, the northern front commander, was uneasy about this potential threat to his right flank. Proposing that the Jordanian tanks be attacked from the air, he said, "We've got to stop treating them as guests."

After two days, Assad, fed up with Hussein's stalling, told him to either join the fight or withdraw his tanks. Hussein had little choice. Prince Hassan still hoped to avoid casualties, but Jordanian prime minister Zeid Rifai acknowledged to Ambassador Brown that "what is required is that there be Jordanian martyrs."

The brigade was attached to a Syrian division. Its orders now came not from Jordanian officers but from Syrian officers. Ever the gentleman, Hussein, a graduate of the Royal Military College at Sandhurst, informed Prime Minister Meir through a telephone link that his tanks could no longer remain uninvolved. "Israel should consider the Fortieth Armored Brigade hostile as of yesterday morning," he said. Israeli ambassador Dinitz in Washington passed on to Jordan a message from Tel Aviv suggesting that the brigade be advised "not to engage heavily in battle."

At a meeting in Mrs. Meir's office with Dayan and the military chiefs, it was decided that if the Jordanian tanks attacked they would be dealt with like any adversary but that there would be no attack on Jordan proper. Likewise, if Jordanian planes joined in the battle over Syria, their bases in Jordan would be spared. The Israelis understood that Hussein was making a gesture by not attacking into the West Bank and they were willing to reciprocate.

Unlike the other Arab forces on the battlefield, Jordan was equipped with Western tanks—Centurions and Pattons—identical to the tanks used by Israel. Only when Israeli officers looking through binoculars the next day spotted small green pennants flying from the antennas of two columns of approaching Centurions did they realize it was an enemy force. Fire from Ran Sarig's brigade stopped one column. The other was hit by Ori Orr's brigade.

Syrian tanks and Iraqi artillery also fired at the Centurions, assuming them to be Israeli. The brigade pulled back, leaving twenty tanks and APCs on the battlefield.

The Syrian high command planned a major counterattack on October 19, together with Iraqi and Jordanian forces. However, Israeli tanks the night before captured the village of Um Butna east of Kuneitra. The move inadvertently disrupted the planned counterattack. A fierce fight for the village broke out in the morning between the Syrian Ninth Division and Yaacov Hadar's brigade, with heavy losses on both sides. Jarred by the unexpected development, the Syrians pulled its division back and asked the Iraqi division and Jordanian brigade to launch a combined attack earlier than planned.

Due to lack of coordination, the Iraqis attacked first, with several thrusts across a broad front. At a critical moment, Col. Yossi Peled ordered his brigade's reserve of three tanks to move out into the open on the Iraqi flank. Within five minutes, the force destroyed nine tanks without loss to itself and the surprised Iraqis pulled back. A witness would later say of the commander of the flanking force, a reservist officer from Beersheba named Gozlan, that "he deploys like he dances," presumably a reference to smoothness.

The Jordanian attack began more than an hour later. The recurring difficulty in identifying their Centurions led to a Jordanian force passing unchallenged between two Israeli Centurion companies. When the Jordanians were finally recognized, a slugging match broke out at close range and the Jordanians were driven back. The brigade's total loss in Syria now amounted to twenty-seven dead and fifty wounded.

The Soviets, meanwhile, were wasting no time in following up Sadat's plea for a cease-fire. Ambassador Dobrynin in Washington called Kissinger Friday morning to read an urgent message from Brezhnev to President Nixon. It proposed the speedy dispatch of Kissinger to Moscow, noting that every hour counted, given the fast-moving pace of events. "It would be good," said the message, "if he could come tomorrow, October 20."

It had been Dobrynin who suggested the invitation. The idea was eagerly grasped by Brezhnev. Gromyko suspected that it was in fact Kissinger himself who suggested the idea to Dobrynin. The Soviet foreign minister believed Dobrynin, who had an amiable relationship with Kissinger, would not have dared make such a proposal to Moscow—and expose Brezhnev to the possibility of an embarrassing rejection—unless he was certain the invitation would be accepted. In his memoirs, Kissinger offered no hint of such collusion but expressed delight at the invitation. "I felt it solved most of our problems."

American interests required an end to the conflict on terms that did not undermine its Israeli client, exacerbate U.S. relations with the Arab world, or endanger détente with the Soviets. A cease-fire was plainly in Israel's interests too but it was important for Washington's standing that its client emerge from the conflict looking like a winner. The Soviets had so far been reasonable but it was easy to see how the clash between the client states, if not halted, could lead to a direct confrontation between the superpowers.

The Arabs had unsheathed the oil weapon by announcing cutbacks in oil production and raising prices. Saudi Arabia declared an embargo on the sale of oil to the U.S. a day after Nixon announced a $2.2 billion supplemental appropriation for the military aid being sent to Israel. Europe panicked—distancing itself from American policy and demanding an immediate cease-fire.

This craggy political landscape was the kind of terrain in which Kissinger moved with the deftness of an Indian scout. He saw the importance of stopping the war, but not before Israel had advanced far enough to at least even the score with the Arabs strategically. On the other hand, it would not do to let the Israelis humiliate the Arabs. Moscow would have to be engaged in constructive partnership so as not to leave the Russian bear feeling vengeful. But the Middle East war presented the U.S. with an exceptional opportunity to lure away Moscow's Arab clients by demonstrating the superiority of American arms, as wielded by Israel, and by showing that Washington alone had the ability to make Israel toe the line.

After consulting with Nixon and the president's other senior advisers, Kissinger called Dobrynin to accept the invitation. He would leave the next morning and arrive in the evening, Moscow time. With the Israeli counterattack threatening to bring about an Egyptian collapse, turgid diplomacy had suddenly acquired winged feet. Kissinger informed Dinitz of his upcoming journey and asked the Israeli ambassador to furnish him with detailed reports of the military situation three times a day during his stay in Moscow. He estimated it would be four days before the cease-fire took hold. In discussions that night among Dayan, Mrs. Meir, and Dinitz, it was reckoned more realistically that military operations might have to be concluded as early as Monday evening—that is, another three days.

Elazar was uncertain about what could be achieved in that time, given the stubborn fight the Egyptians were putting up. "What's troubling me about this war," he said in the Pit to Yigael Yadin, a former chief of staff and Israel's most prominent archaeologist, "is that nowhere are we pushing them to the point of complete collapse."

"Because the IDF doesn't have enough strength," said Yadin, now among the former military leaders serving as informal advisers to Elazar.

There were no tank reserves left to throw into the battle. The IDF had achieved what it had until now by nimbly concentrating its limited forces. It established the bridgehead by hurling two divisions at one narrow point in the Egyptian line. Now, by deploying skeleton forces in Sinai opposite the two Egyptian bridgeheads in Sinai, the bulk of Israeli armor could cross into Africa and achieve a ratio of about 1 to 1 for the crucial battles there. At 9:15 Friday night, Elazar met with the inner cabinet in the prime minister's office. The main subject was Kissinger's trip and the options left to Israel. Elazar hoped the Soviets hadn't grasped the extent of the Israeli advance west of the canal and thus wouldn't press for an immediate cease-fire. The Soviet military, however, was reading the battle clearly from its satellites and warning the Kremlin that if the Israeli momentum kept up it could bring about the military and political collapse of Egypt.

Elazar's mistaken belief that the IDF was almost out of ammunition left him uncertain about how much longer it could keep up its drive. Casualties were another limiting factor. When it was suggested that the IDF's main effort be directed at the Egyptian bridgeheads in Sinai, Elazar ruled it out because it meant attacking entrenched infantry. Confrontation would be sought only with enemy tanks. (Bar-Lev told Elazar that flanking tactics now being employed against concentrations of Saggers had substantially reduced their threat.)

Elazar and Dayan curbed commando operations behind enemy lines to keep down casualties. On the night that Major Mofaz's force was set down near the Damascus–Homs highway, a team from the elite Sayeret Matkal reconnaissance unit lifted off in four helicopters to strike at the Egyptian command and control network west of the Suez Canal. The men, exiting the helicopters in eight jeeps, were approaching their target when Dayan heard that Mofaz's force was trapped. Fearing the loss of two commando forces in one night, he asked the chief paratroop officer, Gen. Emanuel Shaked, to call off the raid behind Egyptian lines. Shaked balked, saying he would need an order from the chief of staff. Dayan put the matter to Elazar, who issued the recall order ten minutes before the commandos were to strike.

Dayan called Bar-Lev close to midnight to inform him of Kissinger's trip and of the cease-fire countdown. What are the chances of reaching Suez City, the major supply channel to the Third Army, in the next two days? Dayan asked. Fifty-fifty, said Bar-Lev. Elazar was not sure that the IDF would be able to complete the encirclement of the Third Army in the time available.

Egyptian commandos this night attacked one of Colonel Matt's companies guarding the approaches to the Suez bridges. They were driven back after a battle in which the paratroopers were assisted by effective artillery fire. Three paratroopers died in the fight. In the morning, the bodies of thirty Egyptian commandos were found in front of the position. Matt arrived shortly afterward. Unlike his own troops, who came in all sizes, the Egyptian commandos were all strapping fellows, as if physical build was a criterion for the Egyptian special forces. As he looked down at them, he saw one moving. Thinking of his own son, he ordered that the man be carried to an aid station.

The next day, Saturday, Adan advanced southward thirteen miles against stiffening resistance. His division cut the Suez–Cairo railway line, brought one of the two main Suez–Cairo highways under fire, and destroyed more missile bases. Much of the Egyptian logistical echelon had begun falling back toward Cairo but Egyptian fighting units were remaining in place.

Adan's tanks captured a missile base on the highest point in the Geneifa Hills, which offered a sweeping view. Egyptian troops, urged on by the commander of the Third Army, General Wasel, staged repeated counterattacks.

Dayan made a point of visiting the battlefront every day, generally both fronts, to take the measure of the war. He asked questions of the commanders and offered advice. A senior officer who had witnessed Dayan's depression during the early days of the war was convinced that his frequent passage through the heavily shelled Suez bridgehead reflected a death wish. Dayan's public mood, however, was jaunty and his self-confidence appeared to have returned. On Saturday, he managed to visit all three divisional headquarters west of the canal. Sharon was optimistic and attack-minded as usual. He intended, he said, to seize bridges across the Sweetwater Canal and cut Ismailiya and the Second Army off from Cairo. Dayan did not believe that Sharon had the strength for that but he was nevertheless buoyed by Sharon's upbeat spirit that seemed to have imprinted itself on his whole division. Dayan found Magen's division, which had been spared the breakthrough battle in Africa, fresh and eager to go. The division, under General Mendler, had lost two-thirds of its tank strength on Yom Kippur trying to block the Egyptian crossing but it had since been rebuilt.

Adan too was in a buoyant mood and asked to hear about Kissinger's trip to Moscow. More than ever, the political dimension now guided the Israelis in weighing military moves. Dayan wanted the IDF to be holding a solid line on the western bank of the canal from Ismailiya to Suez when the fighting stopped. This would offset the Egyptian gains on the Sinai bank.

He urged Adan to turn east and capture the flat strip between the Geneifa Hills and the Suez Canal. This area, the immediate rear of the Third Army, was full of intact and well-entrenched Egyptian forces. There were also Arab expeditionary units, including a Palestin- ian brigade and a Kuwaiti battalion. Much of the area was covered with vegetation, marshes, military camps, and villages, which made it ideal for defense. Until now, Adan had chosen to avoid it for precisely that reason. He told Dayan he wanted to keep going south through the desert so as to close off the last escape routes of the Third Army and only then turn toward the canal. Dayan was not sure there was enough time to do both.

"It's a good deed [mitzvah] to eliminate the Egyptian army," Adan said.

"You do good deeds after you've done necessary deeds," Dayan responded. But he did not attempt to impose his will on Adan.

Meanwhile, Raviv's brigade was eliminating the last holdouts in the Chinese Farm and pushing on toward Missouri. The area was covered with fire, smoke, and burned-out vehicles and suffused with the smell of death. The only thing missing, thought tank gunner Avi Weiss, was devils prancing with pitchforks. His energetic platoon commander, Capt. Mendi Feibush, in whose tank Sergeant Weiss served, stopped alongside a truck filled with dead Egyptian infantrymen and brought back three Kalashnikov rifles, which would provide better range than the tankers' Uzis. Both Feibush and Weiss were officers of the Student Union at the Technion in Haifa. Feibush had been on a visit to the U.S. with his wife when the war broke out. His readiness to volun- teer his tank for dangerous missions sometimes upset his crew but they could not help admiring his spirit.

As the brigade pressed methodically northward, Feibush had to scrounge shells from other tanks after using up all his ammunition in two hours. He asked Weiss to keep a list of targets hit. At the end of the day, the list included nine tanks, fifteen trucks, some of them filled with troops, six APCs, and numerous infantry positions. Hun- dreds of Egyptian soldiers took shelter from the tanks by clinging to the canal side of the Israeli rampart. But there they were exposed to fire from Sharon's forces across the canal. According to Col. Yehoshua Sagui, Sharon's chief intelligence officer, Sharon stopped the fire on the grounds that it was too much like a massacre. Sharon, according to Sagui, ordered that the Egyptians sheltering on the ramparts be taken prisoner by the forces east of the canal.

Many Egyptians on Missouri were indeed surrendering. Israeli planes carried out bombing runs over the position and dropped leaf- lets promising good treatment to prisoners. In the afternoon, enemy soldiers began to approach Raviv's forces with leaflets clutched in raised hands. An Egyptian officer who surrendered was sent back in a captured truck to bring out others willing to lay down their arms. The officer returned with thirty men.

Three Israeli artillery officers who made a wrong turn on the Sinai bank south of the bridges were taken prisoner at a Third Army outpost and brought to Fort Botser for interrogation. An Egyptian intelligence officer introduced himself as Major Suleiman. He spoke a reasonable Hebrew and said he also spoke Russian, having studied at a military academy there. Another Egyptian officer present spoke a faultless Hebrew. "If this is the quality of their officers," one of the prisoners, Lt. Allon Kaplan, said to himself, "Israel's in trouble."

The atmosphere was relaxed enough for Kaplan to remark to his captors that life often takes strange turnings. "You know, Major Suleiman, we're in your hands at the moment but tomorrow you might be captured by our soldiers." The Egyptian laughed. "You never can tell," he said. "But it's not going to happen. Your army has received a blow." He seemed unaware of the Israeli crossing.

With darkness, the Israelis were taken across the canal by Suleiman and guards in a rubber boat to a waiting vehicle on the west bank. "I'm taking you to Africa without a passport," joked the Egyptian officer, aware of the way the Israelis were referring to the west bank of the canal. As they drove off, they were suddenly taken under fire. Everyone leaped from the vehicle, the Egyptians running back toward the canal and the prisoners running forward, shouting, "We're Israelis." Kaplan and his colleagues reached the Israeli patrol safely. Their captivity had lasted six hours.

At a cabinet meeting Saturday night, Dayan said the end of the two-week-old war was approaching. He permitted himself a note of congratulations. "A war that began with us being pushed back from the eastern bank of the Suez Canal and ends with us sitting on the west bank is a tremendous victory." Elazar said the Israeli salient west of the canal now stretched thirty-five miles north–south and up to twenty miles to the west. Resistance remained stiff and it was not clear whether there would be time to complete encirclement of the Third Army. The outcome of the war depended now more on Henry Kissinger than on the IDF.

34

KISSINGER TO THE FORE

Secretary of state kissinger had stipulated before his arrival in Moscow that he would not enter into negotiations until he had had a good night's sleep. Apart from the need to rest after a fifteen-hour flight, he reckoned that the delay would add half a day to Israel's military timetable. Shortly after their arrival, however, Kissinger and his party were invited to dinner at the Kremlin. The evening's conversation consisted of diplomatic foreplay that managed to keep just short of negotiations. Brezhnev tried to win Kissinger's assent to a comprehensive peace settlement that would oblige Israel's return to the pre–Six Day War boundaries. Kissinger pointed out that he had come to discuss a cease-fire, not a peace settlement. The dinner, which Brezhnev spiced with his usual hearty anecdotes, ended close to midnight.

Before Kissinger went to bed, he conversed with White House chief of staff Alexander Haig and learned that Washington, normally somnolent on weekends, was in turmoil, and for reasons unconnected to the Middle East. President Nixon had just fired special prosecutor Archibald Cox. Attorney General Elliot Richardson and his deputy had then resigned. It was the Saturday Night Massacre and the climax to Watergate was fast approaching. Kissinger hoped that Brezhnev would not interpret this news as a sign of American weakness and toughen his position.

Brezhnev, however, had other things on his mind. Early the next morning, he assembled his advisers to talk through the Soviet position before his meeting with Kissinger. Defense Minister Grechko and Chief of Staff Kulikov warned that if the Israeli attack continued, the Egyptian army would be completely surrounded and the war lost.

On the northern front, they said, the Syrians, together with Iraqi and Jordanian forces, were planning a major counterattack but it would not succeed. Their assessment increased Brezhnev's determination to reach a cease-fire quickly. He was prepared now to waive the linkage of a cease-fire with return to the pre–Six Day War borders, a position Sadat himself had already abandoned.

The Soviets, with military advisers in Cairo and Damascus, had a clearer view of the plight of the Arab armies than did the Americans. A report received from Dinitz while Kissinger was still airborne offered little indication of the IDF's progress and no hint about its strategic objectives or timetable. A second report from the envoy said that Israeli forces had cut the Suez–Cairo road but that the Egyptians were expected to counterattack. There was no request for Kissinger to stall. There would be no further reports from Dinitz, which Kissinger took to mean that the Israelis themselves were not sure how the fast-moving battle was developing.

When negotiations began at noon Sunday, Kissinger was surprised at Brezhnev's readiness to deal. It took only four hours to arrive at an agreement, one which met every one of Kissinger's demands. There would be a cease-fire in place. A major achievement was the agreement's call for negotiations "between the parties concerned"—that is, Israel, on one hand, and its Arab adversaries on the other. Since Israel's establishment in 1948, the Arabs had refused to negotiate with it directly.

Kissinger understood the Soviet eagerness for a cease-fire to reflect the desperation of the Arabs' situation. But the absence of haggling meant that the clock would start running sooner than expected toward a cease-fire that might well bring the IDF to a halt before it had attained its objectives. Kissinger was able to slow the clock down a bit by proposing to Brezhnev that they allow nine hours for their governments to consult with their respective clients and allies. The cease-fire would go into effect twelve hours after the Security Council adopted its resolution. Brezhnev accepted the timetable.

In a letter to be dispatched to Mrs. Meir in Nixon's name, Kissinger informed her of the agreement. He then lay down to nap. When he woke, he found that all transmission channels from Moscow were garbled and that the message had not gone out. He suspected the Soviets were playing electronic games. Four hours had been lost in transmitting to the Israelis that the cease-fire countdown had already begun.

.   .   .

On the battlefield, both sides attempted to improve their positions before the looming cease-fire went into effect. Sharon sought permission to swing out of the agricultural belt and drive north through the open desert in an attempt to cut off the Second Army. He had planned to launch such an attack the previous night but had been stopped by Southern Command, which was monitoring his division's radio net down to battalion level to keep track of what Sharon was doing.

To his dismay, he was ordered instead to mount an attack on Missouri. When his protests were rejected, he summoned brigade commander Raviv and told him that he must expand the corridor northward through Missouri at all costs. Raviv said that he had only forty-six tanks left, less than half brigade strength. Missouri was a formidable position, which had withstood Israeli attacks since the beginning of the war and it had been augmented now by substantial forces retreating from the Chinese Farm. The order, however, stood. Sharon did not mention that he himself adamantly opposed the attack but Raviv sensed the absence of his usual enthusiasm. Returning to his brigade, Raviv summoned the commanders of the two battalions remaining to him. In a replay of his meeting with Sharon, he passed on the attack order, without acknowledging his own strong reservations. The battalion commanders protested too but, as one of them, Yehuda Geller, would later say, "not strongly enough."

Geller, whose battalion had brought the roller bridge to the canal, knew that his men would regard the order as suicidal, a view he shared. He knew too that they would carry it out. There were many ways a soldier could avoid combat, but the men still on the line were those prepared to fight, regardless of the consequences. Geller, a kibbutznik, had gone from tank to tank the night before to talk to the men. All the tanks and crews that Israel had at its disposal, he told them, were now committed to battle. The battalion had been engaged in constant combat but so had all other units and there was no one else to do the job. Whoever was quicker, smarter, and more aggressive would survive. Tank gunner Avi Weiss, who kept a towel at his position to wipe the cold sweat of fear from his hands, was touched by Geller's words. The prickly truth, he felt, was better than the boasting he had been hearing on the radio.

The brigade had finally, two weeks into the war, received machine guns during the night and the crews were wakened to install them. In Weiss's tank, the men were too tense to go back to sleep. They spent the two hours remaining before dawn chain-smoking and consuming the chocolate and battle rations they had received for the Sabbath. A crewman from an adjoining tank, the unit wit, joined them and began telling jokes. Some of the men found themselves laughing too loudly. At dawn, they cleaned and oiled the tank gun. While going through a burned-out tank the day before, crewmen had found that mess kits had survived the blaze intact. Some crewmen now wrote farewell letters to their families and placed them inside their mess kits.

As the morning fog dispersed, the tanks moved into positions opposite the enemy lines. It was immediately clear to Weiss that the easy victory portended yesterday by the surrender of Egyptian soldiers was an illusion. Missouri was dark with troops. Armored vehicles in large numbers could be seen deploying. Waves of Skyhawks bombed Missouri and hundreds of Egyptian troops fled the area on foot and in trucks. But thousands of others were digging in and preparing to fight.

Across the canal, Bar-Lev visited Adan late Sunday morning and tried to persuade him, as had Dayan the day before, to turn east in order to reach the Suez Canal before the cease-fire went into effect. Adan, however, reiterated his desire to first continue south and cut the main Suez–Cairo road. Bar-Lev did not press him. Unlike with Sharon, whose suggestions were as often as not rejected, Southern Command and Elazar were inclined to accept Adan's views even when it differed from theirs. When Bar-Lev told Dayan of his conversation with Adan, Dayan said of the division commander: "You can let him decide on the spot. He's thorough and sound."

It was now Adan's war. Sharon would indeed win the glory as the man who led the crossing of the canal, but once across the waterway he was tied down on the road to Ismailiya in a slow-moving secondary thrust while Adan was deftly maneuvering large armored forces across a broad landscape in the war's strategic endgame.

Two of Adan's brigades were fighting their way briskly south through the Geneifa Hills and the desert to its west and one was proceeding slowly down the heavily defended strip between the hills and the Suez Canal. Joining this brigade in the afternoon was Maj. Yoram Yair's paratroop battalion, which included the men evacuated from the southern Golan strongpoints on the third day of the war. The paratroopers were a welcome reinforcement for armor officers who were craving for crack foot soldiers for the close-in fighting. The "totality of the tank" concept had been buried in Sinai.

Tuvia Raviv's attack on Missouri got under way at 3:15 p.m. One battalion attacked from the south, destroying twenty tanks and over-running infantry positions before being stopped by minefields and Saggers. Yehuda Geller's battalion attacked from Lexicon Road, southwest of Missouri. His orders were to reach the Artillery Road on the far side of the Egyptian position. When the order was transmit-ted to the crews, gunner Avi Weiss's palms began to sweat again. The order meant that their tanks would have to cross a three-mile-deep for-tified position crowded with antitank weaponry and masses of troops. All that could be done was to reconcile oneself to death. Weiss put a letter from his girlfriend in his pocket and checked his Uzi.

At Geller's command—"Move, move, fire with all weapons, out"— the battalion started forward.

The widely dispersed tanks moved at high speed, firing as they went. In Weiss's tank, Captain Feibush stood in the turret, firing the newly installed machine gun with one hand and a Kalashnikov with the other. The radio was filled with shouted commands—"Keep abreast, fire, target to left, smash them, keep going." Weiss fired at groups of infantrymen as fast as his loader could insert shells. "They're falling like flies," he shouted. The air seemed to be filled with flying body parts. In the midst of the bedlam, the gunner saw a startled gazelle in his sights. Beyond it, two soldiers were kneeling alongside a suitcase. Weiss fired at them but before the smoke of the explosion cleared his tank was hit.

Six adjacent tanks were struck by missiles almost simultaneously. Major Matspun, the deputy battalion commander, who was following in their wake, picked up ten survivors, including Weiss and Feibush. Instead of turning back, however, he continued forward, firing as he went, despite the shouts of the rescued men, most of them wounded, to turn. When he finally did, his tank was hit a glancing blow by a missile, wounding him. A company commander he had taken aboard assumed command but the tank was hit again and set aflame. Most of the men took shelter in an empty Egyptian firing position. Enemy infantrymen closed in but two of the Israelis with Uzis held them at bay, firing single shots to save ammunition. Captain Feibush was killed in the exchange.

The Egyptians called on the men to raise their hands. A crew-man, ignoring the cries of his comrades, ran to Matspun's tank in an attempt to get to the machine gun on the turret. He was killed before he reached it. The other men in the group, including Weiss, surrendered. Weiss's loader had hidden in an abandoned foxhole with the company commander, the two men covering themselves with sand. Emerging after midnight, they made their way toward the Israeli lines, crawling close enough to enemy positions to hear snatches of conversation. After passing through a minefield, they succeeded in reaching the Chinese Farm and safety at dawn.

Assaulting a fortified infantry position with a few dozen tanks was a repudiation of everything that had been learned in two weeks of battle. As the tank crews realized from the start, the attack was doomed. Only commanders far from the battlefield could have ordered such an attack, which may have made sense on a map but not in the field.

Half of Raviv's depleted brigade, twenty-two tanks, were destroyed. Watching from across the canal, Sharon was beside himself as he saw tank after tank burst into flame. "If your mission is necessary, you accept even the worst casualties. But this was meaningless, suicidal," he would write of the battle. But during the following night the Egyptians pulled back almost a mile. Shazly would acknowledge that the withdrawal was necessitated by Sharon's northward advance on the African side of the canal and the fire that Reshef's tanks were directing into Sinai from the Egyptian ramps. After three days of grinding combat, the corridor to the crossing point had been widened from two and a half miles, the original goal, to five miles.

The senior command, however, was not yet done. Gonen ordered Sharon to send Reshef's brigade back to Sinai to resume the attack in the morning together with Raviv's remaining tanks. Sharon bluntly refused.

"This will constitute failure to carry out an order," warned Gonen.

"Now, really," said Sharon. "Don't bother me with things like that." But Bar-Lev, whose authority Sharon did not presume to challenge, took the microphone and repeated the order.

General Elazar was in a helicopter heading for Northern Command at 10:15 p.m. when he was asked to return immediately to Tel Aviv. Kissinger's notification of the imminent cease-fire had just been received. Meeting with Dayan, Elazar agreed that in the time left Adan would continue his attempt to encircle the Third Army and another push would be made on Missouri. But the most important thing, said Dayan, was to complete the recapture of the Hermon this night.

. . .

Since the aborted attempt by the Golani Brigade to recapture the mountain spur on the third day of the war, Northern Command had put the operation on hold as it focused on the Golan plateau below. But it was clear to all that before the war was over another attempt would have to be made and at all costs. Strategically, the mountain was a vital platform from which to monitor Syrian deployment and communications all the way to Damascus. It was just as important to deny the Syrians the ability to monitor from there the Golan Heights and northern Israel. Politically, Israel was determined to prevent the Syrians from winning any territorial gain. Psychologically, it was incumbent upon the IDF to undo the ignominy of the Hermon's fall.

For two weeks, the Golani infantrymen had been heavily engaged in the battle for the Syrian enclave—raiding behind enemy lines, laying ambushes, guarding tank laagers against Syrian commandos at night. All the while, they kept looking over their shoulders at the Israeli Hermon. It struck battalion commander Yudke Peled, who had led his men up the western face of the mountain on October 8, that it would be preferable to stage the next attack from the east, starting up from the Syrian enclave. From this direction, the four-thousand-foot climb was exceedingly steep. But it would bring them directly to the Israeli outpost, perched on the edge of the incline, without the need to fight their way up the ridge again from the west. Brigade commander Drori agreed.

Peled's battalion was pulled off the line and posted in an abandoned Syrian village at the foot of the eastern face. On three successive nights, the battalion commander led his men up a steep spur with full pack to see how they would bear up. He concluded that it could be done. Saturday night, Drori was helicoptered to front headquarters to receive his orders. Northern Command had decided to go for the entire crest, including the Syrian Hermon. While Golani would attempt to recapture the Israeli spur, Lt. Col. Haim Nadel's paratroop brigade would attack the Syrian part of the crest.

Paratroop officers proposed that Nadel's force move down to take the Israeli Hermon after capturing the higher crest. This was rejected by Hofi's deputy, Yekutiel Adam, himself a former commander of Golani, who insisted that the brigade be permitted to retake what it had lost. The paratroop officers then suggested that Golani attack from the east to avoid a recurrence of the October 8 battle—the same view as Peled's and Drori's. This was rejected on the grounds that the eastern slope was too vulnerable to Syrian artillery and too steep to ensure safe evacuation of wounded. A paratroop officer at Northern Command headquarters urged Drori to challenge the order. Two weeks of combat showed on Drori's drawn face. "They're going to slaughter your brigade," the paratrooper said. Drori said he had his orders and would carry them out.

Four hundred Golani soldiers assembled in a grove near the foot of the western slope late Sunday for a final briefing. Drori stressed to them the supreme importance of recapturing the ridge, the only Syrian success not yet erased. The Hermon, he said, was "the eyes and ears" of the country. For the past two weeks, artillery and aircraft had been dropping tons of explosives on the ridge but the effect was not clear. A reconnaissance team led by Yoni Netanyahu had climbed an adjacent spur that morning to observe the Israeli Hermon. It reported seeing only two Syrians on the ridge all day. Air photos likewise offered no indication of a Syrian presence. Either the Syrian paratroopers had been driven off or they were so well disciplined that they kept hidden on the boulder-strewn slopes by day. It was hard to imagine that they had pulled back without a fight, yet there was virtually no sign of them. "This is either going to be very easy," Yudke Peled said to Drori, "or very hard."

An officer told his men that the attack they were about to carry out could be more dangerous than anything they had done until now. Anyone who wanted to stay behind could do so, he said. It would be enough to leave a note in the officers' tent. "We're going up even if we're not coming down," said another officer. Sgt. Meir Elbaz, a recently discharged Golani veteran who had rejoined Peled's battalion at the start of the war, did not feel fear. He had read Plato not long before. What is death? it said there. Either dreamless sleep, which we all desire, or afterlife in which we meet Achilles.

Peled's battalion moved off with darkness to the Druze village of Majdal Shams from where they started their climb. The brigade's reconnaissance company moved up the slopes far to the left. Between the two units, a force led by tanks and a bulldozer prepared to move up the road, waiting until the foot soldiers on both flanks had progressed. A rolling artillery barrage two hundred yards to their front kept pace with the advancing troops but when shells began to hit too close the artillery was called off.

Peled moved at the head of his column, keeping the pace slow so as not to exhaust the men. They would have to climb four thousand feet with seventy-five-pound backpacks before reaching the Hermon outpost and they had to be ready to enter into battle along the way. They were two-thirds of the way to the top, after climbing nine hours, when a heavy burst of fire cut into Peled's column. A parallel ambush of the motorized column knocked out the lead tanks and half-tracks, blocking the road. The reconnaissance men on the left flank were caught up in battle as well and their company commander killed.

The Syrians had kept hidden by day for the past two weeks, waiting for the Israelis to return. Only two Syrians had been wounded by the shelling and bombing, the close-packed boulders offering almost total protection.

The two sides fired at each other at close range. A dozen Golani troopers would be found dead after the battle with bullet holes through their helmets, a penetration made possible because of the high velocity of the bullets fired at close proximity.

The Syrians were using Israeli machine guns they had taken from the outpost. More than once, Golani soldiers, seeing the familiar reddish tracers—readily distinguishable from the greenish tracers of Soviet ammunition—and recognizing the rhythm of the machine gun, shouted "Cease fire," believing it was friendly fire from a unit that had gotten ahead of them. Whoever rose up was hit.

As he neared the point of contact, Sergeant Elbaz could hear commanders to his front calling on their men to charge. A rush forward would be followed by the sound of sniper fire and the sight of falling figures. The sergeant had picked up a Kalashnikov rifle from a dead Syrian. It had a bayonet attached to it, which he tried unsuccessfully to detach. He was with two other soldiers when they came abreast of someone kneeling in the darkness. It was Colonel Peled. "Move on," said the battalion commander. The three men rose and charged up the slope. The man on one side of Elbaz fell dead. A moment later, the other soldier was hit. Elbaz kept running. He had only tracer bullets, which made him uncomfortably conspicuous whenever he fired. To his front, he saw several figures and fired in their direction. There were shouts, apparently from men he had hit. Rounding a boulder, he came on a Syrian soldier also holding a rifle with a bayonet. Both men sank their bayonets into each other. Elbaz also fired, killing his adversary.

His wound was not crippling and he was able to continue forward.

But as firing around him grew heavy, he went flat. Something exploded overhead and he felt shrapnel ripping into his back. Now, he knew, it was over—the war and life itself. The October cold of the mountaintop gripped him. To keep warm, he began crawling toward the rear. He came abreast once more of Colonel Peled, still kneeling. The battalion commander was talking into a radio with a calmness Elbaz found hard to comprehend. The officer had a map on his knee, which he was examining with the aid of a tiny light. Elbaz reached an aid station and was carried down the mountain. Plato had not included the possibility of being wounded among his options.

Peled was maneuvering his three companies by radio through steep, barely passable topography in an attempt to outflank the Syrians. Movement was agonizingly slow. The commander of a company told to move northeast moved northwest instead. Climbing the wrong outcropping, he reported himself in place but with no enemy in sight. Peled moved forward to the line of contact in order to better grasp what was happening. His radioman passed on an urgent request that Peled go back to confer with Drori. Peled ignored it, not wishing to have the men see him pulling back. Unknown to him, Drori was calling because he had been shot in the chest and wanted to pass on his command. Before being carried down on a stretcher, Drori told the officers with him, "You've got to finish this business. Don't dare go down without taking the mountain." A few moments later, Peled was himself shot through the side and was evacuated.

As dawn began to tint the slope, surviving Golani fighters could for the first time glimpse the enemy. A commander called for the men to take immediate shelter in the cover of boulders and then called for artillery fire "on our forces." The fire straddled the battle lines. Some Golani soldiers were hit but Syrian resistance perceptibly weakened. An Israeli raised a helmet above a boulder but it drew no fire. Here and there, Syrian snipers rose from behind rocks with raised hands as the Golani troops pressed forward, eliminating final pockets of resistance. At 11 a.m., an officer announced on his radio: "To all stations, to all stations in the world, the Hermon is in our hands."

The price had been steep—55 dead and 79 wounded. Counting the casualties in the failed attack two weeks before, the brigade had paid with 80 dead and 136 wounded to regain the mountain.

The paratroop attack on the Syrian Hermon was over too. It had been a very different fight. Instead of scaling the mountain on foot,

Nadel's force was airlifted to the crest by helicopter. Two battalions, each of three hundred men, were transported in twenty-seven sorties. The helicopters followed a carefully plotted route through wadis that would get them around the Syrian antiaircraft defenses. Artillery batteries laid down a rolling barrage just to the front of the helicopters to suppress any attempt to down the craft with small arms fire or shoulder-held missiles.

The Syrians on the crest saw the helicopters only when they broached the skyline to their rear. Seven MiGs were downed by patrolling Israeli aircraft when they tried to intercede. The Israeli planes also downed two helicopters carrying Syrian reinforcements. The airlift was completed by 5 p.m., leaving the paratroopers the entire night to operate. Although the distances to be covered were not great, the thin air obliged slow walking. A helicopter placed seven men, including artillery observers, on the peak of the Hermon from where at night they could see the lights of Damascus.

By 3 a.m., after a series of minor skirmishes, the paratroopers were overlooking the main Syrian observation post, four miles from where they had landed. It was from this post, 7,800 feet high, that the Syrian paratroopers had set out on Yom Kippur to capture the Israeli outpost below. Nadel called down artillery on it; when his men attacked, they found that the defenders had fled. Total casualties for the paratroop brigade in the operation were one dead and four wounded.

With dawn, the paratroopers could see smoke from the Golani battle down the slope. At 10 a.m., one of Nadel's battalions began moving along a path leading to the Israeli Hermon to assist. It encountered Syrians fleeing the Golani battle. Some were killed and others taken prisoner. Halfway down, the paratroop force was ordered by Northern Command to return upslope. The retaking of the Israeli Hermon was the Golani's prerogative.

A cabinet meeting to discuss endgame strategy got under way at midnight Sunday. Mrs. Meir told the ministers she would ask Kissinger to stop off in Tel Aviv on his way back from Moscow. Elazar, who had briefed the cabinet, begged leave at 2:15 a.m. to return to the Pit. He had not gone far when unspoken thoughts welled up. Executing an about-face, he returned to the cabinet meeting and asked for the floor.

The cease-fire worried him greatly, he said. It would halt the IDF just as it was gaining stride. More worrisome, it would permit the

Arabs to build up strength for a new round. A resumption of fighting within a few days or weeks was not only possible, he said, but likely. The Egyptians would deploy new SAM batteries, closing off the skies so arduously opened. The Syrians would train crews for the hundreds of new Soviet tanks they had already received and the Iraqis would send another division. A cease-fire that lasted only a few days or weeks was Israel's worst option. The government must therefore seek guarantees that this would not happen. He himself would like to have three or four more days to eliminate the Third Army, capture Missouri, and deploy the army along viable new lines.

After the meeting, Dayan received a call from Sharon pleading to have the order to attack Missouri rescinded. Dayan had hitherto refrained from interfering in the disputes between Sharon and his superiors. This time, however, he called General Tal. An appeal from a division commander who believed that a plan was unworkable, said Dayan, could not be ignored. Tal said he would look into it. He called Elazar, waking him from a deep sleep. The chief of staff decided not to fight it anymore. With his assent, Tal called Gonen and told him to give Sharon the option of attacking Missouri or not. Neither had any doubt what Sharon's choice would be.

Admiral Telem had ordered Captain Almog at Sharm el-Sheikh to attack Ardaka Sunday night. The remaining Egyptian missile boat there constituted a threat to an amphibious operation across the Gulf of Suez that was still an option. Telem suggested that the raiding party this time stand off from the target, which was bound to be protected up close after the previous attack, and use LAW missiles. Almog, a former commander of the naval commandos, decided to lead the operation himself.

Two boats reached the Ardaka channel an hour before dawn and found it unguarded. At 150 yards from their target, fire was opened on them. "Close to firing range," shouted Almog. The designated gunners in the two boats rose at eighty yards and placed the missile launchers on their shoulders. Bracing themselves against the roll, they tried to ignore the enemy fire. Each had five missiles. They both missed with the first four. Almog ordered the boats to close to forty yards. The last two rounds hit, setting the missile boat aflame. As Almog's boat turned, it ran onto a reef, damaging its propeller. The second boat took it under tow. As they reached the open waters of the gulf, Monday morning was dawning. On the Hermon, at the other end of the Israel-Arab battlefield, four hundred miles to the north, Golani fighters were nearing their final objective.

In New York an hour later, the United Nations Security Council adopted a cease-fire resolution. It would go into effect in twelve hours, 6:52 p.m., Israel time.

Israel had until sundown to try to break the back of the Egyptian army.

35
CEASE-FIRE

A DAN BEGAN THE NEW DAY as he had every day for the past two weeks by addressing his brigade commanders on the radio in a parody of Israel Radio's start to its broadcast day—with the date and a reading from the Psalms.

"This is Monday, 22 October, the eighteenth day of the war. On this day the Levites would chant in the Temple 'And you shall strike the Egyptians and pursue them to the end.' Should it come to pass that you do not hurry, you will not finish the task. Prepare for orders. Over." Each commander reported readiness and Adan gave them their assignments in down-to-earth military jargon.

The emphasis this day would indeed be on hurrying. But the race would have to be delayed. The Egyptians had seized the initiative by staging counterattacks in nearly every sector, often before dawn. In addition, neither artillery nor air support would be available to Adan until 8:30 a.m. because they were being directed at the last SAM bases in the area of Suez City. Adan's plan was to grind up the enemy forces to his front, sever the main Suez–Cairo road, and then, before the cease-fire went into effect, sprint for the canal, fifteen miles east across flat terrain.

The Egyptian Fourth Armored Division had been playing a leading role in resisting the Israeli incursion. But now the division commander, Brig. Mustafa Kabil, refused an order from the commander of the Third Army, General Wasel, to force open the Suez–Cairo road from the west to permit the passage of supply convoys. "The Suez road is cut off, Kabil," said General Wasel, in a message intercepted by Israeli monitors. "Open it for me. You are under my command. Why do you refuse? I'm giving you a clear order." Complaining to War Minister

Ismail, Wasel said that Kabil's excuse was that Israeli planes would pounce on him if he left the SAM umbrella still deployed in the direction of Cairo.

Adan had positioned himself on a peak of the Geneifa Hills offering a broad view of the battlefield. To the north, Gabi Amir's brigade was fighting its way down the narrow plain between the canal and the hills. To the south, his other two brigades were approaching the Third Army's remaining supply routes. With the last SAMs in the Canal Zone under attack, the air force was furnishing intensive close support.

Dayan arrived by helicopter in mid-morning. He stressed to Adan the importance of reaching the canal before the cease-fire. Adan reluctantly called off the southern drive at 2 p.m. and ordered his forces to reach the canal before the cease-fire went into effect half an hour after darkness.

Kissinger landed at Lod International Airport from Moscow early Monday afternoon and was driven to the same Mossad guesthouse where less than a month before King Hussein had warned Prime Minister Meir of war. At the start of a fifty-minute tête-à-tête, Mrs. Meir went directly to the heart of her concerns: had the U.S. struck an agreement with the Soviets to force Israel back to the 1967 lines? Kissinger assured her there was no such agreement. When he asked if she thought Sadat would survive the military setbacks of the last days, Mrs. Meir said he would. "He is the hero. He dared."

During lunch, Kissinger was informed by aides that Sadat had accepted the cease-fire. Kissinger told his hosts that he would not make a fuss if military operations continued through the night. He was thus compensating Israel for the four hours lost in forwarding the message from Moscow about the cease-fire agreement. He told Dayan that Israel had been wise not to stage a preemptive strike on Yom Kippur. If it had, he said, it would not have received so much as a nail from the U.S.

Before departing, Kissinger met briefly with Elazar, Benny Peled, and Zeira and scanned a situation map of the battlefield. It showed the Third Army cut off from Cairo except for a secondary road to the south near the mountain known as Jebel Attika. The map was in error since Adan had halted his drive just short of the main Suez–Cairo road in order to turn to the canal. The generals told Kissinger that the Egyptian and Syrian armies had fought well. Zeira said that the Egyptian Sixteenth Infantry and Twenty-first Armored Divisions had been destroyed and two other divisions, the Fourth Armored and Sixth Mechanized, were badly hurt. These losses, he said, removed from the Egyptian army its offensive capability. The Syrians, he said, had lost 1,000 of their 1,600 tanks but Soviet resupply had brought the number back up to 1,400. When Kissinger asked to what they attributed the IDF's successes, Elazar said a wide gap remained between the Israeli army and the Arab armies in leadership and in the quality of the fighting men. Kissinger was impressed by Elazar. "[He] struck me as a man of rare quality, noble in bearing, fatalistic in conduct. He briefed us matter-of-factly, but with the attitude of a man to whom the frenzies of the day were already part of history."

Kissinger would describe his brief stopover in Israel as one of the most moving episodes of his government service. He sensed the nation's exhaustion and the trauma that came with the loss of its sense of invincibility. The way was opening now for diplomacy. But the war and the dying were not over yet.

In Sharon's sector south of Ismailiya, a tank officer looking north along the Suez Canal saw Egyptian soldiers on the African bank shooting deserters trying to swim across from the Sinai bank. However, Israeli paratroopers pushing through the greenbelt toward Ismailiya were encountering heavy resistance. In a dusty village where chickens scattered in front of the armored vehicles, the soldiers came on a farmer, one of the few inhabitants who had not fled. Sharon, himself a farmer, paused to chat. "How many kilos of peanuts do you get to the quarter acre?" he asked.

"One hundred fifty," said the farmer.

Sharon looked surprised. "You should be getting better yields than that," he said. "We get six hundred kilos, at least, in Israel."

At one point, a small Egyptian training plane which had been fitted out for combat appeared above the tree line and made a run at Sharon and others grouped around him on a road. The plane did not fire and a burst from an APC's machine gun brought it down. The pilot managed to bail out and was picked up by Israeli troops. Described by one of the Israelis as a "dandy" with lacquered fingernails, the pilot was brought to Sharon, who asked why he hadn't fired when he plainly had the group on the ground lined up in his sights. The pilot said he hadn't been sure if they were Israelis or Egyptians. "What kind of pilot are you?" asked Sharon dismissively. The Egyptian pilot looked hurt almost to the point of tears.

As his brigades were moving into position for their race to the canal bank, Adan received a message from Southern Command which he passed on to his commanders: Radio Cairo was reporting that Egypt accepted the cease-fire. "We have to hurry," Adan said. They could not begin moving immediately, however, because local resistance had first to be overcome. It was not until 4 p.m., three hours before the cease-fire was to go into effect, that Nir's and Keren's brigades finally began their advance.

It was, Adan would write, a feast for the eyes. "The division was speeding across the plain in a broad, deep structure. The sun was at our back, but vision was obscured by the clouds of dust raised by the charging tanks. The reports were coming in fast and furious, mentioning a thousand and one code names [of locations], so that it was hard to follow. Thousands of Egyptians, I was told, were fleeing every which way." It was the first sign that elements of the Egyptian army were at last breaking under Israel's relentless attacks.

While Egyptian soldiers were raising their hands in surrender, however, they were still gripping their weapons. Adan's officers asked how they should react. There was neither time to teach the Egyptians how to surrender nor time to take them prisoner. Adan said not to fire at them but to keep moving forward and to stay alert in case the Egyptians had second thoughts and started shooting. To the north, Colonel Amir's brigade seized a major army base, the Geneifa camp, where thousands of Egyptians wanted to surrender but were passed by for lack of time.

The air force was no longer available for close support, since it was dealing with masses of planes that Egyptian air force commander Mubarak had thrown into the fray in a desperate effort to block the Israelis' final dash. Tank crews watched parachutes, almost all of them Egyptian, floating down from amidst the swirl of aircraft in the sky.

Dusk was descending as the first tanks neared the agricultural belt. Adan ordered each brigade commander to send a battalion to the canal to stake out an Israeli presence, the other battalions remaining in the desert outside. At 6:50, Bar-Lev asked for a situation report. One unit had reached the canal, said Adan, and two more would soon reach it at other points.

"Okay," said Bar-Lev. "In another two minutes the cease-fire is supposed to take effect."

"Repeat, please," said Adan, feigning deafness. "I can't hear you."

General Magen was replying in the same spirit to a similar message from Ben-Ari. "Are you sure it's today?"

As part of the final drive, Sharon received permission in the afternoon to move toward Ismailiya. He ordered Reshef to break through to the city together with paratroopers in the few hours remaining. Reshef gave preparatory orders but expressed doubts to Sharon about the wisdom of the attack in view of the pending cease-fire, the paucity of forces, and the likely casualties. A ranking member of Sharon's staff urged Reshef in a whisper not to execute the order.

A company of paratroop reservists under Capt. Gideon Shamir led the way in late afternoon across a still intact bridge spanning the Sweetwater Canal a mile south of Ismailiya. The paratroopers were taken under fire by Egyptian commandos lying in ambush and by artillery. Within minutes, Shamir's company had seventeen dead and wounded. Looking behind him, the officer saw four tanks from Reshef's brigade hit almost simultaneously as they prepared to join him. Darkness had already descended when Shamir was ordered to pull back.

Addressing the entourage of reporters accompanying him, Sharon said: "The battle to capture Ismailiya could have been effected last night. The very same forces that conducted it now have been ready for the past forty-eight hours. Had they begun then, we would have brought about a radical change in the situation." The reporters were left to decide how much of this analysis had come from a frustrated soldier and how much from an ambitious politician.

President Sadat had prepared his own endgame gambit—the launch of Scud ground-to-ground missiles. As with the firing of the Kelt missiles in the opening moments of the war, his intention was to demonstrate that he had a strategic option in case Israel contemplated future attacks on his cities or economic infrastructure. He would not fire them now at Israel itself but into the battle zone. He wanted the missiles fired just moments before the cease-fire went into effect, too late for the Israelis to retaliate. The Israeli Air Force had indeed drawn up a long list of economic targets including power plants as potential targets, but the high command had decided to execute them only if the Egyptians first fired Scuds into Israel.

The Scuds were in the hands of Soviet units training Egyptian crews and could not be fired without Moscow's permission. The Soviet military advisers in Cairo were inclined to accept Sadat's request but the Politburo had heretofore refused the use of the Scuds as long as they were under Soviet control. According to the only inside account of events in the Kremlin during the war, Ambassador Vinogradov in Cairo called Gromyko to ask what to do but the foreign minister was not available. The ambassador then asked to speak to Defense Minister Grechko. "Go the hell and fire it," said the marshal, angered at the loss of Soviet lives in the Israeli attack on Damascus and the sinking of a Russian freighter in Latakia during an exchange of fire between Israeli and Syrian missile boats.

According to Sadat's memoirs, two Scuds were fired. According to Shazly, three Scuds were fired at Deversoir. Israeli sources speak of only one Scud hit. It exploded amidst supply vehicles of Yehuda Geller's battered battalion near Missouri, touching off an explosion in an ammunition truck that killed seven soldiers. When Gromyko learned what Grechko told Vinogradov, he was furious and tried to get permission rescinded. But it was too late. Minutes before the cease-fire went into effect, Egyptian artillery, mortars, and Katyushas unleashed a massive bombardment on both banks of the crossing point, inflicting sixty casualties.

The silence that settled over the battlefield would not last long.

The cease-fire had gone into effect after dark so that not even satellite photos could determine the precise location of the combatants at the moment, particularly since the Israelis had been in the midst of a headlong charge. Adan was frustrated at being stopped just as his forces were in position to deliver a knockout blow. "One way or the other," he would write, "I did not believe the cease-fire would be observed." The impulse among Israeli military leaders after the shock and humiliation of the war's opening days was to go for the kill. Sharon called Begin and asked him to press the government to delay the cease-fire, which, he said, was intended only to save the Egyptian army from destruction. Elazar, in a statement to the fighting forces announcing the cease-fire, added: "From the viewpoint of readiness, you must act as if the war is still going on."

Gen. Dov Tamari, however, believed the troops had had enough. Climbing onto tanks to talk to crewmen, Adan's deputy saw their exhaustion. They had been going virtually around the clock for close to three weeks and it was difficult just staying awake. "Their eyes said, 'We've gotten this far and we're still in one piece. Let's end it already,'" he would later say. "With some it wasn't just in the eyes. They actually said it." For tank company commander Rami Matan, who had been in the thick of the fighting since the first day, the most onerous aspect was not physical exhaustion or even the constantly shortening odds of survival but the accumulated sense of loss from comrades killed and wounded. He was flooded with relief at the cease-fire but would have been ready to go on to Cairo without a qualm if the order were given.

The unit Adan referred to as having reached the canal before the cease-fire was Elyashiv Shimshi's battalion of Centurion tanks, which had participated in the destruction of the Twenty-fifth Brigade. It had this morning overcome an Egyptian ambush, destroying more than twenty tanks without suffering a loss. The battle was a tactical jewel of fire and maneuver, a fitting end to two weeks of war in which the unit had been shaped into a seamless fighting machine. At 4 p.m., Shimshi was informed by brigade commander Arye Keren that he had one more mission. In the three hours remaining before the cease-fire, he was to proceed eastward ten miles and reach the point where the canal touched the southern end of the Bitter Lake. The final stretch of their route would take them back through the agricultural strip. Shimshi wanted to get across the strip, filled with potential ambush points, before darkness set in at 6:30. However, the battalion had to fight its way through an Egyptian position on the way and it was not until 6:45 that the tanks entered the strip.

Finding a suitable place for a night laager proved difficult. All about them were bogs and mines, not to mention an enemy army whose attitude toward the cease-fire was not yet clear. As they drove north along the canal-side road, Shimshi saw an open field to the left, the size of a soccer pitch. The tanks entered and formed a rectangle, guns pointing outward. Shimshi positioned himself in the hollow center, with APCs carrying an infantry company lined up behind him. Engines were cut and absolute silence descended. The darkness of the night gave way to the deeper darkness of shrubbery and trees beginning twenty to forty yards west of the field. To the east, the waters of the Bitter Lake glittered. Shimshi had wanted to remain outside the agricultural belt for the night but Colonel Keren refused. If international observers arrived in the morning, it was important that they find Israeli forces on the canal.

Shimshi assembled his company commanders. They had been through a trying day of battle, he said, but there could be no sleep this night. There was no telling, he said, what forces were out there in the shrubbery and what their intentions were. Shimshi ordered the commander of the infantry company to take two APCs and check escape routes in case they had to hastily pull out. A few minutes after the personnel carriers departed, fire was heard from their direction and a flaring could be seen through the trees. The infantry commander reported that they had been ambushed and one APC set aflame. Shimshi told him to evacuate the men in the burning vehicle and return. The surviving APC had just made it back with one man dead when fire opened from the shrubbery on the laager itself—RPGs, small arms, and mortars. The crashing response of the tanks brought silence. Shimshi contacted Keren and asked permission to pull out. The brigade commander checked with division and again refused. Once more the Egyptians opened fire and once more the tanks' response silenced them.

In the coming hours, the cycle would be repeated periodically. Shimshi feared that they would run out of ammunition and again requested a pullout. Again denied. Many of the tanks reported being hit but all continued to function. About 11 p.m. a tank reported penetration of an RPG and two wounded. There was a nightmarish helplessness to their predicament—immobilized and surrounded by Egyptian forces they could not see. Shimshi made a point of keeping his voice confident-sounding on the radio net, as if this was just another tactical difficulty of the kind they had overcome so often in the past two weeks. At 1:30 a.m. Shimshi again asked Keren for permission to pull out. There was no point in remaining, he said; the cease-fire was clearly being violated and if they stayed the results could be disastrous. At 2 a.m., permission was finally granted.

"Start engines," said Shimshi. "Prepare to move out." It was an order the men had been eagerly awaiting. "We'll mount the road and move north," Shimshi said. "At the first junction, we turn left." The map showed a side road there leading across the Sweetwater Canal and on out of the agricultural strip. Several crews reported being unable to move their tanks because of damage from RPGs. Shimshi ordered them to abandon the tanks and find a place on others. Delivering a parting volley at the Egyptian infantry, whose fire had intensified with the engine starts, the tanks began filing out onto the road. They had not gotten far when Shimshi's tank was struck by RPGs. The driver swerved and the tank mired in a bog. Shimshi and his crew evacuated the tank and boarded another. Egyptian soldiers were firing at them now from trenches alongside the road. The Egyptians were too close to be hit by the tank's weapons, which could not be depressed sufficiently. An officer standing in the turret next to Shimshi was wounded as he threw grenades. Shimshi himself fired an Uzi.

A personnel carrier ahead of him was set aflame and its occupants scampered aboard other vehicles. As the line of vehicles swung around the burning APC, two tanks and an APC ran onto mines at the side of the road. Another tank was caught in a bog and could not extricate itself. Shimshi said to abandon all vehicles that could not be moved rather than try to tow them out.

The company commander with the lead tanks, Maj. Zimran Koren, reported that he had reached the turning but that the side road was blocked by an earthen barrier. Shimshi looked at the map and saw another turning a few hundred yards farther north. It too led across the Sweetwater Canal to the desert. He told Koren to head there. The company commander soon called back: "The first tank has reached the canal but there's no bridge."

Shimshi could sense the tension along the column. They had started out only a few minutes before but already half the tanks and APCs were gone and the fire coming at them from the darkness was increasing. The battalion commander looked once more at the map. Koren was clearly at the point marked "Crossing." Telling him to remain where he was, Shimshi reported his predicament to Brigade. The reply from intelligence, after a pause to check maps, was that there should be an Irish bridge, a causeway, just under the surface of the water. Shimshi told Koren to order the lead tank to descend into the water. The crew should open hatches and be prepared to jump if the tank went under. A few moments later came the exultant cry—"We're across." The remaining vehicles, firing to either side of the dirt road as they went, hurried across the bridge and out of the greenbelt.

Two miles into the open desert, Shimshi called a halt. The claustrophobic nightmare was over. Around them now were endless expanses. At his request, the men gathered around his tank. They had lost nine tanks and several APCs and every one of the surviving tanks had suffered at least five hits from antitank weapons. But there were only two fatalities and seven wounded. Shimshi commended the crews on their professionalism. The crewmen briefly abandoned professionalism to vent their relief by embracing him.

Other Israeli units were also busy this night. Bar-Lev had ordered his division commanders to start mopping-up operations to achieve territorial continuity between the southern approaches to Ismailiya and Suez City. "If they don't shoot at us," said Bar-Lev, "we won't shoot at them. If they open fire, of course, we'll respond."

Major Brik was ordered to take the five tanks remaining to him and "steal ground." The cease-fire prohibited shooting but said nothing about movement, according to Brik's battalion commander. (The cease-fire did, in fact, call upon the parties to halt all military activity "in the positions they now occupy.") Brik was told to get as far as he could, without firing, before U.N. observers arrived in the morning.

Brik's company had been fighting from dawn to sunset for the past five days. The nights had been given up largely to preparations for the next day's battle and the tanks had moved off well before dawn. There had been no more than an hour or an hour and a half for sleep each night inside the tanks. Sleep deprivation caught up with them now as they rolled through the night. About 2 a.m., Brik could fight it no longer and ordered the tanks to halt. "Let's rest for fifteen minutes," he said. They were too weary even to post guards outside, although they were deep inside Egyptian territory. Within a minute, all were sound asleep in their seats.

When Brik opened his eyes, he saw pale blue sky through the hatch. His watch told him it was 5:30 a.m. Rising up in the turret, he saw that they were in the center of a large Egyptian logistics depot. The encampment had shown no lights at night, which is why the Israelis had driven into it without noticing. The Egyptian sentries assumed the arriving tanks were their own. Around Brik now were at least a hundred vehicles, including fuel trucks, but no tanks. The Egyptian soldiers in the Israelis' vicinity paid no particular attention to them. After wakening his crews, Brik beckoned to an Egyptian captain nearby. The officer approached and was taken aback when Brik announced to him, through one of his crewmen who spoke Arabic, that they were Israelis. Tell your superior, said Brik, that he must evacuate all this equipment toward Cairo. Sorry, said the Egyptian officer, we were here before you. Brik asked him to call the commander of the encampment. The officer returned with a colonel to whom Brik repeated his demand. The colonel said Brik could not give him orders. "There's a cease-fire," he said.

"Don't get me angry," said Brik. "I have tanks and I can shoot. You with these vehicles can't. I will fire if you don't pull out."

The colonel assembled his officers and within an hour the Egyptian vehicles started to move off. A truck driver whose path Brik was blocking honked his horn and the Israeli tank obligingly moved aside. This relatively civil encounter would soon prove an anomaly as the Egyptians began to challenge Israel's interpretation of the cease-fire.

Word of the near-destruction of Shimshi's battalion made its way up the Israeli chain of command, feeding the unhappiness with which the cease-fire was being viewed by almost the entire military hierarchy. It was Adan, as general in command of the most active front, who felt it most keenly. An order was an order but the destruction of the Third Army was a historic opportunity. Adan was aware that Dayan, in the Six Day War, had ordered the IDF to halt six miles short of the Suez Canal but that officers in the field had nevertheless brought the army to the water's edge. Elazar himself, as commander of the northern front in that war, had stretched the cease-fire time limits in order to complete the capture of the Golan Heights. Adan concluded that he too would "finish the job" if afforded an opening. About midnight, he informed Gonen of the plight of Shimshi's battalion and noted that there were also other incidents of Egyptian fire. In these circumstances, said Adan, he intended to continue fighting the next day. Gonen replied that Adan was to maintain the cease-fire unless the enemy violated it. Adan took it as a pro forma response from a commander who in fact wanted to continue the fight as much as he did. He spent the remainder of the night preparing his brigades for continuation of the battle the next day on the assumption that the high command would in the end authorize an all-out advance. Shortly after dawn, Colonel Nir reported Egyptian tank fire in his sector. When he suggested checking to see if this was merely a local incident or something broader before reacting, the division commander replied: "Don't make me any armistice here. If they've opened fire at you, take up positions and fire back."

At 8 a.m., Elazar informed Dayan of the Shimshi episode and other shooting incidents. "Last night they destroyed nine of our tanks and now they're attacking in a number of places, trying to grab territory back from us. I want to tell Southern Command that it's free to act in the Third Army's sector." Dayan gave his approval. Just make sure, he said, that the army spokesman points out that Israel is reacting to Egyptian violations. Unlike Elazar, who believed the cease-fire would prove only a temporary lull, Dayan was convinced that Soviet interest in a cease-fire meant that it would last once it took hold. However, if Israel had its way, it would not take hold just yet.

Dayan's approval opened the way for resumption of an all-out offensive in the southern sector. Magen was ordered to cut the remaining road links between Cairo and Suez. Implementation was delayed because his division was engaged with Egyptian forces trying to break through from the direction of Cairo to the beleaguered Third Army. Intelligence reported that beyond the attack force, only two armored brigades—Libyan and Algerian—remained to defend the road to Cairo. Magen's division included Dan Shomron's brigade as well as Ran Sarig's, which had come down from the Golan after thirty-three hours on tank transporters. It numbered thirty tanks—less than one-third its normal size.

Adan's division, located between Magen and the Suez Canal, began its own drive south shortly after noon, routing scattered Egyptian forces in its path. An hour after dark, the lead elements reached the outskirts of Suez City, at the southern end of the canal.

Magen's division was by this time on the move. As it approached Adan's sector in the darkness, Adan suggested that its vehicles switch on lights in order to be able to move faster. Hundreds of headlights suddenly lit up the desert. Passing between Adan's tanks lining the road like an honor guard, Magen's force continued the rest of the way in darkness. At midnight, it reached the port of Adabiya at the northern end of the Gulf of Suez, headquarters of Egyptian naval forces in the gulf. The last road link to the thirty thousand men of the Third Army in Sinai was now severed. A major new strategic reality had been imposed on the Egyptian front, with far-reaching implications.

Meanwhile, on the northern front, the Syrian high command was preparing an attack this day—Tuesday, October 23—that was to be the most massive since the initial incursion into the Golan Heights. The Iraqi expeditionary force now numbered two divisions. These forces and the Jordanian brigade would be thrown into the battle together with all five Syrian divisions, which had been resuscitated with the arrival of hundreds of tanks from the Soviet Union. A brigade of Iraqi mountain troops normally stationed in Kurdistan had reached the front as well as smaller detachments from Saudi Arabia and Kuwait. Palestinian guerrilla units had also arrived. The Moroccan brigade which had been fighting alongside the Syrians since the beginning of the war was still in action.

According to the Syrian plan, the attack would begin with the landing of special forces, including Palestinian commandos, by helicopter behind the Israeli lines. The tank forces would then attack the Israeli enclave from two directions. The Arabs, by their own estimate, had a 5 to 1 advantage in tanks and artillery and a 4 to 1 advantage in infantry. Assad believed the counterattack would drive the Israelis from the enclave within two days. The plan envisaged a second stage in which the Golan would be recaptured as well. Israel was aware of the pending attack and braced for it. Its units had rested and refitted and were deployed along most of the line on dominant hills with TOW antitank missiles newly arrived in the American airlift.

The acceptance by Egypt of the cease-fire the day before created a major dilemma for Assad. The cease-fire did not bind Assad but its implications could not be ignored. Some on the Syrian General Staff favored going ahead with the attack, arguing that if it did so Egypt would feel obliged to continue fighting as well. Even if Egypt stopped fighting, it would take the Israelis several days to shift forces northward from Sinai. Others, however, argued that continuation of the war on the northern front would legitimize Israel's efforts to destroy the Egyptian Third Army. In that case, Egypt would not come to Syria's assistance when Israel turned its full might northward, destroying Syria's infrastructure and perhaps attacking Damascus.

In the end, Assad and his advisers decided that the risks outweighed the opportunities. Instead of the day beginning with a massive artillery barrage heralding the Arab counterattack, it passed quietly and ended with Syria's announcement of its acceptance of the cease-fire. The Iraqi government, which objected to a cease-fire, ordered its forces to return home immediately.

With the satisfaction due a man who had been instrumental in wrapping up the Middle East war, Henry Kissinger dropped off to sleep for four hours upon his return home from Moscow and Tel Aviv in the early hours of October 23. He arrived at his office in late morning to find that the cease-fire agreement had already started to unravel. A message from Hafez Ismail in Cairo informed him that Israel was occupying new positions in disregard of the cease-fire. Another message, from Ambassador Kenneth Keating in Tel Aviv, reported a troubling conversation with Mrs. Meir. The prime minister said that she had initially rejected a request from her military leaders for two or three days to finish off the Third Army. However, she added, the Egyptians had broken the cease-fire during the night in several places and she had therefore ordered the IDF to resume fighting until the Egyptians stopped shooting.

An alarmed message followed from Brezhnev. Soviet reconnaissance flights had confirmed that Israeli forces were moving south along the canal toward Suez City in what the Soviet leader called "flagrant deceit." Brezhnev wanted the Security Council swiftly convened in order to call on both sides to withdraw to the cease-fire lines. When Golda Meir came on the line a few minutes later, Kissinger suggested that the IDF simply pull its troops back a few hundred yards and announce that it had returned to the cease-fire line. "How can anyone ever know where a line is or was in the desert?" he asked.

"They'll know all right," replied Mrs. Meir.

Kissinger found out what she meant soon enough; the last road links between Suez and Cairo had been severed and the Third Army was trapped. The urgency of the situation was reinforced by still another message from Brezhnev, this one addressed to Nixon. Accusing Israel of "treachery," he asked for joint action to stop the fighting. Kissinger now realized that the Egyptians' plight must be more serious than the CIA, or the Israelis, had indicated. He informed the Soviets that the U.S. would support a Security Council resolution reconfirming the cease-fire. "We had no interest in seeing Sadat destroyed," he would write. "Even less so via the collapse of a cease-fire we had co-sponsored." Nor did Kissinger wish to lose a heaven-sent opportunity for the U.S. to elbow aside the Soviets in the Arab world.

In mid-afternoon, a message addressed to Nixon was received from Sadat himself, the first time since the Six Day War that an Egyptian leader had directly addressed the American administration. He asked for American intervention—even, if necessary, the use of force—to implement the cease-fire. After obtaining from Dinitz an Israeli pledge to observe a new cease-fire if Egypt did, Kissinger informed Brezhnev and Sadat of that in Nixon's name. With the president trapped in the mire of Watergate, Kissinger was signing Nixon's name to diplomatic notes almost as frequently as his own.

At 4 p.m. Tuesday in New York, the Security Council met to reconfirm the cease-fire and direct that U.N. observers be dispatched to the front. Two hours later, Dayan received a call from the head of the U.N. Emergency Force in Cairo, Gen. Ensio Siilasvuo. He had received instructions from New York, said the Finnish officer, to send observers to the front to delineate the cease-fire line. Siilasvuo accepted Dayan's suggestion that the new cease-fire take effect at 7 a.m., local time, that is, thirty-six hours after the initial cease-fire was to have gone into effect. Israel's interpretation of cease-fire, however, would continue to prove more flexible than everybody else's.

In the Pit that evening, Elazar mused aloud on the dilemma posed by the cease-fire. Militarily, Israel needed only a few more days in order to bring about the Third Army's surrender and cut off the Second Army as well, bringing about a total Egyptian military collapse. Politically, however, the debt to the U.S. was too great to ignore. Israel had already received in the past few days forty Phantoms and thirty-two Skyhawks, two-thirds the number of planes that had been lost since the beginning of the war. "That's why we accepted the cease-fire that the United States decided on," he said.

An hour after midnight Adan received from Uri Ben-Ari at Southern Command his operational orders for the following day, October 24. He was to complete mopping up the greenbelt, cut water pipes laid across the canal to the Third Army, and capture Suez City— "provided it doesn't become a Stalingrad," in Ben-Ari's words. Israel took the view that the attack would not violate the new cease-fire if it was launched before 7 a.m., even if the fighting continued after that hour. The Arabs had determined when the war would start and when to call for a cease-fire and the Israelis felt no qualms about adjusting the rules a bit now in their own favor. They also maintained that the cease-fire did not apply to "mopping up" since these operations were not altering the front line, only rear areas not in contention.

Adan requested information on the Egyptian military presence in Suez. Intelligence was aware of a commando battalion, two infantry battalions, and an antitank missile company in the city. These were enough forces to put up formidable resistance, particularly in a built-up area, but Adan thought it unlikely to happen. "We were just too tired to think clearly," his deputy, General Tamari, would say later.

During the previous two days, Egyptians had been surrendering in masses, including many officers. Adan believed that the fight had gone out of the Egyptian army and that resistance in the city would collapse with the first strong shove. It was an assumption he would have cause to deeply regret.

36

SUEZ CITY

L IKE A CAVALRY OFFICER impatiently tapping his leg with a riding crop, Col. Arye Keren urged paratroop commander Yossi Yoffe to move at "armor pace."

The two men were conferring on the western outskirts of Suez City where Keren had set up his command post. The tank brigade commander was in charge of the attack on the city. He informed Yoffe that his paratroop reservists would lead the way. He was to start immediately since they were already past the new cease-fire deadline of 7 a.m.

Yoffe protested. He had only one small map of the city that showed little detail. Nor had he seen air photos. He was being asked to drive straight up the main street of Suez in the nine captured Soviet APCs put at his disposal as if there would be no resistance. It was not clear to him on what that confidence was based. The battalion was being sent in blind, the way Mordecai's paratroopers had been at Tirtur Road.

Suez had been almost emptied of its 260,000 residents during the War of Attrition four years before. But enough residents remained to form a local militia which assisted the army in defending the city.

Pressed by Adan to finish the job before the international observers arrived, Keren had little patience with Yoffe's request to study the situation and draw up a plan. "In the armored corps," said the brigade commander, "we take our orders while we're on the move." Nevertheless, he gave Yoffe half an hour to organize his force. A tank battalion commanded by Lt. Col. Nahum Zaken would lead the attack instead, accompanied by its own infantry detachment. Yoffe would follow, dropping off platoons to secure major intersections.

In the battle for Jerusalem in the Six Day War, Yoffe's battalion had captured Ammunition Hill in a night action that was the turning point

Cease-fire Lines on the Egyptian Front

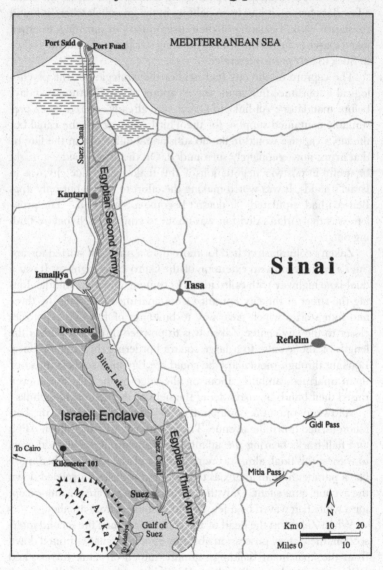

in the battle. In this war, it had broken the commando ambush on the road to Fort Budapest. Since being helicoptered across the canal a few days before, it had been fighting in the greenbelt where it found resistance weak. Learning of their assignment this morning, the men joked that they might save time by driving straight to the mayor's office in Suez to accept his surrender.

The capture of the city had neither the strategic nor the psychological importance that made the recapture of the Hermon two days before mandatory. All links to Cairo were already severed. Suez presumably contained supplies for the Third Army across the canal but the city's capture would make no substantial difference in the fate of that army, now completely surrounded. On the positive side, it might be useful in postwar negotiations if this major canal-side city was in Israel's hands. It was worth making the effort to take it but only if, as Ben-Ari had stipulated, "it doesn't become a Stalingrad." The problem was that Adan's division was about to commit itself before finding out.

Zaken's column stretched for more than a mile as it started toward Suez's main avenue, an extension of the Cairo–Suez highway. It was a dual-lane highway with railroad tracks running down the middle. Lining the street at the city entrance were apartment buildings of three and four stories which gave way to buildings of five and six stories closer to the city center. Zaken was to proceed three miles down the length of the avenue to a large square bordering the Gulf of Suez. Looking through binoculars, he could see Egyptian soldiers, most of them unarmed, ambling about on the edge of the city. Some even raised their hands in surrender at the sight of the approaching tanks.

All twenty-one tank commanders stood in their turrets as the battalion turned down the avenue. The commanders of the fifteen APCs and half-tracks bearing the infantry detachment likewise stood erect to witness this final, almost ceremonial, act of the war. It looked more like a parade than an attack as the armored vehicles proceeded down the avenue, guns silent. Only the crowds and flags were missing except for a white flag waved by a few Egyptian soldiers from an alley.

When Zaken, at the head of the column, reached the second intersection, the victory procession abruptly ended. Grenades rained down from the apartment buildings, gunfire rattled off tank turrets, and RPGs were fired from the alleys. Within seconds, almost all the tank and infantry commanders were hit. Zaken was unhurt. But looking back down the avenue, it seemed that his entire battalion had been wiped out at one blow. Not a single head protruded from the turrets and there was no reply when he tried to reach his company commanders on the radio. Zaken called to crewmen. "Whoever is still alive, enter the commander's compartment and answer." Voices of gunners and loaders began to be heard. They named commanders who had been killed or wounded. Zaken could hear panic in their voices. "Keep moving," he shouted over the din. "Fire all weapons. Get out of the ambush. Keep moving forward."

Maneuvering around two tanks which had been set afire, the rest of the battalion made it to the square at the end of the avenue. They deployed with their backs to the gulf and their guns facing the surrounding buildings and alleys. The lead company commander, Capt. Menashe Goldblatt, had lost consciousness after being hit in the shoulder. He recovered now and at Zaken's request made his way on foot from tank to tank to talk to the crews. He found many in shock, with their commanders, and sometimes other crewmen, lying inside the tank wounded or dead. Goldblatt appointed gunners or loaders as tank commanders, assigned them sectors of fire, and directed them to switch their radios from their company frequencies to the battalion frequency so that Zaken could talk directly to them. With fire sweeping the square and no one else afoot in it, Goldblatt moved carefully, trying to keep tanks between him and the enemy.

He found one tank commander who had not been wounded but was afraid to lift his head out of the turret. When persuasion failed, Goldblatt warned him that if he did not begin to function he, Goldblatt, would fire a shell at his tank. As he moved off, he turned and saw the sergeant's head rising slightly above the turret. The captain, who would make several rounds on foot during the day, well understood the men's fear. For months after the war he himself would be unable to sleep except in his tank because of the vulnerability he felt outside it.

Zaken organized the transfer of casualties to an APC which sped back up the main street. The Egyptians were taken by surprise and the vehicle made it out of the city unharmed. After depositing the casualties at an aid station, the crew members decided to run the gauntlet again and rejoin the battalion. They made it halfway back before the vehicle was hit by an RPG. One soldier was killed and almost everyone else wounded, but the driver managed to turn the vehicle and make it back to the city's outskirts. When a second APC with dead and wounded tried to leave the square it was turned back by heavy fire. Its commander, however, heard a report on the radio net that offered a measure of encouragement: "Red boots entering the area." The paratroopers were moving in.

Fire hit the paratroopers' column as soon as it started down the avenue. Yoffe ordered his APC to halt alongside the two burning tanks but found that their crews had already been evacuated. The Egyptian fire was too intense for the APCs to continue. An RPG hit Yoffe's vehicle, killing four men and wounding the others, including the battalion commander himself. The vehicles pulled to the side of the street and the paratroopers took cover in adjacent buildings. Most converged on a two-story structure which turned out to be a police station. Two policemen were killed in an exchange of fire as the paratroopers burst in but the rest were permitted to leave.

Fifty of the paratroopers congregated in the station. There were many wounded. Lt. David Amit, the ranking unwounded officer, organized the defenses. Men posted at windows and behind a low stone wall outside blocked attempts to storm the building. Egyptians penetrated a side entrance and reached a room being used as an aid station. The battalion doctor, Maj. Gabi Canaan, rose up from tending the wounded and opened fire on them with his Uzi. Medics joined in the fight.

Yoffe, whose leg had been badly ripped, refused morphine in order to remain alert. At one point, enemy fire suddenly ceased. He listened to the silence for a moment and said, "They're preparing to attack." A hail of RPGs and grenades struck the building, setting a fire on the second floor. Yoffe told Dr. Canaan, "It's time to burn the documents." He was referring to maps and papers that might be useful to Egyptian intelligence. The men, however, repulsed the attack and doused the fire. Yoffe had lost much blood and periodically lost consciousness. During his intervals of wakefulness, Lieutenant Amit consulted with him.

The paratroopers believed that armored forces would break through to rescue them before long. Several attempts were indeed made. As one force of tanks and APCs approached, the trapped paratroopers threw furniture out the window to signal their location. But the vehicles were traveling with closed hatches and sped by. The rescue detachment, however, spotted a second paratroop force commanded by Lt. Col. Ya'acov Hisdai, which had entered behind Yoffe's battalion. Hisdai's force consisted of eighty men, most of them by now wounded. The rescuers succeeded in taking aboard all the wounded but six. Enemy fire curtailed further rescue efforts.

As night approached, Adan ordered armored forces out of the city. They were too vulnerable in the darkness to RPG teams. The evacuation route was a back road along the Gulf of Suez shore which had been cleared of enemy troops. Zaken's battalion, which suffered eighteen dead and thirty-five wounded, left three disabled tanks behind.

The two paratroop forces—Yoffe's and Hisdai's—were the only Israelis remaining in the city. Adan wanted them to make their way out on foot rather than risk armor in a rescue attempt. Communicating with Keren in the Hebrew equivalent of pig latin to foil Egyptian eavesdroppers, Hisdai asked to have tank projectors beam their lights skyward to provide orientation. He himself scouted the route before returning to lead his men out, including the six remaining wounded. As they approached the Israeli lines, Hisdai led a full-throated rendition of the Hebrew song "Hevainu Shalom Aleichem" ("We've brought peace unto you") to identify themselves.

For Yoffe's men, evacuation was more complex since they were twice as deep inside the city—more than two miles. After dark, the group in the police station was joined by other paratroopers who had been sheltering in nearby buildings. There were now ninety men, of whom twenty-three were wounded. With darkness, soldiers dashed out several times to the stranded vehicles to bring in ammunition, medical supplies, and a jerrican of water.

Even though shooting had ceased, the men were reluctant to leave the security of the building. Colonel Keren tried to persuade Amit to lead them out, but the lieutenant said he preferred to wait for armor to reach them in the morning rather than proceed on foot past buildings filled with enemy troops. He finally succumbed to Keren's increasingly insistent demand, saying he would send the men out in small groups. Keren ruled that out. They must leave in one large group, the brigade commander said, capable both of supporting the wounded and defending itself if attacked. Keren passed the microphone to Hisdai, who encouraged Amit to do it.

At this point, General Gonen, who was closely following the imbroglio on the radio net, spoke to Amit directly. When the lieutenant explained his reluctance to move out on foot, Gonen told Colonel

Keren to attempt an armored rescue in the morning. Exasperated, Keren called Adan to complain that Gonen had spoiled it all after Amit had been persuaded to leave on foot. The division commander called Gonen and explained that a rescue attempt would be too costly. Gonen called Amit back and said it would be best after all to leave on foot.

"Do you have a paper and pencil?" asked the general. Looking at an enlarged air photo of Suez, he proceeded to dictate to Amit the route he should follow out of the city. "Two hundred meters south to the third block of buildings from the corner, then 200 meters west along the alley, then, before the end of the street there's an alley and you go on it 200 meters north, afterwards 250 meters west through a bunch of huts, turn north towards the railroad track, northwest 700 meters you reach a bridge on the [Sweetwater] canal, then you pass a cemetery, then 1,400 meters northwest you reach a crossroad held by our forces. What you have to decide is whether you want artillery or not."

Amit, sitting on the floor of the darkened police building with a flashlight, had stopped writing halfway through. What Gonen was proposing would have been difficult enough to follow with a good map by day but he had no map and it was night. Furthermore, the proposed route would take them through an area south of their location that Amit knew to be dense with Egyptian troops. He accommodated Gonen by muttering "Yes, sir" periodically but he had no intention of heeding his advice. He would later be told by a sergeant at Umm Hashiba who was with Gonen at the time that the general seemed to see his direct involvement in the rescue as personal vindication for his maladroit performance at the beginning of the war. Amit asked Gonen for an artillery bombardment around the police station to clear the immediate area for their departure but said he preferred to move through the city quietly. He organized the men into squads, each responsible for three wounded men. The squads were to keep distance between each other, so as not to constitute a suspiciously large grouping, but not to lose eye contact. The men gathered outside the building and awaited the order to start. However, lookouts reported activity in the buildings around them and said that Egyptian soldiers had set up positions down the street. Amit ordered everyone back inside.

The situation looked hopeless. It was becoming apparent that no rescue attempt would be made, even by day. After the casualties they had inflicted on the Egyptians, the paratroopers did not think prisoners would be taken. Some of the men determined to finish themselves off with a grenade or bullet at the last minute if the Egyptians broke in. When Dr. Canaan responded "I'll tell you tomorrow" to a question put to him by a soldier, the soldier said, "Gabi, there won't be tomorrow." The doctor mustered a smile and said: "You've fought well until now and you'll have the privilege of fighting in many more wars. This story isn't over."

At 2 a.m. Keren cut through the deliberations. Raising Amit on the radio, he said, "Move out. Report implementation [of the order] in ten minutes. Out." This was what the lieutenant needed—not a suggestion but an unambiguous order. At this point, Yoffe woke and Amit consulted with him. The battalion commander agreed it was best to leave on foot rather than await the dubious prospect of rescue. As his men watched, the colonel struggled to his feet for the first time since being carried into the building in the morning and took a few tentative steps. "I can walk," he announced. In a scene resembling a mass resurrection, other wounded men, including some in even worse condition than Yoffe, began to rise and hobble about to test their limbs.

Amit ordered the men again to move out. Just two of the wounded had to be carried on stretchers. The remainder walked, some of them supported by comrades. With an artillery barrage keeping down the heads of Egyptians in the vicinity, the column set out behind a point squad unencumbered by wounded. Instead of heading south, as Gonen had suggested, the men moved north across the broad avenue and then turned left to follow narrow side streets paralleling it. Broken glass and other debris made it impossible to walk quietly. Cigarettes glowing in the dark revealed the presence of men in surrounding buildings. Several times, Egyptian soldiers passed close, sometimes even emerging from side streets and cutting through gaps in the column. The Egyptians did not challenge the Israelis, either believing they were Egyptian or preferring not to know.

After an excruciating passage lasting almost two hours, the men reached the Sweetwater Canal. They walked along its inner face toward a vehicular bridge marked on the map, ready to fight their way across. A few score yards before the bridge, they came on a railroad bridge not indicated on the map. They could hear the voices of Egyptian soldiers guarding the vehicular bridge beyond. But the railroad bridge was unguarded. The paratroopers made their way across it without incident. The Egyptians at the vehicular bridge may well have seen the column, which included men shuffling from their wounds. But if so they chose not to become entangled in a firefight with the war as good as over. Just before dawn, the paratroopers reached Keren's tank force awaiting them on the outskirts of the city.

The price paid by the IDF for the Suez misadventure was heavy— 80 dead and 120 wounded. The last major action of the Yom Kippur War was over. But the final shots had not yet been fired.

Although all roads to Suez had been cut, Israeli forces had still not established a presence in a six-mile stretch along the Suez Canal north of the city. At first light on October 25, just after Yoffe's men reached safety, Major Brik and his five remaining tanks were dispatched south through the agricultural strip to close this gap. The company commander was told not to fire unless fired upon. The second cease-fire was officially in effect but the Israeli command was not interpreting it to mean cease-movement. At the rear of Brik's tanks, was an APC with a squad of paratroopers. Halfway, the commander of the lead tank reported Egyptian tanks amidst trees to the front. A moment later, a shell hit Brik's tank, the second in line, destroying the machine gun and antenna alongside his head but causing him only a face cut. "Move left," he shouted to his driver, but there was no response. "He's dead," called the loader. (The driver, the last Israeli fatality in the war, was the son of a future Israeli Supreme Court justice.) Brik and the other two surviving crewmen leaped from the tank before it could be hit again. Meanwhile, the paratroopers raced through the shrubbery toward the Egyptian tanks. They found them with hatches open and tossed grenades inside. But they had been abandoned by their crews. Brik shifted to another tank, his seventh since the war started, and led the column on to the outskirts of Suez.

On the first morning of the war, Brik, a future general, had barely escaped when an RPG brushed his shirt and set it afire during the commando ambush near Baluza—the first Sinai fight involving reservists. He had survived the charge of Assaf Yaguri's battalion on October 8, initiated the improvised defense line that stopped the subsequent Egyptian attack, and participated in the ambush of the Twenty-fifth Brigade and in many other clashes. He had now barely escaped again in the very last skirmish of the war. Of the 120 men of the battalion who had started out on Yom Kippur, only seven were still in action, including Brik and his gunner. Of the original battalion members and their replacements, 80 had been killed and close to 100 wounded—a casualty rate of 150 percent.

The resumption of fighting in the Third Army sector raised the possibility that it might spread to the Second Army sector as well. Paratroop forces, including Mordecai's battalion, prepared to renew the drive on Ismailiya by capturing bridges across the Sweetwater Canal. Stiff resistance was expected. The units were moving to their start positions when the attack was called off.

Mordecai ordered his units to make an immediate U-turn in order to avoid accidental clashes. As the young paratroopers turned back, the tension in their faces melted into grins. Men slapped each other on the shoulder. Some had tears in their eyes. "We made it," said one.

The war was over.

Despite the disastrous opening of the war for Israel, it held more territory at the end than at the beginning—more territory, indeed, than it had ever held. The Egyptians had captured 1,200 square kilometers in Sinai but the IDF held 1,600 square kilometers west of the canal. The IDF was now within 50 miles of Cairo, 12 miles closer than before. In the north, it had captured 500 square kilometers beyond the former Golan cease-fire line and was likewise 12 miles closer to Damascus.

But even before the Arabs and Israelis could begin debating who won the war and who would pay the price, the superpowers had begun mustering their own armed forces in a menacing confrontation.

37

NUCLEAR ALERT

BELIEVING THE WAR already behind him, Chairman Brezhnev was looking forward on the afternoon of October 24 to the festive opening in the Kremlin the following day of the World Congress of Peace Forces, a prestigious conclave in which he would have the kind of starring role he relished. A team of speechwriters submitted drafts of his keynote speech for review and he conferred with colleagues about resolutions to be adopted. Late in the day, an annoyingly dissonant note was sounded in a message from Ambassador Vinogradov in Cairo. The Israelis were ignoring the cease-fire, Vinogradov reported, and the Egyptian Third Army was cut off. The Egyptians feared that the Israelis were about to descend on Cairo. Militiamen had been mobilized and the population was called upon to resist any incursion.

Brezhnev wondered aloud whether Kissinger had made some kind of deal during his stopover in Tel Aviv, a concern that mirrored Mrs. Meir's fear that Kissinger had made a deal at Israel's expense in Moscow. Reinforcing Vinogradov's report was a message from Sadat asking for Soviet observers or troops to be sent this very night. Sadat said he was asking the same of the Americans.

The Politburo would agree to send fifty observers but the request for troops stirred little enthusiasm. To become embroiled in a military adventure in which the U.S. stood with the opposite camp was not in Moscow's interest. Chief of Staff Kulikov said that by the time Soviet forces had been organized and flown to Egypt, Cairo would have fallen. Nevertheless, there was a consensus that something meaningful had to be done to help Sadat, and quickly. According to Kremlin chronicler Victor Israelyan, it was decided to hint to the Americans that the Soviets might intervene unilaterally, in the hope that this would make the Americans worried enough to pressure their Israeli clients. In other words, to bluff.

A message from Brezhnev to Nixon was composed in the chairman's study after midnight. It called for American and Soviet contingents to be dispatched to the Middle East to ensure implementation of the cease-fire. Then came the trumpet blast. "I will say it straight that if you find it impossible to act jointly with us in this matter, we should be faced with the necessity urgently to consider taking appropriate steps unilaterally. We cannot allow arbitrariness on the part of Israel." If Brezhnev intended to catch Kissinger's attention, he succeeded.

Kissinger had spent the day trying to placate Sadat and the Soviets by assuring them that he was exerting maximum pressure on the Israelis. He was indeed in constant contact with Dinitz, who relayed unconvincing messages from Tel Aviv claiming that it was the Egyptians who were attacking. Kissinger expressed indignation at Israel's violation of the cease-fire.

In Tel Aviv, Elazar was summoned urgently to Mrs. Meir's office. He found her and her senior advisers agitated. Calls were coming in to Dinitz from the White House "every five minutes" to complain of the Israeli actions, he was told. Dinitz had been warned in Nixon's name by Haig that if the fighting did not stop immediately the president might "disassociate himself" from Israel. Furthermore, Sadat had asked for superpower intervention and there were indications that the Soviets were planning to comply. The chief of staff, still unaware of the extent of the snafu in Suez, called Gonen to pass on the order. "They're shouting in Washington and howling in New York," he said. However, when Gonen requested air support at two points near the Cairo–Suez road where Egyptian tank forces were trying to break through to the Third Army, Elazar gave his approval.

In Washington, Kissinger rejected Cairo's bid for the dispatch of U.S. and Soviet forces to the region. "We had not worked for years to reduce the Soviet military presence in Egypt," he would subsequently write, "only to cooperate in reintroducing it. . . . We were determined to resist by force if necessary the introduction of Soviet troops into the Middle East." At 9:35 p.m. he took a call from Ambassador Dobrynin, who said he had received a letter for Nixon from Brezhnev so urgent that he would read it on the phone before sending it over. When Kissinger heard that the Soviets were considering "taking appropriate steps unilaterally," he understood that a major crisis was at hand.

A superpower confrontation was for presidents to manage, not cabinet secretaries, talented though they might be. And Nixon was superb at handling international crises. But it was all the president could do now to hold himself together as the final humiliation of Watergate closed in. In a conversation with Nixon earlier in the evening, Kissinger had found him agitated and talking about the desire of his political enemies not just for his ouster but for his physical demise. By the time Brezhnev's letter arrived, the president had gone to bed. When Kissinger asked Haig whether he should be wakened, the White House chief of staff replied firmly, "No." Haig shared Kissinger's feeling that Nixon was in no condition to make weighty decisions.

But decisions had to be made. Kissinger called for an immediate meeting of the senior officials who had been monitoring the Middle East crisis with him since its outbreak. They included Defense Secretary Schlesinger, CIA director Colby, chairman of the Joint Chiefs of Staff Adm. Thomas Moorer, presidential assistant Gen. Brent Scowcroft, and Haig. At Haig's suggestion, the meeting was held in the White House with Kissinger presiding. It got under way at 10:40 p.m. in the Situation Room in the basement of the West Wing. What followed would be described by Kissinger as "one of the more thoughtful discussions that I attended in my government service."

The forum took the Soviet threat seriously. The CIA reported that the Soviet arms airlift had unexpectedly stopped early that morning. This could mean that the planes were being reconfigured to carry troops. Airborne divisions were known to have been put on heightened alert status and the Soviet Mediterranean fleet had been reinforced to unprecedented size.

The forum decided to formulate a conciliatory-sounding reply to Brezhnev's letter aimed at drawing the Soviets into talks. At the same time, America's determination not to be stampeded would be signaled by increasing the state of alert in the armed forces from DefCon (Defense Condition) 4 to DefCon 3, the highest state of readiness in peacetime. At 11:41 p.m., Admiral Moorer issued orders to that effect. Kissinger left the meeting several times during the night to confer with Dinitz in the empty lobby of the West Wing. The Israeli ambassador was asked to keep the Israeli government abreast of developments and to report back its reactions. Informing Dinitz of the heightened alert status, Kissinger said it would have a greater impact if Soviet intelligence detected it on its own before a U.S. announcement.

At 11:55 the forum approved a message to Sadat in Nixon's name intended to cut the legs out from under the Soviet threat by persuading Egypt to drop its request for Soviet intervention. The U.S., warned the message, would challenge any Soviet force that appeared in the area. "I ask you to consider the consequences for your country if the two great nuclear countries were thus to confront each other on your soil."

During the meeting, it was learned that eight giant Soviet transports were due to fly from Budapest to Cairo within the next few hours to evacuate Soviet families which had not left during the prewar evacuation. In addition, elements of the East German armed forces were being put on alert. At 12:20 a.m. the forum decided to alert the Eighty-second Airborne Division for possible movement. Five minutes later, orders went out for a carrier task force in the Atlantic to join the two others already positioned in the Mediterranean. At 1:45 a.m., the commander of American forces in Europe was told to delay the scheduled return to the U.S. of troops participating in a NATO exercise. At 3:30 a.m., the Joint Chiefs ordered the Strategic Air Command to have its Guam-based B-52s, capable of carrying nuclear bombs, repositioned to the U.S. It was decided not to deliver the reply to Brezhnev until 5:30 a.m. so as to give Soviet intelligence time to pick up the readiness measures and time for the American military to begin implementing them.

Conferring with Dinitz during a break, Kissinger asked how long it would take Israel to destroy the Third Army if there was a showdown. The suggestion that the U.S. might tolerate, even encourage, such a move astonished Mrs. Meir and her cabinet, which had assembled to receive Dinitz's reports. According to Dinitz, the Americans estimated that if the Soviets intervened, they could fly 4,500 soldiers a day to Cairo. In four or five days, when sufficient troops would have been assembled, the force was expected to begin moving toward the front. Kissinger wanted to know if Israel could destroy the Third Army before then. The Israelis were certain they could, since the besieged army no longer had air defenses. Kissinger suggested that the attack not be launched the day the Soviets began to arrive in Cairo but the day after so that it was clear to all which action came first.

Kissinger said he expected Soviet troops to begin landing in Cairo in two days. The Israeli envoy expressed doubt that the Soviets would intervene, noting that since the Second World War Soviet troops had never fought in countries which did not border their own. There's always a first time, said Kissinger. Nevertheless, he asked for Israel's intelligence assessment regarding Soviet intervention. When General Scowcroft, who was party to the conversation, said that Israel had placed Egypt in an impossible position by trapping the Third Army, Dinitz replied that one side or the other had to be in that position. Now that it was Egypt, Israel had negotiating clout. Kissinger nodded. In Tel Aviv, Mossad chief Zamir reported to Mrs. Meir that there was no sign from his sources that the Soviets were intending to send troops to the Middle East.

Close to midnight Israeli time Dayan called Bar-Lev at Southern Command and was told that all was quiet except in one corner of Suez. Bar-Lev was referring to Yossi Yoffe's trapped battalion. Egyptian pressure on the Cairo–Suez road had ceased and there was no shooting elsewhere at this hour.

It was the first quiet night since cantors had chanted Kol Nidre on Yom Kippur eve nineteen days before. Bar-Lev asked if Dayan could come south in the morning to talk to the division commanders about the political implications of the cease-fire. Dayan agreed but said he might be delayed. "I can't leave Tel Aviv before Golda goes to sleep and she doesn't go to sleep before Kissinger does."

Kissinger was already in bed when a messenger arrived at the Soviet embassy at 5:40 a.m. Washington time to deliver the reply to Brezhnev's note. Composed in Nixon's name, it said the U.S. would not tolerate unilateral action. It expressed hope, however, for cooperation and accepted the idea of a U.N. truce supervisory force. The message was soft-voiced. The big stick was left dangling behind Washington's back for the Soviets to discover.

Aboard his flagship, the USS *Little Rock*, Adm. Daniel Murphy, commander of the U.S. Sixth Fleet, was showering when an aide knocked on his cabin door shortly before 6 a.m. to inform him of the Def-Con 3 alert. The message added that the carrier *John F. Kennedy* had been ordered through the Gibraltar Strait to join the two carrier task forces already under Murphy's command in the Mediterranean. The *Franklin D. Roosevelt*, which had been maintaining a discreet distance with its escorts in the western Mediterranean, would now join up with the *Independence* task force south of Crete. Transport ships bearing two thousand marines, anchored in Suda Bay on the northern side of Crete, were to join the carrier fleet south of the island, closer to the war zone.

For more than two weeks, the Sixth Fleet had been playing tag with the Soviet Mediterranean squadron as each positioned itself for possible intervention in the Israel-Arab conflict while keeping an eye on the other. Murphy's fleet had increased from fifty vessels to sixty. Lookouts monitoring ship movements through the Dardanelles reported many surface ships and submarines streaming south; the Soviet squadron's strength had increased from fifty-seven ships to ninety-seven since Yom Kippur. This included sixteen submarines as well as landing craft for several thousand marines with the Soviet fleet. As the *Kennedy* sailed in from the Atlantic, it was picked up by a Soviet submarine shadow.

The American rules of engagement in this naval face-off, the most massive ever between the superpowers, left it to Murphy's discretion to strike if he determined a Soviet attack imminent and there was no time to consult with Washington. Murphy calculated that if the Soviet fleet attacked first, it could get off forty sea-to-sea missiles and 250 torpedoes. If it came to it, however, he was confident that information provided by naval intelligence would enable him to fire the first shots. Murphy reckoned that there was a 40 percent chance of the Soviets attacking. If hostilities commenced, it was his intention, he would say in an interview years later, to hunt down and destroy every Soviet warship in the Mediterranean, above and below the surface.

Electronic monitors detected Soviet missile systems constantly tracking the American carriers. Murphy kept the *Roosevelt* and *Independence* seventy-five to a hundred miles apart, close enough for their planes to provide mutual support but far enough to determine which one was being painted by Soviet radar. The Americans kept constant air patrol over the Soviet ships. The Soviet fleet, lacking a naval air arm, shadowed the American vessels with submarines and with destroyers, dubbed "tattletales." Soviet admirals, who had not in the past participated in these close encounters, could now be seen on the bridges of the tattletales, indicating the seriousness with which the Soviets were taking the game. The admirals did not attempt to hide their signs of rank. Murphy and his commanders reviewed standing orders for the evacuation of American citizens in the region in an emergency. Of the 60,000 Americans estimated to be in the belligerent countries, 45,000 were in Israel. The marines would play a role in any evacuation.

The closest approach by the Sixth Fleet to the war zone was the positioning of a destroyer off Cyprus, the last in a string of picket vessels down the length of the Mediterranean aiding navigation for planes participating in the airlift to Israel.

Within hours of the DefCon 3 alert, Murphy was informed of a change in the deployment of the Soviet fleet. The destroyer tattletales had been joined by first-line missile-carrying warships. Washington's alert had been picked up.

At the regularly scheduled meeting of the Politburo this morning, the American alert displaced all items on the agenda. Brezhnev expressed astonishment at the move and rejected a suggestion that it might be connected to his message to Nixon. "What has this to do with the letter I sent to Nixon?" he asked. Podgorny believed it did. "Who could have imagined the Americans would be so easily frightened?" he asked. Marshal Grechko said the Americans had no right under the 1972 Treaty for the Prevention of Nuclear War to alert its nuclear forces. However, none of the Soviet leaders saw a casus belli. "It is not reasonable to become engaged in a war with the United States because of Egypt and Syria," said Kosygin. KGB chief Yuri Andropov echoed that thought. "We shall not unleash the Third World War."

The Kremlin decided to increase military readiness but, except for Marshal Grechko, there was no support for sending troops to the Middle East. Instead, the Soviet leaders reconciled themselves to an Arab defeat. Brezhnev predicted the imminent fall of Ismailiya. "We must tell Sadat that we were right [about the inadvisability of Egypt going to war], that we sympathize with Egypt but we can't reverse the course of military operations." This sentiment was echoed by Andropov. "We tried to hold the Arabs back from starting military operations, but they didn't listen. Sadat expelled our military advisers, but when the Arabs started the fighting we supported them." Brezhnev expressed concern about the possibility of anti-Soviet demonstrations in Cairo.

The meeting was still in session when the reply to Brezhnev's letter formulated in Nixon's name arrived. Its conciliatory tone struck a responsive chord. Brezhnev seized on the message's call for the two powers to act jointly for peace in the Middle East. "That's exactly what we are trying to do," he cried. The Soviet leaders took heart from the statement that the American government was pressing the Israelis to ensure full compliance with the U.N. resolutions. This, Brezhnev said, was all he had been after.

Then came the key paragraph. "We must view your suggestion of unilateral action as a matter of the gravest concern involving incalculable consequences. It is clear that the forces necessary to impose the cease-fire terms on the two sides would be massive and would require closest coordination to avoid bloodshed. This is not only clearly infeasible but it is not appropriate to the situation."

Defense Minister Grechko responded first. "Why is it infeasible? A gesture of Soviet-American joint action would have led to an immediate halt to the fighting. Is it not clear? The Americans want to impose their own scenario."

Brezhnev also expressed indignation. "We only said that if the Americans don't agree to act jointly we would have to *consider* taking steps unilaterally. And now, after having unilaterally declared a nuclear alert, they dare to criticize us. Something is wrong with the American logic." There was bewilderment at the absence of any explanation for the nuclear alert, which was not alluded to in the American message.

It was Brezhnev who came up with the most constructive response to the American move—no response at all. "Nixon is too nervous," he said. "Let him cool down." A conciliatory message was drafted, reaffirming Moscow's objective of bringing an end to the war through joint Soviet-American action and noting that Nixon's agreement for the dispatch of observers obviated the need for unilateral Soviet action.

In Washington, the issue had been defused even before receipt of the new Brezhnev message. Returning to his office at 8 a.m., Kissinger found a message from Hafez Ismail saying that Egypt was dropping its request for Soviet troops in view of the American opposition and would ask the U.N. instead for an international force. Since U.N. rules excluded the superpowers from such peacekeeping missions, there would be no Soviet troops.

Nixon woke to discover that while he had been sleeping a global alert had gone out over his name. When briefed by Kissinger and Haig, he expressed elation at the way events had played themselves out. The crisis, it seemed, was over. Almost forgotten in the sense of relief wafting over both Washington and Moscow was that an army of thirty thousand men was trapped in the Sinai desert and that Israel had cut off its water supply.

For Israel, the encirclement of the Third Army was psychological nourishment of the kind it had been desperately seeking since Yom Kippur, a reaffirmation of strength after the severest testing in its history. The Israeli cabinet decided Wednesday night to offer passage for the men of the Third Army through the Israeli lines without their weapons. Officers, however, were to be held as prisoners of war until exchanged, together with the other 8,300 Egyptian POWs being held by Israel, for 230 Israeli POWs in Egyptian hands, mostly from the Bar-Lev Line. An alternative proposal put to Kissinger was for both sides to pull back across the canal to their prewar lines. Kissinger said the withdrawal of the Third Army from Sinai would not be acceptable to Sadat. He proposed instead that the Israelis permit food, water, and medicines to reach the beleaguered force while maintaining its encirclement. That way the Third Army would remain Israel's hostage for future bargaining but would not be forced into a humiliating surrender.

There was little sympathy in Israel for that idea. Attempts on Friday by the Egyptians to break out of the pocket and to put a bridge across the canal at Suez City were exploited by Israel to shell and bomb priority targets like command posts and water reserves. American officials reacted angrily. "I hope it's clear to you that you're playing with a superpower confrontation," a Defense Department official said to the Israeli military attaché, General Gur. Kissinger told Dinitz "as a friend" that Israel was playing a dangerous game.

Although Kissinger pressed Israel not to destroy the Third Army, its entrapment was a gift to American diplomacy. It made Sadat totally dependent on the U.S. if he wished to prevent the army's annihilation. Kissinger told Dinitz that Washington would not countenance the Third Army's destruction. Nixon saw the survival of the Third Army as both an American obligation and the key to luring Egypt from the embrace of the Soviet Union.

Beyond that, the Third Army had become the delicate fulcrum of the endgame that Kissinger was attempting to contrive, one in which Egyptian honor would be restored and Israeli deterrence reasserted. He had pushed Israel during the war to strike hard—harder, in fact, than it had initially been able to—in order to demonstrate its military superiority. But once the Israelis had begun smiting the Egyptians, he worked toward a speedy cease-fire that would leave the Egyptians with their dignity intact. Israel, in short, was to emerge quasi-victorious, not triumphant.

The Defense Department proposed that American planes parachute supplies to the beleaguered force. Kissinger preferred to win Israel's acquiescence to supplies passing through its lines and thus possibly open a door to a dialogue between Israel and Egypt. However, Israel was fixated on evening the score with Egypt. Not even the normally farsighted Dayan was ready to see the linkage between the Third Army's fate and the possibilities of peace.

Mrs. Meir took her time—half a day—before responding to Kissinger's urgent call for immediate lifting of the siege. Instead of acquiescing, she suggested that Egyptian and Israeli representatives meet face-to-face to discuss the fate of the Third Army and of the POWs. The Egyptians, she said, could fix the place, the time, and the rank of the representatives. Kissinger saw this as a further stall—no one could expect the Egyptians to agree to direct talks with Israel at this early a stage—but he passed the offer on to Hafez Ismail.

Meanwhile, two developments threatened to undo the delicate web being woven by Kissinger. Nixon, in a desperate bid to shore up his image, called a press conference to describe how he had sure-handedly managed the crisis which touched off the American alert—the crisis he had in fact slept through. Referring to Brezhnev's threat of unilateral Soviet intervention, he said, "Rather than saying that his note to me was rough and brutal, I would say it was very firm and it left very little to the imagination as to what he intended. My response was also very firm and left little to the imagination of how we would react." Brezhnev, said Nixon, understood American power and understood Nixon. He, Nixon, had after all been the president—continued Nixon—who bombed North Vietnam against all expectations. Kissinger winced as he listened, fearful that Brezhnev would feel called upon to prove his manhood by replying in kind. Haig warned Kissinger not to express his reservations to the president. "He's right on the verge," he said.

The second development was another message from Brezhnev. It did not echo Nixon's swaggering tone and was much milder than Brezhnev's "unilateral action" note two days before. But it expressed deep concern about the Third Army and asked for an American response within a few hours. Brezhnev, having learned his lesson, did not threaten consequences, a restraint that did not imply impotence.

It was time, Kissinger decided, to come down on the Israelis. Calling Dinitz at 11 p.m., he said he was passing on a message from the president. Firstly, the destruction of the Third Army "is an option that does not exist." Secondly, the president wanted an answer by 8 a.m. the next morning, Saturday, October 27, as to whether Israel would permit nonmilitary supplies to reach the trapped force. If the reply was negative, the U.S. would regretfully support the U.N. demand for an Israeli pullback to the October 22 lines. This would open the supply routes to the Third Army and in the process significantly worsen Israel's tactical deployment.

In Tel Aviv, Dayan had been telling Elazar and Mrs. Meir that permitting supplies through was the worst of all options since it would keep the Third Army intact as a viable fighting force. This would leave Adan's and Magen's divisions hung up between the Third Army in Sinai to their east—which still had bridges capable of carrying it back across the canal—and a new army forming on their western flank, toward Cairo. The preferable option would be to hammer the Third Army into submission. The next best option was to let it pull back, leaving behind its weapons. If it came to it, however, Dayan was prepared to let the army take its weapons, as long as it abandoned Sinai. All these thoughts were rendered irrelevant when word was received from Dinitz of Kissinger's ultimatum delivered in Nixon's name.

Reflecting on the war to date, Dayan told the cabinet that the Arabs had surprised him by their steadfastness. "They didn't run, not even when they were defeated in a battle." The minister said the Israeli troops had been superb. They had fought wisely and with determination but too boldly. "It's a wonderful thing and a terrible thing. We have to slow down and think what we're fighting about. When I'm on the other side of the canal I am constantly thinking, 'What are we doing here? This isn't the Western Wall.'" Recalling the Australian cavalrymen lost in the battle for Gaza in the First World War, he said, "We generally understand these things a generation later. We should not be shedding blood unless it's necessary."

Five hours before Kissinger's ultimatum expired, a message arrived in Washington from Hafez Ismail saying that Egypt accepted Israel's offer of direct talks. Kissinger was flabbergasted. "You're from a land of miracles," he told Dinitz. The meeting point set by Cairo was Kilometer 101 on the desert road between Cairo and Suez. The Egyptians designated General Gamasy as their representative and stipulated two preconditions for the meeting—a complete cease-fire and the passage of a convoy bearing nonmilitary supplies to the Third Army.

Mrs. Meir accepted both conditions and designated General Yariv as Israel's representative. The meeting was scheduled for 3 p.m. Saturday. However, General Gamasy and his party were held up ten miles farther west on the Cairo–Suez road by Israeli troops who had not received word of the meeting. It was 1:30 a.m., Sunday, October 28, when the generals finally shook hands in a large tent that had been set up, the first time that representatives of the two countries had met for direct negotiations.

More substantive talks would be going on in Washington in the coming days. Acting Egyptian foreign minister Ismail Fahmy showed up in Kissinger's office on October 29 without an invitation and was followed two days later by Mrs. Meir.

On the eve of her departure for Washington, the prime minister helicoptered south with Dayan and Elazar for her first visit to the front. At Southern Command and at each of the divisional headquarters, she met with the commanders, who described the war from their vantage points. At each division, the prime minister also met with the troops and answered their questions. When she visited Sharon's division and made her entrance alongside Dayan, Elazar, and Sharon, the troops began chanting, "Arik, King of Israel." It was a spontaneous display of affection for a commander at the successful end of a war but it had political implications not lost on Mrs. Meir and Dayan.

When asked by a soldier why supplies were being permitted to reach the Third Army before Israel's POWs had been freed, the prime minister explained that American pressure left no choice. "It's easier to fight enemies than friends." From time to time, the grandmotherly nature of the visit gave way to disturbing questions. When a soldier asked, "How could we have been so unready?," Mrs. Meir said that she could not give an authoritative answer. She was not an expert on military matters, she said, and relied in this area on the two men sitting alongside her, the chief of staff and the defense minister. Her answer infuriated Lt. Col. Yom Tov Tamir, who still bore emotional scars from the destruction of his tank battalion on the northern canal front the first day of the war. "Because you don't understand these things I lost fifty-eight men?" he shouted. General Gonen, standing alongside him, calmed him down. Anger suppressed during the weeks of combat was beginning to vent.

The question raised by the soldier about the nation's unpreparedness was being asked on the home front with increasing stridency. The two men to whom Mrs. Meir had referred, Elazar and Dayan, would offer conflicting answers to the question the following day. In an appearance before the Knesset Foreign Affairs and Defense Committee, Elazar laid the blame for the initial setbacks on the failure to mobilize the reserves in time. "If we had mobilized," he said, "the war would have lasted three, four, six days. From a terrible opening, the IDF went on to victory, and if there were enough time it would have magnified it in a way that would have startled the world." There had been mistakes, he admitted, but the structure of the IDF and its preparations for the war had proven sound. There were no previously unknown factors that affected the outcome of the war, he said. It was a statement that ignored the stunning surprise of the Egyptian antitank tactics, the unexpected resilience of their infantry, Israel's neglect of combined arms operations, and the fact that the air force, in which the IDF had invested so much of its resources, had been impaled by the SAMs over the front lines.

Dayan disagreed with Elazar on every point. His hard-nosed assessment was that the problem went much deeper than the element of surprise and the failure to mobilize. "The army's operational concept proved incorrect," he said in a meeting with the country's newspaper editors in Tel Aviv. "Even if there had been full mobilization, the tanks could not approach [the enemy without being hit] and the planes could not approach. We estimated that if we have 300 tanks in Sinai and 180 on the Golan it would be enough. But it was not enough."

Having overcome its initial problems, the IDF had become a formidable fighting machine, he said. "We have three divisions in the south, the likes of which the Israeli people have never seen. If we wanted to, we could reach Cairo. The question is whether that's desirable." Asked whether he feared a renewal of the war, he said, "On the contrary. I very much want a renewal of fighting with Egypt." Israel's present deployment west of the canal—sandwiched between two Egyptian armies and with an overextended supply line—was too awkward to maintain. Dayan wanted to pull back across the canal but only for a price—the reopening of the waterway and the repopulation of the abandoned canal cities as a guarantee that Egypt would not readily go to war again. If the Egyptians refused, he said, Israel would destroy the Third Army and try to do the same to the Second.

After seeing off Mrs. Meir to Washington, Dayan flew south to consult with the senior command there. He told the generals that he expected the war to flare up again in the next few weeks. This time "we will have to preempt." The army was strong, he said. Damaged tanks had been repaired "and the fellows have rested." He did not favor a move toward Cairo, which could provoke Soviet intervention.

Instead, he was eager to finish off the Third Army and then tackle the Second Army. He proposed attacking the Third Army even at the cost of a crisis with the U.S. since the present situation was untenable.

Adan said he believed the Third Army could be overcome in a single night. Sharon advocated steering the talks with Egypt into a dead end and then attacking. Instead of hitting the Third Army, however, he favored attacking the Second Army, which, he said, posed the more serious threat to the Israeli bridgehead. He agreed that it was unwise to move on Cairo. Israeli doctrine had never advocated the capture of an Arab capital in an attempt to impose its will. Colonel Reshef favored a feint toward Cairo and then hitting the Second Army. A small number of men under his command, he said, had lost their motivation. Some had been wounded five times already. However, most wanted to bring the war to a decisive conclusion and were prepared to press on, refreshed now after several days' rest. General Tamari did not believe they had the strength to subdue the Second Army.

At a meeting of the General Staff, almost all speakers favored resumption of fighting. There were two dissenters. Tal did not see any point in risking additional lives. Zeira said he did not think that destruction of the Third Army would make Sadat more amenable to a settlement.

Close to midnight November 2, Elazar ordered Adan to take his division back into Sinai and prepare to attack the Third Army. By dawn, the division had disengaged on the west bank and was streaming eastward across the bridges. The command decision, however, was made in Washington. "You will not be permitted to capture that army," Kissinger told Dinitz. As long as the U.S. called the tune, there would be no decisive victory. What the Americans were determined to achieve, indeed, was a decisive tie.

The American airlift had been no less important to Israel symbolically than militarily. It brought 22,000 tons of supplies compared to 15,000 tons airlifted by the Soviet Union to Syria and Egypt. Only a small part of the matériel reaching Israel was actually used in the war. But the knowledge that the armaments were coming permitted Israel to use its own stockpiles more freely and cushioned it psychologically in a significant way. The sight of the giant American transports landing at Lod International Airport, some forty a day, was a reminder to Israelis that they were not alone at a time when Europe—indeed, the world—

was intimidated by the oil boycott. Of the eleven thousand sorties carried out by the Israeli Air Force in the war, only some three hundred were by planes that arrived from the U.S. during the war. Only a dozen tanks were flown to Israel during the war. However, long-range artillery shells and antitank missiles for infantrymen met critical needs.

The Americans had initially hoped to carry out the airlift discreetly so as not to offend the Arabs. The planes were to land at night and depart before dawn. Against the background of the Soviet airlift, however, the operation came increasingly to be seen in Washington as a reassertion of America's ability to project power. In the post-Vietnam era this was not something to be bashful about. The delivery of tanks in giant Galaxies was only a symbolic addition to Israel's arsenal. But the muscular preening before the foreign media successfully burnished America's "can do" image.

An indirect benefit of the airlift was that it made it easier for President Sadat to ask for a cease-fire by saying he was no longer fighting Israel but the United States—a statement that conveniently ignored the Soviet airlift, which had begun before the American airlift. American planes had in fact begun landing only late on October 14, after the battle with the Egyptian armored divisions that marked the turning point in the south and after Israel had already shelled the outskirts of Damascus.

The strain of the past three weeks was clearly visible on Mrs. Meir's face when Kissinger greeted her upon her arrival in Washington. "The war had devastated her," he noted. On her official agenda were a POW exchange, the fixing of the cease-fire line, and the fate of the Third Army. However, the real purpose of her visit was to discern whether America's ties to Israel were threatened by Washington's efforts to bring Egypt into its orbit. There had been a worrying development when Kissinger in Moscow worked out the cease-fire resolution with the Soviets without consulting Israel. Was that an omen? In Israel's current state, the prospect of being jilted by its one friend and benefactor was not easy to contemplate.

Kissinger explained that once an Arab country signaled willingness to negotiate peace, America's position shifted to a mediating role that no longer necessarily overlapped all of Israel's positions. If there were no Israeli concessions—such as permitting supplies to get through to the Third Army—there would be no incentive for Egypt to move forward. "Arab intransigence and Soviet pressure had created the illusion that Israel did not have to conduct a foreign policy, only a defense policy," Kissinger would write. "Egypt's turn toward moderation had ended that simple state of affairs. Golda was railing not against America's strategy but against a new, more complicated reality."

The key to future developments lay in Cairo with the man who had just turned the region upside down. Kissinger set out for his first meeting with Sadat two weeks after the fighting stopped. Rapport between the two men was immediate, both appreciating the other's shrewdness and vision and both finding the other worthy of trust.

"I sensed that Sadat represented the best chance to transcend frozen attitudes that the Middle East had known since the creation of the State of Israel," Kissinger would write. The American diplomat tried to convince Sadat that his insistence that Israel pull back to the October 22 line would just lead to protracted debate. Instead, he said, the focus should be on a disengagement of forces in which Israel would pull back from the west bank altogether. The Third Army would meanwhile remain encircled but Israel would be persuaded to permit supply convoys to get through.

"Sadat sat brooding, saying nothing for many minutes," Kissinger would recall. "I was saying in effect that the key to peace was his acquiescence in keeping an Egyptian army cut off in the desert for weeks on end, relying on the assessment of an American he had just met. And then he astonished me. He did not haggle or argue. Violating the normal method of diplomacy—which is to see what one can extract for a concession—he said simply that he agreed with my analysis and my proposed procedure." Kissinger's proposal, which profited from his earlier talks with Fahmy and Mrs. Meir, included the following points:

- A formal cease-fire agreement.
- The supply of the Third Army via U.N. checkpoints which would replace Israeli checkpoints on the Cairo–Suez highway. Israeli officers could examine the supplies together with U.N. officers to ensure their nonmilitary nature.
- A POW exchange.

For Israel, the agreement meant that it would be getting its prisoners back without being required to loosen its grip on the Third Army. Egypt, for its part, was ensured that the Third Army would remain intact and that an Israeli pullback across the canal was in the offing. For the U.S. it meant displacement of the Soviet Union as the dominant foreign influence in Egypt. The agreement was signed on November 11 at Kilometer 101 by Generals Gamasy and Yariv, who were left to work out implementation.

The dialogue begun by the two generals in a desert tent was transformed a month later into a formal international conference in Geneva attended by Kissinger and the foreign ministers of Israel, Egypt, Jordan, and the Soviet Union. For the first time, Arab foreign ministers sat at the same table with their Israeli counterpart. Syria declined to attend but an empty chair at the table hinted at possible attendance in the future. The conference on December 21 provided the formal framework for a peace process which would unfold in the coming months—not in the stately halls of Geneva but in a sparkling tour de force by Kissinger that came to be known as shuttle diplomacy.

Flying between the capitals of the Middle East—sometimes several capitals in one day—he achieved his first major breakthrough when Egypt and Israel signed a disengagement agreement on January 18 calling for Israeli withdrawal across the canal to a line that would leave the Gidi and Mitla Passes in its hands. Egyptian forces on the Sinai bank would not be required to pull back, as Israel had initially demanded, but the two sides would be separated by a U.N. buffer zone.

The agreement put an abrupt end to the uneasy cease-fire that had prevailed for ten weeks. Israeli casualties during this postwar war totaled fourteen dead and sixty-five wounded. Egypt's casualties were higher, particularly in the sector commanded by Sharon, who ordered his forces to respond with massive artillery barrages to any perceived transgression. (A different take on Sharon's character was his reaction to the sight of an Israeli reservist major striking a prisoner in a POW camp. According to his senior intelligence officer, Col. Yehoshua Sagui, who said he witnessed the incident, Sharon summoned the major to a tent, out of sight of the prisoners, and slapped him.)

The partial Israeli pullback and Sadat's agreement to reopen the Suez Canal and repopulate the canal cities was what Dayan had proposed in 1970 as the most stable solution in Sinai. Golda Meir had rejected it then. In a talk a few months after the war to the Labor Party Central Committee, she appeared to express contrition. "I must confess that I didn't understand what he was talking about," she said. "That we should just propose pulling back from the canal?" She did not elaborate but the implications were enormous. If she had grasped the implications, then the war, if it came, would have taken a very different course.

A month after the disengagement agreement, the last Israeli troops pulled back from Africa across the bridges. It was not without nostalgia that the reservists pulled up their tent stakes. "We'll miss being together," a paratroop sergeant from Colonel Matt's brigade told a reporter at an outpost being evacuated near Ismailiya. "I think some of us wouldn't mind going on living together like in a small kibbutz." In a ceremony next to the roller bridge before it was pulled back, Lt. Eli Cohen, the first Israeli to step ashore on the west bank four months before (and a future Israeli ambassador), lowered the Israeli flag from a pole as his comrades set off colored smoke grenades and released balloons.

Israel prepared now to begin the arduous task of rebuilding its army for the next round, which could come at any time. Sadat, however, was still one step ahead. In a gesture that startled Mrs. Meir, the Egyptian leader sent her a personal note through Kissinger. "You must take my word seriously. When I threatened war, I meant it. When I talk of peace now, I mean it. We never had had contact before. We now have the services of Dr. Kissinger. Let us use him and talk to each other through him." Sadat recognized that the recovery of the rest of Sinai was likelier through the allure of peace than the threat of war.

Mrs. Meir's first reaction was suspicion—"Why is he doing this?" she asked Kissinger—but she recovered quickly. In a reply that Kissinger took back with him to Cairo, Mrs. Meir wrote, "I am deeply conscious of the significance of a message received by the prime minister of Israel from the president of Egypt. I sincerely hope that these contacts . . . will continue and prove to be an important turning point in our relations."

For Syria's Assad, there would be no such civilities. Committed to the idea of Israel's nonlegitimacy, he found it hard to negotiate with it, even indirectly. However, he had no alternative if he wanted his territory back. Before returning home, Kissinger stopped off in Damascus to test the waters. Assad said he was prepared to enter into a cease-fire agreement on condition that Israel pull back not only from the enclave it had captured in this war but from half the territory it had captured on the Golan Heights in the 1967 war. Israel had just surrendered to Egypt territory in Sinai that it had captured in 1967 and Assad demanded a similar concession. He had to show his people, he said, that the thousands of Syrian soldiers killed in the war had not died in vain. Making the best of it, Kissinger told the Israelis that Assad had at least shown willingness to negotiate.

A month later, the secretary of state returned to the Middle East briefly after Assad agreed to transmit through him the list of Israeli POWs in return for an Israeli counteroffer on the cease-fire. Until now, Syria had refused to say how many prisoners it was holding, let alone give their names. In Jerusalem the next day, Kissinger handed over the list to Mrs. Meir. She wept and Kissinger put a comforting arm around her. Israel had not known how many of the 140 men missing on the Syrian front had survived. The list contained 65 names, mostly men captured on the Hermon on the first day and downed airmen. Israel held 380 Syrians. The Israeli counteroffer envisioned only a minor withdrawal in the newly captured enclave and none at all on the Golan. Rather than risk negotiations being broken off by transmitting that offer, Kissinger told Assad that the Israelis still needed time to think about it and flew back home. Meanwhile, a war of attrition had broken out between Syrian and Israeli forces like the one that occurred on the Egyptian front before disengagement.

When Kissinger returned to Damascus at the beginning of May, it was for a make-or-break effort that would set new standards for the diplomatic art. Over the course of thirty-four days he shuttled between Damascus and Jerusalem, with frequent side trips to other Arab capitals. He was able to narrow differences down to a strip of territory about a mile wide around Kuneitra. But at that point both sides refused to budge any further. Accepting defeat, Kissinger flew to Damascus to take leave of Assad. He had made his farewells and was heading for the door when Assad indicated that he was prepared to make a final concession, a negotiating technique familiar to any bazaar patron in the Middle East. Kissinger flew back to Jerusalem to wrest a final concession there as well.

The agreement arrived at called for Israel to withdraw from the entire enclave captured after Yom Kippur and also from the abandoned town of Kuneitra, which had been on the Israeli side of the Purple Line. Israel gave up smaller patches of land as well along the southern part of the line, including the site of Outpost 116, which had been on the Syrian side of the 1967 line, and those parts of the Hermon crest—the Syrian Hermon—it had not held before the war.

The Syrians, in turn, agreed to a prisoner exchange, a limitation on the forces both sides could maintain in their forward areas, and a U.N. observer force between the two lines.

The Syrian army would no longer deploy major forces up against the Israeli line, capable of springing without warning. Assad also pledged that Syria would prevent guerrilla incursions. Syria would honor this unwritten agreement in the ensuing decades, turning the Golan into the quietest of Israel's borders. On June 5, 1974, military representatives of the two sides signed the disengagement agreement in Geneva. The Yom Kippur War—or the October War or Ramadan War, as the Arabs referred to it—was officially over on both fronts.

With disengagement in the south, Israel had withdrawn twenty miles from the canal but it still held the bulk of Sinai, to be used as a buffer against war or as a trade-off for peace.

There was time now to begin thinking through the lessons of the war. In an unsparing analysis, an armored corps general, Moshe Bar-Kochba, concluded in an article he wrote for an Israeli military journal that the IDF's senior command, wielding formations far larger than any in Israel's history, had insufficient training in the complex art of war. This, he said, was why it had decided on static defense lines held with minimal forces instead of on a flexible defense. "Future wars will oblige a university level [military education] and our senior officers are still in grade school," wrote Bar-Kochba, who had served as deputy commander of Laner's division on the Golan. There were generals who had never had formal military training more advanced than a company commander's course.

Major IDF assumptions had collapsed within forty-eight hours of the war's opening, he wrote, like belief in the reliability of AMAN, in the air force's mastery of the skies over the battlefield, in the low fighting qualities of the Arab armies. Investing more than half the defense budget on the air force, he said, meant that the armored corps was not able to keep pace with the Arab armies. If the air force had been allocated twenty fewer planes, Bar-Kochba wrote, this would have left money for the creation of two more armored divisions, which could have made a critical difference on both fronts.

Given the strategic, operational, and psychological dimensions of the Arab surprise, Israel's recovery from the edge of the abyss was epic.

The IDF destroyed or captured 2,250 enemy tanks. Hundreds were captured intact after being abandoned by their crews, mostly on the Syrian front. The IDF would incorporate four hundred of them into its own order of battle, enough for more than one division. Four hundred Israeli tanks were destroyed. Another six hundred were disabled but returned to battle after repairs. Virtually every tank had been hit and many were hit several times. Acknowledging the serious strategic errors that had been made, Gen. Herzl Sapir, a member of the General Staff (manpower), said that as a fighting force the army had been superb, with experienced commanders who had fought in all of Israel's wars. "It's the best army the IDF has ever had or will have." A former commander of military intelligence, Gen. Mordecai Gazit, said the war was a phenomenal victory. "We recovered from our Pearl Harbor not after two years but after two weeks."

Although largely neutralized over the battlefield by the SAMs, the air force had performed spectacularly in air combat. It shot down 277 Arab aircraft against the loss of six Israeli planes in dogfights, a 46 to 1 ratio compared to the 9 to 1 ratio of the Six Day War. Israel's recovery from the war's shattering opening was a testament to the vigor of its society. Avigdor Kahalani would note that those who stopped the Syrian onslaught were not members of elite units but ordinary tank crews who represented a cross section of the population. They proved strong enough to overcome the grievous failures of the leadership.

Had the superpowers not imposed a cease-fire, Israel's success would doubtless have been even more striking as it prepared to roll up the Third Army and perhaps try to do the same to the Second Army. But the price had been heavy. Israel had 2,656 dead and 7,250 wounded. (Col. Haim Erez's prediction on Yom Kippur day that the war would end with 2,500 to 3,000 dead proved accurate.) Arab figures for their own casualties were 8,528 dead and 19,540 wounded. Israel estimated Arab casualties to be almost twice those figures—15,000 dead (11,000 of them Egyptian) and 35,000 wounded (25,000 Egyptian).

Who won?

Egypt did. So did Israel.

Like a jeweler cutting a precious stone, Sadat had struck with his military mallet perfectly, producing a political process that would lead to the recovery by Egypt of all of Sinai. More important even than territorial gain was the performance of the Egyptian army, which wiped clean the Arab humiliation of 1967.

Politically, Egypt's victory was stunning. But it would bring with it an Israeli political victory even more stunning—namely, peace with Egypt itself and the long-awaited breakthrough, however tenuous, to the Arab world beyond.

In terms of morale, Egypt was the clear winner. It had seized the initiative, risking the shattering prospect of another defeat, and emerged honorably. In Israel, the abrupt fall from supreme confidence, not to say arrogance, shook the nation to its core. The brutal surprises of the war had confronted it with the prospect not just of defeat but mortality. The psychological shock found insufficient remedy in military success. Despite the entrapment of the Third Army and the momentum Israel had built up on the road to Cairo, it was Egypt, not Israel, that sensed triumph when the shooting stopped.

Time would bring a different perspective. In military terms, Israel would recognize its reversal of fortune on the battlefield as having few historic parallels. Reeling from a surprise attack on two fronts by armies twice as large as its own and confronted by battlefield realities it had not prepared for, Israel was in a situation that could readily bring strong nations to their knees. Yet within days it had regained its footing and within less than two weeks it was threatening both enemy capitals. Israel confronted not just the Egyptian and Syrian armies but much of the Arab world and it did so with the arm it had most relied on, the air force, tied behind its back. As a military feat, the IDF's performance in the Yom Kippur War dwarfed that of the Six Day War. Victory emerged from motivation that came from the deepest layers of the nation's being.

In retrospect, the performance of the Arab armies came to be seen in Israel as less impressive than at first perceived. Still viewing the Arabs through the spectrum of the Six Day War, the Israelis in 1973 were startled by the daring they displayed and by the way they held their ground. With the passage of time, however, Israel would come to see the Arabs as having "fought bravely, not well," as one armor colonel put it. Disdain for the Arab fighter had given way to respect, but not to a sense that the balance of power was shifting.

As for Syria, it had been saved by the intervention of Iraq. Key elements of Syria's physical infrastructure were smashed and the country would suffer blackouts for months after the war. But it won at the negotiating table what it had failed to gain on the battlefield—Kuneitra. And it did so without having to pay a political price in the form of recognizing Israel. Syria would subside once again after the war into sullen insularity. Unlike Egypt, which rebuilt its heavily damaged canal cities, Syria left Kuneitra in ruins—a monument to ongoing hostility. But it adhered to its pledge to keep the border quiet.

Despite Israel's striking recovery on the battlefield, its mood at war's end was anguished. It had lost almost three times as many men per capita in nineteen days as the U.S. lost in Vietnam in close to a decade. For the first time in one of Israel's wars, a significant number of its nonfatal casualties—between 10 and 23 percent, according to different studies—suffered from battle trauma, in good measure deriving from the initial surprise.

As the reservists returned home, public squares began to fill with crowds—not celebrating Israel's military achievement but giving vent to the deepest trauma in the nation's history.

38

AFTERMATH

IT WAS A RAINY MORNING when Motti Ashkenazi took up position across the road from the prime minister's office in Jerusalem. Drivers passing through the government center slowed down to read the placard held aloft by the bespectacled figure in a windbreaker.

"Grandma," it read, "your defense minister is a failure and 3,000 of your grandchildren are dead."

Four months had passed since the Egyptian attack on Budapest, the Bar-Lev fort under Ashkenazi's command. The notion of demonstrating against the government had been with him since he had flung himself down in the sand under the opening Egyptian barrage. Anger at the failure to anticipate the war was reinforced by anger at the operational unreadiness to deal with it. Now, just two days after his discharge, Ashkenazi had embarked on a campaign of his own.

On the second day of his solitary demonstration, a news photographer happening by took his photograph. The day after the picture was published another discharged reservist wordlessly took up position some distance away with his own placard. With every passing day, more demonstrators arrived.

Two ministers looking out a window before the start of a cabinet meeting studied the growing forest of placards. "They want Dayan's head," said one.

"They want all our heads," said the other.

The returning soldiers all bore memories of comrades who did not come back. The friend with whom Ashkenazi had discussed the inevitability of war in a Jerusalem café a few months before, Gideon Giladi, was killed trying to open Tirtur Road with two tanks on the first night of battle in the Chinese Farm. The kibbutz mate with whom Yitzhak

Brik had gone off to war Yom Kippur afternoon, Meir Hatsfoni, was killed alongside him in Yaguri's charge at Hizayon on October 8. Yisrael Itkin, the commander of Sharon's APC, had been picked up at Kibbutz Givat Haim by a mobilization bus on Yom Kippur afternoon together with Yehuda Geller, who would lead the final attack on Missouri, and tank commander Yisrael Dagan. Itkin and Geller returned to the kibbutz without Dagan, killed in his tank an hour before the cease-fire in the final attempt to reach Ismailiya.

Kibbutz members had a highly disproportionate place on the casualty lists. At Bait Hashita in the Jezreel Valley, 120 men went off to the war. Eleven did not return, the highest per capita loss for an Israeli community.

A month after Ashkenazi's one-man protest opposite the prime minister's office, more than twenty thousand persons assembled there to call for the government's resignation. The painful process of working through the nation's trauma was under way.

For Amnon Reshef, the process had begun as soon as the shooting stopped. His brigade suffered more fatalities than any other Israeli brigade in the war, more than three hundred, including replacements. It had borne the brunt of the Egyptian crossing on Yom Kippur and of the battle for the Chinese Farm nine days later. Following the cease-fire, the brigade was posted at a captured airbase where it remained for two months. On Friday nights, after the unit's Sabbath meal, Reshef would retire to a bunker with his officers and choose two of them to share with him a bottle of whiskey. He would insist that the pair drink until drunk, until they danced or laughed or cried. Some shouted at him for having let their friends die. In every unit, officers and men vented their feelings in endless discussions. How could they have been surprised? Why were they so unprepared?

For the nation as a whole, the major instrument of therapy was an inquiry commission appointed by the government to answer those questions. It was clear to Dayan and Mrs. Meir even before the war was over that heads would have to roll—perhaps their own—and that only an inquiry conducted by a body enjoying the highest repute could hope to restore public confidence in the government and the army. Three weeks after the cease-fire, the president of the Israeli Supreme Court, American-born judge Shimon Agranat, was asked to head a five-man commission to investigate the events leading up to the war and the setbacks of the first days.

The appointment of the prestigious commission provided a breathing space for the nation to begin pulling itself together. Knesset elections, postponed from October because of the war, were held on December 31. It was too soon for deep-seated voting patterns to have significantly changed. The Labor Party, headed by Mrs. Meir, won again, although with five fewer seats, 51, in the 120-seat Knesset. Mrs. Meir asked Dayan to stay on as defense minister in the new government. He told her that if the Agranat Commission found him in any way responsible for the failings of the war, he would resign. The public, not waiting for the commission's report, focused its anger on the defense minister, the dashing figure on whom it had rested its sense of security. The anger was brought home to him at military funerals when grieving relatives shouted at him "Murderer."

Attempting to better understand the public mood, Dayan accepted an invitation from a philosophy professor at Hebrew University to meet with one of his students, Motti Ashkenazi—the man who had come to symbolize the protest movement. To the meeting at the professor's home in Jerusalem Dayan brought the heads of the Mossad and Shin Bet, the internal security service. The meeting of the philosophy student with the country's three top security officials lasted for more than an hour. Only Ashkenazi and Dayan engaged in the dialogue. Neither left a favorable impression on the other.

The IDF, preparing itself for a renewal of fighting, absorbed the massive American arms shipments, most of it arriving now by sea. Accelerated courses for tank crews to fill the depleted ranks of the armored corps were held just behind the front lines. Half the war dead had been tank crewmen. Within a few months, the army was back to its prewar strength.

Haim Bar-Lev took off his uniform and returned to the cabinet two weeks after the cease-fire but Southern Command was not entrusted again to Gonen. At Dayan's insistence, Gonen was shifted to the command of remote southern Sinai until completion of the final Agranat Report, General Gavish leaving that post to return to civilian life. Southern Command was turned over temporarily to General Tal.

Sharon was elected to the Knesset on the Likud ticket but he told Dayan that he would return to the army if he were appointed chief of staff. Dayan dismissed that possibility although he supported Sharon's bid to retain his reserve commission as a division commander despite Elazar's opposition. In Sharon's farewell address to his troops, he said that victory had been won "despite the blunders and the mistakes, despite the loss of control and authority"—a clear slap at the high command. When Dayan learned of it, he revoked Sharon's commission.

On April 2, 1974, the Agranat Commission published its eagerly awaited preliminary findings. The commission demanded six heads, foremost that of Elazar. "We have reached the conclusion that the Chief of Staff, Gen. David Elazar, bears direct responsibility for what happened on the eve of the war, both as to the assessment of the situation and the IDF's preparedness." The commission recommended dismissal of Zeira as chief of intelligence "for grave failures," and the removal of his deputy, General Shalev, from his post as well. Transfer from intelligence duties was recommended for two other officers, Colonel Bandman, head of the Egyptian desk at AMAN, and Colonel Gedalia, the chief intelligence officer of Southern Command. General Gonen, said the commission, should be relieved from active duty until the conclusion of its investigation. The IDF as a whole was chastised for permitting its military doctrine to "stagnate" since the Six Day War.

As for Mrs. Meir and Dayan, the commission cleared them of all responsibility. Dayan, it noted, had no independent method of assessing the possibility of war. "The defense minister was never intended to be a 'super chief of staff' who would guide the chief of staff in the latter's operative area of responsibility," it declared. Mrs. Meir, the commission found, had "used her authority properly and wisely when she ordered mobilization of the reserves on Yom Kippur morning despite the weighty political factors involved." The commission stressed that it was judging the ministers' responsibility for security failings, not their parliamentary responsibility, which was outside its mandate.

The absolution of Dayan and Mrs. Meir aroused widespread anger and made public calls for their resignation, particularly Dayan's, even louder. Mrs. Meir had twice during the war rejected his offer to step down and she had defended him against cabinet colleagues calling for his resignation. After the commission's report, Dayan asked her again whether she wanted him to resign. This time she said that the Labor Party leadership must decide. In her memoirs, she would suggest that the commission's harsh findings regarding Elazar and Zeira should have led Dayan to "stick by" his comrades-in-arms and step down. "But he was following a logic of his own," she would write, "and I didn't feel that on such a weighty matter I should give him advice."

She followed her own logic. A week after the report, she announced her resignation, saying she could not ignore the public mood. Her move obliged the resignation of the entire cabinet, which became effective in June after disengagement on the Syrian front. The new government was headed by Yitzhak Rabin, with Shimon Peres as defense minister.

The Yom Kippur War continued to claim its victims long after the shooting stopped. General Elazar left the army deeply hurt that the Agranat Commission had placed the onus of failure upon him while sparing Dayan. He felt that the commission had failed to give proper weight to the critical stabilizing role he had played during the war. It was an assessment that was widely shared. A general who had worked alongside him would compare his performance to that of a cruise missile which maintains a fixed altitude relative to the ground no matter how uneven the terrain. This was no mean feat given the gusts of gloom around him, the need to prop up the front commanders, especially in the opening days, and the effort expended calming the political leaders. All this in addition to dealing with the initially calamitous situation on the battlefields. His cardinal sins were committed before the war, not during the war. As chief of staff he failed to recognize the distortions in Israel's military posture. His strategy of stopping the Egyptians on the waterline proved disastrous. So too his appointment of Gonen as southern front commander. He did not challenge the analysis of his intelligence chiefs despite ample evidence that something about it was amiss. He did not grasp the import of Egypt's accumulation of Sagger missiles. Elazar was the linchpin who held the high command together in a time of awesome stress but there was a price to be paid by the man at the top of the pyramid for what happened on Yom Kippur.

He left the army with the admiration of his peers and of Mrs. Meir and was appointed head of Israel's national shipping line, Zim. Foreign Minister Abba Eban reportedly planned to offer him the ambassadorial post in Washington before he himself was dropped from the cabinet. But the war and his dismissal bore heavily on Elazar. His biographer, Hanoch Bartov, records that shortly after the cease-fire Elazar entered the secretaries' room at army headquarters to look for a document. A transistor radio was playing a poignant song sweeping the country, "Would That It Were," which captured the pain of the war. It was the first time Elazar had heard it and he stood transfixed. When it was over he strode swiftly back to his office without taking what he had come for. The chief secretary hurried after him. Opening his door, she saw the man whom Mrs. Meir and others had termed "a rock" sitting at his desk, holding his head between his hands and sobbing. She closed the door without his having seen her. Two years after the war, at age fifty-one, he died of a heart attack while swimming.

Although Dayan symbolized for the demonstrators the arrogance that brought the nation to the precipice, he was the most far-seeing of the nation's leaders. His ability to think creatively was of the same order as Sadat's. His proposal in 1970 for a pullback from the canal and creation of a buffer zone between the two armies, rejected by Mrs. Meir, would have averted the kind of attack Egypt launched on Yom Kippur, although perhaps not war itself. Without his insistence on reinforcing the Syrian front in the days before Yom Kippur with additional tank units, the Golan would have fallen, something that would have rendered Israel's military position truly catastrophic. His boldness was hemmed by caution but in the end he had not been cautious enough, failing to press the military to rethink basic assumptions.

If the Six Day War had imbued Dayan with a sense of Israel's power and Arab dysfunction, the Yom Kippur War determined him to explore the road to peace. Changing his parliamentary colors by joining the right-wing government of Menahem Begin in 1977 as foreign minister, Dayan played a major role in the breakthrough to peace with Egypt.

General Zeira, whose gross misreading of Arab intentions was the most palpable personal failure of the war, had a rewarding career after his forced retirement from the army as a consultant to foreign governments. In the week before Yom Kippur, Zeira's perverse dismissal of a multitude of war warnings brought Israel to near-disaster. In a book he wrote two decades later he argued that Ashraf Marwan was a double agent, an allegation which in effect placed responsibility for the surprise Arab attack on the Mossad, his institutional rival. His claim would be rejected by virtually all Israeli intelligence analysts. If Marwan was a double agent, why would he have warned Mossad chief Zvi Zamir on Yom Kippur eve of the coming attack? He had in fact given the code word for war by telephone thirty-eight hours before the war.

In a rare public appearance by Zeira, on the fortieth anniversary of the war—on a panel that also included his nemesis, Mossad chief Zvi Zamir—Zeira acknowledged having underestimated the threat of war but blamed others for what went wrong on Yom Kippur. His analysis would have been more insightful, he said, if there had been a poet on his staff capable of understanding the soul of the enemy. During the war itself, he performed well as intelligence chief, offering sound insights.

As for Mossad chief Zamir, his performance before and during the war was applauded by all. Much of the information he obtained from Marwan about Egypt's intentions was nullified by Zeira, but enough got through to the high command to make a decisive difference. His insights and balance made him an important support for Mrs. Meir.

Ashraf Marwan became a billionaire businessman based in London. When his identity was revealed in a book published in England in 2002, which echoed Zeira's contention that he was a double agent, Marwan was hailed in Egypt as a national hero who had fooled Israel. Ex-Mossad chief Zamir threatened to bring Zeira to court for violating a basic code of the intelligence community by revealing Marwan's identity to journalists. When the matter was brought to a retired Supreme Court judge for arbitration, he ruled in Zvi Zamir's favor, indirectly confirming that Marwan was an Israeli spy, not a double agent. Shortly afterward, Marwan fell to his death from the balcony of his luxury apartment in London. A witness reported seeing two men "of Mediterranean appearance" looking down from a balcony at the body.

Israeli historian Uri Bar-Joseph, who would write a book on the Marwan episode, suggests that the finding by an Israeli judge of repute meant that Egyptian authorities could no longer avoid the conclusion that Marwan had indeed been an Israeli spy. British police would make no finding about whether his death was a suicide or murder.

Marwan's warning in London on Yom Kippur eve of imminent war almost certainly saved the Golan Heights for Israel by setting mobilization in motion hours before the war began, giving Ori Orr's reserve brigade just enough time to block the Syrians near Nafakh.

Despite criticism in the Pit of General Hofi's performance as northern front commander, his staff officers would maintain that he had performed coolly and competently in extremely trying circumstances. He went on to become a successful head of the Mossad.

Deputy Chief of Staff Tal had repeatedly differed with Elazar during the war. After Tal's brief tenure heading Southern Command, Elazar refused to take his old friend back as his deputy. Instead, Tal devoted himself to development of the innovative Merkava tank.

Ariel Sharon emerged from the war with the glory he had sought.

Although he had pressed for a canal crossing from the first day, he was not the man who initiated it. The decision to cross was made by Elazar and Bar-Lev and it was they who chose the timing. Sharon was a bane to his superiors but an inspiration to his officers and men, a born leader. He was able to lift morale by his very presence.

Sharon was one of the only commanders not to be stunned by the surprise attack although he knew moments of despair. On the second night of the war, one of his APC crewmen heard him talking with brigade commanders outside. The enormity of the hole that the IDF had dug for itself had by now become apparent. "He was very down," recalled the sergeant, who had been part of Sharon's headquarters staff for years. "He said there was danger of a disaster. Of course he said we will win in the end but it was very hard to hear." Unlike other senior officers, however, he did not freeze. Within hours of his arrival at the front he was pushing for a canal crossing and he would continue to press for aggressive action. Clausewitz had someone like him in mind when he wrote: "Happy the army in which an untimely boldness frequently manifests itself. . . . Even foolhardiness, which is boldness without an object, is not to be despised."

Once the army crossed into Africa, it was General Adan's war. Sharon would be tied down on the road to Ismailiya in a slow-moving secondary thrust while Adan was deftly maneuvering large armored forces across a broad landscape in the war's strategic endgame. It was Adan who pushed for abrogation of the first cease-fire in order to complete encirclement of the Third Army—a move which fundamentally altered the outcome of the war. What Israel was able to bring to the negotiating table was not just Egyptian territory but the fate of the Third Army.

For General Gonen, the ignominy of being superseded at Southern Command at the height of the war was compounded when he was forced to leave the army after the final Agranat Report. Gonen believed Dayan responsible for his disgrace and told reporters that he had considered walking into Dayan's office and shooting him.

Instead, he spent thirteen years in the jungles of the Central African Republic searching for diamonds. His intention, he said, was to become wealthy enough to hire the best lawyers in Israel to clear his name. He reportedly made and lost one or two fortunes but rejected appeals by family and friends to abandon his obsession. A reporter who visited him in the jungle after nine years found him somewhat mellowed, self-aware, not without sardonic humor, and still sprinkling his conversation with apt quotes from the Talmud. The tough soldier appeared to find satisfaction in coping with the challenges of the steamy jungle rather than nursing his grievances in the cafés of Tel Aviv. He died of a heart attack in 1991 during one of his periodic business trips to Europe. Among the few possessions returned to his family were maps of Sinai on which he had apparently refought the war during his jungle exile, and a copy of a kabbalistic work in which the former yeshiva student may have sought an explanation, beyond what maps could tell, for the catastrophe which had overcome him.

On the Egyptian and Syrian sides too, the heads of senior officers were not often garlanded with wreaths. General Shazly, who had so ably prepared his army, irrevocably angered Sadat by opposing a push to the passes and by his demand that forces be withdrawn from Sinai to meet the Israeli incursion west of the canal. After the war, Shazly was informed that Sadat had decided to terminate his service in the army. To avoid the public scandal of dismissing a war hero, he was named ambassador to London and later to Portugal. After publicly criticizing the 1978 Camp David peace agreement with Israel, he was forced into exile, spending most of the next fourteen years in Algeria. During this period he wrote his account of the war, for which he was sentenced in absentia to three years' imprisonment for revealing military secrets. Returning to Egypt in 1992, he was imprisoned for half his term. He died in 2011. The commanders of the Second and Third Armies, Generals Wasel and Khalil, were eased out of the army after the war and appointed to civilian governorships.

On the Syrian front, the Druze commander of an infantry brigade that had collapsed during the Israeli breakthrough was executed even before the war ended. The Seventh Division commander, Gen. Omar Abash, who had failed to break through Ben-Gal's brigade, was alternately reported to have been killed in the fighting or to have died of a heart attack.

The supreme victor in the Yom Kippur War was the man who initiated it—President Sadat. He had dared, as Mrs. Meir said. Risking all, he parlayed an audacious military move that restored Egypt's dignity into an audacious diplomatic process that restored its lost lands. Addressing the Egyptian parliament in November 1977—four years after the war—he said, "I am prepared to go to the end of the earth, and Israel will be surprised to hear me say to you, I am ready to go to their home, to the Knesset itself, and to argue with them there." It was a flourish no less breathtaking than his crossing of the Suez

Canal. Within days he received an invitation from Israeli prime minister Menahem Begin. Sadat's arrival in Israel was one of the most charged moments in modern Middle East history. Introduced on the airport reception line to Sharon, now agriculture minister, the Egyptian leader smiled and said, "If you attempt to cross to the west bank [of the Suez Canal] again, I'll have you arrested." From the Knesset podium, Sadat proclaimed, "No more war."

Until a few months before his visit, Sadat had seen peace with Israel in the form of a nonbelligerency pact. Normalization and diplomatic relations, he said, were to be left to future generations, given the bloodiness of the recent past. However, in the end he decided to seek a psychological breakthrough with Israel by going all the way diplomatically. Although he reiterated in the Knesset his commitment to a comprehensive agreement that included the Palestinians, he settled in the end for a separate agreement with Israel, expressing the hope that it would set in motion a broader peace process. Four years after his visit to Jerusalem, Islamic fundamentalists gunned him down as he reviewed a military parade marking the anniversary of the war.

The other major victor of the Yom Kippur War was a man who had been six thousand miles from the battlefield. Henry Kissinger had with dazzling statesmanship stage-managed a scenario in which both sides could claim victory while acknowledging, to themselves at least, victory's awful price. In the process, he deftly managed to nudge aside the Soviet Union and tie the leading country in the Arab world to the U.S.

The Yom Kippur War had a major impact on the world's armies. The success of the Sagger and RPG in the early days of the war evoked widespread eulogies for the tank. Closer study brought revision. With better armor, defenses against antitank missiles, and different tactics, the tank would continue to play a major role on the battlefield.

Two senior American armor generals arrived in Israel shortly after the war to walk the battlefields and confer with their Israeli peers. For a decade, the U.S. had been mired in Vietnam, mentally as well as physically. The Soviets advanced their military doctrine and weaponry during this period but the American military had skipped a cycle of upgrading. The Vietnam War had ended early in 1973 and the Americans wanted to learn what the Middle East conflict had to teach about the shape of future wars.

The generals found Yom Kippur War tank battles to have been of unprecedented intensity. The fighting in Sinai and the Golan involved more tanks than any Second World War battle with the possible exception of the battle of Kursk in the Soviet Union and the Allied breakout from Normandy. The intensity stemmed not just from the number of tanks but from the lethality of the weapons, their extended range, and their improved accuracy. Entire tank battalions were consumed on the battlefield within hours. What the generals learned would play a role in the reshaping of the American armored corps in the decades leading up to the first Gulf War.

The future battlefield, they warned, would be far more crowded with tanks and antitank weaponry than any hitherto known. Combined tank losses on the Arab and Israeli sides in the first week of the war, they noted, exceeded the entire U.S. Army tank inventory in Europe. "Because of the numbers and the lethality of modern weapons, the direct fire battle will be intense; enormous equipment losses can be expected in a relatively short period of time," wrote Maj. Gen. Donn Starry.

Whereas tanks in the Second World War had fought at an average range of 750 yards, in the Yom Kippur War Israeli tanks were engaging at 2,000 and even 3,000 yards. This meant a far broader killing ground.

General Starry's conclusions concerning the human element in battle were strongly influenced by the Israeli performance. "In modern battle, the outcome will be decided by factors other than numbers," he wrote. "It is strikingly evident that battles are yet won by the courage of soldiers, the character of leaders, and the combat excellence of well-trained units."

For Israel, however, one of the major lessons of the war was that numbers count. Brigade commander Ben-Gal, who overcame great odds in the Kuneitra Gap, and General Adan were among Israeli military leaders who would make this point. As Adan put it, "Quantity is quality."

In the Six Day War, the Israeli Air Force had achieved one of the most stunning air victories in history. In the Yom Kippur War, to the surprise of all, the IAF's impact on the outcome was less than decisive. It overwhelmed the Arabs in air combat, conducted strategic strikes against Syria, prevented the Egyptians from foraying out from under their missile umbrella, and kept enemy air forces from Israel's skies. But it was the battered armored corps that turned the war around in the end and forced the Arabs to seek a cease-fire.

In the years after the war, the air force would devote itself to coming up with an answer to the Soviet SAMs. By 1978 it had devised a plan employing new weaponry and electronic devices, some made abroad and some produced in Israel. Instead of overpowering the missile system, as Tagar was designed to do, the IAF would attempt to outsmart it. When the Lebanese War came in June 1982, the new tactics were put to the test in Lebanon's Bekaa Valley where the Syrians deployed a missile system more formidable than the one opposite the Golan Heights in the Yom Kippur War.

Unlike in 1973, when inability to identify the location of the SAM-6s led to the failure of Dougman 5, the IAF was now able to track the deployment of the Syrian batteries at all times. Most important, it had the standoff weapon lacking in the Yom Kippur War—smart bombs with cameras that could be launched from beyond the range of the SAM missiles and guided onto target.

The IAF opened the battle by dispatching drones to send back images of the nineteen SAM-6 batteries in the valley as well as of the radar-controlled antiaircraft guns guarding them. In an elaborate scenario, planes and drones sent electronic signals activating SAM radars which were being deliberately kept dormant by the Syrians to avoid being targeted. When the radars came alive, their electronic parameters were recorded and instantly fed into airborne and ground-launched missiles that homed in on them before they could be closed down.

With the radars blinded, Israeli warplanes swarmed over the valley and destroyed fifteen of the nineteen batteries and severely damaged three others. When Syrian warplanes rose to challenge them, dozens were shot down, as Israeli air controllers in surveillance planes directed waiting fighter squadrons to the attack. At this stage, with not a single Israeli plane downed, Air Force Commander David Ivri recalled his planes to ensure that the day would not be even slightly marred. Air battles would resume the next day. A total of eighty-two Syrian planes were downed over the two days in dogfights. Israeli losses were one Skyhawk and two helicopters downed by conventional antiaircraft fire.

The Israeli response to the SAMs in the Bekaa Valley involved an integration of technology and tactics which American military analyst Anthony Cordesman would call "uniquely efficient." With this stunning display nine years after the frustrations of the Yom Kippur War, the Israeli Air Force took back the technological and psychological high ground which had been lost with the introduction of the SAMs in Egypt and Syria more than a decade before.

The air force's success also had extraordinary political fallout, senior officers in Warsaw Pact armies would tell Israeli colleagues years later. A day after the destruction of the SAM array in the Bekaa Valley, the Soviets dispatched the deputy head of their air defense system to Syria to find out how the Israelis had done it. The incident severely shook the Soviet leadership, which relied on the SAMs as a shield for the Soviet Union itself against Western air attack. A deputy chief of staff of a Warsaw Pact country told General Ivri that the vulnerability of the SAMs revealed by the Bekaa clash was one of the factors in the changed Soviet mind-set that led to glasnost and the opening to the West.

For soldiers on both sides of the war, the battles left mental scars that would be long in healing, if healed at all. Lt. Shimon Maliach, who had fought at the Chinese Farm with Colonel Mordecai's paratroopers, was haunted by the memory of Lieutenant Rabinowitz and by his own unfulfilled promise to rescue him. But Rabinowitz had in fact survived. One of the doctors in the hospital where Maliach was being treated for combat stress found Rabinowitz in a Beersheba hospital and brought Maliach a tape recording from him. After Maliach woke him from his stupor, Rabinowitz related, he managed to crawl to the rear.

Two years later, returning from a visit to the Golan Heights, Maliach stopped off at a restaurant in Haifa and noticed a mother and young boy sitting at the far end of the room. Across the table from them was a man with red hair, his back to the door. The boy was about two years old. Maliach thought of the red-haired lieutenant who had told him his wife was about to give birth. He could not see the man's face but ran up to him shouting, "Rabinowitz." It was indeed he. The two men embraced and wept and told each other their stories and wept again.

Maliach stopped praying on Yom Kippur after the war. He would spend the day alone, sometimes in an empty apartment, sometimes in the Judean Desert, where he would upbraid God for what he had permitted to happen.

Sgt. Mahmud Nadeh did not despair of God but he had come to despair of life. Even after the cease-fire, the soldiers of the Third Army remained surrounded in the desert for months on limited rations. Nadeh's company at Botser was isolated from the main body of the Third Army and supplies were uncertain. "We're cut off and entirely dependent on God and the U.N.," he wrote in his diary. On the same day, in a fanciful bit of escapism, he drew up a list of favorite music, plays, films, and books. Almost all were Western. "Tchaikovsky, 1812 Overture, Napoleon's war" headed the music list. Robert Bolt's *A Man for All Seasons* headed the list of plays with *The Koran and Its Modern Interpretation*, third on his literary list, the only Arabic entry.

On November 27, a month after the cease-fire went into effect, Nadeh recorded that his commander had demoted him to private and struck him for refusing to work because he was ill. Ten days later, he and six comrades slipped away from their unit and crossed the canal at night in an effort to infiltrate through the Israeli lines. In an encounter with an Israeli patrol they were all killed. The diary found on Sergeant Nadeh's body was handed over to intelligence officers. Six years later, two Israeli journalists, who obtained the diary from the army, traveled to a slum dwelling in Alexandria to hand it over to Nadeh's parents. The parents agreed to publication of excerpts. These included a last will and testament in English. "When the moment comes, remember me," it said. "I fought for my country. Millions of my countrymen dream of peace. It may be that the unknown is beautiful. But the present is more beautiful."

The Yom Kippur War marked a major turning in the Israel-Arab confrontation: a terrible war with a perfect ending. By restoring pride to Egypt and a sense of proportion to Israel, it opened the way to the Camp David peace agreement. Fifteen years after that, Israel signed a peace agreement with Jordan. In the ensuing years, the Jewish state would weave discreet economic and political ties with other Arab countries, from Morocco to the Gulf states, as demonization gave way, at least among elites, to a measure of realpolitik. These relations would wax and wane but a psychological barrier had been breached.

The possibility of renewed war in the Middle East would remain ever-present, particularly when the unresolved Palestinian issue inflamed passions. But the Yom Kippur War, despite its disastrous opening for Israel, had enhanced its military deterrence, not diminished it. It is hard to imagine a more propitious opening hand than the one Egypt and Syria dealt themselves in October 1973—achieving strategic and tactical surprise in a two-front war, fought according to plans they had rehearsed for years under the tutelage of a superpower.

Yet the war ended less than three weeks later with the Israeli army threatening their capitals. The chances of Israel permitting itself to be surprised like that again would appear unlikely.

Even before the shooting had completely stopped, there were glimmers of recognition among the combatants on the Egyptian front, of the human face in the foxhole opposite. Infantrymen attached to Amir Yoffe's tank battalion, positioned at the edge of Suez City, exchanged fire with Egyptian troops opposite them despite the cease-fire until a U.N. contingent inserted itself between the two forces. As the blue-helmeted peacekeepers deployed, soldiers on both sides raised their heads above their firing positions and looked across at the men they had just been shooting at. The Egyptians were the first to react, dozens of them setting their weapons down and passing through the U.N. line to the Israeli company opposite.

The company commander radioed Yoffe to report that his position was being inundated with Egyptian soldiers. "Take them prisoner," said Yoffe, assuming that was the reason they had come over.

"They don't want to surrender," said the company commander. "They want to shake hands." Some of the Egyptians kissed the Israeli soldiers. Shouts from Egyptian officers brought the men back.

When an army entertainment troupe performed for Yoffe's battalion a few days later, their songs included one dating from the Six Day War. It mocked Egyptian soldiers who fled the battlefield, leaving behind their boots in the sand. Afterward, soldiers went up to the performers and suggested that they drop that song from their repertoire. Such easy derision of the enemy was jarring after three weeks of grueling battle.

The most striking fraternization occurred at the other end of the line, near Ismailiya. The morning after the first cease-fire went into effect, Capt. Gideon Shamir was deploying his paratroop company along a spur of the Sweetwater Canal when he saw Egyptian commandos encamped in an orchard one hundred yards away. They were apparently part of the unit with which he had clashed the previous night. The cease-fire was already being violated elsewhere along the line and Shamir, from a religious kibbutz in the Beisan Valley, wanted to ensure that there would be no more killing in his sector.

Telling his men to cover him, he entered an empty irrigation ditch leading toward the orchard, taking with him a soldier who spoke Arabic. Shamir shouted to the Egyptians as he approached—"Cease-fire, peace." The ditch provided ready cover if needed but the commandos signaled the two Israelis to approach. They summoned their company commander, who introduced himself as Major Ali. Speaking English, Shamir told him that he wanted to avoid unnecessary casualties. The war was over, he said, and it would be foolish for anyone on either side to get hurt now. Ali agreed. He surprised Shamir when he said that Sadat wanted not just a cease-fire but peace with Israel.

In the coming days, soldiers from both sides ventured into the clearing between the two positions and fraternized. When shooting broke out in adjacent sectors, they hurried back to their respective lines. Initially, when there was shooting at night, the Egyptians fired at Shamir's positions, although they did not do so by day. The paratroopers held their fire and after a few nights the Egyptians opposite no longer fired either. Before long, the commandos and paratroopers were meeting daily to brew up coffee and play backgammon. Soccer games followed. Men came to know each other's first names and showed off pictures of wives and girlfriends. There was an occasional kumsitz, with the Egyptians slaughtering a sheep and Shamir's men contributing food parcels from home.

Word of the local armistice spread and similar arrangements were forged in other sectors. Even Sharon came by to see what was going on. One day, Ali told Shamir he had permission to take him on a visit to Cairo. However, Israeli intelligence officers, fearful that their Egyptian counterparts intended to get information from him, ruled it out.

In a discussion with Ali one day, Shamir asked about an editorial in a Cairo newspaper asserting that Cairo would never recognize Israel. The editorial had been reported on Israel Radio.

"That's just propaganda," said the commando major. "The truth is that we want peace and that we're moving towards it."

"Why doesn't Sadat say so?" asked Shamir

"Sadat can't say so explicitly. He's a new leader, and although some of the intelligentsia support him, his problem is to win the support of the common people, who are still hypnotized by the figure of Nasser."

A year before, said Ali, he had participated in a meeting of officers with Sadat. Ali was then a captain and the lowest-ranking officer present. "Sadat said that we have to concern ourselves with Egypt's internal development; if Israel would only show serious intentions of withdrawing from Sinai he would talk with it." Matters had to progress in stages, said Ali. "First the war has to stop. After a year or two we will travel to Tel Aviv and you to Cairo." According to what the Egyptian soldiers told their Israeli counterparts, Ali's uncle was a very senior officer. Some suggested it was Shazly himself.

The day after the disengagement agreement was signed, Ali brought his battalion commander as well as a colonel whose branch was not made clear. They wanted to hear from the Israeli captain what he thought about the agreement, evidently to probe at field level the seriousness of Israel's declarations. They seemed satisfied by Shamir's assurance that Israel really intended to pull back. Before departing, the Egyptian officers said they hoped that relations between the two countries would come to resemble the relations between Shamir's and Ali's men.

The Egyptian commandos and the Israeli paratroopers were at the spearheads of their respective armies. That these motivated fighters, left to themselves, chose at first opportunity to lay aside their weapons and break bread together on the battlefield said something about what the war had wrought.

After the 1967 war, Egypt perceived that its honor could be retrieved only in a renewed war, while Israel, certain of victory, was not overly intimidated by the prospect. In 1973, both sides emerged from the confrontation with honor intact and a desire not to taste of war again.

The Yom Kippur War had begun with a surprise attack but history, that master of paradox, provided an even more surprising ending, one that left behind on the furrowed battlefield the seeds of peace, however fragile. Not even Sadat, dreaming under his tree in Mit Abulkum, would have conjured up a vision as surrealistic as his journey to Jerusalem.

For Egypt, the war was a towering accomplishment that enabled Sadat to fly to Jerusalem as an equal, not a supplicant. For Israel, the war was an existential earthquake, but one whose repercussions were ultimately healthier than the euphoria induced by the Six Day War. The trauma was not a nightmare to be suppressed but a national memory that would be perpetuated, a standing reminder of the consequences of shallow thinking and arrogance. Israel's battlefield recovery reflected a will to live and a capacity to improvise amidst chaos. Israel would bear its scars but it would be sustained by the memory of how, in its darkest hour, its young men had mounted the nation's crumbling ramparts and held.

NOTES

1. Footprints in the Sand

Interviews with Motti Ashkenazi, Meir Weisel, and Mossad officer Reuven Merhav.

Dayan on inherent Arab weakness—address at Israel's Staff and Command College, August 1973.

2. The Man in the Peasant Robe

Sadat reshapes Dayan proposal—remarks by Ashraf Gorbal, Sadat's spokesman, at Yom Kippur War symposium in Washington, D.C., published in Parker's *The October War: A Retrospective*.

Saying it with flowers—Sisco in Parker.

All information on Kremlin discussions in this and other chapters, other than those involving Henry Kissinger, is from Israelyan's invaluable *Inside the Kremlin During the Yom Kippur War*.

Ismail's report on his conversation with Kissinger—Gamasy's *The October War*.

Sadat's conversation with Vinogradov—Anwar Sadat's *In Search of Identity*.

Interview with Jehan Sadat—*Yedioth Achronot*, November 6, 1987.

3. Dovecote

Quotes from Elazar throughout the book are mainly from Bartov's *Dado*, Shimon Golan's *Decision Making of Israeli High Command in Yom Kippur War*, and the Agranat Report.

Dovecote plan—mainly from "Shovakh Yonim" (Dovecote), an article in *Ma'archot* 276 by Dr. Ze'ev Eitan.

Dusky Light—article by Col. Shaul Shai in *Ma'archot* 372.

Officer uneasy about Zeira's self-confidence—Col. Danny Matt at Ramat Efal symposium.

Information on Ashraf Marwan throughout the book is principally from Bar-Joseph's *The Watchman Fell Asleep* and *Hamalach (The Angel)* and from the autobiography of Mossad chief Zvi Zamir, *B'ainaim Ptukhot (Eyes Wide Open)*, and an interview by the author with Zamir.

Dayan's comment on Marwan—interview with Rami Tal, published in *Ma'ariv*, April 27, 1997.

4. Badr

Egyptian preparations are based mainly on Shazly's *The Crossing of the Canal;* Gamasy; and Sadat.

On Israeli awareness of Egyptian use of water cannon—article by Roland Aloni, *Ma'archot* 361.

Intelligence not being passed on to the decision makers—*Israel Today,* March 10, 2015.

Meeting in Mrs. Meir's residence—Zamir.

5. Illusions

Background on air force—interviews with Benny Peled, Avihu Bin-Nun, Eitan Ben Eliyahu, David Ivri, Motti Hod; Ehud Yonay's *No Margin for Errors.*

Prewar estimate that the Israeli Air Force could lose one plane per missile battery attacked—interview with Benny Peled.

Bar-Lev's comments on Arab capabilities—Kermit Guy's *Bar-Lev.*

"Totality of the tank"—Wald's *The Curse of the Broken Vessels;* Luttwak and Horowitz's *The Israel Army;* and a series of articles by Binyamin Amidror in *Ha'olam Hazeh* in 1974–1975. Also, Shimon Naveh, "The Cult of the Offensive Preemption and the Future Challenges for Israeli Operational Thought," in Efraim Karsh, ed., *Between War and Peace.*

American general on Israeli gunnery—interview with Gen. Donn Starry.

Armored corps had doctrine for dealing with Sagger—interview with General Adan.

General Tal dismissing request for better antitank weapons—interview with Gen. Emanuel Shaked.

Material on Israeli Navy—from *The Boats of Cherbourg* by the author.

6. Summer Lull

Brezhnev-Nixon summit—Kissinger's *Years of Upheaval.*

State Department official sees better than 50-50 chance of war—Parker.

April 18 meeting at Mrs. Meir's home—Bartov, Bar-Joseph.

Paratroop general—interview with Danny Matt.

Gorodish inspections—interview with Dan Meridor.

Adan on Gonen—interview with Adan.

Egyptian secrecy about the coming war—article in *Ma'archot* 373 by Col. (Res.) Yohai Shaked.

7. A Royal Visit

Meeting of Mrs. Meir and King Hussein—interviews with Lou Kedar, Zussia Keniezer, and Mordecai Gazit.

Zeira's prediction of no war for another ten years—interview with Shmuel Askarov.

8. Sword from the Scabbard

Figures on Israeli and Arab armies—Carta's historical atlas.

Eleven warnings received by Israeli intelligence in September—Bar-Joseph in *Ma'archot* 361.

General Tal's warning—Bar-Joseph, *Ha'aretz*, December 18, 2002.

AMAN material—Yoel Ben-Porat's *Locked On;* Bar-Joseph; interviews with Avi Ya'ari and Zussia Keniezer.

Pearl Harbor—article by Robert Wohlstetter in *Foreign Affairs,* July 1965, as cited in Agranat Report.

"special means"—"The Special Means of Collection: The Missing Link in the Surprise of the Yom Kippur War," by Uri Bar-Joseph, *Middle East Journal*, Autumn 2013; "The Ears of the Country Weren't Listening," by Naama Lanski, *Yisrael Hayom*, September 13, 2013.

On Shabtai Brill—article in *Kol Hair* by Yair Sheleg, September 24, 1993.

Sergeant Nadeh's diary, translated and excerpts published in *Yedioth Achronot*, September 14, 1975.

9. Countdown

Shalev at meeting with Mrs. Meir—Agranat Report.

Forty-seventh Syrian Brigade—Amos Gilboa at Ramat Efal symposium.

Lieutenant Siman-Tov—Agranat Report.

American satellites and CIA—interview with Bruce Reidel.

Sadat-Vinogradov meeting—Israelyan.

Radio monitors pick up evacuation of Soviet families from Syria—film documentary, *Lo Tishkot Haaretz*.

Zeira's avoidance of ambiguity—Agranat Report.

Meeting in Dayan's office with Mrs. Meir—Agranat Report.

Zeira's need for closure—Uri Bar-Joseph and Arie W. Kruglanski, "Intelligence Failure and the Need for Cognitive Closure: On the Psychology of the Yom Kippur Surprise," *Political Psychology*, Vol. 24, No. 1, March 2003.

Intelligence bulletin, Friday morning—Bar-Joseph.

General Havidi—interview by Oded Granot in *Ma'ariv Sofshavua* magazine, October 1993.

Elazar would have mobilized if he had received the warning—Bartov.

Gamasy fears Israeli trick—Interview with Gamasy by Shmuel Segev in *Ma'ariv*, September 24, 1985.

Interception of Iraqi ambassador's message about evacuation of Soviet civilians from Syria and Egypt—*Yediat Hazahav (Golden Information)*, by Amos Gilboa, The Meir Amit Intelligence and Terrorism Information Center, July 2015.

General Elazar on October 1–6 being "the most normal week"—Agranat Report.

Zamir missing Kol Nidre—conversation with Zamir.

Zamir's meeting with Marwan—Zamir's autobiography, *Eyes Wide Open*.

10. Yom Kippur Morning

Conversation between Elazar and Benny Peled—interview with Peled.
Elazar's "almost ceremonial" look—Bartov.
Elazar's brothel joke—interview with Shlomo Gazit.
Dayan's refusal to preempt—article in *Ma'archot* 393 by Shimon Golan.
Mrs. Meir and General Lior—Haber's *War Will Break Out Today.*
Meeting of Zeira and senior staff—interview with Keniezer.
Cabinet meeting—interview with Victor Shemtov.

11. The Egyptian Crossing

Account of Egyptian crossing—Shazly and Gamasy.
Account of forts—interviews with Motti Ashkenazi, Shaul Moses, Yaacov Tros-
    tler, Avi Yaffe, Meir Weisel, Shalom Hala, Dr. Avi Ohri, Pinhas Strolovitz,
    Arye Segev, and Menahem Ritterband.

12. The Humbling of the Tank

Most of this chapter is based on the war diary compiled by Amnon Reshef's
    brigade and the unit history of Dan Shomron's brigade. Also *Albert* by
    Aviezer Golan—an account of General Mendler; and the unit history of
    Amir Yoffe's battalion.
Article by Amiram Ezov in *Yom Kippur War Studies.*
Egyptian antitank defenses—Shazly.
Oded Marom's story—from talk by Marom at Ramat Efal symposium.
Interviews with Eyal Yoffe, Rami Matan, Gabi Amir, and Reshef.
Air photos the air force didn't see until several days later—interview with Benny
    Peled.
Israel's shortage of firepower—Yisrael Tal's *National Security.*

13. Mobilization

Interviews with Yeshayahu Gavish, Uri Ben-Ari, Yitzhak Brik, Gabi Amir, Yom
    Tov Tamir, and Rami Matan.
Ariel Sharon's *Warrior;* Carta's historical atlas; Golan; Adan; and unit histories.
Some reserve units reaching front in half the planned time—Lt. Col. (Res.)
    Roland Aloni, *Ma'archot* 361.
Ben-Ari keeping an eye on Gonen—interview with Ben-Ari.
Appraisal of Abu Agheila—Binyamin Amidror, *Ha'olam Hazeh,* 1975.
Dayan saying there will not be war in the coming year—article by Sharon in
    Yedioth Achronot, September 24, 1993.
Erez's prediction of 2,500 to 3,000 dead—interviews with Haim Erez and Ami
    Morag.
Destruction of the Egyptian ambush near Baluza—article in *Ma'ariv Sofshavua,*
    October 1980, by Menahem Rahat.
Conversation between Sharon and Weisel—tape recording by Avi Yaffe.
Sharon moved by conversations with forts—interview with Yisrael Itkin, who
    served in Sharon's command personnel carrier.

14. Syrian Breakthrough

Interviews with Raful Eitan, Avigdor Kahalani, Avigdor Ben-Gal, Yair Nafshi, Uri Simhoni, Motti Hod, Dennie Agmon, Haim Barak, Shmuel Askarov, Oded Beckman, Zvi Rak, David Eiland, Shmuel Yakhin, Avraham Elimelekh, Yossi Gur, Nir Atir, Yoram Krivine, Amir Drori, Yudke Peled, Yoram Yair, Moshe Zurich, Hanan Schwartz, Zvika Greengold. Also Agranat Report, Kahalani's *Oz 77*, and "The Syrian Attack on the Golan Heights," by Lieutenant Colonel (Res.) Zvi (no last name given), in *Ma'archot* 314.

Acquisition of latest Syrian plan a week before war—Bar-Yosef's *The Watchman Fell Asleep.*

Outline of Syrian plan—Brig. Gen (Res.) Amos Gilboa, former head of AMAN's Syrian desk, at Ramat Efal symposium, October 2001.

Ben-Shoham not warning of war—Agranat Report, interview with Nafshi.

Intelligence officer who revealed too much—interview on Israel's Channel Two, 2016.

Erez not knowing that Barak's battalion was behind him—Agranat Report.

Interrogation of Lieutenant Al-Joju—article by Alex Fishman, *Yedioth Achronot*, September 19, 1999.

Ben-Gal reluctant to detach one of his battalions—interview with Ben-Gal in *Shirion.*

15. Darkest at Dawn

Poor reporting from the field—Shimon Golan at Ramat Efal symposium.

"I'm an atheist"—Sabbato's *Adjustment of Sights.*

Yotser's ascent—interview with Yotser.

Laner: "The fighting is over in the southern part of Golan"—Bartov.

Dayan's hands shaking from *Lo Tishkot Haaretz,* film documentary by Amit Goren.

Tagar—Yonai and interviews with Bin-Nun, Giora Furman, David Ivri, Benny Peled, Amos Amir, Eitan Ben-Eliyahu, Giora Rom.

16. The Fall of the Southern Golan

Interviews with Yair, Krivine, Kahalani, Ben-Gal, Gil Peled, and Drori; Kahalani's *Oz 77.*

Kalish—interview on Israel's Channel Two, May 20, 2001.

Ben-Shoham: "We've done our bit."—Agranat Report.

17. The Beanstalk

Interviews with Sarig, Bierman, Agmon, Yair, Ben-Porat, Orr, Greengold, Avraham Elimelekh, Shmuel Yakhin, Benny Michaelson, and Drori.

18. The Battle for Nafakh

Interviews with Greengold, Yotser, Barak, Orr, Haim Danon, Ron Gottfried, Agmon, Hanan Anderson, and Zurich. Also the unit history and film produced by Orr's brigade.

Agranat Report.

Zurich—Some of Ben-Shoham's staff officers, including Zurich, would contend that Zvika Greengold saved Nafakh and the Golan by blocking the Syrian drive up the Tapline Saturday night. However, it is not clear that the Syrian force had stopped because of its encounter with Greengold. Article by Yehuda Wagman in *Yom Kippur War Studies*.

19. Cut Off

Interviews with Moussa Peled, Avraham Rotem, Beckman, Gur, Yair, Atir, Orr, Motti Katz.

Written sources: Sabbato and unit histories.

Dayan on the need to replace Hofi—Arie Braun's *Moshe Dayan and the Yom Kippur War*.

Dayan weeping—Oral history interview with Moussa Peled, Armored Corps Library, Latrun.

Bar-Lev ordering radios at Northern Command to be shut—Guy's *Bar-Lev*.

Tel Fares bunker—Interview with Nir Atir; Uri Millstein's *The Collapse and Its Lessons*.

20. Hand on the Tiller

"Let the line be the Artillery Road or the Lateral Road"—Braun.

Conversation between Mrs. Meir and Lou Kedar—interview with Ms. Kedar.

Phantom pilot describing Syrian army on Golan—article by Sima Kadmon in *Ma'ariv*, September 24, 1993. Years later, Ms. Kadmon met the pilot, who did not recall his words but apologized for them.

The absence of "anticipatory fear"—Dr. Reuven Gal's *The Yom Kippur War: Lessons from the Psychologist's Perspective*.

Battle of San Simon—Bartov.

"Take a good look at each other"—article by Ravit Naor in *Ma'ariv*, September 24, 1993. The speaker, Maj. Ron Huldai, would be elected mayor of Tel Aviv in 1998.

Elazar's telephone conversation with Gonen—Agranat Report.

Dayan and the nuclear issue—"When Israel Stepped Back from the Brink," by Avner Cohen, *New York Times*, October 3, 2013; "Dayan Suggested Israel Prepare Nukes," by Amir Oren, *Ha'aretz*, October 3, 2013; article in *Yedioth Achronot* magazine, October 4, 2013 (in Hebrew), by Ronen Bergman.

Description of meeting of Dayan with ministers and Mrs. Meir in latter's office—The Avner Cohen Collection, Woodrow Wilson Center.

Sharon's conversation with Gonen—Sharon's *Warrior*.

Events at Fort Orkal—Arye Segev's *Unfulfilled Mission;* interviews with Segev, Ritterband.

IDF lacking sound staff work—Binyamin Amidror, in *Ha'olam Hazeh*.

21. Failed Counterattack

Interviews with Adan, Nir, Gabi Amir, Yitzhak Brik, Yom Tov Tamir, Haim Adini.

Adan's book offers a detailed description of the agonizing day, as does the Agranat Report. Other published material includes "October 8," by Colonel Ze'ev (no complete name given), in *Ma'archot* 268, Bartov, Elyashiv Shimshi's *Storm in October*, Millstein, unit histories, and article by Assaf Yaguri in *Yedioth Achronot*, October 10, 1978.

Commando officers who eliminate artillery spotters—interview with Lt. Col. Amazia Chen.

Elazar: "The sky's the limit"—Agranat Report.

Radio communications between Gonen and Adan—Agranat Report.

Gonen not commanding from the saddle—Binyamin Amidror.

Adini comparing a tank charge to an orgasm is from Millstein.

22. Bomb Damascus

"But in war it's forbidden to tell the truth"—Shimon Golan, p. 555.

"There isn't a single tank from there to Haifa"—Bartov.

Attack on Hermon—interviews with Drori and Yudke Peled.

Sharon on seeking votes in Cairo—Braun.

Meeting at Umm Hashiba—Bartov, Adan.

Dayan on need for "brutal effort" to drive Syria out of war—Braun.

Dayan on entering Damascus—interview with Dayan's aide-de-camp, Arie Braun, by Yigal Sarna in *Yedioth Achronot*, September 17, 1991.

Kissinger quip to Dinitz—article by Yigal Sarna in *Yedioth Achronot*, Yom Kippur edition, 1996.

Disappointment within air force at poor showing of Israeli armor—interview with David Ivri.

Attack on Damascus—interview with Lapidot.

Description of Joel Aronoff—interview by Arieh O'Sullivan in *Jerusalem Post*, February 4, 2000.

Basement of Syrian army headquarters—interview with Barber.

23. Touching Bottom

General Tal on war of survival—Bartov.

Israel's nuclear arsenal—Hersh's *The Samson Option*.

Debate in the Pit on nuclear issue from *Lo Tishkot Haaretz* film documentary.

Hizayon—Interviews with Ohr and Strolovitz. Ohr became a professor of rehabilitation medicine at Tel Aviv University. He recalled his ordeal as he sat at his swimming pool in the upscale Tel Aviv suburb of Savion.

Egyptian cameraman—interview with Gohar in Cairo.

"Silent patrol"—interview with Matt.

Brom's patrol—interview with Brom's deputy, Zvi Avidan.

24. Golan Counterattack

Interviews with Kahalani, Gidi Peled, Ban-Gal, Rak, Nafshi, Sarig.

Entry of rescuers into bunker at Tel Saki—The story was related on Israel Radio by Motti Aviram, one of the men in the bunker. As an archaeologist twenty years later he excavated the site of Yodfat in the Galilee where the

Jewish general and historian Josephus hid in a cave with others after the city's fall to the Romans, an experience paralleling that of Aviram and his comrades.

Kahalani's *Oz 77,* unit histories.

Assad exhorting division commanders—interview with Mohammed Bassiouni, Egyptian liaison at Syrian General Staff headquarters.

Shmuel Askarov's wound—The bullet entered his forehead and emerged from the rear of his skull. Three doctors said it was hopeless but a fourth decided to operate. Askarov recovered. Though partially paralyzed and speech impaired, he would walk unaided and be able to drive.

General Jehani—Amos Gilad at Ramat Efal symposium.

25. Iraqi Intervention

Bierman would remain unconscious for two months and undergo fourteen operations but recover. He became a senior official with the Israel Antiquities Authority, headed by Amir Drori, former Golani commander.

Ben-Gal acceding to Ben-Hanan's request to attack Tel Shams—Herzog.

Ben-Hanan would eventually become commander of the armored corps. Netanyahu was killed in the Entebbe rescue operation in 1976.

Mofaz's raid behind Syrian lines—article by Moshe Zonder, *Ma'ariv Sofshavua* magazine, October 1992.

26. Powers That Be

This chapter is based largely on Kissinger and Israelyan.

27. Change in Command

Interviews with Benny Peled, Gavish, Moses.

"Positions of the Chief of Staff and the Political Level on a Canal Crossing and Cease-Fire," by Lt. Col. Shimon Golan, *Ma'archot* 327.

Bartov's *Dado.*

Dayan on Sharon: "'What will I be getting out of this business?'"—*Yedioth Achronot,* August 2003.

Ben-Ari on Gonen—Ezov, p. 79.

Egyptian brigade moved out from under SAM umbrella—Shazly.

Israeli Arabs in war—author's reporting for *The Jerusalem Post.*

Naval account based on *The Boats of Cherbourg* by the author.

28. Decision to Cross

"Positions of the Chief of Staff and the Political Level on a Canal Crossing and Cease-Fire," by Lt. Col. Shimon Golan, *Ma'archot* 327.

Bartov, Braun, Dayan's *Milestones.*

Talk by Zvi Zamir at Ramat Efal symposium.

Mossad receives message from Egyptian agent on pending armor attack—from documentary *Lo Tishkot Haaretz (The Land Will Not Be Silent),* produced by Amit Goren.

The ongoing debates within the Israeli high command and with the commanders of the northern and southern fronts is spelled out in detail by Shimon Golan in his 1,300-page compilation on the General Staff during the war, *Milkhama B'Yom Hakipurim (Decision Making of the Israeli High Command in the Yom Kippur War)*.

29. Stouthearted Men

"Kissinger almost tore his hair out"—from documentary *Lo Tishkot Haaretz (The Land Will Not Be Silent)*, produced by Amit Goren.

Mendler and navy—Golan's *Albert*.

Extracts from Nadeh's diary were published in *Yedioth Achronot* on September 30, 1979.

Material on bridges from interviews with Avi Zohar, Yishai Dotan, Amikam Doron, Menashe Gur, Ya'acov Even. Also books by Adan, Tal.

Sharon conversations with Yael Dayan and Ezer Weizman—Uri Dan's *The Bridgehead*.

"The Crossing," article by Gen. Ariel Sharon in *Shirion [Armor magazine]*, October 1998.

Battle with Egyptian commando force—interview with Lt. Col. Amazia Chen.

Estimates of Egyptian tank losses in October 14 attack—oddly enough, Shazly and Gamasy cite the higher figure while Israeli analysts tend toward the lower.

Mrs. Meir had recovered her composure—interview with Victor Shemtov.

Soviet involvement in planning canal crossing—Soviet journal *Novia Vrema* as cited in *Bamahane*, May 3, 1989.

"They believed"—article by Sharon in *Yedioth Achronot* on twenty-fifth anniversary of the war.

"The computer would have burned up"—Ezov.

Scene at Umm Hashiba on night of the crossing—article in *Ma'ariv* by Aharon Priel, September 9, 1985.

Hanan Erez threatening to shoot colonel—interview with Erez.

Mitzna briefing his men—article in *Yedioth Achronot* by Yael Gevirtz, June 17, 1995.

30. The Chinese Farm

Most of this chapter is based on the war diary compiled by Colonel Reshef's brigade. Also Yuval Neria's *Aish*. Interviews with Reshef, Matan, Doron, Matt, Eli Cohen, Natan Shunari, Even, Giora Lev, Itkin, and Neria. The latter, awarded Israel's highest medal for his performance in the war, would become a psychologist and a prominent member of Israel's peace movement.

Rabin's nephew—Reshef's *Lo Nechdal*. Ochayon would in time become a senior officer in the Israeli police.

Article on Danny Matt by Simha Aharoni in *Yedioth Achronot*, October 6, 1985.

Sharon adjusting his beret—Itkin.

31. The Bridges

Bridges—interviews with Even, Avi, Dotan, Doron, Gur.

Morag's ride—interviews with Morag, Yehuda Tal, and company commander Amnon Amikam.

"If they don't get a bridge up soon"—*October Days,* edited by Mordecai Naor and Ze'ev Aner.

Sharon's division—interviews with Erez, Reshef, Lev, Geller.

Dayan angry at Mrs. Meir's Knesset revelation—Braun.

Paratroopers—interviews with Matt, Yitzhak Mordecai, Yehuda Duvdevani.

Colonel Razon and his wounded son—article in *Shirion* by Col. Shaul Nagar, September 2000.

Adan's division—interviews with Adan, Tamari, Nir, Amir.

Article by Eitan Haber, in *Yedioth Achronot,* October 1985.

"Lail Hapritsa L'Chava Hasinit" ["Night of the Break—into the Chinese Farm"], article by Shimon Manueli, published by Israeli Defense Forces in 1977.

32. Crossing into Africa

"Three infiltrating Israeli tanks"—Mohammed Heikal's *The Road to Ramadan.*

Israel learns that Sadat has taken personal command—Braun.

Sharon at crossing point—interviews with Itkin, Yehoshua Sagui, and Reshef.

Sergeant Barnea's account—article by Barnea in *Ma'archot* 361.

Dayan and Elazar discuss Sharon—Ezov.

Sharon wanting to smack Bar-Lev—Sharon's *Warrior.*

Yitzhak Brik—interview. As an IDF general in the 1990s, Brik visited an armor training school in Russia where he discovered that the ambush of the Twenty-fifth Brigade was part of the curriculum.

Warning not to use poison gas—Braun.

Attack on Banha—interview with Benny Peled.

33. Breakout

Books—Adan, Carta, Sharon, Heikal, Shazly, Gamasy, Sadat.

Interviews—Brik, Bin-Nun, Yehuda Geller, Adan, Nir, Reshef, Lev.

Gillois—interview with deputy Gillois commander, Amikam Doron.

Saudi force lost in Jordanian desert and rescued by camel patrol: Asaf David.

Casualties in Chinese Farm—from *Tzliha [Crossing],* by Amiram Ezov.

Bomb explosion near Dayan's APC; Sharon firing Kalashnikov—interview with Itkin.

Chief of Staff Elazar dresses down air force commander for insufficient ground support—*Milkhama B'Yom Hakipurim,* by Shimon Golan.

Israeli skeleton forces in Sinai only one-fourth Egyptian forces there—Adan in Ofer and Kober's *Aichut v'Kamut.*

Jordan's participation in the war is based mainly on an article by Asaf David—"Jordan's War That Never Was"—which appears in a collection of articles edited by Asaf Siniver, *The October 1973 War: Politics, Diplomacy, Legacy.*

Major Suleiman—article by Yigal Lev in *Ma'ariv,* October 10, 1981.

34. Kissinger to the Fore

Southern Command monitoring Sharon's units—Braun.

Avi Weiss's *Prisoner of Egypt* provides an intimate view of Israeli tank crewmen at the battle for Missouri.

Final assault on the Israeli Hermon—interviews with Yudke Peled, Drori.

Paratroop officer's conversation with Drori—Uri Millstein, *Hadashot,* September 24, 1985.

Elbaz's account—interview on Israel Radio.

Paratroop assault on the Syrian Hermon—interview with brigade commander Haim Nadel.

Naval commando assault on Ardaka—interviews with Almog and Gadi Kol.

35. Cease-fire

General Wasel complaining about General Kabil—"Aircraft in Ground Support," by Major Y. and Colonel Y. (full names not given), in *Ma'archot* 266.

Israel wouldn't have received so much as a nail—Braun.

Egyptian soldiers shooting deserters—interviews with Matan, Col. Yehoshua Sagui.

Sharon and Egyptian pilot—interview with Yisrael Itkin.

"Their eyes said, 'We've gotten this far' "—interview with Dov Tamari.

Ready to go to Cairo—interview with Rami Matan.

Shimshi's battalion—*Storm in October.*

Arab odds against Israel on northern front—Iraqi war diary.

36. Suez City

Article by Aviezer Golan, *Yedioth Achronot,* September 14, 1975.

Adan, unit histories.

Interviews with David Amit, Amiram Gonen, Brik, Yitzhak Mordecai.

37. Nuclear Alert

Interview with Admiral Murphy from *The Boats of Cherbourg* by the author.

Dayan: "They didn't run"—Braun.

Yom Tov Tamir shouting at Mrs. Meir—interview with Tamir.

Sharon slapping major—Sagui.

Mrs. Meir regrets not pulling back in Sinai in 1970—Dayan's autobiography.

Kissinger's comforting arm—interview in *Yedioth Achronot,* September 9, 1991, with Eli Mizrachi, former director of Mrs. Meir's office.

IDF incorporates 400 Syrian tanks into its ranks—Roland Aloni in *Ma'archot* 361.

400 Israeli tanks destroyed in war, 600 damaged and repaired—Tal.

"The best army the IDF has ever had"—interview with Gen. Herzl Sapir.

Arab casualty figures—Col. Trevor Dupuy, *Elusive Victory.*

Israelis in battle trauma—Gal's *The Yom Kippur War: Lessons from the Psychologist's Perspective.*

38. Aftermath

Ashraf Marwan—Uri Bar-Joseph is the major source on this episode. Mossad chief Zamir also shed light on the affair in an interview with the author and he referred to it in a lecture given in Tel Aviv to mark the fortieth anniversary of the war.

Reporter who visited Gonen in Africa—Adam Baruch of *Ma'ariv.*

General Shazly, in a telephone interview in Cairo with the Israeli newspaper *Yedioth Achronot* on the thirtieth anniversary of the war, said he refused to meet with Israelis but that he followed developments in Israel closely.

IAF attack on the Bekaa in 1982—Yonay, Amos Amir's *Flames in the Sky*, interview by author with former air force commander David Ivri.

Shimon Maliach episode—article in *Ma'ariv* by Avihai Becker, September 24, 1993.

Fraternization outside Suez City—unit history of Amir Yoffe's battalion.

Israeli paratroopers and Egyptian commandos fraternizing south of Ismailiya—interview with Gideon Shamir; 1974 documentary on Israel Television Channel One by Motti Kirschenbaum.

A SELECTED BIBLIOGRAPHY

The two-thousand-page report of the Agranat Commission is basic to any study of the war, as is Hanoch Bartov's wartime account of Chief of Staff David Elazar. Bartov was provided access to extensive records by Elazar.

An invaluable text published in 2013, forty years after the war, is *Milkhama B'Yom Hakipurim (Decision Making of the Israeli High Command in the Yom Kippur War)* by Shimon Golan, who was an IDF historian. The 1,300-page book, in Hebrew, is a day-by-day compilation of decisions by the Israeli high command during the war based on written protocols and recordings. It captures the shifting moods through verbatim exchanges.

Relevant excerpts from cabinet and General Staff protocols are contained in Moshe Dayan's autobiography and the account written by his aide-de-camp, Arie Braun.

The colossal failings of Israeli military intelligence prior to the war are detailed in two highly illuminating books by Prof. Uri Bar-Joseph, himself a former intelligence analyst. The then Mossad chief, Zvi Zamir, provides in *Eyes Wide Open (B'ainaim Ptukhot)* the ultimate insider's account, in Hebrew, of the dramatic reports he received from Egyptian informers that changed the course of the war and of his disputes with the chief of military intelligence.

Gens. Avraham Adan and Ariel Sharon offer illuminating accounts of the war on the Egyptian front in their memoirs.

Scores of highly useful accounts and analyses of the war have been published in *Ma'archot,* Israel's leading military journal, as well as other Hebrew periodicals. Unit histories were invaluable in reconstructing battles. An often poignant personal dimension is provided in memoirs by combatants, from tank sergeants to pilots, and by the diary of an Egyptian soldier, Sgt. Mahmud Nadeh, found on the battlefield.

Eight daylong symposiums conducted by the Israeli Society for Military History in 1999–2001 produced important insights.

The Arab side is far less well documented than the Israeli. The best English-language book on Egypt's performance is by Gen. Saad el Shazly, wartime chief of staff. There is no substantive account from Syria of its part in the war although some light on the Syrian performance is offered in an Iraqi account of the war translated into Hebrew and in articles by former Israeli intelligence officers. Most Israeli combatants noted significant improvement in the Arabs' battlefield performance. Virtually none of the Arab accounts translated into English has a good word to say about the remarkable recovery by the Israeli army, although the Iraqi account is straightforward and professional.

Victor Israelyan's inside view from the Kremlin nicely augments Henry Kissinger's account of the war.

Two multipart film documentaries—*Lo Tishkot Haaretz [The Avoidable War]*, an Israeli production directed by Amit Goren, and *The War in October* by Al Jazeera English, are worthy and informative accounts.

Much of this book rests on interviews by the author with more than 130 participants in the war. Talks with senior officers sometimes involved several sessions.

Books

Adan, Avraham. *On the Banks of the Suez*. San Francisco: Presidio Press, 1980.

Amir, Amos. *Aish ba'shamayaim [Flames in the Sky]*. Tel Aviv: Defense Ministry, 2000.

el Badri, Hassan, Taha el Magdoub, and Mohammed Dia el din Zohdy. *The Ramadan War*. Dunn Loring, Va.: T. N. Dupuy Associates, 1979.

Bar-Joseph, Uri. *The Angel: The Egyptian Spy Who Saved Israel*. New York: HarperCollins, 2016

———. *The Watchman Fell Asleep*. Albany: SUNY Press, 2005.

Bartov, Chanoch. *Dado*. Tel Aviv: Ma'ariv Book Guild, 1978.

Ben-Porat, Yoel. *Neila [Locked On]*. Tel Aviv: Edanim, 1991.

Benziman, Uzi. *Sharon: An Israeli Caesar*. Tel Aviv: Adama, 1985.

Bergman, Ronen, and Gil Meltzer. *Zman Emet [Real Time]*. Tel Aviv: Yedioth Achronot and Chemed, 2003.

Braun, Arie. *Moshe Dayan v'Milkhemet Yom Kippur [Moshe Dayan and the Yom Kippur War]*. Tel Aviv: Edanim, 1992.

Carta. *Atlas l'Toldot Medinat Yisrael [Atlas of the History of the State of Israel, 1971–1981]*. Jerusalem: Carta, 1983.

Cohen, Avner. *Israel's Worst Kept Secret*. New York: Columbia University Press, 2010.

Cohen, Eliot, and John Gooch. *Military Misfortunes*. New York: Vintage, 1991.

Cordesman, Anthony H., and Abraham R. Wagner. *The Lessons of Modern War, Vol. 1: The Arab-Israeli Conflicts 1973–1989*. Boulder, Co.: Westview Press, 1990.

Dan, Uri. *Rosh Gesher [The Bridgehead]*. Tel Aviv: A. L. Special Edition, 1975.

Davis Institute for International Relations. *Milkhemet Yom Hakipurim [The Yom Kippur War, a New View*. Symposium on the War's twenty-fifth anniversary.] Jerusalem: Hebrew University, 1998.

Dayan, Moshe. *Avnei Derekh [Milestones]*. Jerusalem: Edanim, 1982.

Dupuy, Trevor. *Elusive Victory*. New York: HarperCollins, 1978.

Ezov, Amiram. *Tslicha: Shishim Sha'ot [Crossing: 60 Hours]*. Tel Aviv: Dvir, 2011.

Gal, Dr. Reuven. *The Yom Kippur War: Lessons from the Psychologist's Perspective*. Zikhron Ya'acov: The Israeli Institute for Military Studies, 1987.

el-Gamasy, Gen. Mohamed Abdel Ghani. *The October War*. Cairo: The American University in Cairo Press, 1993.

Gelber, Yoav, and Hanni Ziv. *Bnai Keshet [Sons of the Bow]*. Tel Aviv: Defense Ministry, 1998.

Golan, Aviezer. *Albert*. Tel Aviv: Yediot, 1977.

Golan, Haggai, and Shaul Shai. *Milkhama Hayom [Yom Kippur War Studies]*. Tel Aviv: Defense Ministry, 2003.

Golan, Shimon. *Milkhama B'Yom Hakipurim [Decision Making of the Israeli High Command in the Yom Kippur War]*. Tel Aviv: Modan Publishing, 2013.

Gordon, Shmuel. *Shloshim Sha'ot B'October [30 Hours in October]*. Tel Aviv: Ma'ariv Book Guild, 2008.

Guy, Kermit. *Bar-Lev* (Hebrew biography of Haim Bar-Lev). Tel Aviv: Am Oved, 1998.

Haber, Eitan. *Hayom Tifrots Milkhama, [War Will Break Out Today]*. Tel Aviv: Edanim, 1987.

Haber, Eitan, and Zeev Schiff. *Lexicon Milkhemet Yom Kippur [Yom Kippur War Lexicon]*. Or Yehuda: Zmora-Bitan-Dvir, 2003.

Heikal, Mohammed Hassenein. *The Road to Ramadan*. New York: Ballantine, 1975.

Hersh, Seymour M. *The Samson Option*. New York: Random House. 2013.

Herzog, Chaim. *The War of Atonement*. Tel Aviv: Steimatzky, 1975.

Hirst, David, and Irene Beeson. *Sadat*. London: Faber & Faber, 1981.

Insight Team of *The Sunday Times*. *Insight on the Middle East*. London: André Deutsch, 1974.

Iraqi Defense Ministry. *Zva Iraq b' Milkhemet Yom Kippur [The Iraqi Army in the Yom Kippur War]*, translation from Arabic to Hebrew. Tel Aviv: Ma'archot, 1986.

Israelyan, Victor. *Inside the Kremlin During the Yom Kippur War*. University Park: Pennsylvania State University Press, 1995.

Kahalani, Avigdor. *Oz 77 [77th Battalion]*. Tel Aviv: Schocken, 1975.

Karsh, Efraim, ed. *Between War and Peace: Dilemmas of Israeli Security*. London: Frank Cass, 1996.

Kedar, B. Z. *Sipuro Shel Gdud Makhatz [Story of a Strike Battalion]*. Tel Aviv: Tamuz Press, 1975.

Kissinger, Henry. *Years of Upheaval*. Boston: Little, Brown, 1982.

Kober, Avi. *Hakhara Tsvait [Military Decision in the Arab-Israeli Wars]*. Tel Aviv: Ma'archot, 1996.

Kumaraswamy, P. R., ed. *Revisiting the Yom Kippur War*. London: Frank Cass, 2000.

Lanir, Zvi. *Hahafta'a Habasist [The Basic Surprise]*. Tel Aviv: Kav Adom, 1983.

Luttwak, Edward, and Dan Horowitz. *The Israeli Army*. New York: Harper & Row, 1975.

Meir, Golda. *My Life*. Tel Aviv: Ma'ariv, 1977.

Meital, Yoram. *Egypt's Struggle for Peace*. Gainesville: University of Florida Press, 1997.

Michaelson, Benny, and Effi Meltzer. *Milkhemet Yom Kippur [The Yom Kippur War]*. Israeli Military History Association, a compilation of articles presented at an eighteen-day seminar, Tel Aviv, 1998.

Millstein, Uri. *Krisa V'lekacha [The Collapse and Its Lessons]*. Kiron: Sridot, 1993.

Morris, Benny. *Righteous Victims*. New York: Vintage, 1999.

Naor, Mordecai, and Ze'ev Aner, eds. *Yemai October [October Days]*. Tel Aviv: Defense Ministry, 1974.

Neria, Yuval. *Aish [Fire]*. Tel Aviv: Zmora Bitan, 1989.

Ofer, Zvi, and Avi Kober, eds. *Aichut v'Kamut [Quality and Quantity]*. Tel Aviv: Ma'archot, 1985.

Oren, Elhanan. *Toldot Milkhemet Yom Hakipurim [The History of the Yom Kippur War]*. Tel Aviv: Israel Defense Forces History Department, 2004.

Orr, Ori. *Elah Ha'achim Sheli [These Are My Brothers]*. Tel Aviv: Yedioth Achronot and Chemed, 2003.

Parker, Richard B., ed. *The October War: A Retrospective*. Gainesville: University Press of Florida, 2001.

Peled, Yossi. *Ish Tsava [Soldier]*. Tel Aviv: Ma'ariv, 1993.

Pretty, R. T. *Weapon Systems*. London: Jane's, 1979.

Rabinovich, Abraham. *The Boats of Cherbourg*. Annapolis, Md.: Naval Institute Press, 1988.

Rafael, Gideon, *Destination Peace*. Jerusalem: Edanim, 1981.

Reshef, Amnon, *Lo Nechdal [We Will Not Cease: The 14th Brigade in the Yom Kippur War]*. Tel Aviv: Dvir, 2013.

Sabbato, Chaim. *Tium Kavanot [Adjustment of Sights]*. Tel Aviv: Yediot Achronot, 1999.

Sadat, Anwar. *In Search of Identity*. New York: Harper & Row, 1978.

Safran, Nadav. *Israel, the Embattled Ally*. Cambridge, Mass.: Belknap Press of Harvard University Press, 1978.

Seale, Patrick. *Assad: The Struggle for the Middle East*. Berkeley: University of California Press, 1988.

Segev, Arye. *Lo Bitsati et Hamesima [Unfulfilled Mission]*. Tel Aviv: Seder Tselem, 2001.

Sharon, Ariel, with David Chanoff. *Warrior: The Autobiography of Ariel Sharon*. London: MacDonald, 1989.

Shashar, Michael. *Sikhot Im Rehavam Ze'evi [Talks with Rechavam Ze'evi]*. Tel Aviv: Yedioth Achronot, 1982.

Shay, Shaul, ed. *The Iraqi-Israel Conflict, 1948–2000*. Tel Aviv: Defense Ministry, 2002.

el Shazly, Gen. Saad. *The Crossing of the Canal*. San Francisco: American Mideast Research, 1980.

Shimshi, Elyashiv. *Aifo Ani Nimtsa [Where I Stand]*. Tel Aviv: Defense Ministry, 2002.

———. *B'Koach Hatachbula [By Virtue of Stratagem]*. Tel Aviv: Defense Ministry, 1999.

————. *Seara b'October [Storm in October]*. Tel Aviv: Defense Ministry, 1986.

Shirion magazine, a compilation of articles published by the magazine of the Armor Corps on the fortieth anniversary of the war in 2013.

Siniver, Asaf, ed. *The October 1973 War: Politics, Diplomacy, Legacy.* London: Hurst & Co., 2012.

Spector, Yiftakh. *Khalom B'tchelet-Shakhor [A Dream in Blue and Black]*. Jerusalem: Keter, 1991.

Tal, Israel. *Bitachon Leumi [National Security]*. Tel Aviv: Dvir, 1996.

Wald, Emanuel. *Klalat Hakailim Hashverum [The Curse of the Broken Vessels]*. Tel Aviv: Schocken, 1987.

Weiss, Avi. *B'Shevi Hamitsri [Prisoner of Egypt]*. Tel Aviv: Defense Ministry, 1998.

Wohlstetter, Roberta. *Pearl Harbor: Warning and Decision*. Stanford: Stanford University Press, 1962.

Yonay, Ehud. *No Margin for Errors: The Story of the Israeli Air Force*. New York: Pantheon, 1983.

Zaloga, Steven J. *Armour of the Middle East War*. London: Osprey Publishing, 1981.

Zamir, Zvi. *B'ainaim Ptukhot [Eyes Wide Open]*. Or Yehuda: Kinneret, Zmora-Bitan, Dvir, 2013.

Zeira, Eli. *Milkhemet Yom Kippur: Mytos Mul Metsiut [The Yom Kippur War: Myth vs. Reality]*. Tel Aviv: Yedioth Achronot, 1993.

Other Sources

Four-part documentary produced for Israel Television by Amit Goren—*Lo Tishkot Haaretz [The Land Will Not Be Silent;* released in English as *The Avoidable War]*.

Three-part documentary produced by Al Jazeera English—*The War in October.*

War diary of Col. Amnon Reshef's brigade.

Tape recordings from Fort Purkan, including conversation with Gen. Ariel Sharon, made by radioman Avi Yaffe.

A summation of the Israeli Air Force's role during the war compiled by Lt. Col. Yossi Aboudi, made available by Gen. Benny Peled.

Films produced by Yitzhak Mordecai's battalion, Ori Orr's brigade, and the Engineering Corps.

Israel Radio broadcasts.

Israel Television.

Unit Histories (listed by names of unit commanders)

Division histories—Raful Eitan; Dan Laner

Brigade histories—Ori Orr; Yossi Peled; Haim Erez; Tuvia Raviv; Dan Shomron; Danny Matt; Natke Nir; Mordecai Ben-Porat

Battalion histories—Amir Yoffe; Emanuel Sakel; Yitzhak Mordecai; Shimon Ben-Shoshan; Ami Morag

Israeli Military Magazines

Ma'archot
Shirion
Bamahane

Israeli Newspapers and Magazines

Yedioth Achronot
Ma'ariv
Ha'aretz
The Jerusalem Post
Hadashot
Ha'olam Hazeh (an incisive series of articles by military analyst Binyamin Amidror in 1974–1975)

Persons Interviewed (ranks given were those held at the time)

Northern Command

Gen. Rafael (Raful) Eitan—division commander
Gen. Moussa Peled—division commander
Col. Avigdor Ben-Gal—armored brigade commander
Col. Mordecai Ben-Porat—armored brigade commander
Col. Ori Orr—armored brigade commander
Col. Ran Sarig—armored brigade commander
Col. Haim Nadel—commander paratroop brigade
Col. Amir Drori—commander, Golani Infantry Brigade
Col. Avraham Rotem—deputy division commander
Lt. Col. Uri Simhoni—operations officer, Northern Command
Lt. Col. Avigdor Kahalani—tank battalion commander
Lt. Col. Yudke Peled—Golani battalion commander
Lt. Col. Yair Nafshi—tank battalion commander
Lt. Col. Ron Gottfried—tank battalion commander
Lt. Col. Motti Katz—intelligence officer, Moussa Peled's division
Lt. Col. Chagai Mann—Northern Command intelligence officer
Lt. Col. Pinhas Kuperman—deputy commander, Golan District Brigade
Lt. Col. Aldo Zohar—artillery battery commander
Maj. Shmuel Askarov—tank battalion deputy commander
Maj. Giora Berman—tank battalion commander
Maj. Haim Barak—tank battalion commander
Maj. Haim Danon—tank battalion commander
Maj. Hanan Schwartz—communications officer, 188th Brigade
Maj. David Caspi—deputy tank battalion commander
Maj. Zvi Rak—tank company commander
Maj. Yoram Yair—commander of paratroops manning frontline outposts
Capt. David Harman—intelligence officer
Lt. Avraham Elimelekh—commander of Strongpoint 107

Lt. David Eiland—tank platoon commander
Lt. Nitzan Yotser—tank platoon commander
Lt. Zvika Greengold—tank officer
Lt. Gidi Peled—tank battalion operations officer
Lt. Oded Beckman—tank platoon commander
Lt. Hanan Anderson—tank platoon commander
Lt. Yehuda Wagman—deputy tank company commander
Lt. Yossi Gur—commander of Strongpoint 116
Lt. Shmuel Yakhin—tank platoon commander
Sgt. Nir Atir—tank commander
Sgt. Yoram Krivine—paratrooper

Southern Command

Gen. Avraham Adan—division commander
Gen. Yeshayahu Gavish—commander of southern Sinai
Brig. Gen. Barukh Harel—deputy to General Mendler
Brig. Gen. Dov Tamari—deputy to General Adan
Brig. Gen. Avraham Tamir—assistant to General Sharon
Brig. Gen. Uri Ben-Ari—deputy southern front commander
Col. Asher Levy—southern front staff
Brig. Gen. Ya'acov Even—deputy to General Sharon
Col. Haim Erez—armored brigade commander
Col. Amnon Reshef—armored brigade commander
Col. Natke Nir—armored brigade commander
Col. Gabi Amir—armored brigade commander
Col. Danny Matt—paratroop brigade commander
Lt. Col. Amazia Chen—commando officer
Lt. Col. Yehuda Geller—tank battalion commander
Lt. Col. Yitzhak Mordecai—paratroop battalion commander
Lt. Col. Ami Morag—tank battalion commander
Lt. Col. Giora Lev—tank battalion commander
Lt. Col. Yom Tov Tamir—tank battalion commander
Lt. Col. Haim Adini—tank battalion commander
Maj. Meir Weisel—commander of Fort Purkan
Maj. Yehuda Tal—deputy tank battalion commander
Maj. Yehuda Duvdevani—deputy paratroop battalion commander
Maj. Natan Shunari—paratroop battalion commander
Maj. Ilan Oko—deputy to General Even
Maj. Yitzhak Brik—tank company commander
Maj. Zvi Avidan—deputy commander, armored reconnaissance battalion
Maj. Gabi Komissar—General Adan's communications officer
Capt. Gideon Shamir—paratroop company commander
Capt. Hanan Erez—paratroop officer
Capt. Amnon Amikam—tank company commander
Capt. Yaacov Trostler—commander of Fort Milano

Capt. Motti Ashkenazi—commander of Fort Budapest
Capt. Rami Matan—tank company commander
Capt. Menashe Goldblatt—tank company commander
Lt. Yuval Neria—tank company commander
Dr. Avi Ohri—Fort Hizayon
Lt. Shaul Moses—tank platoon commander
Lt. David Amit—paratroop platoon commander
Lt. Eli Cohen—paratroop platoon commander
Sgt. Avi Yaffe—radioman, Fort Purkan
Sgt. Pinhas Strolovitz—Fort Hizayon
Sgt. Shalom Hala—Fort Milano
Sgt. Yisrael Itkin—commander of Sharon's APC
Sgt. Eyal Yoffe—tank commander
Sgt. Arye Segev—Fort Orkal
Pvt. Menahem Ritterband—Fort Orkal

Air Force
Gen. Benny Peled—Israeli Air Force commander
Gen. Motti Hod—liaison to front commanders
Col. David Ivri—deputy air force commander
Col. Giora Furman—chief operations officer
Col. Avihu Bin-Nun—air strike planning
Col. Eitan Ben-Eliyahu—planning staff
Col. Amos Amir—planning staff
Lt. Col. Giora Rom—Skyhawk squadron commander
Lt. Col. Yuval Efrat—helicopter squadron commander
Maj. Yossi Aboudi—intelligence
Maj. Arnon Lapidot—deputy Phantom squadron commander
Capt. Avraham Barber—Phantom pilot

Navy
Adm. Binyamin Telem—Israeli Navy commander
Capt. Ze'ev Almog—commander of Gulf of Suez theater
Lt. Cmdr. Gadi Kol—naval commando

Engineering Corps
Lt. Col. Aldo Zohar—pontoon bridge battalion commander
Maj. Yishai Dotan—deputy commander, pontoons
Capt. Amikam Doron—deputy commander, Gillois raft company
Lt. Col. Menashe Gur—commander of roller bridge
Lt. Eilon Naveh—deputy commander, rubber boats

Military Intelligence
Lt. Col. Zussia Keniezer—head of Jordanian desk, AMAN
Lt. Col. Avi Ya'ari—head of Syrian desk, AMAN

Lt. Col. Dennie Agmon—chief intelligence officer, Eitan's division
Lt. Col. Yehoshua Sagui—chief intelligence officer, Sharon's division
Lt. Col. Chagai Mann—chief intelligence officer, Northern Command
Maj. Amos Gilboa—Syrian desk, AMAN
Maj. Moshe Zurich—188th Brigade intelligence officer
Maj. Ilan Shahar—Seventh Brigade intelligence officer
Capt. David Harman—intelligence officer
Sgt. Amiram Gonen—Southern Command

Others
Zvi Zamir—head of Mossad
Brig. Gen. Emanuel Shaked—chief paratroop and infantry officer
Lou Kedar—assistant to Golda Meir
Mordecai Gazit—director of prime minister's office
Prof. Yuval Nee'man—physicist, member of defense establishment
Mohammed Bassiouni—Egyptian liaison to Syrian General Staff
Gen. (Ret.) Shlomo Gazit—Israeli military intelligence
Victor Shemtov—health minister
Gen. (Ret.) Donn Starry—U.S. Army
Bruce Reidel—CIA
Mohammed Gohar—Egyptian photographer
Reuven Merhav—Israeli intelligence community
Dan Meridor—served under General Gonen in Six Day War
Benny Michaelson—former chief IDF historian
Prof. Uri Bar-Joseph, Haifa University
Prof. Edward Luttwak
Prof. Martin van Creveld, Hebrew University
Prof. Shimon Shamir, Tel Aviv University

INDEX

Note: Page numbers in *italics* refer to maps.

ABOUT THE AUTHOR

Abraham Rabinovich worked as a reporter for *Newsday* before joining *The Jerusalem Post*. His work has also appeared in *The New York Times*, *The Wall Street Journal*, *The Christian Science Monitor*, the *International Herald Tribune*, and *The New Republic*, among other publications. He is the author of five previous books, including *Jerusalem on Earth*. Born in New York City, he lives in Jerusalem.

A NOTE ON THE TYPE

This book was set in Baskerville. The face itself is a facsimile reproduction of types cast from the molds made for John Baskerville (1706–1775) from his designs. Baskerville's original face was one of the forerunners of the type style known to printers as "modern face"—a "modern" of the period A.D. 1800.